Adventure Guide™

Montana

Genevieve Rowles

HUNTER PUBLISHING, INC,
130 Campus Drive, Edison, NJ 08818
732-225-1900; 800-255-0343; Fax 732-417-1744
hunterp@bellsouth.net

The Boundary, Wheatley Road, Garsington
Oxford, OX44 9EJ England
01865-361122; Fax 01865-361133

ISBN 1-55650-856-5

© 2000 Genevieve Rowles

Cover photo: View from Going-to-the-Sun Road,
Glacier National Park (© Donnie Sexton)

Photos on pages 117, 277 and 518 © Victor Bjornberg; on page 163 © Lonie Stimac; on page 175 © Georgia Maclean. Other photos © Donnie Sexton. All photos courtesy Travel Montana.

Maps by Kim André, © 2000 Hunter Publishing, Inc.

1 2 3 4

Contents

Introduction

It kinda sneaks up on you, Montana does. You come to fly-fish a world class stream – say the Madison or Blackfoot. Or to take a hike on the wild side; check into a guest ranch. Or maybe you're here to explore the state's fabled ghost towns, or visit Glacier National Park. Whatever, the place grabs you and won't turn loose. The beauty of it makes your head reel. Curiosity sets you to wondering

what's around the next twist in the trail; wondering what other adventures await in this broad-shouldered, sprawling place called Montana. This book will clue you in.

Discovering Montana

In order to simplify outlanders' quests for adventure, *Travel Montana*, the state's official welcome mat and magazine, divided the state into six travel regions: Missouri River, Charlie Russell, Glacier, Gold West, Yellowstone and Custer Country. This book follows these logical divisions.

Colorful as these monikers may be, they can't match the swagger of Montana's famous sobriquets: The Treasure State, Big Sky Country, The Headwaters State, The Last Best Place... tall claims all. Montana measures up to these and a heap more.

A passel of adventure opportunities reinforces the Treasure State nickname: sapphire mine pack trips, gold panning, hunting fossils and agates. All are doable.

The "Big Sky Country" claim was popularized by A.B. Guthrie, Jr. in his novel by that name. Montana's wide azure sky is a fitting foil for the High Plains' whispering wheat; for the soaring mass of the Rocky Mountain Front kicking the far distance.

"Headwaters State" is no idle boast. More rivers (81 to be exact) rise in the Montana Rockies than in any other state, inviting splashing good adventure. Rushing downslope from the Continental Divide, these rivers and streams feed the Mississippi to the east and the Columbia to the west.

Some might argue that the "Last Best Place" appellation is a tad outmoded. Montana's attraction for visitors, transplants and the rich and famous, all riding the coattails of a spate of highly hyped films, coat that sobriquet with irony. But Montanans have complained of over-crowding ever since prospectors and settlers gave the nudge to Indians and Mountain Men.

One constant no one refutes: Montana invites adventure.

■ Mountain Adventures

Montana is Latinized Spanish for "mountainous." A partial misnomer, that. Only in the western third of the state do jagged peaks rise above valleys spiced with seductive streams.

The mountain mystique draws visitors as bears are drawn to berries. Adventuring here can be as tame as exploring Gold West Country ghost towns or driving Glacier National Park's Going To The Sun Highway. It can be as edge-pushing as rock climbing above Lolo Pass or kayaking the Yaak River in spring spate. It can be as exciting as exploring the Bob Marshall Wilderness on horseback or as challenging as fishing the sun-glinted Big Hole River.

With so many adventure opportunities, this up-thrust third of Montana attracts the most visitors. At times, it seems downright crowded. Not so, the eastern two-thirds.

■ High Plains Adventures

This is cowboy country, and there's plenty of that breed itching to make the acquaintance of adventurous city slickers. Guest ranches, often sidelines to working cattle ranches, welcome folks with a yen to sample the storied West. You can ride on a real cattle round-up, complete with branding and steering. The latter isn't something you do with a pickup; fried Rocky Mountain oysters are the byproducts. At least one eatery stages noisily-touted testicle festivals. Yee-haw! Fishing is big here, as it is throughout Montana. So is watching an ever-changing wildlife show while canoeing the fabled Missouri. These plains, where buffalo once roamed in their thousands, heft a richly endowed passel of history. Landmarks and trails celebrate the courage of men and women who live in legend: the Nez Perce Trail, Lewis and Clark's Journey of Discovery, Little Bighorn, the dashed hopes of hard-working homesteaders.

■ Native Culture

Indian tribes were here first. Though brutally shouldered aside, forced onto reservations comprising but a fraction of their sacred ancestral lands, Native peoples' enduring presence stands proud in today's Montana.

Montana has seven reservations: Blackfeet, Crow, Flathead (Salish and Kootenai), Fort Belknap (Assiniboine and Gros Ventre), Fort Peck (Assiniboine and Sioux), Northern Cheyenne and Rocky Boy's (Chippewa-Cree). Most welcome visitors. Some offer opportunities to explore tribal culture and traditions.

Visiting Montana without exploring its history and the people shaped by that history is akin to climbing a mountain blindfolded.

■ Taking Off

On the premise that there's no appreciating today without a handle on yesterday, this book includes plenty of Montana's swaggering history, plus insight into the people who made Montana the last best place and who want to keep it that way.

This book's title promises to steer you toward the state's adventure opportunities, which translates differently for every traveler. Some prefer to test their mettle. Others want adventures of the mind. Some prefer to carve out personal adventures. Others prefer to be guided by savvy outfitters. Many seek a middle ground.

So hang on tight. Pack a passel of curiosity and an open mind. We're off, adventuring to museums, on national forest trails, to historic landmarks, to guest ranches, on cultural safaris, to wildlife refuges and fly fishing streams, on lazy river floats, through white water rapids, on backpacking forays into the high mountains. And much more.

But whoa! First, read this book through. Savor the choices. Decide on the experiences that most intrigue you. Then allow plenty of time. One Montana adventure inevitably leads to another. Every road and trail ends at a place called serendipity.

Geography & History

■ Prehistoric Montana

Montana's geography and topography molded its human history. Some 12,000 years ago the ancestors of today's Blackfeet, Flathead and Kootenai Indians chased buffalo to their deaths over the High Plains' steep river breaks. For centuries, the meat and hides harvested in this manner sustained the people. The buffalo formed the foundation of the Plains Indians' rich culture and deep reverance for the land, for the creatures and plants that grace it.

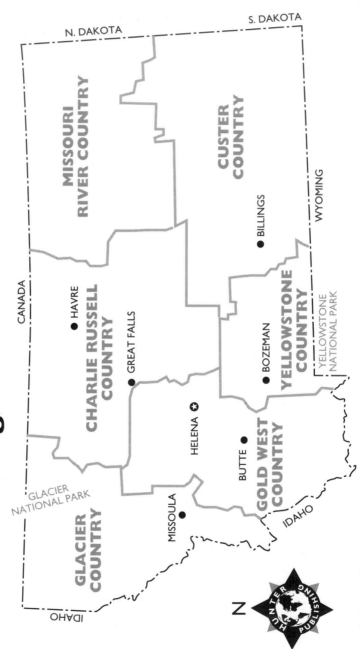

Regions of Montana

Much earlier, dinosaurs roamed plains formed from ancient seas and lakes. Their bones keep turning up, delighting paleontologists. Over time, cataclysmic earthquakes and explosive lava spurts formed the mountains that we know as the Rockies.

Montana's geological history is written in these mountains' rocks and minerals. The gold digs that excited 19th-century prospectors have given way to a few commercial mines. But sapphires, one of two official Montana gemstones, can still be found in placer deposits. Some two million years ago huge ice sheets ground across the northern half of Montana. Cycles of freezing and melting created the deep valleys, the mountain lakes and river courses that comprise today's landscape. Most of these glaciers retreated 20,000 years ago. Remnants, such as Glacier National Park's Grinnell Glacier, are legacies of that age. Global warming has caused them to retreat.

■ The First Montanans

The hype surrounding the bicentennial of Meriwether Lewis's and William Clark's Voyage of Discovery suggests that it marked the dawn of Montana's human history. Not so. No one really knows from whence came the first Montanans. Recent discoveries suggest that the Bering Sea land bridge theory may be as full of holes as a scatter-shot hide. It's generally agreed that pre-historic buffalo hunters were the ancestors of many of the Plains Indians encountered by Lewis and Clark: Sioux, Blackfeet Piegans, Shoshone (Sacajawea was a Shoshone). Their descendants live in Montana today.

Most had made previous contact with Caucasians, trading with French fur trappers and British traders who had filtered down from Canada. Friendly toward whites (except for the wary Blackfeet), these people had little inkling of the dangers those contacts posed to their culture – to their very existence.

The first intimation came in the shape of death-dealing smallpox. Traders' rot gut (raw alcohol doctored with tobacco and capsicum) degraded a proud people to objects of derision. White men's ignorance of and disdain for Indian ways led to misunderstandings that spawned cruelty in both camps. The result was a trail of broken promises and abrogated treaties. The legacy yet lingers.

■ The Legacy of the Slaughtered Buffalo

By the mid-1870s, a few erstwhile miners and trappers had become cattlemen. Some trailed Oregon stock over the Continental Divide. Others drove herds up from Texas. The cattle thrived on the native grasses that had long sustained the buffalo. Perhaps buffalo and cattle might have co-inhabited these vast plains. But it was not to be. In the ensuing decades, the bleaching bones of systematically slaughtered buffalo littered the land. For eons, the shaggy hump-backed beasts had provided plains tribes with meat, hides and bone tools. Buffalo were the foundation of their culture and sense of place on the Earth. Then, in the space of two decades, the buffalo were gone. The killing of the buffalo and the arrival of settlers coincided, climaxing decades of gradual white intrusion onto tribal hunting grounds. The corral gates slammed shut, confining a once-free people.

Defeated, devoid of land and livelihood, the people had no choice but to move onto reservations. Even these were reduced in size over the decades. Contravening treaties, land was ruthlessly sliced from reservations to make way for railroads and the homesteaders they brought in.

Indian agencies, answering to Washington bureaucrats, could not or would not provide sustenance to replace the buffalo. A very few, such as Peter Ronan, agent to the Flathead Reservation, made honest efforts to help. More often, agents robbed their charges of what little the government allotted to them.

The people were starved and demoralized; their cultural and spiritual heritage violated. Traditional dance, music and worship were forbidden in the name of Christianity. Children were forced to attend schools designed to "civilize" them. Speaking their own language was a punishable offense. This cultural genocide lasted well into the 20th century. Bitter memories of these schools and of the punishments meted out there still linger.

Today's strong resurgence of Native culture and spirituality is instrumental in restoring the people's dignity and pride. Pow-wows, once forbidden, are joyful celebrations of Native spirit and culture. The buffalo remains a powerful symbol of identity.

■ The Homestead Boom

A combination of circumstances fueled Montana's homestead boom. By the turn of the 20th century, the fertile and relatively well watered mountain valleys had been pre-empted by a few prosperous cattle barons. The High Plains, vacated by Indian removal and the slaughter of the buffalo, sustained large free-ranging herds of sheep and cattle belonging to mountain valley ranchers. The grazing was free until railroads bought up large tracts along their rights of way. And until Congress passed the Desert Land Act.

Tidy 160-acre farms might sustain a family in well-watered Iowa and Minnesota, but not on the semi-arid high plains. So, in 1877, Congress amended the 1862 Homestead Act by passing the Desert Land Act. This allowed the sale of 640-acre sections of land at $1.25 per-acre – four times the acreage allowed by the Homestead Act. Then, in 1909, Congress passed the Enlarged Homestead Act, upping allowable free acreage to 320.

Earlier homesteaders, a.k.a. sodbusters, had pretty well settled the lands east of central North and South Dakota. By 1909, a second generation, augmented by would-be farmers riding the crest of an immigration wave from Germany and Scandinavia, sought new land.

A South Dakota farmer named Hardy Webster Campbell developed a highly hyped system for conserving water in the soil. It worked, in years of adequate rainfall.

The Milwaukee Road, the Great Northern and Northern Pacific lines seized on "the amazing Campbell System of dryland farming" to convince land seekers of the fertility and promise of Montana's Great Plains.

The railroads' promotional efforts, circulated in fatally seductive packets, would cause today's brashest ad writers to blush. Today's ads contain kernels of truth. Those promoters didn't tweak the truth, they invented it. Glossy four-color brochures and extravagant promises inflamed gullible imaginations with visions of land ownership and prosperity beyond their wildest dreams.

Propaganda packets coined Montana's "Treasure State" sobriquet. Ironically, precious metals were Montana's proven treasures. The "treasures" of eastern Montana's high plains were as ephemeral as those greedy railroad barons' hype.

The weather cooperated with the railroads. Few realized that high plains rainfall comes in cycles. Montana's peak homesteading years coincided with a wet period averaging an annual 16 fortuitously timed inches of precipitation.

Between 1909 and 1923, homesteaders, derisively labelled honyockers and scissorbills by irate stockmen, filed 114,620 claims on nearly 25 million acres of Montana land. Untold thousands of miles of barbed wire fencing destroyed the open range. But the cattlemen got their revenge in the end.

Everything was hunky-dory for awhile. Towns and close-knit farming communities developed and thrived. Crops flourished. Montana's hard wheat was in high demand on the international market. World War I brought increased demand and assured prices. Times were so good that farmers mortgaged their land in order to purchase the shiny new tractors that would enable them to produce yet more wheat on yet more mortgaged land.

Then the rains stopped. The homestead boom went bust.

Demoralized families watched their fields turn to dust. They left their lands, houses, barns – all the results of incredibly hard work. They left those shiny new tractors to rust in the fields. Soon the steel rails tracked through near-deserted towns. Most folks headed for Oregon, for Washington and California. Some hung on. Some sold out to cattlemen. Some became cattlemen.

Today, the original "Treasure State" appellation has been affirmed through advanced soil technology and mechanization, larger farms, diversified farming, drought-resistant wheat varieties and shelter belts planted to cut damaging winds. Agriculture is Montana's number one industry.

■ Trails Through Montana

The trails trod by Montana's people and animals are outlines of her history. Many are still visible. Some remain in use, though in much altered forms. Each shaped a facet of history that impacts the state and its people even now, at the dawn of the 21st century.

Trails enter the state from each of the four directions: following the rivers, threading the mountain passes, traversing the plains.

The earliest tracks were made by deer and antelope seeking water, by bears and wolves in search of food. Native peoples' moccasins trod trails threading the mountains to the plains and back. They also trod trails forking down from the land that would become Canada. These trails were followed by trappers of beaver and mink, the legendary Mountain Men of the late 18th and early 19th centuries.

It is fitting that Lewis and Clark blazed their trail at the turn of a new century. Yet, the Voyage of Discovery followed existing trails. Most of what we know as the **Lewis and Clark Trail** traversed routes along river courses and over mountain passes traveled by Indians for centuries. You can follow the route today, driving or hiking snatches of it, canoeing the Missouri and Yellowstone, looking in on many of the landmarks that caused Lewis and Clark to marvel.

Gold Trails

The **Bozeman Trail** is less well known. In 1864, John Bozeman and John Jacobs mapped what they perceived to be an easy wagon route from the Oregon Trail near present-day Casper, Wyoming to the newly discovered gold digs on Grasshopper Creek, a tributary of the Beaverhead River. Angling into Montana east of the Bighorn River, the road skirted the Bighorn Mountains and ran along the Yellowstone River before crossing Bozeman Pass into the Gallatin Valley.

This "easy" route cut smack through the Sioux and Northern Cheyenne's prime buffalo hunting grounds. A few emigrant wagons got through despite Indian attacks. Others were less fortunate. After a couple of years, emigrants ceased using the trail. It was used as a military road until 1868, when it was abandoned following the Fort Laramie Treaty. The short-lived trail's legacy surfaced a decade later at Little Bighorn. Mostly traversing private lands and the Crow Indian Reservations, the route's Montana's stretch is difficult to follow until it parallels I-90 through Bozeman Pass.

The **Corinne Road**, an easy route over Monida Pass, opened the way to Montana's gold mining spree. Hundreds of prospectors and supply wagons crowded the road between 1862 and the 1880s, to-ing and fro-ing between Salt Lake City and rip roarin' gold towns whose names still resonate: Bannack, Virginia City, Nevada City.

Today, I-15 enters Montana from Idaho over the original route of the Corinne Road.

Highways roughly parallel many of the old trails, making some fairly easy to follow. Feasible highway routes through western Montana are generally limited to valleys and passes. Road building and rough mountain terrain are incompatible even today.

Though pleasant to muse upon, it's a stretch to think that Montana's glorious mountains and valleys, its shining rivers and bounteous wildlife, would have remained inviolate to large-scale mining had not the **Mullan Road** picked up where Missouri River steamboat navigation left off at Fort Benton.

The Corinne Road served gold camps from the south. The Mullan Road provided a link to the east, opening up mining opportunities to the north of those early digs. The road was conceived as a link between the head of navigation at Fort Benton and the Columbia River. The Columbia link never panned out as planned, the Bitterroots proving nearly impassable for wagon travel.

In the 1860s and 1870s, freight wagons loaded with heavy mining equipment lumbered over the Mullan Road to the gold camps spreading northward from Bannack to more lucrative digs. Last Chance Gulch, one of the few Montana gold camps to survive as a city, later shed its inelegant moniker in favor of Helena. Helena crowded out Anaconda in the capital city sweepstakes in 1889, when Montana became a state. Gold, silver and copper mines thrived, providing Montanans with jobs while heedlessly polluting both soil and politics. Butte dallied with gold and silver mining until, in 1882, the world's richest body of copper sulphide was discovered on its very doorstep. The world's largest copper smelter polluted nearby Anaconda.

Immigrants answered the promise of jobs in the mines, streaming into Butte and Anaconda from Ireland, Italy, Eastern Europe and elsewhere. Powerful political interests vied for control of Butte's copper, and thereby of the fledgling state. The Anaconda Copper Mining Company won, creating a far-ranging business empire that hogtied Montana's newspapers, and through them state politics, until the mid-20th century. Other mining conglomerates shouldered into the state. Anaconda and Butte became synonomous with heavy metal pollution. It's a dirty story that threw an ugly shroud over a state better celebrated for its great natural beauties.

The Nez Perce Trail

A very different trail seared across Montana in the fall of 1877. A year earlier, the trail followed by the vainglorious Col. George Armstrong Custer had led the US Cavalry to defeat at Little Bighorn. Both were steeped in tragedy.

Chief Joseph

The Nez Perce (Nee-Me-Poo) Trail was blazed by Chief Joseph, leader of a non-treaty Nez Perce band banished from their ancestral lands in northeastern Oregon's Wallowa country. Accompanied by some 100 warriors, 800 women and children and 2,000 head of stock, Chief Joseph sought refuge in Canada rather than accept confinement on a reservation. He almost made it. Trapped, his people sick, cold and hungry, Joseph surrendered in the Bears Paw Mountains, some 30 miles short of the Canadian border.

A National Historic Trail, the Nez Perce Trail enters Montana from Idaho at Lolo Pass and parallels US 93 to the Big Hole National Battlefield site. Here, with much loss of life, Nez Perce warriors defeated some 2,000 soldiers and civilian volunteers before they re-entered Idaho. In all, the band traveled over 1,100 miles while successfully engaging the US Cavalry in some 20 battles and skirmishes. Ironically, the band had preferred not to fight. Kind and peace-loving, Chief Joseph sought only freedom for his people. After traversing northeastern Idaho and part of Yellowstone National Park, the Nez Perce Trail follows the Clark's Fork of the Yellowstone River back into Montana west of the Crow Reservation. From here, it heads north into the Bears Paw Mountains. Much of this portion of the trail is on private land and is difficult to follow.

Trails of the Iron Horse

It was inevitable that railroad routes would trace those trod by the horses of Indians, trappers, traders and miners. In 1881, the Utah Northern reached Butte from the south. Over the next two decades, locomotives of the Northern Pacific, the Great Northern and the Milwaukee Road began pounding rails that straight-lined across the width of Montana. Box cars spilled homesteaders and their goods and chattel onto the prairie. Railroad towns sprang up beside the tracks. Much as the Indians were deceived by the so-called Great White Father, so homesteaders were deceived by railroad promoters. Jim Hill and other railroad barons visualized shining steel tracks linking a network of towns and farms.

The tide of homesteaders began to abate about the time a new class of people came to ride the rails: tourists bound for Yellowstone and Glacier National Parks. Their descendants still ride rails through Montana. (See *Railways*, page 65).

Today's Trails

Montana's trails metamorphosed into the highways, roads and scenic byways linking the diverse facets of this huge state. Many roads cover the tracks that wrote the history of Montana's people. Many of the hiking trails threading Montana's wilderness and national forest lands link riders and hikers with the diverse peoples who trod them for centuries.

Climate

Montana has nine weather zones that roughly correspond with the state's six travel regions. Refer to regional chapters of this book for information on localized weather trends and extremes.

Montana's weather often pushes the envelope. Extremes are as dramatic as its jumbled mountains and high plains.

DID YOU KNOW? *The lowest recorded temperature in the contiguous 48 states occurred on January 20, 1954 when the mercury fell to a numbing -70° at 5,470-foot-high Roger's Pass. Montana's highest reading, a sweltering 117°, was tied at Glendive on July 20, 1893 and at Medicine Lake on July 5, 1937.*

The old saw, "if you don't like the weather, wait five minutes," could have been a Montana original. Warm Chinook winds from the Pacific sometimes sweep in over the Front Range of the Rockies in winter, raising temperatures dramatically and quickly melting snow cover. Chinooks have dropped temperatures by as much as 30° in as little as seven minutes. The warming usually occurs more gradually, over a day or so.

The most rapid Chinook-generated temperature increase occurred at Great Falls on January 11, 1980 when the mercury rose from -32° to 15° in seven minutes. The greatest change over a 24-hour period occurred at Browning on January 23, 1916 when temperatures plunged from 44° to -56°. On Christmas Eve, 1924, Fairfield folks shivered when the temperature plummeted from a balmy 63° at noon to -21° at midnight. Such extremes aside, the weather is pretty much what you might expect at an average elevation of 3,400 feet, between the latitudes of 44 and 49 degrees north. Translation: be prepared for any kind of weather at any time.

■ Seasons

The air over Montana is squeezed of moisture as it passes over the Rockies. If you are accustomed to a moist climate, your skin will develop a sudden craving for heavy-duty lotion.

Springs tend to be brief and capricious. Sudden April or even May snowstorms give the lie to the calendar. Spring comes earliest to the lower elevations. Grasses green up and trees bud while snow still clings to the high country. Sunny, warm weather generally revs up in late June, though earlier warm spells aren't uncommon. Summer daytime temperatures in the mountains usually hover in the 70s to 80s; nighttime lows can dip into the upper 40s. The plains tend to be 10 or more degrees warmer. Three-digit heat waves are fairly common on the high plains.

Autumns bring glorious weather – clear sunny days and frosty nights. Snow can swirl through mountain passes as early as late September or October. Then come golden Indian summer days when the chokecherries are ripe and the air is crisp.

Winters play hardball. Snow can come as early as October and can linger into May. The cold is intense enough to freeze the ears off a cougar, particularly on the high plains.

Northern Lights

Northern Montana skies sometimes host the phantasmagorical displays known as the Aurora Borealis, common to Alaska's and Canada's far north. Referred to as northern lights, they have been variously described as dancing lights, a kaleidoscope of lights, or ghost lights. Not all are dramatic; they can be gentle as a breaking dawn. Sometimes they resemble paint brush streaks scooting across the sky.

These nocturnal displays occur at times of sunspots and solar flares. Most take place during the March and September equinoxes, but may happen any time of year.

The best time to see them is around midnight on a clear night. City lights interfere.

Any exposed area, be it campground or trail, is ideal.

Don't look straight up, but rather about halfway between the North Star and the horizon.

AUTHOR TIP *Stretch the season when packing for your Montana trip. Add a couple of sweatshirts and sweaters, wool socks, a jacket and gloves to your usual summer gear. Roll a blanket into your sleeping bag. Rain gear is a must, particularly in the mountains, where sudden summer rain squalls and thunderstorms are facts of life. In winter, add a t-shirt or two and a pair of lightweight pants to your snuggy cache.*

Flora & Fauna

Montana abounds with plant and animal life. Many species went unrecorded until Lewis and Clark made meticulous drawings and descriptions during their 1805-06 expedition.

Much has changed since that time. Except in Yellowstone National Park, buffalo graze only on ranches and reservations. Mountain streams are no longer thick with beaver, though the resourceful rodents have made a comeback of sorts since being nearly trapped out in the mid-19th century. Trout aren't what they used to be either. Non-native trout have been introduced, native bull trout are on the endangered species list, whirling disease has infested most streams, and in some waters mandatory catch and release nixes the pleasure of dining on a mess of fresh-caught fish.

The virgin forests that once covered the Rocky Mountain slopes have been burned over by wildfires. The most destructive was the benchmark 1910 fire. Logging has also taken a toll. But forests recover quickly. Strong second growth, both natural and planted, soon sheltered a vigorous undergrowth of shrubs, wildflowers and berries. Montana boasts an unimaginable range of animal and plant diversity. Wildlife refuges offer opportunities for birding and for watching and photographing other wildlife and flora. These refuges are just a beginning. You can't set foot on a trail or dip a paddle into a river without spotting animals and birds.

Bison

Many people associate buffalo with news reports of Montana Fish and Wildlife officers destroying Yellowstone National Park bison straying beyond park boundaries in search of winter forage. Some 1,100 bison were killed in the severe winter of 1996-97, about 100 in the mild winter of 1997-98. The controversial practice is prompted by concerns that the buffalo may spread brucellosis among cattle. Brucellosis is a bovine disease that causes pregnant females to abort. In humans, it's a nasty called undulant fever.

While the intent of allowing Yellowstone bison to range free is to return them to their native habitat, today's reality suggests the wisdom of managed herds where animals can be tested for brucellosis and vaccinated against it. Buffalo ranches are increasing as the meat gains in popularity. It tastes like beef, but is leaner. The hardy animals thrive on natural rangeland.

Where to see them: Media mogul Ted Turner runs buffalo on his 107,000-acre **Flying D Ranch** near Bozeman. Some 500 buffalo roam the **National Bison Range**, near Moise on the Flathead Indian Reservation. Residents of the **Fort Belknap Reservation** also manage a herd of buffalo.

■ Montana Flora

Homesteaders' plows destroyed many of the high plains' native grasses. Only scattered stands of tuft-growing bunchgrass, sagebrush, buffalo grass and bluejoint remain. **Cottonwoods** grow to tremendous size along prairie water courses, affording habitat for numerous species of birds.

 Where there are cottonwoods, you can bet on finding shade, water and lush grasses.

Conifers march up Montana's high mountains and eastward-facing slopes, casting green-black shadows. Balsam, Western red cedar, lodgepole pines, yellow pine, red fir, Western larch (also referred to as tamarack), ponderosa pines and other conifers thrive on congenial soil and weather conditions. Lodgepole pines continue to be highly prized as tepee poles.

Deer and elk graze on **alpine meadows** amid scatterings of wildflowers. Moose and wildfowl enjoy copious wetlands. Mountain stream courses are lush with grasses, alders, woods roses, berries, and chokecherries. **Huckleberry** bushes ripen in woodlands and on disturbed terrain, bringing out droves of pickers to supply Western Montana's thriving wild huckleberry preserves industry.

Come autumn, stands of **aspen** and **Western larch** glow golden against conifers' contrasting green. Early-changing **sumac** and **mountain maple** paint the slopes with red. **Chokecherries** are ripe and as sweet as they'll ever be, to the delight of both bears and humans.

Indian Plants

Plains Indians once included some 70 plants in their diets and recognized the medicinal properties in 50 plants. Eight plants were used to freshen and cleanse tepees and campsites. Fifteen sacred plants were used in war and hunting preparations.

Montana's Native Peoples still gather wild plants for healing and religious ceremonies. Chokecherries have long been valued as a principle ingredient in pemmican. These cakes, made of dried chokecherries and bear grease, were winter staples that staved off scurvy when game was the only other item on the menu. Mountain men and settlers also relished the fruit. Their descendants make chokecherry jellies, syrups, even wines. Lewistown stages a fall chokecherry festival (see page 539 for details)

▪ Montana Fauna

You're right on if you associate Montana with high profile wild animals such as grizzly bears, mountain lions and wolves.

Bears

Montana has more grizzlies than any other state in the Lower 48. An estimated 100,000 roamed the area in Lewis's and Clark's time. Today, some 500 to 600 live in the mountains of northwest Montana. Decimated by hunters, grizzlies became almost as scarce as hair on a duck. The bruins have been making a comeback since 1975, when they were listed as threatened under the Endangered Species Act.

Bear sightings are increasing. Grizzlies like the taste of sheep and young stock, especially in autumn when they gorge to store fat for winter hibernation. Both grizzly and black bears sometimes venture near ranch buildings. Reports of ranchers killing bears in defense of themselves or their stock seem to be increasing.

Hikers' encounters of a scary kind are also occurring more frequently. In May, 1998 a hiker in Glacier National Park's Two Medicine area was killed and partially consumed by a grizzly sow and her half-grown young. The sow and one cub were tracked down and destroyed. The other cub was shot after eluding rangers for weeks, and bluff charging a group of hikers.

More grizzlies may be moved from Canada to the Bitterroot Mountains along the Montana-Idaho border. The goal is to transplant five grizzlies each year for five years. Conservationists like the proposal. Ranchers and rural residents are vehemently opposed. Montana is a magnet for disenchanted city folks who regard the "last best place" sobriquet as gospel truth. That factor, plus the normal growth of towns and cities, is causing housing developments and ranchettes to encroach on many animals' traditional feeding territory. Deer, coyotes and bears are sometimes seen checking out life in the suburbs. Even sightings of usually reclusive mountain lions have increased.

Co-Adventuring With Grizzlies

Grizzlies are BIG. They weigh 250 to 500 pounds and measure six to eight feet when standing upright. They are almost twice the size of black bears. You can identify a grizzly by its dished face, prominent shoulder hump and long curved claws. Grizzly fur is often brown, tipped with blonde, causing the grizzled or silvertip appearance that prompts their name. Bears sense fear. If you are uncomfortable hiking in grizzly country, choose another area. But bear-savvy behavior on your part can help to alleviate that fear.

■ Take sensible safety measures when hiking or camping in grizzly country. Never hike alone. Leave Rover at home – dogs attract bears. Make lots of noise by singing and talking. Some hikers carry bells, but old timers say the human voice is a better deterrent.

■ Be especially wary when near berry patches or upon seeing signs of grizzly activity such as tracks, droppings, clawed trees or partially consumed animal carcasses. Camp away from trails or areas where grizzly signs are apparent.

■ A fed bear will soon be a dead bear. Ergo: once a bear tastes "people food" he'll seek out more. Used to human smells, he'll cease avoiding humans, become a threat and eventually have to be shot.

■ Never allow a grizzly to get at your food. He'll associate it with snacks. You don't want to be a snack. Avoid cooking smelly foods and keep a clean camp. That means hanging all food, trash, personal cosmetics and other strong smelling items at least 10 feet up in a tree, on a branch that's at least four feet away from a vertical support. Or store these items in a bear-proof container. That goes for livestock feed, too. Don't sleep in the same clothes you wore while cooking or eating. Set up your tent at least 300 feet from your cook site in order to discourage bears from nosing about your sleeping area. To leave fish entrails beside lakes or streams is to invite trouble.

■ Women traveling in grizzly country during their menstrual periods must take special precautions. Use pre-moistened unscented cleaning towelettes, use tampons instead of pads, and never bury them. Place used tampons or pads in double zip-lock bags and store them 10 feet up, as you would food. Use only unscented feminine products.

- Bear-resistant panniers, backpacker food tubes and rope and pulley hoisting systems can be rented for nominal fees at the Hungry Horse, Spotted Bear, Lincoln, Seeley Lake, Missoula and Rocky Mountain Ranger District offices of the Flathead, Helena, Lewis & Clark and Lolo National Forests. These items are also available at the Augusta Information Station in the Lewis & Clark National Forest, and the Flathead National Forest Condon Work Center and Kalispell Office. Poles or bear-resistant boxes are provided at all Glacier National Park campgrounds.

Encountering a Grizzly

So what to do if, after taking all the above precautions, you encounter a grizzly? The Montana Department of Fish, Wildlife and Parks suggests the following:

- Maintain a safe distance and behave in a non-threatening manner. Drop something like a hat or gloves on the ground in front of you, then slowly back away. Avoid eye contact. Speak in a soft monotone. Hopefully, the bear will lumber off into the bush. Don't climb a tree unless you can get at least 10 feet up before the bruin reaches the tree. **Don't run**. To run is to invite attack. It's surmised that the young man killed in Glacier National Park in May, 1998 made two big mistakes: he hiked alone and he ran from the bear.

- If a bear charges, remain standing in the hope that it's a bluff charge and the bear will run past you. Otherwise, assume a cannonball or fetal position. Some rangers advocate lying flat on your stomach in order to make it harder for the bear to turn you over. Either way, the idea is to protect your vulnerable front. Play dead. Keep your pack on to protect your back. Cover your neck and head with your arms and hands. Don't look up until you are certain the bear has gone away. The object is not to appear threatening. If you do, the bear will likely charge.

- Many experts recommend carrying a spray made of cayenne pepper extract. It's intended to be sprayed directly into the face of a charging bear. Do not use it as a bear repellent. Oddly, bruins are attracted to the stuff like kittys to catnip when it's sprayed around a campsite or wherever. The sprays are available at sporting goods stores.

- If you carry a weapon, use it only as a last resort and at close quarters. It takes a heap of firepower to stop a bear. A wounded grizzly is an enraged grizzly.

- If a bear attacks at night when you are in your tent he may be seeking food rather than trying to neutralize a threat. It's recommended that you fight back to show that you are dangerous.

- Finally, report all encounters. In Montana, grizzlies are managed jointly by the Montana Department of Fish, Wildlife and Parks, the US Fish and Wildlife Service, and tribal wildlife managers. Much of their habitat is managed by the US Forest Service and other public and tribal land management agencies. Report grizzly encounters to the US Fish and Wildlife Service, Endangered Species Field Office, PO Box 10023, Helena, MT 59626 (☎ 406-449-5225), the Montana Department of Fish, Wildlife and Parks, 490 N. Meridian Road, Kalispell, MT 59901 (☎ 406-752-5501), or to the nearest Forest Service ranger station or Indian reservation.

Wolves

Wolves, as numerous as needles on a pine tree before being hunted almost clear out in the last century, have been reintroduced in some mountainous areas of eastern Idaho and to Yellowstone National Park. Occasionally, a wolf wearing a telltale radio collar wanders into Montana, or someone reports sighting a collarless native wolf. The chances of seeing one of these reclusive characters ranges from unlikely to nil. More wolves may extend their range into Montana as time goes on.

Wolfing

The rampant "wolfing" of the 1880s and 1890s was, depending on which side of the fence you stand on, a black mark on Montana's escutcheon or good riddance. These viewpoints color the differences of opinion surrounding the re-entry of Canadian wolves into Northern Idaho and Yellowstone.

Environmentalists, delighted with the transplanted wolves' quick adjustment to their new habitat, downplay occasional stock killings. Ranchers are compensated for their losses, yet are adamant in wanting the wolves out. In 1998, US District Judge William Downes ordered non-native wolves removed from the region. Canadian officials refuse to accept the wolves. Environmental groups claim the order amounts to the wolves' death penalty. So goes the see-saw. Stay tuned.

In 1880, some 200,000 gray wolves roamed Montana. The killing of the vast buffalo herds forced the wolves to scout out new dinner entrées. Young cattle made tasty substitutes. *Canis lupus nubilus* prefer fresh meat. They eat to satiation, often devouring only a portion of a kill. This fastidious habit leads to more kills than would occur if wolves dined on a carcass over the course of a few days. Stockmen wanted the wolves gone.

Enter wolfers, a motley crew comprised of seasonal Missouri River steamboat workers, hard luck miners, discontents. Prime wolf pelts harvested in winter brought high prices, plus bounty money.

A wolfer would track down the few remaining bison and shoot them at intervals of a few miles, leaving them to lie in a circular pattern. He would implant each carcass with strychnine and wait. Wolves would feed on the poisoned meat and drop dead. Wolfers got their pelts and bounty money and stockmen had one less pack of wolves to worry their young animals.

Stockmen also got into the wolf eradication act. In spring, they would destroy she wolves and pups in their dens, effectively cutting down on the propagation of the species. Today's native wolf population is estimated at less than 100.

Though it's unlikely that you'll glimpse a wolf, you're bound to see other animals. Elk, moose, beaver, eagles, black bears, mule and white-tailed deer, racoons, great horned owls, river otters, prairie dogs, proghorn antelopes, rattlesnakes, waterfowl – all enjoy Montana's prime habitat. Hiking is a good way to see them.

Mountain Lions

Mountain lions, the legendary "ghosts of the Rockies," are also known as cougars or pumas. They range through all the mountainous areas of Montana and in the vicinity of the Missouri River breaks. Lions are big, stealthy and vicious. They vary in weight from 85 to 180 pounds and measure six to eight feet from nose to tip of tail. The reclusive cats were once almost never seen, but encounters are becoming more frequent. These guys are a far leap from your playful pussy cat. While grizzlies attack when they feel threatened and often leave when they think the attackee is dead, lions regard humans as dinner.

■ Lions are most active at dusk or dawn, but they sometimes travel in the daytime. When hiking in lion habitat, go in groups, make noise and carry a walking stick. Keep children close to your side. **Never approach a mountain lion.** If you do come onto one, offer it a way out. Don't expect your dog to act as a deterrent. A dog can act as a decoy. The lion may be more likely to attack if a hiker is accompanied by a tasty looking dog. This horrific possibility may be acceptable if it comes down to the dog's life or yours.

■ If you do encounter a mountain lion, stay calm. Talk to the lion in a quiet, confident voice. Immediately pick young children up off the ground. Rapid movements of a frightened child may provoke an attack. Don't run. Slowly back away from the lion. The idea is to move slowly at all times. Sudden movement or fleeing behavior often triggers instinctive predatory attacks. **Never turn your back on a lion**. Face it and remain upright. Try to project a large image.

■ If the lion behaves aggressively, seize a big stick, throw rocks, raise your voice. Don't turn or crouch. You want him to think you are dangerous. If the lion attacks, remain standing and fight.

■ If you have a confrontation with a mountain lion, immediately report it by calling the nearest office of the Montana Department of Fish, Wildlife and Parks. Kalispell, ☎ 752-5501; Missoula, ☎ 542-5500; Bozeman, ☎ 994-4042; Great Falls, ☎ 454-3441; Billings, ☎ 252-4654; Glasgow, ☎ 228-9347; Miles City, ☎ 232-4365; Helena, ☎ 444-4720.

The People

Montanans are a hardy, individualistic breed reflecting an adventurous history and the state's rugged topography. Granted, some religous cultists and militant survivalists carry individualism to extremes. Some are clearly wacko. Some are scary. For the most part, these way-out types simply interject spice and color in the state's cultural brew.

High Plains ranchers and farmers, mountain folk, Native Peoples, fishing and hunting guides, townsfolk, emigrant outlanders: each is distinct; all take pride in being Montanans.

DID YOU KNOW? *Montana's natural wonders, its ghost towns and wild animals, ranches and cattle drives, are the genuine items. No room here for Disneyesque pseudo anything. This sense of genuineness is one of the reasons visitors return to Montana again and again. Disney artists and imagineers number among these visitors. They come seeking inspiration from the real thing. Ironically, many a theme park or thrill ride had its genesis in Montana's on-the-edge reality.*

Montanans harbor a deep love of the land – of mountain grandeur and the changeable luminosity of the plains. Most every individual values some special place in the vast outdoors. It might be a haven in the wilderness or a certain lake or stretch of river. Montanans guard the land jealously. Voters reacted to proposals permitting oil and gas leasing on the sensitive Rocky Mountain Front with a resounding "No!"

The Creator lavishly distributed riches both under and across the land that would be known as Montana. A penalty must be payed for disturbing Mother Earth to extract the gold, silver, copper, coal, oil, gas, precious stones, timber and other materials. So it is that deep scars and ugly slag piles mar the surface of the land. A hot topic is how to ameliorate the damage and prevent further depredations without endangering Montanans' livelihoods.

Also of concern is the disposition of Montana's large historic ranches. Some occasionally come on the market. The sigh of relief can be heard statewide when a buyer declares his intention to continue running a ranch as a cattle operation. Such was the case in 1997 when the 70,000-acre-plus Dearborn Ranch was purchased by a California millionaire who made that intention clear.

Latter-day emigrants' rosy fantasies of life in rural Montana often succumb to reality over the first harsh winter. Some haven't a clue as to rural etiquette. They tangle with the neighbors when their dogs chase stock, or wrinkle delicate noses when it comes time for a neighboring farmer to spread the manure that's been piling up in the corral all winter. Or they feed those cute bears and raccoons, then complain when their garbage cans are overturned.

Not that Montanans mean to be inhospitable. It's just that they prefer that visitors spend their money and go home. Montanans have an innate aversion to crowding – a protectiveness toward the beautiful places that feed the soul. Emigrants coming in droves make folks a mite edgy. They bring their high-falutin' lifestyles and pricey tastes with them. And there's the jobs crunch. Some towns, Kalispell comes to mind, out and out tell people not to come unless they can bring their jobs with them. Land-gobbling religious cults and weirdos like the Montana Militia and Ted Kaczynski have given rise to a wariness akin to that of a skunk-sprayed dog. Nobody needs that kind of notoriety.

How to Tell a Montanan From a Dude

Telling a real Montanan from a dude is easy. With tongue firmly planted in cheek, I offer the following tips:

■ Who else arrives at a symphony concert in a pickup truck? Or accepts a compliment on her "outfit" as referring to the pickup she's driving, not the clothes she's wearing? Or whose outfit's accessories include a gun rack, gun and dog?

- Most Montanans' best friends have four legs and either whinny or bark. The barkers' job descriptions include waiting in their masters' pickups outside a bar named The Mint or The Stockman.

- Real Montanans think it's odd that some people have to pay sales taxes and observe a numerical speed limit. Up until the law changed as this book went to press, only a Montanan would speed down the Interstate at a reasonable and prudent 80 mph while talking on a cellular phone and waving at the Highway Patrol. But he willingly gives herds of cattle or sheep the right of way.

- Montana's city police officers direct more than vehicular traffic, such as persuading an errant moose or elk to mosey on out of town. You can tell a born and bred Montanan by his or her eagerness to inform a stranger that grandma and grandpa settled in the Deer Lodge Valley in 1888, or that great-gramps proved a mining claim on Grasshopper Creek in 1863.

- But there's hope for you. You're a bonafide adopted Montanan if you moved into the state a year ago from California and now gripe about all those dang-blasted Californians invading Montana.

▪ Montana's Native Peoples

Sometimes, you might think you'd been plunked down in a foreign country. Which, in a sense, you have if you visit one of Montana's seven Indian reservations.

Native Americans are United States citizens, but their reservations are sovereign nations and are governed as such. The Bureau of Indian Affairs serves as a guardian of sorts, holding moneys in trust. And Congress has more say over Indian affairs than most think is just. This situation is gradually changing as more young Indian men and women seek higher educations. Some are becoming attorneys with a mandate to serve as advocates for their people.

Most tribal members retain strong ties to their reservations. Respect for Mother Earth and all life is basic to Native beliefs. Indians traditionally hunted and fished for food, not for sport.

DID YOU KNOW?

When an Indian kills a deer or other creature, he thanks the Creator for the food and begs the animal's forgiveness.

On the surface, reservation life may appear similar to that of any rural town. Below the surface runs a strong current of cultural re-identity. Each tribe struggles in its own way with vital issues such as employment, housing, educational opportunities for young people, health care and alcohol abuse.

Crow Fair, Hardin, MT.

Ever since it was introduced by white traders, alcohol has been Indians' most deadly enemy. Its grip tightened when tribes were forced onto reservations. Men could no longer hunt and wage war, but they knew no other life. Adapting to white ways and occupations wrenched the pride clear out of them. Today, sobriety is a mark of pride.

Balancing tribal traditions with tourism is a complex issue. Some reservations discourage tourists. Others welcome visitors with traditional hospitality. The Flathead, Blackfeet and Fort Belknap reservations are in the vanguard of a cultural tour concept designed to foster understanding between Indians and non-Indians. Some reservations maintain museums with exhibits highlighting tribal history and traditional skills. Some Indians, particularly on the Crow and Blackfeet reservations, work as fishing guides.

Today's Indians are a proud people fighting to abolish the stereotypical image that has dogged them for too long. Poverty is an on-going problem. Alcohol addiction remains a problem of tragic proportions that's being fought in the schools and through recovery programs. Alcohol and drug-free pow-wows are the rule rather than the exception.

Visitors are welcome at pow-wows. A pow-wow will likely serve as your introduction to reservation life. People will be dressed in colorful regalia (outfit is an acceptable term, but costume is not). Each person's regalia has special cultural and religious significance. You will meet friendly people who will treat you with courtesy. But you may sense a cultural barrier, much as you would when visiting any foreign country. It takes time to get to know Native People, but once you are accepted they are warm friends.

■ Plains Folk

Smile lines are etched deeply in their suntanned faces. You sense an almost ingenuous friendliness upon meeting these ranchers and farmers and their families – an honest, open friendliness honed by long dusty miles between farms and towns.

If the traditional rural values of honesty and integrity, of making do and cobbling together, are alive in any corner of the US, they surely are here. Ask a plains dweller why Montana is called the last best place and he'll likely give credit to the ranch and farm families who hold it together.

Grain farmers till and harvest hundreds of acres with computerized tractors boasting air-conditioned and heated cabs. Ranchers are as apt to herd cattle and ride fencelines on ATVs as on horseback. Pickup trucks are indispensible and come in all guises, from battered, beat up and held together with baling wire to late models sporting chrome wheels and extenda-cabs. Every pickup has a coating of fine road dust, a dog or two in the bed, and a driver sporting a 10-gallon hat.

Farm and ranch families live in comfortable homes equipped with the latest in household gadgetry. Yet, they retain spiritual ties to forebears who literally coaxed a living from the soil with their bare hands and raised families in flimsy shacks or drafty log cabins. Identification with the heartache and hardship that rode in with the homesteading bust is palpable in plains country.

Tractors, ATVs and pickups aside, horses remain central to prairie life. Some tasks, like roping young stock for branding, cannot be accomplished without horses. And folks just plain like 'em. Kids grow up on horseback, learning to rope and barrel race as naturally as city kids learn to shoot baskets. Every crossroads town hosts a rodeo and boys' heroes are more apt to be rodeo champions than basketball greats.

Times Have Changed

The days are pretty well gone when a cowboy could ride his horse into town and tie him outside a saloon without causing a second look from passersby. Wayne Ellsworth found that out one November day when he loped into Great Falls, tied his pony to a succession of parking meters and proceeded to sample the local watering holes. The bemused constabulary took a dim view of the cowpoke's bar-hoofin' spree, but failed to find a law prohibiting parking a pony downtown. They strongly suggested that the pair ride out of town before sundown. Pretty well tanked up by then, Ellsworth treated Great Falls's finest to some blazin'-hot language before he and his horse moseyed off into the sunset.

It's tough to make a living farming or ranching. Some ranchers augment their livelihoods by operating guest ranches on the side or by inviting dudes on cattle drives. Some farmers, thinking city folks may not have a clue as to how a farm works, offer farm tours.

Hometown pride and cohesiveness are integral to the small towns scattered across the plains. Some barely survived the homesteaders' bust. Most maintain cherished historical museums, some quite exceptional, some ho-hum. Each town projects a sense of community that kicks up its heels in 4th of July parades, festivals reflecting their heritage, and the ever-popular rodeos.

The high point of the year for plains families is the county fair, held in late summer. That all-time, all-American institution thrives out here where kids show off their 4-H steers and horses, women still vie to see who makes the best pickles or jellies, girls enter cookie baking contests, and fancy chickens strut their stuff.

▪ Mountain Dwellers

Mountain dwellers, and that includes residents of most of Montana's larger cities, often grouse about over-crowding. No surprise there. Plains people are spread as thinly as flowers on a desert, but residents of the state's mountainous third often feel downright cramped, especially at the height of the summer tourist season. Mountain country is irresistibly attractive to outlanders with a wanna-be Montanans complex. Until fairly recently, only weathered log cabins leaning thataway blended into the contours of slopes and draws. Now raw new log houses perch on hillsides like so many interlopers. The two extremes make strange companions. I wonder how many hard winters will pass before the newcomers and their owners weather as well as their humble counterparts. Or will protective coatings keep them ever raw?

Formerly self-contained small towns like Belgrade, a ramble down I-90 from Bozeman, are being transformed into bedroom communities complete with bland housing developments and trendy shops.

Montana's city folk are pretty much like city folk elsewhere. With a difference. Others tend to look toward the city center for relaxation and entertainment. Montana's city dwellers look outward. Ask a resident of, say, Missoula or Helena, what aspect of the city he or she most enjoys. Eleven out of a dozen will cite the close proximity of hiking trails, lakes or fly fishing streams. Not that music and the performing arts go unappreciated. Some cities support active arts communities.

At one time, gold was heavily mined in Montana's mountain country. Today's motherlode is visitors. Tourism being Montana's number two industry, many mountain dwellers make their livings from some aspect of it. Every town, no matter how small, boasts shops featuring Montana souvenirs, wild huckleberry products, and items bearing images of bears and moose. Most souvenirs are in good taste. The array of imaginatively rustic items, many hand fashioned, is truly staggering. The output of Montana's talented artists is also impressive.

Like anywhere, you'll come across a few people who regard visitors as nothing more than cash cows. But most take a genuine interest in the people who entrust their vacations to them. Sharing the places that make their hearts sing is their privilege. Some hosts are relative newcomers to

Montana, but the majority are Montanans born and bred. Montana's mountain country is beautiful and picturesque, a place of river-scored valleys and calendar-art ranch spreads displayed against craggy mountains. Working ranches were established in mountain valleys such as the Deer Lodge and Beaverhead well over 100 years ago. Their modern counterparts are apt to be guest ranches. Outfitters and guides are as thick in these mountain communities as needles on a larch tree. Especially fly fishing guides. Robert Redford's *A River Runs Through It* put Montana at the top of every fly fisher's dream stream list. Sometimes, it seems you could cross the Blackfoot River by stepping from one dory to another. I wouldn't be surprised to learn that the Madison spawns fly fishers like river waters do trout. That makes the choices more difficult. Many guides claim to know secret fishing spots where solitude is guaranteed. Some really do.

AUTHOR TIP *Montana's licensed outfitters have increased so rapidly over the past few years that the state has placed a moratorium on new licenses. Prospective licensees must now wait until a slot opens up due to an outfitter's retirement or death. If an outfitter or a guide in his employ baits a hook or shoots a bullet, he or she must be licensed by the Montana Board of Outfitters. No license is required for guides leading river, hiking, horsepacking or other types of trips that don't entail fishing or hunting.*

Montana's mountain people feel a deep affinity with the place they call home. Most appreciate visitors who exhibit a sincere desire to learn more about the country they love.

How to Use this Book

Montana's size defies a whole gulp approach. With that in mind, this book is organized around six travel regions delineated by Travel Montana, the state tourist organization. Each reflects the geographical and cultural characteristics of a portion of this varied state. However, logic sometimes falters. The travel regions being predicated on zig-zagging county lines rather than on mountain ranges or rivers, these natural features sometimes overlap regional boundaries. For example, both Custer Country and Yellowstone Country can logically claim the Pryor Mountains National Wild Horse Range, and both do.

This book's chapters are arranged in a sequence reflecting the arbitrary supposition that most visitors driving to Montana would enter from the east via I-94. So we begin with Custer Country before heading westward through southern Montana to Yellowstone and Gold West Countries. We swing north to Glacier Country before traveling east to Charlie Russell and Missouri River Countries.

■ Custer Country

Custer Country occupies southeast Montana and is accessed via two interstate highways. I-94 enters Montana from North Dakota, west of Glendive. I-90 enters Montana some 20 miles north of Sheridan, Wyoming and scoots across the Crow Indian Reservation. Three major airlines, Delta, Northwest and United, serve Billings. The Yellowstone River flows through the region from west to east. Custer Country includes **Billings**, Montana's most populous city with some 86,000 residents, and **Miles City**, the self-styled Cowboy Capital of Montana.

Points of interest include the **Northern Cheyenne and Crow Indian Reservations, Little Bighorn Battlefield National Monument**, and **Bighorn Canyon National Recreation Area**.

■ Yellowstone Country

Yellowstone Country claims the slim slice of **Yellowstone National Park** falling within Montana. The principle access route is east-west I-90. Or enter from Yellowstone Park, traveling northward through the scenic Gallatin Valley via

Beartooth Highway from Red Lodge to Yellowstone National Park.

US 191, or through the gorgeous Paradise Valley via US 89. **Bozeman**, the region's largest city, is served by Delta and Northwest Airlines. Yellowstone Country's northern half is rolling rangeland punctuated by the **Crazy Mountains** in the **Gallatin National Forest**. The **Absaroka Mountain Range** and numerous rivers and wilderness areas pack the southern half. Some of Yellowstone Country is in the **Custer National Forest**, but the majority of the public lands between I-90 and Yellowstone National Park are in the Gallatin National Forest.

Points of interest include **Hailstone and Halfbreed National Wildlife Refuges**, the confluence of the Jefferson, Madison, and Gallatin Rivers at **Missouri Headwaters State Park**, the sky-high **Beartooth Highway** linking Red Lodge and Cooke City, and **Greycliff Prairie Dog Town**.

■ Gold West Country

Gold West Country is a brawny place of mountains, valleys and rivers. It borders Idaho on the south and thrusts northward to nudge the huge **Scapegoat/Bob Marshall Wilderness Areas**. I-90 makes a northwesterly tack across the region. I-15 enters from Idaho south of Dillon. It streaks northward to **Butte** and **Helena**, Montana's capitol city. Both cities are served by Delta and Northwest Airlines. The **Madison**, a world renowned fly fishing stream, flows through Gold West Country from Hebgen Lake and Yellowstone. The area is also scored by the **Big Hole**, **Beaverhead** and numerous other rivers. Points of interest reflecting the region's Gold West moniker include the gold rush town of **Bannack** and the historic **Grant Kohrs Ranch** at Deer Lodge.

■ Glacier Country

Glacier Country was named for **Glacier National Park** in the region's far north. Glacier Country shares the **Bitterroot Range** with Idaho and borders British Columbia on the north. A "thumb" of land extends southward to include the trendy **Bitterroot Valley**. I-90 crosses the region, taking a northwesterly tack into Idaho after looking in on **Missoula**, Montana's most eclectic city. Several scenic highways wind north from I-90, following natural valley contours. Delta and Northwest Airlines serve Missoula. Amtrak serves Glacier National Park and several communities between the Park and the Idaho border. Soaring mountains, pleasant valleys and deep blue lakes characterize Glacier Country. The region includes the **Blackfeet and Flathead Indian Reservations**, popular **Flathead Lake** and the adjoining **Bob Marshall**,

Scapegoat and **Great Bear Wildernesses**. Numerous points of interest, recreational opportunities and guest ranches reflect the wild and historic features of Montana's most visited region.

■ Charlie Russell Country

Charlie Russell Country vies with Custer Country as Montana's most spacious region. Sandwiched between Glacier and Missouri River Countries, it brushes up against Alberta and Saskatchewan. Prairies dominate the landscape. The **Little Belt, Big Belt, Bears Paw, Highwood** and **Big Snowy Mountains** thrust abruptly skyward – islands in the prairie. I-15 heads northward from Helena to **Great Falls** before continuing on to Alberta. State highways link Great Falls, Russell Country's largest city, with **Lewistown** and **Havre**. Great Falls is served by Delta and Northwest Airlines.

The excitement of the Old West is reflected in this region named for Charlie Russell, the artist whose paintings preserved the spirit of that chapter in Montana's history.

Scored by the Missouri River, the region includes numerous Lewis and Clark landmarks. The **Rocky Boy and Fort Belknap Indian Reservations** are in Russell Country. The **Lewis and Clark National Historic Trail Interpretive Center** in Great Falls and historic **Fort Benton** are paramount among the region's many historic attractions.

■ Missouri River Country

Missouri River Country, Montana's most remote and least visited region, is a seemingly endless expanse of high plains edged by Bad Lands spilling over from North Dakota and by Saskatchewan on the north. No interstates here, just narrow state highways. **Glasgow**, **Wolf Point** and **Sidney**, the largest city with some 5,100 residents, are served by Big Sky, a regional feeder airline.

Almost half of the Missouri River, where it crosses this region, has been dammed to create sprawling **Fort Peck Reservoir**. The **Fort Peck Indian Reservation** lies northeast of the reservoir. Points of interest include the **Medicine Lake National Wildlife Refuge** and the impressive **Fort Peck Dam**.

■ Chapter Organization

Each chapter begins with an introduction and a run-down of the region's history, culture, topography and climate. This is followed by *Getting*

Around, designed to give you a fix on the region's travel basics, scenic highways and byways and what to look for, or to watch out for, along the way. *Getting Around* also includes *Information Sources* with contact numbers for chambers of commerce, US Department of Agriculture Forest Service ranger district offices and other helpful contacts.

Touring sections elaborate on the routes outlined in *Getting Around*. Museums, historic sites, natural history and wildlife-watching sites and other points of interest are highlighted.

Subsequent sections describe specific adventures in each region. These include options for both independent travel and guided adventures. Fishing outfitters and guides licensed by the Montana Board of Outfitters are listed. This book also includes guides who lead a variety of other adventures, such as river, horseback, horsepack, hiking, cattle drives and others. Also listed are guest ranches, with both working cattle and dude ranches.

The following are brief descriptions of the adventure categories included in this book and what they may include.

Adventures on Foot

Hiking & Backpacking

 Montana's extensive national forests and wilderness areas provide virtually limitless opportunities for On Foot adventures, both independent and guided. This category will clue you in on how to locate trails that fit your interests and abilities. Enjoying the state's fabulous natural beauties on foot is Montanans' favorite recreational activity.

A wide variety of trails traverse terrain ranging from mountains laced with silver streams to prairies carpeted with wildflowers. Montana's epochal history strides alongside. Constant companions are that amazingly wide and changeable Big Sky and achingly beautiful vistas unfolding at each bend in the trail. Wild animals are never far away. You may come face to face with a moose or grazing elk, complete with natural hatracks, when you least expect it. Or glimpse a curious mountain goat watching you from a craggy outcropping. So varied is the wildlife along Montana's trails that you hardly know whether to look down, up, or sideways.

Montana's hundreds, maybe thousands, of miles of trails are as diverse as the strenuous Continental Divide National Scenic Trail and Great Falls' paved River's Edge Trail. Some are easy paths of a mile or two, others strenuous multi-day wilderness adventures requiring specialized equipment and finely honed mountaineering skills. Trails to suit every taste and fitness level fall between these extremes. It's impossible to list all of them. This book includes a cross-section of both well known and little known trails for all ability levels and information on obtaining helpful brochures and purchasing topographical and/or trail maps.

AUTHOR TIP *Trails or portions of trails may be closed or impass-able from time to time due to avalanches, land-slides or other natural causes. Some forest roads and trails may be closed to certain kinds of traffic on a temporary basis. Your hike will be more enjoy-able if you first inquire about closings and other trail conditions at the local ranger district office. Forest Service personnel are there to help you. Make use of them. Ask questions, no matter how hesitant you may be to display your ignorance. No question or concern about back country travel lacks merit.*

Purchasing a topographical map of your area of interest is money well spent. Once available free at ranger district offices, these maps now cost a few dollars.

Travel With Respect

Treat Indian reservations as you would any privately owned land. Permission to use tribal land is a privilege. Each reservation's tribal council determines rules and regulations pertaining to non-Indian land use. Thus, hiking and camping regulations vary from reservation to reservation. Some areas are designated for tribal use only. If you wish to hike on a reservation, you must first contact the tribal office for a permit or permission. Discuss the area in which you wish to hike with the tribal representative on duty, making sure you understand which areas may be off-limits. Tribal office addresses and phone numbers are listed in Information Sources and in regional chapters of this book.

Special Concerns

- Be sure to match your abilities to the trail, then stay on it. Don't take chances. Hiking alone is not a bright idea. Never hike alone in grizzly or mountain lion country. That trans-lates to all of Montana's mountainous areas.

- Be sure to advise someone of your route and when you expect to return. You want to be found if something goes wrong. For-est Service ranger stations seldom offer this service, but someone there may agree to note your name and route. Don't forget to check in with the person with that person on your re-turn. Causing a search party to beat the bushes for you while you quench your thirst at a watering hole is a serious no no. Paying the search and rescue bill might be the least of your worries.

■ Most short trails are boot-worn and well marked. Even so, it's easy to get lost. On long back country trails you can get off the trail and lose your sense of direction in a heartbeat. A compass is essential. Make careful preparations, covering all possible bases, before venturing into a wilderness area.

■ Altitude sickness is no fun – it can even be fatal. If you live at a low altitude, take a day to become accustomed to Montana's 3,000- to 10,000-foot elevations before even thinking about hiking that trail. Mountain trails seem to be all uphill when you are out of condition. Make sure your fitness level matches the activity you have in mind. Wear sturdy, waterproof, broken-in hiking boots with lug soles over two pairs of socks, preferably wool. Blisters have spoiled many a hiking trip. I've seen people on trails wearing sneakers, even flip-flops. They're the ones who are carried down on stretchers.

■ Even if you're off on a day-hike on a sunny summer morning, be sure to pack a rain poncho and basic cold weather gear. Every year, hikers become lost or caught short of trail's end at sundown. Nights are cold in the mountains, sometimes dipping to freezing even in July. Never hit the trail without sufficient water to see you through. A gallon per day per person is a good rule. Don't drink from a stream, no matter how sparkling clean it looks. Chances are it contains the microscopic critters that cause *giardia*, a nasty intestinal illness that lays you low and lingers long after you return home. Pack food and water for a couple of days longer than you expect to remain out.

■ Only experienced back country hikers with solid orienteering and survival skills should backpack into the Bob Marshall/Great Bear/Scapegoat Wilderness on their own. This also goes for the Absaroka-Beartooth Wilderness. Don't overestimate your back country skills. It may be preferable to hire an experienced back country guide or to join a hiking tour.

Rock Climbing

Montana is rock climbers' heaven. The prime climbing areas are concentrated in the mountainous western third of the state. Rock climbing is an extremely dangerous sport. Only experienced climbers and novice climbers under the tutelage of experienced mountaineers and/or rock climbing guides need apply.

This writer has, and/or does, engage in most of the adventure categories included in this book. An exception is rock climbing. I have no intention of scaling the bare face of any mountain over six feet high. For that reason, this book's rock climbing coverage does not include technical details. Travel region chapters include easily accessible climbing areas known to Montana climbers, plus climbing equipment shops and climbing clubs and guides.

The assumption is that readers seeking out these climbing areas will be familiar with rock climbing safety measures and special concerns.

 If you wish to seriously pursue rock climbing in Montana, I suggest you obtain a copy of *The Rock Climber's Guide to Montana*, edited by Randall Green (see *Bibliography*).

Caving

Montana has almost 300 caves. Though most lack significant decorations, some do boast ice formations and fanciful crystalline deposits of calcite and gypsum. Guided cave tours are scarce. An exception is **Lewis and Clark Caverns**.

 The majority of these caves should be approached only by experienced cavers. This book lists guided cave tours and caves suitable for casual exploration. Serious cavers are advised to obtain a copy of *Caves of Montana* from the Montana Bureau of Mines & Technology, Attn: Publication Sales, Montana Tech, 1300 W. Park St., Butte, MT 59701-8997; ☎ 406-496-4167.

Rockhounding

Many a rockhound has thought he'd died and gone to heaven in Montana, so varied is the state's wealth of precious, semi-precious and just plain unusual or curious gems, stones and fossils.

The list reads like a jewelers' show window: garnets, amethysts, sapphires, rubies, quartz diamonds. Or like a rock shop's banner: moss agates, jasper, chromite, quartz, selenite crystals. And tons of fossilized plants and creatures.

 Many skeletal dinosaur remains have been found in Custer Country and Missouri River Country.

A word or two about rockhounding ethics is in order before you head out. Observing the rockhound's golden rule should be a given: "treat the land as if it were your own, and leave it as you would like to find it."

Rockhounding on Private Lands

Some additional caveats are in order. Expect to be rockhounding on private, tribal, BLM, US Forest Service or state lands. If on tribal or other private land, it's imperative that you ask permission of the tribal office or landowner and carefully follow any instructions regarding where and where not to search. If on federal or state lands, contact the local BLM, Forest Service or state lands office for pertinent information. All have specific rules and regulations for which you will be held accountable. Contact addresses and phone numbers are listed under Information Sources.

This book's regional chapters will clue you in on where to search for gems, stones and fossils.

 Serious rockhounds may want to purchase a copy of Robert Feldman's *Rockhounding Montana* (see *Bibliography*).

Adventures on Horseback & Travel with Pack Animals

 Horses and mules are as much a part of Montana's cultural heritage as are its diverse peoples. The sturdy, surefooted animals are ideal for trekking and packing into Montana's wilderness areas and national forests. So are llamas. These amiable South American pack animals are used by a handful of Montana guides offering llama-supported treks. On the assumption that few will do so, this book only touches on advice for travelers who trailer their own horses or llamas into Montana. If you do plan on bringing Old Dobbin along, before leaving home contact the appropriate Forest Service Supervisor's office. Getting a fix in advance on equine rules and regulations, plus trail and campground information, will result in more fun for both you and your steed. Forest Service contacts are listed under *Information Sources* (page 67).

Outfitters' pack-supported trips include the option of totally guided multi-day trips or drop treks. On the latter, a guide takes you into an area with a pack string, helps unload your plunder, then returns to take you out at an agreed upon time.

Horses are sometimes available to rent, but guided horseback and pack trips are more common. Montana has no shortage of guides offering horseback and/or pack supported multi-day wilderness trips reflecting a variety of interests such as fishing or photography. Many will customize a trip to your interests.

Selecting a Horseback Guide

Take care in choosing a guide. Horseback guides need not be licensed in Montana unless they double as hunting or fishing guides. Most are experienced professionals, but you may run up against one who takes unnecessary chances or is downright incompetent. Ask if the guide you are considering is bonded and carries liability insurance. Request references from persons who have used his services, then follow up on them. Ask the guide lots of questions, particularly if you are contemplating a multi-day trip. You may want to ask about his policy concerning liquor, especially if it's a family trip.

Some guides offer trail rides and/or dinner rides featuring traditional Western barbeque or Dutch oven fare. Cattle drives and wagon train trips are exciting fun. Most operate in eastern Montana's cattle country.

Most guides provide horses suitable for kids, for novice riders, for experienced riders, and those who fall somewhere in-between.

Be sure to clue your guide in on your riding experience and ability. Be honest. That New England trail ride three years ago didn't make you an experienced rider. You might harbor cowboy aspirations, but reality may rear up as fast as a spirited steed can sashay sideways.

A Cautionary Tale

I still shudder at the memory of a Montana wagon train trip I went on that included the option of riding horseback. I don't know what certain dudes told the guide about their riding abilities, but it sure as shootin' weren't the gospel truth. Everything went along peaceably enough until after chow when someone suggested a ride into the sunset. All hell broke loose when a liquored up numbskull whipped her horse into a flat-out run. The other horses, instinctively aware of their riders' lack of control, seized the moment. Riders tumbled off horses as fast as bad guys in a Hollywood Western. The fallout included broken bones and a woman who couldn't sit down for a week. Even worse, a horse was lamed.

One: Certain guests were less than honest about their riding ability, or lack thereof. Two: The outfitter didn't set up guidelines at the trip's git-go. He failed to control both the wrangler involved in the mêlée and the paying guests. Three: Hard liquor and horseback riding don't mix.

This book sometimes lists horseback and pack trip guides under the region in which they are headquartered, rather than the locations of the trips on offer. This might be the same region, but sometimes a guide headquartered in, say, Bozeman, will offer trips in both Yellowstone and Gold West Country national forests. Trip locations are noted. Cross referencing is a good idea.

Guest and dude ranches featuring horseback riding are listed under *Adventures on Horseback.*

Adventures on Wheels

Back Country Roads

Don't even think about driving a passenger car on many of Montana's Forest Service and remote dirt roads. Even some sports utility vehicles may not cut it.

Sturdy high clearance 4WD vehicles are musts in negotiating most of Montana's unimproved back country Forest Service roads even in dry weather, let alone in wet weather.

Montana, particulary its mountainous areas, has hundreds of miles of roads, some of which have switchbacks and steep grades. Many are minimally maintained, if at all. Some are on the Official Montana Highway Map, others only on topographical maps and Forest Service travel maps covering individual national forests or sections thereof. Unimproved roads and private ranch roads may look similar.

 Most private roads post No Trespassing signs. When in doubt, err on the conservative side by avoiding roads that may be private.

Montana landowners can be prickly as a cactus with an interloper. Request permission if you feel you must enter private land, then be sure to close any gates you open. Nothing raises ranchers' ire faster than cattle straying because some city fella lacked the courtesy to close a gate. Cattle guards confine most free-ranging stock to a rancher's land or sections of BLM grazing land. These are parallel metal rods placed over a ditch or depression at the entrance to grazing areas. If cattle and horses were to cross these guards, their feet would slip between the rods. Driving over a cattle guard will alert you to the fact that you may encounter free-ranging cattle, i.e., cattle in the road. Slow down and drive cautiously. If mama cow is on one side of the road and her calf is on the other, it's a good bet that baby will cross to mama's side at the exact moment your vehicle approaches.

Off-Highway Vehicles

Some US Forest Service and BLM lands include trails open to motorcycles, ATVs and other off-highway vehicles (OHVs). Whether or not to allow OHVs on portions of the Continental Divide Trail is a hotly debated topic. Most hiking trails are closed to OHVs. Most ranger districts encourage OHV users to ride on Forest Service and logging roads. Be alert to closures. A chain with a "Closed" sign indicates that a road is closed to mechanized vehicles due to lack of maintenance, to protect certain animals in the area or for other reasons. All types of wheeled vehicles are prohibited in designated wilderness areas.

Regional chapters of this book identify some trails open to OHVs. Check with the local Forest Service or BLM office for current trail restrictions and conditions.

All OHVs driven on Forest Service and BLM roads must be registered and display a current OHV decal. A non-resident using an OHV that is not registered in his or her home state must purchase a non-resident temporary-use permit.

Off-Road! Montana, available at Montana Fish, Wildlife and Parks offices, includes valuable information on OHV regulations and permits.

Mountain Biking

Most Forest Service trails are multi-use, open to mountain bikes as well as hikers and horses. Exceptions are steep mountain trails unsuited to bikes. This book identifies many of the state's best mountain biking trails. Before setting out, stop at the applicable ranger district office to purchase a topo map and to obtain updated trail information.

Montana's best biking trails aren't trails at all, but rather scenic byways and little used country roads linking small towns.

The Montana to Mexico Great Divide Mountain Bike Trail runs through Montana from Glacier Park to the Idaho line. The trail is a succession of dirt roads and single-track trails roughly paralleling the Continental Divide.

Guided mountain biking trips are listed in this book, usually in the chapter covering the region where the trip begins or takes place. The **Adventure Cycling Association**, headquartered in Missoula, is an excellent mountain biking resource. 150 Pine St., Missoula, MT 59807-8308; ☎ 406-721-1776, fax 406-721-8754.

Adventures on Water

The Rivers

The Headwaters State boasts more icy-cold snowmelt rivers than 'most any other state. All feed into North America's major drainages.

Lewis and Clark's expedition put the Missouri, the Yellowstone, Clark's Fork of the Columbia and the Marias on the national historical map. More recent exposure has highlighted the pleasures of rafting and fly fishing the Blackfoot, the Gallatin and a galaxy of other rivers.

With 81 rivers, Montana satisfies every level of riparian adventure. And it's hard to ignore most rivers' soul-satisfying beauty.

AUTHOR TIP

As this book goes to press, the Smith River Gorge and the Upper Missouri National Wild & Scenic River are the only riparian stretches requiring permits for all types of recreation. Contact the Montana Department of Fish, Wildlife & Parks for permit info (see page 66).

Montana's Stream Access Law (H.B. #265 - 1985) states that all surface water capable of recreational use may be so used by the public without regard to ownership of the land underlying the waters, and that recreationists may use rivers and streams up to the high water mark. Flood plains next to streams are considered to be above the ordinary high water mark and are not open to recreation without permission from the owners.

Crossing private land, including Indian reservation lands, without permission is prohibited. Public river access sites are identified by signs depicting a fish approaching a hook, or by signs indentifying a boat ramp or raft/kayak put-in site. Overnight camping is permitted at many of these sites.

A booklet summarizing the 1985 Stream Access Law is available from any Montana Department of Fish, Wildlife and Parks office.

Whitewater Rafting

Montana's rivers splashed onto the whitewater rafting map in 1993, when *The River Wild* hit movie theatres. Suddenly, everyone wanted to do what Meryl Streep did. Few people realize that the ride through the infamous Gauntlet depicted in the film was a cinematographer's creation involving a helicopter and invisible harnesses, allowing them to run the unrunnable Kootenai Falls.

Montana has comparatively few serious whitewater rivers. However, stretches of the Kootenai, the Yaak, the Middle Fork of the Flathead, the Gallatin, the Stillwater, the Clarks Fork through Alberton Gorge, the Boulder feeding the Yellowstone, and the Madison kick up enough Class III to V rapids to raise rafters' and kayakers' adrenalin levels.

Rating Rapids

Rapids are rated on a I through VI scale. **Class I** means relaxed floating. **Class II** means gentle waves that a savvy kid can negotiate in a kayak. **Class III** rapids are considered intermediate with some high-splash waves. **Class IV** rapids get serious, requiring a knowledge of river dynamics. **Class V** rapids are dead serious, requiring advance scouting by expert river runners. **Class VI** rapids are flat-out unrunnable. Most rivers' rapids and character change according to weather conditions and time of year. Flows increase in spring, when snow runoff is high.

Experienced kayakers and river rafters can enjoy Montana's whitewater on their own. Half- or full-day guided whitewater trips are available. Some guides offer pack-in/float-out packages or combination whitewater/ horseback trips. This book lists whitewater guides under regional chapters.

Selecting a River Guide

River guides need not be licensed in Montana. Most are reliable, experienced river runners, but there remains the occasional exception. Exercise care in choosing a whitewater river guide. Guides with proven track records are generally your best bet. Ask for references, then follow up on them. Ask lots of questions. Be especially picky if a member of your party has never run a river, is under 10 or elderly.

Floating & Canoeing

Most of Montana's rivers are ideal for lazy-day floating and canoeing. The Yellowstone, the Madison, the confluence of the Jefferson, Madison and Gallatin, the Missouri and many others offer delightful floating and canoeing. Usually anything goes: rafts, tubes, canoes, dories. Guided float and canoe trips are available on some rivers. Several river guides offer multi-day trips on the Upper Missouri National Wild & Scenic River. Popularized by the current Lewis and Clark bicentennial hoopla, these trips trace a portion of the explorers' route in reverse.

AUTHOR TIP *Information on self canoeing and floating most of Montana's rivers is included in regional chapters. Surprisingly few canoe and kayak rentals are available. Bring your own craft if you are seriously into canoeing or kayaking. Local inquiries may turn up someone who will agree to shuttle you back to your car from a take-out point.*

River guides and the types of trips they offer are listed under the travel regions in which they operate.

Fishing Mechanics

There's nothing new about fishing Montana's rivers and streams; men and women have pulled glistening trout onto grassy banks since time out of mind. Early adventure travelers had no need for exaggerated fish stories. This has changed very little.

The Madison, Blackfoot, Big Hole, Beaverhead, Jefferson and a swash of other rivers and streams offer fabulous fly fishing. Lakes, reservoirs and warm water rivers also offer great fishing.

Fishing Licenses & Regulations

Montana's fishing rules and regulations are quite simple:

- Non-residents age 15 and older must obtain a license to fish. The licensing season runs from March 1 through the following February. Non-residents under age 15 must obtain a fishing license unless he or she fishes in the company of an adult license holder.

- The fish take limit for an unlicensed youth and accompanying adult combined may not exceed the limit for one adult. A non-resident of any age may obtain a fishing license and be entitled to a legal take limit.

- A conservation license is required before a fishing license may be issued. License fees are subject to change, but as this book goes to print the charge for a non-resident conservation license is $5. A non-resident seasonal fishing license costs $45. A non-resident two-day fishing license costs $10. Residents pay $4 for a conservation license and $13 for a fishing license.

Conservation licenses and fishing licenses may be purchased at any Montana Fish, Wildlife and Parks office and at sporting goods and other stores designated as licensing agents.

AUTHOR TIP *This book describes fishing opportunities under regional chapters, but it is imperative that anglers obtain current copies of Montana Fishing Regulations and the supplementary Montana Fishing Guide, available free from Montana Department of Fish, Wildlife and Parks (see Informatin Sources) or wherever fishing licenses are sold. FWP's hotline has information on a variety of recreational topics. Charge: $1.50 per minute. ☎ 1-900-225-5397.*

The Montana Department of Fish, Wildlife and Parks maintains more than 300 pubic fishing access sites identified by roadside signs depicting a fish about to grab a hook. Additional fishing access sites are maintained by the Bureau of Land Management and National Forest ranger districts. FWP publishes a free brochure listing fishing access sites.

Whirling Disease

Whirling disease is afflicting young salmonoids in every Western state except Arizona. The often fatal ailment is caused by a microscopic parasite that attacks the cartilage of young fish, causing deformities rendering the fish unable to feed. The name is derived from the tail-chasing motions of stricken fish. This disease is every fishing outfitter's worst nightmare. Rainbow trout are the most vulnerable, while bull trout seem to resist the disease. Whirling disease is present in numerous Montana rivers, prompting changes in fishing regulations limiting the number and size of trout that may be taken in certain streams. Throw away that outdated Montana Fishing Regulations booklet, obtain a current one and read it through. So far, the Whirling Disease Foundation and Montana Fish, Wildlife and Parks biologists are keeping ahead of the disease.

Some species of fish in some waters are catch and release only. Catch and release regulations are subject to annual changes. Many fly fishing guides advocate releasing fish whether mandated or not.

Catch and Release Guidelines

- Do not play a fish to total exhaustion.
- Keep the fish in the water as much as possible when handling and removing the hook. Resist the temptation to hold the fish out of water for more than a few seconds while you photograph and admire it; two minutes is the maximu.

■ Remove the hook gently without squeezing the fish or putting your fingers in its gills. If the fish is deeply hooked, cut the line.

■ Release the fish only after its equilibrium is maintained, gently holding the fish upright facing upstream and moving it gently back and forth in the water. Release the fish in quiet water close to where it was hooked. Larger fish take longer to recover after being caught and handled.

AUTHOR TIP *Catch and release is no fun for the fish. Fish are vertebrates with nervous systems similar to ours. This means they feel pain. A fish's mouth parts are especially nerve-rich. A caught and released fish is severely, often fatally, traumatized. One person's sport is another's anathema. My personal ethic abhores killing any creature except for food or clothing, but your ethic may differ from mine.*

Fly Fishing

The gentle art of fly fishing has long been practiced on the Madison and assorted other rivers and streams. Now, thanks (or no thanks, according to some Montana anglers) to the film, *A River Runs Through It*, fly fishing is big business.

It's a good idea to hire a guide to acquaint you with the best holes and least crowded streams. At the very least, drop in at a fly shop to inquire about local conditions. Some outfitters have exclusive access to privately owned streams and spring creeks.

If you could line Montana's fly fishing guides up side by side, they'd likely stretch along both banks of the Gallatin all the way from Gardiner to Livingston. An exaggeration, but close enough to the mark to be confusing.

 CAUTION *So many fishing guides have applied to the Montana Board of Outfitters for licensing that a moratorium has been declared on new licensees. This and other factors have spawned a breed of rogue outfitters, i.e., unlicensed guides operating on the shady side of the law. Contact the Montana Board of Outfitters, Department of Commerce, 111 N. Jackson, Helena, MT 59620; ☎ 406-444-3738, if in doubt regarding the status of a given guide. It may also be helpful to request a copy of the Board's current directory.*

This book lists fishing outfitters in the chapters covering the regions in which they are headquartered. Some fish waters in several regions. Most fly fishing outfitters freelance, guiding individuals or small parties by the day. Others operate in conjunction with fly shops or fishing lodges, ranging from back woodsy to posh. Some offer other types of accommodations. Lodgings catering exclusively to anglers are listed under *Fishing*.

Selecting a Fishing Outfitter

It makes sense to request references and to ask lots of questions in order to assure that a given outfitter can deliver the angling experience of your dreams. Some fly fishing outfitters guide experienced anglers only. Others stress their willingness to guide novices. Some offer fly fishing lessons. Make sure to choose the right outfitter for your level of expertise.

Lake Lore

Montana's mountain lakes are legion. Many, carved by retreating glaciers, appear as sparkling blue as they did in the mountain man era. They could have been lapping for eons in mountain cirques, awaiting your visit. Some are stocked with trout. Others have no fish. See *Adventures on Foot* in the chapters covering Yellowstone, Glacier and Gold West Country for tips on finding these gems.

Flathead Lake is the largest natural freshwater lake west of the Mississippi. Enfolded by the soaring snow-clad peaks of the Salish, Swan and Mission Mountains, the lake's transcendant beauty is legendary. This popular resort lake affords a big splash of aquatic fun. This book's chapter on Glacier Country lists Flathead and other regional lakes' marinas, charter fishing boats and state parks. **Fort Peck Lake** is to eastern Montana what Flathead Lake is to Glacier Country. The Fort Peck Dam holds back the lake, which extends for 135 miles through Missouri River Breaks country. This lake is famous for record walleye catches. Turn to the chapter on Missouri River Country for fishing information and a list of Fort Peck Lake fishing outfitters.

Alcohol and water don't mix when you drink the former while recreating on the latter. Numerous water-related injuries and deaths are annually attributed to alcohol consumption. Wait for down time in camp to quaff that beer. And always wear a life jacket no matter how calm the water. It won't do you any good if it's in the boat while you're flopping helplessly in the water. Always wear a life jacket when water skiing or operating personal watercraft.

Adventures on Snow

Snow begins wafting across the Rockies from the Pacific Northwest and fluttering down from Alberta in late October or early November. By December, thick sheets of the white stuff howl across the plains, clog mountain passes and cloak high peaks. On clear winter days, the peaks appear to be encrusted with millions of glittering diamonds. Sunrises set them afire with scintillating shades of pink and red. Winter packs a big-shouldered wallop in Montana, and offers big-shouldered fun.

Downhill Skiing

Montana's 14 downhill ski resorts are conveniently sprinkled across the state's mountainous regions. Some, like **Big Sky Ski Resort** in Yellowstone Country, project as glitzy a profile as Utah's Park City or Idaho's Sun Valley. Big Sky, The Big Mountain and Bridger Bowl appear regularly among *Snow Country Magazine*'s 50 best ski areas in North America. Others, like **Bear Paw Ski Bowl**, owned and operated by the Chippewa-Cree Business Committee of Rocky Boys Reservation, are refreshingly laid back and inexpensive. Some, like **Big Mountain** in Glacier Country, are destination resorts. Others, like **Marshall Mountain** near Missoula, are spur-of-the-moment day-use areas. All welcome snow boarders. Openings vary according to snow conditions, but most open by mid-December or earlier and are in full swoosh by Christmas.

This book describes Montana's downhill ski resorts and includes the information you need to make an informed choice.

Cross-Country Skiing

Montana's topography offers ideal cross-country skiing and snowshoeing conditions. Glacier and Yellowstone National Parks, nine national forests and 12 wilderness areas, plus several privately owned cross-country ski resorts have hundreds of miles of groomed and ungroomed trails.

There's lots of varied terrain. Difficulty ratings range from easy to most difficult. Trail lengths vary from 2.5 km, taking a couple of hours to cover, to mountain touring trails requiring a day or longer to traverse.

Most trails include inclines of varying degrees, especially in the mountains. Some trails penetrate the back country, where snow conditions are often unstable and avalanches are a possibility in certain areas.

Preparing for Cross-Country Skiing

■ It is strongly recommended that you check with the local National Forest ranger station before striking out on back country trails. Apprise someone of your itinerary and when you expect to return.

■ Be prepared for wide weather variations, with temperatures swinging from below zero into the 30s. Conditions can and do change rapidly.

■ Be sure to dress warmly and carry high energy foods. Don't wear cotton, which retains moisture. Do wear waterproof outerwear.

■ Be realistic about matching your ability level to the proposed route. Wear a ski mask and wrap a warm scarf around your neck.

■ Carry along a basic first aid kit, a compass, a knife, a flashlight, matches and food to last a couple of days. Be sure to include signal devices: a SOS transceiver, flares, a mirror and a whistle. Taking sensible precautions when skiing in Montana's back country can literally mean the difference between life and death. Don't ski alone. Mountain country is avalanche country. Let someone know where you are going and when you plan on returning

Avalanche conditions are dependent on air temperature and snow conditions. Conditions are ripe when a heavy snowfall covers a layer of snow that has melted on top and then frozen. Avalanche injuries and fatalities occur in Montana every winter. See *Snowmobiling* (below) for further avalanche precautions. This book will clue you in on Montana's cross-country ski trail options. Resorts and lodges catering to cross-country skiers are listed under *Adventures on Snow*.

Snowmobiling

Montana boasts 3,700 miles of groomed snowmobile trails through valleys and over mountain passes, mostly on public lands. That's not counting ungroomed areas on public land. Some designated trails cross pri-

Snowmobiling Huckleberry Pass Trail, outside of Lincoln.

vate land. Montana's snowmobiling season generally runs from mid-December to April. Expect powder early in the season. Hardpacking occurs as the season progresses.

Snowmobiles riding on public lands must be registered and display a decal. Snowmobiles registered in another state are not required to show a Montana registration decal. A non-resident, temporary-use permit is available for unregistered snowmobiles by contacting Montana Fish, Wildlife and Parks Department at ☎ 406-444-2535. Snowmobilers riding on plowed streets or roads open to snowmobile traffic must have a driver's license or possess a Montana-approved snowmobile safety certificate. Youngsters under driving age must travel with a person 18 years of age or older.

Taking sensible precautions when snowmobiling in Montana can literally mean the difference between life and death. Mountainous areas of heavy snowfall are not to be trifled with. Don't snowmobile alone. Mountain country is avalanche country. More than one life has been saved because riders have had the foresight to wear SOS transceivers, also referred to as avalanche beacons, and to carry probe poles and shovels. Let someone know where you will be riding and when you plan to return.

Sometimes a snowmobile can stay on top of the snow and ride out of a slide. But don't bet on it. If your sled begins to tumble, get away from it and make swimming motions.

It's a given that you should wear an insulated one-piece wind- and water-repellent snowmobile suit, gaiters, boots and gloves. Wear a ski mask-type knitted hat under your helmet and wrap a warm scarf around your neck. Carry along extra fuel, basic tool and first aid kits, a compass, a knife, a flashlight, food to last a couple of days, matches and possibly a spirit lamp or stove. And be sure to include signal devices such as the above mentioned transceiver, flares, mirror and whistle.

Using Beacons

Snowmobiles can trigger avalanches, so carrying a transceiver/beacon is a must. But just carrying a transceiver isn't enough. Practice using it well before heading out so you can activate it within seconds of a slide. Set it on transmit while skiing or snowmobiling so that if you are buried by a slide the device will signal your location to rescuers. When searching for someone, set it on receive. Time is vital to avalanche survival. If a victim is uncovered within 15 minutes, there is a 92% chance of survival. Chances plunge with every additional minute under the snow.

This book describes Montana's snowmobile areas and trails and lists snowmobile rental and service shops. Resorts and lodges catering to snowmobilers are listed under the *Adventures on Snow* sections.

Ice Fishing

Come winter, cold-hardy Montanans exchange fly rods for set lines. Lakes generally freeze over in December and remain frozen until March. This book offers tips on ice fishing and identifies the best ice fishing lakes.

Good ice fishing is available on several Blackfeet Reservation lakes. Anglers must obtain a tribal fishing permit, a tribal recreation and conservation tag and a ice house permit. Similar permits are necessary to ice fish lakes on other Indian reservations.

Follow Montana Fish, Wildlife and Parks regulations for licenses to ice fish non-reservation lakes and reservoirs.

Dog Sledding & Sleigh Rides

Dog sledding is available in some areas, particularly in Glacier Country. Ditto, horse drawn sleigh rides. This book will steer you to these and other winter adventures.

Wildlife Watching

Birds & Animals

Montana's wildlife is legion. Wildlife viewing areas, both managed and informal, are scattered across the state. These include such varied attractions as the huge **Charles M. Russell National Wildlife Refuge**, pretty **Spring Meadow Lake** inside the Helena city limits, Flathead Lake's **Wild Horse Island**, The **National Bison Range**, the wildly beautiful **Blackfeet Indian Reservation** and many, many more. Some you must drive through. Others welcome hikers, cross-country skiers, bicyclers and canoers. Some permit camping.

Watch for highway signs stating "Wildlife Viewing Area" and depicting white binoculars on a brown background.

A memorable adventure trip can be planned around viewing Montana's changing wildlife scene. The state is roughly divided into four habitats: coniferous forests, lowland river forests, inland marshes and prairie grasslands.

Birders will be struck speechless by the numerous species of songbirds, waterfowl, raptors and migratory birds awaiting identification along streams, on uplands, in forests, marshes and mountains. Canyon Ferry Lake and Rogers Pass afford prime bald eagle watching.

> *The Western meadowlark is Montana's state bird.*

Montana is synomous with wild animals in the minds of many people. You can expect to catch sight of deer, elk, moose, possibly river otter or beaver, black bear, coyote, and pronghorn antelope. You are less likely to see a grizzly bear or a mountain lion. You might be lucky enough to photograph those quintessential Montana animals, bison and prairie dogs. Or perhaps a ferruginous hawk will wing its way into your lens.

This book identifies and describes a passel of wildlife viewing areas in each travel region, how to derive the most enjoyment from them, and the activities permitted in each area.

Flora

Montana's flora are equally fascinating. Many plants that appear to the uneducated eye as merely pretty flowers or tasty berries were, and often continue to be, valued by Native Peoples for food or medicine.

DID YOU KNOW? *Montana's state flower is the bitterroot, familiar as the name of a mountain range, a valley and a river. The lovely pink and white flowers spread across mountain meadows and prairie lands in spring. Though bitter, as the name implies, the Indians have long valued the root as a food and for making bitterroot tea, thought to be good for a variety of ailments. Bitterroot was traditionally dug in May, before the annual pine bark harvest.*

The ponderosa pine, Montana's state tree, once afforded Natives a sweet and nourishing treat. Women peeled the outer bark away from the tree and separated the inner bark, which was eaten like candy. This book identifies varieties of flora in regional chapters.

State Parks

Montana's state parks are mostly concentrated in Yellowstone, Gold West, Glacier and the western part of Charlie Russell Country. However, **Hell Creek State Park** on Fort Peck Lake is a mecca for water sports enthusiasts, and **Makoshika State Park** near Glendive in eastern Montana's Badlands is a must if you are fascinated by prehistoric animal digs.

Many are multi-use parks with campsites that can accommodate RVs. Only one, Finley Point on Flathead Lake, has RV hookups. Some parks have RV dump stations, but most do not and offer dry camping only. Several, such as Chief Plenty Coups State Park on the Crow Indian Reservation, are day-use parks commemorating a facet of Montana's history or cultural heritage. Others, such as Clark's Lookout State Park near

Dillon, reflect the Lewis and Clark Expedition's impact on Montana. Many offer activities and special events in keeping with the park's theme.

Fees/Passes

A small fee, usually 50¢ per person or $4 per vehicle, is charged to visit most state parks' day-use areas. A passport entitling the bearer to a year's unlimited access to all state parks costs residents $20, non-residents $24. Fees are subject to change. Camping fees vary according to services provided but are usually in the $12 to $15 range. Passport holders receive a discount. Camp sites are available on a first-come, first-served basis. Most include a picnic table, a fire ring or grill and parking for one vehicle and an RV.

Special Interest Adventures

Montana's natural and cultural history is incredibly rich and varied. Numerous experts offer adventure trips reflecting their specialized areas of knowledge. These include archaeologists, geologists, Native Americans, paleontologists, historians and botanists.

Whether such tours are conducted in a vehicle, on foot, in canoes or on horseback, this book lists them under *Special Interest Adventures*. Most are listed in the travel regions in which they take place. Those that overlap regions may be listed more than once.

Kid Stuff

KID-FRIENDLY Some of the adventures described in this book are suitable for kids younger than eight. More are not. Therefore, except in rare cases, we'll assume that you won't attempt most of these with your under-eight child. An exception is downhill skiing at resorts offering instruction for young children. Other exceptions might include floating Montana's quieter rivers, short hikes and guest ranch stays. The assumption is that most kids over eight or nine will enjoy the same adventures that their parents do. Of course, there are exceptions – rock climbing for instance.

AUTHOR TIP *Know your child's limitations. Try not to over- or under-estimate his abilities and taste for adventure. Remember that a youngster's idea of adventure may not mesh with yours. Take time to do kid stuff like visiting a water park or town park playground. Relax. Your kids' outdoor interests will evolve as they grow.*

My daughter Amy has accompanied me on fact finding trips since she was quite young. When she was seven, we visited playgrounds across a wide swath of Arkansas and Oklahoma. A couple of years later, she lugged some 25 pounds of rocks home from Alaska. On a plane, yet. The summer Amy turned 11, her obsession was panning for gold. We must have hit every mountain stream in Idaho. A year later, she got into canoeing Northern Saskatchewan's lakes. Now 14, her idea of fun is swimming and horseback riding. She's a fairly typical kid. I learned early on that when I indulged Amy's definition of adventure, she would happily participate in mine.

This guide picks up on especially-for-kids stuff and throws it out for parental perusal. Many adventures, notably horseback trips, river floats and guest ranch visits, have strong appeal for both parents and tagalongs. Just-for-kids stuff adds balance.

Festivals & Special Events

Montanans love parties. The Treasure State's many festivals are super-sized parties. They include everything from chokecherries to rodeos, Rocky Mountain oysters to blue grass in the park, Railroad Days to gold mining hoopla. Lewis and Clark and crew are duly commemorated in these bicentennial years. Some of the most colorful festivals are pow-wows and other events staged by Montana's 11 Indian tribes on the state's seven reservations.

Whatever your taste in festivals may be, this book will clue you in on established annual events statewide.

Pow-Wows

Every Montana Indian reservation presents at least one, sometimes several, large annual pow-wows to which the public is invited. Most tribes hold smaller pow-wows throughout the year. Each Native American college association and public school Indian Education program presents at least one annual pow-wow. Non-Natives are welcome at most pow-wows, but some may be by invitation only. Inquire ahead of time by contacting the reservation's tribal office or the area chamber of commerce. Tribal customs differ, but the following insights and rules of etiquette should be helpful when attending a Montana pow-wow. Visitors seldom look beyond the singing, drumming, dancing and colorful regalia. But every pow-wow embodies a spiritual legacy which should be treated with respect and honor. Pow-wows hold deep meaning for Indian People. They are coming together times for families and friends, times of sharing, times for the mingling of laughter and tears, for strengthening cultural identity. Pow-wows are occasions for Native families to reflect on their traditions and pass them on to their children.

Dancers vie for prize money at many of the larger pow-wows. Others are traditional non-competition pow-wows. Discerning visitors will detect subtle differences between the two. Both include inter-tribal dances open to all. Non-competitive pow-wows generally include a Friendship Dance where everyone is invited to the dance circle whether or not they are wearing regalia. Dancers shake hands as they proceed around the circle. Listen closely to the master of ceremonies; he'll be your guide to understanding what's happening. All collegiate and school pow-wows are drug and alcohol free. Others strive to be, but compliance may falter. Respect for elders is a pow-wow basic. Some tribal pow-wows commemorate a historical event of importance to the tribe. Others are held specifically to honor veterans or other personages. A ceremony honoring veterans customarily follows every pow-wow's Grand Entry.

Regalia generally reflect the dances in which an individual participates. Young women's Fast and Fancy Shawl Dance regalia differs markedly from the sedate Women's Traditional regalia. Men's Grass Dance regalia, the long fringes reflecting waving prairie grasses, is quite unlike Men's Traditional regalia, which may include an eagle feather bustle and staff.

Pow-Wow Etiquette

- Never, ever touch an eagle feather! These feathers have deep religious significance.

- Never touch any part of a dancer's regalia. Many items are sacred to the wearer.

- Never photograph persons in regalia without asking permission. That includes those adorable children.

- A word about your own pow-wow attire. Women should leave the short shorts and halter tops at home. Indian women generally dress very modestly. Female dancers' legs are covered with knee-high moccasins or leggings. Jeans and t-shirts or Western-style shirts are appropriate for both sexes.

Understanding pow-wow basics and observing simple rules of pow-wow etiquette will enhance your enjoyment of Montana's colorful pow-wows.

Where to Stay & Eat

This is an adventure guide. It is not a whistle-stop restaurant and accommodations guide. On the premise that any visitor can find a café, only exceptional eateries and those of special historical interest are included herein. Bed and breakfast inns and historical or unusual lodgings are also listed, as are large motels with swimming pools. In towns offering no alternative, small motels may be included for your convenience.

AUTHOR TIP

A word about deciphering Montana restaurant signage. Gambling machines are legal in Montana. So is drinking. They go together. Unless an eatery's sign indicates that it's a family restaurant, you can expect to find both. Conversely, a sign touting an establishment as a family restaurant doesn't mean it's one of those bland chain eateries. A café can fall somewhere between the two.

Montana's eateries and lodgings include both the expected and the surprising. You'd expect the Old West's steak-and-beans culture to be alive and kicking up its heels. But did you know that you can also enjoy trendy gourmet cuisine in Montana?

Small town cafés generally serve up basic downhome fare, particularly in eastern Montana and in areas less traveled. Pies are right up there with steak in the favorite grub sweepstakes. Most are homemade and delicious. Some touristy eateries feature chow purported to be straight from a chuckwagon, but any self-respecting cowboy would shy away from them. Look for gourmet in trendy towns such as Livingston, in the larger cities, and in more heavily visited regions such as Yellowstone and Glacier.

The same principle goes for lodgings. Log cabin rentals and B&Bs range from basic homesteaders'-style to spendy replicas of country digs depicted in glossy home magazines. The decorating bug has definitely bitten Montana innkeepers. Frequently visited areas are awash in log lodges, guest ranches and fly fishing lodges projecting a self-conscious Wild West image. Some towns boast historic hotels that retain their turn-of-the-century integrity. At the opposite extreme, inexpensive bare-bones hostels afford cheap digs near Glacier National Park and in a few other areas where hiking and mountain biking are popular. Forest Service cabins also provide inexpensive lodgings.

This book attempts to steer you through Montana's dining and lodgings thicket. One of the greatest pleasures of adventuring afield is taking time to become acquainted with the folks who own and manage lodges, B&Bs and eateries.

You can find a bed and a meal in every corner of the state save the wilderness areas. Prices vary according to how popular a given area may be. If you feel stymied, a call to a local chamber of commerce or tourist information center will get you a blizzard of lodgings suggestions and other information – probably more than you really want.

Montana Watering Holes

You won't experience Montana in the raw until you drop in at a cow town saloon on a Saturday night. Folks come in from miles around, duded up in clean jeans and boots. Likely, a local band will be proving the old saw, "if you can't be good, be loud." As the evening wears on and the libations flow, someone or other is sure to get up and sing. A codger and his missus might dance a jig. It's a cinch you won't be strangers for long.

Forest Service Cabins

The US Forest Service rents cabins and former fire lookout towers deep in the national forests. Most are primitive, basically furnished accommodations with wood stoves. Expect to bring your own bedding, cooking utensils and possibly water. Some have horse facilities. Some require minimum or maximum stays. All reflect Montana at its most rugged way-out-West best. Cabins available year-round afford memorable ski-in, ski-out experiences.

Contact any Forest Service office to request a current copy of the *US Forest Service's Northern Region Recreational Cabin and Lookout Directory*, to obtain a cabin permit, and for information on what to bring. National Forest addresses and contact numbers are listed under *Information Sources* at the end of this Introduction (see page 67).

Guest Ranches

Guest ranches offering horseback riding and other activities are listed by region, following *Adventures on Horseback*. These ranches offer riding and lots of it. Some may also have fishing, hiking, cross-country skiing, snowmobiling, visits to local points of interest and/or other outdoor activities. Some are working cattle ranches welcoming guests as a sideline. Guests may be included in cattle roundups, fence mending and other ranch chores. Others are large-scale dude ranches with attendant Western hoopla. Yet others are family-run establishments whose hosts take pleasure in making you feel at home. Many are historic spreads owned by descendants of homesteaders.

Most ranches described in this book include meals and all activities in one price, as opposed to those renting cabins and charging extra for horseback riding and other activities. All sit smack dab in the middle of unimaginable natural splendor.

Choosing a Guest Ranch

When contacting a guest ranch, be sure to ask lots of questions. Does the ranch stress horseback riding to the exclusion of other activities? If not, what other activites are on offer? What level of horseback riding instruction is available? Is instruction/orientation mandatory before guests may go on trail rides? Is there a children's program and/or special kids' activities? If so, for what ages? Some working ranches encourage children to participate in routine chores such as collecting eggs and feeding young animals. You'll think of a wagonload of other questions. Don't be bashful about asking.

Camping

Camping's popularity is on the increase. More and more families are trading in tents for trailers ranging from pop-ups to fifth wheels, for motorhomes ranging from converted vans to fancy bus-type vehicles with diesel pushers.

Montana's numerous public and privately owned campgrounds and RV parks reflect this trend. This is especially true in heavily visited areas such as Glacier, Yellowstone and Gold West Countries. The US Forest Service maintains some exceptionally nice campgrounds. Many state parks run a close second. Most of wide-flung Eastern Montana lacks forest service campgrounds and state parks are scarcer here, too. Some communities compensate for this by offering free overnight RV parking in their city parks.

I use a small motorhome while researching my guide books. I racked up over 10,000 miles for this book, re-visiting Montana's every corner over a three-month period. Where possible, I used free town parks, BLM camping areas and Forest Service and state parks campgrounds. Every third or fourth night I stayed at a privately owned campground if I needed to dump, take on water or do laundry. Sometimes a privately owned campground was the only option. Though traveling only with my dog Licorice, I never felt unsafe.

DID YOU KNOW?

Did you know that those ubiquitous Kampgrounds of America (KOAs) originated in Montana and are headquartered in Billings?

KOAs and other privately owned campgrounds vary widely in quality and character. They also vary in price from a low of about $12 to a wallet-busting $30 for camping *sans* utility hookups in some touristy and metropolitan areas. Prices about halfway between are more common. Forest Service and Glacier National Park campgrounds are bargains, most charging under $12 per night. Holders of Golden Age Passports pay half. You can sometimes camp free at fishing access sites and on BLM land.

Regional chapters of this book list state parks, Forest Service and BLM campgrounds. Also, some free camping areas and privately owned campgrounds of merit. Wilderness camping is included in *Adventures on Foot* sections.

■ Travel Strategies & Helpful Facts

Montana is one huge hunk of real estate. For example, the driving distance between Missoula in Glacier Country and Sidney in Missouri River Country is 544 miles. Zipping back and forth from one end of the state to the other in a few hours is hardly feasible. You'll need to be selective unless you have a couple of weeks in which to explore more than one travel region. You can visit other areas and sample other adventures at a later time. And you'll be back. Montana has a way of whetting the appetite for more. Most visitors with whom I spoke had visited Montana before or intended to return.

Car Rentals

Your host may meet you at the closest airport if you book a multi-day outfitted trip or a week at a guest ranch. Otherwise, you'll need a car. Consider renting a high clearance 4-wheel-drive vehicle if you plan on driving in remote areas or on unimproved Forest Service roads. Montana's larger cities have major car rental agencies. Some automobile sales agencies in smaller cities have rental cars.

RVs

You might want to tour Montana in a recreational vehicle, either your own or a rental. The downside of RVing in Montana is that many unpaved mountain roads are less than RV-friendly. A few are off-limits to RVs. Many RVers tow small cars.

AUTHOR TIP

> *I've safely traveled all of Montana, save the gnarliest roads, in a 24-foot motorhome sans tow vehicle. I don't recommend this in a larger RV.*

Airlines

Montana enjoys good air service with three major, two regional and one local airline. Delta and Northwest Airlines serve Billings, Bozeman, Butte, Great Falls, Helena, Kalispell/Whitefish and Missoula. Billings is also served by United Airlines. Horizon links several Western cities with Billings, Bozeman, Butte, Great Falls, Helena, Kalispell/Whitefish and Missoula. Sky West serves Billings, Bozeman, Butte, Great Falls, Helena, Kalispell/Whitefish and West Yellowstone. Big Sky Airline links

Billings with Glasgow, Glendive, Havre, Lewistown, Miles City, Sidney and Wolf Point.

Bus & Train Service

Greyhound provides bus service between most towns and cities. Amtrak's *Empire Builder* stops at Wolf Point, Glasgow, Malta, Havre, Shelby, Cut Bank, Browning, Glacier Park (East Glacier), Essex (Isaac Walton Inn), West Glacier/Whitefish and Libby. It's a great way to go, especially with kids in tow, but cuts render all but the most up-to-the-minute information unreliable. Call Amtrak at ☎ 800-872-7245 before making serious plans to hitch a ride on the Empire Builder.

The Crowd Factor

The summer high season brings out the crowds at Glacier and Yellowstone National Parks and in Glacier and Gold West Countries. It's smart to make lodging reservations well in advance. Hikers can expect fewer companions on the trail as they travel into the back country. But even here, and especially along idyllic fly fishing streams, you can expect to bump up against fellow travelers. If possible, consider visiting more popular areas in late spring or early fall when schools are in session. These can be the pleasantest times to visit. The tourist crush has subsided, days are sunny and crisp and nights are clear and cold. There's always the possibility of a brief May snowstorm or a surprise September blizzard, but this is Montana.

Custer, Charlie Russell and Missouri River Countries represent the flip side of the tourism coin. Except in high profile areas such as Great Falls, Fort Benton and Little Bighorn Battlefield National Monument, you can pretty much expect to have the mountains and wide open spaces all to yourself. Montana's smaller ski resorts offer uncrowded conditions all season long and the ambience is strictly small town Montana. You may even spot skiers sporting 10-gallon hats. Montana's snowfall can be capricous. Contact your chosen resort to request current snow conditions before making firm plans.

Climate

Montana's weather is pretty much what you would expect of a land of mountains and plains north of the 45th parallel. Think unpredictable; be prepared for just about any kind of weather at any time. West of the Front Range, the higher you go the cooler it is. Not that it can't hit 90° at high noon on a mountain meadow in July. It's not unusual for the plains of Eastern Montana to bake under 100°-plus summertime readings or for the mercury to dip well below zero in January.

If average daily high and low temperatures tell you anything (they don't tell me a thing), July's average in Missoula is 84.8° and 50.4°, while Billings shows 87° and 58.4°. Missoula's January average: 29.8° and 14°. Billings shows 32° and 13.3°. This doesn't address wind chill, which can plummet a 20° reading to well below zero.

Winds are facts of life east of the Front Range. They may be hot and dry on summer days, or gentle as a kitten's breath on summer evenings. They can pack a wallop cold enough to freeze a stream of coffee thrown out a cabin door before it hits the ground. Or they can ride in on a January Chinook, melting snowbanks before your eyes. Sounds a bit fearsome, but not to worry. Summers are pleasant, with occasional rain. Springs are late by more temperate standards. Once the weather moderates, the air is soft. Fresh green hues spread across prairielands and down mountain streambeds. Hints of winter may intrude on crisp autumn days, but the changing leaves and air spiced with the tang of wood smoke make it many Montanans' favorite season. Expect the plains to be dry except in spring, when most of the precipitation occurs. Mountain thunderstorms come up quickly and rumble off just as quickly. Snowfall varies from year to year. The mountains receive the most. Yellowstone Country's Big Sky Ski Resort racks up the deepest average annual snowfall at 400 inches. Bear Paw Ski Bowl near Havre racks up the lowest at 140 inches. Other ski areas' annual average snowfalls come between these extremes. Pack for any eventuality. You'll be glad you did.

Clothing & Gear

Casual clothing is *in* in Montana. Spiffy duds look out of place except in the occasional upscale city restaurant. Pack t-shirts, sweatshirts, shorts and jeans. Chances are that once in Montana your vacation clothing will seem pretty tame. You'll want to pick up a fancy Western shirt or skirt, or a 10-gallon hat that you'll never wear at home. And you'll feel undressed without a bandana tied around your neck. Even dogs sport bandanas.

Hiking with Man's Best Friend

Speaking of dogs, you might want to consider a **doggy backpack** if you plan on hiking with Fido. Many sporting goods stores sell packs similar to those used by canine search and rescue units. Take your dog along to be fitted. Dogs may or may not accept a pack as part of the fun of hiking with you. Let them make the decision. Try letting them pack just their food and treats. Keep their comfort in mind. Remember, packs place pressure on a dog's spine. Look for one with padding, adjustable wide straps and double-seamed stitching. Only consider buying a pack for a big dog, say a lab or a German shepherd. If he seems to like the idea, try the pack out on short walks before hitting the trail. Start light and slowly increase the load until Fido seems comfortable. Don't overload him!

Pack **Polaroid sunglasses** for all seasons. The summer sun can be bright enough to stagger a mule. In winter, the glare off the snow can literally blind you. Remember, the higher the altitude, the closer you are to the sun and the more intense the ultraviolet rays.

Packing tons of clothing may seem like overkill, especially if you wind up not wearing some items. But it's essential to take along **warm clothing**, even in summer. Layers are a must for sweaty activities like hiking, biking and cross-country skiing. Planning for severe conditions is the key to feeling comfortable and deriving the most pleasure from your adventure. You can shed layers as the day warms up and your activity level rises, or add a layer if the shivers strike. Montana has numerous hot springs. Pack a **swimsuit** and beach towel, even in winter.

Sneakers and sandals are okay for touring, but not for activities more adventurous than museum cruising and shopping. **Hiking boots** and rubber sandals with woven straps held in place with Velcro do me just fine in summer. Take along a pair of broken-in Western **riding boots** if your plans include more than a couple of hours on horseback. Hiking boots with heels will do for short rides. Watershoes or the above-mentioned **sandals** are indispensible for floating rivers. In winter, take **snow boots**.

Consult with your guide regarding gear if you'll be fly fishing for the first time. You can't pack too many **socks** – wool for hiking, lighter socks for most other activities. Pack **rain gear**, especially if you'll be spending time in the mountains. A light **poncho** will do for summer rainstorms. You could substitute a **slicker** for spring or fall hiking or biking. You'll need a **wetsuit** for serious kayaking. Many sports shops rent kayaks and wetsuits.

AUTHOR TIP *River outfitters generally provide wetsuits and other gear needed on your trip. Before leaving home, ask your guide or outfitter what is included in the package and what you'll need to bring.*

Gathering Information

If you plan on adventuring into the back country on your own, find out everything you can in advance about your destination from US Forest Service ranger stations and/or other sources. Ask about water supplies, firewood availability, restrooms, approved waste disposal practices. Are restrictions in force on camping, group sizes, wood cutting, fires? Ask lots of questions, then plan your gear accordingly. Many national forests offer helpful booklets covering these and other questions about forest usage.

Be sure to match your **skis** to the type of skiing that figures in your plans. New designs in skis and related equipment seem to pop up every winter.

Research the market before making an expensive purchase. Ski rentals are widely available.

Always carry **extra food and water** when venturing into the back country. Don't forget **sunscreen**. Wearing a **hat** or **visor** cuts glare. Pack **insect repellent**, especially if you'll be on a lake or viewing wildlife in marshy terrain.

Driving

In the past few years, Montana's lack of an official speed limit came in for heavy criticism. As this book went to press, the state legislature established a new 75 mph limit on interstate highways day and night and a 70 mph daytime, 65 mph night limit on two-lane roads.

Many roads don't lend themselves to speeding. Most Eastern Montana roads are narrow shoulderless wonders with steep drop-offs on either side. The white cross factor can also inhibit speeding.

DID YOU KNOW? *The State Highway Department erects a white cross at the site of every highway fatality. Friends and relatives of the deceased sometimes decorate these crosses with wreaths and flowers. Approaching a cluster of three or four white crosses can be sobering.*

Fellow Travelers of the Deer Kind

Wildlife in the road can pose a greater danger than speedsters. Where you have deer, elk and other wild animals in abundance (aren't these one of the reasons you chose to visit Montana in the first place?), you have animal road hazards. Roads don't seem to faze animals. This includes adventurous cattle. Deer leap onto roads with unpredictable suddenness. One minute there's no animal in sight. First thing you know, you have a dead deer, a stoved-in right fender and a big repair bill.

I have yet to hit a deer, but I still shudder at the memory of two near-misses, both on curvy mountain roads, one at night, one in daytime. The first time, I swerved just in time to miss a deer leaping from a bank onto the road. The second time a deer appeared out of nowhere in full daylight, crossing the road directly in front of me. I missed both animals by inches.

The greatest number of car-deer accidents seem to occur on I-15 between Wolf Creek and Great Falls, on I-90 between Big Timber and Laurel, on I-94 between Hysham and the North Dakota line, and on US 93 between Lolo and Darby. But they can happen anywhere, any time. There isn't much you can do to avoid collisions of the deer kind, but the following tips from the Montana Highway Patrol might help.

■ Pay close attention to deer crossing signs; they're there for a reason.

- Slow down. Most collisions occur in the evening, around dusk.

- Keep an eye on the roadsides.

- If one deer or elk jumps out, others may follow.

- Don't use cruise control at night or in deer-crossing areas.

- Slow down when encountering another vehicle at night. On-coming cars' headlights diminish your vision.

Getting Around

You'll need a vehicle in order to make the most of your Montana trip. Interstate highways and main arteries are unavoidable at times, but do take lesser traveled roads when possible. By choosing the byways and small towns, you'll gain a feel for the real Montana and its people. Montana's Scenic and Adventure Byways meander through spectacular terrain where each bend in the road reveals a vista more fabulous than the last. US Forest Service and BLM roads also track some fabulous chunks of back country.

Montana Roads

Montana has come a long way since the 1920s when it had only a few miles of paved highway. Granted, most state highways could be improved, and they no doubt will be in time. But Montana is well endowed with interstate highways and other national and state highways. **Interstates 94** and **90** cross the state from east to west, converging at Billings where I-90 comes up from Sheridan, Wyoming. **I-15** splits the state on the west, entering from Idaho and more or less following the Continental Divide to Butte and Helena before looking in on Great Falls, then continuing on to Alberta at the Port of Coutts. **US 93** also splits the state on the west, entering from Idaho and cruising up the Bitterroot Valley to

Rocky Mountain Front, as seen from Hwy 89, near Dupuyer.

Missoula, continuing on to Flathead Lake, Kalispell, and the Port of Roosville, British Columbia.

US 89 enters Montana from Yellowstone National Park, following the Yellowstone River to Livingston before continuing northward to Great Falls.

US 87 describes an arc beginning at Lewistown, sweeping

westward to Great Falls, then heading northeast past Fort Benton to Havre and across the plains to Glasgow before following the Missouri River to the North Dakota line.

US 2, referred to as the **Hi-Line** because it follows the high line route of the Great Northern Railway, crosses the entire state, entering from North Dakota just east of Bainville and entering Idaho west of Troy.

Montana 200 splits the state as it crosses the plains from Glendive to Great Falls, continuing on to Missoula and into Idaho just west of tiny Heron.

US highways are quite good and fairly well maintained. Driving can be a challenge on many paved roads and highways, a test of skill on most unpaved roads. Except for cities and their environs and popular tourist areas, roads tend to be narrow. Apparently, shoulders are a concept foreign to Montana road builders. Unpaved roads often become quagmires in wet weather. High winds and sudden gusts can be scary on the High Plains, especially when driving a high profile vehicle. The legendary crosswinds on I-90 through Livingston have been known to topple brawny semi trucks.

Montana made out like a bandit in Congress's huge 1998 road appropriation bill. Hopefully, this funding windfall will soon mean better roads.

AUTHOR TIP

You might happen on a cattle or sheep drive, especially in spring or fall when stock is moved to or from seasonal grazing lands. Should you approach a stock drive, pull over, stop, reach for your camera and enjoy the show. Drovers, usually on horseback, will appreciate your patience and courtesy. If you're going their way, he or she will signal when it's safe to drive through the herd at five or 10 mph. If the drive is headed for you, he'll likely move the animals to the side of the road before waving you on. Be on the alert for a confused calf darting into the road or an ornery cow determined to do it her way.

Survival Gear

If you plan on driving over unimproved and/or US Forest Service or BLM roads, take along survival gear for both yourself and your vehicle. This should include **extra fuel**, a **spare tire** and **jack** and **water** for your radiator. Consider packing a roll of **duct tape**, the magic stuff that's good for 101 emergency repairs. Most small towns have at least one gas station, but in remote areas top off your tank whenever the opportunity presents itself. Be prepared for muddy conditions in the spring and after rainstorms. Proceed with caution if the road seems to be petering out. Attempting to turn around in a mudhole is no fun. A **CB radio** or **cellular**

phone is an idea, but mountainous terrain can obstruct their range. An up-to-date **map** may be your best traveling companion. The *Official Montana Highway Map* delineates numerous unimproved roads and scenic byways. It also identifies state parks and points of interest. US Geological Survey topographical maps may be purchased at Forest Service offices, at many sporting goods stores and through the US Geological Survey office and the Montana Bureau of Mines & Geology. Or purchase a statewide topo map book at a bookstore or sporting goods store. See *Information Sources* (page 66) for addresses.

Winter Driving

Winter driving is a whole other game. The Montana Department of Transportation makes available an excellent winter survival handbook covering all aspects of winter driving and first aid. Request a copy by contacting **Montana Department of Transportation**, Disaster & Emergency Services, 1100 North Main, Helena, MT 59620; ☎ 406-444-6911.

- Before setting out, check with the nearest state highway patrol office for current information. Remember: current conditions are subject to sudden changes.

- Let someone know where you are going and the route you intend to take.

- Forget about driving unimproved and Forest Service roads unless you're driving a snowmobile. Paved roads are generally plowed, but road clearing can take time in sudden and/or heavy snowstorms. Always expect the worst road conditions.

- Don't even start your engine without stowing a winter survival kit on board. This should include a basic tool kit, snow tires or chains, a shovel, an old rug or mat and kitty litter for traction, an axe or saw, a tow chain, rope, starter fluid, gas line deicer, jumper cables, flashlight or lantern with fresh batteries, matches, candles and high energy non-perishable foods.

- Keep blankets or sleeping bags and emergency food and water in your vehicle at all times.

- If you become stranded, remember that engine oil burned in a hubcap creates smoke that will be visible for miles.

You may never have need of these precautions, but they could mean the difference between living to tell about your adventure or not.

Ecological Etiquette

Montana has struggled with pollution ever since the first gold strike. Mining has left horrendous scars on the face of the land. Smelting has soiled the air with noxious gases. In the past, most Montanans tended to overlook such depradations, considering them a necessary price to pay for jobs. But no longer. Responsible stewardship of the land is a big issue today.

Big Industry was once the good guy. It's now the bad guy. Environmental victories are becoming increasingly common.

Time was when Montanans took a casual attitude toward stewardship of the state's vast expanses of forest and prairie. No longer. Back country rules of etiquette apply to everyone. Observing these rules will help to preserve Montana's beauty for future generations of adventure travelers to enjoy.

- **Take only photographs and leave only footprints**. Everything packed into designated wilderness areas must be packed out. That means everything. In non-designated wilderness areas, human waste can be buried 100 feet or more from a water source and away from possible campsites. Hang garbage high enough in a tree to discourage bears, then pack it out.

- **Fire danger** is often high, especially in late summer and early fall. Most forest fires are caused by lightning, but careless use of campfires and casual disposal of cigarette butts cause too many preventable fires.

- Before setting out, check with the local ranger station regarding current **fire regulations**. Camp stoves are encouraged in some ranger districts, mandated in others. Fire hazard road signs offer a quick fix on current fire danger. An extreme fire danger alert will put a damper on all campfires. Using a camp stove is preferable to building a fire, though admittedly short on coziness. If you must build a fire, use a fire ring if available. Otherwise build your fire in the open, away from combustible materials. Burn only small sticks. Forage for deadwood and never cut a tree. Don't cut snags either; they provide valuable wildlife habitat. Before leaving, make sure your fire is dead out, then scatter the ashes and cover the site with sod or organic materials.

- Take care in **choosing a campsite** if not in a designated camping area. Whenever possible, choose an already impacted site. Failing that, choose one at least 200 feet from trails, lakes, streams and wet meadows. Hide the campsite from view if possible and don't dig ditches around your tent. Avoid using a campsite on consecutive nights. A single night spent in a campsite makes it easier to erase traces when you hit the trail.

- Don't even think about **drinking river, stream or lake water** unless you've boiled it for 20 minutes. You can't see them, but *giardia lamblia* protozoans may be lurking in the water, waiting to lay you low with stomach cramps and diarrhea that will continue even after you've returned home. Pack in water or a water purifier designed for camp use. Do not wash yourself, your utensils or clothing in lakes or streams. Dispose of wash water in a hole dug well away from campsites, lakes or streams. Use only biodegradable soap.

- The US Forest Service offers tip sheets covering wilderness etiquette. Obtain one, read it, then follow it.

- **Respect private property**. Observe *No Trespassing* signs. If, for some very good reason, you must cross private land (some snowmobile trails are on private land), be careful to close any gate you might open. Open range may not be fenced, though metal cattle guards will have been placed across roads to keep animals in. Don't approach cattle. Cows are curious creatures and might follow you at a distance. Ignore them. Bulls are seldom on open range, but be on the alert anyhow. These guys are not to be trifled with.

■ Information Sources

The US Department of Agriculture Forest Service administers Montana's national forests and their networks of trails and unimproved roads and campgrounds. The US Department of the Interior Bureau of Land Management (BLM) lands include some maintained trails, the oversight of several Montana rivers, including the Upper Missouri National Wild and Scenic River, and numerous primitive campgrounds. Regional Forest Service headquarters and ranger district offices are listed below and in regional chapters of this book. State parks are also listed in regional chapters.

Travel Montana, the Montana Chamber of Commerce, and regional tourism offices are listed below. Town and area chambers of commerce are listed in regional chapters.

Many of the following information sources are also included in regional chapters. Listing them below can get you started if you are undecided as to what you want to see and do in Montana. Most contacts will provide lots of free information on sights, activities, where to stay and eat, tours, rental car services, special permits and regulations.

The following air, bus and train companies serve Montana. Automobile rental agencies are listed in regional chapters.

Airlines

Big Sky Airlines: ☎ 800-237-7788.
Delta Airlines & The Delta Connection: ☎ 800-221-1212.
Horizon Airlines: ☎ 800-547-9308.
Northwest Airlines: ☎ 800-225-2525.
Sky West: ☎ 800-453-9417.
United Airlines: ☎ 800-241-6522.

Buses

Greyhound Bus Line: ☎ 800-231-2222.

Railways

Amtrak's Empire Builder pounds the tracks pioneered by the Great Northern Railway. Heading from east to west, the train stops at Wolf Point, Glasgow, Malta, Havre, Shelby, Cut Bank, Browning, East Glacier, Essex, West Glacier, Whitefish and Libby. ☎ 800-872-7245.

Montana Rockies Rail Tours runs a luxury excursion train. It calls at Spokane, Washington and Sandpoint, Idaho before following the Clark Fork River into Montana. It looks in on St. Regis and Missoula before terminating at Livingston. Side tours visit Yellowstone, Grand Teton and Glacier National Parks. Overnights are spent in hotels along the route. 2660 W. Ontario, Sandpoint, ID 83864; ☎ 800-519-7245.

Handy Contacts

Montana Highway Patrol: 2550 Prospect Ave., Helena, MT 59620; ☎ 406-444-7000.
Montana Roadway Condition Report: ☎ 800-226-7623, TTY ☎ 800-335-7592 or 406-444-7696.
Montana Ski Reports: ☎ 800-847-4868 ext. 6WG (out of state), ☎ 406-444-2654 (in Montana).

State Tourism Offices

Travel Montana, Department of Commerce, PO Box 200533 (1424 9th Ave.), Helena, MT 59620-0533; ☎ 800-847-4868 outside Montana, 406-444-2654 in Montana. Internet http://travel.mt.gov/.
Montana Chamber of Commerce, Box 1730, Helena, MT 59624; ☎ 406-442-2405.

Regional Tourism Offices

Custer Country Tourism Office, Rt. 1, Box 1206A, Hardin, MT 59034; ☎ 800-346-1876 or 406-665-1671.
Yellowstone Country Tourism Office, Box 1107, Red Lodge, MT 59068; ☎ 800-736-5276 or 406-446-1005.
Gold West Country Tourism Office, 1155 Main St., Deer Lodge, MT 59722; ☎ 800-879-1159 or 406-846-1943.

Glacier Country Tourism Office, 1507 1st. Ave. W., Suite E, Kalispell, MT 59901; ☎ 800-338-5072 or 406-756-7128.

Charlie Russell Country Tourism Office, Box 3166, Great Falls, MT 59403; ☎ 800-527-5348 or 406-761-5036.

Missouri River Country Tourism Office, Box 387, Wolf Point, MT 59201; ☎ 800-653-1319 or 406-761-5036.

Federal Government Agencies

US Geological Survey, Federal Center, Box 25286, Denver, CO 80225; ☎ 800-435-7627 or 303-202-4700.

US Bureau of Land Management, Montana State Office, 222 N. 32nd St., Billings, MT 59107-0137; ☎ 406-255-2888.

USDA Forest Service-Northern Region Office, Federal Building, 200 E. Broadway, Box 7669, Missoula, MT 59807; ☎ 406-329-3511.

US Army Corps of Engineers, Box 208, Fort Peck, MT 59223; ☎ 406-526-3411.

US Bureau of Reclamation, Montana Area Office, Box 30137, Billings, MT 59107-0137; ☎ 406-247-7313.

US Fish & Wildlife Service, Mountain Prairie Region, Box 25486 DFC, Denver, CO 80225; 303-236-7400.

State Government Agencies

Montana Board of Outfitters, Department of Commerce, 111 N. Jackson, Helena, MT 59620; ☎ 406-444-3738.

Montana Bureau of Mines & Geology, Montana Tech, Main Hall, Room 206, Butte, MT 59701; ☎ 406-496-4167.

To obtain topographical maps: **Montana Bureau of Mines & Geology**, *Attn: Publication Sales, Montana Tech, 1300 W. Park St., Butte, MT 59701-8997;* ☎ *406-496-4167.*

Montana Department of Natural Resources & Conservation, 1625 11th Ave., Helena, MT 59620; ☎ 406-444-2074.

Montana Department of Transportation, Customer Service Unit, 2701 Prospect, Helena, MT 59620; ☎ 406-444-6200.

Montana Fish, Wildlife & Parks, 1420 E. 6th Ave., Helena, MT 59620; ☎ 406-444-2535.

National Parks

Yellowstone National Park, Visitors' Services, Box 168, Yellowstone National Park, WY 82190; ☎ 307-344-7381 or 307-344-7311 (reservations only).

Glacier National Park, Superintendent, West Glacier, MY 59936; ☎ 406-888-7800 or 602-207-6000 for room reservations.

National Park Service, Grant Kohrs Ranch National Historic Site, Box 790, Deer Lodge, MT 59722; ☎ 406-846-2070.

National Forest Headquarters

Beaverhead National Forest, 420 Barrett St., Dillon, MT 59725; ☎ 406-683-3900.

Bitterroot National Forest, 1801 N. First St., Hamilton, MT 59840; ☎ 406-363-7161.

Custer National Forest, PO Box 2556, Billings, MT 59103; ☎ 406-657-6361.

Deerlodge National Forest, 420 Barrett St., Dillon, MT 59725; ☎ 406-683-3900.

Flathead National Forest, 1935 3rd. Ave. E, Kalispell, MT 59901; ☎ 406-758-5200.

Gallatin National Forest, PO Box 130, Bozeman, MT 59715; ☎ 406-587-5271, ext. 4233.

Helena National Forest, 2880 Skyway Dr., Helena, MT 59601; ☎ 406-449-5201.

Kootenai National Forest, 506 Highway 2 West, Libby, MT 59923; ☎ 406-293-6211.

Lewis & Clark National Forest, PO Box 869, Great Falls, MT 59403; ☎ 406-791-7700.

Lolo National Forest, Building 24, Fort Missoula, Missoula, MT 59801; ☎ 406-329-3557.

Indian Reservations

Blackfeet Nation, Box 850, Browning, MT 59417; ☎ 406-338-7276.

Crow Reservation, Crow Agency, MT 59022; ☎ 406-638-2601.

Flathead Reservation-Confederated Salish & Kootenai Tribes, Box 278, Pablo, MT 59855; ☎ 406-675-2700.

Fort Belknap Reservation, Fort Belknap Tourism Office, RR 1, Box 66, Fort Belknap Agency, Harlem, MT 59526; ☎ 406-353-2205.

Fort Peck Reservation, Fort Peck Assiniboine & Sioux Tribes, Box 1027, Poplar, MT 59255; ☎ 406-768-5155.

Northern Cheyenne Reservation, Box 128, Lame Deer, MT 59043; ☎ 406-477-6284.

Rocky Boy's Reservation, The Chippewa-Cree Business Committee, RR1, Box 544, Box Elder, MT 59521; ☎ 406-395-4282.

Activity-Related Organizations

Adventure Cycling Association, Box 8308, Missoula, MT 59807; ☎ 406-721-1776, fax 406-721-8754.

Fishing Outfitters Association of Montana (FOAM), Box 67, Gallatin Gateway, MT 59730.

Montana Department of Transportation, Bicycle/Pedestrian Program Coordinator, Box 201001, Helena, MT 59620-1001; ☎ 406-444-6123, fax 406-444-7671.

Montana Outfitters & Guides Association, Box 1248, Helena, MT 59624; ☎ 406-449-3578, fax 406-443-2439.

Montana Snowmobile Association, PO Box 3202, Great Falls, MT 59403.

Montana Wilderness Association, Box 635, Helena, MT 59624; ☎ 406-443-7350.

State Trails Coordinator, Montana Fish, Wildlife & Parks, 1420 E. 6th Ave., Helena, MT 59620; ☎ 406-444-4585.

Whirling Disease Foundation, PO Box 327, Bozeman, MT 59771-0327; ☎ 406-585-0860.

Custer Country

Introduction

In most Americans' minds, "Custer Country" resounds with images of Lt. Col. George Armstrong Custer's ill-fated Last Stand at the Battle of the Little Bighorn on June 25, 1876. But Custer Country has much more to offer both history buffs and adventure seekers than tours of the Little Bighorn Battlefield National Monument.

The Bighorn River, one of North America's finest fly fishing streams, flows through the Crow Indian Reservation and the Bighorn Canyon National Recreation Area. Bighorn Lake, created in 1965 by the building of Yellowtail Dam, offers water skiing and other aquatic fun.

The Pryor Mountain National Wild Horse Range west of Bighorn Canyon is a must-see.

The Crow and Northern Cheyenne Indian Reservations occupy a 2,679,771-acre chunk of Custer Country. Residents provide opportunities for visitors to become acquainted with their traditions through pow-wows and rodeos.

The Custer National Forest's Ashland Ranger District affords bird and other wildlife watching and some hiking, cross-country skiing and snowmobiling.

DID YOU KNOW? *"National forest" may be a misnomer here. Much of the Ashland District of the Custer National Forest is scrubby grazing land strewn with sagebrush, though forested areas exist at higher elevations and along river and stream beds.*

The bones of the Earth protrude in Custer Country; dinosaur bones, too. Some of the region's remarkable rock formations are historically significant. Many have spiritual significance for Native Americans. The Yellowstone River corridor is noted for a rich trove of agates. Custer Country includes eight state parks, most created around a natural attraction or some aspect of Montana's human history. Medicine Rocks, Makoshika and Tongue River Reservoir State Parks offer camping. Others are day-use parks.

Much of the region is plains country, home to cowboys, cattle drives and working ranches. Some open their spreads to guests.

That ethos is reflected in Billings, the region's largest city and Montana's most populous. The small towns sprinkled across Custer Country, microcosms of a culture unique to the Great Plains, project the unique flavor of this big-shouldered, sprawling region of Montana.

 The Custer Country Tourism Region publishes one of the best regional vacation guides I've seen anywhere. It's available free at area visitor centers or by dialing ☎ 800-346-1876 or 406-665-1671.

■ History

The **Bozeman Trail**, blazed in 1866 as a "safe route" for wagons bound from Fort Laramie to Montana's gold country, sliced through the southwest corner of today's Custer Country. Not a wise move. The route ran smack through the Sioux's prime buffalo hunting country. Two wagon trains got through in 1866, but Indian attacks rendered the trail less than popular. Meanwhile, **Fort C. F. Smith** was constructed two miles below the mouth of Bighorn Canyon in order to protect emigrants on the Trail. So fierce was Sioux harassment that the fort was abandoned after two years. The Sioux had postponed the inevitable spread of settlers for a decade.

The Little Bighorn victory of **Chief Crazy Horse** and his Sioux and Northern Cheyenne warriors over Custer and the Seventh Cavalry was a valiant last hurrah. The 1877 Nez Perce War and the 1890 massacre at Wounded Knee on South Dakota's Pine Ridge Reservation were yet to occur. But the Indians' open plains, buffalo hunting lifestyle was doomed. The slaughter of the buffalo put the quietus on the way of life that had, for

Custer Country

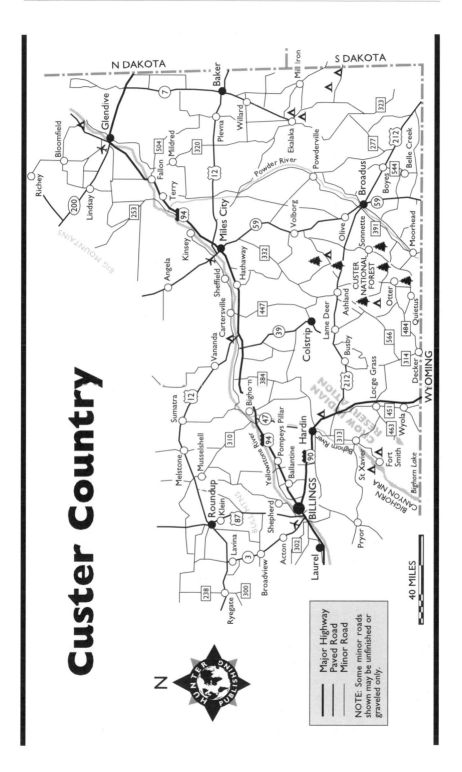

N DAKOTA • S DAKOTA

Mill Iron

Baker

Glendive

Bloomfield

Richey

Lindsay

200

253

504 • Mildred

320

Fallon

Terry

Plevna

Willard

Ekalaka

Powderville

Powder River

277

323

212

Belle Creek

Broadus

Boyes

544

59

Moorhead

391

Sonnette

Otter

Quietus

Olive

Volborg

Miles City

59

Hathaway

332

Angela

Sheffield

Cartersville

447

Ashland

CUSTER NATIONAL FOREST

566

484

Decker

314

WYOMING

Kinsey

Vananda

39

Colstrip

Lame Deer

Busby

Lodge Grass

212

451

Wyola

463

Sumatra

12

Bigho'n

384

47

Pompeys Pillar

94

Hardin

313

90

Fort Smith

St Xavier

Bighorn Lake

BIGHORN CANYON NRA

CROW INDIAN RESERVATION

Bighorn River

Yellowstone River

Ballantine

Melstone

310

Musselshell

Klein

Roundup

87

Shepherd

Acton

302

BILLINGS

Pryor

Lavina

3

Broadview

238

300

Ryegate

Laurel

BIG MOUNTAINS

BULL MTNS

40 MILES

N

HUNTER PUBLISHING

—— Major Highway
— Paved Road
— Minor Road

NOTE: Some minor roads shown may be unfinished or graveled only.

countless centuries, defined Native American culture, religion and tradition.

Northern Cheyenne bands began farming along the Tongue River and several nearby creeks in 1880. The Tongue River Reservation was established in 1884. In 1900 it was enlarged to its present 444,679 acres, some 98% of the land being controlled by the tribe. Today, it is known as the **Northern Cheyenne Reservation**.

The federal government tried initially to assimilate the Northern Cheyenne with neighboring non-Indians and with their traditional enemy, the Crows. The fiercely independent Northern Cheyenne weren't having any of that. Today, though the Northern Cheyenne and **Crow Reservations** share a commmon boundary, the two are completely separate.

DID YOU KNOW?

The Crow Indians were so named by whites in an inept attempt to identify with the tribe's Indian name of Apsaalooke, the "Big Bird People."

The Fort Laramie Treaty of 1851 gave the Crows a huge swath of land covering north-central Wyoming and southern Montana. The second Fort Laramie Treaty, signed in 1868, pared the Crow lands to a big chunk of southern Montana. In 1880, the Crows signed an agreement further whittling the reservation to it's present 2,235,092 acres. It lies south of Billings and includes the shores of the Bighorn River from the Wyoming line north to Hardin.

The **Northern Pacific Railroad** was completed across Montana in 1883, around the time the last of the buffalo were being slaughtered. By 1906, the Chicago, Milwaukee and St. Paul had built road beds across Custer Country, roughly paralleling today's US Highway 12. The Northern Pacific pitched the Montana Plains to farmers, but those efforts paled beside the flim-flam operation launched by the Chicago, Milwaukee and St. Paul. The idea was to sell prospective homesteaders on farming the fertile plains, milking them for transportation to Montana and further milking them for services provided by towns bankrolled by the railroads. The weather cooperated, sending fortuitous rains. Fortuitous for the railroad barons, less so for gullible farmers. Many were foreign immigrants with little or no knowledge of the Plains' harsh weather and cyclical droughts. In time, the wet cycle gave way to a more typical dry cycle. By the 1930s, most of the farms carved out by homesteaders had been abandoned, their fences torn out to allow cattle to range freely. Weeds choked the now-dusty streets of the railroad towns. The Homestead Era was over. The cattle era had returned.

■ Custer Country Today

A few towns survived, notably Baker, Terry and a few one-horse, high-grass towns along US 12. Some still serve farmers. Today's wheat and grain farmers, using modern technology (would you believe satellites?) and machinery, cultivate fields larger than homesteaders' entire farms.

AUTHOR TIP

If you doubt that Custer Country typifies the West's wide open spaces, you have only to glance at a crossroads signpost identifying residents living along the roads snaking into the distance. In more densely populated areas such signs indicate that the Smiths, say, reside at number 54. Here, the Smiths can be found at milepost 13, the Ride-'em Ranch at milepost 21. And so on.

Miles City, the self-styled "Cowboy Capital of Montana," epitomizes the resurgence (it never really went away) of the Montana cattle culture that has captivated America for well over 100 years. It may captivate you, too. The annual **Miles City Bucking Horse Sale** is a must. Equally captivating is the Indian culture; what some consider the flip side of the cowboy ethos. Any made-in-Hollywood cowboy and Indian misconceptions that you may harbor will quickly dissipate if you so much as scratch the surface in Custer Country. Indian people have an innate sense of artistry that is closely connected to nature. Many are exceptionally talented artisans. Most visitors to Indian Country are awed by the beautiful beadwork and traditional artifacts and clothing fashioned of feathers and supple deer and elk hides. Examples are on display at the **Cheyenne Indian Museum** at St. Labre Indian School at Ashland.

■ The Land

Custer Country's seemingly endless prairie spaces, interrupted by green river valleys and punctuated by gumbo buttes, low mountains and oddly shaped rock formations, overlay rich seams of coal. Minerals, both curious and valuable, are intriguing evidences of the region's pre-history.

Coal lies beneath much of the southern half of the region and under all of the Northern Cheyenne Reservation. Believing in the sacredness of Mother Earth, the Northern Cheyenne are loathe to disturb her. The tribe has so far declined mining offers.

Not so the Northern Pacific Railroad, whose lands to the north of the reservation are also rich in coal. The railroad once mined the coal to fuel its locomotives. The advent of diesel locomotives prompted the railroad to sell its coal leases to the Montana Power Co. A subsidiary, Western Energy Co., currently exploits the coal fields. The town of **Colstrip**, built as a company town, continues to be supported by coal.

Custer Country

Pompey's Pillar.

Moss agates can be found in the **Yellowstone River Valley**. The river flows diagonally across the northern half of Custer Country, paralleling I-94 until it veers east at Glendive. Lewis and Clark's 1806 return journey followed the Yellowstone to its confluence with the Missouri River at the Montana-North Dakota line.

Lewis and Clark wrote of being awed by the high rimrocks framing the valley now occupied by **Billings**. A nearby sandstone formation, named "Pompey's Pillar" for Sacajawea's baby, was but one of many other rock formations noted by the explorers.

The **Pryor Mountains'** grassy limestone heights are rich in archaeological sites. And in caves formed by ground water dissolving limestone while slowly dripping through fissures in the rocks. Wild horses move over the natural grazing lands administered by the BLM. The Badlands encroach on Eastern Montana from the Dakotas, littering the landscape with wild and strange shapes. The **Terry Badlands Area's** contrasting colors, caused by alternating seams of gray shale, yellow sandstone and red clinker, gives the lie to the "badlands" sobriquet. Dinosaur bones lie beneath the thin soil. The Sioux name for badlands, or bad earth, is Ma-ko-shi-ka. Hence the naming of **Makoshika State Park**, occupying the site of several important dinosaur digs. You can see the fossil remains of triceratops and fellow travelers excavated here at the park visitor center.

Digging Up Dinosaurs

In August, 1990, Irv Ladish, a Milwaukee Public Museum volunteer on a dig in the Hell Creek formation, decided to take a break. He almost sat on a triceratops brow tine! Milwaukee Public Museum paleontologist Diane Gabriel and Makoshika State Park Manager Mike Sullivan organized a dig that uncovered the skull of a juvenile triceratops measuring five feet from beak to frill. The skull is on display at the Makoshika State Park Visitor Center.

■ Climate

Weather extremes are a given in southeastern Montana. Being prepared has seldom held so much importance. The long harsh winters generally bring heavy snows and chilling winds. Springs are often late, failing to shake the shrouds of winter until May. A soft balmy day can be followed by a spate of driving snow or cold rain. Once summer arrives, it settles in with six weeks or so of baking days when the mercury can climb toward the 100° mark. Autumn may be the most pleasant time of year, with cold nights and crisp days warmed with liquid gold sunshine. Early snows are always possible.

The Badlands of Eastern Custer Country experience all these weather extremes in spades, especially in summer. Rocks reflect heat. That's why rattlesnakes are partial to basking on them.

Getting Around

■ Highways & Byways

I-94 bisects Custer Country from Laurel to the North Dakota line, paralleling the Yellowstone River and providing access to Billings, Miles City, Terry and Glendive. **Interstate 90** dips into Wyoming from Billings, crossing the Crow Indian Reservation and accessing the Little Bighorn Battlefield National Monument. Paved roads lead from I-90 to Bighorn Canyon National Recreation Area.

US 12 roughly follows the old Chicago, Milwaukee and St. Paul roadbed across the northern quarter of Custer Country, looking in on the cattle town of Roundup and slumbering homestead era towns. **US 212** heads east from I-90 at Little Bighorn Battlefield National Monument, slicing across the Northern Cheyenne Indian Reservation and Custer National Forest before crossing the Powder River at Broadus and sloping down into Wyoming. North-south **Montana Highways 3, 39, 59, 7** and **US 87** divide Custer Country into more or less manageable parcels. Most other roads are gravelled or unsurfaced. Many of the latter are closed to vehicles other than snowmobiles in winter.

■ Road Etiquette

Custer Country has more miles of gravelled and minimally maintained roads than paved highways. The Interstates offer smooth driving, but most other roads, paved or unpaved, are narrow and lack adequate shoulders. Gravel roads cross national forest lands and Indian reservations, linking ranches and towns that may consist of a post office and little more.

Your inclination may be to slow down on gravel roads, but don't expect rural Montanans to do so. Vast distances between towns breed speed. If you see a dust cloud approaching, shut your windows and get as far to the right as possible. If you see a dust cloud bearing down on you from behind, give the pickup a chance to pass. (Dust clouds on gravel roads almost always contain pickups.)

Watch for **horses** on all rural roads, paved or unpaved. Slow down when encountering riders on horseback and give them a wide berth. The horses are probably accustomed to cars, but don't chance it.

Most roads passing through open range have **cattle guards** designed to prevent cattle from straying. These are the metal bars placed across the road that your tires rumble over. Cattle guards delineate property lines and sometimes take the place of cross fences. Watch for stock in the road, whether or not cattle guards are in place or the animals are confined (theoretically) by fences. A cow whose calf has wandered to the other side of the road will respond to maternal instinct. Slow down and ease past her.

You may encounter a **cattle drive**. If you do, obey the drover on horseback. He or she will make an effort to clear a path and will signal when it's safe to go through. Always move cautiously; cows are unpredictable critters. You don't want to buy one. Be alert for deer, elk and other **wild animals** when driving any Montana road. They are even faster and more unpredictable than cows. And they make every bit as big a dent in your car.

Beware of **black ice**! If nighttime temperatures dip below freezing, and if there's fog, you can bet the roads will be coated with that invisible hazard come morning. It may melt off when the sun hits the pavement, but shaded areas can remain treacherous. Freezing daytime temperatures can also result in black ice. While this no-see-'um ice is a greater hazard on smooth surface roads, gravel roads can also be slick. If you feel your vehicle sliding, tap the breaks and steer gently into the slide. County highway crews try to keep roadways clear of snow, but wind-driven blizzards can overwhelmg maintenance crews. The more remote the road, the longer it will take for plows to arrive.

Use common sense when heading out on winter roads. Before setting out, dial the Montana Road Condition Report hotline (see Information Sources) for a report on current highway conditions. Remember that "current" is just that and conditions change quickly.

Information Sources

Getting There

Big Sky Airlines serves Billings, Glendive and Miles City: ☎ 800-237-7788.

Delta Airlines serve Billings: ☎ 800-221-1212.

Horizon Airlines serves Billings: ☎ 800-547-9308.

Northwest Airlines serves Billings: ☎ 800-225-2525.

Sky West Airlines serves Billings: ☎ 800-453-9417.

United Airlines also serves Billings: ☎ 800-241-6522.

Greyhound Bus Line: ☎ 800-231-2222.

Greyhound offers good between-city bus service – worth considering if you wish to travel from town to town and don't have access to a car. In Montana, ☎ 406-252-4169 to obtain scheduling information. Outside Montana: ☎ 800-231-2222.

Powder River Trailways: ☎ 800-442-3682.

On the Road

Montana Highway Patrol, 2550 Prospect Ave., Helena, MT 59620; ☎ 406-444-7696.

Montana Road Condition Report: ☎ 800-226-7623, TTY ☎ 800-335-7592 or 406-444-7696 (CB'ers: Emergency Channel 9).

Local Road Reports

Billings: ☎ 406-252-2806.

Glendive: ☎ 406-365-2314.

Miles City: ☎ 406-232-2099.

Car Rentals

Billings

AAA Auto Rental: ☎ 800-423-9049 or 406-245-9759.

Ace/Vintage Rent-A-Car: ☎ 800-362-1100 or 406-252-2399.

Avis Rent-A-Car: ☎ 800-331-1212 or 406-252-8007.

Big Sky Car Rental: ☎ 406-252-2992.

Budget Rent-A-Car of Billings: ☎ 800-527-0700 or 406-259-4168.

Dollar Rent-A-Car: ☎ 800-803-8832 or 406-259-1147.

Enterprise Rent-A-Car: ☎ 800-RENTACAR or 406-652-2000 or 406-259-9999.

Hertz Rent-A-Car: ☎ 800-654-3131 or 406-248-9151.

National Car Rental: ☎ 800-227-7368 or 406-252-7626.

Thrifty Car Rental: ☎ 800-699-1025 or 406-259-1025.

Glendive

Avis Rent-A-Car: ☎ 800-331-1212 or 406-365-8032.

Hertz Rent-A-Car: ☎ 406-353-2331.

Miles City

Mac's Frontierland: ☎ 800-758-1010 or 406-232-2456.

Tourism Offices

Travel Montana, Department of Commerce, PO Box 200533 (1424 9th Ave.), Helena, MT 59620-0533; ☎ 800-847-4868 outside Montana, ☎ 406-444-2654 in Montana. Internet http://travel.mt.gov/.

Custer Country

Custer Country Tourism Office, Rt. 1, Box 1206A, Hardin, MT 59034; ☎ 800-346-1876 or 406-665-1671.

Chambers of Commerce

Montana, Box 1730 Helena, MT 59624; ☎ 406-442-2405.

Baker, PO Box 849, Baker, MT 59313; ☎ 406-778-2266.

Billings, PO Box 31177, Billings, MT 59107; ☎ 800-735-2635 or 406-245-4111.

Broadus, PO Box 47, Broadus, MT 59317; ☎ 406-436-2818 or 436-9976.

Colstrip, PO Box 1100, Colstrip, MT 59323; ☎ 406-748-5046.

Ekalaka, PO Box 297, Ekalaka, MT 59324; ☎ 406-775-6658.

Forsyth, PO Box 448, Forsyth, MT 59327; ☎ 406-356-2123.

Glendive, PO Box 930, Glendive, MT 59330; ☎ 406-365-5601.

Hardin, 21 East 4th, Hardin, MT 59034; ☎ 406-665-1672.

Hysham, PO Box 63, Hysham, MT 59038; ☎ 406-342-5457.

Laurel, PO Box 395, Laurel, MT 59044; ☎ 406-628-8105.

Lavina, Lavina, MT 59046; ☎ 406-636-2722.

Miles City, 901 Main St., Miles City, MT 59301; ☎ 406-232-2890.

Richey, PO Box 279, Richey, MT 59259; ☎ 406-773-5580.

Roundup, PO Box 751, Roundup, MT 59072; ☎ 406-323-1966.

Terry, PO Box 6, Terry, MT 59349; ☎ 406-637-2126.

Wibaux, PO Box 159, Wibaux, MT 59353; ☎ 406-795-2412.

Government Agencies

State BLM Office, Box 36800, Billings, MT 59107; ☎ 406-255-2885. Billings BLM Resource Area, 801 East Main, Billings, MT 59105; ☎ 406-238-1540.

Miles City District BLM Office, 111 Gary Owen Road, Miles City, MT 59301; ☎ 406-233-2800.

Custer National Forest, Supervisor's Office, Box 2556, Billings, MT 59103; ☎ 406-657-6361.

Custer National Forest, Ashland Ranger District, PO Box 168, Ashland, MT 59003; ☎ 406-784-2344.

Regional Information Officer, Dept. Fish, Wildlife & Parks, PO Box 2004, Miles City, MT 59301; ☎ 406-232-4365.

Regional Information Officer, Dept. Fish, Wildlife & Parks, 2300 Lake Elmo Dr., Billings, MT 59105; ☎ 406-247-2940. 24-hour information: ☎ 406-247-2970. Internet http://fwp.mt.gov.

Bighorn Canyon National Recreation Area Headquarters, PO Box 458, Ft. Smith, MT 59035; ☎ 406-666-2412.

Montana Board of Outfitters, Department of Commerce, 111 N. Jackson, Helena, MT 59620; ☎ 406-444-3738.

Indian Reservations

Crow Reservation, Crow Agency, MT 59022; ☎ 406-638-2601.

Little Bighorn College Micro-Tourism, PO Box 370, Crow Agency, MT 59002; ☎ 406-638-7223.

Northern Cheyenne Reservation, Box 128, Lame Deer, MT 59043; ☎ 406-477-6284.

Northern Cheyenne Chamber of Commerce, PO Box 991, Lame Deer, MT 59043; ☎ 406-477-8844.

Touring

 Custer Country's size discourages the sort of leisurely touring that offers serendipity at every turn in the road. Fact is, turns in the road are scarce, given relatively level terrain broken by occasional breaks, coulees and gumbo buttes resembling baby volcanic cones.

 Gumbo buttes got their name from the local soil's tendency to turn into a gooey morass when it rains. They are generally 200-500 feet high.

As there's no way to do a circle tour of the entire region, this *Touring* chapter loosely follows west-east corridors.

The southern corridor encompasses Bighorn Canyon National Recreation Area, the Little Bighorn Battlefield National Monument, the Crow and Northern Cheyenne Indian Reservations and a chunk of the Custer National Forest, ending at Broadus.

The I-90/I-94 corridor includes the Lewis and Clark Trail, identifiable by signs depicting the two captains pointing in true explorer fashion. The corridor begins on I-90 west of Billings, zips through Miles City and Glendive and ends at Wibaux. We'll tack on side trips to Baker, Ismay and Ekalaka.

Last, we'll take a swing through cattle country via US 12, looking in on Roundup and following the Musselshell River.

AUTHOR TIP *As you drive, be sure to pull up to read the entertaining and informative historical highway markers that the Montana Department of Transportation has erected along the state's highways and byways. Exceptionally well written, these signs offer valuable fixes on local history, geology and culture.*

Custer Country

■ The Southern Corridor

Chief Plenty Coups State Park

It's fitting that the first stop on a tour of Custer Country's southernmost corridor should be this park. Take the Hardin Road Exit (#452) off I-90. Drive about 12 miles to the Pryor Creek Road (MT 416). Follow this road for 23 miles to the small Crow Reservation town of Pryor. A sign direct drivers to the day-use park.

Chief Plenty Coups

Plenty Coups, the last chief of the Crow tribe, is revered by both Indians and whites. As a child, he had a vision predicting the coming of the white man and the killing of the buffalo. Subsequent spiritual quests directed him to lead his people down the paths of education for all Crow children and of friendship with whites. He advised his people thusly: "With education you are the white man's equal, but without it you are his victim." In 1928, he dedicated his homestead as a park not only for the Crow people, but for all people, saying, "This park is not to be a memorial to me, but to the Crow Nation. It is given as a token of my friendship for all people both red and white." Plenty Coups died in 1932 at the age of 84.

The park includes an interpretive center/museum displaying many of the chief's belongings, Plenty Coups' hewn log house, and the Medicine Water Spring where his childhood vision occurred. It's a peaceful place where, if you listen, you can sense the drumbeats of history.

Park personnel, including a descendant of Plenty Coups, are on hand during the summer to relate Crow Creation stories and accounts of Plenty Coups' eventful life. Special events include the annual Plenty Coups Day of Honor in early September.

The park is open daily, May 1-Sept. 30, 8-8. The visitor center is open daily, May 1-Sept. 30, 10-5 and the rest of the year by appointment. Plenty Coups State Park, Box 100A, Pryor, MT 59066; ☎ 406-252-1289.

Bighorn Canyon National Recreation Area

Strike eastward across the Crow Reservation to access the Bighorn Canyon National Recreation Area. The scenery along the approximately 35-mile stretch of road between Pryor and the junction of MT 313 at St. Xavier is starkly beautiful, all chiseled coulees, swales and rounded hills. Chances are you'll not see another living being, save an occasional deer.

Head south on MT 313 at St. Xavier. The road follows the Bighorn River to Yellowtail Dam and the straggling town of Fort Smith. Fly fishing lodgings, fly shops and other services cater to anglers attracted to one of the finest tail water fisheries in the country. You must stop at the visitor center to purchase a permit before entering the Recreation Area.

 Most of the area is on the Crow Reservation and off-limits to visitors. Signs at Reservation boundaries make this abundantly clear.

Attractions other than fishing include a visit to the **Yellowtail Dam Visitor Center**, water sports and admiring the stupendous scenery afforded by the deep lake at the bottom of a dramatic 2,200-foot-deep gorge. The lake stretches south from Yellowtail Dam into Wyoming. The **Pryor Mountains National Wild Horse Range** rises across the lake. The northern half of the lake is surrounded by the Crow Indian Reservation and is inaccessible by road. WY 37 enters Montana on the west side of the lake and continues to Barry's Landing. The Bighorn Canyon Visitor Center is at Lovell, Wyoming.

The best way to appreciate the magnitude of the lake and gorge is to drive the twisty 10-mile mountain road from Fort Smith to the Ok-A-Beh Marina. Views of the shimmering lake reflected in chiseled red-rock gorge walls, forever changing with the light, surpass magnificent.

Hardin

Retrace your treads to St. Xavier and continue on MT 313 to **Hardin**, a tidy agricultural town that makes hay by being the gateway to the Crow Indian Reservation, Bighorn Canyon and the Little Bighorn Battlefield National Monument. A big job for a little town. A brochure states that "celebrations rage here." The biggest and most highly hyped of these (see

Custer's Last Stand Re-enactment, Hardin, MT.

Custer Country

Festivals & Special Events) is **Little Bighorn Days/Custer's Last Stand Re-enactment** in June. Hardin has ample accommodations for Battlefield visitors.

Hardin also has a couple of interesting museums. The **Bighorn County Historical Museum and Visitor Center**, at Exit 497 off I-90, features a "village" with several historic structures. A summertime Indian exhibit includes several tipis, one of which belonged to the late Robert S. Yellowtail, Sr., Bureau of Indian Affairs Superintendent at Crow Agency and Crow Tribal Council Chairman. Free admittance. The museum is open year-round, 8-8 from May 1 to Sept. 30 and 9-5 Mon.-Sat. from Oct. 1-Apr. 30.

The **Jailhouse Gallery** at 218 Center Ave. is maintained by the Big Horn Arts & Crafts Association. Revolving monthly art exhibits reflect the local heritage. The museum and shop are open Tues.-Fri., 10-5, in Jan. -Apr. and Mon.-Sat., 9:30-5:30, May-Dec. **Crow Agency**, 11 miles south of Hardin on I-90, is the real gateway to the Little Bighorn Battlefield National Monument. The Crow tribal offices are also at Crow Agency. The **Reno-Benteen Monument** and the **Reno Battlefield Museum**, open year-round, are at **Garryowen**, off I-90 six miles south of Crow Agency. Battlefield sites of interest to Little Bighorn buffs link the monument sites and continue south of the Reno-Benteen Monument.

Little Bighorn

The Little Bighorn site offers much of interest, regardless of your stand in the controversy that continues to swirl around George Armstrong Custer and the famous battle in which his 7th Cavalry was defeated by Lakota and Cheyenne warriors.

At first glance the cemetery and visitor center lawns, their sanitized appearance extending to the undulating battlefield, belie the battle that raged here on June 25, 1876. I had to jolt myself into a visceral feeling for those bloody events.

The 7th Cavalry Obelisk and markers identifying where soldiers fell take a polarized approach to the battle's interpretation despite slow changes since Congress's 1991 decision to remove Custer from the Battlefield's name. Congress also authorized the construction of a monument to honor all fallen American Indian people.

At the opposite pole, visiting Custer buffs may take umbrage at the efforts of Monument Supervisor Gerard Baker to recognize the Indians who fought here. Indians now fill about half the Monument's summer tour guide jobs and the Crow Tribe's Little Bighorn College has been awarded a bus tour contract. The new attitude has created a climate conducive to the holding of Indian ceremonies at the Battlefield, and more Native Americans feel comfortable about visiting.

Crow Fair, Hardin, MT.

The visitor center store stocks many of the estimated 1,000 books that have been published about Custer and the battle that did him in. Regardless of whether you regard him as frontier hero or genocidal maniac, you'll find a book to satisfy your curiosity.

The amount of time you spend at the Battlefield depends on your level of interest. You could easily spend days tracking down every battle position and route. The Battlefield tour road and the Reno-Benteen Entrenchment Trail are open daily until 7:15 pm.

Daily visitor center talks and tours interpret the battle and cover a wide variety of related subjects. Living History Contact Stations are set up daily to interpret Plains Indian life and that of the US Cavalry, Indian scouts and attached personnel in 1876. A Junior Ranger program for kids is also available. Refer to *Special Interest Tours,* page 122, for information on private Battlefield tours.

The Crow & Northern Cheyenne Reservations

The Crow Nation welcomes non-Indians to its biggest annual event. The bang-up three-day Fourth of July pow-wow, parade and rodeo has achieved international fame. The huge tipi encampment at Lodge Grass draws visitors from all over the world to purchase Indian arts and crafts of exquisite workmanship and to enjoy the swirl of color surrounding this big competition pow-wow. See *Festivals & Special Events*, page 124, for information on other pow-wows and celebrations.

US 212 heads east across the Crow and Northern Cheyenne Reservations' common boundary. The reservations' topographical differences are as diverse as the tribes' traditional cultures and approaches to modern life. While the Crow Reservation consists largely of upland grazing lands, the Northern Cheyenne is a place of dry, rugged pine-clothed hills.

Lame Deer is the Reservation's principal town. Impressive new tribal offices stand in contrast to exceedingly modest homes.

DID YOU KNOW?

The town was named for Chief Lame Deer, killed here in a raid by Gen. Nelson A. Miles of Fort Keogh (now Miles City) on May 8, 1877. Lame Deer and his warriors were surprised on a peaceful hunting foray.

Ashland, on US 212 just off the reservation's eastern boundary, is a sad straggle of a town offering basic services. The Ashland District of the Custer National Forest office and St. Labre Indian School are located here. Begun in 1884 by four Urseline nuns, the school currently provides K-12 education to 700 children at three locations on the Crow and Northern Cheyenne Reservations. The Ashland campus includes a unique tipi-style church and the excellent **Cheyenne Indian Museum**. On display is a large collection of Native American artifacts representing several Plains Indian tribes. Photos of tribal elders and school children from times past hang on adjoining hallway walls. I wondered at the thoughts seething behind those childrens' impassive faces. How did they feel about being forced to attend a school designed to erase their culture in the name of Christianity? Museum hours vary, but you can generally find someone to open up for you. ☎ 406-784-2200.

Colstrip

The Northern Cheyennes' poverty, exacerbated by their reluctance to allow coal mining on their sacred lands, contrasts sharply with tidy Colstrip. Residents of this planned community, 22 miles north of Lame Deer via MT 39, depend on Western Energy Co. for their jobs. Colstrip's big draw, from a kid's perspective, is a huge municipal swimming pool featuring a labyrinthine waterslide.

Parents may want to check in at the Visitor Information Center at 6200 Main Street to join a free guided tour of the power plant and surface mine. Center hours are Mon.-Fri., 9-5. Tours run from April to October, weather permitting. ☎ 406-748-2990 for tour times.

Broadus

From Ashland, US 212 slopes southeastward to Wyoming over almost 100 seemingly interminable miles. A halfway point is Broadus, in the Powder River Valley. One of the arid West's mile-wide, inch-deep, too-wet-to-plow and too-thick-to-drink rivers, the Powder made more impact on the history of the region than it does on recreationists, other than hunters and wildlife watchers. Tellingly, the **Powder River Historical Museum** displays a buggy designed to ford streams. The **Powder River Cattle Drive** (see *Adventures on Horseback*, page 105) has made Broadus the self-styled Wagon Train Capitol of the World; a boast as big as area stockmens' 10-gallon hats.

■ The I-94 Corridor

The Lewis & Clark Trail

The Lewis and Clark Trail is easily traced through Custer Country. Just follow the Yellowstone River and watch for Lewis and Clark signs and Montana Historical Markers.

On the 1806 return trip to St. Louis, the party split at the site of present day Missoula. Captain Meriwether Lewis and most of the party explored northern Montana before heading down the Missouri River. Clark and nine men, accompanied by their Shoshone guide Sacajawea and her baby, followed the Yellowstone, rendezvousing with Lewis below the confluence of the Yellowstone and Missouri Rivers in today's North Dakota. Clark's journals record many exciting events on this leg of the trip.

Pompey's Pillar is the route's only readily identifiable landmark, but you can visit the approximate site where Clark and company carved out two dugout canoes to use in continuing their journey downriver. From I-90, take Exit 426 at Park City. Follow Lewis and Clark signs seven miles east on the frontage road, then six miles on a country road to the undeveloped Buffalo Mirage Access fishing site.

Pompey's Pillar National Historic Landmark, maintained by the BLM, is 28 miles east of Billings on I-94 at Exit 23. Rising from the surrounding prairie, the massive sandstone outcrop has a venerable history. The remains of animal drawings on the rock face indicate that people have long camped and hunted in the area. The Crow Indians called the rock "Where the Mountain Lion Lies."

AUTHOR TIP *The Clark party came upon the landmark on July 25. Clark was awestruck, naming it Pompey's Tower for Sacajawea's baby. The child's name was Jean Baptiste, but the explorers fondly called him Pompey, meaning "little chief" in the Shoshone language.*

"I marked my name and the day of the month and year," wrote Clark in his journal. And so he did, unwittingly providing the only verifiable on-site reminder of the Voyage of Discovery. A boardwalk climbs to the inscription and continues to the top of the rock.

Interpretive tours are available on request in summer. The visitor center is open daily from Memorial Day weekend to Sept. 30. Call ☎ 406-875-2233 for current hours. The gates are closed during the remainder of the year, but the site is open to walk-in access.

At the mouth of the Bighorn River, the party was kept awake by the bellowing of buffalo bulls. At Castle Rock, near today's **Forsyth**, Clark noted that the elk on the riverbank were so abundant that he had not been out of sight of elk that day. Near present day **Miles City**, Clark remarked upon the coal in the hills. On July 30, after negotiating Buffalo and Bear Rapids, the group came upon the **Makoshika Badlands**, described by Clark as "birnt hills." Camping near present day **Glendive**, Clark recorded seeing an unusually large grizzly bear eating a buffalo. On August 1, the party saw thousands of buffalo crossing the river ahead of their canoes. A quarter of a mile wide, the herd took an hour and 15 minutes to cross. While setting up camp near today's **Sidney**, they saw two more big herds crossing the river. The next day they crossed into present day North Dakota.

I-94 Corridor Cities & Towns

Billings

Billings, nestled in the Yellowstone River Valley, has been a thriving metropolis since its 1882 founding as a Northern Pacific Railway head. Instead of suffering the decline typical of railway towns at the close of the homesteading era, Billings just hummed along. Its population grew with the times, working in oil refineries and a variety of other industries. Today Billings is Montana's most populous city, boasting upwards of 100,000 residents.

Billings heartily embraces the cowboy ethos. Some $150 million in livestock is sold annually at the city's Public Auction Yards.

Billings Fun Facts

The city named for Northern Pacific Railroad promoter Frederick Billings has an eclectic history. Charles Lindbergh once lived here, repairing bicycles and performing as a barn-storming stunt flyer. Earlier, Calamity Jane drove a stagecoach and sold baked goods near Billings. Kampgrounds of America (KOA) headquarters occupy a Billings highrise; the first KOA campground is east of town on the Yellowstone River.

Except for some leafy residential areas bordering the river, Billings is not a pretty city. The refineries west of town sprout bulbous structures and nasty spewing stacks. Downtown is a grey forest of highrises. The rimrocks are somewhat dramatic and the view of the city from that eminence is worth the uphill drive.

Bedroom developments have long since spilled out of the valley onto the tablelands topping the 300- to 500-foot-high rimrocks north and east of town. I-90 runs along the southern edge of downtown, veering off toward Hardin and the Crow Indian Reservation east of the city. I-94 jump-starts where I-90 leaves off, zipping eastward to the North Dakota line.

Billings is an easy city to get around in. The one-way streets follow logic and are more of a help than an annoyance. A handsome Visitor Center, just north of Exit 450 off I-90, serves as a foil for a huge bronze mounted cowboy urging on two bronze Longhorn steers. The statues commemorate the Great Centennial Cattle Drive of 1989 and celebrate the importance of cattle to Montana history.

The **Visitor Center** is on 27th Street, the main artery through downtown, affording easy access to museums and the rimrock area. Friendly and knowledgeable Visitor Center/Chamber of Commerce personnel will steer you where you wish to go. Pick up a Billings Scenic Drive brochure. The Visitor Center is open daily in summer, 8:30-6. Winter hours: weekdays, 8:30-5.

Ride a **Billings Trolley** for a guided a tour of the city. Reserve a seat by calling ☎ 888-618-4FUN or 406-254-7180 or fax to 406-245-5699.

The amount of time you ought to spend in Billings is largely dependent on your interest in museum-hopping. Billings has a bunch. The **Peter Yegen, Jr. Yellowstone County Museum** is on the rimrock north of downtown, adjacent to the Billings Logan International Airport. Housed in a circa 1893 log cabin, the museum displays a collection of Native American artifacts, cowboy memorabilia, dinosaur bones, old photographs, antique clothing and other artifacts reflecting area history. An assortment of horsedrawn vehicles is also on display. Free admission. The museum is open Mon.-Sat., 10:30-5, ☎ 406-256-6811.

Pick up the rimrock-edge **Black Otter Trail** east of the museum, following it about four miles to Boothill Cemetery and Kelly Mountain.

In-town museums include the **Yellowstone Art Museum**, at 401 N. 27th St., exhibiting Western and contemporary art. Call ☎ 406-256-6804 for current hours. The **Western Heritage Center**, at 2822 Montana Ave., offers changing exhibits reflective of the Western ethos. Open Tues.-Sat., 10-5 and Sun. 1-5. ☎ 406-256-6809. The **Moss Mansion**, the elegant turn-of-the-century home of a prominent Billings family and a filming site for the movie, *Son of the Lonesome Dove*, offers tours year-round. 914 Division St. ☎ 406-256-5100 for current hours.

Two museums, west and east of downtown respectively, offer a fix on the Yellowstone Valley's homesteading era and the agricultural machinery that drove it. **Oscar's Dreamland**, a private museum at 3100 Harrow Dr., displays over 500 units of steam, gas and horse drawn farm machinery and some 5,000 other antiques and artifacts. A "pioneer town" includes several original structures. You can spend an entire day here, revisiting the "good old days" of sweat and toil. Modest admittance fee. Open daily, 9-6, May 1-Sept. Take I-90 west from downtown to Exit 446, then drive west on S. Frontage Road. ☎ 406-656-0966 or 245-4598 for further information.

The **Huntley Project Museum of Irrigated Agriculture**, three miles east of the homesteading-cum-bedroom town of Huntley on US 312 (take Exit 6 off I-94), is another nostalgic showcase of homesteading tools and memorabilia. Open daily, 9-4, Memorial Day-Labor Day. ☎ 406-967-2680 (evenings).

Billings residents, proud of the **Alberta Bair Theatre for the Performing Arts**, are quick to inform visitors that it's the largest performing arts theatre between Minneapolis and Spokane. You might catch a

Custer Country

Broadway musical, a ballet or a Billings Symphony performance. ☎ 406-256-6052 for schedule information.

Nearby **Pictograph Caves State Park** preserves three caves containing over 100 pictographs drawn some 10,000 years ago by prehistoric hunters. Archaeologists excavated the caves' floors to reveal over 30,000 artifacts from four distinct prehistoric time periods. The remarkably well preserved pictographs, reflecting several painting methods and dyes, may record successful hunts or raids, or may relate to certain ceremonies. Images of shields may have been painted on rocks before battles by warriors wishing to gain rock-like strength. Your conjecture is as good as anyone's. A visit to the Pictograph Caves can be deeply moving as you place the caves and yourself in perspective with those long ago artists. Bring your binoculars. Steep paved trails link the three caves. A pleasant picnic area is provided.

The park is seven miles south of Billings by way of Coburn Road. The first four miles are paved, but the final three miles are gravel with no turn-arounds and may be too hilly and winding for large RVs and vehicles towing trailers. My 24-foot RV had no problem. The park is open daily, 8-8, April 15-Oct. 15. Snow or heavy rain may shorten the season. For further information, ☎ 406-245-0227 in season, 406-247-2940 out of season.

Small riverside and/or railroad towns, some worth a look-see, others little more than dusty has-beens with post offices, pop up at intervals along I-94.

Forsyth

I-94 more or less follows the Yellowstone River east of Pompey's Pillar, but interstate and river get close and personal at Forsyth, a typical homestead-cum-cattle town and county seat. To visit is to look backward to the 1930s. The **Roxy Theatre** boasts that it has been showing films since 1930. The weathered brick **Howdy Hotel** looks much as it did in 1905 when it opened to accomodate drummers swinging off trains carrying sample cases.

The **Rosebud County Courthouse** is Forsyth's pride. Listed on the National Register of Historic Places, it boasts a copper dome as well as numerous murals and stained glass windows. Next door is the **Rosebud County Pioneer Museum**, a repository for "olden days" artifacts and photographs. Open May 15-Sept. 15, 9-7, Mon.-Sat., 1-7 Sundays.

Miles City

A scattering of has-been towns line the 42-mile route between Forsyth and Miles City. Miles City folks don't refer to their town as "The Cowboy Capitol of Montana" just to wag their tongues. This is the ultimate cow town. It's also one of those Western towns whose pride kinda rubs off on you. It even has bragging rights to a park with a real old-fashioned, honest-to-goodness swimming hole.

Named in honor of Gen. Nelson A Miles, commanding officer of nearby Fort Keogh, the town was birthed by the Indian wars and teethed on Montana's railroad and free-range cattle boom. By 1884, when the Montana Stockgrowers' Association was formed here, the railroad had transformed the raw new town into an important cattle and sheep market. Miles City's rollicking cowboy history is an integral part of the city's outlook today.

Sheep & Cattle

The successful introduction of sheep to the Fort Keogh area presaged the co-existence of cattle and sheep on today's range, giving the lie to a common belief that cattle and sheep don't mix because sheep crop forage to the roots. Many of Montana's cattle barons, such as Charles M. Bair (see *Russell Country* for information on visiting his home near Martinsdale) successfully managed both sheep and cattle. At one time, sheep were important cash crops. Today's stockmen often introduce sheep to their ranges to keep noxious weeds in check. Sheep will eat weeds while finicky cattle prefer grass.

KID-FRIENDLY Remnants of **Fort Keogh** still stand on the western edge of town. The **Range Riders Museum**, a fascinating repository of cattle country memorabilia, occupies the original site of Fort Keogh cantonment #1, built to secure the area following the Battle of the Little Bighorn. The museum owes its existence to the Range Riders Organization, a group of cowboy/stockmen who felt that area history should be preserved. The complex's nine buildings house artifacts representing every facet of life on the range, from the early days to the present. Exhibits include Plains Indian artifacts, a typical frontier town with 11 representative shops, the Bert Clark Gun Collection featuring over 400 firearms, pioneer era conveyances, and a gallery of photos honoring area stockmen. That's just for starters.

You absolutely must visit the Range Riders Museum. Small admission fee. Open April 1-Oct. 31, 8-8, or by appointment. ☎ 406-232-4483. Take Exit 136 off I-94 and follow US 12 toward town. The museum is on your left. You can't miss it.

The **Fairgrounds**, across the street from the museum, is often the site of the brand of country auction that you may have thought went out with the good old days. Farm machinery, household goods or livestock – one could be in progress the weekend you are there. Every third weekend in May, folks for miles around turn out for the **Miles City Jaycee Bucking**

Horse Sale. Not just a sale, the event is also a thrill-a-minute rodeo and downhome wing-ding. Rhinestone cowboys need not apply. It's a slice of real life, Western-style. Yeehaw! See *Festivals & Special Events* (page 125) for listings of other Miles City events.

Don't think Miles City eschews art. The **Custer County Art Center**, on Waterplant Road off US 12, a half-mile west of downtown, displays an eclectic assortment of permanent, special and traveling exhibits. This is truly "underground art." No, nothing contraband. The gallery is housed in the former Miles City Water Works' underground concrete tanks. When I visited, one entered through a huge corrugated steel pipe. There was talk of constructing a more conventional entrance. Too bad. Entrance fee. Open year-round, Tues.-Sun., 1-5. ☎ 406-232-0635.

Though Miles City has the type of fast food and motel strip common to all larger American towns, it still has a Main Street with a dime store lunch counter, an early-days saloon and no parking meters.

Terry

I-94 jaunts along the Yellowstone for 70 miles before pulling up at Glendive. Halfway is Terry, a must-stop. The **Prairie County Museum**, housed in the old State Bank of Terry building, is the repository of Evelyn Cameron's homestead era photographs. The museum also features room displays, artifacts relating to the homestead era, and some of Cameron's possessions. Open Memorial Day-Labor Day, Wed.-Mon. Call the Terry Chamber of Commerce for current hours. Free admittance. If the museum is closed when you arrive, a board member will open it for you. A list of phone numbers is posted on the door. Terry is also a popular agate hunting site.

Evelyn Cameron

Evelyn Cameron accompanied her husband Ewen to a Montana ranch in 1889. Her impractical spouse envisioned raising polo ponies on nutritious Montana grass and shipping them to England where he would sell them for large sums of money. After the pony business foundered, Ewen turned naturalist, observing and writing about birds. His wife took to the hardships of ranch life like a frog to a lilypad, cheerfully performing the chores incident to running a ranch. She found time to keep diaries in which she expressed her admiration for the resourcefulness and pluck of her neighbors. Today, these diaries are invaluable records of the joys and hardships of life on a homestead.

Financial setbacks reduced Evelyn to selling vegetables and taking in boarders. One such, a well-to-do Irishman named Adams, introduced her to photography. She quickly became proficient. Photographers developed their own negatives in those days of heavy, unwieldy equipment. Evelyn mastered the art. She photographed every facet of rural life, from the bounteous wildlife to the peoples – especially the people. She was soon charging for her pictures, 25¢ apiece or $3 per dozen. Ewen died in 1915. Evelyn became a US citizen and continued ranching and photographing. She died in 1928, leaving 35 leatherbound diaries and thousands of photographs.

Donna Lucey, author of *Photographing Montana 1894-1928: The Life and Work of Evelyn Cameron*, described the photographs as "a virtual home movie of life on the frontier." In 1970, Lucey discovered thousands of photo-negatives in the basement of Evelyn's best friend's home. She spent years sorting the photographs and studying the diaries that faithfully chronicled a vivid chapter in Montana history.

Custer Country

Glendive

Glendive, a city of some 5,000 residents, thrives on dinosaurs, paddlefish and agates. Though indirectly named by a British anachonism (see below) and owing much of its prosperity to anachronistic creatures, Glendive enjoys an economy that is also based on grains and forage crops. And on tourists.

Sir St. George Gore

Glendive was named for Glendive Creek, a corruption of Glendale, the name given to the stream by the aptly named Sir St. George Gore. In 1854, Gore turned up in the area with a gaggle of companions, 40 servants, 112 horses, 12 yoke of oxen, 14 hunting dogs, 21 carts loaded with luxuries, and an arsenal that would excite the envy of an army. Gore hired Jim Bridger as guide and proceeded to shoot every animal and bird that moved. So excessive was the slaughter that he earned the scorn of both Indians and whites.

Paddlefish, prehistoric throwbacks, have proved profitable for Glendive. The roe, or caviar, graces upscale tables and commands upscale prices. Anglers are encouraged to donate their catch's roe to the common good. A fish weighing 60 lbs. will have 10 lbs. of roe. This processes to eight pounds of caviar. Proceeds are divided between Montana Fish, Wildlife and Parks and non-profit services in the Glendive area.

At the processing plant in the Chamber of Commerce building, the roe is worked through a screen, sorted and lightly salted before being weighed, placed in containers, stored in a cooler for three weeks, then quick frozen.

The Chamber, occupying former supermarket digs at 313 S. Merrill Ave., houses displays of paddlefish and agates (see *Rock Hounding*). Chamber hours are Mon.-Fri., 9-5. Hours may be extended in summer. ☎ 406-365-5601 for current hours.

Makoshika State Park cozies up to a residential area on Glendive's west side. See *The Land* (page 73) for insight into prehistoric creature digs in the park. The 8,000-acre park is a weird wonderland of conical grey rock formations and juniper-studded badlands overlaying as-yet-undiscovered dinosaur fossils. Several roads and trails traverse the park (see *Adventures on Foot*, page 100). The visitor center doubles as an interactive museum displaying a triceratops skeleton, head and frill and numerous other fossils. A target shooting range is a mere half-mile from the park entrance. Is this Montana, or what? The Makoshika Visitor Center is open daily, Labor Day-Memorial Day, 10-6. Off-season hours are 9-5 Mon.-Sat., 1-5 Sunday. ☎ 406-365-6256.

Glendive's **Frontier Gateway Museum**, on Belle Prairie Road north of town, is a complex of seven buildings that includes the ubiquitous original log cabin, schoolhouse and blacksmith shop, plus a replica of Glendive's main street in the 1890s. Other exhibits include reminders of the Northern Pacific Railroad upon which the town was founded, and other local memorabilia. Open Mon.-Sat., June-Aug., 9-12 and 1-5 and 1-5 on Sundays and holidays. Open daily in May and Sept., 1-5. For an off-season appointment, ☎ 406-365-8168.

The **Yellowstone River** runs tan and turgid through Glendive. It pretties up a bit as it cruises along MT 16 for 17 miles to the Yellowstone Intake Diversion Dam and the adjacent fishing access site. Here, you can attempt, in season, to snag a paddlefish, a gen-u-ine pre-historic gamefish. Dubbed paddlefish because of long paddle-like "snouts," the fish weigh 40-100 lbs. and are quite tasty. Learn how to catch one in the *Fishing* section of this chapter.

Wibaux

I-94 veers due east at Glendive, looking in on Wibaux before entering North Dakota. This proud old town of some 600 residents bills itself as the eastern gateway to Montana. It's more than that. Called Mingusville before Pierre Wibaux strutted into town 1895, the burg was the Wild West personified. Liquored-up cowboys sported with greenhorns, making them dance to sprays of bullets. One such "sporting event" earned nearby rancher Teddy Roosevelt the nickname Old Four Eyes after the bespectacled future president successfully defended himself. A Huguenot cattleman named Pierre Wibaux civilized the town after lending it his name in an exercise of political flim-flam. Learn all about it at the **Pierre Wibaux Museum Complex**, hard by the railroad tracks off Wibaux Street. Guide Marlene Welliever showed me around, as she does all visitors. A veritable fount of Wibaux lore, Marlene brought the town's salad days and the doings of its first citizen entertainingly to life. In addition to Pierre Wibaux's home, the museum includes artifacts recalling the days when men like Wibaux and Roosevelt lived the romance of the open range.

The museum complex is open May 1-Oct. 1, Mon.-Fri., 9-5, and on weekends and off-season by request. ☎ 406-796-9969, 795-2381 or 796-2253 for an appointment.

Baker

Head swirling with fascinating tid-bits of historical lore, I headed south on MT 7 for the 45-mile drive to Baker. Narrow and high-centered, the road invites reflection on the historic trail that once wound through here, linking the Missouri in Dakota Territory with Fort Keogh on the Yellowstone. A historical marker some 12 miles north of Baker reads, "Around these gumbo buttes and across these ridges, the old trail wended its way.... " It goes on to describe the colorful assortment of people who traversed the trail before the coming of the Northern Pacific Railroad and homesteaders' fences caused it to be abandoned. Grassy trail ruts are still visible off to the southwest.

Baker enjoyed an oil boom before settling down to a ranching economy. A serendipitous lake, complete with boat launch, beach and pleasant park, lies just south of town. Baker is a good stop-off en route to Ismay off US 12, or to Medicine Rock State Park, Ekalaka and the Sioux Ranger District of the Custer National Forest.

Plevna

US 12 heads west from Baker to Miles City. The lonely 77-mile drive through cattle country is broken midway by a nice rest stop. Some 13 miles west of Baker is Plevna, a homestead era town named for the Bulgarian home of immigrants who worked on the Milwaukee Railroad and settled nearby. Russians and Germans also settled here, making it a pocket of Eastern European culture. Plevna's heyday is history. Today, abandoned storefronts and neatly kept houses cluster like frightened quail around the town's grain elevators.

Ismay

Twenty-five miles west of Baker on US 12, a sign announcing "Ismay, 6 miles" points down a dusty gravel road.

A Town Called Joe

Ismay, alias Joe, Montana, was a typical on-the-skids homestead-era railroad town; the kind of place where dust rides

Custer Country

prairie winds through gaping doors. The Official Montana Highway Map lists Ismay (not Joe) as having 20 residents.

Back in 1993, a gimmick-hungry Kansas City radio station contacted Ismay's mayor (salary: $4 per month), to inquire if the city fathers would consider changing the town's name to Joe, Montana for the duration of the football season. Townsfolk, thrilled with the implied association with the famous Kansas City Chiefs quarterback, agreed. Just one catch: it seems to have escaped the locals that the change would be only temporary.

Delighted with its 15 minutes of fame, Ismay thirsted for more. Residents launched a bang-up celebration that included a July 4th parade, rodeo and fireworks wing-do that drew some 2,000 spectators. Darned if the town didn't net almost $70,000! Flushed with success, the town's leading (well... almost only) citizens, the Gerbers and the Nimitzes, decided to recreate their moment of victory the following year.

Assured of a spot on the David Letterman show, Ismay (er... Joe) made elaborate preparations. But the spot never materialized. Neither did the expected hordes of outlanders. It's anyone's guess if Joe will hold another wing-do, but the town is worth a visit just for the... well, you know.

Ismay seems to have resigned itself to rural anonymity. Almost. The rodeo arena and firehouse still bear signs recalling its Joe, Montana fling. Grain elevators and steel storage bins lining the railroad tracks indicate that the townsite is surrounded by a large farming operation. Forlorn wooden signs identify buildings and householders long since gone. The inevitable junk cars keep company with some dilapidated houses. A community church set against low buttes is well kept and in use.

Medicine Rocks State Park

Medicine Rocks State Park, off MT 7 25 miles south of Baker, is a place of oddly shaped eroded sandstone formations. Depending on your preference, it's either fantastically beautiful or disturbingly desolate. As the name implies, it was a place of "big medicine" where Indian warriors listened to spirit voices. The park offers primitive camping and picnicking.

Ekalaka

Just down MT 7 is Ekalaka, a small town where not much happens. The Meadowlark Club's celebration of the annual arrival of Montana's state bird is about it. The town offers basic services.

The nearby **Sioux District** of the Custer National Forest, which includes the Chalk Buttes, Long Pines and Ekalaka Hills, is a good place to spot nesting raptors. See this chapter's sections on *Adventures on Foot*, *on Wheels*, *on Snow* and *Wildlife Watching* for recreational opportunities.

■ Ranch Country Via US 12

US 12 swings north and west from Forsyth, meeting up with the Musselshell River at Melstone. It continues past Roundup and a clutch of fading homestead-era towns, passing into Charlie Russell Country near Deadman's Basin Reservoir.

Here, homesteaders' frame shacks seem not to rest easy on the land, settling to earth in splintered heaps. You can almost hear their sharp-edged sighs. By way of contrast, weathered log cabins and barns seem skewed by time, but not defeated – content to settle gently to the earth from whence they came.

Ingomar

If you blink, you won't notice Ingomar. Don't blink. If there was ever a remnant of those old-time cow towns, this is it. The streets are still dirt-dusty. The boardwalk sidewalk is still in place outside the Jersey Lily Saloon & Eatery. There are outhouses, too, identified as "Heifer Pen" and "Bull Pen." But hold up there, pardner: Ingomar was once hailed as the sheep-shipping capitol of the world. In Montana, sheep and cattle do mix.

Beginning near White Sulphur Springs, the cottonwood-fringed **Musselshell River** flows through farm and ranch lands for 365 miles before emptying into Fort Peck Reservoir. It's a fairly pretty river, offering canoeing (see *Adventures on Water*) and affording pleasant bucolic views through the heart of Montana's cattle country.

Melstone

With 155 residents and a ramshackle general store, Melstone is the most populous of the string of dying towns between Forsyth and Roundup. The **Hougen Ranch** (see *Adventures on Horseback*) enjoys a romantic view of river and town.

Roundup

An annual cattle drive (see *Adventures on Horseback*) capitalizes on Roundup's name and is one of the town's best-known events. With over 2,000 residents, the Musselshell County seat is the trading center for folks from miles around.

DID YOU KNOW?

Named Roundup for the herds of cattle that were gathered here prior to the homesteading era, the town later enjoyed a coal mining boom.

Custer Country

The **Musselshell County Historical Museum** celebrates Roundup's coal mining era with a realistic coal tunnel. Photos of past roundups and memorabilia reflecting area history are also on display. The museum is open daily, April-Sept., 1-5.

The **Cowbelle Campground**, across the river from the Musselshell County Fairgrounds, offers free camping and picnicking in a grove of mature trees.

Lavina

Lavina, 21 miles west of Roundup, nuzzles the river in a leafy glade. The old **Adams Hotel** gleams white in the sun, its rows of windows seeming to reflect on the town's and hotel's salad days. A restoration effort is afoot, but those glory days remain ever illusive. So it goes.

Adventures

■ Adventures on Foot

Hiking & Backpacking

Hiking and backpacking opportunities in Custer Country are fewer than in the mountains to the west. But they hold a special appeal for those who enjoy the mystique of rock formations and near-desert country.

> *Observe the "leave no trace" ethic in the Custer National Forest, the Pryor Mountains, the Bighorn National Recreation Area, and on BLM lands. That means pack out what you pack in. Leave trails and other sites exactly as you found them.*

Bighorn Canyon National Recreation Area

Bighorn Canyon is almost next door to the battleground, as distances are measured in this place of far-flung landmarks. Head south on Rt. 313 from Hardin for the 44-mile drive to the **National Park Service Visitor Center at Fort Smith** and the nearby **Yellowtail Dam Visitor Center**. The nearby site of **Fort C.F. Smith** is on the Crow Indian Reservation. The Fort area and Reservation lands bordering Bighorn Canyon National Recreation Area are generally closed to the public. The Park Service offers summer programs and tours.

The Recreation Area extends into Wyoming. This book confines itself to the portion within Montana. Much of the canyon is not served by road. If you wish to visit the area between the Wyoming line and Barry's Landing on the west side of the canyon, you must drive north from Lovell, Wyoming on Rt. 37. In Montana, this road is known as the Bad Pass Highway. You can use this "highway," recommended for 4WD high clearance vehicles, as a take-off point for cross-country backpacking forays to and beyond Barry's Landing.

Cross-country backpacking is permitted in all sections open to public use within the 120,000 acres of the National Recreation Area. Custer National Forest Ranger stations and visitor centers issue free, mandatory back country permits.

You will need an area map (obtainable at ranger stations and visitor centers for a small charge), a compass, drinking water, a first aid kit with snakebite kit, and sufficient provisions for the time you intend to be out. This area is notorious for sudden weather changes. Bring rain gear and other appropriate clothing for high country weather extremes. Become informed regarding private property lines and areas closed to public access.

You'll see lots of wildlife; bighorn sheep, black bears and wild horses. Take normal precautions while in bear country. Black bears are less intimidating than grizzlies, but guidelines applying to grizzlies apply to black bears as well:

- Never feed a bear.
- Never leave food or garbage where a bear can get at it.
- Don't leave empty food containers or dirty dishes or cooking utensils outside or stored in a tent.
- Black bears are generally more afraid of you than you are of them, but make tracks if you come upon a sow with her young.

Prairie rattlesnakes and black widow spiders abound in high desert country. Watch where you place your feet and hands in brushy areas and around rocks. One evening at dusk, I sat right next to a coiled rattlesnake. Luckily for me, I departed faster than the sluggish snake, no doubt sleeping off a meal, could strike.

Always inform someone of where you are going and when you plan to return. And don't hike alone.

Pryor Mountain National Wild Horse Range

The Pryor Mountain National Wild Horse Range butts up against Bighorn Canyon National Recreation Area, but they are not joined by a public road. The best access to the Wild Horse Range is from Laurel via US 310. Watch for signs about a mile south of Bridger. From there, a gravel road passes through the Custer National Forest to Dryhead Overlook. From here on, the road deteriorates to little more than a trail. A 4WD high-clearance vehicle is recommended if you wish to continue on to Penn's Cabin at the northern edge of the Wild Horse Range. The Burnt Timber Ridge Road and the Sykes Ridge Road circumnavigate the Range southward from Penn's Cabin.

 WATCHABLE **WILDLIFE** The Wild Horse Range is in the Pryor Mountains, an extension of the Bighorn Mountains. Annual rainfall variants from less than five inches in the foothills to 20 inches in the high country indicate the types of plants you can expect to find: from native high desert grasses to stands of ponderosa pine. These nourishing grasses afford grazing for the wild horses, descendants of European Spanish horses. Bighorn sheep, mule deer and some elk also thrive here. **Dry Head Overlook** is a good place to see golden eagles and other raptors. Bats roost along limestone cliff ledges.

Hiking opportunities abound in the Pryor Mountains, but there are no maintained trails. Access is from the aforementioned roads surrounding the Range. From Sykes Ridge, you can enjoy a sweeping view of the Bighorn Basin. All concerns regarding back country hiking hold true here.

Southeast Custer Country

 WATCHABLE **WILDLIFE** Custer Country's southeastern corner also offers some hiking opportunities. The three **Camps Pass Trails**, ranging from 1.7 to 3.7 miles in length, are in the Ashland Ranger District of the Custer National Forest. This district has been described as an island of pine in a sea of grass. Proghorn, mule deer and sagegrouse are often seen. The trailhead is 18 miles east of Ashland on the south side of US 212, off Road 785. The trails are also open to horses and mountain bikes, but these are reportedly seldom encountered.

Another Ashland Ranger District trailhead, culminating at a fire lookout tower affording views of the Tongue River Breaks and the distant Bighorn Mountains, is five miles south of Birney. Drive south of Ashland on the Tongue River Road for about 25 miles to the intersection with the highway to Lame Deer. Bear left on Poker Jim Road. Continue until the road becomes impassable (about two miles). Park here. Follow cow paths along the South Fork of Poker Jim Creek. Head for the highest spot after reaching open meadows above the breaks and climb to the Lookout. The hike is 14 miles round trip.

Buffalo Creek Wilderness Study Area

This area, administered by the BLM in the Powder River Country south of Broadus, virtually guarantees a back country experience sans crowds. Take the Powder River East Road south from Broadus off US 59. Choose a dry sunny day unless you are driving a 4WD vehicle. The wilderness study area is marked by brown posts, visible on the south side of the road. Park and hike wherever you like in the trailless area.

A north-south ridge of some 4,000 feet above sea level rises above the Powder River on the west and Buffalo Creek to the east. Raptors and deer are among the wildlife commonly seen. This area provides an opportunity to poke around and explore while enjoying the area's unspoiled beauty.

Pompey's Pillar, off I-94 at Exit 23, offers good hiking. See *Touring* and *Wildlife Watching* (pages 85 and 118).

Strawberry Hills Recreation Area

 DID YOU KNOW? *The Strawberry Hills derive their name from a red layer of rock, called "clinker," formed when underlying coal seams caught fire, baking upper layers of sedimentary rock.*

If you visit **Miles City** and wish to enjoy a short day-hike, hie to the Strawberry Hills Recreation Area in the BLM's Powder River Resource Area. Take US 12 east from Miles City for about eight miles. Watch for the sign. Park and set your feet on the rough jeep track climbing from the parking lot. After passing through a gate, you'll cross an eroded basin on the north side of Strawberry Hill. From here, you may wander at will. Low ridges afford a view of the Lower Yellowstone River Valley.

CAUTION *These hills can be baking hot in summer, so bring plenty of water and a snakebite kit: prairie rattlers bask on the exposed rocks.*

The Sioux Ranger District

The Sioux Ranger District of the Custer National Forest, on the far eastern edge of Custer Country, lacks hiking trails. However, numerous primitive roads and jeep trails are open to hikers. Badlands hiking is not for everyone, but if you are intrigued by sometimes fanciful, often daunting eroded sandstone rocks and buttes you will enjoy exploring Medicine Rocks State Park, 10 miles north of Ekalaka on Montana 7. These rock formations have long held religious significance for Native Americans.

Hiking in Custer National Forest, north of Red Lodge.

Makoshika State Park

At Makoshika State Park near Glendive, you can combine an interest in pre-historic critters with hiking in an upland prairie habitat punctuated by hogback ridges, fluted hillsides, pinnacles and caprocked buttes. Brochures describing hiking and nature trails meandering through the park's 8,123 acres are available at the park Visitor Center.

Organized Walks/Hikes

Members of the Montana Wilderness Association offer a new schedule of Wilderness Walks every year. Everyone is invited, but group sizes are limited, so sign up early. Walks/hikes range from easy to strenuous and may occur anywhere in the state. For example, a 1998 hike, rated "moderate," explored the Custer National Forest wildlands of eastern Montana, taking in a prairie dog town, a wide lush valley, and lots of wildlife and birding. To obtain a booklet listing the current year's walks, contact the association at PO Box 635, Helena, MT 59624; ☎ 406-443-7350.

Caving

Where you have limestone formations, you'll likely have caves. Over the course of eons, ground water dripping through cracks and fissures in the rock dissolved the limestone, forming cavernous spaces within the rocks. These can vary from caves barely large enough to wiggle through to large caverns.

Exploring such caves is fun, but can be dangerous. Never explore by yourself. It's always best to err on the side of caution, especially if you are an inexperienced spelunker.

The Pryor Mountains

These mountains have numerous caves, most of a solution type formed in the Madison Limestone of the Mississippian age. None of the "discovered" caves have large rooms with copious amounts of stalactites and stalagmites. However, some comparatively unspectacular decorations are present.

Contact the BLM or US Forest Service to obtain a caving permit, and for information on necessary caving equipment and cave accessibility. BLM Public Lands in Montana *map 36 Pryor* can be useful in determining the locations of these caves, many of which are quite challenging. The best known of the Pryor Mountain caves is **The Big Ice Cave** on the east rim of East Pryor Mountain, 12 miles southeast of the Sage Creek Campground. A thick layer of ice covers the floor of the cave's second "room." A third level is suspected, but the ice on the second level blocks exploration. The Forest Service sometimes conducts tours of this cave on summer weekends. A locked gate covers the entrance. Contact the Custer National Forest office in Billings if you wish to explore this cave.

Mystery Cave may be one of Montana's better decorated caves, having attractive flowstone, delicate speleothems and soda straw stalactites and stalagmites. The entrance to Mystery Cave is gated to prevent vandalism. Again, contact the Forest Service if you wish to explore it. The cave is near the crest of East Pryor Mountain.

Pictograph Caves State Park

A softer caving experience can be enjoyed at Pictograph Caves State Park, seven miles south of Billings on Coburn Road (see *Touring*, page 88). For thousands of years, the trio of shallow caves in the Eagle Sandstone formation was used as a place to rest, repair weapons and tools, and to dry meat. And to record images via a method of inscription that we refer to as pictographs. While petroglyphs are images made by incising rocks, pictographs are painted on rock surfaces. Researchers have documented 106 paintings in **Pictograph Cave**, the larger of the three caves. The others are referred to as **Ghost Cave** and **Middle Cave**.

Sizeable rock shelters can also be found in **Medicine Rocks State Park** and on **Starvation Butte** southeast of Ekalaka.

Rock Hounding

Rock hounding in Custer Country, as well as in the rest of Montana, can be educational, fun and rewarding. But only if you follow the rules. Determine which individual or governing entity owns or maintains the land where you wish to search, then contact the appropriate office for regulations and a permit, if mandated. The following rockhounding site descriptions barely scratch the surface and are intended for the casual collector.

Serious rockhounds and geology buffs are advised to purchase a copy of Robert Feldman's *Rockhounding Montana* (see *Bibliography*).

The **Yellowstone River** between Billings and Sidney is prime agate hunting territory. The **Terry** area is especially fertile. Montana agates, often called plume or moss agates, are prized for the scenic designs sealed

Custer Country

inside the stones. The rough-skinned translucent rocks occur in terraced gravel deposits on the hills above the Yellowstone and its tributaries, as well as in the streams' and rivers' sand and gravel bars. The latter, constantly shifting, are the best places to look at times of low water. Montana agates resemble potatoes before being cut and polished.

Most of the lands along the Yellowstone and its tributaries are privately owned. Obtain permission from the landowner before setting foot there. The proprietors of rock shops in area towns are often helpful in providing information regarding accessible areas. A guided **Yellowstone River boat tour** offers a great way to search for agates. LeMar Schock is happy to oblige. His customized agate trips meander upriver for a distance of 18 to 30 miles, using a pontoon boat or an outboard runabout. Trips are of one or two days' duration. Schock can be reached at 213 N. Merrill, Glendive, MT 59330; ☎ 406-365-5601.

An **outdoor recreation vehicle site** adjacent to the Yellowstone River Bridge on South Billings Boulevard often yields fossils and crystals. It also yields off-road vehicles, so be alert. You may find petrified wood and possibly an agate in the gravels in and near the Yellowstone southwest of Billings.

Fossilized leaves are often found in red shale about eight miles east of **Miles City** on US 12. Leaf prints are revealed by carefully splitting layers of shale with a hammer and chisel. Area roadcuts may also produce fossil leaves.

Fossil oysters (*Crassotrea subtrigonalis*) can be found in road cuts about 9.7 miles west of **Lavina** on the north side of US 12.

If you know what you are looking for, and can identify geologic formations, you may expect happy rockhounding in the **South Pryor Mountains**. Numerous jeep trails penetrate this area accessed by US 310 south of Bridger.

Rock Shops & Clubs

Collectors Emporium, 114 N. 29th St., Billings, MT 59101; ☎ 406-259-2338 or 656-5707.

Greenleaf's Jewelry, Inc., 312 8th St. W., Billings, MT 59104; ☎ 406-245-7424.

Hobby Cab Rock Shop, 1912 Old Hardin Rd., Billings, MT 59101; ☎ 406-259-6284 or 256-5044.

Big Sky Agates, owned by Oscar Mastvelton, 817 Jefferson School Rd., Glendive, MT 59330; ☎ 406-365-3888.

Mart's Agates, 602 E. Borden, Glendive, MT 59330; ☎ 406-365-5154.

Billings Gem & Mineral Club, PO Box 477, Billings, MT 59103. Visitors are invited to attend meetings held the first Thurs. of each month, July, Aug. and Dec. excepted, at 7:30 pm at the First Christian Church, 522 N. 29th St.

Yellowstone Agate Club, Inc., Miles City, MT 59301.

■ Adventures on Horseback

Horseback-friendly trails in Custer Country are handy for Montana horse owners. On the assumption that readers of this book will not be trailering Old Dobbin clear out to Montana, this book skips do-it-yourself trail riding information in favor of insight into guided riding opportunities. If you do plan on visiting Montana complete with steed, you should contact area BLM offices and the Custer National Forest headquarters and/or the Ashland or Sioux ranger station for detailed information on horse trails and equine etiquette on BLM lands and in the Custer National Forest.

The following riding opportunities include cattle roundups, wagon trains and working cattle operations that double as guest ranches. These are listed for your convenience and are not endorsed by me in any way. I recommend requesting the names of persons who have experienced the particular trip or ranch, then following up with them before reaching a decision. A taste of the West via horseback can be a week of heaven or seven days of hell. Your advance preparations may well determine which it will be.

Selecting an Outfitter

Ask questions and more questions of both yourself and the ranch owner or cattle drive director under consideration. Do you and your family have sufficient riding experience to spend hours in the saddle? If not, you might prefer a guest ranch offering a range of other activities. This way, you can ease into the riding bit.

The questions you ask the ranch owner or cattle drover should reflect your personal concerns. Don't be hesitant to ask, no matter how trivial the question might seem. They've heard it all. They are as anxious as you are to make your visit a success.

Good questions include:

- How much riding experience should you have to keep up?
- Are horses suitable for beginners as well as for intermediate and experienced riders provided?
- How much instruction is provided before neophyte riders are permitted to hit the trail?
- Are the horses owned by the ranch or drover, or are they rented for the season? (Owned is the preferred answer.)
- How many hours will you be in the saddle each day?

- Do plans allow for easing into riding? Plunging into hours of riding can cause soreness in muscles you never knew you had. Best to begin with an hour or two and work up from there.

Other concerns need to be addressed if you plan on taking the kids:

- What ages are accommodated?
- Will others in your kids' age ranges be there?
- Are there other fun things to do besides riding?
- Any special kids' activities? What safety rules are in place pertaining to kids?
- Are helmets provided? If not, pack Junior's bicycle helmet and see that he wears it.

Unlike some high-toned guest ranches in Montana's trendier areas, Custer Country cattle drives and guest ranches are not places to make a fashion statement. Worn jeans, shirts and a denim jacket are in. Spiffy designer jeans and dazzling Western-style shirts are out. There's a reason why cowboys wear 10-gallon hats. Buy a hat with a brim wide enough to shade your eyes from the sun's glare. Inexpensive straw will do. You will also need Western riding boots with heels; not to swagger around in, but to help keep your feet in the stirrups. If your wardrobe doesn't include such boots, purchase a pair well ahead of your trip and break them in. Few things are more painful than blisters caused by chafingly new boots when you must wear them on the trail tomorrow and the next day and the day after that.

Trail Rides

Refer to *Special Interest Adventures* (page 123) for information regarding **Cheyenne Trailriders**, an outfit that offers culturally based trail rides and other adventures on the Northern Cheyenne Indian Reservation.

Cattle Drives & Wagon Trains

Custer Country is cattle drive country. Yee haw! The annual **Roundup Cattle Drive**, originating from (where else?) Roundup, has put the town on Montana's Wild West map. Staged in mid-August, the six-day drive gathers and sorts stock on a working cattle ranch. Participants may choose between riding 'em cowboy or watching the action from a wagon seat; between sleeping in a tent or snoozing under the stars. Side trail rides, hearty chuckwagon meals, a rodeo and dancing Western-style are included in the fun. Contact Roundup Cattle Drive, Inc., Roundup, MT 59072; ☎ 800-257-9775.

Krayton and Druann Kerns hold their **Double Rafter cattle drives** whether or not any tender feet come to join in. The Double Rafter is a working ranch. In June, the cattle are moved from the foothills to summer range high in the Big Horn Mountains on the Montana-Wyoming line; then moved back down in September. 'Tween times, visitors are welcome to join the Kerns and their hands on the mountain as they go about such cattle tending chores as cutting out strays, scattering salt by pack horse, roping and doctoring sick cattle.

DID YOU KNOW? *Krayton Kerns is proud of the fact that the home ranch near Parkman, Wyoming was homesteaded in 1887 by his great great grandfather. Family members have trailed the Double Rafter herd to summer range in the Big Horns since 1895. Guests have been invited to trail along since 1989.*

The seven-day June cattle drives cover 60 miles. The six-day September drives cover 40 miles. Summer cow camp trips are of five days' duration. One singles trip is planned each summer.

The Double Rafter Ranch is headquartered at 521 Pass Creek Road, Parkman, WY 82838. The ranch maintains an office at 419 E. Main, Laurel, MT 59044. The Kerns can be reached by phone at ☎ 800-704-9268 or 406-628-2320.

Myers Ranch Wagon Trains offers three-day trips over the prairie east of Miles City. Guests ride in buckboards and other wagons reminiscent of rural transportation 100 years ago. The Myers family, Wayne, Sharon and Shannon, provide hearty meals, fiddlin' around a campfire, and stories related to the history of the area. Wildlife viewing, hiking and rock hunting come as part of the package. Guests sleep in tents. Trips run from June 1 through Labor Day. HC 80-Box 70, Ismay, MT 59336; ☎ 406-772-5675.

Powder River Wagon Trains, Cattle Drives & Ranch Vacations (see page 108 for a description of the outfit's ranch vacations) offers the Premiere Drive in early August. Operated by a group of ranchers and townsfolk from the Broadus area, the six-day wagon train and cattle drive trails a herd of 80 to 100 longhorn cattle over country rich in history. Guests can ride horseback or hitch a ride in a covered wagon. Evenings feature campfires and country music and dancing under a big tent. Box 676, Broadus, MT 59317; ☎ 800-492-8835, ☎ 800-982-0710 or 406-436-2404.

Schively Ranch offers cattle drives. See entry under *Working Guest Ranches* below.

X Hangin' H Ranch, Inc., a working cattle ranch near Glendive, stages multi-day June and August cattle drives on the gently rolling prairie of eastern Montana. Special drives can be arranged for groups of 10 or more. 221 River Road Loop, Glendive, MT 59330; ☎ 406-365-5839.

Working Guest Ranches

Visit a working stock ranch if you want an inside view of life on a real Western spread. The following Custer Country ranches are working cattle and/or sheep ranches that welcome guests. All provide bounteous country-style meals. Accommodations vary from rustic to down-home comfortable. Guests become acquainted with ranch families, gaining a perspective on rural life, Montana cow country-style. Some hosts invite guests to explore the ranch and to tag along or help with ranch chores. Others offer day trips to local points of interest. Ask about activities before deciding on a ranch.

Portrait of Two Ranches

"Typical" isn't an apt term for a Montana cattle/guest ranch. Each is as individualized as the family that runs it. But in many ways the Hougen and Drga Ranches typify those Montana ranches that combine stock operations with hospitality. Like the Drgas, most ranch families began welcoming guests as a "cash crop" to augment ranching's sometimes iffy monetary returns. Most found that they take to the experience as readily as do their guests. Karen Drga enjoys getting to know guests from as far away as Switzerland. She says that most remember farm life and want to expose their kids to it.

Like many ranches, the Hougen spread is run by two generations. Son Alan and wife Kayleen live just beyond hollering distance from parents Helen and Tom.

The Hougens are atypical in that they haven't been on this land for generations. They purchased the ranch some 25 years ago, building a handsome ranch house on a hill commanding views of the distant Little Snowy Mountains. They run 1,200 head of cattle on 35,000 acres and raise alfalfa in the fertile Musselshell River Valley. Their two daughters have grown up and moved away. Alan and Kayleen combine ranch work with competing at rodeos throughout the West.

Typically, the Hougen Ranch has seen a bunch of Montana history. Indians were here long before cattlemen. Tom surmises that the flat rock outcropping above the river is an old buffalo processing site. Bones and arrowheads have been found in the vicinity.

"I enjoy people," says Helen, who began her guest ranch venture by hosting hunters in the fall of 1997. "We have game just galore," she adds. Helen especially enjoys watching guests' reactions to ranch life. "They want to know how the ranch works.

Sprinklers and hay balers fascinate them." While guests are welcome to ride horseback, the Hougens make it clear that they "don't just do trail rides... ranching is a fulltime job."

Like most ranch women, Helen deftly combines seeing to her guests' comfort with turning out down-home meals, keeping an immaculate house, tending a bountiful garden, and lending a hand with ranch chores. She typifies all working guest ranch hosts when she says, "we love what we do and love where we are."

Anvil Butte Ranch near Wibaux in the eastern Montana badlands is a third generation family cattle ranch. Accommodating just one family or group of two to five at a time, Claudia and Leif Bakken offer personalized tours as part of the ranch package. Guests may choose between sleeping in the ranch house or in a tepee, priced on a per-day basis. Soaking up ranch life is an option. Tours offer an Indian Culture experience that may include a pow-wow; a Custer's Seventh experience offering insight into the Battle of Little Bighorn which may include the Custer's Last Stand Re-enactment; or a Dinosaur Experience, with agate hunting on the Yellowstone and visiting Makoshika State Park and the Dakota Dinosaur Museum. HC 71 Box 7335, Wibaux, MT 59353; ☎ 406-795-2341.

Buffalo Creek Ranch, 49 miles east of Billings near Custer, is an 8,000-acre grain and cattle ranch situated in an area of pine-covered hills and grasslands studded with rock formations. The extended Myhre family welcomes guests who wish to enjoy the simple pleasures of country life such as horseback riding, wildlife watching, fishing, swimming and chuckwagon cookouts. Guests are invited to participate in or watch seasonal ranch activities such as moving cattle on horseback, branding calves, fixing fence and haying. There are also campouts and covered wagon trips. The ranch features a guest lodge with four bedrooms, a living room, kitchen and laundry room. HC 76, Pineview Road, Custer, MT 59024; ☎ 406-947-2424 or 406-947-5547.

Cowboy Crossing is 60 miles north of Gillette, Wyoming, on the Wyoming-Montana line.

*The 45,000-acre cattle spread is known locally as the **3Bar Ranch**. Sprawling over timbered ridges, redrock buttes and broad valleys, the ranch includes three creeks draining into the Powder River. Wildlife abounds.*

Hosts Julie and J.D. Hewitt strive to create a wholesome family atmosphere. Guests are invited to join the hands in seasonal ranch activities such as branding calves, moving cattle and gathering yearlings for shipping. Accommodations are in a separate three-bedroom home at ranch headquarters. Home-cooked meals feature ranch-raised beef. Per-day all-inclusive rates. Cowboy Crossing, Recluse, WY 82725; ☎ 888-643-9488 or 406-427-5056.

Drga Ranch, in pine-studded hills 45 miles east of Miles City, is an 11,000-acre working cattle ranch – a no-frills family ranch. The Drgas also do some farming and raise much of their own food. Fred and Karen Drga and their three teenagers welcome one family or small group at a time. Guests can try their hand at milking the family cow, collecting eggs, picking berries or caring for 4-H animals. Other activities include horseback riding, going on a picnic in a team-drawn wagon, hiking, wildlife watching, fishing and watching or participating in rounding up cattle and other ranch chores. Accommodations are in the family home. Meals feature home-grown meats and produce. HC 80 Box 20, Ismay, MT 59336; ☎ 406-772-5715.

O Spear Guest Ranch, Ltd., on the Little Powder River between Broadus and Biddle, is a working sheep and cattle ranch homesteaded in 1890 by Ted Elgin's grandfather. Unlike most guest ranches, the O Spear bills guests separately for lodging, meals, horseback riding and assisting on the ranch. Guests determine their length of stay. Lodgings include a guest house and a guest bungalow. Route 82, Box 50, Broadus, MT 59317; ☎ 406-427-5388 or 406-421-5406.

 Hougen Ranch is a 35,000-acre cattle spread near Melstone, off US Highway 12. The Hougen family's slogan, "Ranching is our business, guests are our pleasure," rings true here, where guests feel like family. Guests may participate in ranch activities determined by the time of year. For example, calf branding is finished by early June. Stock is moved between pastures in summer. Cows and calves are corralled in mid-September. Watching deer, antelope, bald eagles, beavers and other wildlife is an anytime experience. Private accommodations in the ranch house's spacious walk-out basement transcend comfortable. Home-cooked meals are served family-style. Most guests book for three to five days, but the Hougens will accept guests on a per-night basis. PO Box 127, Melstone, MT 59054; ☎ 406-358-2204 or 406-358-2209.

Powder River Ranch Vacations, in the Broadus area, offers a chance to participate in cattle ranching chores in a five-day "Cowboy Life" package as an alternative to the group's Powder River Wagon Trains & Cattle Drives. Contact the group at PO Box 676, Broadus, MT 59317; ☎ 800-492-8835 or 800-982-0710.

Rose Ranch near Ekalaka invites guests to participate in trailing cattle and other ranch chores. The area also offers hiking and wildlife viewing. Accommodations include a cabin and guest rooms in the main house. All-inclusive rates are on a per-day, per-person basis. Guests may accompany the Brence family to area rodeos, roping events and Western dances. Paul and Nancy Brence, PO Box 492, Ekalaka, MT 59324; ☎ 406-775-6204.

Schively Ranch is so far off the beaten path that you'll need a 4WD vehicle to reach it via a two-hour-plus drive from Billings. Or the ranch will pick you up in Billings on a Saturday, returning you a week later on Sunday. The ranch's cattle are wintered on farm lands in northern Wyoming. After calving season is completed in mid-April and grasses have begun to grow along the eastern slopes of the Pryor Mountains, the cattle are trailed across the Big Horn Recreation Area and the National Wild Horse Range to grazing lands on the Crow Indian Reservation. Guests are invited to join the cattle drive, sleeping in tepees along the trail. Then the ranch experience begins. Rustic cabins are provided at the higher ranch. The lower ranch has a log bunkhouse. Both feature hot showers and home-cooked ranch-style meals. Guests are assigned registered quarter horses trained for ranch chores. 1062 Road 15, Lovell, WY 82431; ☎ 307-548-6688 or 406-259-8866 (July-October).

DID YOU KNOW? *The Allotment Act of 1887 enabled individual tribal members to own some Reservation lands. Between 1922 and 1962, many allottees sold their lands to non-Indians, resulting in some 34% of the Crow Reservation being owned by non-Indians. The tribe is making an effort to purchase back such lands, but is having little success due to the expense involved.*

The **Wald Ranch** is on the Crow Indian Reservation near Lodge Grass. Ron and Donna Wald's 400-cow working ranch along Lodge Grass Creek accommodates a single family or group at a time. Guests are invited to participate in ranch chores. Horse care and riding instruction are included. Other activities include watching horse trainer Nate Wald in action, plus hiking, creek wading, hot tub soaking and overnight cookouts. Accommodations are in the ranch house. Star Route, Lodge Grass, MT 59050; ☎ 406-639-2457.

■ Adventures on Wheels

Jeep tracks in the **Pryor Mountains** are well suited for four-wheeling. Indeed, you'll need a 4WD vehicle to negotiate them, especially in wet weather. But stay on the roads.

Most of Custer Country is open prairie and rangeland that might look ideal for mountain biking, powered trail bikes or ATV riding. Not necessarily so. Contact the Ashland or Sioux Ranger District of the Custer National Forest, the Miles City or Billings BLM office, the reservation tribal office or private landowner before you even think about unloading that ORV. Regulations vary from place to place and from season to season. All wheeled vehicles, including mountain bikes, are prohibited in wilderness areas.

■ Adventures on Water

Rivers

Custer Country has four canoeable and floatable rivers, the Yellowstone, Bighorn, Little Bighorn and Tongue. Considering the floatability of these relatively lazy rivers, you'd expect to find numerous canoe and raft rentals. Not so. You may stumble on a roadside canoe or raft for rent (I didn't), but don't count on it. Perhaps it's because the locals have their own craft and most tourists focus on other attractions. So, if you are into canoeing or rafting, you must bring your own. By asking around, you may be able to find someone who will agree to shuttle you back to your vehicle from your take-out point.

 If you want to do some serious river floating, I recommend purchasing a copy of the extremely well researched and comprehensive *Floating and Recreation on Montana Rivers* by Curt Thompson. See *Bibliography*.

The Yellowstone

The Yellowstone is considered a navigable river below the Billings Hwy. 87 bridge, but six big wall-to-wall diversion dams requiring portaging give the lie to this designation. If portaging is not an option for you, consider floating sections of the river between the dams. You might want to combine your float with agate and fossil hounding. The Custer Country stretch of the Yellowstone is a wide, deep prairie river moving slowly between sandstone breaks with scenery to suit. Suitable for both canoes and rafts.

 Be alert for hidden currents and snags, especially in spring and early summer.

Marked public access sites are at Pompey's Pillar, Captain Clark, Isaac Homestead Bridge, Fort Alexander Site, US 12 Bridge, Forsyth, Hathaway, Tongue River, Roche Jeune, Powder River, Fallon Bridge, Glendive Bridge, Intake Diversion Dam, Elk Island Recreation Area and Seven Sisters Recreation Area.

The Bighorn

The Bighorn is famed as a fly fisher's river. Between Yellowtail Dam and Hardin, the river runs through the Bighorn Canyon Recreation Area and the Crow Indian Reservation. The quiet, scenic warm water river may be dewatered in fall. Suitable for dorys, canoes and small rafts. Marked access sites include Bighorn, below the blue ribbon fishing stretch, Mallard off Hwy. 313, Arapooish near Hardin, and Grant Marsh at river mile 26. There are two diversion dams between here and the confluence with the Yellowstone.

The Little Bighorn

The Little Bighorn enters Montana south of Lodge Grass and merges with the Bighorn at Hardin. The entire river is on the Crow Indian Reservation and lacks access sites other than bridges. If you float this river you must stay on the water unless you have permission from the Tribal Agency.

Intermediate paddlers can easily float the entire river in a canoe or small raft or boat. The catch: the river may not be floatable in autumn low-water months. Obstructions include two diversion dams, fences and log-jams.

The Tongue River

Opinions vary as to how the Tongue River came by its name, but all agree that Indians named it. Tongue may be a euphemism for "talking river." "Crooked as the tongue of the white man" may be more accurate.

The Tongue River, near Miles City.

The river flows north from the Tongue River Reservoir near Decker, just over the Wyoming line. See *Boating*, below, for Tongue River Reservoir and Tongue River Reservoir State Park information.

The entire 206.7 miles of the Tongue in Montana can be canoed or floated by a beginner. Expect numerous wildlife sightings, but beware of rattlesnakes on rocky banks. The gravel Ashland-Birney Road, becoming the Tongue River Road south of Birney, accesses the river from Ashland to the dam. North of Ashland, MT 447 follows the river to Miles City where it empties into the Yellowstone. Designated access sites are non-existent except for the T-Y Diversion Dam Access at river mile 20.4, but you can put in the river at numerous bridges. No matter where you put in, you can look forward to a leisurely float through prairie terrain. Possible campsites are at the Tongue River Dam, a park at the Ashland Bridge, and downriver at the T-Y Diversion Dam. You'll need to portage around several diversion dams.

Boating

Bighorn Lake

Bighorn Lake, confined between steep 2,000-foot-high canyon walls, is popular with boaters and water skiers. The lake, created in 1965 by the construction of the Yellowtail Dam, is 70 miles long, 22 miles wide at its widest point and 500 feet deep at the dam. Marinas and boat launch ramps are at **Horsehoe Bend** in the South District in Wyoming and at **Ok-A-Beh Marina** in the North District. Pick up a boating regulation sheet at National Recreation Area headquarters if you're trailering a boat. No permit is required for boating on Bighorn Lake, but craft must carry valid registration for the states in which they are registered.

Ok-A-Beh Marina has a boat ramp, a restaurant and a store selling groceries, ice and such. Boats and recreation equipment available for rent include pontoon boats, outboards, runabouts and a 34-foot party barge. The marina is open weekends 8-8, weekdays 10-7, Memorial Day-Labor Day. Winter, ☎ 406-665-2216. May-Sept., ☎ 406-666-2349.

Tongue River Reservoir

Tongue River Reservoir, set on southern Montana's rolling prairie, offers boating, fishing and other water sports. **Tongue River State Park** has primitive camping, swimming and a boat ramp. You can reach the lake via I-90 and WY 238 from Sheridan, Wyoming, via MT 314 from US 212 near the Crow/Northern Cheyenne Reservation line, by MT484 from just east of Ashland, or by a gravel road following the river south from Ashland.

MT 314 passes the site of the **Rosebud Battlefield**, a day-use state park commemorating the June 17, 1876 Battle of the Rosebud. Interpretive signs describe the battle that occurred a week before the better known Battle of the Little Bighorn.

Fishing

Bighorn Lake has good walleye fishing, plus rainbow, brown trout and black crappie. The **Tongue River** has a healthy population of smallmouth bass. The 12-mile-long **Tongue River Reservoir** is noted for record walleye and northern pike. Tongue River Reservoir State Park has a boat ramp, camping and other anglers' facilities.

The **Lower Yellowstone River** is a warm-water fishery supporting bass, walleye, pike and perch as well as shovelnose sturgeon, sauger, big channel catfish and paddlefish.

Refer to the FWP publications below for information on other Custer Country fishing waters.

AUTHOR TIP

If you want to fish in Custer Country, or anywhere in Montana, you should obtain copies of Montana Fishing Regulations *and* Montana Fishing Guide *at any store selling state fishing licenses or by contacting Montana Fish, Wildlife & Parks. Be sure they are current; some fishing regulations may change from year to year. Read them through. They not only include fishing rules, regulations, seasons and water conditions, but information on where to catch which species of fish, plus facilities at given sites. Fishing access site maps are also available from FWP. Obtain a reservation fishing license if you want to fish on an Indian reservation.*

Paddlefishing

The paddlefish is a relative of the sturgeon and similarities to fossil records of their distant ancestors, the *Polyodon Spathula*. Their name is derived from paddle-shaped snouts that sometimes reach two feet in length. Adult paddlefish weigh from 60 to 120 pounds. Fish of this heft are usually associated with ocean waters. A heavy surf rod 8-12 feet long, a heavy-duty salt water spinning reel or star-drag reel, 4-6 ounce weights, and 40-80# test line is needed to snag one. Snag is the operative word. Paddlefish feed on microscopic organisms and do not rise to bait.

The fish thrive in the roily waters of the **Yellowstone River Intake Diversion Dam** 17 miles north of Glendive. The May 15 through June 30 season is subject to curtailment, should the joint Montana-North Dakota paddlefish quota be reached ahead of the cut-off date. Limit: one paddlefish per licensee per season. You must purchase a special paddlefish tag in addition to a Montana fishing license. Contact the Glendive Chamber of Commerce for further information on how you can snag a paddlefish.

Paddlefish can also be caught in other stretches of the **Yellowstone** and **Missouri Rivers**. See *Montana Fishing Regulations* for specific waters.

Caviar Capitol of Montana

Glendive has earned the title of Caviar Capitol of Montana. Paddlefish roe are processed and marketed to cruise ship lines and upscale eateries throughout the country.

Tasty paddlefish can be frozen, canned, poached, smoked, baked or grilled. One fish will yield a daunting quantity of meat. The Glendive Chamber of Commerce and the Montana Fish, Wildlife & Parks Department will clean your catch free of charge and process the roe into caviar. Fishermen are encouraged to donate the roe to the Chamber. Proceeds from cavier sales are split between Eastern Montana's historical, cultural and recreational projects and Montana Fish, Wildlife & Parks.

Fly Fishing

The Bighorn River

The Bighorn River between Hardin and Fort Smith is a world famous blue ribbon fly fishing stream. Anglers consider it the best tail water fishery in North America. The river's brown and rainbow trout population is estimated at 6,000 browns per mile of river and 1,000 rainbows averaging 16 to 19 inches long. The river is open to fishing year-round. The prime dry fly season is April through November. This is the up side. The down side is that boatloads of anglers have discovered the Bighorn, making it one of the most crowded rivers you're likely to find in Montana.

Catch and release is the preferred practice and is mandatory for some species. Barbless hooks are recommended. Obtain a copy of *Bighorn River Fishing Regulations* from any Montana Department of Fish, Wildlife & Parks office or wherever fishing licenses are sold. **Fort Smith** is the Bighorn's fly fishing hub, supporting businesses offering everything an angler might want.

Fort Smith is on the Crow Indian Reservation. The sale of alcohol is prohibited on the Reservation, so if you wish to imbibe you must BYOB. And be discreet, out of courtesy to and respect for your hosts. Even though you might be an experienced angler, it's a good idea to hire a guide for your first day out in order to become acquainted with the river. Less experienced anglers will surely prefer a guided fishing experience.

Guides vary in services offered and in fishing philosophies and methods. Some operate out of fishing lodges, some out of fly shops. Some prefer to work with experienced anglers, some welcome neophytes. Some offer wade fishing, though float fishing is preferred on the Bighorn because the land above the high water line is owned by the Crow Indian Reservation. The river belongs to the State of Montana. Be sure to ask lots of questions before committing yourself to a day's fishing or longer. Be honest regarding your experience or lack of same. Inquire regarding the level of instruction offered. Most, but not all guides, offer some fly fishing instruction. Don't be bashful about talking prices. Fly fishing can be pricey, especially when you stay at a posh lodge.

A word about rogue fishing guides: The popularity of fly fishing in Montana has spawned a school of guides that should be avoided. These "guides" circumvent the Montana Board of Outfitters, guiding anglers without benefit of licensing. A guide must work under the supervision of an outfitter licensed in the State of Montana, or be an outfitter so licensed. Licensed outfitters are bonded and insured. Most rogue guides are not. Ask a prospective guide if he is licensed. If in doubt, contact the Montana Board of Outfitters to check. If you come upon a rogue guide, you will be doing everyone in the angling fraternity a favor by reporting him to the Board. See Information Sources, page 78.

Bighorn River Fly Fishing Outfitters & Lodges

The following guides are a good representation of the fly fishing outfitters guiding on the Bighorn. Many have been in business since 1981, when the river was opened to fishing following the US Supreme Court's decision that, although it flows through the Crow Indian Reservation, riparian rights belong to the State of Montana.

Bighorn Angler's Don Cooper offers a complete Bighorn fly fishing experience with a variety of services that include a fly fishing shop, lodging, meals, boat rentals, day-long float fishing trips and experienced guides. PO Box 7578, Fort Smith, MT 59035; ☎ 406-666-2233.

Bighorn River Country Lodge enjoys a secluded location on the Crow Indian Reservation near Fort Smith. The lodge accommodates singles, couples and groups. The cuisine has been described as "comfortable gourmet." Guided float trips are offered with licensed outfitters using McKenzie-style drift boats. PO Box 7795, Fort Smith, MT 59035; ☎ 406-666-2331.

Big Horn River Lodge is on the river bank some 12 miles downstream from Fort Smith. The log lodge is charmingly rustic, as befits this remote area. The full-service lodge is designed especially for anglers and offers guide service in addition to gourmet meals. Owner Phil Gonzalez prides himself on offering guests easy access to the river. Phil or Patty Gonzalez, PO Box 756, Fort Smith, MT 59035; ☎ 800-235-5450 or 406-666-2368.

Big Horn River Outfitters' Gael Larr and family are Fort Smith residents and offer guided fishing trips all year. PO Box 483 YRS, Fort Smith, MT 59035; ☎ 406-666-2351 or (mobile) 406-665-5113.

Big Horn Trout Shop, owned and operated by Steve Hilbers and Hale Harris, offers a full fly fishing experience that includes lodging and meals, a fly fishing shop, float fishing in McKenzie drift boats, and a com-

Custer Country

plete guide service. Catch and release is advocated. Box 477, Fort Smith, MT 59035; ☎ 406-666-2375.

Eagle Nest Lodge, an Orvis-endorsed log lodge on the river a few miles south of Hardin, offers complete fly fishing packages. An Orvis fly shop is on the premises. Amenities reflecting the Montana outdoors include comfortable surroundings and delicious meals. PO Box 509, Hardin, MT 59034; ☎ 406-665-3711.

Elk River Outfitters & Guide Service's Don and Trudy Tennant, professional biologists as well as fishing guides, operate out of Billings. Their fishing packages include lodging at the Northern Best Western Hotel in Billings, transfers to and from the Big Horn River, a night's lodging at a riverside motel, two lunches and two days of guided fishing. Contact the Tennants at 1809 Darlene Lane, Billings, MT 59102; ☎ 406-252-5859.

Montana Adventures in Angling's Jim McFadyean offers guided fishing on the Bighorn and on private streams on the Crow Reservation. He also fishes the Yellowstone, Stillwater and Boulder Rivers and Glacier Country streams (see *Glacier Country*, page 434). 1845 Bannack Drive, Billings, MT 59105; ☎ 406-248-2995.

Montella From Montana Outfitter Service's Richie Montella specializes in float fishing the Big Horn River, using McKenzie River driftboats. Montella has over 45 years experience fly fishing for trout. He offers guide service and can put clients up overnight. Richie Montella, PO Box 7553, Fort Smith, MT 59035; ☎ 406-666-2360.

Quill Gordon Fly Fishers' Gordon and June Rose offer customized float fishing trips, boat rentals, motel accommodations, flies and fishing gear. PO Box 7597, Fort Smith, MT 59035; ☎ 406-666-2253.

■ Adventures on Snow

You won't be downhill skiing in Custer Country, but cross-country skiing and snowmobiling are possibilities. However, options are more plentiful in other parts of Montana.

Custer Country's dry, windy climate and prairie terrain translate to powder snow and lots of drifting. Daytime temperatures are in the 10-25° range. The wind chill is penetrating, so don the same protective clothing that you would for mountain country winter sports.

Cross-Country Skiing

Camps Pass Trail in the Ashland District of the Custer National Forest (see *Hiking*, page 98, for directions) does winter duty as a cross-country ski trail. Parking is at the trailhead. The trail has two loops of two kilometers each. Trails are groomed intermittently and are rated "easy" and "more difficult."

You also might try cross-country skiing on **Two Moon Park** trails (see *Wildlife Watching*, below).

Snowmobiling

 Before even thinking about snowmobiling anywhere in Montana, obtain a copy of the ***Snowmobile Law & Safety Guide*** from the Department of Fish, Wildlife & Parks (see *Information Sources,* page 66).

The **Tongue River Trail** near Miles City is popular with local snowmobilers. Put in at **Spotted Eagle Recreation Area** for a ride on the shallow frozen river.

If you plan on visiting **Makoshika State Park** near Glendive in winter,
you can snowmobile an eight-mile trail through the badlands, snow conditions permitting.

Cross-country skiing.

Eco-Tours & Cultural Excursions

▪ Wildlife Watching

Watching wildlife is one of the principle draws for visitors to Montana. If wildlife watching is your thing, you are following in the footsteps of Lewis and Clark. The explorers were wowed by the number and diversity of birds and animals they encountered on their epic journey. If alert, you will see wildlife wherever you may be hiking, horseback riding or fishing. Or make special forays to one or more of Custer Country's 12 designated wildlife viewing areas. Two are situated close to Billings.

Two Moon Park

Over 200 species of birds have been recorded at this park on the Yellowstone River. Waterfowl and beavers can be seen in a slough on the north side of the park. You may see bald eagles in winter and spring. Mammals include deer, racoons and foxes. A designated nature trail circles the park. The park is open from a half-hour after sunrise to 10 pm. In Billings, take Main Street (US 87) north. After the airport intersection, turn right on Lake Elmo Road. Drive 0.6 mile and turn right onto Two Moon Road. ☎ 406-256-2701.

Norm Schoenthal Island

This island is rich in wildlife inhabiting grasses and dense willow thickets. **Barbara's Oxbow**, a shallow lake near the Yellowstone River, also offers good viewing. From turtles and leopard frogs, to great blue herons to white-tailed deer, the variety of wildlife is seemingly limitless. In Billings, take South Billings Boulevard (County Road 416) south 0.4 miles past the I-90 interchange. Turn right onto a dirt road and proceed for 0.3 miles to Wendel's Bridge over Barbara's Slough. Park here and cross the bridge on foot. A 2.5-mile path loops the island. ☎ 406-657-8372.

Lake Mason National Wildlife Refuge

If you are in the vicinity of Roundup, you may wish to hie yourself to Lake Mason National Wildlife Refuge. This prairie marsh's reeds, cattails and mudflats attract numerous nesting populations of waterfowl that include mallards, teal and pintails. A variety of shorebirds can also be seen, plus migrating Canada geese and American white pelicans in spring and fall. Pronghorn herds roam the uplands. A prairie dog town borders the Refuge's southeastern edge. Some areas are closed to the public, but the balance is open to hiking and non-motorized boating. A high clearance 4WD vehicle is recommended. From Roundup, take US 87 to 13th Avenue. Turn west, proceed for one block, turn west onto Golf Course Road. After 6.5 miles, turn right and continue for about three miles. ☎ 406-538-8706.

Pompey's Pillar

This sandstone bluff that William Clark named for Sacajawea's baby is a National Historic Landmark administered by the BLM. Numerous birds, from raptors to wildfowl to wrens and orioles, can be sighted here. Yellow-bellied marmots scamper over the pillar. There is also a small wetland. The entire area is open to hiking and wildlife viewing. Leave I-94 at Exit 23 and follow the signs to the trailhead. ☎ 406-657-6262.

Howrey Island

Howrey Island is a primitive bottomland area on the Yellowstone east of Pompey's Pillar. A 1.3-mile trail affords opportunities for viewing a variety of birds that include bald eagles, great horned owls, red-headed woodpeckers, great blue herons and wild turkeys. Beavers, foxes and fox squirrels are also commonly seen. Exit I-94 at Hysham. Follow Rt. 311 west for 6.9 miles to the Myers Bridge Fishing Access Site. Walk to the island. ☎ 406-232-7000.

Yellowtail Dam Afterbay

Thousands of mallards are sustained at this area on the Bighorn River. Raptors include nesting bald eagles, rough-legged hawks and prairie falcons. As many as 47 bird species have been recorded on the two-mile-long body of water below Yellowtail Dam. You can view the afterbay from either the north or south side. ☎ 406-666-2412.

The William L. Matthews Recreation & Habitat Management Area

This is a riparian area along the Yellowstone River in the viciity of Miles City. A short loop trail from the parking lot affords opportunities to view a variety of birds. Ring-necked pheasants, red foxes, deer and racoons may be seen in a shelterbelt. From I-94 at Miles City, drive northeast on Old US 10 for about 10 miles to the Kinsey Road turnoff. ☎ 406-232-7000.

The Terry Badlands

The rugged Terry Badlands adjacent to the Yellowstone River afford opportunities to see a wide variety of dryland wildlife. Raptors prey on an abundance of desert cottontails and white-tailed jackrabbits. Hike in from the overlook, or from the south along the old Milwaukee Road grade. The area is administered by the BLM. From Terry, follow Rt. 253 north for a couple of miles. Turn left onto a dirt road (impassable when wet) and go west for six miles to a scenic overlook.

The Black's Pond Drive Route

A high-clearance 4WD vehicle is recommended for this 23-mile route in the Ashland District of the Custer National Forest. The route is impassable from November through April. This is a great place to view deer, wild turkeys, songbirds, pronghorn and more. Six species of bats have been identified in the area. Watch for them in the evening near Black's Pond and O'Dell and Cow Creek Reservoirs. A brochure describing the auto tour route is available at the Ashland Ranger District office. From Ashland, drive east on US 212 for three miles. Follow Otter Creek Road (Rt. 484) south for 19 miles to Cow Creek Road (Road 95) where the drive begins. ☎ 406-232-7000.

Makoshika State Park

Makoshika State Park near Glendive is fine habitat for desert wildlife such as horned lizards, bull snakes and prairie rattlesnakes. A surprising variety of wildlife not generally associated with a desert habitat may also be seen. Look for rock wrens and turkey vultures from the 0.6-mile **Cap Rock Nature Trail**.

Medicine Rocks State Park

Raptors and cliff swallows abound at this park. Use binoculars to watch the residents of a large prairie dog town on private property west of the park. 25 miles south of Baker via MT 7.

Long Pines

This area of ponderosa pine forests and aspen-lined draws south of Ekalaka has the nation's highest reported nesting density of merlins. It's also a good place to see great horned owls and golden eagles. Songbirds abound around springs. Ovenbirds, wild turkeys and peewees are of special interest. A tour route brochure is available at Custer National Forest offices. This area includes both public and private lands. High clearance 4WD vehicles are recommended. From Ekalaka, drive south 23 miles on Rt. 323. Go east (left) on Tie Creek Road for 11.3 miles to Forest Road 118. Drive north (left) one mile to the forest boundary and the beginning of the driving route. ☎ 406-365-6256.

■ State Parks

Custer Country has eight state parks. The five day-use parks have been developed around points of historical or natural interest. The three full-service parks offer camping. Campsites are available on a first-come, first-served basis. Contact the park to make group campsite reservations. Montana has no comprehensive statewide reservation system. Most campsites have a picnic table, a fire ring or grill, and parking for one vehicle and an RV.

Most state parks have disabled access toilets and some have disabled access trails. If in doubt, call the park for further information.

Day-Use State Parks

Chief Plenty Coups State Park

Located on the Crow Indian Reservation, this park preserves the home of Plenty Coups, the last chief of the Crow Indians and a man revered by his people. His log house and store are reminders of the chief's efforts to lead the tribe toward peace with all people. Afternoon interpretive tours of the home, museum and grounds are offered daily in July and August. On Saturdays in July and August, Crow Elders and historians offer interpretive programs and discuss a variety of Crow ceremonies and traditions. September 5 is Chief Plenty Coups Day of Honor and features day-long festivities that include drumming and dancing and a buffalo feast. One mile west of the town of Pryor. ☎ 406-252-1289.

Lake Elmo State Park

This park, on the edge of Billings, has a 64-acre reservoir used for swimming, non-motorized boating, windsurfing and fishing. A nature trail circles the lake. From Billings, take US 87 north to Pemberton Lane, then drive west 0.5 miles. ☎ 406-247-2940.

Pictograph Caves State Park

This park (see *Caving*, page 101), also near Billings, offers fascinating insight into prehistoric rock paintings. Take the Lockwood Exit off I-90. ☎ 406-247-2940.

Piroque Island State Park

Situated in the Yellowstone River near Miles City, this park is set aside for floaters to watch wildlife and search for moss agates. In low water, usually in late summer, a small channel can be forded by vehicle to obtain access from the mainland. Drive one mile north of Miles City on Montana 59, then two miles east on Kinsey Road, then two miles south on Route 28. ☎ 406-232-0900.

Rosebud Battlefield State Park

Rosebud Battlefield State Park is on the site of the June 17, 1876 battle between the Sioux and Cheyenne and General Crook's infantry and cavalry. Unless you are a battle buff, there's little to see except rolling prairie. Drive 25 miles east of Crow Agency on US 212, then 20 miles south on Rt. 314, then three miles west on an unmarked country road (watch for signs). ☎ 406-232-0900.

Full-Service State Parks

Makoshika State Park

Makoshika is good for a couple of days of exploring, hiking and checking out the visitor center exhibits. These include the fossilized triceratops found near the park in 1990 (see *Touring*, page 92). The Museum of the Rockies in Bozeman hosts summer digs at Makoshika as part of their research into the causes of the dinosaurs' extinction tens of millions of years ago. Summer interpretive programs are presented in the park's amphitheatre. Small primitive campground. ☎ 406-365-6256.

Medicine Rocks State Park

This park preserves an area of eroded sandstone formations in eastern Montana that are sacred to many Native Americans. Primitive campground. Twenty-five miles south of Baker on Montana 7. ☎ 406-232-0900.

Custer Country

Tongue River Reservoir State Park

Tongue River Reservoir State Park takes advantage of a 12-mile-long reservoir in the impounded Tongue River. Boating and other water sports, plus fishing, make this prairie park popular with eastern Montanans. Primitive campground. Drive six miles north of Decker on Rt. 314, then one mile east on Route 382. ☎ 406-232-0900.

■ Special Interest Adventures

 The site of the Battle of Little Bighorn and the Crow and Northern Cheyenne Indian Reservations are Custer Country's major points of interest. They offer unique opportunities for cultural adventures. You can visit Little Bighorn Battlefield National Monument, museums associated with the famous battle, and a few points of interest on the Reservations on your own (see *Touring*). But signing on for a tour adds a special dimension.

Little Bighorn Battlefield National Monument

An industry has sprung up around the battle that has captured the public's imagination for over a century. Conjecture still swirls around Custer the man and soldier. Tacticians are still "fighting" the battle that led to the deaths of Custer and all 210 of his cavalrymen and afforded the Indians a back-against-the-wall victory. Feelings still run high among history buffs and descendants, in fact and in spirit, of warriors on both sides.

There is much to learn here regardless of your point of view and depth of interest regarding this chapter in Western history. Between Memorial Day and Labor Day, the Battlefield Visitor Center offers daily live programs and talks, plus living history presentations interpreting the lives of Plains Indians and of US Cavalrymen and Indian scouts in the 1876 time period.

Self-guiding Little Bighorn Battlefield road tapes are available at the Visitor Center and area outlets.

Tours

Jim Court, superintendent of Custer Battlefield from 1978 to 1986, offers all-day **Battlefield tours**. The customized tours include visits to Sitting Bull's village site, Last Stand Hill, Custer's lookout point, Custer's June 24 campsite, and archaeological interpretations of Battlefield digs. Extended tours can be arranged. Contact Jim Court at Action Travel, 416 N. Cody Ave., Hardin, MT 59034; ☎ 800-331-1580 or 406-665-1580.

Frontier Adventures offers a variety of tours that include the Little Bighorn and Rosebud Battlefields and other sites that played prominent parts in Western history. Tours offer insight into the Native point of view. Guides include local Indians who relate oral histories offering insight into Native American cultural beliefs. Customized tours available. PO Box 85, Colstrip, MT 59323; ☎ 800-684-5469 (pin 2937). Internet www.exploremontana.com.

The Crow & Northern Cheyenne Indian Reservations

The Crow Nation shares its culture and traditions in numerous ways. Tours and lecture referrals are available through **Little Bighorn College's Micro Tourism Department**.

Tours

Cheyenne Trailriders, owned and operated by Northern Cheyenne Tribal members Zane and Sandra Spang, offers horseback rides on the Northern Cheyenne Reservation. Rides of from an hour to several days feature the natural beauty of this home of the Northern Cheyenne people. Participants see tipi rings, a buffalo jump and other sites. Optional experiences include ethnobiology courses, Cheyenne history/culture courses and Cheyenne storytelling. PO Box 206, Ashland, MT 59003; ☎ 406-784-6150.

Ethnobotany on Horseback, sponsored by the Billings Western Heritage Center, offers day-long workshops on Fridays and Saturdays in June. Workshops on horseback addressing the indigenous and Native uses of plants are guided by Northern Cheyenne tribal members. Visits to cultural and historical landscape sites are included. ☎ 406-256-6809.

Sacred Ground is a week-long camp experience in the Pryor Mountains designed to appeal to a limited number of participants who wish to gain insight into Native American culture and spiritual beliefs. Guests live in tipis, learn about plants and wildlife from the Indian perspective, join in drumming and singing, and study under elders and storytellers from the Northwest and Canada. PO Box 78, Pryor, MT 59066; ☎ 406-245-6070.

■ Kid Stuff

KID-FRIENDLY In reading through this chapter you will have picked up on a number of activities fit to capture your offspring's interest. Most kids get into activities offering a "trophy" to take home. Agate hunting is a good example. My daughter Amy and I enjoy finding neat stuff on hikes; agates, chunks of beaver-chewed wood, a bear-clawed pole. Many kids "dig" dinosaurs. Hands-on exhibits at the **Makoshika State Park Visitor Center** (see page 121) allow kids to get a feel for ancient bones. Most kids thrill to the colorful aspects of Indian culture. **Pow-wows** featuring drumming, singing and dancers in full regalia are fun and exciting for kids. They also offer opportunities to learn about a culture that may be very different from their own. **Rodeos** represent another aspect of Western life that seldom fails to appeal to kids. See *Festivals and Special Events* below for both activities.

Many Custer Country towns have public **swimming pools**. Colstrip's waterslide and Miles City's old-time swimming hole are standouts. **Little Bighorn Battlefield National Monument's Junior Ranger program** is a fun way for kids to learn some history and earn a badge. Many of the festivals and events listed below feature children's activities.

Festivals & Special Events

 It may come as no suprise that many of Custer Country's special events are centered around rodeos, pow-wows and other celebrations reflecting the region's distinctive heritage. But they don't stop there. Doin's listed below are annual events with proven track records. Other musical and cultural events may take place on relatively short notice throughout the year. Chambers of commerce are good sources of information on local events.

The dates listed below are approximate or subject to change. Before making definite plans, check the exact date with Custer Country Tourism, local chambers of commerce or the number listed opposite the festival entry.

Billings's **Alberta Bair Theatre** presents plays and musical events throughout the year. ☎ 406-256-6052 for current listings.

January
New Years Pow-Wow on the Crow Reservation at Lodge Grass and Crow Agency. Crow Tribal Office, ☎ 406-638-2601.

February
Cowtown Beef Breeders Show, Craft Expo & Ag Trade Show, in Miles City (Cow Capitol of the World) in early February. Yearling bulls are on display in corrals set up on Main Street. Art & crafts. ☎ 406-232-2890. Fax 406-232-6914.

Northern Rodeo Association Finals, held in early February in Billings' METRAPARK Arena, features top bucking horse riders, steer wrestlers and others competing in one of the state's largest rodeos. ☎ 406-252-1122. Fax 406-252-0300.

Montana Agri-Trade Exposition, in Billings in mid-February, is the biggest agricultural trade show between Minneapolis and the West Coast. There's something for everyone: farm equipment, ATVs, computer programs, ostriches, boots. ☎ 406-245-0404. Fax 406-245-3897.

Washington's Day Pow-Wow on the Crow Reservation at Lodge Grass and Crow Agency. Crow Tribal Office, ☎ 406-638-2601.

March

MSU-Billings Annual Inter-Tribal Pow-Wow, in Billings in late March, attracts drummers and dancers from Canada to Oklahoma. This large collegiate pow-wow is available to all Nations and non-Indians to enjoy and benefit from. ☎ 406-657-2561. Fax 406-657-2388.

Montana Outdoor Recreation Exposition is held in Billings in late March. ☎ 406-256-8676. Fax 406-252-5872.

April

Nile Budlight Cup Series Bull Ride is a mid-April event in Billings. The world's top professional bull riders compete on the gnarliest bulls from across the US. ☎ 406-256-2495. Fax 406-256-2494.

May

Glendive's Buzzard Day celebrates the return of the buzzards to Makoshika State Park with nature walks, 10K, 5K and fun run, orienteering, children's fun fest, area-wide garage sales and more. Mid-May. Makoshkia State Park, ☎ 406-365-6256.

Montana Woman's Run is held annually at Billings the first Saturday before Mother's Day. Runners of many abilities include walkers, joggers, women in wheelchairs and women pushing strollers. Deaconess Billings Clinic Health System, ☎ 406-657-4677. Fax 406-657-3779.

Hardin High School Rodeo in mid-May features bareback riding, steer wrestling, saddle bronc riding, calf roping, goat tying, barrel racing and more. ☎ 406-666-2330.

Miles City Bucking Horse Sale in mid-May features bareback and saddle bronc riding, bull riding, wild horse races. All this in addition to the famous bucking horse auction. Also street dances and a parade. Miles City Area Chamber of Commerce, ☎ 406-232-2890.

Nile Spring Horse Show in Billings in mid-May features three complete American Quarter Horse shows. Kevin Dawe, ☎ 406-256-2495. Fax 406-256-2494.

Heart & Sole Run in Billings in mid-May features 5K, 10K and two-mile Health Walk. Medals awarded to first five finishers in seven age divisions. ☎ 406-657-7666. Fax 406-657-3211.

June

Forsyth Rodeo Days are celebrated in Forsyth the first weekend in June. A typical small town rodeo plus Cattle Women's Chuckwagon Breakfast, Main Street Parade & Western Trade Show, Bullmania, dancing under the stars to country music favorites. Penny Teeters, ☎ 406-356-7325.

Custer Country

Festival of Cultures, in Billings in early June, celebrates area heritage and cultures with 100 arts & crafts exhibits, cultural displays, storytelling, art show and food. ☎ 406-657-1105. Fax 406-259-9751.

Billings Strawberry Festival in mid-June offers over 90 arts & crafts vendors, live entertainment, storytelling, dancing, children's activities. Downtown Billings Association, ☎ 406-259-5454. Fax 406-248-6228.

Montana Seniors Olympics, a mid-June event in Billings, features sports for men and women 50 years of age and over. No residency requirement. Montana Seniors Olympics, ☎ 406-252-2795.

Western Days, held in Billings in late June, features two days of street dancing and other fun events. Jaycees, ☎ 406-652-8494 or 256-6961.

Zoograss Festival, in Billings in late June, is a ZooMontana fund raising event featuring an outdoor concert. ☎ 406-652-8100. Fax 406-652-9281.

Badlands Drifters Car Club Eighth Annual 'Cars in the Park' Show is held in Glendive in late June; fun run, dance, car show. ☎ 406-365-8925.

Custer's Last Stand Reenactment and Little Big Horn Days, in Hardin the last weekend in June, offer hoopla galore. Over 250 reenactors replay the events that led up to Custer's Last Stand. Also nightly entertainment, cultural cuisine, parades, arts & crafts, a rodeo and a military ball. Hardin Chamber of Commerce, ☎ 406-665-1672.

Miles City Balloon Roundup in late June features numerous hot air balloon events. Colorful balloons ascend every morning at 6 am if the wind is right. On Saturday night, the balloons are inflated and lit up. Miles City Chamber of Commerce, ☎ 406-232-2890. Fax 406-232-9415.

Concert in the Park and Picnic on the Green is a late June event featuring a Billings Symphony Concert playing pop and light classical music. ☎ 406-252-3610. Fax 406-252-3353.

July

Laurel 4th of July Celebration features all the hometown USA activities that you would expect of a 4th of July celebration. Laurel Chamber of Commerce, ☎ 406-628-8105. Fax 406-628-8260.

Valley of the Chiefs Pow-Wow & Rodeo is held at Crow Agency over the 4th of July weekend. A rodeo adds to the fun of this major pow-wow. Crow Tribal Office, ☎ 406-638-2601. Fax 406-638-7283.

St. Xavier Amateur Rodeo, a 4th of July event in Hardin, includes participatory events for children and adults. A cattle drive through town on July 3 at 11 am drives the rodeo stock into town. ☎ 406-666-2386. Fax 406-666-2045.

Eastern Montana 'Ski Festival isn't about skiing on water or snow. This ethnic celebration honors Norskis and Polish families whose names end in "ski." Festivities include a parade, a Polish barbeque, music and dancing. Polka, anyone? Held in Wibaux over July 4th. ☎ 406-795-2412.

Big Sky State Games, in Billings in mid-July, is a multi-sport event for Montana athletes of all ages and abilities. Modeled after the Olympic Games. ☎ 406-254-7426. Fax 406-254-7439.

Sleepy Hollow Bluegrass Festival, in Glendive in mid-July, features a full day of bluegrass music, food and a crafts fair. ☎ 406-365-2556.

Summerfair, at Billings' Yellowstone Art Center in late July, features artisans from 20 states selling quality work. Ethnic and American food, children's activities and art/craft demonstrations. ☎ 406-256-6804. Fax 406-256-6817.

Richey Rodeo, held in that town in late July, is an amateur rodeo. Kids' games prior to the rodeo. ☎ 406-774-3467.

Wendy's Family Fun Day, at Billings' ZooMontana in late July, is a day of family fun and activities. ☎ 406-652-8100. Fax 406-652-9281.

Clark Day, held in late July on the Yellowstone River at Pompey's Pillar, honors William Clark. Interpretive programs, historic canoe float, music, food. ☎ 406-238-1541.

Big Skyfest, at Corporate Air in Billings in late July or early August, is a gathering of competitive hot air and special shaped balloons. Carnival and circus, evening concert. ☎ 406-245-6294. Fax 406-259-9751.

August

Billings Hispanic Fiesta, in South Park in early August, is a two-day festival of food, music, dancing, games and curios. Mexican dance on Saturday night. ☎ 406-259-0191 or 406-248-8492.

Dawson County Fair in Glendive in early August is a typical county fair featuring a rodeo, tractor pull, antique tractor and machinery display, country western concert and more. ☎ 406-355-6781. Fax 406-365-2022.

Montana Fair, in Billings in mid-August, features all the fun you would expect at a Western state fair. Rodeos, horse racing, parade, chili cookoff and more. ☎ 406-256-2400 or 256-2422. Fax 406-256-2479. Crow Fair & Rodeo, held in mid-August at Crow Agency, bills itself as the tipi capital of the world. This is **the** big pow-wow and rodeo on the Crow Reservation. Jerome White Lip, PO Box 78, Lodge Grass, MT 59722, or call the Crow Tribal Agency at ☎ 406-638-2601.

Theatre in the Park, in mid-August, is a dinner theatre production in the Makoshika State Park outdoor amphitheatre. ☎ 406-365-6256. Fax 406-365-8043.

Annual Threshing Bee, in Worden in mid-August. This is your chance to watch steam-powered threshing as it was done in the early years of this century. Also a working blacksmith shop, sawmill, shingle mill, horse-drawn machinery, old time music and a hearty threshers' lunch. ☎ 406-967-6687.

Taste of Billings in mid-August is an outdoor dinner party smack dab in the middle of downtown Billings streets. Dancing and entertainment. ☎ 406-259-5454. Fax 406-248-6228.

Custer Country

Eastern Montana Fair at Miles City is held in late August. Rodeo and all the trimmings. ☎ 406-232-2502.

Wibaux County Fair in late August features an amateur rodeo and a demolition derby in additon to county fair staples. ☎ 406-795-2486. Fax 406-795-2625.

September

Canyon Creek Battlefield Pipe Ceremony, September 13 at the Canyon Creek Battlefield north of Laurel. Twenty-six men, including Nez Perce Indians from Lapwai, Idaho, participated in the first pipe cere-mony at the Canyon Creek Battlefield on September 13, 1996. The cere-mony honors all veterans of the 1877 battle between the Nez Perce and the US Army. The Nez Perce perform this ceremony at every site along the Nez Perce Historical Trail. They believe that the pipe smoke will carry their prayers to the heavens. ☎ 406-628-8105. Fax 406-628-8260.

Billings Riverfest is held in mid-September along the Yellowstone River. The fundraising event to help build trails along the Yellowstone features competition walking, biking, running and boating. ☎ 406-652-5523 ext. 2.

Historic Bell Street Bridge Day is held in Glendive in late September to celebrate the bridge's preservation as a walking and biking bridge across the Yellowstone River. Boat and jet ski parade, bridge stroll, horse and buggy rides, outdoor musical entertainment. Glendive Chamber of Commerce, ☎ 406-365-5601. Fax 406-365-5602.

Laurel Herbstfest, held in late September, celebrates German dancing, music and foods. ☎ 406-628-8306.

October

Nile Stock Show & Rodeo is a week-long Billings event in mid-October. Professional rodeo performances, youth events, livestock show and sales featuring cattle, sheep, swine, horses, llamas and stock dogs. Farm and home trade show with over 150 exhibitors. ☎ 406-256-2495. Fax 406-256-2494.

JK Ralston Studio & Art Gallery Auction, held in Billings in early October, features quality historic and contemporary Western art. ☎ 406-254-0959.

November

Festival of Quilted Wonders/Winter Wonderland, in Miles City in mid-November, is a true wonderland of handmade quilts. ☎ 406-232-0254.

Billings Holiday Parade, held downtown in late November, brings Santa to town. ☎ 406-259-5260. Fax 406-248-6228.

Forsyth Christmas Walk & Parade of Lights is held in late November. ☎ 406-356-2134.

December

Billings Annual Festival of Trees, held in early December, features a Santa's workshop, holiday boutique, decorated trees and a tree auction benefitting the Billings Council of the National Committee for the Prevention of Child Abuse. ☎ 406-252-9799.

Laurel Christmas to Remember, held in early December, ushers in the holidays with caroling, carriage rides and a parade complete with Santa. ☎ 406-628-8105.

Annual Chase Hawks Memorial Cowboy Gatherin' Dinner, Dance and Rough Stock Invitational Rodeo is held at Billings in mid-December. ☎ 406-248-9295. Fax 406-252-7259.

Where to Stay & Eat

Other than a few posh fly fishing lodges along the Big Horn River, a clutch of bed & breakfast inns, and some top drawer Billings restaurants, Custer Country's lodgings and eateries can best be described as basic. Most local residents live active no-nonsense lives. Billings offers big city amenities, but otherwise you must look elsewhere for trendy restaurants and fancy digs. You will find downhome food served up Western-style, and clean motels.

On the premise that lodgings should be fun wherever possible, smallish motels are listed only for towns lacking an alternative. Chain hostelries are listed on the premise that some travelers, especially those with children, might prefer these. Most have swimming pools. Look for fly fishing lodges under *Fishing* (page 112) and guest ranches under *Adventures on Horseback* (page 106).

Lodging Prices	
$	dirt cheap
$$	moderate
$$$	pricey, but oh well
$$$$	hang onto your checkbook

Most lodgings accept major credit cards, but inquire to be sure. Reservations are also a thought, especially in small towns with limited accommodations. Small town prices are usually quite moderate. Custer Country eateries run heavily to cafés and every small town has at least one. This book concentrates on eateries offering something special, be it the atmosphere, the food or whatever.

Folks hereabouts really like pie. If a café offers homemade pies you can bet they're lip-smackin' good.

■ Hotels, Motels & B&Bs

Ashland

Be thankful that Ashland has a motel. It's the 19-room **Western 8 Motel** on US 212. $. ☎ 406-784-2400.

Baker

Lodgings are pretty much of a toss-up here.

Roy's Motel & Campground at 327 W. Montana Ave., has apartments, 22 rooms, a gift shop, a hot tub and cable TV. $. ☎ 800-552-2321 or 406-778-3321.

Sagebrush Inn, at 518 US 12 West, caters to truckers, as do most small town motels. Many travelers consider this to be an asset. A restaurant is next door to this 40-room motel. $. ☎ 800-638-3708 or 406-778-3341.

Billings

Billings' full complement of chain motels include two **Best Western**s (☎ 800-528-1234 or 406-248-9800, 800-628-9081 or 406-259-5511), **Clarion** (☎ 800-228-2828 or 406-248-7151), **Holiday Inn** (☎ 406-248-7701 or 248-7701), **Howard Johnson** (☎ 800-654-2000 or 406-248-4656), **Radisson** (☎ 800-333-3333 or 406-245-5121), **Ramada** (☎ 800-2-RAMADA or 406-252-2584) and **Sheraton** (☎ 800-588-ROOM or 406-252-7400).

Charter House, at 21 Nightingale Road, has two guest rooms, one with private bath. $$. ☎ 800-447-4370 or 406-252-0733.

The Josephine Bed & Breakfast, at 514 N. 29th St., has five guest rooms, three with private baths, in a historic home within walking distance of downtown. Romantic and elegant are the buzzwords. The inn is named for a historic paddlewheeler that made it up the Yellowstone to Billings. $$. ☎ 800-552-5898 or 406-248-5898.

Pine Hills Place Bed & Breakfast, at 4424 Pinehill Drive, offers a cozy two-bedroom cabin in the piney hills. $$. ☎ 406-252-2288/0313 or 259-5132.

Sanderson Inn, 2038 S. 56th St. W. This B&B occupies a clapboard homestead-era farmhouse situated between Laurel and Billings. Guests can watch sheep frolic in the adjacent barnyard. The three guest rooms have private baths. $$. ☎ 406-656-3388.

Broadus

Oakwood Lodge is a on a ranch bordered by the Custer National Forest at S. Pumpkin Creek Road. This bed & breakfast has three guest rooms and full breakfasts are served. $$. ☎ 406-427-5474. Fax 406-427-5475.

Broadus Motel, at 101 N. Park St., has 51 rooms, some with kitchenettes, a Jacuzzi room and cabins. $$. ☎ 406-436-2626.

Colstrip

This coal town's two motels cater to Little Bighorn Battlefield visitors. A lakeside B&B rounds out the lodgings.

Fort Union Inn, 5 Dogwood St., has 20 guest rooms. $. ☎ 406-748-2553.

Lakeview Bed & Breakfast, at 7437 Castle Rock Lake Dr., has three guest rooms, one with private bath. Full gourmet breakfasts. $. ☎ 888-LAKEBNB or 406-525-3262.

Super 8 of Colstrip, at 6227 Main St., has 40 rooms. $$. ☎ 800-800-8000 or 406-748-3400.

Ekalaka

This remote eastern Montana town has two very small lodgings. What they lack in size they make up for in friendliness toward hardy folks who venture this far off the beaten track.

Guest House, at 4 Main St., has five rooms. $. ☎ 406-775-6337.

Midway Motel, also on Main St., has six rooms. $. ☎ 406-775-6619.

Forsyth

Forsyth's I-90 location no doubt accounts for its numerous motels. **Best Western Sundowner Inn**, at 1018 Front St., has 40 rooms and the expected amenities. $$. ☎ 800-332-0921 or 406-356-2115.

Howdy Hotel & Lounge, at 807 Main St., has been putting up strangers since 1905. There's a sauna, a 24-hour café, and an antiques store. $. ☎ 888-23 HOWDY.

Rail's Inn Motel at 3rd and Front St. is a sizeable establishment with 50 guest rooms. $$. ☎ 800-621-3754 or 406-356-2242.

Westwind Motor Inn, a 33-room hostelry at the west end of Main Street, is Forsyth's newest hostelry. $. ☎ 888-356-2038 or 406-356-2038.

Fort Smith

Fort Smith's lodgings reflect the town's dedication to fly fishing. Refer to *Fly Fishing* if you prefer one catering almost exclusively to anglers.

The following small no-frills places welcome all comers with a laid-back ambience.

The Bighorn River Motel ($$) (☎ 406-666-2458) and **Polly's Place** ($) (☎ 406-666-2458) each has five guest rooms and a restaurant.

Custer Country

Glendive

This bustling town, large by rural Montana standards, does double duty as the gateway to Makoshika State Park and the area's paddlefishing site.

Best Western Jordan Inn, at 223 N. Merrill St., occupies a historic hotel that's been a Glendive landmark since 1901. The 69 rooms and suites are augmented by an indoor swimming pool and a restaurant. $$$. ☎ 800-824-5067 or 406-365-5655.

Charley Montana Bed & Breakfast, occupying a fine old home on the Historic Register at 103 N. Douglas Ave., has four guest rooms with private baths and serves full breakfasts. $$$. ☎ 406-365-3207.

The Hostetler House Bed & Breakfast, at 113 N. Douglas Ave., has two guest rooms, a hot tub, a sun porch and secretarial services. Full breakfasts. Shared bath. $$. ☎ 406-365-4505.

Hardin

Hardin capitalizes on an I-90 location, the Custer's Last Stand reenactment, and proximity to the Big Horn River and the Little Bighorn Battlefield National Monument. The town boasts two B&Bs, one in a historic hotel.

American Inn, at 1324 N. Crawford Ave., has 42 rooms, a restaurant, a casino, and an outdoor swimming pool with a looping slide. $$$. ☎ 800-582-8094 or 406-665-1870.

Lariat Motel, at 709 N. Center Ave., is small but nice with 18 rooms. $. ☎ 406-665-2683.

Historic Hotel Becker Bed & Breakfast, at 200 N. Center St., recalls days gone by. The hotel is complete with a street corner cupola. Seven guest rooms, full breakfast. $$. ☎ 406-665-2707.

Kendrick House Inn, at 206 N. Custer Ave., has five guest rooms with shared baths. Full breakfast. $$. ☎ 406-665-3035.

Laurel

Best Western Locomotive Inn, at 310 S. 1st Ave., is a full-service 51 room hostelry. $$$. ☎ 800-528-1234 or 406-628-8281.

Riverside Bed & Breakfast, at 2132 Thiel Rd., has two guest rooms with private baths in a rural setting beside the Yellowstone River. Full breakfast. $$$. ☎ 800-768-1580 or 406-628-7890.

Lodge Grass

Lodge Grass, on the Crow Indian Reservation, offers a taste of reservation life at two small lodgings.

Cottage Inn, at 22 Hester Ave., has five guest rooms and an eatery. No credit cards. $. ☎ 406-639-2453.

Westwood Ranch Bed & Breakfast, a 15-minute drive from the Bighorn Battlefield (ask for directions), has three guest rooms with private baths and a ranch setting. Full breakfast. $$. ☎ 800-551-1418 or 406-639-2450.

Miles City

Miles City, as befits a cattle country hub, accommodates periodic influxes of cattlemen and other visitors with two notable chain hostelries and a B&B.

Best Western War Bonnet Inn, at 1015 S. Haynes, is a 54-room full-service hostelry. $$$. ☎ 406-232-4560.

Rodeway Inn and Historic Olive Hotel, at 501 Main St., is, as the name suggests, in historic digs reeking of Miles City's yip-yiing good old days. There are a highly regarded restaurant and 72 guest rooms. $$. ☎ 800-228-2000 or 406-232-2450.

Helm River Bend Bed & Breakfast is south of town on the Tongue River Road. Three guest rooms, two with private baths. Full breakfast. $$. ☎ 406-421-5420.

Roundup

Best Inn, at 630 Main St., has 20 rooms. $. ☎ 406-323-1000.

Big Sky Motel, at 740 Main St., has 22 rooms. $. ☎ 406-323-2303.

St. Xavier

This small town on the Crow Indian Reservation boasts a six-room hostelry with an ambitious name: **Royal Big Horn Lodge**. No credit cards. $$$. ☎ 406-666-2340.

Terry

Terry is an interesting place to visit for its homesteading history, but accommodations are limited.

Diamond Motel, at 118 E. Spring St., has 12 guest rooms. $. ☎ 406-637-5407.

The Historical Kempton Hotel, at 204 Spring St., has 15 guest rooms. $. ☎ 406-637-5543.

Wibaux

If you are traveling from the east on I-94, Wibaux will serve as your introduction to Montana. Accommodations are limited.

Nunberg's N Heart Ranch Bed & Breakfast, seven miles south of town on MT 7, has four guest rooms, each with shared bath. Full breakfast. The antiques-filled ranch home includes a gallery of host Fred Nunberg's original art works. $$. ☎ 406-795-2345.

Wibaux Super 8 Motel, at the west exit of I-94, has 35 guest rooms. $. ☎ 800-800-8000 or 406-795-2666.

Custer Country

■ US Forest Service Cabins

One rental cabin is available in the Ashland Ranger District of the Custer National Forest. Located 18 miles east of Ashland near Beaver Creek, **Whitetail Cabin** accommodates four persons and rents for $20 per night. Available year-round, the maximum stay is four nights. There's a corral for horses but no water or power. Wood is provided for the heating stove. A cook stove and refrigerator are also furnished. You may have to hike 100 yards to the cabin, depending on road conditions and the type vehicle you are driving. Bring your own bedding and cooking utensils. Contact the Ashland Ranger District office, ☎ 406-784-2344, for reservations.

■ Camping

 Custer Country campgrounds come in several guises: small town parks offering free overnight RV parking, US Forest Service campgrounds, BLM fishing access sites, state parks (see *State Parks*, page 120) campgrounds, private campgrounds with RV hookups, and FWP (Montana Fish, Wildlife and Parks) fishing access sites. Reservations are not accepted at state parks and other public campgrounds. Except in peak tourist season, you can also show up on the spur-of-moment at private campgrounds. Most Forest Service and other public campgrounds enforce a 14-day-stay limit. Camping is permitted at many fishing access sites. Camping fees range from zero to $12. Golden Eagle card holders pay half the posted price at US Forest Service and BLM campgrounds.

Public Campgrounds

Ashland Ranger District

The Ashland Ranger District of the Custer National Forest maintains four primitive campgrounds: **Cow Creek** (has a fishing pond), **Holiday Springs**, **Red Shale** and **Blacks Pond**. Red Shale and Cow Creek accommodate trailers up to 32 feet. Contact the Ashland Ranger District office, ☎ 406-784-2344, for current information.

Beartooth Ranger District

The Beartooth Ranger District of the Custer National Forest maintains **Sage Creek Campground**, off Highway 310 in the vicinity of the Pryor Wild Horse Range (☎ 406-446-2103).

Bighorn Canyon National Recreation Area, North District

There are two campgrounds, at **Afterbay** near Fort Smith and **Black Canyon** (boat-in camping only) five miles south of Ok-A-Beh boat ramp. Self-contained vehicles may overnight in the upper parking lot at Ok-A-

Beh and in the parking lot above the boat ramp at Barry's Landing. Primitive campsites for backpackers exist in a variety of environments within the Recreation Area. Inquire regarding the current status and availability of these campsites at the Yellowtail Visitor Center, open April, May and Sept., 9-4:30; Memorial Day-Labor Day 9-6. Closed Oct.-March (☎ 406-666-2412).

Ekalaka

The Ekalaka vicinity has two no-fee public campgrounds, open May 1-Nov. 15. **Ekalaka Park** is three miles southeast of town on Route 323, then one mile west on Beaver Flats Road. Nine spaces. Trailers up to 16 feet. **Macnab Pond Forest Service Campground** is seven miles southeast of Ekalaka on Rt. 323 and one mile east on Prairie Dale Road. Trailers up to 22 feet.

Forsyth

In the Forsyth area, FWP manages two public campgrounds with boat launch ramps and Yellowstone River fishing access. The **Rosebud (East Unit)** is off I-94 at Forsyth (Exit 93). The Rosebud West unit is west of Forsyth on US 12 at the end of the Yellowstone River Bridge, Milepost 270. No drinking water.

Glendive

A pleasant shady campground is north of Glendive at the **Intake Diversion Dam**. It hums with activity in paddlefishing season. The fishing access site is 16 miles north of Glendive on MT 16, then a mile south on a county road. There are 40 spaces and a boat ramp. The **Huntley Diversion Dam**, on a gravel road one mile west of I-94 Exit 6, allows camping. Boat launch ramp (requires 4WD vehicle) and fishing.

Laurel

Laurel has a community campground at **Riverside Park**, on US 212 South on the banks of the Yellowstone River; 100 tent and RV spaces, some with hookups. Fee campground.

Baker

Baker allows free overnight RV parking in its pleasant City Park.

Broadus

Broadus has camping facilities in the town park, complete with swimming pool, playground and tennis courts.

Roundup

The **CowBelle Campground** at the Roundup fairgrounds offers no-fee camping and RV parking. Barbeque pits and plenty of shade beside the Musselshell River. Call the Roundup Chamber of Commerce at ☎ 406-323-1966 for information.

Other small towns may offer free overnight camping and/or RV parking if there are no nearby public or private campgrounds. If you find yourself in a small Custer Country town at dusk, ask the local constabulary if parking is available at the town park or wherever. Most townsfolk are gracious toward visitors, realizing that they bring much-needed dollars to the local economy.

AUTHOR TIP *A problem with dry camping in a self-contained RV is locating a dump station. A few public and most private campgrounds have dump stations and will allow access for a fee. Some truck stops have dump stations and will let you dump for free if you buy gas.* Montana Fish, Wildlife and Parks *makes available a booklet,* Waste Disposal Stations for Recreational Vehicles, *listing RV dumps throughout the state. I found it to be reasonably accurate. Request a copy by contacting any FWP office.*

Private Campgrounds

Custer Country's private campground situation is somewhat spotty. There are plenty in the more popular tourist areas, few or none off the beaten track. These range from a few slots beside a motel to pleasant well run campgrounds offering such amenities as swimming pools, showers and laundries. Full hookup rates vary widely, from around $10 at low end campgrounds to well over $20 in tourist areas. Recommendable private campgrounds are listed below, under the nearest towns.

Billings

Billings is the headquarters of Kampgrounds of America, those KOAs dear to the heart of every kid who ever rolled into a sleeping bag. The world's first **KOA** is pleasantly situated beside the Yellowstone River south of downtown. Generous spaces on lush lawns under mature trees give a country estate feeling. Every amenity, plus Kamping Kabins. Worth the high end price. Take I-90 Exit 447 or 450. 547 Garden Ave., Billings, MT 59101; ☎ 800-KOA-8546 or 406-252-3104.

Glendive

Green Valley Campground, like many Montana campgrounds both public and private, is close to a set of railroad tracks. But never mind. It's a pleasant place to lay your head, surrounded as it is by farm fields. Trout pond, playground, tipi rentals. Open year-round. Take I-94 Exit 213. Box 1396, Glendive, MT 59330; ☎ 406-365-4156.

Hardin

Grandview Campground is a block from a park with an Olympic-size pool, playground and tennis courts. Large pull-through sites. 1002 N. Mitchell Ave., Hardin, MT 59034; ☎ 406-665-2489.

Hardin KOA is also surrounded by growing crops. This well run KOA has a swimming pool and lots of grass. Follow the KOA signs from I-90 Exit 495. RR1, Hardin, MT 59034; ☎ 800-KOA-1635 or 406-665-1635.

Sunset Village RV Park is sparkling new with all services. 920 3rd St. So., Hardin, MT 59034; ☎ 406-665-1100.

Miles City

Miles City KOA boasts more than 70 cottonwood trees over 50 feet tall. That's one valuable asset on the prairie in high summer. Heated pool, grassy tent sites and other amenities. Take I-94 Exit 135 and follow the KOA signs. 1 Palmer, Miles City, MT 59301; ☎ 800-KOA-3909 or 406-232-3991.

Terry

Terry RV Oasis has shade and grass. Take I-90 Exit 176. PO Box 822, Terry, MT 59349; ☎ 406-635-5520.

Wibaux

Beaver Valley Haven, on MT 7 south of town, offers RV and tent camping and rustic cabins within walking distance to downtown. Shade and a picnic area. 500 S. Wibaux St., Wibaux, MT 59353; ☎ 406-795-2280.

■ Where to Eat

Dining in Custer Country can be an adventure, for sure. Don't expect trendy California dishes, or haute cuisine either, unless you come to roost in Billings. The pickings tend to be on the bland side at the family restaurants popped up like dandelions in the vicinity of major tourist attractions. But Custer Country is cattle country; go for the steak and burgers. It's also Indian country; go for the buffalo steaks, Indian tacos and fry bread. And it's homestead country; go for the pies. You'll find these in tasty abundance at small town cafés catering to the locals. 'Most every town has at least one of these, often with saloon attached – a combination that guarantees good food and a high old time.

Uninspired eateries earn no mention here. You can find mediocre on your own. Each of the restaurants and cafés listed below has something interesting to recommend it, be it only a steak, homemade pies or great cow country atmosphere.

Custer Country

Baker

Sakelari's Kitchen has good downhome food and interesting antiques. Weekdays 5 am-8 pm, Sundays 6 am-3 pm. ☎ 406-778-2202.

Heiser's Bar boasts that "we brought the world's largest steer home to Baker." Find out what that means while chowing down on beef or broasted chicken. ☎ 406-778-2001.

Billings

Billings restaurant offerings range from cowboy corn to upscale sophisticated.

Acton Bar & Cowcamp Steak House claims that they won't give you a bum steer. Corny? Yes, but this Western-style eatery does serve up good charbroiled steaks and other ranch-type chow. It also serves chuckwagon cookouts, hay rides, dummy roping and rip-roarin' live entertainment. Touristy? Yes, but fun. Call for a reservation. At Acton, 16 miles northwest of Billings on MT 3. ☎ 406-652-9438.

The Golden Belle Restaurant, in the Radisson Northern Hotel at 19 N. 28th St., combines local color with an upscale menu. ☎ 406-245-2232.

Jim's Smokehouse, at 145 Regal St., spices Western fare with line dancing to country music. On summer weekends, there's live bull riding in a pen outside the bar. ☎ 406-254-0885.

The Lucky Diamond Restaurant & Lounge, at the top of the Sheraton Hotel, the world's tallest free-standing brick building, serves up fine city views with your dinner. 27 N. 27th St.; ☎ 406-252-7400.

Montana Brewing Company typifies today's trendy cottage industry breweries. Enjoy pasta or wood-fired pizza while quaffing handcrafted ales. Open daily, 11 am-midnight. 113 N. Broadway; ☎ 406-252-9200.

The Rex is an upscale Montana-style restaurant (no, that's not an oxymoron) serving great steaks. 2401 Montana Ave.; ☎ 406-245-7477.

Walkers Grill (movie people hang out here) has a California-style menu. Lower Level, 301 N. 27th St.; ☎ 406-245-9291.

Broadus

The Judge's Chambers boasts that it serves up "the best food in 500 miles." That may be so, considering the dearth of settlements in extreme southeast Montana. ☎ 406-436-2002.

Montana Bar & Café is worth a stop for the homemade rolls and pies; if you can stand the red velvet dining room. ☎ 406-436-2454.

Forsyth

Speedway Diner, at 811 Main, features fresh-baked caramel rolls and serves breakfast all day. ☎ 406-356-7987.

Fort Smith

See *Hotels, Motels & B&Bs*.

Glendive

Glendive residents shake their heads when the subject of interesting eateries arises.

By consensus, the best dinner in town is at **Bacio's**, specializing in Northern Italian cuisine. The restaurant at 302 W. Towne St. resembles a KFC on the outside because it was one. Dinner only. ☎ 406-365-9664.

Two casinos serve food: **Doc & Eddy's** at the West Plaza Shopping Center (☎ 406-365-6782) and **Silver Dollar Casino** at 1101 W. Towne St. (☎ 406-365-6120).

Hardin

Don't expect to find exotic fare in Hardin. Eateries run to family and touristy restaurants *sans* atmosphere – the type that post "buses welcome" signs.

Merry Mixer Restaurant & Lounge, at 317 N. Center Ave., advertises "daily homemade specials" and features pastas, steaks and home-baked desserts. Breakfast, lunch and dinner. ☎ 406-665-3735.

Miles City

The fare in this ultimate cow town reflects Western tastes: steaks, more steaks, and pies.

Montana Bar, at 612 Main, so strongly reflects a turn-of-the-century watering hole ambience that it's listed on the National Historic Register. ☎ 406-232-5809.

Visiting cattlemen and their families have been dining at the **Historic Olive Hotel**, at 501 Main, for decades. ☎ 800-228-2000 or 406-232-2450.

Roundup

Pioneer Café on Main Street features such downhome ranch country dietary staples as chicken fried steak, biscuits and gravy, homemade cinnamon rolls. Open daily, 6 am-8 pm. ☎ 406-323-2622.

Wibaux

No visit to Wibaux is complete without stopping in at the **Shamrock Club** at 101 S. Wibaux. You'll be so busy looking at the brands on the ceiling, at the antique bits and spurs and the log cabin complete with cowboy gear, that you may forget to order. Don't. There's steaks and trimmin's, barbeque and lots of other good stuff. Bring an appetite; plates come heaped with more food than any normal person can eat. Lunch and dinner. ☎ 406-795-8250.

Custer Country

Yellowstone Country

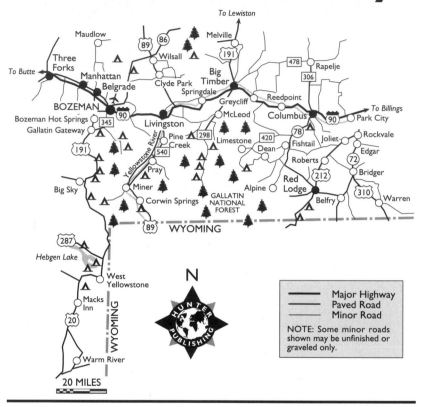

Yellowstone Country

Introduction

 **T**his travel region takes its name from the slim slice of **Yellowstone National Park** lying within Montana. Most of the park is in Wyoming. Yellowstone Country is a compact chunk of Montana spiced with forested mountains and lush valleys. In the north and east, the mountains give way to windswept prairie supporting cattle and sheep ranches. The region's beauty transcends poetic imagery. It reaches its peak on the **Beartooth Scenic Byway**, dubbed by Charles Kuralt "The most beautiful highway in America." No surprise that Yellowstone Country has been "discovered" by movie folk and other trend setters. The **Gallatin National Forest**, the **Beartooth Ranger District** of the Custer National Forest, the **Lee Metcalf Wilderness** and the **Absaroka Beartooth Wilderness** afford more hiking, backpacking, horseback riding, rock climbing and snow adventures than any one person could explore in a lifetime.

The rivers lacing Yellowstone Country, the **Upper Madison**, the **Stillwater**, **Yellowstone**, **Clarks Fork** of the Yellowstone, **Boulder** and **Gallatin**, attract fly fishers, canoers, kayakers, floaters and whitewater rafters.

Missouri Headwaters State Park, marking the place where the Madison, Jefferson and Gallatin Rivers join to form the Missouri, is in the

Yellowstone Country

northwest corner of the region near the appropriately named town of Three Forks.

Two national wildlife refuges, **Hailstone** and **Halfbreed**, occupy the region's extreme northeast corner. **Greycliff Prairie Dog Town**, home to thousands of comical burrowing creatures, is near Big Timber. This is a region in transition. Crusty ranchers and swaggering outdoorsmen are less visible these days than high-profile corporate and entertainment personalities. A profusion of businesses catering to well-heeled vacationers has followed as inevitably as trout follow a fly. Yellowstone Country is awash in guest ranches, fly fishing shops, river guides and back country outfitters. Many are expensively low-key. Other tourist-oriented businesses, particularly in West Yellowstone, come on strong. Not that Yellowstone Country slights less well-heeled adventurers. You can still name your adventure here, but you may have to search for it.

The Church Universal & Triumphant

Yellowstone Country's trendiness is tempered by survivalism. But apparently not for long. Since 1986, the Gallatin country near Corwin Springs and Gardiner has been home to a New Age religious sect called the Church Universal & Triumphant. A rumpus transpired when spiritual leader Elizabeth Clare Prophet warned of an imminent nuclear holocaust and directed her followers to build an enormous fallout shelter high in the Gallatin Range. Stocked with food, water, vehicles, fuel and weapons, the shelter and the faithful awaited the apocalypse. After the predicted March, 1990 date came and went peacefully, the church hit the skids. The sect's 12,000-acre Royal Teton Ranch is considered a hot property among the movie star and Wall Street set. Poised like vultures, they await the declining sect's decision to sell snippets of the ranch.

Area towns are abloom with trendy shops and eateries. **Bozeman**, the region's hub city with over 25,000 residents, projects a mixed image. The historic gateway to gold country named for John Bozeman of Bozeman Trail fame is fast succumbing to '90s-style trendiness. Once sleepy Old West towns like Livingston and Red Lodge have been "discovered" by the chic set, causing prices and native Montanans' blood pressure to rise.

Value shifts aside, Yellowstone Country offers weeks' worth of adventure for sightseers, serious adventure seekers, and carloads of folks in-between.

■ History

History is comparatively quiescent in Yellowstone Country. Indian tribes lived, warred and hunted here for centuries. In the early 19th century, mountain men befriended the Shoshone and mixed it up with the Blackfeet. But most of the events were more closely associated with Montana's other regions.

There was some gold prospecting, but it couldn't hold a miner's canary to the mining that changed the face of the mountains of Gold West Country. The **Bozeman Trail**, built partially to serve the mines, passed through the region.

Legendary mountain men moved through these mountains and river valleys, trapping beaver and other fur-bearing animals. They traded directly with the Indians, or at trading posts established to the north and along the Missouri River.

Lewis and Clark traveled through today's Yellowstone Country on their 1805 expedition. They were overcome with awe at their first view of the converging forks of the Jefferson, Madison and Gallatin Rivers. Lewis's description of the bowl in which the rivers converge holds true today: "The country opens suddenly to extensive and beautiful plains and meadows which appear to be surrounded in every direction with distant and lofty mountains."

DID YOU KNOW! *Lewis named the Jefferson and Madison Rivers for President Thomas Jefferson and Secretary of State James Madison, the Gallatin for Secretary of the Treasury Albert Gallatin.*

In 1877, the Nez Perce crossed Yellowstone Park on their epic flight to freedom before angling northward across the prairie.

Yellowstone Country has long been a place of quiet settlement. The first mountain men to trap here encountered bands of Crow Indians hunting in the Abasaroka Mountains. Later came a few hardy settlers, farming and ranching the fertile valleys and rolling prairie lands north and east of the mountains.

Meanwhile, **Yellowstone Park** was being promoted by the Northern Pacific and Milwaukee Railroads. Established by Congress and President Ulysses S. Grant in 1872, the park captured the imagination of a credulous public. Railroad connections provided the first convenient access. Spur lines extended from Livingston to Gardiner at the park's northern entrance. Visitors still pass under Gardiner's massive stone arch, dedicated by President Theodore Roosevelt in 1903.

The town was named for early mountain man Johnston Gardiner.

By the 1930s, Yellowstone Park was **the** place to visit. In response to the tourist boom, numerous dude ranches were established among the mountains and valleys north of the park. These were the precursors of today's booming guest ranch business.

■ A Volcanic Geology

Volcanic activity created many of the interesting rock formations and petrified forests in Yellowstone National Park and the mountains north of the park. Over the course of the past few million years the landscape has been shaped and modified by episodes of glaciation accompanied by continuous water action. Though retreating, some glaciers remain.

These mountain building processes continue, as was evidenced by the massive earthquake and landslide that hit the Madison River Canyon in 1959.

Geology in the northern part of Yellowstone Country approximates that of other parts of Montana with Cambrian limestones and shales. The Three Forks area overlays Mississippian Madison limestone. There are exposures of Devonian Three Forks Shale. Mica is mined at Sappington Junction near Three Forks. Exposures of Livingston Formation in Bozeman Pass yield zeolite minerals and calcite. See *Rock Hounding* (page 101) for descriptions of minerals, rocks and fossils in Yellowstone Country and where to find them.

■ Weather

Yellowstone Country seldom experiences the extreme heat that can plague eastern Montana. Summer days are generally warm and pleasant. Temperatures are apt to be cooler in the mountains, hotter and dryer in plains areas. It cools down rapidly at night, becoming downright crisp in the higher elevations.

Expect fast-moving summer rainstorms in the mountains. Rain gear is a must. The upside: raindrops clinging to leaves like tiny sparkling cocoons.

Spring's early signs vary according to elevation. The snow disappears and the land starts greening up by late April in the lower elevations, gradually spreading to mountain valleys by early May. Some sheltered valleys may green up earlier. Late spring snowstorms are not unusual. Snows remain until July on 12,799-foot-high Granite Peak; year-round in high north-facing Absaroka-Beartooth Wilderness elevations. Ditto: the Beartooth Highway's highest points. Fall comes early to the mountains. Scattered September snows are harbingers of winter. Autumn is a glorious time in Yellowstone Country, with brilliant foliage, crisp nights and sun-washed days. Winter often brings thick curtains of snow by November, covering the ground by mid-December. Higher elevations experience longer winters. And it's teeth-rattling cold. The cold is visible in millions of ice crystals sheeting the snowy slopes, shining like stars fallen to earth.

AUTHOR TIP *Bring your snuggies when visiting Yellowstone Country in any season. Just because it's July does- n't mean you can leave your long johns, sweat shirts and windbreakers at home. Here, as in any moun- tainous country, the key is to be prepared. If you err, make it on the side of overkill. This is especially true if backpacking and camping are on your agenda.*

If you sign on for a guest ranch visit or a fly fishing or other expedition, follow the clothing suggestions included in the packet sent you by the ranch or outfitter. If you don't receive such a list, be sure to ask. They know about the vagaries of the weather and the type of clothing that will keep you comfortable.

Getting Around

■ Highways & Byways

Getting around in Yellowstone Country reveals a fabu- lous vista at every turn of the road. The Lee Metcalf and Absaroka-Beartooth Wilderness Areas are closed to ve- hicles, but US Forest Service roads penetrate national forest lands. High clearance 4WD vehicles make good sense on these often mountainous roads.

I-90 wriggles east to west across Yellowstone Country like a snake dodging a coyote. The artery enters Yellow- stone Country at Laurel and exits at Three Forks, looking in on Bozeman, Livingston, Big Timber and a scattering of smaller towns. Exits connect with several national and state highways. Many head south, skirting the Beartooth and Absaroka Mountains and accessing Yellowstone National Park. A few head north into the Gallatin National Forest.

Among those heading south is **US 212**. The stretch linking Red Lodge with the northeast entrance to Yellowstone Park at Silver Gate is the highly hyped **Beartooth Scenic Byway**. The highway splits north of Red Lodge. US 212 continues north to Laurel. **Montana 78** follows a northwesterly course to I-90 at Columbus.

Montana 306 shoots north from Columbus to access Halfbreed and Hail- stone National Wildlife Refuges.

The enormous chunk of splendid mountain country comprising the Absaroka-Beartooth Wilderness lies between US 89 and a confusion of unimproved roads west of MT 78.

After crossing Yellowstone National Park, **US 89** enters Montana at Gardiner and follows the Yellowstone River to I-90 at Livingston. North of Livingston, US 89 continues on to Great Falls in Charlie Russell Country.

At the western edge of Yellowstone Country, **US 191** heads north from West Yellowstone and lazes along the Gallatin River, through the Gallatin National Forest to Bozeman. After merging with I-90, US 191 heads north from Big Timber into Charlie Russell Country.

Most of these highways track idyllic rivers through mountain country. But not all. The prairie laps the mountains in eastern Yellowstone Country, opening up distant vistas. Heading west, your sense of adventure is whetted by jumbled mountains rising like crenelated towers against a cobalt sky.

"Driver beware" should be the byword on Yellowstone Country's mountain roads and blind curves. An abrupt acquaintance with free-roaming wildlife is among the hazards of excessive speed. Deer and other animals can appear out of nowhere in a flash.

Summer is a window of driving opportunity. Winter is another matter altogether. Many mountain roads, including secondary and Forest Service roads and the Beartooth Scenic Byway, are closed when winter snows sock in. Snow can force a closure of the Beartooth even in mid-summer.

Winter Driving

If you are thinking of driving mountain roads between Labor Day and Memorial Day, dial the Montana Road Condition Report hotline for current road closures (☎ 800-226-7623). Roads may be free of snow in the shoulder seasons, but beware of black ice. The very words send shivers up the spines of Western drivers. I've encountered this demon on more than one occasion. The scariest one rolled us. We were lucky to walk away. Others aren't so lucky. Black ice kills folks every winter.

Drive extra cautiously if nighttime temperatures dip below freezing, especially when there's fog. If you feel your vehicle sliding, tap the brakes gently and steer into the slide.

Road crews make heroic efforts to plow and sand major roads and highways, plus access roads to ski resorts and other winter sports localities. But sudden snowstorms can delay maintenance crews. Keep a winter survival kit in your vehicle at all times. This should include snow tires or chains, a shovel, a board, an old rug or mat, kitty litter for traction, a flashlight or lantern with fresh batteries, blankets or sleeping bags, and enough food for several days. A cellular phone is an idea, but it may be useless in the mountains. If you do become stuck in the snow, be careful to keep the exhaust clear. A snow-clogged exhaust can result in carbon monoxide fumes entering your vehicle.

Information Sources

Getting There

Delta Airlines serves Bozeman: ☎ 800-221-1212.

Horizon Airline serves Bozeman: ☎ 800-547-9308

Northwest Airlines serves Bozeman: ☎ 800-225-2525.

Sky West Airline serves Bozeman and West Yellowstone: ☎ 800-453-9417.

Greyhound Bus Line offers service between Yellowstone Country towns and cities: ☎ 800-231-2222 or 406-252-4169.

On The Road

Montana Highway Patrol, 2550 Prospect Ave., Helena, MT 59620; ☎ 406-444-7696.

Montana Road Condition Report: ☎ 800-226-7623, TTY ☎ 800-335-7592 or 406-444-7696. (CB'ers: Emergency Channel 9.)

Local Road Report, Bozeman: ☎ 406-586-1313.

Montana Ski Reports and Travel Information: ☎ 800-VISIT MT, ext. 3WG outside Montana or 406-444-2654.

Car Rentals

Belgrade

Budget Rent-A-Car: ☎ 800-952-8343 or 406-388-4091.

Thrifty Car Rental: ☎ 406-388-3484.

Bozeman

Avis Rent-A-Car: ☎ 406-388-6414.

Enterprise Rent-A-Car: ☎ 800-RENTACAR or 406-586-8010.

Hertz Rent-A-Car: ☎ 406-388-6939.

National Car Rental: ☎ 406-388-6694.

Practical Rent-A-Car: ☎ 800-722-4618 or 406-586-8373.

Rent A Wreck: ☎ 800-344-4551 or 406-587-4551.

Simpson Honda: ☎ 800-246-0761 or 406-587-0761.

Yellowstone Country

Livingston

Cranky Ranky: ☎ 800-497-1001 or 406-222-8600.
Livingston Ford: ☎ 800-367-4451 or 406-222-7200.
Rent A Wreck: ☎ 406-222-0071.

Red Lodge

Anderson Chevrolet: ☎ 800-608-2720 or 406-446-2720.
Ray Judd Ford: ☎ 406-446-1400.

West Yellowstone

Big Sky Car Rentals: ☎ 800-426-7669 or 406-646-9564.
Budget Rent-A-Car of West Yellowstone: ☎ 800-231-5991.

Tourism Offices

Travel Montana, Department of Commerce, PO Box 200533 (1424 9th Ave.), Helena, MT 59620-0533; ☎ 800-847-4868 outside Montana, ☎ 406-444-2654 in Montana. Internet http://travel.mt.gov/.

Yellowstone Country Tourism Office, Box 1107, Red Lodge, MT 59068; ☎ 800-736-5276 or 406-446-1005.

Chambers of Commerce

Belgrade, Box 1126, Belgrade, MT 59714; ☎ 406-388-1616. Fax 406-388-4996.

Big Sky Resort Association, Box 100, Big Sky, MT 59716.

Big Timber (McLeod), Box 1012, Big Timber, MT 59011; ☎ 406-932-5131.

Bozeman, 1205 E. Main, Box B, Bozeman, MT 59715; ☎ 800-228-4224 or 406-586-5421. Fax 406-586-8286.

Bridger, Box 99, Bridger, MT 59014; ☎ 406-662-3728.

Columbus, Box 783, Columbus, MT 59019; ☎ 406-322-4505.

Cooke City, Box 1071, Cooke City, MT 59020; ☎ 406-838-2244 (winter), ☎ 406-838-2272 (summer) or 406-838-2495.

Cardiner, Box 81, Gardiner, MT 59030; ☎ 406-848-7971.

Livingston, 212 W. Park, Livingston, MT 59047; ☎ 406-222-0850. Fax 406-222-0852.

Red Lodge, Box 988, Red Lodge, MT 59068; ☎ 406-446-1718. E-mail redlodge@wtp.com. Internet www.net/redlodge.

Three Forks, Box 1103, Three Forks, MT 59752; ☎ 406-285-3198.

West Yellowstone, Box 458, West Yellowstone, MT 59758; ☎ 406-646-7701.

Outdoors Associations

Adventure Cycling Association, Box 8308, Missoula, MT 59807; ☎ 406-721-1776. Fax 406-721-8754.

Fishing Outfitters Association of Montana (FOAM), Box 67, Gallatin Gateway, MT 59730; ☎ 406-763-5436.

Montana Outfitters & Guides Association, Box 1248, Helena, MT 59624; ☎ 406-449-3578. Fax 406-443-2439.

Montana Wilderness Association, Box 635, Helena, MT 59624; ☎ 406-443-7350.

Government Agencies

Montana Department of Fish, Wildlife & Parks Offices

FWP State Headquarters, 1420 E. Sixth Ave., Helena, MT 59620; ☎ 406-444-2535. Fax 406-444-4952. TDD ☎ 406-444-1200.

FWP Bozeman Region, 1400 S. 19th, Bozeman, MT 59715; ☎ 406-994-4042. 24-hour information: ☎ 406-994-5700.

Custer National Forest, Supervisor's Office, PO Box 50760, Billings, MT 59105; ☎ 406-657-6361.

Custer National Forest, Beartooth Ranger District, HC 49, Box 3420, Red Lodge, MT 59068; ☎ 406-446-2103.

Gallatin National Forest, Supervisor's Office, PO Box 130, Bozeman, MT 59771; ☎ 406-587-6701 or 406-587-6920.

Gallatin National Forest, Big Timber Ranger District, Highway 10 East (PO Box 196), Big Timber, MT 459011; ☎ 406-932-5155.

Gallatin National Forest, Bozeman Ranger District, 3710 Fallon St., Suite C, Bozeman, MT 59718; ☎ 406-587-6920.

Gallatin National Forest, Gardiner Ranger District, Highway 89 (PO Box 5), Gardiner, MT 59030; ☎ 406-848-7375.

Gallatin National Forest, Hebgen Lake Ranger District, Highway 287 (PO Box 520), West Yellowstone, MT 59047; ☎ 406-646-7369.

Gallatin National Forest, Livingston Ranger District, 5242 Hwy. 89 South, Livingston, MT 59047; ☎ 406-222-1892.

Bureau of Land Management, Montana State Office, 222 N. 32nd St. (PO Box 36800), Billings, MT 59107-6800; ☎ 406-255-2885.

Bureau of Land Management, Butte District, 106 N. Parkmont (Box 3388), Butte, MT 59702; ☎ 406-494-5059.

US Geological Survey, Federal Center, Box 25286, Denver, CO 80225; ☎ 800-435-7627 or 303-202-4700.

Yellowstone Country

Touring

■ East of the Absaroka-Beartooths

Touring Montana's most compact travel region is a snap when compared to the considerable distances between towns and points of interest in the three easterly travel regions. It's possible to breakfast in Bozeman, lunch in Big Timber and wind up dining in Red Lodge. I don't recommend this telescopic approach. There's too much spectacular scenery to enjoy along the way; too much to do. The **Absaroka-Beartooth Range**, which includes the so-named wilderness, juts northward from Yellowstone National Park almost to I-90. North of I-90, the **Crazy Mountains**, the **Bridger Range** and expanses of rolling rangeland, cut through by US 89 and 191, merge with Charlie Russell Country. Thus has nature divided Yellowstone Country into two logical touring entities south of I-90 and a broader, less visited area north of I-90.

Working from east to west and using I-90 as a starting point, we begin by exploring the creek- and river-scored valleys on the lee side of the Beartooths. Here, all roads eventually lead to **Red Lodge**. Choose between three routes: **MT 72** to Belfry with a westward jog on County Rt. 308; the more direct **US 212**; scenic **MT 78**. All three offer bucolic river valley scenery backdropped by the looming snow-tipped peaks of the Beartooth Range.

Take I-90 Exit 34 at Laurel to access both US 212 and MT 72. The routes branch 11 miles later at Rockvale. This is where the scenery perks up. MT 72 follows the Clarks Fork of the Yellowstone River, pulling up at the tiny town of Bridger before hanging a right at a crossroads named Belfry and cruising through Bearcreek to Red Lodge.

Bridger

The former coal mining town of Bridger owes its name to mountain man/guide/explorer Jim Bridger, one of the first white men to explore Yellowstone Park. Seems that Bridger forded the Clarks Fork of the Yellowstone in 1864, while guiding a wagon train to Virginia City. Dubbed Bridger's Crossing, the name was shortened to Bridger after a town sprang up.

Bearcreek

Pig Races

Bearcreek has assured itself a place on the map of only-in-Montana quirks because of the local saloon's periodic pig races. Real live pigs race for food and applause. Montana's answer to the Triple Crown benefits a scholarship fund for Carbon County 4-H and Future Farmers of America youths. Proceeds come from two-dollar bets wagered by onlookers. The Montana Legislature has officially sanctioned sports pool pig racing. Half the pool money goes to the winners. Half goes into the scholarship fund. The Bearcreek Saloon stages the races all summer long. In winter, the show moves indoors and features gerbil and hamster races.

US 212 is a more direct route to Red Lodge. The road follows aptly named Rock Creek through several small towns. **Cooney Reservoir** and the state park by that name is reached via FS Road 4074 from Boyd. The reservoir's near proximity to Billings boosts its popularity quotient on summer weekends. See *State Parks* and *Fishing*.

Take I-90 Exit 408 at Columbus to access MT 78. Columbus has the dubious honor of being the home of the only precious metals smelter in the Western Hemisphere. The drive to Red Lodge is surpassingly beautiful. The first leg parallels the lower Stillwater River, after which the route meanders through the foothills of the Beartooths. Like many of Yellowstone Country's most scenic pockets, the bucolic Stillwater River Valley is fast filling with ranchettes complete with raw new log houses and sleek hobby horses.

Absarokee

Pause in Absarokee, a pleasantly shaded small town with touristy ways awash in antiques shops and attractive old homes. Situated on part of the original Crow Indian Reservation, Absarokee is just up the road from the site of Old Crow Agency, c. 1875-1883. A plaque identifies the site.

The Crows

Absarokee is the name by which the Crows were originally known. Of Siouxan origin, the Crows were once part of the Hidatsa tribe living around the Great Lakes. In the Hidatsa tongue, Absarokee is derived from absa, meaning "large-beaked bird" and rokee, meaning "off-spring." These words, expressed in sign language by the flapping of arms to simulate wings, were interpreted to simulate crows. Thus came "Crow."

A network of interlinked paved and unpaved county and Forest Service roads branches west into the Beartooths from Absarokee and two other points along MT 78. Watch for signs. Rt. 420 follows the Stillwater to the edge of the Absaroka-Beartooth Wilderness. Turn onto RT. 419 at Nye and follow the gravel road through Dean to reach **Mystic Lake**. The small reservoir supplying Red Lodge's water is surrounded by wilderness. See *Adventures on Foot* and *Camping*.

Red Lodge

MT 78 sneaks into Red Lodge, unlike US 212 which runs a gauntlet of ancillary services as it enters the town. A self-consciously quaint town sans stop lights, Red Lodge's turn-of-the-century houses testify to a former life as a thriving coal mining town. Much of Red Lodge is on the National Register of Historic Places. On the cusp of becoming touristy, Red Lodge has been "discovered" by artsy trend setters. Interesting shops line two or three blocks of Broadway.

The town enjoys a dramatic situation in a deep declivity defined by high ridges rising on two sides. Nearby Rock Creek gurgles through **Bearcreek Canyon**.

You have to admire Red Lodge's movers and shakers. They have the promotion angle down pat, welcoming visitors with an attractive Chamber of Commerce visitor center in plain view of folks driving in from the north. The town throws one wing-ding after another, either in town or at nearby **Red Lodge Mountain Ski Area**. The annual **Festival of Nations** honors the numerous cultures that have called Red Lodge home. Other events include a rodeo, a mountain man rendezvous, music festivals, Round Barn Theatre productions, even a can-can troupe high-kicking

Main Street, Red Lodge, MT.

under the name of the Red Lodge Grizzly Peek-a-Boos (see *Festivals & Special Events*, page 222).

Several attractions, plus a self-guided historic walking tour, augment shops and special events. Pick up a walking tour guide at the visitor center.

The **Carbon County Arts Guild** digs are in Red Lodge's original railroad depot at the north end of town. Changing exhibits representing area artists keep the gallery fresh and alive. The Depot Gallery is open Tues.-Sat., 11-5. Also open summer Sundays from 11-3. Donation.

 KID-FRIENDLY The **Beartooth Nature Center**, dedicated to protecting injured or orphaned animals unable to survive in the wild, is a great place for kids to see bears, mountain lions, wolves and other beasties up close. There's a petting zoo for tots. Educational programs are presented. Open daily in summer, 10-6. ☎ 406-446-1133 for feeding times.

All this keeps folks coming, but the area's most highly touted asset keeps 'em both coming and going. The **Beartooth National Scenic Byway** (US 212), linking Red Lodge with Cooke City and Yellowstone National Park, has received much press, thanks to the late CBS commentator Charles Kuralt's ecstatic coverage. The 65-mile stretch of road is slated to receive some much-needed upgrading, thanks to a recent mega-bucks Federal highway appropriation.

The approach to the byway is innocent enough. The first 20 miles or so run through gently undulating terrain above burbling Rock Creek. Several Forest Service campgrounds are situated along the creek and hiking trails abound (see *Adventures on Foot* and *Camping*).

Just as you're thinking that tales of the byway's gnarlier aspects may be so much ballyhoo, the road narrows and climbs steeply, executing a series of dizzying switchbacks until, poised at 10,942-foot Beartooth Pass, it has switchbacks all the way down. There are places to park and play in the snow (yes, snowbanks are here year-round), and to admire views stretching forever. Above-the-treeline alpine meadows sloping from the byway host drifts of tiny wildflowers in late summer. Alpine lakes shimmer amongst the meadows. Glaciers lie in cirques among distant peaks. A highway seems an intrusion here. Wouldn't it be best left to the eagles and an occasional intrepid backpacker?

President Herbert Hoover apparently didn't think so when, in 1931, he signed a bill authorizing the building of "approach highways" to certain national parks. Yellowstone's northeast entrance was one of them. Construction on the Beartooth Highway took five years and cost $2.5 million in Great Depression money.

Yellowstone Country

Driving the Beartooth

Driving the Beartooth is not for sissies. Drivers see more pavement than distant vistas. Best to cross in a passenger car or mini-van. It can be negotiated in a motorhome or a vehicle pulling a trailer (buses travel it every day in season), but it's no picnic in the park. I went across in my 24-foot RV, but wished I'd been driving a car. Switchbacks are tight and some grades slope alarmingly. Large vehicles may need the entire road on steeply graded switchbacks. Guardrails are scarce as snakes in a snowfield.

Large slow-moving vehicles must turn out when possible to let fast-moving local vehicles pass. Red Lodge and Cooke City residents regard the route only as a way to get from point A to point B and take a dim view of being stuck behind a 40-foot "camper." This may seem the last place in the world to find yourself in a traffic jam, but traffic can and does stack up here at the height of the summer travel season.

If in doubt regarding the safety of driving your outsize rig over the Beartooth, inquire at the Beartooth Ranger District office south of Red Lodge on US 212.

Baby your brakes. Shift down to second or even first on some downhill stretches. This goes for uphill climbs, too. Vapor lock has sidelined more than one vehicle here.

Expect windy, even snowy, weather. Drifting snow sometimes forces closure of the Beartooth even in summer. The byway closes for the winter as early as September and remains closed until mid- to late May. Inquire regarding closures at the Red Lodge Chamber of Commerce or the Beartooth Ranger District office.

Much of the byway traverses Wyoming, returning to Montana just short of Cooke City. Yellowstone Park's mountains beckon long before the rustic mountain settlement heaves into view. Cooke City and nearby Silver Gate are barely in Montana. Inside the Park, the road straddles the state line for a short distance before dipping into Wyoming. Get set for a pothole-dodging slalom if you plan to travel this apallingly bad road to Mammoth Hot Springs.

Cooke City

Cooke City's gold mining days are over, except for the occasional die-hard prospector. Only a few precarious moss-covered log huts remain to tell the story. Gold digs came a cropper in 1877 when Chief Joseph and his band swept through and burned the gold mills. Today, gold is gleaned from tourists.

Most of Cooke City still consists of log structures, giving it a frontier ambience despite numerous tourist services. The town seems to exist to serve travelers, swelling in summer and waxing somnolent in winter. People must be tough and have a well-honed sense of humor in order to live here year-round. Tiny **Silver Gate** is more rustic and less touristy. Both augment summer tourist gold with winter snowmobile gold (see *Adventures on Snow*, page 211).

■ I-90: Columbus to Three Forks

Reedpoint

Heading west on I-90 from Columbus, you'll pass the hick town of Reedpoint. Doesn't look like much from the Interstate, but it's worth a stop. The town could have given up and blown away with the demise of the homestead era, but sheep came to the rescue. The annual Reed Point Sheep Drive (see *Festivals & Special Events*) draws gawkers galore to watch the woolies and quaff a few at local watering holes. The false-front high-grass town tolerates the upscale pretensions of the renovated **Hotel Montana**, now a B&B with attached **Wild Horse Saloon**. Local farmers still chew the fat at the log **Water Hole Saloon**. I dropped in after a five year absence and know what? Same old dudes straddling the same barstools nursing the same beers. If you're into junk shops, this town's for you; junk looks like its been here forever, too.

Greycliff Prairie Dog Town State Park

Next stop: Greycliff Prairie Dog Town State Park at Exit 377. That's a mouthful for a few arid acres hard on the Interstate. But the blacktailed prairie dogs popping in and out of their burrows and squeaking shrill warnings when you approach make it well worth a stop. Interpretive signs relate the story of these "dogs" enjoying the protection of the Nature Conservancy and the Montana Department of Transportation and Fish, Wildlife and Parks.

 The engaging little critters are best seen in early morning or at dusk.

These prairie dogs are among the protected few. Since the varmints' burrows are hazardous to horses and cattle, the rodents are heavily hunted. Many Montana boys grow up using prairie dogs for target practice.

Big Timber

Big Timber is most notable for the restored **Grand Hotel** and as the access point for a jaunt down County Rt. 298 to Boulder River Falls and Natural Bridge. The Boulder River empties into the Yellowstone at Big Timber.

Yellowstone Country

McLeod

After closely following the Boulder River for some 16 miles, the paved road looks in on the quaint settlement of McLeod. Consisting of a post office, prettily-shaded riverside cabins and camp sites and a small clutch of houses, McLeod seems to have changed little since its trading post days back in the last century.

The pavement continues for several more miles before giving way to gravel a short distance before the falls. The ructious boulder-strewn river has several fishing access sites (see *Adventures on Water*, page 196). Numerous campgrounds are spaced on Forest Service roads branching off the main road, and between the falls and trailheads along the Absaroka-Beartooth Wilderness border (see *Adventures on Foot* and *Camping*). The spectacular falls are a popular day trip destination. Picnic areas and interpretive signs border the gorge. The river squeezes through a narrow canyon in a torrent of foaming water. The natural bridge below the falls is not so much a bridge as a broad shelf of rock hindering the river's passage. Over eons, the river has burrowed a channel under the rock shelf. In high water, the cataract flows over it. In low water, it chutes underneath, emerging in a rage. The 27-mile stretch of I-90 between Big Timber and Livingston follows the Yellowstone. The river is mostly out of sight, but occasionally surprises with attractive vistas.

Be alert for high cross-winds as you approach Livingston. I'd swear my wheels were once lifted off the ground by a capricious wind gust; a sobering experience.

Livingston

It seems fore-ordained that Livingston should have been seized upon by the trendy set. The old Northern Pacific railroad town served as the original gateway to Yellowstone National Park. Passengers would change trains at Livingston, boarding the Park Branch Line for a scenic jaunt through Paradise Valley to Gardiner and Yellowstone's North Entrance. Threaded by US 89, Livingston remains a popular Yellowstone gateway via Paradise Valley.

DID YOU KNOW?

Actor / director Robert Redford chose Livingston as the locale for A River Runs Through It *and* The Horse Whisperer. *Movie folk took to Livingston like bears to a berry patch, hailing it as a veritable shrine of Western culture and values. Anglers and rodeo buffs descended in their multitudes. Fly shops and guides proliferated. See* Fishing *(page 203).*

Once projecting a pleasant middle class image with modest residential districts clustered around railroad-facing Main Street, the town began putting on airs. To Livingston's credit, numerous fine old buildings, many dating to or before the turn of the century, have been restored. In excess of 400 structures have qualified for listings on the National Register of Historic Places.

The **Northern Pacific Depot**, restored to a fare-thee-well, remains Livingston's most impressive structure. It's fitting that the hub of activity in days gone by should continue to be the town's focal point. The Livingston **Chamber of Commerce** is housed in the Depot. So is the **Livingston Depot Center**, a museum celebrating Western history and art. Open daily, mid-May through mid-Oct. ☎ 406-222-2300 for current hours. Ample parking and a shady park parallel the tracks adjacent to the Depot.

A truncated version of Livingston's early train service has returned via **Montana Rockies Rail Tours**. Once more, passengers alight at the historic Depot. Those bound for Yellowstone board tour buses instead of another train.

The Livingston Wind

Livingston's gales rate first in a state known for high winds. The town's average annual wind speed is 15.3 mph. The wind speed instrument at Mission Field doesn't register higher than 115 mph, so one can only guess at the velocity of Livingston's mightiest gale.

Weather experts believe that winds funneled down Paradise Valley are compressed through the canyon south of town and scatter-shot over Livingston. The situation is exacerbated by wind-flow coming down over the mountains and collecting over Livingston.

Wind stories are legion. Cow paddies frisbie across pastures, tractor trailer rigs flip like toys, signs fly for miles, roofs take on lives of their own.

Sometimes the wind causes the closure of I-90. The worst stretch is the five miles between Livingston's east interchange and the city center interchange.

Livingston is gallery happy. Over a dozen art galleries feature the works of artists creating in a wide range of genres. **Gallery Walks** are scheduled in summer. Contact the Chamber of Commerce for dates. If you are into history, you may enjoy a visit to the **Park County Museum** at 118 W. Chinook St. Historic memorabilia pertinent to Park County include dioramas, photographs, artifacts and more. ☎ 406-222-3506 for current hours.

Yellowstone Country

The **International Fly Fishing Center**, at 215 E. Lewis St., is a museum given over to all things fishy. An education center for fly fishing enthusiasts, or folks just curious about the sport, the Center traces the evolution of fly rods and displays some 10,000 flies, trout eggs and more. Open daily, May 25-Sept. 15, 10-6. ☎ 406-222-9369.

I-90 follows the old Bozeman Trail through Bozeman Pass (see *Rock Climbing*, page 176) directly west of Livingston.

Bozeman

Bozeman, home of Montana State University, is a fairly typical mid-size college town. The city is purported to have some 25,000 residents, but a burgeoning string of bedroom communities extending along I-90 to the west boosts the count. Ranchettes, carving niches in the surrounding hills, help to make Bozeman one of Montana's fastest growing communities.

It's an attractive place, with the Bridger Range on the north and east, the Gallatin Range on the south, and a broad valley spreading westward. Residential areas lap a vibrant downtown. Main Street, the quintessential Main Street USA, invites strolling. Historic buildings house interesting shops, galleries and eateries.

Bozeman has three fine museums, each as different from the other as dinosaurs from buffalo.

 KID-FRIENDLY The **Museum of the Rockies** is outstanding. A riveting series of exhibits, opening up one after the other, takes you on a trip through four billion years of Rocky Mountain life. "T. Rex on Trial" showcases the fierce Tyrannosaurus Rex with moving and growling robotics and the kinds of hands-on exhibits that kids love. Tots can even ride a triceratops! The origins and development of the indigenous peoples who have occupied Montana for over 11,000 years are explored through artifacts, photographs and textiles. A 3-D presentation and the **Taylor Plantetarium** complete the museum complex's offerings.

The museum is on the Montana State University campus at 600 W. Kagy Blvd. From I-90, take the 19th Street exit, drive until you reach Kagy Blvd. and follow the signs. Admittance fees in the $6 range are good for two days. Open daily Memorial Day-Labor Day, 8-8 with planetariium shows throughout the day. The rest of the year, the museum is open Mon.-Sat., 9-5 and Sunday, 12:30-5. ☎ 406-994-DINO.

The **Gallatin County Pioneer Museum**, in a historic jail at 317 W. Main, showcases more recent history. There's a 12x14 log home, a model of the Bozeman Trail's Fort Ellis, numerous Indian artifacts, and mementoes of John Bozeman. A resource library, available to the public, has family histories and over 8,100 photographs archived for quick viewing.

Summer hours: Mon.-Fri., 10-4:30, Sat. 1-4. Open Oct.-May, Tues.-Fri., 11-4. Free admission. ☎ 406-582-3195.

The **American Computer Museum**, at 234 E. Babcock St., presents a 4,000-year timeline covering "computer technology" from ancient Babylonian and Egyptian times to the present. Quite a challenge, considering the zillions of escalating ancillary computer-connected technologies. This museum meets the challenge and does it well. Open Sept.-May, Tues., Wed., Fri., Sat. noon-4. Open daily June-Aug., 10-4. Admission. ☎ 406-587-7545.

The **Emerson Cultural Center**, in downtown Bozeman at 111 S. Grand, has galleries, working artists' studios, specialty shops, an acclaimed café and a performing arts stage. Open Tues.-Sat., 10-5.

Bozeman hosts an array of musical, theatrical and other cultural events, plus various other festivals. See *Festivals & Special Events* (page 222).

Belgrade & Manhattan

Belgrade and Manhattan, agricultural towns strung along I-90, are fast becoming bedroom communities. Belgrade, in particular, has assumed a suburban coloration. Manhattan, being a bit farther from Bozeman, retains its rural character. For awhile. Founded as a malting center, Manhattan has long capitalized on the valley's grain-growing capability.

Big Sky Carvers is a sign of Manhattan's gradual change. The firm employs talented artists to create Ducks Unlimited folk art decoys, bears and other animal carvings, winsome signs, decorative mirrors and such. Browsing through the store at 324 E. Main is an adventure. ☎ 406-284-6067.

Take a side trip to **Madison Buffalo Jump State Park** from I-90, five miles west of Manhattan. Take the Logan Exit (283) and travel seven miles south on Buffalo Jump Road.

 DID YOU KNOW? *For centuries prior to obtaining horses in the mid-1700, Shoshone, Flathead and Blackfeet hunters stampeded buffalo over steep precipices to their deaths. Waiting below, the women skinned and dressed the carcasses. The Madison Buffalo Jump was a favored bison harvest site.*

The day-use park has interpretive signage and hiking trails. Impressive views of the Madison River Valley from the top of the Jump.

Three Forks

Three Forks has much to celebrate. It was near here that Lewis and Clark marveled over the convergence of the Gallatin, Madison and Jefferson Rivers to form the headwaters of the storied Missouri. Situated

Yellowstone Country

but four miles from the confluence, the bland agricultural town's only interesting features are the creaky old **Sacajawea Inn**, and the **Headwaters Heritage Museum** at 124 Main St. The museum's most notable artifact is a small anvil salvaged from the ruins of Manuel Lisa's Missouri River Trading Post, constructed near Three Forks in 1810. The museum is open in summer. ☎ 406-285-4556 for current hours.

John Colter

John Colter, a member of Lewis and Clark's Voyage of Discovery, opted out of returning with the company to St. Louis. Enthralled by the wild mountain country, he chose to remain and trap furs. In November, 1807 he joined up with trader Manual Lisa. Later that winter, carrying only a 30-pound pack, Colter made an epochal journey through the uncharted mountains and valleys south of the Yellowstone River. He is credited with being the first white man to explore the wilderness that would become Yellowstone National Park. His tales of the area's geysers and hot springs earned Yellowstone the name, "Colter's Hell."

It was near the Headwaters that, in 1808, Colter and John Potts encountered a band of Blackfeet Indians while trapping near a stream. Known for their fierceness, the Blackfeet had yet to smoke the peace pipe with white men. Potts was killed in a hail of arrows. Colter was captured, stripped, given a head start and told to run for his life. That he did, across flats covered with prickly pear, with fleet braves in swift persuit. He outran his pursuers over the six miles necessary to reach cover in the timber along the Jefferson River. The story goes, and this may be apocryphal, that he killed an Indian who had gained on him with his own spear. However that may be, Colter dove into the river and came up under a driftwood jam. He laid low until nightfall, when he lit out for Fort Lisa at the mouth of the Big Horn River. He arrived seven days later, naked and bleeding. Two years later, Manuel Lisa's partners, Andrew Henry and Pierre Menard, built a trading post on a spit of land between the converging Madison and Jefferson Rivers. The Blackfeet weren't having any of that. Repeated attacks forced the abandonment of the post in a matter of months.

The main attraction hereabouts is the **Headwaters of the Missouri River**, the confluence of the three rivers. The Headwaters are reached via a frontage road on the north side of I-90, between Exits 278 and 283. Watch for signs.

Headwaters State Park comprises the confluence and surrounding area. The area's history and natural attractions are celebrated through interpretive signs at points of interest along the access road. This excellent park affords at least a couple of days of camping, canoeing, wildlife watching and picnicking in achingly beautiful surroundings (see *Adventures on Water, Wildlife Watching* and *Camping*).

The History of the Headwaters

Native American tribes used the Headwaters as a meeting place long before Lewis and Clark "discovered" the area on July 25, 1805. It was near here that the child, Sacajawea, was captured during a battle between the Shoshones and the Minatarees. Arriving here with the Lewis and Clark Expedition, she recognized it as being close to the home grounds of her tribe, the Shoshone.

Meriwether Lewis was so taken with the meeting of the rivers that he wrote in his journal, "...the beds of all these streams are formed of smooth pebble and gravel, and their waters are perfectly transparent; in short they are three noble streams."

Fur trappers came into the region shortly after Lewis and Clark's passage. Settlers came on the heels of the trappers. Two towns, first and second Gallatin City, established in the 1860s, enjoyed brief prosperity. The c. 1870 **Gallatin City Hotel** structure stands in an empty field, eloquent testimony to the ephemeral nature of progress. Eons of silt build-up has made prime agricultural land of the wide valley through which these rivers ramble to form the Missouri. Flooding occurs periodically, changing the rivers' courses and spelling the demise of "permanent" settlements. The spit of land on which Henry and Menard built their fort has long since been washed away. You may think you are viewing the very confluence point that enraptured Meriwether Lewis, but chances are you are not. Be that as it may, just being there is a heady experience.

■ Paradise Valley

Backtrack to Livingston to pick up US 89, threading through Paradise Valley to Yellowstone National Park's north entrance.

The bucolic beauty of this valley carved by the Yellowstone River occasioned its extravagant name. Numerous outlanders have taken the name at face value, choosing to settle here. No matter. It would take more than a scattering of expensive homes to mar the valley's loveliness. For an especially idyllic drive, turn off US 89 onto MT 540 three miles south of I-90. The country road winds through **Pine Creek**, a place my grandmother would characterize as "a darling village."

Another route to Pine Creek is **Trail Creek Road**, reached by exiting I-90 at the Trail Creek Exit (#316). The gravel road was once the main road to Yellowstone Park. The railroad also followed this route, serving the valley's coal mines and delivering tourists to Gardiner. Suburbanization is creeping in, but if you look sharp you can see the remains of an old hotel, a stage house leaning thataway and some dilapidated houses.

Some 12 miles south of Pine Creek, MT 540 comes up short at a crossroad posing a choice between Chico Hot Springs and Emigrant, on US 89.

Chico Hot Springs Resort (see *Hotels, Motels & B&Bs,* page 234) is a venerable all-season resort tucked back in the hills. A tasteful facelift has preserved its charm. The re-

Chico Hot Springs Lodge.

sort has somehow managed to remain rustically homey while aspiring to upscale toniness. Fun activities are available year-round at this haunt of both home folks and corporate and show business personalities.

Emigrant

Emigrant, situated below 10,921-foot Emigrant Peak and 10,195-foot Chico Peak, enjoyed a brief fling as a gold camp. Situated in Yellowstone's "thermal zone," Emigrant's hot springs were enjoyed by prospectors and trappers by way of vats thrown up around the springs. Emigrant trains passed through here, no doubt giving rise to the town's name. Emigrant remains a pass-through kind of place. South of Emigrant, the rivercourse deepens, descending into a deep canyon. Numerous fishing access and boat put-in points are sited along the river (see *Adventures on Water*). US Forest Service roads and trails (see *Adventures on Foot*) branch off the Paradise Valley stretch of US 89. The verdant terrain of the lower valley gives way to arrid hillsides as you approach Gardiner.

Gardiner

Gardiner does full justice to a prime location at the north gate of Yellowstone National Park. Conveniently arranged on breaks above the Yellowstone River, Gardiner makes no apologies for being a tourist town providing amenities ranging from lodgings to river trips. Many a backpacker has come off a week in Yellowstone's back country to gratefully avail herself of a laundromat only paces away from the Roosevelt Arch. As the only park entrance open to auto and truck traffic year-round (the Park Service keeps the Gardiner-Cooke City road open all year), The town caters to snowmobilers and cross-country skiers as well as summer visitors.

The road between the Roosevelt Arch and Mammoth Hot Springs describes a sweeping, five-mile uphill curve. This northerly slice of Yellowstone is in Montana; Mammoth Hot Springs is in Wyoming.

US 191's 89-mile stretch between Bozeman and the US 287 junction, eight miles north of West Yellowstone, is more commercialized than the

Paradise Valley route to Yellowstone National Park. US 287 continues on to Hebgen and Quake Lakes from the junction with US 191.

The **Gallatin River** has gurgled more or less within earshot since veering toward the highway above the Axtell Bridge. The river crosses under the highway at the mouth of Gallatin Canyon and continues up close and personal to within a few miles of West Yellowstone. It's in full spate on this stretch, kicking up rapids and taking drivers' eyes from the road. (See *Adventures on Water* and *Camping* for river access sites and campgrounds.) If exhiliarating scenery sends your spirit soaring, here's your chance to revel.

Whitewater rafting on the Gallatin River near Big Sky.

Traveling as it does through national forest lands, US 191 is free of towns from a few miles south of the tourist service town of Gallatin Gateway to West Yellowstone. The one exception is the **Big Sky Resort** complex (see *Adventures on Snow* and *Hotels, Motels & B&Bs*). The development of this upscale resort has resulted in a spate of condo and seasonal home building with attendant services, lending the corridor a distinctly upscale tone.

West Yellowstone

Time was when West Yellowstone defined the term tacky. No longer. Today the streets are wide and clean, the shops are in good taste (there are even two well-stocked bookstores), and most lodgings have shed the grungy look of yore. If the newest attractions aren't exactly low-key, they are well done.

West Yellowstone once depended solely on summer traffic through Yellowstone Park's West Entrance. The isolated town huddled under tons of snow in winter. Enter the snowmobile. West Yellowstone seized upon the sled that roars with high enthusiasm.

AUTHOR TIP *I spent a night in West Yellowstone six or seven years ago while on a multi-day snowmobile trip through the Park. At that time, the community was just waking up to the benefits of winter recreation. Only some so-so motels and an eatery or two were open. Today, the place is wide awake year-round. Winter may be the best time to visit. Those humongous RVs are gone and you can drive your snowmobile right up to your inn door.*

No doubt, the **Yellowstone Imax Theatre** and the adjacent **Grizzly Discovery Center** contributed to West Yellowstone's cleaned-up act. The Imax's six-story screen is the perfect showcase for *Yellowstone*, a dramatic film that accomplishes the daunting task of presenting the story of the Park in its many guises. The theatre complex is open daily in summer from 9-9. ☎ 406-646-4100 for off-season hours. Admission to the Grizzly Discovery Center is in addition to Imax Theatre admission. If you don't happen to see a bear in the Park, you can see some here.

The **Museum of the Yellowstone**, across the main drag from Imax, is a splendid showcase of the many facets of Yellowstone Park, both yesterday and today. There are exhibits centering on the fires of 1989 and on the 1959 earthquake that changed the landscape. Also numerous historical artifacts. Open daily, Memorial Day-Labor Day, 8-10. Hours are 8-9 in May and from Labor Day through Oct. ☎ 800-500-6923 or 406-646-7814.

The **Madison River** swings northwestward out of Yellowstone Park, allowing itself to be swallowed up by **Hebgen** and **Quake Lakes** before emerging in a froth of whitewater and taking a more northerly course to the Headwaters of the Missouri. US 287 follows the river all the way from West Yellowstone to Ennis, entering Gold West Country after leaving Quake Lake.

Driving along the north shore of these fir-lapped mountain-framed lakes, it's difficult to imagine the ruckus that occurred here during the moonlit night of Monday, August 17, 1959.

The Quake

At 11:37, the earth woke up and burped. The earthquake, measuring 7.8 on the Richter Scale, was centered north of West Yellowstone at the junction of US 191 and 287. The effects were felt throughout Yellowstone Park and much of Montana, and as far west as Seattle. The concrete Hungry Horse Dam, 250 miles away near Columbia Falls, showed measurable displacement. The water level in some Idaho wells fluctuated by as much as 10 feet. Part of the historic Old Faithful Inn's massive chimney fell into the dining room.

The quake caused enormous waves that sloshed like water in a tub and overtopped the dam at the north end of Hebgen Lake. Though damaged, the dam held. US 287 and a lakeside resort were submerged. The worst damage occurred downstream.

Below Hebgen Dam, the river lazed through a scenic canyon popular with campers. That night, the campgrounds were full of trailer and tent campers, and an overflow camping area was in use. No sooner had the sleeping campers been jolted awake by the quake than a 20-foot-high surge of water roared over the dam and tore through the canyon. At about the time the water reached the mouth of the canyon, seven miles downstream, half of a 7,600-foot-high mountain crashed into the valley with such force that soil-borne rocks cascaded up the opposite canyon wall. House-sized dolomite and quartzite boulders were hurled onto the lower end of Rock Creek Campground. The slide plugged the river, forming Quake Lake. Heavy machinery was later brought in from Butte's mines to cut a channel through the debris, a necessary measure to equalize the water in the two lakes and prevent slide debris from imperiling downstream communities.

Numerous adults and children, many injured, were trapped in the canyon. In the dark, with chaos all around, they scrambled to high ground. The rescue efforts were heroic. Eight persons were found dead below the slide. Two women later died of quake injuries. The bodies of 21 campers lie under the mountain that fell.

A monolith honoring the dead lying somewhere beneath stands on the slide. An impressive visitor center offering insight into the geology and human drama of the earthquake is also here. Interpretive signs along US 287 identify quake points of interest.

Adventures

▪ Adventures on Foot

Hiking & Backpacking

Yellowstone Country is one of the most splendid hiking and backpacking regions in a West renowned for hundreds of miles of mountain and forest trails. Day-hikes abound. Back country adventures await hikers of every level of conditioning and expertise. The trails described in this chapter represent but a sampling. Casual hikers will also find trail suggestions. Also refer to *Wildlife Watching*.

If you are a backpacker embarking on a multi-day adventure, you should contact the Custer or Gallatin National Forest Ranger District office overseeing the area in which you choose to hike for current trail/route information, and to obtain topographical maps. Contact the Livingston, Big Timber and Gardiner Ranger Districts of the Gallatin National Forest and the Beartooth Ranger District of the Custer National Forest for information on a myriad of other Yellowstone Country trails.

Topographical maps are available from the US Geological Survey and from US Forest Service offices and ranger districts. The charge is currently $4 per map.

Most ranger districts offer free handouts describing popular trails and including advice on back country hiking and camping.

Special Concerns

Altitude conditioning is important if you hail from a place under, say, 1,500 feet. Some people take high altitudes in stride with nary a dizzy spell. Altitude sickness strikes others with a vengeance, causing headaches, upset stomachs, and in rare cases collapse and death. The surest remedy is to move down to a lower altitude. The best preventative is to gradually accustom yourself to high altitudes. Plan on arriving a day or two before hitting that up-sloping trail. Rest, walk around a bit. Try to give yourself more time if you feel dizzy or headachey at, say, 7,000 feet and the hike will take you to upwards of 10,000 feet.

Mountain country is bear and mountain lion country. Be alert and follow the advice in *Co-Adventuring with Grizzlies* and *Encountering Mountain Lions*, under *Fauna* in this book's opening chapter.

Open fires are prohibited in the following Absaroka-Beartooth Wilderness areas: the Black Canyon drainage off the Lake Fork Trail and the Fossil Lake/Dewey Lake area of the upper end of the East Rosebud Trail. Leave No Trace fires are permitted elsewhere. Check on the current open fire status with the appropriate ranger district office before setting out.

The Forest Service recommends that backpackers carry a small camp stove with bottled fuel. This is not only to minimize fire danger, but because wood is scarce in high elevations.

Instead of making a fire ring of rocks, make a Leave No Trace fire pit. Dig a hole about 8" x 18" that's deep enough to cut through to mineral soil. Remove all twigs, etc., plus a block of sod. Keep the latter moist so that it can be replaced in viable condition. Dig to the desired depth. Tip: dig the length of the pit parallel to the wind direction.

Use only plain white toilet tissue – not scented paper or facial tissue. Bears are attracted to sanitary napkins. Pack them out with your other trash.

Don't gut fish in streams. The cold water environment permits very slow decomposition. Bury fish waste well away from water, away from your campsite and at least eight inches deep. In grizzly country, pack out fish guts with other pack-out garbage.

One more thing: have a great time!

Beartooth Ranger District of the Custer National Forest

Day-Hikes Off the Beartooth Scenic Byway

You can spend several idyllic days camping and hiking along US 212, the Beartooth Scenic Byway. Many of the following trails lead to the edge of the Absaroka-Beartooth Wilderness Area. These trails have the advantage of offering young children a wilderness experience without exposing them to the rigors of an extended hike over rugged terrain. Driving south from **Red Lodge** on US 212, watch for **Forest Service Road #71**. If you come to the Red Lodge Ranger Station you've gone too far. F.S. #71 is the road to Red Lodge Mountain Ski Area. It also goes to **Wild Bill Lake**. A barrier-free trail leads to the lake and continues part way around it. Two barrier-free decks over the water make it easy for wheelchair users to fish.

Just beyond the lake is the trailhead for the **Basin Creek Lakes Trail** (Trail #61), a National Recreation Trail. The trail is closed to horses except in the fall hunting season. It's about 2.5 miles to Lower Basin Creek

Hiking in Custer National Forest.

Lake and another 1.5 miles to Upper Basin Creek Lake. You can camp at either lake. The upper lake shimmers in a glacial cirque. The route follows an old logging road, then switchbacks up the tight Basin Creek Valley. The trail goes around the south side of the lower lake before climbing a ridge to the upper lake.

Watch for the **Lake Fork Road** (Road #346) sign on the right after leaving Red Lodge. If you reach the Beartooth Byway switchbacks you have gone too far. The **Lake Fork Trailhead** is 1.25 miles up this road. You can head either upstream or downstream along Lake Fork Creek. A half-mile upstream you'll come upon pretty **Lake Fork Lake**; 1.5 miles farther on is **Keyser Brown Lake**. Downstream, the trail parallels the creek for 1.25 miles to the **Lions Camp**.

Twelve miles south of Red Lodge, turn into the first campground area. Park at the **Parkside Picnic Area** and walk up **Hellroaring Road**. After some 100 yards, the road makes a sharp left turn. On the right, a trail parallels burbling **Rock Creek** for 2.5 miles to the Lake Fork Road.

 KID-FRIENDLY The **Parkside National Recreation Trail** also begins at the Parkside Picnic Area. The 2.2-mile trail heads north up the canyon to small, shallow **Greenough Lake**. Bring the kids' fishing poles.

A bit farther down the Beartooth Scenic Byway, watch for the **Rock Creek Road** to Glacier Lake. The trailhead is seven miles up this road. You'll need a high-clearance 4WD vehicle to negotiate the last few miles. From the trailhead, it's a two-mile uphill hike to lovely **Glacier Lake** in the shadow of 12,350-foot-high **Mount Rearguard**.

 AUTHOR TIP *Watch for a large, steep down-sloping meadow just across the Wyoming State Line on your right. You can hike down to charming **Twin Lakes**, out of sight in a pocket below the meadow. Once there, you can admire wildflowers while wandering through a wooded landscape.*

Backpacking in the Absaroka-Beartooth Wilderness

The 944,060-acre Absaroka-Beartooth Wilderness, the third most visited wilderness area in the United States, projects a beauty fit to stun chatty folks into worshipful silence. When viewed from on high, the mountains seem to fold one upon another, reaching into infinity. The Wilderness's over 950 lakes and nine major drainages spell heaven for anglers and wildlife watchers. Because much of the Beartooth and Absaroka uplift exceeds 10,000 feet, you'll likely pass over alpine tundra, a particularly fragile ecosystem. These extreme altitudes mean a short summer window of opportunity. Snow lingers into July and returns in September. August snows are not unusual. Motorized vehicles are not allowed in the Wilderness. Park at a trailhead outside the Wilderness and hike in.

The trails listed below represent some of the many backpacking possibilities in and around the Absaroka-Beartooth Wilderness Area. Contact the appropriate ranger station for topo maps and detailed information.

These trails are described more fully in *Hiking Montana* by Bill Schneider (see *Bibliography*).

The **Elbow Lake/Mount Cowen** hike (the trailhead is some 20 miles south of Livingston off US 89) is a rugged overnighter suitable for July through Sept. Contact the Livingston Ranger District of the Gallatin National Forest.

The **Lake Pinchot** hike is ideal for a week-long backpacking vacation from July through Sept. The trailhead is at the Box Canyon Guard Station, 49 miles south of Big Timber on Road #298. Numerous lakes offer splendid campsites. Contact the Big Timber Ranger District of the Gallatin National Forest.

The **Aero Lakes** hike, on the Beartooth Plateau, promises overnighters some good fishing in a region three miles northeast of Cooke City near the northeast entrance to Yellowstone Park. Weather window opportunity: late July through Aug. Contact the Gardiner Ranger District of the Gallatin National Forest.

The **Rock Island Lake** hike is an easy day-hike or overnighter to sprawling Rock Lake. The trailhead is on Road #306, 12 miles east of Cooke City off US 212. Go on this hike from July through Aug. Contact the Gardiner Ranger District of the Gallatin National Forest.

The **Spogen Lake Loop** is a moderate three- to four-day, late July through August, lake-tour hike on the Beartooth Plateau. The trailhead is on the Clay Butte turnoff from US 212, about 20 miles east of Cooke City. Contact the Gardiner Ranger District of the Gallatin National Forest.

The **Sundance Pass** hike is for experienced hikers. The trailhead is off the Beartooth Scenic Byway, 10 miles southwest of Red Lodge at the Lake Fork of Rock Creek. The trail tracks the northeast side of the Beartooth Range. Great fishing and wildlife viewing. Weather window: mid-July to Sept. Contact the Beartooth Ranger District of the Custer National Forest.

The **Tempest Mountain** hike is a take-off point for climbers who wish to scale Granite Peak, Montana's highest mountain (see *Rock Climbing*, page 176). The trailhead is next to the Mystic Lake Power Plant, 14 miles south of Absarokee off Montana 78 (take the right fork). The long steep backpack for experienced hikers has a tight weather window: mid-

August to mid-September. Contact the Beartooth Ranger District of the Custer National Forest.

AUTHOR TIP *Contact the Big Timber Ranger District of the Gallatin National Forest (☎ 406-932-5155) to request a printout describing numerous Absaroka-Beartooth Wilderness trails accessed from trailheads in the East and West Boulder River drainages. Contact the Livingston Ranger District of the Gallatin National Forest (☎ 406-222-1892) for further information on trails in the Absaroka Range. Some are accessed through private property. All involve extreme elevation changes.*

Hiking the Gallatins & Absarokas

The mountains south of Bozeman offer a somewhat "friendlier" appearance than do the rugged Beartooths. But don't be fooled. They include some wonderful and wild back country watered by sparkling streams. The opportunities for viewing bighorn sheep, elk and bear are virtually unparalleled. Spending a night or longer in one of the Forest Service cabins scattered throughout the Gallatin National Forest can enhance your hiking experience (see *Hotels, Motels & B&Bs*).

AUTHOR TIP *Contact the Livingston Ranger District of the Gallatin National Forest (☎ 406-222-1892) for detailed directions to trailheads serving the following trails. While some are comparatively short, they may be steep. Be familiar with your youngsters' abilities before setting their feet on one of these trails. US Geological Survey Topographical maps are available at the ranger district office and area sporting goods stores.*

The **Gallatin Divide**, Devil's Backbone, is a 27-mile mostly unmarked trail traversing the top of the Gallatin Range. It can be accessed from the top of most Gallatin Range trails. Much of this hike is rugged and rocky, but the beauty begs description.

The 12-mile **Big Creek Trail** (#180), reached from Big Creek Road, off the west side of US 89 about 30 miles south of Livingston, passes through meadows and talus slides under rock cliffs and is boggy near the top. The trail provides access to a network of trails. The six-mile **Bark Cabin Trail**, reached six miles up Trail #180 from Big Creek Road, follows a cascading stream through peaceful meadows. The three-mile **Windy Pass Trail**, accessed 10 miles up Trail #180, connects with the **Gallatin Divide Trail**.

The six-mile **Cliff Creek Trail**, one mile up Trail #180, also connects with the Gallatin Divide Trail. It follows a creek within steep canyon walls.

The six-mile lower elevation **Trail Creek Trail**, reached from the lower end of Trail Creek Road off US 89, leads to a Forest Service cabin before descending to Bear Canyon.

The five-mile **Pine Creek Trail**, accessed from the Pine Creek Campground east of the town of Pine Creek, is a steep scenic Absaroka Range trail ending at an alpine lake in a glacial basin.

The five-mile **South Fork Deep Creek Trail**, accessed via Deep Creek Road north of Pine Creek, follows a rushing creek. It's pretty and well graded, but meadows may be boggy.

Bozeman Area Hikes

The Bozeman Ranger District of the Gallatin National Forest maintains numerous trails offering spectacular scenery. Many are accessed from Gallatin Canyon. Others are close in and offer pleasant day hiking. Stop at the Bozeman Ranger District office to obtain maps and information regarding current trail conditions.

KID-FRIENDLY **Palisade Falls** is ideal if you have young children in tow. The half-mile paved path leads to a cascading waterfall in deep woods. Take South 19th Ave. to Hyalite Canyon Road. Cross the reservoir dam and follow the dirt road to the Palisade Falls parking lot. The **Mount Blackmore** hike is accessed from a trailhead at the north end of Hyalite Reservoir. The five-mile trail passes **Blackmore Lake** before climbing to 10,154-foot Mount Blackmore. The views of the Hyalites and Gallatins are outstanding.

History Rock Trail is also off Hyalite Canyon Road. The 1.2-mile trail climbs steeply. Take the History Rock turnoff on the west side of the road, a mile north of Hyalite Reservoir.

The 2.5-mile **Painted Hills Trail** is accessed via a parking area off Kagy Blvd. The trail crosses some roads and several small creeks.

Hiking the Bridger Range

The steeply peaked Bridger Range rises just north of Bozeman and slopes almost to the Big Belts in Charlie Russell Country. **Bridger Bowl Ski Area**, frequented by both skiers and eagles (see *Wildlife Watching*) is in the Bridgers. So is 9,965-foot-high **Sacajawea Peak** and a bevy of pretty mountain lakes. The Bridgers are in the Bozeman Ranger District of the Gallatin National Forest.

The 24-mile-long **Bridger National Recreation Trail** traverses the range's spine and is accessed via numerous trailheads on both sides. The trail begins at the "M" parking lot on Bridger Canyon Road and ends at Fairy Lake.

The **Sacajawea Peak Trail** leads to the tallest peak in the Bridger Range. Starting at the Fairy Lake Campground, the steep two-mile trail switchbacks to a mountain cirque. The view is a stunner and mountain goats gambol hereabouts.

The **Fairy Lake Campground** is reached via Forest Road #74, approximately 24 miles up Bridger Canyon Road (MT 86). Turn west on the gravel road and drive seven miles to the campground.

Hiking the Crazies

 The Crazy Mountains lie north of Livingston and Big Timber and are maintained by the Livingston and Big Timber Ranger Districts of the Gallatin National Forest. These mountains are often overlooked by hikers and backpackers enthralled by the sweeping, soaring beauty of the Absaroka-Beartooth Wilderness and the adjoining Gallatins. But the Crazies are every bit as interesting, offering hikes to alpine lakes, waterfalls, meadows, lush drainages and distant viewpoints. Two peaks, **Conical** at 10,737 feet and **Crazy** at 11,214 feet, command respect. Wildlife abounds. Native wolves (the ones not wearing radio collars) have been spotted in the Crazies. On the flip side, cattle graze in the foothills and on adjoining rangeland.

How the Crazies Got Their Name

There are several versions of the story of how the Crazies came by their odd name. One version maintains that a woman crossing the plains in an immigrant wagon train going insane and escaping from the party, to be later found wandering in these mountains. So they were dubbed the Crazy Woman Mountains, later shortened to Crazy.

The Crazies are favorites with local horseback riders and packers. Most trails are limited to hikers and horses. Except in the higher elevations, the hiking season is longer here than in the Absaroka-Beartooths and the Gallatins. You can pretty well count on good hiking and backpacking weather from late June through September; possibly longer, depending on local weather conditions. Hunters may be encountered in late fall.

Some trails have easy grades, but most are as challenging as any in the higher profile mountains to the south. Many trails are in fair to poor condition and are difficult to follow. Since roads are scarce in the Crazies, and those that do exist are marginal at best, trail access directions can be confusing. Contact the Livingston and/or Big Timber Ranger District offices for detailed trail access information and current trail conditions.

Livingston Ranger District Trails in the Crazies

The five-mile **Tresspass Creek Trail**, accessed via Cottonwood Creek Road and one mile of private road (no cars), offers an easy grade through scenic meadows and forest. "Easy" is relative: the altitude change is 1,800 feet.

The 10-mile **Rock Creek North Trail** has some steep grades and stream crossings, but the difficulty may be worth it to view waterfalls, pretty meadows and a lake.

The 2.5-mile **Smeller Lake Trail** is a steep back-country route encompassing a variety of features: a lovely stream, a lake, a basin and meadows.

The three-mile **Sunlight Trail** ascends a ridge before dropping into an alpine basin containing a lake. This trail is rocky near the pass.

Big Timber Ranger District Trails in the Crazies

Most Big Timber Ranger District trails are in fair to poor condition. The **Middle Fork Sweet Grass Trail** is in good condition and is rated moderate. The five-mile trail travels from the junction of Sweet Grass Creek Trail (#122) to the Middle Fork of the Sweet Grass Divide above Campfire Lake.

See *Wildlife Watching* (page 216) for other Yellowstone Country trails.

Guided Hiking & Backpacking Trips

Hassle-free guided hikes and backpacking trips are an option if you are new to backpacking, if you don't care to strike out on your own, or if you want someone else to attend to meal preparation and other details.

Selecting an Outfitter

As when considering a guest ranch or any other outdoor adventure, be sure to ask questions and more questions. At the top of the list should be the level of conditioning required for a given hike. Ask very specific questions if you plan on bringing your preteen tag-alongs. Some guides offer special family trips tailored to kids' abilities and interests. The trips described below include a range of choices.

Back Country Ltd. Guided Hiking & Adventure Trips, based in Missoula, offers a variety of inn-to-inn hiking and other adventure trips. Offerings include: *Exploring Big Sky Country*, a six-day hike beginning in the Gallatin Mountains and ending at Yellowstone Park. Each day takes you through some of Montana's most gorgeous country. *Beartooth Mountain Adventure Trip* is a six-day excursion that includes hiking, biking, horseback riding and river rafting around and through the

Beartooths. *The Best of the Big Sky* is a five-day hiking, biking, horseback riding and river rafting trip beginning at Bozeman and ending at Yellowstone Park. A five-day Yellowstone Park adventure trip is also on offer. The *Family Adventure Trip* is for families with children between six and 12 years. It includes hiking, biking, horseback riding, river rafting, pond fishing, a gondola ride and fun arts & crafts. PO Box 4029, Bozeman, MT 59772; ☎ 800-575-1540 or 406-586-3556. Fax 406-586-4288. E-mail vacation@bckcntry.com. Internet www.backcountrytours.com.

Country Walkers, based in Vermont, offers trips that are a shade on the soft side. From a base at the 320 Guest Ranch, participants strike out for six-day walks through the surrounding countryside, i.e., Yellowstone Park and the Gallatins. PO Box 180, Waterbury, VT 05676; ☎ 800-464-9255 or 802-244-5661. Internet www.Country Walkers.com. E-mail Ctrywalk@aol.com.

Madison River Outfitters offers guided hiking trips in the back country of Yellowstone Park. PO Box 398, West Yellowstone, MT 59758; ☎ 800-646-9644 or 406-646-9644.

Off the Beaten Path offers multi-day small group hiking/walking adventures. Their *Exploring the Beartooths and Yellowstone* trip winds over the wildflower-filled trails of the 11,000-foot Beartooth Plateau and explores Yellowstone's wildlife-rich northern range. 27 East Main St., Bozeman, MT 59715; ☎ 800-445-2995 or 406-586-1311. Fax 406-587-4147.

Paintbrush Adventures' Wanda Wilcox offers day hikes in the Stillwater Valley and Beartooth Mountains. RR1 Box 2830, Absarokee, MT 59001; ☎ 406-328-4158.

Sun Raven Guide Service's Katherine Howe, a licensed Montana and Yellowstone Park outfitter and guide, offers low-key alternatives to multi-day hiking and backpacking adventures with customized day and half-day hikes in the Yellowstone and Paradise Valley areas. Trips match hikers' ability level. 73 Chicory Road, Livingston, MT 59047; ☎ 406-333-4454.

Walking Stick Tours' David Gentholts offers full- and half-day hiking trips in the Big Sky area. Their day-long *Lone Peak Summit Climb* is probably not for kids, but the half-day *Andesite Mountain to Panorama Point Hike* surely is. Also on offer are a wildflower walk and a forest trek. Box 160451, Big Sky, MT 59716; ☎ 406-995-4265.

Special Interest Hikes

If you are searching for a gay and lesbian trip, **OutWest Adventures** may be for you. The International Gay Travel Association group offers two trips in Yellowstone Country. *Back Country Bliss* is a rugged seven-day backpacking trip in the Beartooth Mountains. *Montana Big Sky Adventure* offers seven days of hiking, biking and river rafting through Yellowstone Country's most fabulous scenery. They also offer *Outwestern Trails*, a ranch stay combining hiking, horseback riding and river rafting. PO Box 2050, Red Lodge, MT 59068; ☎ 800-743-0458 or 406-446-1533. Fax 406-446-1338. E-mail OutWestAdv@aol.com.

Hiking With Llamas

If you've never hiked with a llama, you are in for a delightful surprise. Not only will these docile, furry creatures pack your stuff on the trail, they will provide you with affectionate companionship. Llamas' softly padded feet have almost no impact on fragile terrain. The sure-footed animals are well adapted to high altitudes. And they are so friendly!

KID-FRIENDLY Susanne Hulsmeyer's **Free Spirit Llamas** will accompany you on naturalist-guided day trips. Great for families. 8950 Chapman Rd., Bozeman, MT 59718; ☎ 406-582-0224. Fax 406-582-0226. E-mail llamasusi@aol.com.

Richard and Louise Corbin's **Outback Llamas** offers guided llama day trips into the Tobacco Root Mountains backcountry. 2045 Trail Crest Dr., Bozeman, MT 59718; ☎ 406-587-7964. E-mail Outbacklam@aol.com. Internet www.outbackllamas.com.

Renee and Will Gavin's **Yellowstone Llamas** offers three- to six-day llama-supported trips through the northwest corner of Yellowstone National Park, the Crazy Mountains and the Tobacco Root Range in Gold West Country. The leisurely pace covers about five miles each day. Meals, with wine chilled in mountain streams, define gourmet. High dome tents and inflatable pads assure comfortable snoozing. The season runs from July 1 to mid-Sept. Box 5042, Bozeman, MT 59717; ☎ 406-586-6872. Fax 406-586-9612. E-mail llamas@mcn.net.

Llama trekking in Yellowstone Country, south of Big Sky.

Caving

Yellowstone Country is studded with caves. Several may be found along the Boulder River southwest of Big Timber, and in the Mill Creek area south of Livingston, both in the Absaroka Range. Caves in the Gallatins include some that are accessible from Bozeman.

If you are out for a hike and think it would be cool to check out a cave or two, forget it. For the most part, anyway. Most of these caves, save a few shallow "Indian caves," are not for casual spelunkers but should be explored by experienced cavers only. Some require the use of ropes and/or wetsuits. Many have never been fully explored. Experienced cavers will find plenty of adventure in this upthrust country.

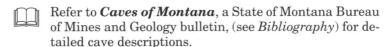 Refer to *Caves of Montana*, a State of Montana Bureau of Mines and Geology bulletin, (see *Bibliography*) for detailed cave descriptions.

The following Yellowstone Country caves can usually be explored by casual cavers.

Montana Hwy. 298 cruises along the Boulder River southwest of Big Timber, providing access to pretty Boulder Falls. Two caves in the vicinity are fun to explore: **Boulder River Cave** is on the side of a cliff south of the falls. A 10-by-20-foot opening accesses a passage leading back into the hill. **Boulder River Indian Cave** is on cliffs above the river. The one-room cave has a large opening not easily missed.

Chestnut Cave is about five miles east of Bozeman. Look for it on a limestone cliff south of I-90. Two small entrances lead to a 20-foot room and 325 feet of narrow passages. Look for cave popcorn and calcite crystals.

Rock Climbing

If you are a rock climber, you'll flip over Yellowstone Country. Several fairly accessible climbing areas within 30 miles of Bozeman have over 230 established climbing routes for experienced rock climbers using technical support equipment.

Bozeman Pass's Frog Rock, in Rocky Canyon off I-90, is well known to Montana climbers. Routes are equipped with lead protection bolts and chain rappel anchors. Drive six miles out of Bozeman on I-90 and watch for a pullout on the right, 2.3 miles past the Bear Canyon Road interchange. Walk across the railroad tracks (use caution!). Cross the creek on a two-log bridge and follow a path across the slope to an avalanche gully. Follow the gully to the base of the wall.

The first known technical ascents in the Bozeman area were scored about 25 miles south of the city in Gallatin Canyon. **Gallatin Tower** leads a confusion of rock formations with names such as Skyline, Buttress, Watchtower, Sparerib and Elevator Shaft. Most are accessible from US

191. Gallatin Tower is on the west side of the Gallatin River, facing off the bulky formations across the river.

 The Rock Climber's Guide to Montana, edited by Randall Green (see *Bibliography*), describes these and numerous other Yellowstone Country climbing routes in technical detail.

Local Climbing Equipment Shops

Northern Lights Trading Company, 1716 W. Babcock, Bozeman, MT 59715; ☎ 406-586-2225.

The Base Camp, 1730 Grand Ave., Billings, MT 59102; ☎ 406-248-4555.

The Great Outdoors, 25 N. Willson Ave., Bozeman, MT 59715; ☎ 406-585-7204.

Climbing Guide Services

Peak Adventures, PO Box 427, Big Sky, MT 59716. No phone.

Reach Your Peak, Attn: Ron Brunckhorst, 405 S. 19th, Apt. C, Bozeman, MT 59715; ☎ 406-587-1708.

Climbing Organization

Beartooth Mountaineering and Climbing Club, 931 Ginger, Billings, MT 59105. No phone.

Rock Hounding

Yellowstone Country offers some adventure for serious rock hounds and fossil freaks, but casual searchers for semi-precious and other pretty stones and minerals will be better served by traveling on to Gold West Country.

The **Gallatin Petrified Forest**, a few miles north of Yellowstone Park, has one of the West's most spectacular concentrations of petrifed wood. Here, fossil forests lie one atop the other. Over millennia, forests were buried by volcanic ash and steam-carried volcanic sediment. New forests emerged, only to be buried in like fashion. And so on. The result: a wild and weird landscape of well preserved petrified stumps and logs. You must climb rocky slopes to find collectible examples.

AUTHOR TIP

Don't even think about collecting a petrified wood sample unless you have a use permit. Request one by mail from the Gardiner Ranger District, Box 5, Gardiner, MT 59030. Cost: free. Limit: one small sample.

The Forest is 15 miles south of Emigrant via US 89, then seven miles west on the Tom Miner Basin Road. Park at the campground and start climbing. Be on the alert for grizzly bears.

Bozeman Pass, about 10 miles east of Bozeman on I-90, can provide happy rock hounding for calcite and laumontite crystals. Search in railroad and highway cuts east of the pass. Break the rocks to reveal crystals.

The **Three Forks area** is so rich in fossils and geologic features that university geology departments use it as an outdoor classroom. Rocks vary in age from Precambrian to recent.

The land is privately owned, so it's imperative to gain landowners' permission before setting foot thereon.

Digging into Cambrian limestone and shale exposures about four miles north of Manhattan along **Nixon Gulch** may produce some trilobytes of the genus Bathyuriscus. The shale layers must be split with a chisel.

■ Adventures on Horseback

Horseback riding opportunities abound in Yellowstone Country. Pack-supported horseback trips offer the best opportunities to explore the fabulous hidden fastnesses, the lakes and streams, of the Gallatins and the Absaroka-Beartooth Wilderness.

Assuming that few readers will be trailering personal steeds, this book skips over tips for self-guided horseback forays in favor of guided trips. If you do plan on bringing Old Dobbin along, contact the Gallatin and/or Custer National Forest Headquarters or the ranger district office maintaining the area in which you intend to ride. Request information on bringing a horse into Montana, a list of back country equine rules, and trails and campgrounds permitting horses.

Yellowstone Country riding choices include hourly and day rides, guided wilderness pack trips, wagon and sleigh rides and stays at guest or working cattle ranches focusing on riding. Because they emphasize riding, such ranches are described in this section. You can generally expect to rough it on pack trips. Book a week at a guest ranch if you prefer a softer riding vacation. Yellowstone Country has a few working cattle/guest ranches where the livin' falls somewhere between pack trip roughing it and dude ranch luxury. Most are out-and-out guest ranches.

Many of the guest ranches listed below are family-operated. Some have absentee owners. All the working cattle ranches are family-owned and -run. Some are sophisticated commercial enterprises. If you crave a warm fuzzy atmosphere and personal interaction, go with a family-owned ranch. While most guest ranches are satisfyingly remote, others are situated on major highways. If this is an issue for you, be sure to ask about the location.

One- and Two-Day Trail Rides

Montana offers so many adventures that you might prefer to be on the move, dabbling in a bit of everything. Riding a horse through meadows carpeted with wildflowers and along frisky mountain streams sounds idyllic, but you may not want to devote a week to it. The following guides will ride to your rescue, offering trail rides by the hour, day or overnight.

Bridger Outfitters offers two-hour to all-day family rides from the family ranch in the foothills of the Bridger Range. (See *Multi-Day & Wilderness Pack Trips*, page 181, for more information on this veteran outfitter.) David Warwood, 15100 Rocky Mountain Rd., Belgrade, MT 59714; ☎ 406-388-4463.

Broken Hart Ranch, at Gallatin Gateway off US 191, raises and trains most of their horses. You can sign on for an all-day ride in the Gallatin National Forest or an overnight pack trip in the Gallatins or the Lee Metcalf Wilderness. They also offer fishing trips via horseback and base camp pack trips. 73800 Gallatin Rd., Gallatin Gateway, MT 59730; ☎ 406-763-4279.

BW Outfitters' Bob Wetzel operates in the Gallatin National Forest. His trip choices include one-day horseback outings complete with steak fry, overnight fishing pack trips, a day-long fishing outing on horseback, and two-day pack trips with overnights at a rustic mountain cabin or back country camp. PO Box 471, Manhattan, MT 59741; ☎ 406-284-6562.

Brothers Jack and Martin Davis of **Flying Diamond Guide Service** are primarily hunting guides when they're not running the family ranch. They also offer hourly horseback riding and overnight pack trips in the summer months. Rte. 38, Box 2116, Livingston, MT 59047; ☎ 406-222-1748 or 222-7362.

Jake's Horses, run by Jake and Katie Grimm, offers one-hour to all-day trail rides, two-hour steak fry dinner rides, and two- or three-day tent camping wilderness pack trips. Also hay rides; wagons in summer, sleighs in winter. Pack horses are available for transporting float tubes and waders to the Gallatin River. The corrals are three miles south of Big Sky on US 191. Mailing address: 5645 Ramshorn, Gallatin Gateway, MT 59730; ☎ 800-995-4630 or 406-995-4630.

Paintbrush Adventures' Wanda Wilcox offers one-hour to full-day trail rides. Saddle and paddle trips are also available. RR 1 Box 2830, Absarokee, MT 59001; ☎ 406-328-4158.

Parade Rest Ranch, on US 287, nine miles north of West Yellowstone, offers one-hour to full-day rides; also Western dinner cookouts reached

Yellowstone Country

via horseback or a surrey ride. 7979 Grayling Creek Rd., West Yellowstone, MT 59758; ☎ 800-753-5934 or 406-646-7217.

Range Riders Ranch at Reed Point, 2.5 miles south of Exit 384 on I-90 (80 miles east of Bozeman), offers customized one- to six-hour trail rides and campouts. All-day rides include Cowboy Trail lunches. HC 57, Box 519, Reed Point, MT 59069; ☎ 406-932-6538 or 932-5107.

Slip & Slide Ranch & Outfitting Service mostly guides fishing trips, but also offers one-hour to full-day horseback rides. Franklin J. Rigler, PO Box 970, Gardiner, MT 59030; ☎ 406-848-7648.

Slow Elk Trails, west of Red Lodge near the Absaroka-Beartooth Wilderness, offers 1½-hour and full-day rides. They will also pack your gear to a drop camp. Also, overnight accommodations in a Sioux-style tipi or an authentic sheep wagon. PO Box 66, Roscoe, MT 59071; ☎ 406-446-4179 or 446-3926. Mobile: ☎ 406-860-0355.

Gary and Sam Duffy's **Wilderness Connection, Inc.** offers half- and full-day trail rides and overnight camping and fishing trips from their ranch at Gardiner. They also offer short pack trips of from two to four days. 21 Shooting Star Trail, Gardiner, MT 59030; ☎ 800-285-5482.

Multi-Day & Wilderness Pack Trips

The following guides and outfitters will take you on the ultimate Western adventure: a multi-day wilderness pack trip to high mountain lakes, frisky mountain freshets, forests abounding in wildlife. This is Montana at its best. In high altitudes the air is fresher than a newborn fawn. The sky is higher and wider than your imagination. Bring your camera, but no photo can do justice to the splendid scenery. Or to the mingled aromas of steaks sizzling over an open fire, horse sweat, and pungent pines. Pack trip prices hover in the neighborhood of $150 per night, but can cost more or less depending on services and accommodations.

Bear Paw Outfitters owners Tim and Cindy Bowers, both fourth-generation Montanans, offer multi-day horseback trips into the Absaroka Mountains and Yellowstone Park. They maintain a high country camp in the Gallatin National Forest, adjacent to the Absaroka Beartooth Wilderness. Elbow Creek Camp's tents and restroom facilities are as luxurious as a tent camp can get. Guests can choose between fishing, sightseeing, photography and rock hounding trips. 136 Deep Creek Rd., Livingston, MT 59047; ☎ 406-222-6642.

Beartooth Plateau Outfitters' Ronnie Wright primarily guides Orvis Endorsed fishing trips. Wright also offers weekly and customized pack trips in the Absaroka-Beartooth Wilderness and Yellowstone Park back country for folks who want a little ridin', fishin', relaxin', sightseein' and photo shootin'. PO Box 1127, Cooke City, MT 59020; ☎ 800-253-8545 or 406-838-2328 (June-Sept.) or 406-445-2293 (Oct.-May).

Black Otter Guide Service's Duane Neal is licensed by the State of Montana and a member of the Montana Outfitters & Guides association and the North American Outfitters Association. The Neal family has led wilderness pack trips since 1968. They offer several trips in the Absaroka-Beartooth Wilderness of from seven to 10 days duration. Nights are spent at tent camps on high mountain meadows. They promise great food and sightings of moose, mountain goats, deer, elk and maybe a bear or two. PO Box 68, Pray, MT 59065; ☎ 406-333-4362.

Bridger Outfitters' Dave Warwood has back country outfitting in his blood. His great-grandfather guided trips into Yellowstone Park at the turn of the century. While the Warwood family's emphasis is on hunting trips, they offer summer pack trips into the Bridger Mountains and the Lee Metcalf Wilderness. Most of their horses are Montana Travlers, a smooth-riding gaited breed developed for use in the mountains. 15100 Rocky Mtn. Road, Belgrade, MT 59714; ☎ 406-388-4463.

Madison River Outfitters offers pack trips in the Yellowstone area. PO Box 398, West Yellowstone, MT 59758; ☎ 800-646-9644 or 406-646-9644.

Medicine Lake Outfitters' Tom and Joan Heintz and Dan Hamman offer a wide choice of multi-day high country pack trips in the Lee Metcalf Wilderness, the Absaroka-Beartooth Wilderness, and Yellowstone Park. They define these as "progressive pack trips" utilizing routes through exceptionally scenic terrain. Each day's ride covers a distance of six to 18 miles, depending on the terrain. Alternate travel and layover days provide opportunities to fish, hike, go on a day ride or relax. PO Box 3663, Bozeman, MT 59772; ☎ 406-388-4938.

Paintbrush Adventures' Wanda Wilcox offers pack trips ranging from two to seven days. Rides to drop camps are also on offer. RR 1 Box 2830, Absarokee, MT 59001; ☎ 406-328-4158.

Western Treasures Discovery Vacations' Stan Hoggatt offers seven-day pack trips over the Nez Perce Trail through Yellowstone Park and the Absaroka-Beartooth Wilderness. 4533 Palisades Park Drive, Billings, MT 59106; ☎ 888-801-1212 (7946 at prompt) or 406-652-8955. Internet www.nezperce.com. E-mail stan@nezperce.com.

Wagon & Sleigh Rides/Wagon Trains

Wagon and sleigh rides are a blast, especially when a Western-style cookout is involved. Overnight wagon train trips are even more fun. **Absaroka Drafthorse Works** uses Percherons to pull wagons on hayrides, chuckwagon cookouts and three- and five-day wagon train adventures in the foothills of the Absarokas. Mark and Sharon Nardin, PO Box 134, Pray, MT 59065; ☎ 406-222-4645.

Beartooth Mountain Wagon & Sleigh Rides offers multi-day wagon train trips along the historic Meeteetsee Trail. You can ride on horseback

Yellowstone Country

or in a wagon. Don Coutts, PO Box 63, Red Lodge, MT 59068; ☎ 406-446-2179.

Guest Ranches

Yellowstone Country guest ranches include working cattle ranches, dude/guest ranches, and ranches with per-night pricing that straddle a fence between guest ranches and rustic lodgings. Resorts fall off into the lodgings corral and are listed under *Hotels, Motels & B&Bs*.

Most ranches observe Sundays as horse holidays. Largely for this reason, week-long ranch adventures generally begin Sunday afternoon and end on Saturday. Most small family-run ranches, particularly working cattle ranches, do not accept credit cards. Per-person prices for a week's stay begin at around $850 and can exceed $2,400. Children usually receive a discount. Working cattle ranch prices are generally lower. Ditto: family-owned and -run guest ranches. Dude ranches in trendy areas command higher prices.

Ranch listings are broken down into categories for your convenience.

Working Cattle/Guest Ranches

Yellowstone Country's working cattle/guest ranches tend to have roots sunk deep in Montana's homesteading and stock ranching history. Most are owned and operated by descendants of the original owners, occasioning a deep pride in the sweep of landscape that has been their home for generations. All take pride in home-cooked meals served family-style. Translation: hearty Western-style chow and plenty of it.

Diamond "S" Guest Ranch is a working cattle and horse ranch near Big Timber commanding views of the Crazy, Beartooth and Absaroka Mountain Ranges. Guests are invited to join the cowboys in ranch chores ranging from calving in spring, branding in May and roundups in May, June and Sept. Fly fishing on the ranch pond, hiking, cross-country skiing, wildlife watching and other activities are on offer. Accommodations are in log cabins, or in a restored 100-year-old homestead cabin. Country chow includes pancakes made from 107-year-old sourdough starter. PO Box 1244, Big Timber, MT 59011; ☎ 406-932-5760.

G Bar M Ranch, a 3,200-acre spread owned by the Leffingwell family, is in the Bridger Mountains near Livingston. The family runs 120 mother cows and a string of saddle horses accustomed to ranch work. The cattle operation dates back to 1900. Guests began signing on in 1934. Guests, limited to a lucky dozen or so at a time, are invited to ride along on ranch chores such as checking fences, doctoring calves and packing salt to cattle grazing the high country. Brackett Creek runs through the ranch and offers fishing and wildlife viewing. The G Bar M is probably as close to a week's worth of ranch life as you can get without owning your own spread. Accommodations are in the ranch house, a family size cabin or a smaller rustic cabin. Clyde Park, MT 59018; ☎ 406-686-4687.

Keenan Ranch is a 6,500-acre spread in the Paradise Valley, 18 miles north of Gardiner and Yellowstone Park. Log cabin bunkhouse stays are priced by the day, including meals and participation in whatever seasonal events are on tap at the time of your visit. Cows are driven to new summer range periodically throughout the summer; in mid-October a roundup and cattle drive brings them down to winter pasture. This conveniently located ranch is an option if you wish to sample cowboy life, yet don't care to commit to a full week. PO Box 1060, Emigrant, MT 59027; ☎ 406-848-7525.

Lazy E-L Ranch, owned by the Mackay family and established in 1901 by a New York City banker for family recreation, began raising beef cattle in the 1930s. Today, fourth-generation descendants Derek and Maureen Kampfe welcome one group of guests at a time to the 15,000-acre ranch. This is a feeding operation, meaning that young steers arrive at the ranch in May to feed on succulent mountain meadow grasses until September, when they are shipped out. The ranch is surrounded by heart-stoppingly beautiful country in the foothills of the Absarokas. Guests are invited to join in moving cattle and other ranch chores, but other activities also beckon. You can hike to wolf dens and dinosaur bones, watch birds and other wildlife, fish West Rosebud or Morris Creeks, roam wildflower meadows. Lodgings are in a cabin. Roscoe, MT 59071; ☎ 406-328-6830.

Lonesome Spur Ranch is beautifully situated in the Clarks Fork Valley between the Pryor and Beartooth Mountains. Owners Lonnie and Darlene Schwend are the fifth generation of a family whose Montana

Lonesome Spur Ranch, Bridger.

Yellowstone Country

roots hark back to 1888, when Gregor Schwend leased an emigrant car for the railroad journey from Missouri to a homestead near Deer Lodge. The present ranch was started as a cattle spread in 1906. The Schwends began welcoming guests in 1993. Pricing is on a per-night basis with all ranch activities included. You are invited to participate in ranch chores and a variety of fun activities. Basic riding and horse safety instruction are offered. Accommodations include cabins, tipis and rooms in the family home. RR 1, Box 1160, Bridger, MT 59014; ☎ 406-662-3460.

Sweetgrass Ranch, owned and operated by William and Shelly Carroccia, is nestled in a valley at the base of the Crazy Mountains. Horseback riding is the main activity at this working cattle ranch. With no TV and no social organization, this is for folks who really enjoy ranch life. Guests may take as active a part as they like in ranch chores, from feeding pigs to mending fences. Rides range to high alpine lakes and over meadows and foothills. Also dinner rides, creek swimming, fishing and hiking. Guests ride and care for "their" horses. The ranch, listed on the National Register of Historic Places, offers a range of accommodations that include rustic cabins without baths, family cabins with baths and rooms in the ranch house. Per-person, per-week rates include lodging, meals and horses. Melville Rt., Box 173, Big Timber, MT 59011; ☎ 406-537-4477.

Dude/Guest Ranches

The ranches listed below offer modern versions of the classic dude ranch vacations that put Montana on the Wild West map in the early decades of the 20th century. All offer horseback riding, comfortable accommodations and bounteous meals. Activities may include fishing, hiking, square dancing, kid stuff, wildlife watching and more. Some offer organized activities, some don't. Most provide home-cooked Western-style meals. But a few take pride in "gourmet cuisine." Ask for specifics when making your inquiries. All are on the American Plan, meaning that the weekly rates are all-inclusive.

Boulder River Ranch, owned by Jeane and Steve Aller, is on the feisty Boulder River, a blue ribbon trout stream. Located 28 miles south of Big Timber, the ranch is in the Gallatin National Forest and is bordered by the Absaroka Mountains. The Aller family has operated the Quarter Horse ranch since 1918. Log ranch buildings reflect this history. Horseback riding and trout fishing are the major activities. Accommodations are in rustic, yet comfortable, cabins. The casual ambience invites you to bring along those saddle-worn jeans. McLeod, MT 59052; ☎ 406-932-6406 or 932-6411.

Covered Wagon Ranch characterizes itself as "a mountain dude ranch in scenic Gallatin Canyon... for a comfortable vacation." That pretty much says it. This venerable ranch has been welcoming guests, no more than 24 at a time, since 1925. Horseback riding is augmented by hiking, fishing the Gallatin River and cookouts. Accommodations are one- and two-bedroom log cabins. Pricing is by the day or week. Non-riding guests save money by not being charged for horse and wrangler service. The ranch is also open from December to April to accommodate cross-country and downhill skiers and snowmobilers. Big Sky Ski Resort is just down the road. 34035 Gallatin Road, Gallatin Gateway, MT 59730; ☎ 406-995-4237.

 KID-FRIENDLY **DeadRock Guest Ranch** welcomes guests year-round. The ranch is situated in the Shields River Valley, between the Crazy and Bridger Mountains. Here, the raw ambience of a 19th century Western frontier town merges with 20th century luxury. The ranch buildings' facades are dead ringers for raw frontier town structures, but inside are comfortable accommodations and facilities. Summer activities stress, but don't mandate, horseback riding. Children as young as seven may go on trail rides; younger tykes are rein-led in a corral. Other activities include hiking, mountain biking, canoeing and float and wade fishing. Winter activities include snowmobiling, cross-country skiing and ice fishing. PO Box 343F, Clyde Park, MT 59018; ☎ 800-DEADROCK or 406-686-4428. Fax 406-686-4176. E-mail deadrock@sunrise.alpinet.netwww.patchnet.come/deadrock.

Hawley Mountain Guest Ranch is the last ranch at the end of a paved road bordering the Abasaroka-Beartooth Wilderness. Hiking, fly fishing, tubing the Boulder River and exploring Indian caves and pictographs augment horseback riding. Accommodations are in one of four lodge rooms or two family size cabins. July and August are the best times to visit this high mountain ranch. PO Box 4, McLeod, MT 59052; ☎ 406-932-5791.

Lazy K Bar Ranch, the Van Cleve family's 22,000-acre spread near Big Timber, was founded in 1880. Guests began coming in 1922. Though the ranch is a working cattle and horse ranch producing its own beef and milk, from guests' perspective it more closely resembles a typical guest ranch. There's actually a swimming pool – as rare in these parts as blisters on a rattlesnake. There's plenty of riding but organized activities are limited to Saturday night square dancing and a Sunday breakfast walk. Lodging is in log cabins accommodating one to eight guests. Box 550, Big Timber, MT 59011; ☎ 406-537-4404. Fax 537-4593.

 KID-FRIENDLY **Lone Mountain Ranch**, situated near Big Sky, is an all around guest ranch in summer, a cross-country ski resort in winter and a fly fishing lodge in all seasons. Accommodations include cabins with fireplaces and rooms in the ranch's Ridgetop Lodge. The Schaap family offers a wide range of activities, including kid stuff. PO Box 160069, Big Sky, MT

Yellowstone Country

59716; ☎ 800-514-4644 or 406-995-4644. Fax 406-995-4670. www.lonemountainranch.com. E-mail lmr@lonemountainranch.com.

Mountain Sky Guest Ranch is a high profile vacation paradise that's reeled in favorable comments from the likes of *Gourmet, Travel & Leisure* and *Fly Rod & Reel* magazines. Situated in the Gallatin Range, the full-service ranch offers horseback riding, fly fishing and a galaxy of other Western activities. Accommodations are in 27 cabins. PO Box 1128, Bozeman, MT 59715; ☎ 800-548-3392 or 406-587-1244.

Nine Quarter Circle Ranch has been owned and operated by the Kelsey family for upwards of a half-century. This ranch in the splendid high country overlooking Yellowstone Park comes about as close to the quintessential dude ranches of yore as you can get.

DID YOU KNOW? *The Kelseys breed, raise and train the ranch's horses, many of them Appaloosas. This breed, sporting distinctive spotted rumps, was originated well over 100 years ago by Chief Joseph of the Nez Perce.*

KID-FRIENDLY Summers are family times with plenty of riding and supervised kids' activities. Every parent will applaud the practice of seating kids and teens at separate tables for dinner. Organized activities. Indian summers are for trout fishing. Accommodations are in comfy log cabins. 5000 Taylor Fork Road, Gallatin Gateway, MT 59730; ☎ 406-995-4276 or 406-586-4972. Internet www.duderanch.org/9quarter/index.htm.

Parade Rest Ranch, nine miles north of West Yellowstone, offers home cooked meals and on-ranch fishing and horseback riding in high country forests. A good choice for families who wish to sample ranch life while visiting Yellowstone Park. 7979 Grayling Creek Rd., West Yellowstone, MT 59758; ☎ 800-753-5934 or 406-646-7217.

63 Ranch has been owned and operated by the Christensen/Cahill family since 1929, but the spread's history harks back to 1863. It was the first Montana dude ranch to be declared a National Historic Site. Sited at 5,600 feet below Elephanthead Mountain, the ranch straddles Mission Creek Canyon and laps the Gallatin National Forest. Riding is the activity du jour, but you can hike and fish, too. And there are wagon rides, square dancing and games. Your stay can also include a pack trip led by a licensed outfitter. The ranch welcomes cross-country skiers in January and February. Accommodations are rustic log or frame cabins nestled among aspens and pines. PO Box 979, Livingston, MT 59047; ☎ 406-222-0570. Winter only Fax 406-222-9446.

Guest Ranches Offering Per-Day Pricing

The following guest ranches bill guests by the night. Meals, riding and other activites are included in the price. Ranches like these are a good idea if time doesn't permit you to commit an entire week to a ranch stay, or if you aren't sure if a ranch vacation is for you. Some establishments ride a fine line between ranch and resort, charging extra for riding and other activities. See *Hotels, Motels & B&Bs* (page 227) for these fence straddlers. Meals may or may not be included in the per-night price.

Firehole Ranch, on the Madison River at the west entrance to Yellowstone Park, includes gourmet meals, horseback riding, boating, canoeing, mountain biking, and hiking in its per-night per-person charge. Guided fly fishing is extra. A minumum four night stay beginning or ending on a Saturday is requested. Cabin accommodations. PO Box 686, West Yellowstone, MT 59758; ☎ 406-646-7294. Fax 406-646-4728. Business address: PO Box 360, Jackson Hole, WY 83001; ☎ 307-733-7669.

Sugarloaf Mountain Hideout, in the foothills of the Absarokas, includes ranch-style meals, guided trail rides, nature hikes, wildlife viewing and stream fishing in reasonably priced per-day packages. Sleep in the main lodge, a bunkhouse, a canvas wall tent or a tipi. Bring a sleeping bag if you choose a tent or tipi. Rt. 1, Box 2620, Absarokee, MT 59001; ☎ 406-328-4939. E-mail smo@mcn.net. Internet www.mcn.net/-smo.

■ Adventures on Wheels

OHV, ATV & Powered Mountain Biking

Wheels of all kinds are prohibited in the Absaroka-Beartooth and Lee Metcalf Wilderness Areas. That's a hard and fast rule.

Off-highway vehicle use in the Custer and Gallatin National Forests is confined to designated trails and US Forest Service roads. Trail use by ATVs is controversial. Some ranger districts are widening certain trails for ATV use, others are sharply restricting ATVs on their trails in order to prevent damage to fragile terrain. Forest Service roads generally lend themselves well to OHVs and ATVs. That's the upside. The downside: you must be a licensed driver and your OHV or ATV must be licensed and registered in Montana or in the state in which you live in order to legally travel on Forest Service roads. That shuts kids out.

If you wish to ride your OHV, ATV, powered trail bike or non-powered mountain bike, contact the Beartooth Ranger District of the Custer National Forest in Red Lodge, or the Gallatin National Forest Ranger District office maintaining the area in which you wish to ride or bike. A ranger will tell you where you can and cannot go and clue you in on approved road and trail practices.

Non-Powered Mountain Biking

Forest Service roads are great for mountain biking. The scenery is fabulous, the road surfaces are generally good except in wet weather when slippery conditions are possible, and the chances that you will encounter heavy vehicular traffic are virtually nil. Many secondary roads also offer superb cycling. MT 540, the **East Yellowstone River Road** beginning three miles south of Livingston and extending to Chico Hot Springs, comes to mind.

Cycling the famed **Beartooth Scenic Byway** is a thrilling challenge, but heavy traffic may offer an unwelcome challenge. As on many Yellowstone Country roads, intermediate and advanced cyclists can expect plenty of challenging hairpin curves and long, steep ascents and descents. Beginners should confine their cycling to the valleys. Mountain biking is permitted on some trails, but conditions can change in a lightning flash. Restrictions are also subject to change. Contact the local ranger station (see *Information Sources*) for current conditions, route suggestions and maps. Local sporting goods stores often provide maps and trail information.

The 19-mile **Meeteetse Trail**, in the Red Lodge vicinity, offers interesting cycling through dramatically changing terrain that includes river bottom, arid prairie, rolling foothills clothed with aspen and sagebrush flats. Ride one mile south of Red Lodge on US 212 and take the dirt road headed southeast. If you pass the ranger station, you've gone too far.

 Another idea: ride the Big Sky Ski & Summer Resort gondola or lifts and bonk down.

Some trails are multi-use, meaning that hikers, mountain bikers and horses share the route. See *Hiking* (page 165) for specifics on the following trails on which mountain bikes are permitted. In the Gallatins: **Gallatin Divide/Devil's Backbone**, **Big Creek**, **Trail Creek**. In the Crazies: **Smeller Lake**, **Trespass Creek**, **Rock Creek North**. Guided mountain biking trips through Yellowstone Country are less plentiful than you might expect. One reason may be that the terrain may leave most beginners huffing and puffing in the dust.

Guided Mountain Biking Trips

Adventure Cycling Association sponsors multi-day cycling trips through some of Montana's most enjoyable and challenging country. Trips change annually. The seven-day *Rivers, Parks and Peaks* trip, covering a wide swath linking Bozeman, West Yellowstone, Ennis and Whitehall, is a classic that bears repeating. Contact the organization for current trip schedules. Bikecentennial, PO Box 8308, Missoula, MT 59807; ☎ 800-755-2453 or 406-721-1776. Fax 406-721-8754. E-mail acatours@aol.com. Internet www.adv-cycling.org.

Adventure Skills Guide Service's Clark Alexis offers mountain bike tours of the Bozeman area, plus biking tours in the Big Sky area. Box 6007, Bozeman, MT 59771; ☎ 800-347-1478 or 406-587-2912.

Backcountry, Ltd. offers six-day inn-to-inn cycling trips through the northern edge of Yellowstone Park, over the Beartooth Scenic Byway, up the west summit of 10,947-foot-high Beartooth Pass, and over remote back roads. The descent from Beartooth Pass covers 5,000 feet in 19 miles. Levels: mostly intermediate and advanced. Energetic beginners may need to shuttle some sections. Backcountry, Ltd., PO Box 4029, Bozeman, MT 59772; ☎ 800-575-1540 or 406-586-3556. Fax 406-586-4288. E-mail vacation@bckcntry.com. www.backcountrytours.com.

Lewis & Clark Trail Adventures offers customized multi-day mountain biking trips. Box 9051, Missoula, MT 59807; ☎ 800-366-6246.

Bike Rentals

Adventures Big Sky rents mountain bikes by the day or half-day. PO Box 161029, Big Sky, MT 59716; ☎ 406-995-2324.

Chalet Sports, 101 W. Main, Bozeman, MT 59715; ☎ 406-587-4595.

Freeheel & Wheel, 40 Yellowstone Ave. (PO Box 634), West Yellowstone, MT 59758; ☎ 406-646-7744.

Gallatin Alpine Sports, Big Sky, MT 59716; ☎ 888-325-7463 or 406-995-2313.

Saddle Sore Cycles, 117 W. Callender St., Livingston, MT 59047; ☎ 406-222-2628.

Yellowstone Rental & Sports, 1630 Targhee Pass Hwy., West Yellowstone, MT 59758; ☎ 888-646-9377 or 406-646-9377. Fax 406-646-9288.

■ Adventures in the Air

Viewing the mountains of Yellowstone Country from the air offers a fresh new perspective on this gorgeous chunk of Montana. The following flying services offer this option.

Paradise Valley Flying Service, 17 miles south of Livingston on US 89 at Pray, offers flights over the Gallatin Range, Yellowstone Park, the Absaroka-Beartooth Mountains and a bird's eye view of Livingston. 3693 Hwy. 89 South, Pray, MT 59065; ☎ 406-333-4146.

Sunbird Aviation, Inc., an FAA approved flight and glider school, offers scenic flights over the Bridger Mountains, soaring flights and three-flight glider mini-courses. They also offer sailplane rentals and glider tows. Reservations required. Sunbird Aviation, Gallatin Field, Belgrade, MT 714; ☎ 800-700-5381 or 406-388-4152.

■ Adventures on Water

Rafting/Kayaking/Floating

The **Stillwater, Clarks Fork of the Yellowstone, Gallatin and Boulder Rivers** thunder out of the Absarokas and Yellowstone Park, kicking up juvenile tantrums. The **Madison River** flows northward from Yellowstone, spilling over Hebgen Dam into **Quake Lake** (see *Touring*, page 164) before getting serious. It wanders off into Gold West Country, flowing through that region until reentering Yellowstone Country south of Three Forks.

You can expect Class II and III rapids on these rivers, plus some Class IV and V whitewater during spring runoffs. See page 39 for rapids classifications. Self-floating is an option if you are familiar with river dynamics and have experience handling a raft. Permits are not necessary. Quiet stretches are ideal for leisurely family floats. Rafts are available for rent in Gardiner, Big Sky and some other riverside towns.

Northern Lights Trading Co., with outlets in Bozeman and Big Sky, claims to offer "complete outdoor rentals." 1716 W. Babcock, Bozeman, MT 59715 (☎ 406-586-2225) and Meadow Center, Big Sky (☎ 406-995-2220).

Panda Sports Rentals in Bozeman has kayaks and canoes for rent. 621 Bridger Dr., Bozeman, MT 59715; ☎ 406-587-6280.

The Stillwater River

The misleadingly named Stillwater River rises at Goose Creek, in the Beartooth Mountains southwest of Absarokee. Mountain freshets fill the streambed to a gnarly river with Class V and VI rapids above the Old Nye Access. These are unrunnable at peak runoff. At other times, only experienced kayakers should attempt the seven-mile romp. From Old Nye to Swinging Bridge, the river offers 31.4 miles of Class I to III rapids. In high spate, low bridges present hazards. By picking your waters and watching out for hazards, you can have a blast either kayaking or rafting this river. Below Swinging Bridge, the Stillwater fits its name, slowing to a sedate ramble for the last five miles before merging with the Yellowstone at Columbus. There are numerous access points and campgrounds along MT 78 and FS #420 paralleling the river.

The Yellowstone River

Only a few diversion dams break the Yellowstone's 678.2-mile run. Diversion dams aside, the Yellowstone is the longest free-flowing river in the lower 48. Flowing through Yellowstone Park, it rollicks through the Grand Canyon of the Yellowstone before leaving the park at Gardiner.

Don't expect great whitewater – just Class II and III rapids with a few fun kickers in Yankee Jim Canyon, between Gardiner and the Carbella Access. Experienced kayakers and rafters can handily negotiate this stretch.

From Carbella to Livingston, the Yellowstone jaunts gently through beautiful Paradise Valley. East of Livingston, it's a prairie river flowing through fields interspersed with steep breaks. These stretches offer enjoyable floating. There are numerous access points from highways paralleling the river from Gardiner to Columbus and beyond.

The Yellowstone River, Grand Canyon, in Yellowstone National Park.

The Gallatin River

The Gallatin is generally the feistiest of this riparian trio. It has more continuous whitewater and is more challenging, with some Class IV rapids and continuous Class II and III whitewater just below the Cascade Creek Bridge Access. The "rock garden" river rises in the high meadows of Yellowstone Park before frisking picturesquely through Gallatin Canyon. From there, it rambles along to Three Forks where it joins the Madison and Jefferson Rivers to form the Missouri. Experienced kayakers and rafters putting in at Big Sky can expect a 16-mile romp to take-out at Squaw Creek Bridge above the mouth of Gallatin Canyon. Below the canyon mouth, several diversion dams, logjams, fences and many channels frustrate floaters.

Guided whitewater rafting and scenic float trips are available on all three of the high-profile rivers described above.

The Boulder River

The Boulder River keeps a lower profile, but offers splashing good fun. Rising in the high country of the Absaroka-Beartooth Wilderness, this river could be the standard by which all scenic high country watercourses are measured. MT 298 parallels the river between Big Timber and the Wilderness boundary some miles above the fall. The river's "boulder garden" reputation discourages commercial river rafting companies from offering floats.

Recreationally, the Boulder comes in two sections. Above the falls, from Hells Canyon Campground to Falls Creek Campground, kayakers can enjoy a gnarly 12-mile run through Class IV-V whitewater.

Yellowstone Country

Below the falls, floaters can put in at the East Boulder Road Bridge or Boulder Forks Campground for a bouncy ride all the way to the Hwy. 10 bridge at Big Timber. Some of this stretch may appear to run deep and quiet, but only floaters with Intermediate or better skills need apply.

Several rafting companies offer half-day and full-day floats. Most include floods of whitewater hype in their brochures. If you are a beginner or some-time rafter, your expectations will likely be met. If you are an experienced river runner, the hype may seem a tad overblown. Go expecting a fun day on a scenic river and you won't be disappointed.

River Rafting/Floating Guides

The following companies offer rafting on Yellowstone Country rivers. Most trips are suitable for all but very young children; make inquiries regarding suggested ages. All-day trips include lunch; half-day trips may also include lunch. Inquire before stepping aboard. Some guides furnish wetsuits for early season floats. They may provide helmets. All furnish life jackets. Most guides are trained in first aid and CPR; ask to be sure. Some firms also offer combination rafting/horseback riding and/or hiking trips.

These companies have good track records, as far as can be determined. Montana requires only hunting and fishing outfitters to be licensed. Lobbying is afoot to persuade the Montana State Legislature to license rafting companies. As this book goes to press, the public does not have the assurance of hiring a licensed river rafting guide. Safeguards include a given firm's longevity on the river, its safety record, and the training required of its guides.

Absaroka Rafting Adventures offers half-day and full-day Yellowstone River floats originating at the Absaroka Lodge in Gardiner. PO Box 10, Gardiner, MT 59030; ☎ 800-755-7414 or 406-848-7414.

Absaroka River Adventures' head guide Matt Holtz has floated and fished the Stillwater for over 20 years. The company offers half-day and full-day trips on the Stillwater River. All are paddle raft trips, meaning that you are part of the action. Oar trips, where a guide does all the work, are available. Also offered are sit-on-top inflatable kayaks. Absaroka also runs full-day combination horseback/rafting trips. PO Box 328, Absarokee, MT 59001; ☎ 800-334-7238 or 406-328-4608. E-mail absriver@mcn.net. Internet www.mcn.net/-absriver.

Adventures Big Sky Raft Company has half- and full-day Gallatin River trips. The full-day trip includes both quiet floating and whitewater. Half-day trips offer a choice between quiet water floats or negotiating Class II and III rapids. PO Box 161029, Big Sky, MT 59716; ☎ 406-995-2324. Internet www.adventuresbigsky.com.

Adventure Whitewater is owned by Marek Rosin, a 17-year veteran whitewater guide. You have your choice of oar boats rowed by guides, paddle rafts paddled by you, or inflatable cat-yaks. Half-day and full-day Yellowstone River trips from Red Lodge. Also Paddle 'n Saddle trips. PO Box 636, Red Lodge, MT 59068; ☎ 800-897-3061 or 406-446-3061.

Beartooth Whitewater invites you to experience three rivers in a half-day: the Rosebud, Stillwater and Yellowstone. Quite a feat. Rafts ride the high volume section of the Yellowstone where a one-sided canyon creates big waves. They also lead full-day Yellowstone trips, combination rafting/riding trips, and multi-day river floats. PO Box 781, Red Lodge, MT 59068; ☎ 800-799-3142 or 406-446-3142.

Geyser Whitewater Expeditions runs scenic floats on the lower Gallatin River and whitewater trips on the upper stretch where the river pours into Gallatin Canyon. You can also ride downriver via sit-on-top inflatable kayaks. Raft/horse combination trips are also on offer. 4700 Gallatin Rd., Gallatin Gateway, MT 59730; ☎ 800-922-RAFT or 406-995-4989. East Coast: ☎ 800-914-9031. Fax 406-995-3249. Internet www.avicom.net/geyserexp.

Lewis & Clark Trail Adventures offers Yellowstone River floats, as well as multi-day wilderness river trips. Main Office: Box 9051, Missoula, MT 59807 (☎ 800-366-6246) or Box 14, Gardiner, MT 59030 (☎ 888-842-7292 or 406-848-7292).

Montana Riverworks owner Gary Padgham is primarily a licensed fishing guide, but he does offer rafting trips on the Yellowstone and other rivers. He also offers multi-day river sampler floating and fishing trips that do just that: sample several rivers. 520 N. Grand Ave., Bozeman, MT 59715; 888-744-FISH or 406-586-4826. E-mail riverwrx@aol.com.

Montana Whitewater, Inc. runs scenic and whitewater trips on the Gallatin and Yellowstone Rivers that can be half- or full-day. Also "beyond espresso" breakfast whitewater trips, "Montana Madness" dinner floats, and full-day Paddle and Saddle trips. They also have two- to five-day guide clinics teaching basic rescue techniques and the paddling and river reading skills required to safely navigate Class II and III rivers. PO Box 1552, Bozeman, MT 59771; ☎ 800-799-4465 or 406-763-4465. E-mail mww@whitewater.com. Internet www.whitewater.com/-garland/mww.html.

Wild West Whitewater Rafting's Shawn Perry and Mike Barlow offer two-hour Classic Whitewater and Spectacular Scenic trips on the Yellowstone. Gardiner, MT 59030; ☎ 800-862-0557 or 406-848-2252.

Yellowstone Raft Company offers half-day and full-day trips on the Yellowstone and Gallatin Rivers. Box 46, Gardiner, MT 59030; ☎ 406-848-7777 or 995-4613.

Yellowstone Country

Kayaking

Refer to *River Rafting/Kayaking/Floating* for river descriptions. If you hanker after short swift spurts of swirling whitewater and plentiful playtime pools, you'd best load your kayak on board when heading for Yellowstone Country. The rivers spilling out of the Park offer fun times for all levels of kayaking skills.

Sometime kayakers can head down quieter rivers in an inflatable kayak in a half-hour or less. You sit on top of these craft. When it flips, you fall out. That's half the fun.

Learning to handle a real kayak is another game altogether. The basic introduction includes mastering the Eskimo roll. In hard-sided river kayaks, you wear a wetsuit and a "skirt" that fastens to the kayak's deck and keeps your lower half dry. It also keeps water out and you in when the kayak rolls. Your basic introduction to kayaking will emphasize mastering the Eskimo roll.

AUTHOR TIP

Learning to handle a traditional kayak requires time and concentration and demands some skill, but even kids can do it. My daughter Amy learned basic kayaking skills at age 10, but many kids learn earlier. The Eskimo roll is best learned in placid water.

Kayaking Outfitters

The following river guides offer kayaking instruction. Some rent kayaks and wetsuits. Some offer guided kayaking trips.

Adventures Big Sky Raft Company has guided inflatable kayaking trips on the Gallatin River. PO Box 161029, Big Sky, MT 59716; ☎ 406-995-2324. Internet www.adventuresbigsky.com.

Montana Whitewater, Inc. operates a kayak and canoe school. A half-day of Eskimo roll lessons are followed by half-day to two-day paddling excursions. PO Box 1552, Bozeman, MT 59771; ☎ 800-799-4465 or 406-763-4465. E-mail mww@whitewater.com. Internet www.white-water.com/-garland/mww.html.

Yellowstone Raft Company gives kayaking instruction that includes two-hour roll practice, a half-day clinic, and a full-day combined clinic and river trip. Box 46, Gardiner, MT 59030; ☎ 406-848-7777 or 995-4613.

Canoeing

The quieter stretches of Yellowstone Country rivers are as irresistible to canoers as a trout hole is to anglers. Flowing between river banks lined with rocky cliffs, grazing lands and cottonwood stands, and often thick with cover for all manner of feathered and furred wildlife, these riparian stretches promise endless hours of pleasant canoeing. Wildlife are often more visible from the water than from land. Think about canoeing in the hours just after dawn, or in the evening, when deer, elk and other animals come down to drink. Waterfowl seem to regard canoes as fellow creatures, allowing you to glide close in for once-in-a-lifetime views of mama ducks trailing vees of babies, or of great blue herons executing one-foot balancing acts.

Gliding over gentle waters, it's no stretch to identify with the Indians, explorers and trappers who traveled these rivers in dugouts and canvas craft, forerunners of today's fiberglass canoes. A good bet is the **Yellowstone** below Livingston, lazing through valleys framed by distant mountains.

To canoe the confluence of the **Jefferson, Gallatin and Madison Rivers** is to shake hands with history, to see nature as Lewis and Clark saw it. Put in on the Madison, off MT 205, the access road to Headwaters State Park.

 The rivers have braided and rebraided here, where the land lies flat. Head your canoe into the current and sit back for an hour or so, until you reach a take-out well downstream in the park. This is a bird watcher's paradise. Avocets fly up in flocks, their wing action resembling tiny windmills. Pelicans pose, Canada geese honk, snipes run about onshore, ospreys sit on stick nests high in cottonwood trees.

 I met up with a laid-back guy named Tim Pattison reading a book on a riverbank while his dog, Lady, snoozed nearby. We struck up a conversation while Lady and my Licorice, played tag. I owned that the history surrounding the confluence had so impressed me that I'd half-expected a drum roll. He invited me to canoe through the confluence. I accepted with alacrity. Come to find out that Tim is so taken with the meeting of the rivers that he lives within hollaring distance. This, despite Montana's paucity of living wage jobs. Teaching country dancing puts food on the table while the rivers feed his soul. Not bad.

Long, Island and **Beartooth Lakes**, studding the Beartooth Scenic Byway, offer enjoyable mountain lakes canoeing. Most other high mountain lakes are accessible only by portaging long distances. Several reservoirs score Eastern Yellowstone Country, where the Beartooths and the Crazies make way for the prairie. **Big Lake**, some 38 miles west of Billings, offers great wildlife watching from your canoe. **Cooney Reservoir**, al-

Canoeing the "Wild and Scenic" Missouri River.

most in the shadow of the Beartooths, invites canoeing. Be warned that motorized boats are also permitted on this popular lake.

Canoe Rentals

Renting a canoe is an option if you didn't bring your personal craft. **Canoeing House Rental** will provide shuttle service to the Headwaters. US Hwy. 10, Three Forks, MT 59752; ☎ 406-285-3488.

Madison Arm Resort & Marina, on the south shore of Hebgen Lake, rents canoes and rowboats. PO Box 1410, West Yellowstone, MT 59758; ☎ 406-646-9328. Fax 406-646-4367.

Northern Lights Trading Co., with outlets in Bozeman and Big Sky, boasts that it offers "complete outdoor rentals." 1716 W. Babcock, Bozeman, MT 59715 (☎ 406-586-2225) and Meadow Center, Big Sky (☎ 406-995-2220).

Panda Sports Rentals in Bozeman has canoes and kayaks for rent. 621 Bridger Dr., Bozeman, MT 59715; ☎ 406-587-6280.

A Guided Canoe Trip

Russell Young, owner of **Montana River Expeditions**, specializes in guided ecologically responsible multi-day canoeing trips on some of Montana's most storied rivers. He invites children aged eight and over to join their parents on trips on the Yellowstone and Jefferson Rivers. Young also offers canoe trips on the Madison and Missouri Rivers. 26 Cedar Bluffs Road, Livingston, MT 59047; ☎ 800-500-4538 or 406-222-5837. Fax 406-222-4718.

Boating & Wind Surfing

Lakes large enough for power boating and wind surfing are rare in Yellowstone Country. Exceptions are **Cooney Reservoir**, off Montana 78, and **Quake** and **Hebgen Lakes**, just north of West Yellowstone.

Fishing

If you want to fish Montana, you should first obtain current copies of *Montana Fishing Regulations* and *Montana Fishing Guide*. You will find them in stores selling state fishing licenses. Or order them from Montana

Fish, Wildlife and Parks (see *Information Sources*, page 66). The publications include current fishing rules and regulations and water conditions, information on where to catch which species of fish, available facilities at fishing sites, catch and release regulations and more. A valid Montana fishing license is a must before venturing streamside.

Lake Fishing

Yellowstone Country's lakes may not be very large, but they're numerous. Most are aleap with rainbow and other species of trout. Warmwater fish are almost as scarce here as scales on a pig. However, **Three Forks Pond** has a population of largemouth bass. You can angle for walleye and yellow perch at **Dailey Lake**, off US 89 north of Miner. **Cooney Reservoir** will also test your walleye angling skills. Coldwater fish abound in Yellowstone Country's mountain lakes. The Beartooth Plateau alone has over 400 alpine lakes where rainbows swim fin to fin with cutthroat, brook and even rare golden trout. That's the upside. The downside is that these lakes are inaccessible to all save backpackers on multi-day hikes. Hiking is generally required to access alpine lakes in the Gallatins and the Crazies. All offer challenging angling for trout.

Lower elevation coldwater lakes accessible by car include **Hyalite Reservoir**, south of Bozeman on MT 345, **Emerald Lake** off MT 78, and **West Rosebud** and **Mystic Lakes** at the end of a Forest Service road on the eastern slopes of the Beartooths. To reach Mystic and Rosebud, take Road 419 off MT 78 and keep heading south after Fishtail. There are some primitive campsites near the lakes. Rainbows are as plentiful as violets in May in all these lakes. Emerald Lake is famous for mountain whitefish. Brown, cutthroat and brook trout, plus mountain whitefish, swim in West Rosebud Lake.

Fly Fishing

Fly fishing is the aristocrat of fresh water angling. The sport has long been associated with British lords flicking flies over cold Scottish streams. Given Montana's swift-flowing mountain rivers and streams, it was inevitable that this gentlemen's sport would become popular here. Few had an inkling of just how popular.

Fly fishing aficionados have cast lines here for decades, but the sport was properly low-key, even hush-hush. Montana fly fishing was mostly the province of well-heeled vacationing flycasters and local folk dipping their waders in jealously guarded secret streams. Enter Robert Redford and his film, *A River Runs Through It*. Suddenly, fly fishing was the "in" sport. Everyone wanted to cast flies over sun-splashed rivers, just like the guys in the movie.

Outfitters who had been introducing flatlanders to the elegant art of fly fishing for years were swamped with requests. The Montana Board of

Outfitters fielded a flood of fly fishing applicants. It seemed that everyone and their bird dog aspired to glean gold from neophyte flycasters. Some delivered as promised, some did not.

Veteran outfitters looked askance at these newcomers; not so much as a threat to their livelihoods as out of concern for their competency. There was soon such a glut of fly fishing outfitters that the Montana Board of Outfitters placed a moratorium on new licensees except by attrition. Then began a gradual weeding out process as less successful guides dropped by the steamside.

 The terms "guide" and "outfitter" are not interchangeable. Only outfitters are licensed. Guides work under the direct supervision of licensed outfitters.

Fly fishing remains incredibly popular. A veteran guide told me, with tongue held firmly in cheek, that the driftboats are so thick you can walk a mile on the Madison without getting your feet wet. Yellowstone Country has so many fly fishing outfitters – fly shops complete with guides, fly fishing lodges with fly shops and guides, plus combinations of the above – that making the right choice is as challenging as catching a record trout.

Then there's choosing the ideal river or stream. There's hardly a one in Yellowstone Country that doesn't pose an irresistible lure for fly fishers. Don't discount high mountain coldwater lakes. Yellowstone Country's best fly fishing waters are in fairly close proximity, meaning that if you plan on fishing without a guide you can target a central destination like Livingston, Bozeman or Gallatin Gateway. Stop in at a fly shop and scope the rivers and streams according to the scuttlebutt. Don't be afraid to ask for advice.

Time of year has much to do with preferred holes. Fly fishing knows no seasonal restrictions. And yes, you can fly fish Montana's storied streams in winter, after summer anglers have long since gone home. An old fly fishing saw says it all. Question: "When is the best time of year to fish?" Answer: "Whenever you are here."

An Interview with Howard Bethel

I met Howard Bethel, past president of Fishing Outfitters of Montana (FOAM) at his home above bucolic Trail Creek. A kindly man whose years lie lightly on his shoulders, Bethel has been outfitting in Montana for some 16 years. He ran mountaineering programs in the Adirondacks prior to coming to Montana. His intention was to guide Montana backpacking trips, but fly fishing soon took precedence. Until recently, Bethel's wife, Joan Coffin, also a guide and rod builder, took an active part in Hawkridge Outfitters & Rod Builders (see *Fly Fishing Outfitters,* below). Bethel champions fly fishing as a women's sport, feeling that women naturally understand the philosophy of fly fishing.

"It is a committment for some, just an experience for others. You get the people who just want to catch a big fish. I have a different philosophy." Bethel often starts neophytes in his sunroom, talking about fishing philosophy.

I asked Bethel's opinion on the impact of fly fishing's double whammy: whirling disease and runaway popularity. "Many outfitters feel that *A River Runs Through It* brought almost too many anglers into the state. Whirling disease may have driven people away, but I haven't seen fishing drop off because of it."

Bethel actively promotes the efforts of the Whirling Disease Foundation, headquartered in Bozeman, to research and eradicate the debilitating disease that kills rainbow and other trout species. He explained that Montana does no stream stocking of fish, thus preventing the possible spread of the disease. Hatchery fish go into high country lakes where they cannot reproduce. "Catch and Release is for the most part encouraged." He adds, "There's a pretty strong push in the state to bring back native fish."

Choosing a Fly Fishing Outfitter

It makes sense to hire a guide for at least your first day or two out unless you are experienced and are familiar with Montana's rivers, lakes, streams and Paradise Valley's spring creeks. Some outfitters have access to secret streams on private lands, giving their clients an edge over crowded sections of river. Still more specialize in certain rivers, or sections of rivers. Others customize trips according to clients' wishes.

The licensed outfitters listed below are a fair representation of Yellowstone Country fly fishing guides. A few outfitters I contacted requested that I not include them in this book, citing a loyal repeat clientele that brings them all the business they can handle. As the Madison River flows mostly through Gold West Country, outfitters who specialize in that blue ribbon river are listed in the Gold West Country chapter of this book. Some guides offer fly fishing in several travel regions.

Fly fishing outfitters are listed in the regional chapters of this book according to their specialty waters. The other rivers they fish are also listed. Admittedly, this can be confusing. Cross-reference fly fishing outfitters by also referring to chapters dealing with Custer, Gold West, Glacier and Charlie Russell Countries.

Choosing a fly fishing outfitter is similar to choosing other adventure experiences. Decide if you prefer an outfitter who personally guides trips, or

Yellowstone Country

one who hires a few carefully selected guides. Or would you rather work through a fly shop offering a wide range of products and trips? You may want to approach from the lodgings-first direction, choosing a fly fishing lodge that arranges guided trips.

Choosing an outfitter who is a member of Fishing Outfitters Association of Montana (FOAM) is a good start. First aid certification is no longer a licensing requirement. Ask if the outfitter under consideration keeps such certification current for himself and his guides. Also ask if he is bonded. Do not knowingly hire a rogue, or unlicensed, guide. If you do so unwittingly, report him to the Montana Board of Outfitters.

Ask questions, and more questions. Does the outfitter guide trips himself or does he employ guides? What rivers and/or streams does the outfitter fish? Does the guide offer instruction for beginners, or does he prefer to guide only experienced fly fishers? Will the trip include wade or bank fishing, driftboat or float fishing, or a combination? What is the guide's specialty? What gear do you need to bring and what is furnished? What is included in a day's fishing? Is instruction included in the cost? What does the outfitter charge and what is included in the price? Request referrals, then follow up on them.

There's much more to fly fishing than simply flicking a fly over a glistening stream. A virtual cult has grown up around the sport. Ergo: it can be a pricey pastime. A day's guided fly fishing outing, on a per-person basis, is in the $230 to $280 range with lots of variables. The per-person price is generally lower if you are two or more. Instruction may be extra: ask. Understanding what a day's fishing will set you back and what extras you may need to purchase can mean the difference between a can't-wait-to-go-back experience and an adventure in debit financing.

For your convenience, outfitters are listed in three categories: Fly Fishing Outfitters, Fly Shops and Fly Fishing Lodges.

Fly Fishing Outfitters

KID-FRIENDLY   Al Gadoury's **6X Outfitters** specializes in fishing spring creeks. He also takes clients to private lakes and offers McKenzie-style driftboat fishing on the Yellowstone and Missouri. He welcomes neophyte anglers and will accommodate both youngsters and older less active anglers. A year-round Montana resident, Gadoury started 6X Outfitters in 1979. PO Box 6045, Bozeman, MT 59715; ☎ 406-586-3806.

Big Timber Guides' Bob Bovee and Mike Lovely offer both wade and float fishing on the Yellowstone and Boulder Rivers. Also available are float fishing trips on the Big Horn, Madison and Missouri Rivers. Wilderness day fishing and extended wilderness fishing trips with pack horses are also available. The partners also offer charter boat trips on Holter,

Hauser, Canyon Ferry and Fort Peck Lakes/Reservoirs. PO Box 328, Big Timber, MT 59011; ☎ 406-932-4080.

Black Butte Outfitters' J.O. Hash is a fourth-generation Montanan born and raised in the shadow of the Beartooths. He offers multi-day pack-supported horseback fly fishing trips from a summer and fall base camp on the West Rosebud River. This kind of fishing trip makes sense if some members of your family prefer to hike, watch wildlife, ride horses and just enjoy the alpine scenery. Box 171, Red Lodge, MT 59068; ☎ 406-446-3097. Fax 406-446-2513.

Dave Handl, native Montanan and veteran fly fisher, offers float fishing on the Yellowstone River, spring creek wade fishing, mountain lake fishing and stream fishing in Yellowstone Park. Dave will also make arrangements for back country horse pack trips. 83 Loch Leven Rd., Livingston, MT 59047; ☎ 406-222-1404.

Fly Fishing Montana Co., owned and operated by Randell Ziegler, focuses on the Yellowstone and Gallatin Rivers and Paradise Valley spring creeks. They also guide on the Madison and in Yellowstone Park. Ziegler offers both half- and full-day walk/wade or float/drift boat trips. Walk/wade trips are suggested for beginners, who can expect to learn fly casting, aquatic insect entomology, fly selection and how to read water. 8491 Lupine Lane, Bozeman, MT 59715; ☎ 406-585-9066.

Grossenbacher Guides is a mom-and-pop guide service. Brian and Jenny Grossenbacher treat guests to insight on area history, geology and ecology on their fly fishing trips to Yellowstone Country's rivers, spring creeks and alpine lakes. The couple offer adventurous back country fishing/hiking trips. They also fish the Madison River over in Gold West Country. PO Box 6704, Bozeman, MT 59771; ☎ 406-582-1760. Fax 406-582-0589. E-mail grossenbacher@gomontana.com. Internet www.gomontana.com/Grossenbacher.html.

Hatch Finders' Dean Reiner specializes in flycasting the Yellowstone River and DePuy's and Armstrong's spring creeks. He also guides in Yellowstone Park. 120 South M St., Livingston, MT 59047; ☎ 406-222-0989.

Hawkridge Outfitters & Rodbuilders' Howard Bethel, past president of FOAM, has decades of experience as a master fly fisherman, award winning photographer and mountaineer. And he is a custom rod builder and instructor specializing in the repair and restoration of cane rods. He likes to work with beginning anglers, including women and young people. His customized trips include float tube fishing mountain lakes and fishing the Yellowstone, Gallatin and Madison Rivers. He also guides trips into Yellowstone Park. 8000 Trail Creek Road, Bozeman, MT 59715; ☎ 406-585-9608.

Headwaters Guide Service, owned and operated by Robin and Pat Cunningham, offers driftboat fishing on the Gallatin and Yellowstone

Rivers, as well as the Madison, Jefferson, Missouri, Bighorn and Big Hole. They also offer walk/wade trips on the Gallatin and spring creeks and in Yellowstone Park. Box 311, Gallatin Gateway, MT 59730; ☎ 800-827-2087 or 406-763-4761.

Macgregor Fogelsong Fly Fishing Outfitters specializes in Montana Sampler trips in which clients fish several rivers, lakes and streams over two to several days. Rivers include the Gallatin, Yellowstone, Madison, Jefferson and Beaverhead. They offer full- and half-day float trips and walk/wade trips. 6067 Moose Hollow Rd., Bozeman, MT 59715; ☎ 406-585-5545. E-mail flycast@imt.net. Internet www.imt.ney/-flycast/flycast.html.

Madison River Outfitters, owned by Dan Hull and Brad Richey, maintains a complete fly shop in West Yellowstone but specializes in guiding single- and multi-day fly fishing trips on the Madison, Gallatin and Yellowstone Rivers and Hebgen Lake. PO Box 398, West Yellowstone, MT 59758; ☎ 800-646-9644 or 406-646-9644.

Montana Maritime Adventures' John Kirby and Dan Todd have been fly fishing Montana waters seemingly forever. John has been guiding since 1971, with time out to earn a degree in fisheries and limnology (fresh water & bugs) from Colorado State University. Dan followed in his father's and grandfather's waders, fishing Western waters since the late 1940s. He spent summers learning the waters of Yellowstone Park while studying invertebrate paleontology at Princeton. Later, he owned an Orvis shop in the Paradise Valley. Dan and John do not employ guides; you get one or the other. They specialize in float, wade and tube fishing in the Yellowstone drainage. Contact John Kirby at Box 1181, Big Timber, MT 59011-1181; ☎ 406-932-4449. Fax 406-932-4442. Contact W.B. "Dan" Todd at Box 1447, Livingston, MT 59047-1447; ☎ 406-222-0398. Fax 406-222-8517.

Paul Tunkis Fly Fishing Guide Service is an owner-guided service. Paul takes out one or two anglers, bringing in others to help with larger parties. He offers customized trips on the Yellowstone, Madison, Big Horn, Beaverhead and Big Hole Rivers according to the hatches on each river. 128 S. "F" St., Livingston, MT 59047; ☎ 406-222-8480. E-mail mtfly fish@imt.net. Internet www.imt.net/mtflyfish/fbsky.htm.

River Quest Anglers outfitter Bob Swain and guides Cliff Gerrells and Ike Maynard specialize in customized float trips on the Yellowstone, Stillwater and Big Horn Rivers. They also offer walk-in wade trips. PO Box 385, Columbus, MT 59019; ☎ 800-356-2850 or ☎ 406-322-4838.

Rocky Fork Guide Service's Ernie Strum reports: "it is my great pleasure to take fishing trips tailored to the client's desires." He uses a 16-ft. McKenzie drift boat for float trips on the Yellowstone and rigid framed rafts on the Stillwater. Ernie is a FFF (Federation of Fly Fishers)-certified flycasting instructor. He has discontinued trips on the Big Hole because "it is getting more crowded every year." He also guides hiking/wading trips to small local trout streams and high country lakes. HC 50, Box 4849, Red Lodge, MT 59068; ☎ 406-446-2514.

Roy Senter also self-guides clients. He offers float trips on the Yellowstone near Livingston using McKenzie-style drift boats. He also guides trips to nearby private lakes. 726 North D St., Livingston, MT 59047; ☎ 406-222-3775 or 222-0904.

Slip & Slide Guide Service, Inc., owned and operated by Franklin Rigler, offers a variety of fishing adventures that include private lake fishing, back country fishing trips and guided float trips on the Yellowstone River. Rigler also offers a lodge rental. PO Box 970, Gardiner, MT 59030; ☎ 406-848-7648.

Running River Fly Guide outfitter Stuart Howard guides most of his clients, bringing in additional guides for large groups only. He offers walk/wade trips on the Gallatin River and McKenzie driftboat float trips on the Yellowstone, Gallatin, Madison and Jefferson Rivers. He also takes anglers to private ponds and spring creeks in the Paradise Valley and has a Yellowstone National Park guiding permit. 113 W. Villard, Bozeman, MT 59715; ☎ 406-586-1758.

Wild Trout Fly Fishing Outfitters & Guide Service guides are professional anglers and year-round Montana residents. They offer full- and half-day walk/wade trips on the Gallatin, full-day float trips on the Yellowstone above Springdale, full-day float tube trips on Hebgen and Quake Lakes and full-day alpine lake horsepack/float tube trips. They also run trips on the Upper Madison above Varney Bridge and full-day Yellowstone Park excursions. Beginners are welcome on selected trips. Casting instruction. PO Box 160003, Big Sky, MT 59716; ☎ 800-423-4742 or 406-995-4895. Fax 406-995-3678. Internet www.gomontana.com/Business/WildTrout/wildtrout1.html.

Fly Shops

Fly shops come in several guises. Small shops owned by fishing outfitters serve as an adjunct to the outfitting business and may be little more than a place to get acquainted, purchase fishing licenses and pick up some needed items. At the opposite end of the spectrum are Orvis-authorized shops that publish catalogs and offer complete fly fishing packages. Somewhere in between fall lower profile shops offering fishing necessities and flies, plus guided trips and instruction.

 Trips arranged through fly shops may be pricier than independent outfitter-guided trips.

Arrick's Fishing Flies fits comfortably into the last category. Instruction, equipment rentals, custom-tied flies and fly-tying supplies are offered by this small full-service shop. Fishing trips are arranged on rivers and lakes within easy driving distance of West Yellowstone. 125 Madison Ave., West Yellowstone, MT 59758; ☎ 406-646-7290.

Big Sky Flies & Guides, in Emigrant on the Yellowstone River, offers all of the above, plus made-in-Montana gift items and name brand clothing. Owners Pam and Garry McCutcheon will also arrange accommodations. PO Box 4, Emigrant, MT 59027; ☎ 406-333-4401.

Blue Ribbon Flies is a full-service fly and guide shop that publishes a combination newsletter and catalog. Getting on their mailing list will assure you of some vital local fishing information. Their guided fishing trips go as far afield as Argentina and Belize, but the best remain close to their West Yellowstone base. Box 1037, West Yellowstone, MT 59758; ☎ 406-646-7642.

Bud Lilly's Trout Shop, also in West Yellowstone, is a complete tackle and guide shop with a twist – a basement gallery featuring artwork and gifts. 39 Madison Ave., West Yellowstone, MT 59758; ☎ 800-854-9559 or 406-646-7801. Fax 406-646-9370.

Dan Bailey's Fly Shop, family-owned and -operated since 1938, bills itself as "the choice of serious fly fishers." They put out an enticing color catalog packed with fishing goodies. Fishing trips on offer include a sampler, designed to acquaint you with several waters near Livingston, and a Yellowstone Valley Ranch stay full of fishing and other Western outdoor activities. Fishing excursions in far-flung climes are also on offer. 222 South Main (PO Box 1019), Livingston, MT 59047; ☎ 800-356-4052 or 406-222-1673. Fax 406-222-8450. E-mail info@dan-bailey.com. Internet www.dan-bailey.com.

East Slope Anglers owners Brad Parsch and Wayne Rooney consider their full-service fly shop as incidental to the sport of fly fishing. Their Big Sky location is convenient to the rivers and private waters their guides will take you to. PO Box 160249, Big Sky, MT 59716; ☎ 888-359-3974 or 406-995-1369.

Gallatin Riverguides, also on the Gallatin River in Big Sky, is a full-service fly shop and guide service. They can provide a wide range of accommodations for clients. Hwy. 191 (Box 160212), Big Sky, MT 59716; ☎ 406-995-2290.

George Anderson's **Yellowstone Angler** takes pride in offering a fly selection that includes over 1,200 patterns and sizes in a full-service tackle shop. Anderson offers a fly fishing school in addition to guide services on Yellowstone Country rivers, plus the Madison, Bighorn and Missouri. Hwy. 89 South (PO Box 660), Livingston, MT 59047; ☎ 406-222-7130. Fax 406-222-7153.

Greater Yellowstone Fly fishers' small Cooke City shop offers a wealth of information on area rivers. Owner Chad Olsen also guides back country fishing trips, belly boat trips and float trips on the Yellowstone, Madison and Missouri Rivers. Summer: PO Box 1150, Cooke City, MT 59020; ☎ 406-838-2468. Year-round: 8471 Lupine Lane, Bozeman, MT 59715-9584; ☎ 406-586-2489. Internet www.flyshop.com.

Jacklin's Fly Shop owner Bob Jacklin has fished the West Yellowstone area for over 30 years. Jacklin's guide service includes walk/wade and river float trips. The shop offers individual and group instruction in the finer points of fly fishing. 105 West Yellowstone Ave. (PO Box 310), West Yellowstone, MT 59758; ☎ 406-646-7336.

Montana's Master Angler Fly Shop, an authorized Orvis dealer, makes available some excellent get-acquainted information sheets on the Yellowstone, Gallatin and other great fly fishing streams. Hatch charts are included – helpful when making fishing trip decisions from the comfort of your home. They also offer guided trips to most of Montana's major rivers. 107 S. Main St. (PO Box 1320), Livingston, MT 59047; ☎ 800-543-4665 or 406-222-2273. Fax 406-222-9433.

Montana Troutfitters, an Orvis dealer established in 1978, is Bozeman's oldest fly shop. Dave Kumlien has been directing Troutfitters' four-day fly fishing school for 20 years. He also offers individual instruction and fishing trips on a few exclusive private waters. Full-day walk and wade trips are offered on numerous high profile rivers. 1716 West Main, Bozeman, MT 59715; 800 646 7847 or 406-587-4707. Fax 406-586-0724. E-mail mttrout@troutfitters.com. Internet www.troutfitters.com.

Park's Fly Shop, founded in 1953 by Merton Park, has been managed for the past 20 years by son Richard, co-author of *Tying and Fishing the West's Best Dry Flies*. Fly fishing schools are offered for novice and experienced fly fishers. Park guides many of the trips, bringing in independent guides when his schedule fills up. Yellowstone Park waters are his specialty. Box 196, Gardiner, MT 59030; ☎ 406-848-7314.

RJ Cain & Co. Outfitters offers day-long walk/wade and float trips that include Yellowstone Country rivers, plus the Upper Missouri. They also offer four-day combo trips and back country fly fishing. 23 East Main, Bozeman, MT 59715; ☎ 406-587-9111.

The River's Edge Outfitters' log fly shop in Bozeman provides an introduction to a company offering one-day "For Ladies Only" fly fishing instruction taught by women. The full-service fly shop offers a variety of other instructional workshops and clinics, as well as walk/wade and float trips. 2012 N. 7th Ave., Bozeman, MT 59715; ☎ 406-586-5373. Fax 406-586-5393. E-mail rvrsege@mcn.net.

Fly Fishing Lodges

A few lodges, guest ranches and bed & breakfast inns cater exclusively (or almost exclusively) to fly fishers.

Firehole Ranch, picturesquely situated between Yellowstone Park's west entrance and Hebgen Lake, has a full Orvis tackle shop and makes every effort to accommodate fly fishers with guided trips, comfortable rustic log cabins and scrumptious food. PO Box 686, West Yellowstone, MT 59758; ☎ 406-646-7294. Fax 406-646-4728. Business address: PO Box 360, Jackson Hole, WY 83001; ☎ 307-733-7669.

High Country Outfitters Fly Fishing Lodge, owned and operated by Francine and Chip Rizzotto, also goes by the name of Rizzotto Ranch. By whatever name, the Rizzottos offer single-party exclusivity. Chip fishes with guests while Francine cooks up fabulous food. Fly fishing lessons and wilderness pack-in fly fishing adventures are also on offer. The ranch is charmingly situated in the Paradise Valley. 158 Bridger Hollow Rd., Pray, MT 59065; ☎ 800-678-9098 code 76 or 406-333-4763. E-mail rizzotto@mcn.net.

The Blue Winged Olive is an angler's bed & breakfast convenient to Livingston eateries and shops. Four rooms with private baths can accommodate as many as nine or 10 anglers. Full ranch breakfasts are served buffet-style. Box lunches at an additional charge. 5157 US 89 (PO Box 1551), Livingston, MT 59047; ☎ 406-222-8646.

Troutwest, owned and operated by T.J. and Jean Laviolette, is a guide service that also offers lodging on the banks of the Yellowstone River. 102 Deep Creek Rd., Livingston, MT 59047; ☎ 406-222-8233.

Yellowstone Valley Ranch, 14 miles south of Livingston in the Paradise Valley, offers anglers six-day all-inclusive Montana Sampler packages fishing a variety of Yellowstone Country rivers and streams. Contact Destinations, 422 S. Main St., Livingston, MT 59047; ☎ 800-626-3526 or 406-585-3526.

■ Adventures on Snow

If you think Yellowstone Country is splendid in summer, just wait 'til winter! The contrast hits hard, like turning the pages of an outsize coffee table book. You admire a panoramic shot of the Beartooths, tumbled mountains gorgeously arrayed in greens and craggy grays. You turn the page and gasp. Here's the same view clothed in dazzling white, mountain peaks brushing a sky so blue it had to have been touched up. But it's for real.

If the scenery doesn't make you gasp, the snowcountry fun will. Yellowstone Country offers some of the finest downhill and cross-country skiing in the entire West. Snowmobiling, too. Here, the oldest and newest winter sports co-exist virtually side by side. Snowshoeing hangs tough while 'boarders shred the slopes.

Downhill Skiing/Snowboarding

Take your pick of Yellowstone Country's three downhill ski areas: Big Sky, Bridger Bowl, Red Lodge Mountain. The first two are easily accessible from Bozeman. Red Lodge Mountain is about an hour southwest of Billings via I-90 and US 212.

Whichever you choose, you'll find adequate, even memorable, lodgings and eateries either on-mountain or in nearby towns. You might even think you're in Switzerland. Winter transforms summer's log and frame villages into picturesque alpine hideaways.

Snowboarders, once pariahs, now ride the frozen wave at all Montana downhill skiing venues. Having alley-oopped into the Winter Olympic Games in 1998, shredders are riding the crest of a new found respect.

Big Sky Ski & Summer Resort, 43 miles south of Bozeman on US 91, is a full-service destination and conference resort and Montana's glitziest ski venue. Amenities include over 1,000 rooms and condo units on the mountain, over a dozen restaurants and nearly as many night spots, a plethora of pools, spas and shops, sleighride dinners, ski movies and the Lone Peak tram. You name it, Big Sky has it. This resort also has the greatest vertical drop (4,180 feet) of any in the nation. Base elevation: 6,970 feet. Top elevation: 11,150 feet. Longest run: six miles. Trail and slope ratings: 10% beginner, 47% intermediate, 43% expert. Average annual snowfall: 400 inches. The resort boasts 75 trails on two mountains and three high-speed quads. Season: mid-Nov. to mid-April. Open daily 9 am-4 pm.

KID-FRIENDLY As you might expect, downhill, advanced/extreme and boarding instructions are on offer, plus day ski camps for kids aged 6-14 and 4-5. Torchlight parades wind their way down mountain on Christmas Eve and New Year's Eve.

Ask about Ski Weeks and other packages. Expect to pay for all that glitz and glamour with pricier lift tickets than at smaller mountains. However, families with kids under 10 get price breaks. ☎ 406-995-5900 for ski conditions. PO Box 160001, Big Sky, MT 59716; ☎ 800-548-4486 or 406-995-5000. Fax 406-995-5001. E-mail bigskymail@ mcn.net. Internet www.bigskyresort.com.

Bridger Bowl, 16 miles north of Bozeman on Bridger Canyon Road, offers great skiing and numerous competitions throughout the winter. Call for particulars and dates. And ask about ski packages. Amenities include the Deer Park Chalet, two cafeterias, a full-service bar and grill and a central reservation service for lodgings in Bozeman. Instruction includes downhill, telemark and snowboard, plus kids' skiing and daycare for ages 18 months to six years. Lift tickets are under $30 with breaks for seniors and kids 12 and under. Free skiing for kids under five and folks age 72 and older. Over 60 runs with expansive bowls, powder glades and winding trails. One quad lift and five double chairs. Base elevation: 6,100 feet. Top elevation: 8,100 feet. Vertical drop: 2,000 feet. Longest run: 2.5 miles. Trail and slope ratings: 25% beginner, 35% intermediate, 40% advanced. Annual average snowfall: 350 inches. Season: Dec. 14-April 6. Open daily, 9 am-4 pm.

There are 500 additional vertical feet on Bridger's "ridge." The nearly 400 acres include steep narrow chutes with little or no room to turn. This is for adventurous, expert skiers and boarders only.

AUTHOR TIP *To characterize the climb to the ridge as strenuous is to radically understate. Only jocks in off-the-charts physical shape need apply. Avalanche transceiver, shovel and skiing partner are required.*

15795 Bridger Canyon Rd., Bozeman, MT 59715; ☎ 800-223-9609 or 406-586-1518. Snow phone: ☎ 406-586-2389.

Montana Powder Guides, headquartered down the road from Bridger Bowl, specializes in extreme adventure and powder snow gravity sports. Helicopters and snowcats are available for back country skiing and boarding excursions. Also, ski action photography service. 15792 Bridger Canyon Rd., Bozeman, MT 59715; ☎ 406-587-3095.

Joring

When cowboys and cowgirls want to kick snow they go Joring. The Norwegian term may seem out of place in the Wild West, but it's as good a term as any for a sport that brings skiers and cowpersons together in uproarious fun. Joring involves skiers being pulled by horses around a 250-yard circular track. Holding a rope and pulled by a rider on horseback, the skier must negotiate a minimum of 12 flagged gates and three jumps. Good time is about 14 seconds – more than 50 feet per second. The National Ski Joring Finals, held annually in Red Lodge in March, features some 75 teams in junior, women and open classifications. The carrot on the stick: some $6,000 in prize money. And a wild time for all!

Red Lodge Mountain, six miles into the Beartooths from Red Lodge (access Red Lodge from I-90 via US 212), combines traditional ski mountain challenges with Wild West insouciance.

Red Lodge Mountain's amenities include a central reservations service, two restaurants, two cafeterias and on-mountain ski shop. (Red Lodge town claims to have more eateries per capita than any other city in Montana, fit to satisfy the most gnawing hungries.) Instruction for kids and grownups includes downhill, snowboard, beginner, advanced and

KID-FRIENDLY specialty clinics. First Timers package includes lift ticket, rentals and a lesson. Kids programs: SKIwee for ages 3-6 and Teepee Creepers for ages 7-12. State licensed daycare center tends children, from six-month-old babies to toddlers up to four.

Red Lodge has 60 trails and groomed slopes, 30 acres of extreme chute skiing and 60 acres of gladed tree skiing. Chairs: two high-speed detachable quads, one triple and four doubles. Base elevation: 7,100 feet. Top elevation: 9,416 feet. Vertical drop: 2,350 feet. Longest run: 2.5 miles. Trail and slope ratings: 15% novice, 55% intermediate, 30% expert. Average annual snowfall: 250 inches. Red Lodge has the largest snow manufacturing system in the Rockies, making snow on 40% of the trails. Season: late Nov.-April 13. Open 9 am-4 pm daily.

Lift prices remain affordable despite recent trail and quad expansion. Ask about ski/lodging packages. PO Box 750, Red Lodge, MT 59068; ☎ 800-444-8977 or 406-446-2610. Fax 406-446-3604. Internet www.montana.net/rlmresort.

Cross-Country Skiing/Snowshoeing

If you are a cross-country skier or snowshoer, you'll flip over Yellowstone Country. Temptation to go afield may beckon, but it's best to stick to groomed and established trails in this steeply tip-tilted, avalanche-prone country. Miles upon miles of trails offer fabulous skiing and pristine snowshoeing, but be careful.

Avalanches

Some winters set up more avalanche danger than others. The best scenario is cold winters with steady snowfalls, resulting in stable snowpacks. The worst scenario occurs in relatively warm winters where snow falls on snowpacks that have melted in the daytime and frozen at night, creating unstable snow layers. Snowpacks break loose and plunge downhill, scooping up everything in their paths and burying whatever or whomever happens to be in the way. Spring's flirtatious weather often poses the worst avalanche danger. Avalanches can be triggered by any weight, be it skier, snowshoer, snowmobile, or even an animal passing over an unstable area. Yellowstone Country is prime avalanche territory. Established in 1990, the Gallatin National Forest Avalanche Center covers slopes from Cooke City to the Bridger Mountains to West Yellowstone. Advisories are issued every day except Tuesdays. Recorded avalanche advisories are available at ☎ 587-6981 in Bozeman, 646-7912 in West Yellowstone and 838-2341 in Cooke City.

Perhaps the best known Nordic ski trails lace Yellowstone Park. You can access them from both the North Entrance at Gardiner and from West Yellowstone. The latter offers advantages in gentle, rolling terrain heading into the Park.

The community of West Yellowstone maintains the 30 km **Rendezvous Trail Complex**. Snowmobiles are prohibited. The US Olympic Ski Team trains here every November. In late November, recreational skiers may attend ski clinics led by former Olympics coach Torbjorn Karlsen and other experts.

West Yellowstone ski races include the **Rendezvous Ski Race**, held in March. Contact the West Yellowstone Chamber of Commerce at ☎ 406-464-7701 for a current race schedule.

West Yellowstone skiers make merry at monthly SPAM Cup races offering cans of Spam to the winners. The "in" joke is that one can lasts all season.

Other Nordic Ski Trails

The seven km **Bear Creek Road Trail**, in the Gallatin National Forest five miles above Gardiner at Jardine, is an easy climb through timber along the Bear Creek Road.

The 10 km **Bozeman Creek Trail**, also in the Gallatin National Forest, is rated More Difficult. This trail five miles south of Bozeman is groomed intermittently.

The **Brackett Creek Cross-Country Ski Area**, in the Bridger Mountains north of Bozeman, includes trips (choose your distance) rated roughly 2 on a difficulty scale of 5. Expect to share the area with snowmobilers, tubers and sledders. This is a popular area, so the ungroomed terrain will be scored by well-worn tracks. Follow them up the Middle Fork of Brackett Creek, making loops down the South Fork. Avalanche danger may be present. The parking lot is on MT 86, three miles north of Bridger Bowl Ski Area.

The **Crowfoot Ridge Cross-Country Ski Area** is about 26 miles south of Big Sky Resort. The parking area is on the west side of US 191, just inside Yellowstone Park. You must cross the road to the ski area. The easy terrain gains about 800 feet to the ridge and covers 10 miles in all, going through the eerie 1988 burn area.

The catch: it's easy to get lost in this trailless area, and you must watch for hazards such as downed trees.

The place where you left your car serves as the staging point for the **Telemark Hills** area of open meadows in the Gallatin National Forest. The **Campanula-Springs-Fir Ridge Trail** is just to the south of Crowfoot.

Cross-Country Ski Resorts & Outfitters

Backcountry, Ltd. offers a five-day cross-country ski trip with overnights at Lone Mountain Ranch. Guided tours track trails in the Gallatins and Yellowstone. PO Box 4029, Bozeman, MT 59772; ☎ 800-575-1540 or 406-586-3556. Fax 406-586-4288. E-mail vacation@ bckcntry.com. Internet www.backcountrytours.com.

Bohart Ranch Cross-Country Ski Center, 16 miles north of Bozeman on MT 86, offers 25 km of groomed and tracked trails in Bridger Canyon. Trails on this nationally and internationally recognized ski terrain are groomed for both diagonal and skating techniques. A biathlon range is available for year-round training. Services include rentals, lessons, warming cabin. 16621 Bridger Canyon Rd., Bozeman, MT 59715; ☎ 406-586-9070.

Lone Mountain Ranch, a guest ranch in summer, offers cozy cabins with wood-burning fireplaces, ranch gourmet meals, 65 km of groomed and tracked trails, naturalist guided ski trips, a Nordic ski shop, ski instruction, sleighride dinners and a winter ambience that doesn't quit. One-week packages are all-inclusive. PO Box 160069, Big Sky, MT 59716; ☎ 800-514-4644 or 406-995-4644. Fax 406-995-4670. E-mail lmr@ gomontana.com. Internet www.gomontana.come/lmrhome.html.

Yellowstone Alpen Guides is worth knowing about if you wish to rent cross-country skis or snowshoes, or if you are interested in joining a naturalist-led ski tour into the back country of Yellowstone Park or the Gallatin National Forest. They also offer multi-day ski tours with overnights at Old Faithful Lodge and Stage Coach Inn. PO Box 518W, West Yellowstone, MT 59758; ☎ 800-858-3502 or 406-646-9591. Fax 406-646-9594. E-mail YstoneAlpenGuides@wyellowstone.com.

Snowmobiling

Snowmobiling is BIG in Montana. Not only does the sport offer rip-roaring chills and thrills, it gobbles up miles of winterbound mountainous terrain. Detractors are vocal in decrying the noise (disturbs wildlife), exhaust smells (pollutes the air) and impact (triggers avalanches) of the growly machines. Enthusiasts are vocal in extolling the merits of this sport that almost anyone, in any physical shape, can enjoy.

Yellowstone Country

Snowmobiling - Pro & Con

The two factions squared off a couple of years ago when a move was afoot to restrict snowmobile use on some Yellowstone National Park roads. The Fund For Animals and the Biodiversity Legal Foundation sued Yellowstone Park, claiming that trails groomed for snowmobiles enabled bison to migrate unnaturally through and out of the park. The plaintiffs also claimed that snowmobiles' impact on wildlife has never been formally studied. For a time, the brouhaha approached the flashpoint as West Yellowstone snowmobile businesses cried "foul!" The upshot: Some Yellowstone roads remain open to snowmobiles (as this book goes to press), and the National Park Service is preparing a three-year environmental impact statement.

Take Care

■ Snowmobiling is fun. It can be dangerous, too. It's imperative that you **be prepared** when snowmobiling in avalanche country (see page 45 for snowmobile rules and licensing regulations).

■ Wearing the **proper clothing** and packing sensible emergency supplies can make the difference between a great trip and pure misery, not to mention survival in the event of becoming lost. Clothing should be windproof and water repellent; a one-piece insulated suit is ideal. Wear lightweight layers underneath. The suit should be snug enough not to catch on the machine, but loose enough to allow for freedom of movement. Wear an approved helmet, boots, gaiters, gloves, a ski mask, and a scarf to fill the gap between mask and collar.

■ Carry a **beacon/transceiver**, food to last at least two days, matches and fire starter, a knife, a compass, a flashlight, your snowmobile registration card and first aid supplies.

■ **Don't snowmobile alone**. Before leaving, tell someone where you are going and when you plan to return. Then don't forget to give that person a jingle when you do get back.

Snowmobiling In & Around Yellowstone

If you wish to snowmobile in Yellowstone Park, you can choose between the **West Entrance** at West Yellowstone and the **North Entrance** at Gardiner. The former is favored because of easy access to Old Faithful and other geysers. The North Entrance offers access to Mammoth Hot

Springs and the historic lodge, open all year. Easy access by air and highway, plenty of snowmobile services and relaxed laws permitting snowmobiling in the streets make West Yellowstone a serious snowmobiling center. There are 600 miles of groomed trails, 200 in the Park and 400 outside.

If you hanker after total immersion in the wonderful world of winter, hop a snowcat at Mammoth Hot Springs for a scenic ride to **Cooke City/Silver Gate**, the Northeast Entrance to Yellowstone Park. In winter, Cooke City is isolated from the world except for the snow-packed road through Yellowstone (the road is open to traffic all winter). The **Beartooth Highway** (US 212) is strictly a fair weather route.

Cooke City buzzes with snowmobile activity. Described as "a friendly community of 80 people, dogs, moose and an occasional bison," the town enjoys the longest winter sports season in Montana and boasts a full complement of snowmobilers' services.

Yamaha and Arctic Cat promoters use Cooke City as a test site and promotional film location.

Cooke City area trails include the 12-mile **Daisy Pass/Lulu Pass** trail, five miles of marked/groomed trail on **US 212**, the nine-mile marked **Daisy Cutoff Loop** and several others that, when combined, offer longer trips. Contact the Gardiner Ranger District of the Gallatin National Forest for more details.

You can ride these and other area trails on your own or arrange a guided tour through the **Upper Yellowstone Snowmobile Club**, Box 1037, Cooke City, MT 59020; ☎ 406-838-2246.

Bison like to congregate in Yellowstone's Hayden Valley, but you may well encounter the burly critters elsewhere in the Park or on the northern and western fringes. These winter ranges include National Forest lands designated primarily for wildlife and secondarily for grazing domestic cattle.

Bison seem to take a ho-hum view of noisy snowmobiles. I came upon a group of them as our snowmobile tour emerged from a stand of trees onto the open road near Hayden Lake. We stopped. They looked at us. We looked at them. We waited while a mama bison leisurely nudged her calf off the road. We proceeded slowly, wary lest the animals get it in their heads to stampede. But they ignored us and we roared on.

Don't assume that your introduction to bison will prove as felicitous as mine did. The animals can be aggressive and assume speeds fit to make a locomotive proud. Keep your distance.

Bison vs. Cattle

If bison remained within Park boundaries where they are protected but not fed, most would enjoy longer lives and local ranchers and wildlife management officials could go back to feeding cattle and catching poachers. But it doesn't happen that way. Hard winters mean scarce forage, so hungry bison go in search of better pickings. These pickings are often on the aforementioned winter ranges. That riles the ranchers, who fear that bison might transmit brucellosis to their cattle.

Brucellosis is a nasty disease that causes cows to abort and afflicts humans with ungulate fever. Montana is a brucellosis-free state. Cattle are tested regularly so as to prevent outbreaks. A bovine testing positive gets a one-way ticket to a rendering plant. Some of the Park's 2,000-odd bison do have brucellosis. Whether or not it can be transmitted from bison to domestic cattle is a hotly debated topic. However, strayed bison, as many as 1,100 in the hard winter of 1997-98, are shot by Montana Fish & Game officers. An equal number may die of starvation inside the Park. Many people consider buffalo slaughters to be an outrage. Not the least of these are Plains Indian tribes who revere the buffalo as central to their culture and spiritual beliefs.

The US Park Service has come up with a "Preferred Alternative" plan. This includes the creation of special management areas (SMAs), hazing and shooting bison outside SMAS, recreational hunting of bison, vaccination, the acquisition of additional winter range and the creation of SMAs there.

At the heart of the controversy is whether the indigenous buffalo should be managed, or whether introduced non-indigenous factors which impact the buffalo herd should be managed. That means cattle. The Inter-Tribal Bison Cooperative has developed an alternative to the federal government's plan. This includes, but is not limited to, acquiring additional range land, adjusting cattle grazing allotments adjacent to the Park, and live removal of cow and calf pairs to private reserves. This plan is supported by the Greater Yellowstone Coalition and the National Wildlife Federation.

Other solutions might include feeding buffalo in the park and capturing and shipping strayed bison to Indian reservations and private buffalo ranches. There is no easy answer. The issue will no doubt wax hot and heavy for years to come. Stay tuned.

Other Yellowstone Country Snowmobiling Areas

Starting at Big Bear Creek south of Bozeman, the 120-mile Big Sky Snowmobile Trail extends all the way to West Yellowstone. Watch for snowmobile access signs on US 191. **Buck Creek Ridge**, off US 191 south of Big Sky, offers miles of great play area. North of Big Sky, you can access the **Brackett-Fairy Lake** and **Olsen Creek-Bangtail Ridge** trails. Contact the Gallatin Valley Snowmobile Association for tour information: 409 S. Grand, Bozeman, MT 59715; ☎ 406-586-3437.

Livingston, conveniently situated between the Absarokas and the Crazies, can be your jumping-off spot for over 84 miles of groomed trails. Contact the District Ranger in Livingston for detailed information. Guided tours can be arranged through **Big Sky Snowriders**, 318 S. 5th St., Livingston, MT 59047; ☎ 406-222-1863.

South of Big Timber, in the lovely Boulder River Valley, you can access the 25-mile **Boulder Canyon Trail** leading to the abandoned mining town of Independence. The seven-mile **East Boulder-Dry Fork Trail** offers extensive play areas. Contact the Big Timber Ranger District of the Gallatin National Forest for more detailed information.

Snowmobile Rentals, Tours & Services

Bozeman Polaris offers snowmobile rentals. 403 N. 7th, Bozeman, MT 59715; ☎ 800-327-4825 or 406-587-4671.

Canyon Adventures has guided snowmobile tours on trails radiating from the Gallatin and Paradise Valleys and through Yellowstone Park. Trailer trips are available for larger groups. PO Box 160326, Big Sky, MT 59716; ☎ 406-995-4450.

Cooke City Exxon & Polaris offers snowmobile and clothing rentals as well as park & ride service. Box 1128, Cooke City, MT 59020; ☎ 406-838-2244.

Hi Country Snowmobile Rental has new Arctic Cats with heated handlebars, rental clothing, trail maps and guides. Blaine and Vicki Heaps, PO Box 721 (US 20 and Hayden Ave.), West Yellowstone, MT 59758; ☎ 800-624-5291 or 406-646-7541. Fax 406-646-9647.

Rendezvous Snowmobile Rentals rents new Polaris snowmobiles and clothing packages. PO Box 580 (429 Yellowstone Ave.), West Yellowstone, MT 59758; ☎ 800-426-7669 or 406-646-9564. Fax 406-646-9353.

Soda Butte Lodge offers full snowmobile services including rentals, guided tours and snowmobile packages. PO Box 1119, Cooke City, MT 59020; ☎ 800-527-6462 or 406-838-2251. Fax 406-838-2253.

Team Bozeman Rentals offers several choices in snowmobile rentals, plus helmets, clothing and trailers. Special weekday rates. 2641 Jackrabbit Lane, Bozeman, MT 59715; ☎ 406-388-7529.

Yellowstone Country

Traveler's Snowmobile Rentals has guided tours, cargo sleds, snowmobile and clothing rentals. Box C, West Yellowstone, MT 59758; ☎ 800-548-9551 or 800-831-5741.

West Yellowstone Snowmobile Rentals, Inc. offers guided tours and snowmobile rentals. 215 Canyon St., West Yellowstone, MT 59758; ☎ 800-231-5991 or 406-646-7735.

Yellowstone Arctic-Yamaha offers guided tours, snowmobile and clothing rentals, full lodgings packages. 208 Electric St., West Yellowstone, MT 59758; ☎ 800-221-1151.

Yellowstone Tour and Travel offers full snowmobile vacation packages that include lodging, snowmobile use, guide service and more. They also offer snowmobile and ancillary equipment rentals, instruction and Yellowstone snowcoach tours. PO Box 410, West Yellowstone, MT 59758; ☎ 800-221-1151 or 406-646-9310.

Dogsledding

Dogsledding will never replace snowmobiling, but the sport made famous by the Alaska Iditarod is a natural for Montana. Now you, too, can mush.

Absaroka Dogsled Treks, based at Chico Hot Springs, uses Siberian Huskies to take you into the Absarokas on two-hour, half-day and full-day mushes. Mark and Sharon Nardin will also teach you to mush on your own. If you have ever wondered what running the Iditarod must be like, here's your chance to taste the high. Box 134, Pray, MT 59065; ☎ 800-468-9232 or 406-333-4933. Home phone: ☎ 406-222-4645.

Klondike Dreams Sled Dog Tours owners Dick and Lorraine Schacher were bitten by the sled dog bug when they lived in Alaska in the 1980s. With their three youngsters, the couple and 22 Alaskan Huskies then moved to the Lower 48, establishing Klondike Dreams in 1992. The family offers half-day, full-day and overnight dogsled tours in the West Yellowstone area. PO Box 77, West Yellowstone, MT 59758; ☎ 406-646-4004.

Northwind Dog Sled Adventures will teach you to drive your own team. 12260 Glacier Mountain Ln., Gallatin Gateway, MT 59730; ☎ 406-763-4838.

■ Wildlife Watching

 A chapter on wildlife watching may seem like overkill. You can hardly avoid seeing wildlife when you come to Montana. The most memorable sightings often occur when you least expect them. This is especially true of Yellowstone Country, where serendipity awaits around each bend in the trail; perhaps a doe and her fawn, a surprised moose, a vee of Canada geese overhead. The following wildlife areas are worth noting if you are a bird watcher, or if you enjoy seeking out wildlife as an end in itself.

Hailstone National Wildlife Refuge

This refuge, five miles northeast of Rapelje (take MT 306 north from Columbus), may fulfill that desire. The alkaline lake and open shortgrass prairie dominated by rocky outcroppings and punctuated by grassy hills is a mecca for waterfowl and shorebirds. A small hill overlooking the lake makes a fine viewpoint. Pronghorn sheep and sharp-tailed grouse are frequently seen in the upland areas. Black-tailed prairie dogs inhabit a town on the east side of the lake. The dogs are fair game for golden eagles, burrowing owls, hawks and the occasional peregrine falcon. With luck, you may see these predators at work. Motorized boats are prohibited on the lake. ☎ 406-538-8706.

Greycliff Prairie Dog Town

Montana's best-known concentration of these funny burrowing rodents. The barrier-free site is seven miles east of Big Timber via I-90 (take Exit 377). The prairie dog community is protected through the efforts of the Nature Conservancy and the Montana Departments of Transportation, Fish, Wildlife and Parks. Interpretive signs explain prairie dog behavior and ecology. Best time to see active dogs is from mid-March through Oct. ☎ 406-252-4654.

Missouri Headwaters State Park

This state park is another "tame" place to see wildlife, albeit in far greater variety and with more effort than the dog town. Walk the **Headwaters Trail** or canoe (see *Canoeing,* page 194) through the confluence if birds are your quarry. A special summertime thrill is watching Canada geese with downy goslings. White tailed deer and moose can sometimes be seen in the meadows. Signs of elusive river otter may also be visible. Watch for beavers and painted turtles. Interpretive displays identify wildlife. ☎ 406-994-4042.

Bridger Raptor Migration Route

If you admire raptors, you may wish to check out the Bridger Raptor Migration Route along the backbone of the Bridger Range. The Bridger Bowl Ski Area cooperates with Hawkwatch International and the Gallatin National Forest to maintain an observation platform and monitoring station high in the Bridgers. The two-hour up-mountain hike to the viewing platform is steep and strenuous, but you'll be well rewarded. Personnel are on hand to help identify migrating birds between Sept. 10 and Oct. 30. Bridger Bowl is 16 miles north of Bozeman via Hwy. 86 (Bridger Canyon Road). ☎ 406-587-9265 or 587-6920.

Yellowstone Country

Bozeman Fish Technology Center

Four miles up Bridger Canyon Road en route to Bridger Bowl, this is an excellent location for viewing a wide variety of land birds. It is open daily, 8 am-4 pm for self-guided tours.

Kirk Hill

If you are in Bozeman to visit the Museum of the Rockies, you might enjoy hiking Kirk Hill, a Montana State University-owned natural history area managed by the Museum. The area features a fairly extensive trail system. The main trail begins at a creek favored by songbirds; over 70 avian species have been identified in the area. More extensive trails traverse the foothills, home to black bear, elk and mule deer. Pets, horses and bicycles are prohibited. From Bozeman, head south on South 19th Avenue for about five miles. ☎ 406-994-5257.

Boulder River Falls

These falls call for a visit if you are a serious wildlife watcher. They are 25 miles southwest of Big Timber via Hwy. 298. The limestone canyon contrasts with fir- and pine-strewn foothills. Two trails, each a quarter-mile long, offer opportunities to spot migratory birds in summer. Golden eagles nest here and can be seen year-round. An interpretive sign explains the wintering habits of area elk. **Grouse Creek Trail** begins here, traversing a quaky aspen and Douglas fir forest frequented by black bear, mule deer, ruffled grouse and a galaxy of other avian life. You can reverse the seven-mile hike, starting at the West Boulder Campground. ☎ 406-932-5155.

The Northern Yellowstone Winter Range

The Northern Yellowstone Winter Range begins near Corwin Springs and extends into the Park near Mammoth Hot Springs. From US 89, you can take a snowpacked back road to Gardiner and thence to Mammoth Hot Springs via US 89. Or you can stay on US 89. Either way, you'll likely see part of the Northern Yellowstone elk herd, the world's largest, with some 20,000 individuals. Other hoofed animals, including proghorn antelope, mule deer and the occasional strayed bison also graze here in winter. Look for bald eagles along the Yellowstone River between Corwin Springs and Gardiner. ☎ 406-848-7375.

Yellowstone River Trout Hatchery

If you are an angler, you might wish to visit this place in Big Timber. The brood hatchery for Yellowstone cutthroat trout supplies production hatcheries with eggs taken from adult brood fish. As many as 2,500 fish may be seen swimming in three outside raceways in summer. This is where fish originate that are dropped via helicopter into high mountain lakes. The hatchery is open daily, 8 am-4:30 pm. The outdoor raceways are left open in summer for after-hours viewing. Follow McLeod Street north from the center of town for a half-mile. ☎ 406-932-4434.

Jimmy Joe Campground

If you like to watch butterflies flutter among wildflowers, hie to this campground, some nine miles south of Roscoe. Watch for a directional sign in Roscoe. Wildflowers bloom in profusion here, attracting numerous species of butterflies from May through July. An interpretive sign describes butterfly ecology and habits. The campground is also a good birding area. ☎ 406-446-2103.

State Parks

Yellowstone Country has four state parks, two day-use and two offering camping.

Madison Buffalo Jump State Park

A day-use park on a site where Blackfeet, Shoshone and Flathead tribes stampeded buffalo over a precipice to their deaths. This was an efficient method of harvesting buffalo for food, clothing and shelter before the acquisition of horses. Drive 23 miles west from Bozeman on I-90. Take the Logan exit (#283). The park is seven miles south on Buffalo Jump Road. ☎ 406-994-4042.

Greycliff Prairie Dog Town State Park

Another day-use park, showcases those comic little dogs in their natural habitat. Nine miles east of Big Timber on I-90 at the Greycliff Exit.

Cooney Lake State Park

A popular recreation area in the shadow of the Beartooth Mountains. The fishing is great and the boating is better. Amenities include a primitive campground, boat ramp and wheelchair accessible restrooms. Drive 22 miles southwest of Laurel via US 212, then five miles west of Boyd on a County Road 4074. Summer: ☎ 406-445-2326. Winter: ☎ 406-252-4654.

Missouri Headwaters State Park

This is one of Montana's most important and most beautiful historical parks. It was on this site that Lewis and Clark sensed that they had found the headwaters of the Missouri. The area served as a meeting ground and stopping place for numerous Indian tribes, as well as for fur trappers. The 560-acre park offers opportunities for floaters and canoers, for wildlife watchers and history buffs. Interpretive signs enhance walking trails. Watch for rattlesnakes in summer. Amenities include camp sites, an RV dump station, boat ramps and barrier-free access. Take

Yellowstone Country

Three Forks Exit #278 off I-90, drive east on Rt. 205, then three miles north on Rt. 286. Watch for signs. ☎ 406-994-4042.

■ Special Interest Adventures

Sometimes a different, more in-depth and personal adventure perspective is in order. The following companies provide just that.

Field Guides Birding Worldwide

This company runs trips to places renowned for bird sightings. In Montana, the company offers an eight-day June dude ranch stay featuring birding forays to a variety of central Montana avian habitats. The tour is guided by Terry McEneaney, staff ornithologist for Yellowstone Park, a veteran of over 28 years birding in the Greater Yellowstone area and author of *The Birder's Guide to Montana*. Field Guides, Inc., PO Box 160723, Austin, TX 78716-0723; ☎ 800-728-4953 or 512-327-4953. Fax 512-327-9231. E-mail fgileader@aol.com. Internet www.fieldguides.com.

Mountain Taxi Tours

These guides, Montana natives all, share an extensive knowledge of Yellowstone Park's history, geology, ecology and current events as they lead tours into the park from Big Sky, Bozeman, Livingston or West Yellowstone. They also offer Beartooth Highway tours. This is a good way to gain a quick overview of Yellowstone Park if your vacation time is filled with other adventures. Individuals and larger groups accommodated. PO Box 160003, Big Sky, MT 59716; ☎ 800-423-4742. Fax 406-423-3678. Location: 11 miles south of Big Sky at the 320 Guest Ranch.

Safari for Wildlife & Cultural History

Sponsored by Northern Rockies Natural History, this organization offers half- and full-day natural and cultural history safaris in a rectangle anchored by Three Forks, Bozeman, Livingston, the Gallatin and Yellowstone Rivers and Yellowstone Park. Host Ken Sinay will also arrange outdoor activity naturalist-led tours involving hiking, canoeing, horseback, Nordic skiing and snowshoeing. Sinay created NRNH in order to share his love of Montana's wildland heritage. As a wildlife biologist, he has held a number of positions in the fields of wildlife biology and resource management. PO Box 42, Bozeman, MT 59771; ☎ 406-586-1155.

Sierra Safaris

Sierra Safaris offers single- and multi-day naturalist-led safaris in Yellowstone Park via 4WD Suburban vehicles. Day-hikes and wilderness walks are tour highlights. Host Carl Swoboda, a professional photographer, offers clients tips on light and subject matter. PO Box 963, Livingston, MT 59047; ☎ 800-723-2747 or 406-222-8557.

▪ Kid Stuff

KID-FRIENDLY Yellowstone Country is one big playground for outdoor-oriented kids. Most of the activities you enjoy will also appeal to eight-to-teens tagalongs. Especially horseback riding. Kids take to horses like frogs to lily pads. Like other young teens, my daughter Amy sticks to a horse like Super Glue; has since she was a tyke. "Will we go riding?" is her first question when a trip is in the offing. One of the tragedies of her young life is our inability to house a horse on our forested coastal acreage.

If your tagalong is as horse-crazy as mine, check out this book's **horseback riding** opportunities. They range from hourly rides to guest ranches. Horsepack trips are an option if your youngster is mature enough for what may be a rigorous trip. Carefully check the itinerary and the host's suggestions regarding kids. Most set minimum ages. Most Yellowstone Country **float trips** are okay for kids; even whitewater trips. Know your child's adventure threshold. Rivers and lakes offer plenty of opportunities for splashing, but the water can be goosebump cold.

I discovered a fun diversion while in search of a campground when Amy was eight or nine: the **Big Timber KOA** just off I-90 (see page 238). "Let's stay there!" exclaimed Amy upon spotting the RV park's very visible waterslide. We did. She enjoyed.

Speaking of water, kids of all ages enjoy splashing in safe waters. Most Yellowstone Country rivers and lakes are shivery cold, but **Cooney Reservoir** (see page 195-96) and quiet river stretches in **Headwaters State Park** offer comparatively warm water. **Chico Hot Springs Resort**'s thermally heated pool is open to the public.

In recent years, the West has seen a surge of mini-zoos featuring indigenous wild animals. Red Lodge's **Beartooth Nature Center** (see *Touring*) has a petting zoo as well as opportunities to view wolves and other wild animals. Kids can also see wolves and grizzly bears at West Yellowstone's **Grizzly Discovery Center**. **Greycliff Prairie Dog Town** (page 219), while hardly a zoo, is a natural for kids. When in Bozeman, be sure to take your tagalongs to the **Museum of the Rockies** (see page 158). The hands-on dinosaur exhibits are exceptional; the moving and growling robotics make many kids' days. And don't forget the **Taylor Planetarium** at the museum.

▪ Just for Teens Trips

Bitterroot Montana Adventures' Alissa Farley offers two-week summer teen programs that include riding on a cattle drive, rock climbing, alpine hiking, Yellowstone backpacking, whatewater rafting, fly fishing, ranch adventures and more. PO Box 6282, Bozeman, MT 59771; ☎ 800-

585-7476 or 406-582-8882. E-mail: bma@sharplink.com. Internet www.sharplink.com/bma.

Black Otter Guide Service offers one-week pack trips designed exclusively for teenage boys and girls. Entitled *Teenagers Wilderness Ways*, the excursions are designed to teach kids wilderness camping and survival techniques. Participants learn to ride and pack a gentle horse, set up camp, catch fish and survive in the wilderness. Owner Duane Neal supervises the trip. PO Box 68, Pray, MT 59065; ☎ 406-333-4362.

Festivals & Special Events

Festivals can be quirky in Yellowstone Country and they're always fun. If it's sedate celebrations you're after, you'd better stay home. Come along and kick up your heels at some of these, but first contact the organizers for correct dates and locations.

Impromptu winter ski events are sometimes on offer at the region's three ski resorts. Inquire when making reservations.

Some theatrical and musical events are ongoing; others are one-timers. Contact local chambers of commerce for information on events that may occur in addition to those listed below.

Ongoing Events

Livingston's Firehouse 5 Playhouse presents old fashioned vaudville from May through September. Bill Koch, PO Box 1264, Livingston, MT 59047; ☎ 406-222-1420.

Montana Blues Chuckwagon Dinner Theatre in Gardiner serves up cowboy food and lore. Brian Meyer, PO Box 740, Gardiner, MT 59030; ☎ 406-848-9898. Fax 406-848-2119.

Playmill Theatre, a West Yellowstone family tradition, presents musicals, comedy and melodrama from May through early September. ☎ 406-646-7757.

Red Lodge's Vigilante Theatre Company spoofs the Wild West in summertime hilarity at the Round Barn Restaurant. ☎ 406-446-1197.

Shakespeare in the Parks is a professional theater company in residence at Montana State University in Bozeman. The non-profit touring company presents Shakespearean and other classical theatre in the parks and fields of communities throuogut Montana. Bozeman performances take place at a naturally protected amphitheatre on the MSU campus. Call or write Shakespeare in the Parks for tour information.

SUB Room 354, Montana State University, Bozeman, MT 59717-0400; ☎ 406-994-3901.

February

Montana Powder 8's Championship is held at Bridger Bowl in early February. Bridger Bowl Ski Area, ☎ 406-586-1518.

Wild West Shred O'Fest Snowboard Competition is an annual late February event held at Bridger Bowl's Avlalanche Gulch. ☎ 406-586-1518.

Northern Rocky Mountain Winter Games are held at Red Lodge in late February/early March. Events include cross-country skiing, showshoeing, snowboarding, hockey, figure skating, ski joring, dog sled races, disabled alpine skiing and Special Olympics events. James Graff, Montana Winter Sports Federation, PO Box 262, Billings, MT 59103; ☎ 406-252-8770. Fax 406-252-8869.

March

Winter Carnival continues the fun in the snow in early March with an uproarious parade Red Lodge-style, on-snow events, cardboard classic race, costume contest, fire hose race, obstacle race, kids' treasure hunt, torchlight parade and more. Red Lodge Chamber of Commerce; ☎ 406-446-1718.

The **Yellowstone Rendezvous Ski Race** attracts world-class Nordic racers to West Yellowstone in early March as part of the American Ski Chase. Drew Barney, PO Box 65, West Yellowstone, MT 59758; ☎ 406-646-9379.

World Snowmobile Expo is held in West Yellowstone in mid-March. SnoWest SnowCross Challenge, Radar Runs and Power Pulls. West Yellowstone Chamber of Commerce, ☎ 406-646-7701. Fax 406-646-9691.

National Finals Ski Joring (see *Adventures on Snow*, page 208) takes place in Red Lodge in mid-March. Plenty of high jinks for all. Red Lodge Chamber of Commerce, ☎ 406-446-1718.

Pinhead Classic has been a mid-March costumed telemark racing event at Bridger Bowl for almost two decades. ☎ 406-586-1518.

April

MSU Indian Club Powwow is held on the Montana State University campus in Bozeman in early April. Drumming, dancing, arts & crafts. MSU Indian Club, MSU, Bozeman, MT 59717-2340; ☎ 406-994-4880.

Livingston's Annual Railroad Swap Meet is held at Depot Center in late April. Diana Sieder, Depot Center, 200 W. Park St., Livingston, MT 59047; ☎ 406-222-2300.

Double Pole, Pad & Pedal races involve downhill, cross-country, running and cycle racing from Bridger Bowl to Bozeman. Early April. ☎ 406-587-2111. Fax 406-586-1518.

Yellowstone Country

June

June marks the beginning of Montana's rodeo season. Most rodeos follow traditional parameters; more or less.

The Pig Races

For really way out livestock excitement, head for **Bearcreek**, a one-saloon town (pop. 41) east of Red Lodge on MT 308. The action takes place every weekend night between Memorial Day and Labor Day. The racers: pigs. The incentive: food. Wagers bid two bucks. And it's legal. Sports pool pig racing is sanctioned by the Montana Legislature. How's that for political pork? Half the pool is paid to the winners and half goes into a scholarship fund. Bearcreek Saloon owners Pits and Lynn DeArmond allow the pigs to take the winter off, replacing them with racing gerbils and hamsters.

Gardiner Rodeo, featuring a rodeo, parade, music and dancing, takes place in mid-June. Gardiner Chamber of Commerce, ☎ 406-848-7971.

Big Timber Rodeo is held the last weekend in June. Monte or Buzz Finn, PO Box 1010, Big Timber, MT 59011; ☎ 406-932-6228 or 932-6697.

Annual Beartooth Run, held in late June, is over a 8.2-mile course on the Beartooth Highway. Runners start at 7,000 feet and wind up at 9,000 feet. A party at the Parkside Campground follows the race. Red Lodge Chamber of Commerce, ☎ 406-446-1718. Fax 406-446-2513.

July

Western Days celebrates July 4th in Livingston with a parade, a rodeo and all the fixin's. ☎ 406-222-0850. Fax 406-222-0852.

Home of Champions Rodeo & Parade celebrates July 4th in Red Lodge. The Professional Rodeo Cowboys Association circuit rodeo brings national champions to this acclaimed rodeo. Red Lodge Chamber of Commerce, ☎ 406-446-1718. Fax 406-446-2513.

Musicians Rendezvous takes place in Columbus over July 4th. The acoustical event features stage performances and impromptu jams. Food, arts & crafts, swap and sell musical instruments. Aron Strange, PO Box 489, Columbus, MT 59019; ☎ 406-322-4143.

Yellowstone Boat Float, held annually in mid-July, features floating from Big Timber to Laurel. The Yellowstone Boatfloat Assoc., 2136 Harmon Lane, Billings, MT 59105; ☎ 406-248-7182.

Gallatin County Fair, held in Bozeman in mid-July, offers old fashioned family fun. Sue Shockley, 901 N. Black, Bozeman, MT 59715; ☎ 406-582-3270. Fax 406-582-3273.

All Harley Rodeo brings motorcycles to Red Lodge in late July. Harley-Davidson owners participate in a 'poker run' over the Beartooth Pass and back to Red Lodge over Sunlight Basin. Red Lodge Chamber of Commerce, ☎ 406-446-1718.

Three Forks Rodeo Weekend, held in late July, features an NRA rodeo with all the excitement these rodeos engender. Parade and flea market on Main Street. Three Forks Chamber of Commerce, ☎ 406-285-4556.

Park County Fair, held in Livingston in late July, features tons of fun. Park County Fairgrounds, PO Box 146, Livingston, MT 59047; ☎ 406-222-4185.

Red Lodge Mountain Man Rendezvous, held in late July/early August, embodies all the color and excitement of these quintessential Western celebrations. The fur trapper era comes alive. Authentically costumed mountain men, cavalry, infantry, 'Indians,' traders, buffalo hunters, scouts, whiskey runners, mule skinners and horse traders mingle in colorful pageantry. Rustic camps include tipis, tents, Dutch oven cooking. Trade goods for sale include beads, jewelry and other typical fur-era items. Sherry Fears, PO Box 988, Red Lodge, MT 59068; ☎ 406-446-1718.

Taste of Bozeman serves up dinner on Main Street in company with 2,000 instant friends. Music and entertainment. Reservations necessary for seated dinner. Bite of Bozeman invites casual snacking. Laurie Shadoan, PO Box 159, Bozeman, MT 59715; ☎ 406-586-1314. Fax 406-586-2210.

Annual Sweet Grass County Cutting Competition, held in Big Timber in late July, features horses and riders working together to cut a cow from a herd. Mary Hathaway, PO Box 989, Big Timber, MT 59011; ☎ 406-932-4790.

August

Fiddlers Picnic, held in Livingston in early August, is a local, state and national fiddlers festival. The public is invited to a potluck dinner. Livingston Chamber of Commerce, ☎ 406-222-0850. Fax 406-222-0852.

Sweet Pea Festival, an early August Bozeman event, offers a full schedule of art, music and dance. Also running events. ☎ 406-586-4003.

Yellowstone Rod Run features a gathering of street rods, trucks and hot rod cars at West Yellowstone. Jim Copenhaver, PO Box 334, Livingston, MT 59047; ☎ 406-222-1084.

Festival of Nations is an early August Red Lodge event featuring the customs, foods, crafts, dances and languages of the community's many nationalities. Red Lodge Chamber of Commerce, ☎ 406-446-1718.

Sweet Grass County Fair, held at Big Timber in early August, is a quintessential rural American festival. Extension Office, County Courthouse, 200 W. 1st Ave., Big Timber, MT 59011; ☎ 406-932-5146. Fax 406-932-4777.

Montana Antique Airplane Assn. Fly-In takes place in Three Forks in mid-August. Antique airplanes from all over the US are flown in for display. Allen K. Rickman, PO Box 118, Absarokee, MT 59001; ☎ 406-328-4375.

Burnt Hole Rendezvous Historical Reenactment, held in West Yellowstone in mid-August, adds a historical battle reenactment dimenson

Yellowstone Country

to a classic mountain man rendezvous. A primitive camp features traders selling pre-1840s crafts. Native American dancers, living history encampment. Dan or Brenda Thyer, PO Box 648, Ashton, ID 83420; ☎ 208-652-7835.

Annual Moonlight Tour in Yellowstone Park, held in mid-August, is a Saturday night bicycle tour leaving Mammoth Hot Springs to follow the North Loop and return. Hot mid-ride snack, t-shirt and sag wagon service. Montana Tour Group, PO Box 80163, Billings, MT 59108; ☎ 406-652-5523, ext. #4.

Red Lodge's Fat Tire Frenzy is a mountain bike competition held in late August for both beginners and experts. Downhill, criterium, cross-country. Art Maxwell, PO Box 1384, Red Lodge, MT 59068; ☎ 406-446-1634.

Buffalo Days Celebration is a late August kick-up-your heels festival in Gardiner. Arts & crafts, music, dancing, barbeque. Gardiner Chamber of Commerce, ☎ 406-848-7971.

September

Reedpoint 'Running of the Sheep' Drive over the Labor Day weekend promises hilarious fun for all – except maybe the hundreds of woolies charging down Reedpoint's Main Street. Costume contests include the best Bo Peeps, foxes in sheep's clothing, ugliest sheep, prettiest ewe, and real life smelliest sheepherder. The event raises money for school and community facilities in this frontier-style town of some 100 residents. Diana Hahn, Reedpoint, MT 59069; ☎ 406-326-9911.

Labor Day Arts Fair is a Red Lodge event that includes music, gourmet food, arts and more. Red Lodge Chamber of Commerce, ☎ 406-446-1718. Fax 406-446-2513.

World of Art Show, held in early September, attracts US and Canadian artists to Bozeman's Main Mall. Visitors watch artists paint, sculpt and carve items for sale. Florence McCathy, Main Mall, 2825 W. Main, Bozeman, MT 59715; ☎ 406-586-4565. Fax 406-586-9638.

Old Settlers Days takes place in early September in Clyde Park. It features old fashioned fun for all. Livingston Chamber of Commerce, ☎ 406-222-0850. Fax 406-222-0852.

Oktoberfest is a late September Livingston event. Beer, brats and live music transform Main Street. Art & crafts booths. Livingston Chamber of Commerce, ☎ 406-222-0850. Fax 406-222-0852.

October

Bridger Mountain Raptor Festival, held in mid-October, celebrates the largest known migration of golden eagles in North America (see *Wildlife Watching*, page 217). Presentations on birds of prey include raptor identification and raptor ecology. Participants hike to the summit of Bridger Bowl to view up to 17 different species of raptors soaring to their winter homes. Bridger Bowl, ☎ 406-586-1518.

November

Cross-Country Fall Ski Camp is in session during November at West Yellowstone. Ski clinics are presented at this US Nordic and Biathlon ski team training center. West Yellowstone Chamber of Commerce, ☎ 406-646-7701.

Gardiner Library Bazaar is an annual election day event featuring Montana-made crafts and homemade soups, breads and pies. Marge McCoy, PO Box 211, Gardiner, MT 59030; ☎ 406-848-7596.

December

Red Lodge Christmas Stroll, an early December event, features wagon rides, Santa, music, hot cider, roasting chestnuts and more. Red Lodge Chamber of Commerce, ☎ 406-446-1718.

Bozeman Christmas Stroll, also held in early December, features a children's parade, street performers and more. Kendall Johnson, ☎ 406-586-4008. Fax 406-586-3882.

Livingston's Old Fashioned Christmas Fair in early December promises fun for all with arts & crafts, entertainment, food, contests and Christmas trees. Donna Golder, ☎ 406-222-4185.

Christmas Eve Torchlight Parade & Festivities is an annual event at Big Sky Ski & Summer Resort. Santa and his elves ski down the mountain by torchlight. Huntley Lodge Concierge, ☎ 406-995-5000.

New Year's Eve Fireworks Display and Celebration at Big Sky. Fireworks on top of the mountain ring in the new year. Also: live band, dancing and dinner. Huntley Lodge Concierge, ☎ 406-995-5000.

Where to Stay & Eat

■ Hotels, Motels & B&Bs

As one of Montana's top tourist areas, Yellowstone Country has lodging choices fit to satisfy the most discriminating visitor. It's no accident if that statement conjures up visions of multiple dollar signs. Toney digs and posh self-consciously "rustic Western" lodges abound. So do historic hotels brought back from near morbidity – often a less expensive choice. Attractive alternatives to spendy digs do exist. Some, like Forest Service cabins, define authentic rustic Western and offer heaps of roughing-it fun. Bed & breakfast inns are often, but not always, an economical choice.

Most lodgings are listed under the nearest town. Historic hotels and Forest Service cabins are listed under separate headings.

Yellowstone Country

Lodging Prices
$ . . . . dirt cheap
$$. . . . . moderate
$$$. . . . . .pricey, but oh well
$$$$ . . . . .hang onto your checkbook

Big Sky

Best Western Buck's T-4 Lodge doesn't resemble the ubiquitous road-side Best Western. This affordable 75-room lodging projects a comfort-able Western ambience. Two restaurants, gift shop, outdoor hot tubs. $$$. PO Box 160279, Big Sky, MT 59716; Direct: ☎ 800-822-4484. Na-tionwide: ☎ 800-528-1234. Local: ☎ 406-995-4111. Fax 406-995-2191.

Big Sky Ski and Summer Resort reflects an ersatz mountain village ambience with the 182-room ski-in-ski-out Huntley Lodge and several condominium complexes. Many accommodate families or large parties. $$$$. Ski or other packages can make them affordable. Central reserva-tions. PO Box 160001, Big Sky, MT 59716; ☎ 800-548-4486 or 406-995-5000. E-mail bigskymail@mcn.net. Internet www.bigskyresort.com.

Gallatin Riverhouse is, as the name implies, on the Gallatin River. Lodgings feature two bedrooms/two baths plus loft for parties of six. Spendy, but the surroundings are gorgeous. Three-night minimum stay. $$$$. ☎ 406-995-2290. Fax 406-995-4588.

Golden Eagle Lodge/Condominium Rentals arranges lodging in a variety of condos and homes, plus the affordable Golden Eagle Lodge. Box 160008, Big Sky, MT 59716; ☎ 800-548-4488.

Rainbow Ranch Lodge, on the Gallatin River, boasts that each guest room enjoys a river view. Luxury suites have lodge pole beds; some have rock fireplaces. $$$. Box 160336, Big Sky, MT 59716; ☎ 800-937-4132 or 406-995-4132. Internet www.gomontana.com/-rr.html.

River Rock Lodge is a posh retreat in Big Sky's Meadow Village. $$$$. PO Box 160700, Big Sky, MT 59716; ☎ 800-995-9966 or 406-995-2295. Fax 406-995-2727. Internet www.avicom.net/bigsky.html.

Big Timber

The **Big Timber Inn** is on the banks of the Yellowstone River, three miles northeast of Big Timber. This affordable bed & breakfast has two guest rooms with adjoining sitting room. Full breakfasts. Owners Bob and Donja Bovee also operate a fishing guide service. $$. PO Box 328, Big Timber, MT 59011; ☎ 406-932-4080.

Grand Hotel: See *Historic Hotels*.

Bridger

Circle of Friends is a bed & breakfast offering overnight stabling for your steed on 24 acres near the farming community of Bridger. Hostess Dorothy Sue Phillips, a transplanted Alaska teacher, offers three reasonably priced guest rooms, one with private bath. $$. RR1 Box 1250, Bridger, MT 59014; ☎ 406-662-3264.

Bozeman

Bozeman's bed & breakfasts are augmented by chain hostelries that include **Best Western** (☎ 800-624-5865), **Holiday Inn** (☎ 800-366-5101) and **Comfort Inn** (☎ 800-587-3833). The following listings offer attractive alternatives.

Fox Hollow Bed & Breakfast at Baxter Creek, in a country setting five miles from downtown, offers five large guest rooms with private baths; gourmet breakfasts. $$$$. 545 Mary Rd., Bozeman, MT 59715; ☎ 800-431-5010.

 DID YOU KNOW?

Howlers Inn Bed & Breakfast doubles as a wolf sanctuary. The log and stone home on 42 acres in Bridger Canyon has three guest rooms with private baths and a two-bedroom guest house with fireplace and kitchen. Amenities include a hot tub and sauna. $$$$. 3185 Jackson Creek Rd., Bozeman, MT 59715; ☎ 888-HOWLERS or 406-586-0304.

Kirk Hill Bed & Breakfast is in a c.1905 farm house in the Gallatin Valley, six miles south of Bozeman and adjacent to the Museum of the Rockies Nature Trail. Irish setters, horses, llamas, sheep, ducks and cashmere goats are raised on the property. Three guest rooms, one with private bath. $$$. 7960 S. 19th Rd., Bozeman, MT 59715; ☎ 800-240-3929 or 406-586-3929.

Lehrkind Mansion Bed and Breakfast is seven blocks from Main Street. The Queen Anne Victorian home, decorated with period antiques, is listed on the National Register of Historic Places. Gourmet breakfasts; outdoor hot tub. $$$$. 719 N. Wallace Ave., Bozeman, MT 59715; ☎ 800-992-6932 or 406-585-6932.

Cooke City

Big Bear Lodge bills itself as a fly fishing lodge, but it's also a bed & breakfast featuring log cabins. Open year-round. The lodge's dining room offers home-cooked meals to be enjoyed in front of a big stone fireplace. $$$. PO Box 1029, Cooke City, MT 59020; ☎ 406-838-2267.

Soda Butte Lodge, Hotel & Casino, Cooke City's newest hostelry as this book goes to press, has 32 guest rooms, a restaurant and casino. Rates are surprisingly reasonable. The fancy Jacuzzi Room just tops $100. Ask about snowmobile package rates. $$$. PO Box 1119, Cooke City, MT 59020; ☎ 800-527-6462 or 406-838-2251. Fax 406-527-6462.

Emigrant

Point of Rocks Lodge tries to be all things to all people: B&B, fishing lodge and guest ranch. Pricing is per night and fishing and trail rides are extra, so we'll go with the B&B classification. An option: sleeping in a refurbished early 1900s log cabin. $$$. 2017 US 89 South, Emigrant, MT 59027; ☎ 406-333-4361.

Querencia is an elegantly rustic bed & breakfast inn that's open year-round so that guests can take advantage of area cross-country skiing as well as fly fishing and hiking. Five guest rooms, one with private bath, others with semi-private baths. Full breakfasts. $$$$. Joe and Linda Skaggs, 3674 Hwy. 89 South, Emigrant, MT 59027; ☎ 888-603-4500 or 406-333-4500.

The Schoolhouse, billed as "a paradise retreat," is a personal guest cottage on the banks of Fridley Creek near Emigrant. Bring your own food and settle into the two-bedroom-with-kitchen restored Fridley School. $$. HC 85, Box 4127, Livingston, MT 59047; ☎ 406-222-2527.

Yellowstone Country Bed & Breakfast has two-bedroom log cabins on the river. Private decks, kitchenettes, outdoor grill areas, large sitting rooms. Breakfasts delivered. $$$$. PO Box 1002, Emigrant, MT 59027; ☎ 406-333-4917.

Fishtail

This tiny town is just off MT 78 between Columbus and Red Lodge.

Rosebud River Retreat is a four-bedroom log home on the West Rosebud River available for rent by the night, week or month. $$$$. HC 55, Box 250, Fishtail, MT 59028; ☎ 406-328-4220 or 578-2234.

Gallatin Gateway

Wrangler at 320 Guest Ranch, south of Big Sky.

Cinnamon Lodge, on the Gallatin River, is an idea if you wish to explore the Gallatin National Forest and Gallatin Canyon. Cabin accommodations, some with kitchens. Restaurant. $$$. 37090 Gallatin Rd., Gallatin Gateway, MT 59730; ☎ 406-995-4253.

Gallatin Gateway Inn: See *Historic Hotels*.

320 Guest Ranch offers an all-inclusive seven-night Western Dream Package, but the main thrust of this popular ranch is per-night luxury log cabin lodging. Individually priced horseback rides, chuck wagon breakfasts, dinner rides, camera safaris and full-day horseback/fishing trips. This ranch is popular with tour groups. Winter sports packages are also on offer. $$$$. 205 Buffalo Horn Creek, Gallatin Gateway, MT 59730; ☎ 800-243-0320 or 406-995-4283. Fax 406-995-4694.

The Trout Club Cabins in Gallatin River Canyon are three miles downstream from the *A River Runs Through It* filming site. Completely furnished riverside cabins. $$$$. For brochure, ☎ 213-939-8156.

Gardiner

Gardiner, as one might expect of a busy national park gateway, has a variety of lodgings. Chain hostelries are represented by **Best Western** (☎ 800-828-9080) and **Comfort Inn** (☎ 800-228-5150).

Absaroka Lodge, a triple-decked structure reminiscent of historic park hotels just outside Yellowstone Park and two blocks from Roosevelt Arch, has 41 rooms and suites with private balconies overlooking the Yellowstone River. Suites have kitchens. $$$. PO Box 10, Gardiner, MT 59030; ☎ 800-755-7414 or 406-848-7414.

Maiden Basin Inn, on US 89 five miles north of Yellowstone Park, has suites with river views; some kitchen units. $$$. PO Box 414, Gardiner, MT 59030; ☎ 800-624-3364 or 406-848-7083.

Paradise Gateway Bed & Breakfast and Log Guest Cabin, on the Yellowstone River near the park's north entrance, is open year-round. Guest rooms have private baths; country gourmet breakfasts. The cabin is on 27 acres bordering the river. $$$. PO Box 84, Emigrant, MT 59027; ☎ 800-541-4113 or 406-333-4063.

Livingston

AUTHOR TIP

Beartooth Wilderness Lodge & Llama Ranch offers year-round lodging in deluxe suites and log cabins furnished with lodgepole pine pieces. Huggable llamas enhance the beautiful surroundings. Hiking with the llamas is a popular activity. Choose between the B&B rate or the all-inclusive American Plan. $$$$. PO Box 1038, Livingston, MT 59047; ☎ 406-220-2895. E-mail THEBTWL@ aol.com. Internet http://yellowstone.minns.com/ bearto/bear.htm.

Davis Creek Bed & Breakfast, 16.8 miles south of Livingston, offers three homey log guest cabins on a working ranch. Each cabin, accommodating four persons, has a private bath and limited kitchen facilities. Hearty breakfasts served family-style, beautiful mountain vistas. Special family and weekly rates. $$$. 575 Mill Creek Rd., Livingston, MT 59047; ☎ 406-333-4353 or 333-4768.

The Island Guest House and Bed & Breakfast features stocked trout ponds. Full breakfast at B&B. Guest house, ideal for families, has three bedrooms, two baths, hot tub and sauna. $$$. 9th Street Island Drive, Livingston, MT 59047; ☎ 800-438-3092 or 406-222-3788.

The Murray Hotel: See *Historic Hotels*.

The Pleasant Pheasant Bed & Breakfast and Bunkhouse is 17 miles south of Livingston in Paradise Valley. The B&B has five guest rooms and provides a breakfast bar. The Bunkhouse is a four-bedroom house. Individual rooms are available or rent the entire house. $$$. 126 Elbow Creek Rd., Livingston, MT 59047; ☎ 406-333-4659.

Pray

Chico Hot Springs Lodge: See *Historic Hotels*.

Log Guest Cabin Bed & Breakfast is on the 4M Ranch in Paradise Valley. Rent the cabin or one of two guest rooms. Breakfasts tailored to taste. $$$. 4M Ranch, 194 Bridger Hollow Rd., Pray, MT 59065; ☎ 406-333-4784. E-mail serene@ycsi.net.

Red Lodge

As you might expect, Red Lodge has a wide variety of lodgings. Luckily, there's a **central reservations service** (☎ 800-800-8000) that can put you in touch with private guest houses and other off-the-beaten-track accommodations. The town's showpiece is the historic **Pollard Hotel** (see *Historic Hotels*). Other lodgings run heavily to generic motels – not what might be expected of a fast-growing resort town in the throes of being "discovered" by disaffected Californians and other erstwhile city dwellers.

Chateau Rouge Lodge has an indoor heated pool and hot tub. Sixteen two-floor, two-bedroom units with fireplaces and eight studio units, all with kitchens. $$$. Box 3410, Red Lodge, MT 59068; ☎ 800-926-1601.

Inn on the Beartooth, Inc. is a log inn where views of the Beartooths accompany full breakfasts. Guest rooms have private baths. Open year-round. $$$$. Box 1515 (6648 Hwy. 212), Red Lodge, MT 59068; ☎ 888-222-7686 or 406-446-3555.

Pitcher Guest Houses are decorated country-style and include two charming homes and two cozy three-room log cabins in Red Lodge. One of the houses is a former Finnish lodging house built in 1903, when Red Lodge was a coal mining town. $$$. Box 3450, Red Lodge, MT 59068; ☎ 406-446-2859.

Rock Creek Resort has two restaurants, an indoor pool, a wide range of outdoor activities and comfortable guest rooms. $$$$. Rt 2 Box 3500, Red Lodge, MT 59068; ☎ 406-446-1111.

The Wolves Den, on Rock Creek six miles north of Red Lodge, has two guest rooms with a shared bath and private entrance and sitting room. Full breakfasts. $$$. PO Box 1231, Red Lodge, MT 59068; ☎ 406-446-1273.

Reedpoint

To overnight in Reedpoint is to experience the unvarnished Wild West.

Hotel Montana Bed & Breakfast: See *Historic Hotels*.

Buckin' Horse Bunkhouse is a ways south of town on Bridger Creek. Accommodations include a log cabin with rustic Western decor and a room in the log main house. Optional breakfasts served creekside or in the sunroom. Horseback riding available. $$$. HC 57 Box 521, Reedpoint, MT 59069; ☎ 406-932-6537.

Roscoe

Papa's & Granny's Guest House is salubriously situated just a few feet from the East Rosebud River and across the street from the Grizzly Bar & Restaurant. The two-bedroom house is available by the night, week or month. $$. PO Box 38, Roscoe, MT 59071; ☎ 406-328-6789 or 328-6719.

Silver Gate

Whispering Pines Cabins is about as close to Yellowstone Park's northeast entrance as you can get. Some of these modern log cabins have kitchen facilities. Nestled in a forest with Soda Butte Creek gurgling through it. $$. Open summers. US Hwy. 212, Silver Gate, MT 59081; ☎ 406-838-2228 or 818-339-4812.

Three Forks

Broken Spur Motel is one of a breed of clean, low-profile digs that are mainstays of many small towns. This AAA-rated one may be a cut above the rest. The lobby sports the ubiquitous elk-with-rack. Continental breakfast. $$. PO Box 1009 (Hwy. 2 West), Three Forks, MT 59752; ☎ 406-285-3237.

Sacajawea Inn: See *Historic Hotels*.

West Yellowstone

If you can't locate a bed in West Yellowstone and vicinity, you're not paying attention. The gateway town's numerous hostelries satisfy every taste and price range. Reservations are a must in summer's peak tourist season and when snowmobiling is hot. Solitude can be a stretch here. Some of the better choices:

Bar N Ranch offers bed & breakfast-style accommodations plus guest ranch packages. Choose between comfortable rooms and cabins. $$$. ☎ 800-BIGSKS or 406-646-7229.

Best Western has two inns here; good choices if more individualized lodgings are filled: **BW Executive Inn**, 236 Dunraven; ☎ 406-646-7671. **BW Weston Inn**, 103 Gibbon St.; ☎ 406-646-7373. West Yellowstone's zip is 59758.

Hibernation Station offers luxury log cabins away from downtown noise. Some have kitchens and fireplaces. Cross-country skiing from your cabin door; snowmobile rentals. $$$$. 212 Gray Wolf Ave., West Yellowstone, MT 59758; ☎ 800-580-3557 or 406-646-4200.

Sleepy Hollow Lodge is a full-service lodge open year-round. Affordably priced one- and two-bedroom log cabins have kitchens and individual heating systems. Host Larry Miller, a licensed outfitter, offers guided fishing trips. He can arrange snowmobile rentals, horseback riding and whitewater trips. $$$. PO Box 1080, West Yellowstone, MT 59758; ☎ 406-646-7707.

Yellowstone Holiday Resort has Hebgen lakeside cabins of the oldtime family road trip genre. Also a marina, general store, water sports. $$. Box 759 (16990 Hebgen Lake Road), West Yellowstone, MT 59758; ☎ 800-643-4227 or 406-646-7400.

Yellowstone Village is a quiet retreat with a view of Hebgen Lake. Fully equipped condos open year-round. $$$. Box 973, West Yellowstone, MT 59758; ☎ 800-276-7335.

■ Historic Hotels

Yellowstone Country's if-only-walls-could-talk historic hostelries range from bare bones to posh. All reflect a yesteryear ambience.

Chico Hot Springs Lodge, at the base of Emigrant Peak, has a low-key appearance, but offers upscale amenities. The 100-year-old hotel, built around a natatorium fed by a thermally heated hot spring, has been restored and enlarged without detracting from the original laid-back ambience. Once popular with the likes of Teddy Roosevelt and Charlie Russell, the resort continues to attract artistic and political personalities, yet welcomes everyday folks. The 90 guest rooms, chalets and cabins include digs ranging from high end upscale to eminently affordable. Open year-round, the Lodge offers a wide range of outdoor activities, plus amenities transcending those early guests' wildest dreams. A children's activity program is available. $$$. Post Office Drawer D, Pray, MT 59065; ☎ 406-333-4933. Fax: 406-333-4694.

Gallatin Gateway Inn, a few miles south of Bozeman on US 191, was built in 1927 by the Milwaukee Railroad as a way station for visitors to Yellowstone Park. The restored hotel is on the National Register of Historic Places. The beautiful windows, beamed ceilings and art deco frescos gracing the enormous lobby are alone worth a visit. The 35 guest rooms have been modernized and reflect the inn's casual elegance. $$$. Hwy. 191, Gallatin Gateway, MT 59730; ☎ 800-366-5101 or 406-587-4561.

The Grand Hotel, restored to reflect the original 1890 ambience, is a bed & breakfast. Three of the 11 rooms and suites have full baths. Hearty breakfasts. Reasonable pricing and a gourmet restaurant make this a good choice within easy driving distance of the Boulder River and other recreational opportunities. $$$. 139 McLeod (PO Box 1242), Big Timber, MT 59011; ☎ 406-932-4459. Fax 406-932-4248.

The Historic Pollard Hotel has been a Red Lodge landmark since 1893. Recently rejuvenated, the 40-room hostelry retains its historic Wild West flavor. Guests have included the likes of Calamity Jane, Buffalo Bill Cody, William Jennings Bryan and Jeremiah "Liver-Eatin'" Johnson. $$$$. 2 N. Broadway, Red Lodge, MT 59068; ☎ 406-446-1111.

Hotel Montana Bed & Breakfast takes you back to a "Victorian twilight zone" when men were cowboys and Montana ladies were hardly blushing violets. The restored 1909 hotel's guest rooms, all decorated with period antiques and having full baths, reflect an era of board sidewalks and quick tempers. There's even a 1900s-style saloon. Generous breakfast buffet. $$$. 201 N. Division St., Reedpoint, MT 59069; ☎ 406-326-2288. E-mail hotelmt@ttc-cmc.net. Internet http//www.ttc-cmc.net/-hotelmt.

The Murray Hotel is dear to the hearts of Livingston's trendy set. *The New York Times* burbled, "the historic Murray Hotel appeals to celebrities and to a certain Western disorder." Make what you will of that, but the hotel does offer 32 comfortable rooms and suites and a lounge and grill where you might glimpse some celebrities. $$. 201 W. Park St., Livingston, MT 59047; ☎ 406-222-1350.

Sacajawea Inn in Three Forks has seen better days. It exists in a kind of limbo, having been up for sale for quite some time. More or less restored, it projects a creaky ambience. But don't be discouraged. The 33 guest rooms are clean and reflect the modest expectations of former days. The inn was built in 1882 at the confluence of the Jefferson, Gallatin and Madison Rivers. Flooding forced the inn's relocation. Two wings were rolled on logs to higher ground in Three Forks; a considerable undertaking in those days. In 1910, the inn was enlarged to accommodate Milwaukee Railroad passengers en route to Yellowstone Park. The sprawling structure's front porch still runs the length of the building. $$$. PO Box 648 (5 N. Main St.), Three Forks, MT 59752; ☎ 800-821-7326 or 406-285-6515.

▪ US Forest Service Cabins & Lookouts

Time was when cabins situated in remote corners of Montana's national forests were used by rangers working on trails and other chores that took them into the back country for days at a time. Remote guard stations, once buzzing with activity, are no longer needed. Many cabins were allowed to deteriorate or were destroyed. Their slide into historical oblivion was halted when it dawned on the Forest Service that they would make nifty digs for hikers and cross-country skiers.

The same fate befell fire lookout towers and cabins. Perched on rocky crags affording 90° forest views, they offer spectacular vistas and front-line storm watching. Once the front line of fire fighting defense, spotters in these aries reported whisps of telltale smoke before the fire could roar out of control. Lookouts became obsolete when airplanes took over the job. Though less numerous than cabins, former lookouts also await adventurers who enjoy unique back country lodgings. A most inexpensive approach, with rates in the $25-$30 per-night range.

Full-service digs, they're not. Amenities vary, but most cabins/lookouts offer a snug roof, a wood heating/cookstove, firewood, lanterns, basic furnishings, no drinking water. A few have electricity, but that kinda spoils the fun. Bring your own bedding and cooking utensils. Ask what the cabin of your choice has, or has not, when making your reservation.

Yellowstone Country

What every one of these Forest Service cabins has in abundance is genuine rustic ambience in the midst of some of the finest natural splendor you're likely to find anywhere on Earth.

Recreational cabin permits are issued on a first-come, first-served basis. You can obtain a permit in person, or by contacting the Big Timber, Gardiner, Livingston, Bozeman or Hebgen Lake Ranger District. The maximum stay is usually 14 days, but may be less for some cabins. The Gallatin National Forest has upwards of two dozen cabins, former guard stations, and a lookout cabin. Some can be reached via primitive roads but most require hiking in from a trailhead. Many cabins are used by snowmobilers, cross-country skiers and snowshoers. Some have corrals and appeal to horsepackers.

 The Northern Region Recreational Cabin and Lookout Directory lists cabins in the Gallatin and other Montana national forests. Copies are available from any ranger district, or from the Gallatin National Forest headquarters.

■ Camping

Public Campgrounds

 Yellowstone Country's camping possibilities are as varied as you'd wish them to be, given the wide range of adventure experiences on offer.

Undeveloped campsites are numerous in the back country. One of the beauties of these is choosing the site that best appeals to you. Forest Service campgrounds are the next best bet. There are dozens of these in the Gallatin and Custer National Forests; none in wilderness areas. Some are first-come, first-served no-fee campgrounds; others cost around $8 per night. All have road access, though some are little better than 4WD tracks. All have tent pads. Some, like Falls Creek Campground on the Main Boulder River, accommodate tents only. Most can handle trailers up to 20 feet. At a few, such as Colter Campground two miles east of Cooke City on US 212, you can get away with parking a 48-foot rig. Most are undeveloped with pit toilets. About half have water, firewood and trash pickup.

Many of these campgrounds are at trailheads, offering the advantage of a place to leave your tent and gear while you explore the adjacent trails.

You can reserve camp sites for an extra fee at some Gallatin and Custer National Forest campgrounds. ☎ 800-280-2267 or fax 301-722-9802 to reserve your campsite. Mail-in reservation forms are available at any Forest Service office or by calling ☎ 406-329-3511. Major credit cards are accepted. First-come, first-served sites are also available at these campgrounds.

Reservation campgrounds in the **Gallatin National Forest** are **Baker's Hole** on the Madison River, **Rainbow Point** and **Lonesomehurst** on Hebgen Lake, **Beaver Creek** overlooking the Madison River Canyon and Quake Lake, and **Cabin Creek** near Cabin Creek Trail.

Custer National Forest reservation campgrounds, all south of Red Lodge, include **Parkside**, **Limberpine**, **Greenough**, **Ratine** and **Sheridan** on Rock Creek, and **Basin** and **Cascade** along the West Fork of Rock Creek.

> 📖 Copies of the *Gallatin National Forest Camp and Picnic Guide* are free at all Gallatin National Forest ranger stations. Detailed maps are available for a small charge.

Cooney Lake and **Missouri Headwaters State Parks** offer camping (see *State Parks,* page 48). Cooney appeals to anglers and boating enthusiasts while Missouri Headwaters is the choice of folks who enjoy a smattering of history with their canoeing and wildlife viewing. The former accommodates tents and RV/trailers, while the latter boasts a dump station and other RVers' amenities.

Private Campgrounds

Private campgrounds usually offer full RV hookups, an advantage if you need to dump your holding tank, enjoy some electricty and maybe do a load of laundry.

Many private campgrounds are little more than expanses of cement with hookups or a few spaces beside a motel or saloon. These are numerous as mini-marts and are often attached to same. They'll serve if you are desperate for a place to overnight, but don't deserve a mention here.

KOA (Kampgrounds of America) originated in Montana and is headquartered here. That doesn't mean that individual KOAs are any better in Montana than elsewhere; some are OK, some not. Some, like the one south of Bozeman, are outrageously pricey.

The following private campgrounds have something other than a concrete pad to recommend them. They are usually more expensive than state park campgrounds, which average about $12.

Gallatin Gateway

Cinnamon Lodge, on the Gallatin River, has RV spaces and tent sites as well as cabins and a restaurant. Trail rides can be arranged. 37090 Gallatin Rd., Gallatin Gateway, MT 59730; ☎ 406-995-4253.

Livingston

Paradise Valley/Livingston KOA, on the banks of the Yellowstone, has an indoor heated pool. Bike and raft rentals are available. RV and tent sites. 163 Pine Creek Rd., Livingston, MT 59047; ☎ 800-KOA-2805.

Big Timber

Big Timber KOA is small and often crowded, but is adjacent to a waterslide. I-90 Exit 377; ☎ 800-KOA-5869 or 406-932-6569.

Spring Creek Campground & Trout Ranch is a stunner. Grassy campsites are strung along the Boulder River. Stocked trout ponds, log camping cabins, laundromat, pancake breakfasts. This one invites staying awhile. Convenient to Boulder River Falls. Two miles south of Big Timber on Hwy. 298. PO Box 1435, Big Timber, MT 59011; ☎ 406-932-4387.

West Yellowstone

Madison Arm Resort Campground & Marina on Hebgen Lake may be a good choice if you wish to do some fishing, swimming or boating. Marina has a ramp, docking, fuel and boat rentals. Shaded tent and RV spaces. Box 40, West Yellowstone, MT 59758; ☎ 406-646-9328.

■ Where to Eat

You'd expect "gourmet" and "trendy" to be the operative terms when discussing Yellowstone Country restaurants. For sure, but not always. Family restaurants, beloved of bus tours, proliferate in places such as West Yellowstone and seldom deserve a mention. Casual eateries dishing up honest Western fare and homebaked pies do. Ditto: high end gourmet restaurants. Funky eateries with atmosphere and food to match are serendipitous finds. Saloons featuring super steaks and such are legion.

Success is in the discovery; an attempt at success has been made in this chapter's eatery listings. But be forewarned: this book makes no claim to being a definitive source of restaurant info. Dining is subjective; one person's dream meal is another's disaster. And eateries come and go.

If a town doesn't boast a memorable restaurant, it doesn't get mentioned here. Anyone can find a café. The local watering hole will usually rustle you up a steak.

Big Sky

Big Sky, as befits a trendy resort, has numerous restaurants in its lodging complexes. Dining venues assume a pseudo-Western ranch guise and can be pretty spendy. Go elsewhere if economy dictates.

Lone Mountain Ranch Dining Lodge at Big Sky offers "rustic elegance," if that's not an oxymoron. Rave reviews in high profile publications. ☎ 406-995-2782.

Rainbow Ranch Lodge, on the banks of the Gallatin River, offers high end cuisine in luscious surroundings. On Hwy. 191 five miles south of the Big Sky Resort entrance. ☎ 800-937-4132 or 406-995-4132.

Big Timber

The Grand Hotel's 1890 Room, "serving cattlemen, cowboys, sheepherders and travelers since 1890," serves up "innovative world cuisine with a Montana touch." That it does, with tasty results. No doubt the haute gourmet offerings, with prices to match, would send those old-time dudes skedaddling for the high timber. Rhinestone dudes flock here from the country 'round. 139 McLeod St.; ☎ 406-932-4459. Fax 406-932-4248.

Bozeman

Bozeman's dining-out scene can be described as collegiate with trendy aspirations.

John Bozeman's Bistro, serving up creative cuisine, has been in the same 242 E. Main Street location for 20 years. A favorite with local artists. ☎ 406-587-4100.

Rocky Mountain Roasting Co. offers al fresco munching. Pastries and fresh roasted coffees. 111 E. Mendenhall (☎ 406-586-2428) and 701 W. Main (☎ 406-586-9333).

Spanish Peaks Brewery features micro brews and Italian dishes. Al fresco dining. 120 N. 19th Ave.; ☎ 406-585-2296.

Western Café is a popular local hangout with 1950s decor and downhome fare. 433 E. Main St.; ☎ 406-587-0436.

Cooke City

Cooke City eateries have no pretensions. No pricey menus, either. Spot a sign, read the menu if one's posted, walk in, sit down, order, strike up a conversation, enjoy. That's it. Some offer homemade pies. Take your pick.

Gallatin Gateway

Cinnamon Lodge Restaurant features the brand of unpretentious stick-to-your-ribs fare for which Montana is famous, at prices that won't scare you. Breakfasts include mammoth huevos rancheros and day-starter omelets. Lunchtime sandwiches and Mexican dishes follow suit. Dinner entrées include such Western favorites as liver with onions and bacon, and 20-oz. porterhouse steaks. 37090 Gallatin Road; ☎ 406-995-4253.

Gallatin Gateway Inn offers creative American cuisine in the beautifully restored dining room. Hwy. 191; ☎ 406-763-4672.

320 Guest Ranch offers fine dining in a rustic log setting. Hwy. 191, Mile Marker 36; ☎ 800-243-0320 or 406-995-4283. Fax 406-995-4694.

Yellowstone Country

Gardiner

Gardiner defines casual. It makes sense that eateries follow suit.

Bear Country Restaurant features fresh homemade pies and other goodies made from scratch. They also pack picnic lunches. Main & Third Streets; ☎ 406-848-7188.

High Country Espresso, convenient to the laundromat, serves up coffees, fruit smoothies and muffins. Opposite the Roosevelt Arch.

Red's Blue Goose Saloon, specializing in smoked meats, baby back ribs and mammoth prime rib and steaks, also packs picnic lunches. Hwy. 89 and Park St.; ☎ 406-848-7037.

Livingston

Livingston lays claim to more eateries per year-round resident than any other Montana community. Not surprising, considering that the old railroad town has been discovered by the rich and famous. In Livingston, gourmet cuisine rubs skillets with broad-shouldered Western fare. A sampling:

Buffalo Jump Steakhouse & Saloon features USDA choice steaks and Montana micro brews. Hwy. 89, one mile south of town; ☎ 406-222-2887.

Chatham's **Livingston Bar & Grille**, presided over by renowned chef André Soltner, promises a first-rate dining experience. Corner of Park and Main; ☎ 406-222-7909.

Crazy Coyote specializes in real Mexican food. 206 S. 11th St. (one block off Park Street); ☎ 406-222-1548.

The Stockman Bar (it's a rare Montana town that can't claim a Stockman Bar) serves up predictable fare with predictable ambience. 118 N. Main; ☎ 406-222-8455.

The Sport sports a decor combining nostalgia with old newspaper clips. The fare is of the "downhome" genre. 114-116 S. Main; ☎ 406-222-8221.

Uncle Looies serves up serious Italian cuisine. 119 W. Park; ☎ 406-222-7177.

Pine Creek

Pine Creek Café proves that low-key isn't necessarily low quality. Homemade is the watchword here. Fabulous burgers, chicken 'n dumplings, home baked desserts. Al fresco dining. 2496 E. River Rd.; ☎ 406-222-5499.

Pray

Chico Hot Springs Resort restaurant's classic continental cuisine and extensive wine list attract discriminating diners from throughout Montana. Hotel Manager Craig Lambert reports that well-heeled Montanans fly in to the resort air strip just for the fabulous Sunday brunch. Menus feature produce from the resort's garden, and from a large greenhouse heated with overflow water from the thermally heated pool. Off MT 540. ☎ 406-333-4933. Fax 406-333-4694.

Red Lodge

As you might expect, Red Lodge dines upscale. It dines downscale, too. Lots of variety in this coal mining-cum-trendy town. Funky wander-in eateries in the historic downtown shopping area invite snacking.

Bear Creek Saloon cooks up he-man steaks in addition to its famous pig races. At Bear Creek, seven miles east of town Hwy. 308; ☎ 406-446-3481.

Bogart's (yes, it's named after Humphrey) offers reasonably priced lunches and dinners running to Mexican and pizza. 11 S. Broadway; ☎ 406-446-1784.

Bridge Creek Back Country Kitchen & Wine Bar offers internationally flavored lunches and dinners, smoked meats, pastas. Gourmet picnic lunches. 106 W. 12th St.; ☎ 406-446-9900.

Greenlee's At The Pollard is gourmet and pricey, as you might expect given the historic hotel ambience. Full meal service reflects upscale California cuisine. On the menu are steaks, chops and Montana ostrich. The Pollard Hotel, 2 N. Broadway; ☎ 406-446-0001.

Old Piney Dell is veddy veddy upscale as befits a "something special" dining venue. Four miles south of town on Hwy. 212; ☎ 406-446-1196.

Round Barn Restaurant & Dinner Theatre serves up a predictable menu as asides to Vigilante Theatre Company productions. Two miles north of town on Hwy. 212; ☎ 406-446-1197.

West Yellowstone

West Yellowstone's restaurant scene is unremarkable, running largely to family restaurants and motel dining rooms.

Einos, on Hwy. 191 some eight miles north of town, near the junction with Hwy. 287, is a fun place where you get to cook your own chicken or steaks. ☎ 406-646-9344.

Gold West Country

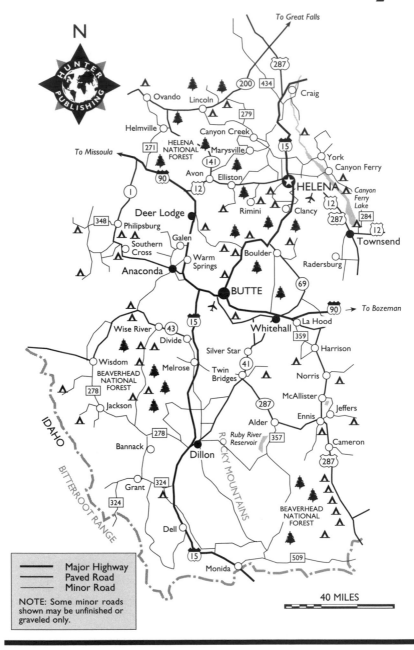

To Great Falls

287

N

HUNTER PUBLISHING

200   434   Craig

Ovando   Lincoln

279

Helmville   Canyon Creek

HELENA NATIONAL FOREST   Marysville

To Missoula   271   141   York

Avon   Elliston   15   Canyon Ferry

90   12   HELENA   Canyon Ferry Lake

1   Rimini   Clancy   12

Deer Lodge   287   284

348   Philipsburg   Galen   Boulder   12

Southern Cross   Warm Springs   Townsend

Anaconda   Radersburg

BUTTE   69

To Bozeman

90

Wise River   43   La Hood

Divide   Whitehall

Silver Star   359   Harrison

Wisdom   Melrose   41

BEAVERHEAD NATIONAL FOREST   Twin Bridges   Norris

278   McAllister

Jackson   287   Ennis   Jeffers

Alder   Cameron

278   Ruby River Reservoir   357   287

Bannack   Dillon

IDAHO

Grant   324

324

BEAVERHEAD NATIONAL FOREST

BITTERROOT RANGE

Dell

ROCKY MOUNTAINS

15   509

Monida

— Major Highway
— Paved Road
— Minor Road

NOTE: Some minor roads shown may be unfinished or graveled only.

40 MILES

Gold West Country

Introduction

The name says it all. The chunk of real estate squeezed between the Gallatins and the Bitterroots taps a rich vein of mountain country adventure opportunities. Gold rush ghost towns drowsing amid hazy memories bring the region's history to life. Some, such as Bannack, are maintained in a state of arrested decay. Others, such as Virginia City, have allowed commercialism to obscure a gritty past. Little more than shadows are left of boomtowns like Confederate Gulch, built overnight on rumors of pay dirt and as quickly abandoned for richer diggings elsewhere. **Butte** and Last Chance Gulch (now **Helena**) upset the norm by hanging on to become thrumming cities. It's easy to get gold fever, exploring these ghost towns to the exclusion of other adventures.

A visit to Gold West Country won't be complete without chasing a rainbow of minerals; gold, sapphires, amethyst crystals, smoky quartz and more.

Pursuing mining era ghosts and the minerals that caused all the fuss is only a beginning.

The **Madison River**, a blue ribbon fly fishing stream, flows mostly through Gold West Country. The **Blackfoot**, of *A River Runs Through It* fame, picks up speed here. Numerous other storied rivers also course through this region: the **Jefferson**, **Big Hole**, **Beaverhead**, **Wise**, **Ruby**, **Red Rock**.

Mountains of unimaginable splendor shoulder above the river valleys. The **Madison Range** lies to the east of the river bearing that name, the **Gravelly Range** and **Tobacco Roots** to the west. The scenic **Tendoy Mountains** anchor the southern tip of Gold West Country. The **Continental Divide** marches across the **Centennial Mountains**, defining the Montana/Idaho line before wiggling north and east to circle Butte and bypass Helena. Northwest of Dillon, the **Pioneer Mountains** gaze over the **Big Hole River** to the craggy **Bitterroots**. The verdant **Deer Lodge Valley** rests in the shadow of the **Garnet Range**. On the west, the **Sapphire Range** straddles an invisible line between Gold West and Glacier Countries. The **Elkhorn** and other pocket-size mountain ranges recall the Earth's sporadic up-thrusting that creating the Rocky Mountain Front.

Gold West Country was at the front of the line when national forests and wilderness areas were created. The region contains all or part of six national forests. The **Beaverhead**, **Deerlodge**, and **Helena National Forests** are in Gold West Country. Portions of the **Gallatin** and **Bitterroot National Forests** lap over the region's eastern and western borders. The **Lolo National Forest** reaches into Gold West Country from Glacier Country.

DID YOU KNOW?

The sprawling Beaverhead National Forest includes nine mountain ranges. The name "Beaver's Head" first appeared in the 1805 journals of Lewis and Clark after the captains passed the distinctive rock. Sacajawea identified it as near the place where the company would meet her people.

The four wilderness areas include most of the **Lee Metcalf** and **Scapegoat Wildernesses** and the **Anaconda-Pintler** and **Gates of the Mountains Wildernesses**. All invite hiking, backpacking, horse packing, cross-country skiing and snowshoeing. Mountain biking and snowmobiling are banned in wilderness areas but are permitted in the national forests.

You can stay in your car (not recommended) and still take in more mountain panoramas, wildlife sightings, wildflowers and frisking rivers than memory can hold. Scenic Byways enhance driving adventures.

The region is fairly bursting with historic sites. I admit it: I'm a history buff. Maybe that explains why Gold West Country is one of my favorite places.

■ History

Promoters characterize Gold West Country as the place where Montana began. In a sense, that's true. Gold and other minerals jump-started the state as we know it today. Montana's first territorial capital was at **Bannack**, the state's pioneering gold rush town.

For centuries, these mountains, valleys and plains supported a thriving Native culture. Lewis and Clark's 1805-06 expedition opened the region to white exploration. Beaver thronged the rivers and creeks, attracting legendary fur trappers and traders.

Modern Montana was born in 1858, when brothers James and Granville Stuart saw the glint of gold in placer deposits at **Gold Creek**, east of present-day Drummond.

The trio couldn't have had a clue to the ramifications of their find. But then, the site never amounted to much. The big rush occurred four years later when one John White found sizeable deposits of placer gold on **Grasshopper Creek**, northwest of present-day Dillon. The hell's-a-poppin' town that sprang up on the site came to be called Bannack.

Bannack might have seemed a mite unsuitable as the seat of the spanking new Territory of Montana, what with scandalous goings-on such as the Plummer Gang robbing and murdering wayfarers. However, Bannack's lack of civilizing influences was typical of that rip roaring era. Given the no-holds-barred political climate of the day (and for many a day well into the 20th century), Bannack's elevation to territorial capital fit like a wet moccasin.

Permanence not being a virtue of 19th-century gold towns, the boom soon rolled over Bannack and stampeded on to new and richer digs. It reined up short at **Alder Gulch**, a 14-mile stretch of rich diggin's between the Tobacco Root and Gravelly Ranges discovered by William Fairweather. Diggin's, it was. Here, the gold was underground; not easily panned placer gold. Shafts and tunnels soon honeycombed the gulch, setting a precedent that would be followed in countless mining areas (Butte comes to mind) and sorely scarring the face of Montana.

■ A Miner's Tale

Bill Fairweather, who discovered gold at Alder Gulch, was the quintessential bust-to-boom-to-bust prospector. He worked his Alder Gulch claim for a year or so, becoming quite wealthy. But he had squandered it all by the fall of 1864, when he sold his mining interests. He squandered that money, too. Like many, he came from nowhere and vanished into oblivion. Unlike others, his name lingers in the Fairweather Mining District.

Virginia City, one of several settlements that sprang up along Alder Gulch, became one of the great gold towns of the American West. Now owned by the State of Montana, the town courts visitors. It awaits on MT 287, between Alder and Ennis.

The next big 1864 strike occurred at **Last Chance Gulch**, soon to bear the respectable name of Helena. These gold deposits proved to be the most extensive in the territory, producing some $19 million over the next four years. The seat of Montana's political life soon shifted north to Helena, with that city serving as territorial capital until 1894, when it won state capital status.

The Plummer Gang

The Plummer Gang was synonomous with lawlessness in Montana's gold country. A restless population of gold-hungry men plunked down in a raw and remote territory out of the federal government's reach provided the perfect set-up for violent gangs of road agents. Henry Plummer seized the opportunity. From mid-1862 through 1863, travelers put their lives on the line. It's estimated that the Plummer Gang murdered over 100 people.

The scion of a respectable Eastern family, Plummer's charm and intelligence masked a psychotic viciousness. He left a trail of lawlessness in California, Nevada and Idaho before lighting out for Bannack and enlisting a band of equally depraved cohorts. It was a cinch to conceal a criminal trail in those days of slow travel through rough country. So it was that Plummer charmed his way into being elected sheriff of Bannack. His authority soon extended to the fledgling Virginia City. As sheriff, he received advance knowledge of gold shipments and lucrative stagecoach runs – knowledge he passed on to henchmen who waylayed the wagons and coaches. Few passengers lived to identify the culprits.

Bannack-Virginia City folk were slow to react. Basically a transient population anxious to make money and leave, they did nothing until late 1863 when young Nicholas Thiebalt was brutally murdered. A posse organized by the youth's friends apprehended George Ives, a Plummer cohort, and promptly hanged him after a quick trial. Feeling ran high after that, and a vigilante committee of some 2,000 men was organized. The vigilantes soon apprehended gang member Erastus "Red" Yeager. Determined not to go to the gallows alone, Yeager fingered Plummer. The sheriff was hanged on January 10, 1864. Between January 4 and February 3, the vigilantes hanged 24 men. The Plummer Gang lives in legend.

Perilous Passage: A Narrative of the Montana Gold Rush, 1862-1863 by Edwin Ruthven Purple (see *Bibliography*) is a first-person account of life in Bannack City. Purple describes his journey from Salt Lake City to Bannack over the trail that would become known as the Corinne Road, and recounts his experiences during the heyday of the Plummer Gang.

The starting gate for Montana's headlong race into the mining age stood wide open. Taking the bit in their teeth, those early prospectors and their inheritors soon transformed themselves into world-class mining moguls. Out front, neck and neck on the long stretch, galloped William Andrews Clark and Marcus Daly.

In the 1860s, Butte was a marginal gold mining camp. In the 1870s, it enjoyed a flirtation with silver, the metal that then dominated the Montana mining scene. As the digs deepened, it became apparent that the Butte mines were incredibly rich in copper. This, at a time when new technologies were demanding large quantities of copper. Prices shot into the blue Montana sky. One of Butte's biggest investors was an Easterner-cum-Montanan named William Andrews Clark.

In 1882, an Irishman named Marcus Daly located a rich copper vein in the Anaconda, a Butte silver mine. The word was soon out: the Anaconda contained the world's richest bodies of copper sulphate

William Andrews Clark

If Bill Fairweather played the part of the quintessential bust-boom-bust prospector, William Andrews Clark (not to be confused with Captain Clark of Lewis and Clark fame), lived a classic rags-to-riches saga. A spare, shrewd man with cold penetrating eyes, Clark followed the mining frontier to Colorado. He saw that the real money lay in providing services to miners. Clark moved through a variety of ventures, opening a bank in Deer Lodge in 1872 before casting an eye on Butte, only 40 miles away and on the cusp of the copper boom. He invested in a large smelting enterprise.

Almost overnight, and still in his thirties, Clark's banks, mines, smelters and other investments catapulted him into the ranks of the Mountain West's leading capitalists. But that wasn't enough for the egotistical little man. He aspired not only to be Montana's richest man, but its foremost statesman. He bargained without Marcus Daly. Daly, as stocky and gregarious as Clark was spare and tight-lipped, left Ireland for America in the 1850s. He learned hardrock mining at Nevada's Comstock Lode, becoming known as a miner's miner. In 1876, Daly came to Butte to manage the Alice Mine. He obtained an interest in the mine, which he later sold, investing the proceeds in the nearby Anaconda Mine. Backed by the Hearst-Haggin-Tevis syndicate (George Hearst, father of William Randolph Hearst, made his pile in the mines of Park City, Utah), Daly came to control over 100 mines, including the Anaconda, the Homestake Gold Mine in South Dakota and Utah's Ontario Silver Mine – America's largest producers of copper, gold and silver.

Passing the Anaconda off as a non-producer enabled Daly to buy adjoining properties at cheap prices. By 1884, the syndicate had built a massive copper reduction plant and smelter on Warm Springs Creek, 26 miles west of Butte. Here, they built a classic company town: Anaconda. From his lavish hotel, Daly sent tentacles throughout the West, investing in timberlands, coal fields and other enterprises. He established a ranch in the Bitterroot Valley, where he raised race horses and built an imposing mansion (open for tours). To work the mines, smelters and other enterprises, Daly brought in Irishmen, Cornishmen, Germans, Finns, English, Chinese and, by the turn of the century, Italians and Eastern Europeans. Rivalries, based in ethnic neighborhoods, were fierce. These ethnic threads eventually became woven together, forming the foundation of the people who today color the fabric of Gold West Country.

Men as wealthy and politically ambitious as Clark and Daly were bound to be on a collision course. The rivals' sparring kept Montanans entertained for two decades. Time and again, the vainglorious Clark went down in defeat before Daly's wiley maneuvers. But Clark had his revenge. In 1894, a runoff election to determine the site of the new state's capital was held between Butte and Helena. Clark favored Helena, where he had investments and connections. Daly stumped for Anaconda. Missiles flew thick and furious. The Daly forces ridiculed Helena's "social airs." The Clark faction condemned the evils of company towns in general and Anaconda in particular.

Helena won by some 2,000 votes. Clark tasted sweet victory. Daly went down in defeat. Montana moved into the 20th century.

The Anaconda's success set off a mining boom that would dominate Montana's Rocky Mountain Front for decades and still does. With mining came strikes, riots and disasters that rent the fabric of the community and claimed hundreds of lives.

Mining's impact on the environment is incalculable even today. The effects are being cleaned up and covered over even as open pit mining continues and factions wrangle over permitting further exploration. In 1985, Butte and environs were declared the biggest Superfund cleanup site in the country. In 1986, the pumps that kept Butte's giant strip mine dry were turned off and the Berkeley Pit was allowed to fill with toxic waters seeping from a maze of old mine tunnels and shafts. The waters rise steadily year after year, creating a "lake" deep enough to swallow an 80-story building.

Mining is but one chapter in Gold West Country's past. **Lewis and Clark's expedition** had a dramatic impact on much of the region, laying down landmarks you can see today. The Lewis and Clark Trail resembles the meanderings of a confused rabbit seeking a hole. It was here, along these rivers, that members of the Voyage of Discovery forged ahead, backtracked and explored wrong routes before Nez Perce guides led them over the Bitterroots.

There is no Indian reservation in Gold West Country, but these mountains and valleys variously sustained the Shoshone, Flathead and Piegan (Blackfeet) tribes. The Nez Perce (Ne Mee Poo) National Historic Trail traverses a portion of the region. After the August 9, 1877 **Battle of the Big Hole**, Chief Joseph and his people followed the Bitterroots south to Bannock Pass and thence into Idaho. The battle site has been awarded National Battlefield and Nez Perce Historical Park status.

 Nez Perce was the moniker given to the tribe by the French. They called themselves the Ne Mee Poo.

Wherever you might wander in Gold West Country, the dramatic events of yesterday will reach out and grab your attention in ways you will long remember.

■ Landscape

Gold West Country includes some of the most exciting features of the Rocky Mountain West. This up-thrust area's mountain ranges could well argue over which is rockier, steeper and richer in hidden gold and precious stones. Spacious river valleys of great beauty relieve the severity of the northwest-southeast-running ranges.

Through these valleys meander rivers whose names evoke dreams of casting a fly on a sunny day, of gently floating the current. The Madison is famous among anglers. The Beaverhead, Big Hole and Ruby, combining to form the Jefferson near Twin Bridges, are equally, some say more, picturesque.

The Continental Divide slithers through this region like a snake on a bender. Stationed like sentinels along the Divide are Fish Peak and Mounts Howe and Evans, each exceeding 10,000 feet.

Gold West Country is a place of contrasts. Gloriously beautiful mountain meadows under a brilliant blue sky contrast sharply with ugly slag piles surrounding old mining digs. Dazzling Canyon Ferry Lake contrasts tellingly with the poisonous "lake" at the bottom of Butte's Superfund cleanup pit. Higher elevations' thick fir forests provide stunning backdrops for Deer Lodge Valley's rich pastures.

This is a geologist's dreamland. The cataclysmic natural events that took place over millenia and contributed to the formation of the minerals underlying much of this region are of inexhaustible interest to both amateur and professional geologists.

■ Weather

Gold West Country is a rugged place of high mountain passes and sheltered valleys. Summers are warm with occasional valley heat and mountain chill. Winters bring heavy snows and below-freezing temperatures. In the northern portion of the region, occasional warm, dry Chinook winds wafting overland from the Pacific provide a moderating influence.

Spring comes gradually, breaking into glorious bloom by late May or early June. In April, critters holed up for the winter begin to stir, and bears emerge from their dens. But May, even June, can bring snow squalls. August means hot days and cool nights. Autumn's hiatus between summer's heat and winter's snows is one of the pleasantest times of the year. Elk bugle their mating calls. Huckleberries ripen in the warm sunlit days and crisp nights, delighting both bears and humans. By October, the aspen have turned to gold and migrating ducks and geese fly against the intense blue sky.

Expect colder temperatures and heavier snows in the mountains, warmer days and possibly rain in the valleys. Summer thunderstorms ride the mountain peaks, kicking up tantrums.

In areas of sparse vegetation the soil underlying trails and dirt tracks can turn to goo in rainy weather. Trails often cross areas of scree. Rain gear and sturdy hiking boots are essential.

Visualize weather extremes as you pack. That means adding sweatshirts and sweaters to your usual summer gear. Add a windbreaker for winter days when the Chinook blows.

AUTHOR TIP *If you're off on an expedition or bound for a guest ranch, follow the outfitter's clothing suggestions no matter how silly some items may seem from your home perspective. They know what conditions to expect. If you don't receive a clothing list, be sure to ask for one.*

Getting Around

■ Highways & Byways

Getting around in Gold West Country is a delight. Scenic routes and back country byways grace the region like gold necklaces on green velvet. Passenger cars are OK on most of these routes, at least in temperate months. If you have a choice, opt for a 4WD vehicle. You never know when the urge will strike to find out where that iffy US Forest Service road goes.

You'll need a 4WD vehicle for sure to explore the **Big Sheep Creek Backcountry Byway**. This rugged Beaverhead National Forest gravel and dirt road traverses the Tendoy Mountains and the foothills of the Beaverhead Mountains. Head west at the Dell exit off I-15 for a plunge into a West that few realize still exists. The byway ends 60-odd wiggly miles later at MT 324.

The following scenic loops, routes and byways take you through the heart of Gold West Country's pioneering and prospecting past. It takes will power to resist branching off to explore forest roads leading to hidden lakes and trailheads. See *Touring* (page 256) for points of interest along these routes.

The 106-mile **Beaverhead Scenic Loop** begins at MT 278, three miles south of Dillon at I-15 Exit 59. A side road leads to Bannack Ghost Town State Park. The loop crosses Big Hole Pass and swings along the Big Hole River. It joins MT 43 at Wisdom, returning to I-15 at Divide. This is mostly good pavement, in contrast to the shoulderless wonders characteristic of many Montana highways.

The 27-mile **Pioneer Mountains Scenic Backcountry Byway** begins at MT 278 and heads north across the Pioneers, ending at MT 43. The road is mostly gravel as I write, but improvements are in the works. Interpretive signs relate the history of the area.

The 63-mile **Pintler Scenic Route** heads west from Anaconda on MT 1. It swings past Georgetown Lake, created by damming Flint Creek, then descends sharply before following the creek through the Deerlodge National Forest, ending at Drummond and I-90.

The 10- to 12-mile **Beaver Creek Canyon Scenic Route**, over MT 280 east of Helena, affords splendid views of the Missouri River's Beaver Creek Canyon. At York, the route continues on an unimproved road through the Helena National Forest to the edge of the Gates of the Mountains Wilderness.

The region's basic getting-around routes include **I-15**, shooting northward from Idaho over Monida Pass, the historic route from Salt Lake City. The semi-desert scenery along I-15 contrasts bleakly with the scenic treasures over the mountains to the west. The scenery looks up a bit some 20 miles south of the I-90 junction, five miles west of Butte. From Butte, I-15 continues to Helena before heading into Charlie Russell Country and on to Great Falls.

I-90 enters Gold West Country some 12 miles east of Missoula, looking in on Deer Lodge, Anaconda and Butte before heading into Yellowstone Country at Three Forks.

From West Yellowstone, **US 287** follows the Madison River to Ennis, then continues on to meet up with I-90 at Three Forks. From here, US 287 heads for Helena, looking in at Townsend at the foot of Canyon Ferry Lake. This alternative to I-15 affords a pleasant change from expressway driving.

Another pleasant alternative is over **MT 287** linking Ennis and Twin Bridges, passing through Alder Gulch and looking in on the Virginia City and Nevada City ghost towns. **MT 41** heads north from Dillon through Twin Bridges and thence to Butte, affording another interesting alternative route.

West of I-15, **MT 43** follows the Big Hole River to Wisdom. From here, it streaks the 26 miles to Idaho over Chief Joseph Pass, looking in on Big Hole National Battlefield/Nez Perce National Historical Park. **US 12** provides a shortcut between the I-90 exit at Garrison and Helena. It follows the Little Blackfoot River before crossing the Continental Divide over the easy (6,320 feet) MacDonald Pass. At Avon, **MT 141** branches off US 12, heading north to meet east-west **MT 200**. Strung along this route are Potomac, Ovando and Lincoln. All along these alternative routes are small-town throwbacks to an earlier era, historic sites, hot springs, scenic overviews, ghost towns, historic highway markers and other points of interest. Turn to *Touring* (page 256) for descriptions of these and other attractions.

■ Road Watch

Driving in mountain country presents built-in hazards. You don't want to miss a single scenic view, yet you mustn't take your eyes off the road lest you miss a curve or hit a deer. (See *Travel Strategies and Helpful Facts,* page 55, for information on avoiding unwelcome contact between your car and wild animals.)

Most Gold West Country roads are reasonably good; generally well maintained and kept clear of snow and ice. But expect the worst when driving in mountain country, even in summer.

With all the space in Montana, you wouldn't expect the state's road builders to be so stingy with shoulders. Perhaps it's the absence of adequate shoulders, but two-lane roadways also seem extra narrow. Not all roads are so handicapped; some, especially new or improved ones, are quite generous.

Slow-moving vehicles, especially trailers and motorhomes, pose the greatest hazards in the summer months. This is when you and a zillion others throng the roads. Everyone wants to enjoy the scenery. Getting behind an RV lollygagging along at 25 mph when you want to go at least 35 can be terminally frustrating. Resist the urge to pass in no-pass zones or over a solid line.

The best remedies are patience and courtesy. Be patient with the slow pokes; there's scenery enough for all to enjoy. The behemoth will no doubt turn off in time.

If you are the slow one, or are pulling a trailer or driving a motorhome, keep an eye on the traffic behind you. It's a courtesy to turn off when possible to allow other cars to pass if three or more stack up behind you.

Watch out for black ice, especially in early morning if you even think the temperature may have dipped below freezing the night before, or if fog has settled in. Be especially cautious on deeply shaded stretches of roadway.

If you'll be driving in winter, be sure to carry adequate survival gear (see *Clothing & Gear* under *Travel Strategies and Helpful Facts,* page 57). The same goes if you plan to venture onto unimproved forest roads. "Better to be safe than sorry" never held truer meaning.

AUTHOR TIP

The best advice when driving in Gold West Country is to make sure you're prepared, then just relax and enjoy. Leave your stresses at home. Isn't that the reason you chose to vacation in the last best place in the first place?

Information Sources

Getting There

Butte and Helena are served by **Delta Airlines** (☎ 800-221-1212), **Horizon Airline** (☎ 800-547-9308), **Northwest Airlines** (☎ 800-225-2525) and **Sky West Airline** (☎ 800-453-9417).

Greyhound Bus Line: ☎ 800-255-7655 or 406-252-4169.

Gold West Country

On The Road

Montana Highway Patrol, 2550 Prospect Ave., Helena, MT 59620; ☎ 406-444-7696.

Montana Road Condition Report: ☎ 800-226-7623, TTY ☎ 800-335-7592, CB'ers: Emergency Channel 9. Helena: ☎ 406-444-6354. Butte: ☎ 406-586-1313.

Weather Conditions: Statewide: ☎ 800-332-6171 or 406-444-6339. Helena: ☎ 406-443-5151.

Montana Ski Reports and Travel Information: ☎ 800-VISIT-MT, ext. 3WG outside Montana or 406-444-2654.

Car Rentals

Anaconda

Payless Car Rental: ☎ 406-563-5256.

Butte

Avis Rent-A-Car: ☎ 406-388-6414.
Budget Rent-A-Car of Butte: ☎ 800-527-0700 or 406-494-7573.
Enterprise Rent-A-Car: ☎ 406-494-1900.
Hertz Rent-A-Car: ☎ 406-782-1054.
Payless Car Rental: ☎ 406-723-4366.

Dillon

Paul's Motor Company: ☎ 406-683-2371.

Helena

Allstar: ☎ 800-722-4485 or 406-443-7436.
Avis Rent-A-Car: ☎ 800-331-1212 or 406-442-4440.
Enterprise Rent-A-Car: ☎ 800-RENTACAR or 406-449-3400.
Hertz Rent-A-Car: ☎ 406-449-4167.
National Car Rental: ☎ 406-442-8620.
Rent A Wreck: ☎ 406-443-3635.

Tourism Offices

Travel Montana, Department of Commerce, PO Box 200533 (1424 9th Ave., Helena, MT 59620-0533; ☎ 800-847-4868 outside Montana, 406-444-2654 in Montana. Internet http://travel.mt.gov/.

Gold West Country Tourism Office, 1155 Main, Deer Lodge, MT 59722; ☎ 406-846-1943.

Chambers of Commerce

Anaconda, 306 E. Park, Anaconda, MT 59711; ☎ 406-563-2400.
Butte-Silver Bow, 2950 Harrison Ave., Butte, MT 59701; ☎ 800-735-6814 or 406-494-5595.

Deer Lodge, 1171 Main, Deer Lodge, MT 59722; ☎ 406-846-2094.

Dillon, PO Box 425, Dillon, MT 59725; ☎ 406-683-5511.

Ennis, PO Box 291, Ennis, MT 59729; ☎ 406-682-4388. Helena, 201 E. Lyndale, Helena, MT 59601; ☎ 406-442-4120.

Lincoln, PO Box 985, Lincoln, MT 59639; ☎ 406-362-4966.

Philipsburg, PO Box 661, Phillipsburg, MT 59858; ☎ 406-859-3388.

Townsend, PO Box 947, Townsend, MT 59644; ☎ 406-266-3176.

Virginia City, PO Box 947, Virginia City, MT 59755; ☎ 800-648-7588 or 406-843-5377.

Outdoors Associations

Adventure Cycling Association, Box 8308, Missoula, MT 59807; ☎ 406-721-1776. Fax 406-721-8754.

Fishing Outfitters Association of Montana (FOAM), Box 67, Gallatin Gateway, MT 59730; ☎ 406-763-5436.

Montana Outfitters & Guides Association, Box 1248, Helena, MT 59624; ☎ 406-449-3578. Fax 406-443-2439.

Montana Snowmobile Association, PO Box 3202, Great Falls, MT 59403. Montana Wilderness Association, Box 635, Helena, MT 59624; ☎ 406-443-7350.

Government Agencies

Montana Department of Fish, Wildlife & Parks, 1420 E. Sixth Ave., Helena, MT 59620; ☎ 406-444-2535. Fax 406-444-4952. TDD ☎ 406-444-1200. **Bureau of Land Management: Butte District Office & Headwaters Resource Area**, PO Box 3388 (106 N. Parkmont), Butte, MT 59702-3388; ☎ 406-494-5059.

Bureau of Land Management, Dillon Resource Area, 1005 Selway Dr., Dillon, MT 59725; ☎ 406-683-2337.

USDA Forest Service, Northern Region, PO Box 7669, Missoula, MT 59807; ☎ 406-329-3511.

Beaverhead National Forest Supervisor's Office, 420 Barrett St., Dillon, MT 59725; ☎ 406-683-3900. 24-hour information: ☎ 406-683-3913.

Beaverhead National Forest, Madison Ranger District, 5 Forest Service Road, Ennis, MT 59729; ☎ 406-682-4253.

Beaverhead National Forest, Wisdom Ranger District, PO Box 238, Wisdom, MT 59761; ☎ 406-689-3243.

Beaverhead National Forest, Wise River Ranger District, Box 100, Wise River, MT 59762; ☎ 406-832-3178.

Deerlodge National Forest Supervisor's Office, PO Box 400 (Federal Building, 200 E. Broadway), Butte, MT 59703; ☎ 406-496-3400.

Deerlodge National Forest, Butte Ranger District, 1820 Meadowlark, Butte, MT 59701; ☎ 406-494-2147.

Deerlodge National Forest, Deer Lodge Ranger District, #1 Hollenback Rd., Deer Lodge, MT 59722; ☎ 406-846-1770.

Gold West Country

Deerlodge National Forest, Jefferson Ranger District, 3 Whitetail Rd., Whitehall, MT 59759; ☎ 406-287-3223.

Deerlodge National Forest, Philipsburg Ranger District, PO Box H, Philipsburg, MT 59858; ☎ 406-859-3211.

Helena National Forest Supervisor's Office, 2880 Skyway Dr., Helena, MT 59601; ☎ 406-449-5201.

Helena National Forest, Helena Ranger District, 2001 Poplar St., Helena, MT 59601; ☎ 406-449-5490.

Helena National Forest, Lincoln Ranger District, PO Box 219, Lincoln, MT 59639; ☎ 406-362-4265.

Helena National Forest, Townsend Ranger District, 415 South Front, Townsend, MT 59644; ☎ 406-266-3425.

Lolo National Forest Supervisor's Office, Building 24, Fort Missoula, Missoula, MT 59804; ☎ 406-329-3750. The Missoula Ranger District is also at this address.

US Geological Survey, Federal Center, Box 25286, Denver, CO 80225; ☎ 800-435-7627 or 303-202-4700.

Touring

Gold West Country defies a one gulp approach. This book divides the region into thirds for touring purposes, using Interstates 15 and 90 as parameters.

■ Madison, Jefferson & Beaverhead Valleys

The rough triangle east of I-15 and south of I-90 abuts Yellowstone Country. This includes two sections of the Lee Metcalf Wilderness, three pockets of the Beaverhead National Forest and part of the Deerlodge National Forest. A portion of the Madison Range and all of the Gravelly and Tobacco Root Mountains lie within this area scored by the Madison, Jefferson and Beaverhead Valleys.

Watch for historic highway markers while traveling through this country. Lewis and Clark passed this way. And it was the tromping ground of crusty characters like the well-traveled Jim Bridger. Long-gone mining towns also sprang up here. Numerous "it happened here" signs put this rich history into perspective.

US 287

US 287 enters Gold West Country at Quake Lake and follows the river through the gentle Madison River Valley. The fir-clad slopes of the

Gravellys rise steeply across the river. On the east, the peaks of the Lee Metcalf Wilderness lord it over the valley. Fishing access and camp sites line the river for some 25 miles. The valley widens out to embrace some of the finest grazing land you'd ever hope to see.

> *Coming onto the highway from a river access one Sunday afternoon in June, I met up with a bunch of ranch hands driving cattle to summer pasture. I'm no stranger to cattle drives, having participated in many in my family's stock raising days. But the thrill is undeniable. Cattle low, mounted cowboys dart to and fro, horses whinny, cars and trucks stack up, Camera-aiming tourists sprout from car windows. I feel let down once the cattlejam has sorted itself out and traffic again begins to move.*

Ennis

KID-FRIENDLY After another 15 miles or so, ranchettes, harbingers of Montana's takeover by outlanders, begin to crown the foot-hills. You zip through **Cameron**, an old cattle town with new fly fishing pretensions. A sign reading, "660 People, 110,000 Trout" announces Ennis. Fishing Access signs point every which way. It doesn't take a crystal ball to gather that Ennis is a flourishing fly fishing center. The Lions Club Park, on the river at the south end of town, even has a just-for-kids fishing pond.

Ennis began as a cattle town and still hypes itself as the quintessential Western town. Main Street's tidy shopping block reflects this collision of fish and cows by way of false fronts over trendy eateries and shops hawking antique creels and rods with price tags steep enough to scare a cowboy back into the hills.

Smack in the middle of the block is a hilarious tableau by metals artist Jim Dolan titled **"A Wreck Waiting to Happen."** Larger-than-life Cowboy Jake has dismounted to adjust the ropes tying an elk hindquarter and rack on his pack horse. Behind him, his wall-eyed saddle horse is fixin' to spook at a cub running toward an approaching mama bear. You fill in the rest.

By way of evening things out, a way-larger-than-life statue of a man fly fishing stands at the intersection of US 287 and MT 287. Proximity to a blue ribbon fly fishing stream, two national forests, the Lee Metcalf Wilderness, and the Virginia City/Nevada City ghost towns has given little Ennis a big reputation. Fair weather outlanders are clearly pushing the limits. Pleasant digs and better-than-most restaurants are easily come by here.

Leaving Ennis, you're faced with a choice: swing west to gander at Montana's most highly hyped ghost towns, or continue north on US 287 to Lewis & Clark Caverns State Park, detouring to the Beartrap Canyon Wilderness en route.

A toss of a coin comes up north. Stay tuned for another route to Virginia and Nevada Cities. Take a right turn on MT 84 at Norris. Drive eight miles to the Madison River bridge. The Beartrap Canyon trailhead is three miles down a gravel road. See *Adventures on Foot* (page 282) for hiking information.

Lewis & Clark Caverns

Lewis & Clark Caverns is a must-do place that belongs on every visitor's list. Touristy, it's not. The caverns tour is too rigorous for that. The park is off US 287 on MT 2. Watch for signs. Ironically, the explorers never saw these caverns, carved in a mountain by geologic forces. Their expedition passed below the site on the Jefferson River in 1805, but had no idea that the caverns existed. Discovery came in 1892 when ranchers Tom Williams and Bert Pannell stumbled on the entrance. Williams and investor Dan Morrison installed 2,000 wooden stairs inside the caves and launched an advertizing campaign. Ownership was later assumed by the Northern Pacific Railroad, which deeded the property to the Federal Government. In 1937, the State of Montana assumed control. The 3,000-acre park includes hiking trails, picnic sites and a grassy campground (see *Adventures on Foot* and *Camping*). The visitor center near the park's entrance has informative exhibits. The caverns parking area, at the top of a steep paved road, includes a small restaurant and shop. Guided tours leave at roughly one-hour intervals between May 1 and Sept. 30. Expect to pay day-use and tour fees. ☎ 406-287-3541 for more information.

The steep one-mile uphill walk to the cave entrance offers wide-angle views of the distant Tobacco Root Mountains. Threading through the caverns' various chambers for about a mile, descending 600 stairs, crouching or scooting on your rump through at least one tight spot, is an adventure not to be missed. You'll pass a fantastic array of speleotherms, dripstones, flowstones, stalactites, helictites and other eerie formations caused by water dripping through limestone. After touring the Caverns, you can continue on MT 2 to tiny **Cardwell**, birthplace of Chet Huntley, TV newscaster and a developer of Big Sky Resort. From here, a detour via MT 359 runs through gold country. **Pony** is sort a of town, sort of gold camp that's been active for some 80 years but has never quite hit pay dirt. However, millions of dollars in minerals have been taken from the nearby **ghost towns** of Strawberry, Clipper, Crystal and Boss Tweed.

Whitehall

Continue on to Whitehall, at the junction of MT 2 and 55. This railroad town is where Chet Huntley grew up and attended school. A pleasant park parallels the tracks. The **Jefferson Valley Museum**, housed in a c.1914 dairy barn at 303 S. Division, is the repository of numerous artifacts and photographs related to the history of the Jefferson Valley. Free admission. Open Memorial Day-Labor Day, 1-4.

Twin Bridges

MT 55 cruises picturesquely alongside the Jefferson River to Twin Bridges, merging with MT 41 about half-way. This town also lives by fly fishing. And why not? The Ruby, Beaverhead and Big Hole Rivers flow into the Jefferson nearby, and the R.L. Winston Rod Company is headquartered here. Some of the town's false front buildings sport fine murals, reinforcing the dusty frontier town ambience. A grassy park on MT 41 south of town invites picnicking.

The Beaverhead Valley

From Twin Bridges, MT 41 lazes through the broad, fruitful Beaverhead Valley to Dillon. Log barns and jackstay fences (the ones that look like this: xxxxx with —— crosspieces) punctuate the valley. Lewis and Clark were much taken with this valley as they traversed it in August, 1805. About half-way, **Beaverhead Rock** looms across the river, though it's difficult to spot. Sacajawea recognized the landmark as the Beaver's Head, a site long known to her people. Watch for an interpretive sign.

We'll save Dillon for the chunk of Gold West Country west of I-15 and south of I-90. Now it's back to MT 287 and a visit to Montana's most over-hyped ghost towns.

MT 287 parallels the Ruby River between Twin Bridges and **Alder**, the center of a talc mining operation. Scenic, Alder isn't. On the way, just south of tiny Sheridan, you might watch for the **Robber's Roost** highway marker. It's private property now, but you can read about the ribald goings-on in olden days and gawk at the former Robbers Roost road house from a turnout.

At Alder, you can pick up MT 357 for the short jaunt to **Ruby River Reservoir**, a water-filled hole surrounded by uninspiring hills (see *Rock Hounding*, page 291).

At Alder, MT 287 swings east along mine tailings-lined **Alder Gulch**. The entire gulch was once thronged with prospectors bent on striking it rich. The hubs of activity were two hellroaring towns spaced a mile apart: Nevada City and Virginia City. Prospecting for tourist gold is the main activity today.

Nevada City

These towns are emphatically not ghost towns in the classic sense. Postpone your dreams of rummaging among abandoned mining-era artifacts. Anything left lying about has long since been picked over. At first glance, Nevada City approaches the classic ghost town image. A clutch of weathered structures invites exploration – for a fee. It turns out that most of

Nevada City ghost town.

these structures, each of which might claim integrity in another setting, were brought to the site by the late Charles Bovey. There's no denying that Bovey performed a valuable service by preserving these old mining shacks and such, but ghost town purists will be disappointed. The townsite was recently purchased by the State of Montana.

Nevada City was built on the creek, below the town's present location. Most of the original buildings fell victim to gold dredges chewing up the creek bottom. A few domiciles eluded the dredges and are included in Bovey's collection. Known as the music man of Alder Gulch, Bovey also collected mechanical music machines. These gaudy reminders of another age are on display. The near absence of shops and such boosts Nevada City's integrity.

A mining museum and gift shop on the eastern edge of Nevada City has a gold dredge on display. You're invited to pan for gold and garnets in sluice boxes set up outside.

Virginia City

Nevada City never could hold a miner's candle to Virginia City. Also owned by the State of Montana, this unghostly ghost town boasts upwards of 100 early structures, many solidly built of stone. The town is of tremendous historic interest, but the touristy atmosphere makes it hard to put the historic angle in perspective. All sorts of riotous goings-on occurred here, not the least of which was the hanging of 32 Plummer Gang varmints over a period of four months.

Town boosters won't let you forget that Virginia City was the site of the second territorial capital, Bannack being the first. Virginia City remains a county seat. Summer weekends bring throngs of visitors to tour the museums, browse the shops and snooze in the old Fairweather Inn or the attendant miners' cabins.

KID-FRIENDLY Hop aboard **Fred Zweifel's 1941 fire engine** for an informative tour of the town. Some of Zweifel's did-you-know facts: Virginia City was a Confederate town, having been settled largely by disaffected Southerners after the Civil War. One third of the original town still stands. In its heyday, Virginia City had three breweries and 76 licensed liquor dealers. Upwards of 25,000 miners worked 100-foot-wide claims along Alder Creek. Some 148 persons, none of them ghosts, live here year-round.

■ West of I-15 & South of I-90

If you descend into Montana on I-15 over Monida Pass, you may well wonder what all the "last best place" fuss is about. Where are the towering mountains, the forests?

Monida town is a cluster of structures huddled together as if for warmth. At Monida, you can hang a right on MT 509, a gravel road leading to the Red Rocks Lakes National Wildlife Refuge (see *Wildlife Watching*, page 316). The road comes out on US 20 in Idaho. It can be dicey going in wet or snowy weather.

North of Monida, the Interstate passes through sere hills and grazing lands strewn with cows. Every five to seven miles, a straggly town arranges itself between the railroad and the shallow Red Rock River. Lima and Dell are the largest, and that's being generous.

Lima & Dell

Lima has the distinction of having been Montana's first railroad town. Little evidence of that left now, but the cemetery's elaborate Victorian-era tombstones are worth a look-see if you're so inclined. Dell resembles an abandoned Western movie set, but there's more going on here than meets the eye. The glaringly white **Red Rock Inn & Lounge**, visible from the Interstate as the largest building in town, was the cowboy-era Dell Hotel. The former Dell Schoolhouse houses **Yesterday's Café-A**, one of Dillon's favorite eateries. Turn into the Dell-Redrock Rest Area to read a tongue-in-cheek historic sign thick with humor.

From Dell, pick up gravel Forest Service Road #302, the **Big Sheep Creek Road**, for a scenic jaunt into the Beaverhead National Forest. This is where a 4WD vehicle earns its keep.

The Red Rock River empties into **Clark Canyon Reservoir** and the Beaverhead River flows northward beneath the dam. Surrounded by piney hills, it's a popular boating and fishing lake. MT 324 heads west across the head of the reservoir to the small town of Grant and pretty much nowhere else unless you count a maze of creeks and gullies. A gravel road heads north to Bannack Ghost Town from Grant, but a smoother route leads west from Dillon.

Dillon

Dillon, the Beaverhead County seat and a major trading center for area ranches, is a prosperous town of over 4,500 residents. I always enjoy visiting Dillon, possibly because it's a straightforward no-frills kind of place. South of downtown, **Montana Western College**'s extravagant Italianate Rennaisance pile dominates a neighborhood of modest well-kept homes. The college features an art gallery and the **Seidensticker Wildlife Collection**. ☎ 406-683-7011 for current hours.

Ranches were well established in the Beaverhead Valley by 1880, when the Utah and Northern Railroad pushed through from Monida Pass. The sleepy settlement of Black Tail grew into a humming railroad terminus dubbed Dillon in honor of Sidney Dillon, president of the Union Pacific Railroad. At one time, Dillon was the largest wool shipping point in Montana. The town still has a frontier feel to it, although cars have replaced buckboards.

The venerable brick **Hotel Metlen** still dominates Railroad Avenue. Skip across the tracks to the former railway station in Depot Park. Here you'll find the **Dillon Information Center**, the **Beaverhead County Museum** and the **Old Depot Theatre**. The boardwalk leading to the entrance sports the registered brands of area ranches. The museum displays a fascinating collection of historical oddments; even a stump on which the infamous Henry Plummer is said to have carved his name in 1862. ☎ 406-683-5511 for current hours.

If you look at a Montana Road Map, you'll see that I-15, Hwy. 278 and MT 43 encircle the Pioneer Mountains northwest of Dillon. Within this circle, and branching outward from it, is a passel of adventures waiting to happen. There's little of interest on the I-15 leg until you come to the **Humbug Spires Primitive Area** some 27 miles north of Dillon at Exit 99. See *Adventures on Foot* and *Rock Climbing*, pages 282 and 289. Forest Service roads lead into the Area.

Bannack

Pick up Hwy. 278 three miles south of Dillon at Exit 50 for a romp into the past. First stop is storied Bannack, huddled above Grasshopper Creek. A sign points the way down a gravel road. Arguably Montana's most significant historical landmark, Bannack is preserved in a state of arrested decay. **Bannack State Park** encompasses the townsite and the adjacent riparian area.

This is a ghost town in the raw. Not a shop in sight, unless you count the small visitor center, which also sells books.

In its heyday, Bannack sprawled across the creek and was divided along partisan lines: Yankees above the creek, Confederates below. Rebel town has long since fallen victim to dredges. The fast-running creek has covered over the tailings. Today, the creek bottom is a haven for elk, deer and songbirds.

DID YOU KNOW? *Two primitive creekside campgrounds are named Road Agent and Vigilante for the nefarious Plummer Gang and the vigilantes who brought it down.*

There's much more to Bannack than the history books tell us: Montana's first major gold strike in 1862, first Territorial Capital, headquarters of the Plummer Gang. Real people lived and worked here for almost 100 years. Sure, the gold strike fever abated with the discovery of richer digs. After that, the town sort of waxed and waned. In the 1930s, several Depression-bit families moved into abandoned houses. The school hung on until 1951, three years before the state took over.

Some 50 original structures remain: the once-posh Hotel Meade, the modest homes of the territorial governor and the town doctor, the sturdy building that housed the Masonic Lodge upstairs over the school, the tumbledown jail. Interspersed among these are simple prospectors' cabins. The gallows, a replica of the original, stands near the hilltop cemetery.

You won't find bits and pieces of the past to pick up, but you will carry home memories of an unvarnished ghost town. No one resides here now save a few park employees and a host of ghosts. The cabins stand empty, wallpaper hanging from the walls in strips, bits of linoleum showing through the grime.

Keeping Up a Ghost Town

Maintaining a structure in a state of arrested decay is not easy. It must be kept from falling down, but it mustn't be fancied up. I came upon a crew shoring up a cabin on Bachelor's Row. There was much head-scratching over how to accomplish this without compromising the structure's integrity. The usual procedure is to brace the cabin with planks, dig out the rotted lower logs and replace the sills with new wood.

Bannack is open year-round, 7-9 in summer and 8-5 the balance of the year. Call ahead for winter road conditions. Guided tours are offered in summer, but you can take a self-guided tour anytime. The visitor center

Gold West Country

Bannack State Park, west of Dillon.

has interpretive displays and historic videos. **Bannack Days**, held the third weekend in July, flushes out the ghosts. See *Festivals & Special Events,* page 325.

You're faced with a choice a few miles west of the Bannack turnoff: swing north on the Pioneer Mountains Scenic Byway or continue west to Wisdom and the Big Hole Valley.

Pioneer Mountains Scenic Byway

The Scenic Byway cuts through the Pioneer Mountains for over 40 miles, traversing ranch lands, mountain meadows, willow bottoms and lodgepole pine forests. At this writing, the road is paved between Elkhorn Hot Springs and the town of Wise River, gravelled between the Hwy. 278 turnoff and the hot springs. However, improvements are under way. The Byway is closed in winter north of Maverick Mountain Ski Area, but open to snowmobiles (see *Adventures on Snow*). There are several Forest Service campgrounds and trailheads along the way (see *Adventures on Foot*). **Maverick Mountain** and **Elkhorn Hot Springs** are in convenient proximity. Don't expect much at the hot springs save outdoor thermal hot springs pools for year-round soaking. A bit farther on is famed **Crystal Park** where you can dig for quartz crystals and amethysts (see *Rock Hounding*, page 272).

The divide between Grasshopper Creek and the Wise River is at 7,800 feet, high enough to assure great views. The narrow guage Montana Southern Railway once rumbled down the divide from the old Elkhorn Mine. You can still make out the railroad bed. Forest Road #2465 branches from the Byway to a trail leading to the site of Coolidge, the town that grew up around the Elkhorn Mine.

The **Wise River** rises in the Pioneers and enjoys a 28-mile tumble to the Big Hole River at the town of Wise River.

DID YOU KNOW?

It's been said that, per mile, there are more campgrounds along this river than any river in Montana; beaver dams, too. The Byway follows the river to the town bearing its name.

If you approach the Scenic Byway from Wise River instead of from Hwy. 278, you can circle the Pioneers, crossing Big Hole Pass into the famed **Big Hole Valley**. The valley owes it's fame to a trio of strange bedfellows: the Blue Ribbon Big Hole River, an unusual way of putting up hay, and the Big Hole National Battlefield-Nez Perce National Historical Park.

West of the pass is Jackson, a bump on the valley floor made notable by **Jackson Hot Springs Lodge**. This place, boasting mineral baths and an indoor pool, seems to have been discovered by the Harley-Davidson bunch.

The **Big Hole River** (variously spelled "Big Hole" and "Bighole") rises in Skinner Lake, in the Beaverhead National Forest south of Jackson. It flows northward through Wisdom, hangs a right below Alder Peak and rolls past Wise River to join the Beaverhead below Twin Bridges. Many anglers consider the Big Hole to be among the best.

Wisdom, at the junction of Hwy. 278 and MT 43, projects a frontier image reinforced by modest log dwellings. In the old days, if a man applying for a haying job in, say, the Deer Lodge Valley, claimed to have helped put up hay near Wisdom, he'd be a shoo-in for the job.

Land of 10,000 Haystacks

The Big Hole Valley has been dubbed "Land of 10,000 Haystacks" for good reason. The nutritious wild hay growing here is legendary. Modern balers are not for these ranchers. For decades, they've stacked hay by way of beaverslides, tall flat contraptions resembling a cross between a catapult and a ladder on steroids. A large rake piled with hay is run up the beaverslide. The hay is then dumped onto the stack. Side gates keep the stack in a neat pile, making it possible for it to reach impressive heights. Tractor or truck power take-offs are generally in use today, but you may see a few ranches using traditional horse teams to lift the rake. Keep your eyes peeled if you travel through this valley in July or August.

Big Hole National Battlefield-
Nez Perce National Historical Park

At Wisdom, head west on MT 43 through the heart of the valley. The towering peaks of the Bitterroot Range, sheltering the valley on the west, seem to beckon like silent sirens. After 26 miles, you'll be there, climbing 7,264-foot Chief Joseph Pass to meet US 93 in Glacier Country. Well short of that, you'll come to Big Hole National Battlefield-Nez Perce National Historical Park.

Gold West Country

The Battle at Big Hole

The Big Hole Valley afforded a pleasant, well-watered area where Indians liked to camp in summer, digging roots and hunting. So, it was a logical place for Nez Perce Chiefs Joseph and Looking Glass to rest their people and horses after being on the run for over two months. The party was a sizeable one, consisting of some 135 warriors, 665 women, children and old men, and 2,000 horses. The five Nez Perce bands had left their sacred homeland in Oregon's Wallowa country in June, 1877. Most Nez Perce had signed an 1863 treaty assigning these lands to the US Government and establishing a reservation in Idaho. Chief Joseph, the "people's chief," refused to sign. Five non-treaty bands remained in the Wallowas. In mid-May, 1877, Gen. Oliver O. Howard gave them 30 days to move onto the reservation. Instead, they chose to travel to Montana where they hoped their old allies, the Crows, would give them shelter. They only wanted to be left alone.

Following several skirmishes in Idaho, the band crossed the Bitterroots over the Lolo Trail with Gen. Howard and his 7th Infantry in persuit. They headed south, pausing in the Big Hole Valley. The women set up their tipis on the North Fork of the Big Hole River on August 7th. The chiefs failed to post guards, thinking Gen. Howard was too far behind to pose an immediate threat. They were unaware that Col. John Gibbon was advancing up the Bitterroot Valley with 162 men. The army attacked the sleeping village before dawn the next day. Men, women and children were shot indiscriminately. The battle continued for two days and nights as "warrior chief" Looking Glass directed his warriors to cover the escape of the surviving women and children.

Military losses included 29 dead and 40 wounded. Some 90 Nez Perce were killed, two thirds of them women, children and old men. Countless others were wounded. Escaping in confusion carrying their wounded, they left many essential items behind.

Depending on your perspective, a visit to the Battlefield and Historical Park can be sobering. For me, it was an emotional experience, empathizing as I do with the peoples' grief and desperation. Other visitors seemed to be caught up in the tactical aspects of the battle.

The Visitor Center museum displays photographs and personal belongings of some of the participants. A video offers insight into the Nez Perce and describes the events. In front of windows affording a wide-angle view of the encampment and battleground, a Park Service representative discusses the massacre/battle and answers questions. You can tour the Nez Perce Camp, considered Sacred Ground symbolizing the strength and spirit of the Nez Perce people. You can also tour the seige area where the soldiers dug in and the site where warriors captured Gibbon's howitzer.

The Big Hole National Battlefield-Nez Perce National Historical Park is open year-round from 8-5 with extended hours in summer. ☎ 406-689-3155.

MT 43

MT 43 heads north at Wisdom, closely following the Big Hole River through Wise River, meeting I-15 at **Divide**. This is one of Gold West Country's most beautiful drives. On your left, the Continental Divide tops the Anaconda-Pintler Wilderness across the narrowing valley. On your right, the forested slopes of the Pioneer Mountains rise abruptly above the deep-flowing river. Numerous fishing access sites line the river.

The small town of Wise River, at the northern end of the Pioneer Mountains Scenic Byway, welcomes anglers and has become somewhat of a mecca for same. Divide is unremarkable save as a fill-'er-up station on I-15.

About 11 miles short of Wise River, Hwy. 273 streaks northward to Anaconda. The 22-mile shortcut is favored by Anaconda anglers. You can also reach Anaconda by traveling north on I-15, then swinging west on I-90.

The latter route offers more direct access to **Fairmont Hot Springs**. The venerable hot springs is at the center of a flossy resort complex having indoor and outdoor swimming pools and a wildlife enclosure. The outdoor pool is distinguished by the mother of all tubular water slides. You may consider the splashy ride worth the steep $20 price. Take I-90 Exit 211. ☎ 800-332-3272 or 406-797-3241.

Anaconda

You'll see the **Anaconda Smelter Stack** well before the city by that name. Aside from enormous slag piles, the 585-foot brick stack is all that remains of the Washoe Smelter, at one time the world's largest nonferrous copper smelter. Because it's a super-fund clean-up site, you must view the stack from a distance.

Anaconda was the quintessential company town. Neatly laid out streets lined with modest homes attest to that. You can get a fix on the town at the visitor center, housed in a replica of the original railway station at 306 E. Park Street. ☎ 406-563-2400 for current hours. **The Copper Village Museum and Arts Center** in the old City Hall Building includes an art gallery offering changing exhibits. ☎ 406-563-2422 for current hours. The basement museum is presided over by curator and historical consultant Jerry Hansen, who enjoys giving visitors personal tours highlighting Anaconda's dramatic history. The museum is open Tues.-Sat., 1-4 pm.

Gold West Country

The Pintler Scenic Highway

The 63-mile Pintler Scenic Highway, over MT 1 between Anaconda and Drummond at I-90, is another of those strikingly beautiful drives that you'd swear is the best – until you come upon the next one. Montana is like that.

The drive breaks you in easy, heading west from Anaconda along Warm Springs Creek. The climb to Georgetown Lakes culminates in a heavily forested area enwrapping three lakes heading Flint Creek. A bunch of Forest Service campgrounds attests to their popularity.

AUTHOR TIP *Warning: the campgrounds can be crowded to the max on summer weekends. I made that discovery late on a Friday evening in June. Campgrounds full, I plummeted down-mountain, not knowing whether to be more intimidated by the steep descent or awed by the beauty of the valley opening up before me. At the bottom of the mountain, I saw the **Flint Creek Campground** sign. A dirt road strung with campsites leads along the burbling creek for a couple of miles. The campground was almost empty; and it was free.*

Just north of the campground is the eastern end of the 54-mile paved and dirt **Skalkaho Road** leading over the pass by that name to Hamilton. It's closed to all but snowmobiles in winter.

Phillipsburg

Phillipsburg is the queen of the 26-mile Flint Creek Valley. A historic silver mining camp that hung on through thick and thin, the hillside town has landed itself on tourism maps by restoring its handsome old structures. The two business blocks are a sight to see. Phillipsburg earned a state tourism award for its storefronts painted in authentic Victorian-era colors. Prominent among the shops and eateries is the **Sapphire Gallery**, featuring gems mined at the nearby Rock Creek Mine and in the Sapphire Mountains. A backdrop of pines cinches Phillipsburg's charm.

The **Granite County Museum & Cultural Center**, at 155 S. Sansome, offers insight into area mining with a miner's cabin, an assay office and mine tunnel. Tours provided. ☎ 406-859-3020 for current hours. You'll need a 4WD vehicle to reach **Granite Ghost Town**, a day-use state park in the Flint Creek Range some five miles southeast of Phillipsburg. Not much here; only memories, the superintendent's house, and the ruins of the old miners' union hall. ☎ 406-542-5500 for road conditions.

The balance of the scenic route follows Flint Creek for several idyllic miles. A stubby grain elevator in the small town of **Hall** attests to the valley's grain growing capacity. Flint Creek empties into the Clark Fork

River at **Drummond**, named for an area trapper. It's easy to imagine the rich trove of beaver that this mountain man trapped from the creek and the river.

From Drummond, I-90 swings westward into Glacier Country and eastward along the Clark Fork River into the fabled Deer Lodge Valley.

■ North of I-90

I-90's swing along the Clark Fork River into the Deer Lodge Valley is a visual treat. Twelve miles east of Drummond at Gold Creek, a gravel road leads to the ruins of **Pioneer**. The site of Montana's first gold strike, this Gold Creek placer mining camp was abandoned in favor of the far richer Bannack digs.

The Interstate chases the river southward from the old railroad town of **Garrison**. From here, you can shortcut east to Helena via US 12 over the Continental Divide at MacDonald Pass.

The Deer Lodge Valley

Indians knew the Deer Lodge Valley as "the Lodge of the White-tailed Deer" long before a canny cattle dealer named Johnny Grant made it one of the first of Montana's verdant valleys to sustain cattle. The valley fattened many a broken-down cow on nutritious native grasses. Today, those grasses have largely given way to introduced forage, but the river-carved valley between the Flint Range and the Boulder Mountains still supports livestock. And tourism.

Deer Lodge has more interesting historic sites and museums within hollering distance of one another than any small town in Montana. Despite this distinction, and its status as the Powell County seat, Deer Lodge remains a modest town of some 3,500 residents. Tourism has clearly not gone to townfolks' heads, a salubrious situation that makes a day or two spent here a delight.

Most attractions are handily grouped together on the main drag south of town. You can't miss 'em. Just watch for crenelated stone towers of the Old Montana Prison.

A single fee gets you into the prison and the adjoining Towe Ford Museum, plus three museums across the street: **Frontier Montana**, **Yesterday's Playthings** and the **Powell County Museum**. The **Montana Law Enforcement Museum**, honoring the men and women who uphold the law and memorializing the fallen, is housed in the prison's Cell House. Montana's first prison building was constructed here in 1871. The prison grew and evolved over the decades until 1979, when convicts were moved to the new prison a few miles west of town (a shop across the street from the Old Prison sells convict-made items). The oldest existing structure in the prison complex is a massive sandstone wall built in 1893 with

Gold West Country

convict labor. The 1912 Cell House was a model of prison efficiency in its day. This and other surviving buildings witnessed such dramatic events as the 1959 riot, as well as the boredom of convicts' daily life. It makes for a fascinating tour. The **Towe Ford Museum** is just steps across a shop and fee area from the prison, but it reflects a slice of America that's leagues distant. I'm not "into" cars, but this collection of over 110 Fords and numerous other vehicles held me enthralled. My car crazy older daughter Heather couldn't be pried loose. The Fords on display range from the first 1903 production model to classics of the 1950s and '60s. All are in mint condition. There are also vintage pickup trucks, a logging truck, a tow truck, and an early motorhome modeled after a luxury railroad coach. The collection, begun in 1952 with a Model T Runabout, was assembled by Edward Towe.

The prison and Towe Ford Museum are open daily year-round from 8 am-9 pm. Hours may be shortened between Labor Day and Memorial Day. The Law Enforcement Museum is open May 15-Oct. 29, Tues.-Sat. from 9-5. ☎ 406-846-3111.

AUTHOR TIP *If you visit in July or August, you may wish to catch a play staged by the **Old Prison Players**. Inquire at the fee area or dial the above number for information and reservations.*

Frontier Montana Museum is what the name implies: a museum given over to the legendary Wild West. The gun collections of Don Cappa and Desert John Bloomquist are housed here. There is also an authentic 1800s saloon bar with hundreds of antique liquor bottles. ☎ 406-846-3111 for current hours.

KID-FRIENDLY **Yesterday's Playthings** contrasts sharply with Frontier Montana's guns and liquor bottles. On display are toys that delighted children of 100 years ago – over 1,000 dolls, working model trains, toy soldiers. Open daily year-round, 9-5; shortened hours after Labor Day.

Powell County Museum tells the story of Deer Lodge from locally excavated mastodon bones to over 22,000 photographs of Powell County people and events. Open summers. ☎ 406-846-3111 for current hours. In summer, you can park in the spacious lot adjacent to the Prison and hop a horse-drawn trolley through town to the Grant-Kohrs Ranch. Or vice versa. Ask about schedules at the fee center. **Pioneer Carriage Service** also offers Deer Lodge historical tours. ☎ 406-846-0026 for reservations.

KID-FRIENDLY The **Grant-Kohrs Ranch National Historic Site** showcases 19th-century ranch life and shakes hands with two storied Montana pioneers: Johnny Grant and Conrad Kohrs.

The ranch's main house, bunkhouse and outbuildings remain much as they were when Conrad and Augusta Kohrs lived here, but insight into the tenancy of Johnny and Quarra Grant lingers. A tour of the house built by Grant and enlarged by Kohrs offers glimpses of the daily life of one of Montana's wealthiest cattle barons.

The Grant-Kohrs Ranch National Historic Site.

Today's ranch no longer fills the valley, but it still supports a small herd of Texas Longhorn cattle of the type that once grazed here, plus several draft and saddle horses. Native grasses are being encouraged. A blacksmith fashions horseshoes, a ranch cook passes beans and coffee and discusses cowboy life around a campfire, a hay wagon stands ready to take youngsters for a ride. On offer are guided ranch house tours, self-guided ranch tours, and a summer living history program. Open year-round, May 1-Oct. 1, 8-5:30, Oct.-April, 9-4:30. Modest fee; kids and seniors free. ☎ 406-846-3388.

The Grant-Kohrs Ranch

Johnny Grant was raised in Quebec, son of a high ranking Hudson's Bay Company trader. In 1847, the boy joined his father at Fort Hall in eastern Idaho. The raw youth matured into an accomplished frontiersman. He married Quarra, a Shoshoni Indian related to Sacajawea's family. In accordance with the Indian custom of the time, Johnny also took other wives, fathering 21 children. His love of children was legendary.

The Oregon Trail transformed Johnny into a cattleman. By the time trail trekkers reached western Wyoming and Idaho, their cattle were well nigh worn out. Johnny bought the animals and drove them to his land in the Deer Lodge Valley to be fattened. The next year, he drove the cattle back to the Trail, trading them to other Oregon Trail folk – one head for two broken-down critters. In that way, he built a herd of some 2,000 cattle.

Throughout the 1850s, Johnny and Quarra lived in what is now the bunkhouse. In 1861, he began building a two-story ranch house, at the time considered the finest in Montana. (Two Grant pieces, a loveseat and a pie safe, remain in the house.) The Grant Ranch became a way-station on the prospectors' route to the Last Chance Gulch gold fields. The Grants' hospitality was legendary; many a down-and-out prospector received free meals and a place to sleep at Johnny Grant's ranch.

In 1867 Quarra, Johnny's favorite wife, died. He was heartbroken. Seeking educational advantages for his children, Johnny sold the ranch to Conrad Kohrs and moved to Manitoba's Red River Valley. He died in 1907.

Lyndel Meikle, blacksmith at the Grant-Kohrs Ranch National Historic Site, has edited and prefaced Johnny Grant's memoirs. *Very Close to Trouble* is available at the ranch visitor center.

Conrad Kohrs was a German immigrant butcher who made a pile selling beef to mining camps. After purchasing the Grant Ranch, Kohrs traveled east to marry 19-year-old Augusta Kruse, a stately woman standing six feet tall. While Conrad built the home ranch and other holdings to over 10 million acres in four states and Canada, Augusta brought culture to a raw land. In 1890, Kohrs added a large two-story brick wing to the rear of the house that Johnny built. Augusta furnished it in opulent-style reflective of the couple's German heritage.

Homesteaders' arrival on the Montana landscape ended the open range era when cattle could be trailed clear across the plains. Kohrs and his partner, half-brother John Bielenberg, began selling off land, reducing their holdings to 1,000 acres around the home ranch by their deaths in the early 1920s. In 1972, Congress designated the ranch a National Historic Site dedicated to "providing an understanding of the frontier cattle era of the nation's history."

Butte

From Deer Lodge, I-90 dips south and east to Butte, a city that actually takes pride in being one huge super-fund cleanup site. Some may consider this the wages of sin; the sin being the grabby nature of Butte's copper boom.

DID YOU KNOW? *In its heyday, immigrants from a dozen or more countries toiled in mine tunnels that so thoroughly honeycombed the city that householders could hear the rumble of pneumatic drills under their kitchens. Over 3,600 miles of tunnels still burrow under Butte and surrounding hills. Many mines exceeded 3,500 feet in depth.*

The **Berkeley Pit** strip mine gobbled up the immigrant neighborhoods. Today, the Pit is a monstrous "lake" brimming with lethal acidic mining residues. The "richest hill on earth" has become the largest pool of contaminated water in America.

Only Butte would flaunt such a place, making it a major tourist attraction complete with viewing area and gift shop.

The Berkeley Pit exerts a perverse pull for wildfowl, too. Some years ago, a vee of migrating Canada geese touched down for a drink. Officials counted 342 carcasses, their insides riddled with burns and sores. Efforts are now being made to scare away wildfowl misled by the sparkling blue waters.

Water began seeping into the pit from a maze of old mine tunnels and shafts after the strip mine's 1982 closure. The water reacts with the ore, creating a toxic soup. There are concerns that the steadily rising water might someday spill over, sending a lethal tide into the city and into already contaminated Silver Bow Creek, a source of the Columbia River. An earthquake fault less than a mile away is another source of concern. But Butte remains bitten by the mining bug. Montana Resources, Inc. operates a pit mine not far from the Berkeley Pit.

The Pit is but one of Butte's points of interest. The city is not a pretty place. It's hard, stark; always has been. It has a history to match: labor riots, mine disasters, political flim-flam. Downtown buildings rise against bare buttes. Gallus frames stand in for trees. These structures resembling a gallows stood over every Butte mine. Housing replacing the ethnic neighborhoods gobbled by the Berkeley Mine sprawl over a wide place in the hills southeast of downtown. A fancy new **Visitor Center** off I-90 at 1000 George Street (take Exit 126) is apparently an effort to dispel the city's gritty image. On display is a collection of fishing flies tied by George Grant, a conservationist devoted to defending and improving the integrity of the Big Hole River. Friendly Visitor Center personnel are on hand to answer questions and direct you to points of interest.

A **tour trolley** originating at the Visitor Center provides an overview of the city. The narrated 1½-hour tour hits Butte's high points, including stops at the Berkeley Pit and the World Museum of Mining. The trolley runs June-September. Admission fee. Contact the Visitor Center for current hours.

The Visitor Center is open daily May-Labor Day, 8-8 and Labor Day-Sept. 30, 8-5. Open weekdays Oct.-May, 9-5. ☎ 800-735-6814 or 406-723-3177. Fax 406-723-1215. Internet www.butteinfo.org.

The **World Museum of Mining**, near the Montana Tech campus, is a must-see. The Orphan Girl Mine's headframe, surface support facilities and adjacent museum offer fascinating insight into the mines that once studded the face of Butte and honeycombed the bedrock under the city. The museum is filled with mining artifacts and machinery. Detailed pen and ink drawings by miner-cum-artist J.C. O'Donnell illustrate, in stark reality, the tough, gritty aspects of hard rock mining. A recreated miners' neighborhood offers insight into the daily lives of miners and their families. Open daily, April 1-Oct. 31, 9-6. Admission fee.

Austere as Butte may appear, the city boasts several opulent homes between downtown and the Montana Tech campus. The **Copper King Mansion**, now a B&B, was built by William A. Clark to showcase his copper wealth. The mansion housing the Silver Bow Arts Chateau was built by Clark as a wedding present for his son, Charles. The arts center and museum is open year-round. Summer hours are Tues.-Sat., 10-5 and Sun., noon-5. ☎ 406-723-7600 for off-season hours.

Hilly downtown Butte projects a seedy appearance; a sad reminder of the vibrant life that once seethed through its streets. The **Dumas Brothel**, at 45 E. Mercury St., reflects that seediness. The last lady of the night packed her bags in 1982. In 1998, the Dumas was purchased by the International Sex Worker Foundation for Art Culture and Education (ISWFACE). Norma Jean Almodovar, a former cop and a former prostitute, heads the foundation with the oxymoronic name. Wander in if the door is open.

Chinese immigrants ran laundries and noodle parlors in Butte, as they did in most Western mining towns. The **Mai Wah** and **Wah Chong Tai Buildings**, on China Alley between Galena and Mercury Streets, once housed such enterprises. Today the buildings offer exhibits interpreting the Asian history of Butte and the Rocky Mountain West. Open June-August, Tues.-Sat., 11-3. ☎ 406-723-3177.

The **Butte-Silver Bow Public Archives**, in the old fire station at 17 West Quartz Street, has extensive records of interest to persons seeking family information and other historical data. You can get a fix on Butte's mine disasters here. The worst disaster occurred on the night of June 8, 1917 when fire killed 163 men in the North Butte Mining Company's Granite Mountain Mine. The Archives are open Mon.-Fri. from 9-5.

Interesting as Butte may be, I'm always happy to shake its dirt from my shoes. I-15 loops around Butte, heading north toward Helena through a scenic patch of the Deerlodge National Forest. Turn off at Exit 164 for a sideshow trip to Boulder on MT 69. From Boulder, the highway follows the Boulder River (not to be confused with Yellowstone Country's river by that name) south through a pleasant valley to Whitehall.

Boulder

Boulder's unassuming appearance is at odds with a brace of enterprises aimed at the health conscious set. The **Free Enterprise Uranium Radon Health Mine** makes claims that put me in mind of those old-time medicine shows. Seems that sitting 85 feet down in the mine can relieve the symptoms of a long list of immune system disorders. Free underground tours are available, but I couldn't quite bring myself to accept. To reach the mine, turn west on Second Street. Follow signs to the top of the hill. ☎ 800-474-8657 or 406-225-3383.

Boulder Hot Springs Hotel, south of town off MT 69, was quite a grand place in 1910, following a renovation that transformed it into a replica of a Spanish mission. Since that time, it has seen numerous uses under many names. The current incarnation is a New Age B&B, health spa and conference facility. The mineral-rich, thermally heated outdoor swimming pool and indoor soaking pools are open to the public. Summer pool hours: Mon.-Thurs, 2-7:30 pm and Fri.-Sun., noon-9. ☎ 406-225-4339.

Helena Approaching

Helena via I-15 from the south is tantamount to knocking on the city's back door. If you do approach from this direction, take an extra half-hour to by-pass the city, continuing on to Exit 209. Turn around here and approach from the north. You'll be glad you did. Seen from the point where the Interstate enters a broad valley, Helena presents the finest sight of any Montana city – especially at sunset when a golden light bathes the city's spires and the Montana State Capitol dome. Like a seductive miss, Helena arranges herself most decoratively against the mountains to her back.

Time and prosperity have transformed the gritty diggin's around Last Chance Gulch into a graceful city of parks and attractive buildings. Helena's showpiece is the gaggle of stone structures snuggling up to the Capitol and surrounded by lawns and flowers. From here, or from any high place in town, you can get a gander at the **Sleeping Giant**, Helena's pet mountain across the valley.

The **Last Chance Tour Train**, pulled by a scaled-down replica of an antique engine, begins hour-long narrated city tours from the Montana Historical Society at 6th and Roberts. Helena is an easy city to navigate, but the overview provided by the open-air train gives you a chance to decide what you want to see more of, and what you don't. Admission fee. The train runs from May 15-Sept. 30. ☎ 406-442-1023 for times.

Don't miss the **Montana Historical Society Museum**, an exceptionally well curated overview of Montana's history, cultures and art. Numerous Charles Russell artworks are on display, as well as Evelyn Cameron photographs. Free admission. Open Memorial Day-Labor Day, weekdays 8-6 and weekends and holidays 9-5. ☎ 406-444-2694 for off-season hours.

The **Montana State Capitol building**'s façade follows the classical trend popular in 19th-century government structures, but inside it's pure Montana. Historical panels portray the miners, cowboys, Indians and others who peopled Montana's history. Most striking is Charles Russell's huge mural titled "Lewis & Clark Meeting the Flathead Indians at Ross' Hole," a reminder that Indians and whites once met as equals rep-

Gold West Country

resenting powerful nations. Free admission. Open daily May 28-Sept. 15 from 8-6. Guided tours on the hour from 9 am to 4 pm. ☎ 406-444-4789 for off-season hours.

Montana's new Governor's Mansion is shaped like a ship, complete with prow and stern: the ship of state. Corny, but nice. The Original **Governor's Mansion** at 304 N. Ewing reflects the opulent tastes of the Victorian era. Built in 1888 as a private home, the mansion housed nine Montana governors and their families before being turned over to the Montana Historical Society. Free admission. Open Memorial Day-Labor Day, Tues.-Sun., noon-5 pm and April, May and Sept.-Dec., Tues.-Sat., noon-5 pm. Tours begin on the hour. ☎ 406-444-2694.

The streets west of the Capitol are lined with fine homes built by Montana's movers and shakers and reflecting the state's wealth. Many of these private residences have been beautifully restored.

DID YOU KNOW?

At the turn of the century, Helena had more millionaires per capita than any other city in the nation.

The homes overlook **Last Chance Gulch**, site of Helena's big gold strike; or what was Last Chance Gulch. Once a raw gash in the ground swarming with prospectors, the Gulch has been filled in and covered over. A tame pedestrian mall lined with shops and eateries offers no hint of the history underfoot. A small park at the head of the mall celebrates the prospectors who made Helena's wealth possible. Helena's first residential area was **Reeder's Alley**, west of Last Chance Gulch. In the early 1860s one Lewis Reeder began constructing a series of small lodgings west of the gulch. The Alley later fell on hard times, but survived the Urban Renewal Project that changed the face of the gulch. Many of the structures have been restored. Craftsmen, artists, shops and restaurants have begun to stake claims where miners once laid their heads.

Helena residents are fortunate in having, almost at their front door, a series of lakes formed by dams on the Missouri River. **Lake Helena**, **Canyon Ferry**, **Holter** and **Hauser Lakes** are popular playgrounds, weekend magnets for many Montanans (see *Adventures*).

Townsend

US 12/287 follows the contour of Canyon Ferry Lake to Townsend at the lake's foot. This very pleasant town prides itself on being "the first city on the Missouri River." Whether or not that's a fact, the **Broadwater County Museum & Historical Library** at 133 N. Walnut Street is well worth a visit for the insight it offers into life here in days gone by. It's apparent that the entire community contributed time and talents to creating their museum. Open daily, 12:30-5 pm.

Hwy. 284, traveling north from Townsend along the east side of Canyon Ferry Lake, affords access to several lakeside BLM campgrounds. You can cross the dam at the head of the lake and return to Helena. The **Gates of the Mountains** that wowed Lewis and Clark as they toiled up the Missouri River in July, 1805 narrow the dammed waters between Canyon Ferry and Holter Lakes. Refer to page 302 for a description of Gates of the Mountains Boat Tours, accessed via I-15 Exit 209. North of Helena, I-15 rides through some spectacular scenery. An even more scenic route begins at Exit 219, jouncing alongside Little Prickly Pear Creek and the Missouri River below the dams. En route back to I-15 and Charlie Russell Country, it passes through the rustic settlement of **Wolf Creek**, an anglers' mecca.

Gold West Country thrusts into the mountainous **Helena National Forest** northwest of Helena. Scored by passes over the Continental Divide and bisected by MT 200, the area is rugged in the extreme. Choose between two ways to get there from Helena. US 12 heads west, topping 6,320-foot MacDonald Pass before descending to tiny Avon. From there, MT 141 follows the shadow of the Garnet Range northwestward to MT 200 west of Lincoln.

If you choose US 12, take time to check out **Frontier Town** at the top of MacDonald Pass. This labor of love represents John Quigley's dream of recreating a microcosm of the communities that made Montana the rugged place it is. Watch for signs.

My favorite is Hwy. 279. Pick it up at I-15 Exit 209. The 39-mile route offers access, via six miles of gravel road, to the **Great Divide Ski Area** (see page 311) and the not-quite-ghost-town of Marysville.

Gates of the Mountains boat trip, west of Helena.

Gold West Country

Marysville

Some mining still occurs in the vicinity of Marysville, and people still live here in picturesque seclusion. While numerous derelict structures remain to be poked about in, the townsite has been tarted up with street signs topped with frolicking wrought iron animals and pickaxe-toting prospectors. The **Marysville House**, the local hangout, is a direct descendant of gold rush-era saloons.

DID YOU KNOW?

Several area mines once produced handsomely, notably Irishman Tommy Cruse's Drumlummon Mine that poured out a cool $50,000,000.

MT 200

MT 200, connecting Great Falls in Charlie Russell Country with Missoula in Glacier Country, enters Gold West Country on the prairie just east of the Rocky Mountain Front. Here, the Rockies rise in abrupt splendor, massive escarpments of tumbled, forested peaks. MT 200 crosses the Continental Divide over windy **Rogers Pass**, a major bald eagle migration route (see *Wildlife Watching*). The storied Blackfoot River begins below the pass at 5,100 feet, bouncing along parallel to MT 200 through Lincoln on its way to meet the Clarks Fork River east of Missoula.

Numerous Forest Service roads radiate from MT 200, exploring the passes over the Continental Divide and the surrounding historic mining country. Many such roads call for a 4WD vehicle, especially in wet weather. The Lincoln Ranger District of the Helena National Forest has available a print-out describing these back roads and their attractions.

Lincoln

Lincoln, the Blackfoot Valley's largest town with about 1,800 year-round residents, could have been plucked from northern Minnesota, so closely does it resemble a northwoods community. Log homes have seemingly been set at random amid scattered pine trees. The sleepy-appearing town seems always to have a bone to chew. No sooner did it live down fame as the Unabomber's hideout than it girded for battle against a proposed cyanide leach gold mine nearby.

Lincoln has much to offer hikers, snowmobilers and campers (see *Adventures on Foot*, *Adventures on Snow* and *Camping*). The Lincoln Ranger District station combines historic ambience with solid information. West of Lincoln, MT 200 continues to the funky crossroads community of **Ovando** before plunging into the Lolo National Forest in Glacier Country.

Adventures

■ Adventures on Foot

Hiking & Backpacking

 Hiking and backpacking adventures in Gold West Country can be as varied as the 1.8-mile Missouri-Beaver Creek Trail below Hauser Dam, or the daunting Continental Divide National Scenic Trail. Between these extremes, dozens upon dozens of US Forest Service and BLM trails lead both casual hikers and serious backpackers on serendipitous adventures. Many trails skirt ghost towns and abandoned mines, moldering reminders of the cataclysmic impact that gold and other minerals have long had on this soaringly beautiful place. In Gold West Country, as well as other travel regions, trailhead directional markers have been placed at most access points along highways. These are of inestimable value in coordinating your present location with trails delineated on travel and topographical maps. The *Special Concerns* advice in Yellowstone Country's *Adventures on Foot* section includes mountain country hiking and camping guidelines that apply to Gold West Country.

 An added caveat: watch for open mine shafts when hiking off-trail. Also watch your step around tumbledown cabins and such. They appeal to rattlesnakes, too.

The Continental Divide National Scenic Trail

You can't help but be struck by the contrast between mining's rape of the land and the pristine beauty of Montana's mountain fastnesses. The Continental Divide National Scenic Trail points up this contrast. The trail was established by Congress under the National Trails System Act of 1968. Much of its 3,100-mile length, stretching from Canada to Mexico, is incomplete. But you can trek all of the northernmost portion, 795 miles over the spine of the Rocky Mountains from the Glacier/Waterton Lakes National Parks border to Yellowstone National Park. Most of these miles meander through Gold West Country. The trail largely traverses current trails and primitive logging and Forest Service roads. Fifty-seven miles are over interim routes that serve as detours pending construction of preferred routes. Over 90% of the trail is within five miles of the Continental Divide, with much of it on the divide. Elevations vary from 4,200 feet at Waterton Lake to approximately 10,000 feet at Red Conglomerate Peaks in the Bitterroot Range.

Gold West Country

Unfortunately for backpackers and horsepackers, 510 miles of the trail's northernmost portion are open to some types of motorized vehicles, including snowmobiles. Some portions of the trail traverse private lands. The trail sometimes crosses highways, affording access if you wish to hike only a portion of it, and providing drop-off points (there are 34 in all) for food and equipment.

From the US/Canada border, the northern segment of the trail follows a route near the divide through the length of **Glacier Park** before crossing a five-mile portion of the Blackfeet Indian Reservation. South of 5,280-foot Marias Pass, the trail passes through the **Bob Marshall** and **Scapegoat Wildernesses**.

These adjoining wilderness areas, their easternmost edges tracing the face of the Rocky Mountain Front, incorporate all that is wild and free in nature. Outdoors-oriented Montanans, and that's most of them, regard these places with fondness and awe; consider them synonymous with the outdoors in its most pristine state. Fortunate is the hiker who seizes the opportunity to trek through them.

After crossing 5,610-foot **Rogers Pass**, notorious for fierce winds and glacial temperatures, the trail looks in on historic mining districts and ghost towns in the Helena and Deerlodge National Forests. West of Anaconda, it traverses the length of the **Anaconda-Pintler Wilderness**. West of the Wilderness, hikers can soak at **Lost Trail Hot Springs** in the shadow of Lost Trail Pass, named for one of Lewis and Clark's more confusing sorties.

The trail winds through the Bitterroot Range, on the Idaho-Montana border, to 7,373-foot **Lemhi Pass**. Here, at the headwaters of the Missouri River, is a memorial to Sacajawea, Lewis and Clark's dauntless Shoshone guide. This route also follows that of Chief Joseph's band of non-treaty Nez Perce during their 1877 flight to elude the US Army.

From Lemhi Pass, the trail continues through the Bitterroots to **Monida Pass**, then winds along the crest of the Centennial Mountains above Red Rock National Wildlife Refuge. It then crosses 6,836-foot **Reynolds Pass** and 7,072-foot **Targhee Pass**, affording views of Henry's Lake in Idaho and Hebgen Lake in Montana. From Targhee Pass, the trail continues to the segment's end at the western boundary of Yellowstone Park.

Hiking the Continental Divide Trail is a once-in-a-lifetime trek. You can't plan too carefully. It's a given that your gear should be designed to serve you well over the most rugged terrains and in the widest weather extremes. You may encounter risky and dangerous conditions that can include lightning, freezing temperatures and snow (even in July), isolation, assorted physical hazards, and minimal communications. Because of the very real possibility of snow, portions of the trail are passable only in July, August and September. The advice given in earlier chapters of this book regarding clothing and emergency supplies, making a campsite, drinking water and other special concerns applies here.

You can expect to see a wide variety of wild animals and birds along the trail – the kinds of thrilling serendipitous sightings that planned wildlife watching can't approach. Be alert for less than thrilling encounters with grizzly bears and cougars. Refer to the introductory chapters of this book for information on how to react to and prevent these confrontations.

Rattlesnakes pose a threat in some areas. Wear long pants with high boots and carry a snakebite kit. And know how to use it.

Exercise respect when crossing private lands and the Blackfeet Indian Reservation.

Special restrictions apply to travel, camping and stock use in Glacier National Park. Backpackers must pay a per-night camping fee (see Glacier National Park info in this book's Glacier Country chapter). Motorized vehicles and biocycles are not permitted in wilderness areas and in Glacier Park's backcountry. Travel and camping permits are not required in wilderness areas, but some restrictions may apply. Contact the appropriate forest service ranger stations for information regarding current restrictions.

The trail crosses the US Sheep Experiment station in two places in the Centennial Mountains. Contact the station for restrictions. You can obtain further Continental Divide National Scenic Trail information by contacting the Northern Region National Forests Regional Office, or offices of any of the national forests through which the trail passes. Topographical maps are available for a small fee, usually $4, from Forest Services offices and the US Geological Survey. Contact numbers for these agencies are found in *Information Souces*. Other agencies, such as Montana Department of Fish, Wildlife and Parks and the Bureau of Land Management, may also be helpful.

 Two books recommended by the USDA Forest Service: James R. Wolf's *Guide to the Continental Divide Trail, Vol. 1, Northern Montana*, Mountain Press Publishing Co., 1976 and *Volume 2, Southern Montana and Idaho*, Continental Divide Trail Society, 1979; Continental Divide Trail Society, Box 30002, Bethesda, MD 20814.

Addresses for Glacier National Park and the US Sheep Experiment Station are as follows: **Glacier National Park**, West Glacier, MT 59936; ☎ 406-888-5441. **US Sheep Experiment Station**, Dubois, ID 83423; ☎ 208-374-5306.

Hiking on BLM Lands

If Bureau of Land Management lands invoke visions of cattle grazing on vast expanses of grasslands, mudhole "lakes" and bumpy primitive roads to nowhere, you're on track. To a point. In Montana, the oft-maligned BLM reaches beyond grazing leases and cow-to-acre formulas. Way beyond. Here, the BLM maintains public access areas that include such diverse places as Garnet Ghost Town (see *Glacier Country*), Humbug Spires (see *Rock Climbing*) and the fascinating Beartrap National Recreational Trail.

All three, plus numerous other BLM sites, invite hiking.

Humbug Spires is well known to rock climbers, but did you know that the 11,175-acre Humbug Spires Wilderness Study Area includes several scenic trails? The main trail follows Moose Creek, passing through stands of 250-year-old Douglas fir trees. Game trails offer access to the spires and to an abandoned miner's cabin. If lucky, you can watch rock climbers resembling tiny lizards as they inch up the Wedge. The Humbug Spires Primitive Area is reached from I-15 via Exit 99, some 38 miles north of Dillon. Drive east about three miles and you're at the trailhead.

The **Beartrap National Recreational Trail**, slicing through the middle of the Beartrap Canyon Wilderness, offers a superb opportunity to follow the famed Madison River on foot. See *Adventures on Water* for more Beartrap Canyon insight.

The nine-mile trail, part of the Lee Metcalf Wilderness, parallels the Madison as it funnels through the 1,500-foot-deep canyon. Hikers' access is from the north, via a three-mile-long gravel road off MT 84. Watch for a road near the bridge over the Madison, eight miles northeast of Norris. Turn south at the Bear Trap Recreation Area sign. The trail begins at the parking area.

The trail's first 3.5 miles to Beartrap Creek is easy going. From here to the southern wilderness boundary, the trail becomes more difficult, often rising above the river. Following the east side of the river, the trail stops well short of the Madison Powerhouse and Overflow Chute. A narrow dirt road links the powerhouse area with Ennis Lake to the south. As it does not provide access to the Beartrap Trail, you must retrace your steps to your starting point.

Poison ivy is common along the river. So are rattlesnakes, ticks and mosquitoes. And this area wasn't dubbed Bear Trap Canyon for no reason. Be prepared.

There are several campsites along the river. Camping in the Wilderness is limited to three consecutive days. Firewood is scarce, so bring a camp stove. Bring along your rod and tackle box, too. All other caveats regarding wilderness camping apply here.

AUTHOR TIP *You'll be glad to learn that pack and saddle stock are limited in the canyon to the period between October 15 and December 15. That's hunting season; good reason to avoid the canyon.*

The Lee Metcalf Wilderness

The Lee Metcalf Wilderness, on the western slopes of the Madison Range, is comprised of four separate units: Beartrap Canyon, Spanish Peaks, Taylor-Hilgard and Monument Mountain. Here, glaciation has produced steep rugged peaks, knife-edge ridges and cirques containing alpine lakes surrounded by high meadows. Numerous trails, most over-nighters or longer, take advantage of this heart-in-your-mouth scenery extravaganza.

The **Spanish Peaks** area includes several trails accessed from trailheads on both the east and west slopes of the Madison Range. The **Spanish Creek trail** is among the most enjoyable. The 26-mile loop hike may take several days to complete. The marked turnoff to the trailhead is on US 191, about 10 miles south of Gallatin Gateway. Take a right up Spanish Creek. The trailhead is at the Spanish Fork Guard Station; five miles up Spanish Creek, then left and eight miles up the South Fork of Spanish Creek. The trail follows the South Fork for eight miles before leaving the creek and climbing past several small sub-alpine lakes, then veering down Camp Creek. The side trip possibilities are virtually endless, the scenery magnificent. For further information on this and other hikes, contact the Bozeman Ranger District of the Gallatin National Forest.

The **Helmet Trail**, a difficult 10-mile loop gaining and losing 3,180 feet as it climbs to and from the saddle below the Sphinx and the Helmet, is not for the casual hiker. The trail starts at Bear Creek Ranger Station, off US 287 at Cameron. After driving three miles, turn right and continue for 2.5 miles to the ranger station. The trail enters the Lee Metcalf Wilderness just beyond the station and follows a series of trails to the saddle between the **Helmet** and the **Sphinx**. Both striking geological formations invite climbing. The vistas are vast, but these are technical scrambles requiring a rope. Moose frequent the area.

AUTHOR TIP *Contact the Madison Ranger District of the Beaverhead National Forest for further information on these trails and to obtain a free booklet describing other trails in the District.*

The Pioneer Mountains

The ruggedly beautiful Pioneer Mountains, encircled by the Big Hole River and split by the Pioneer Mountains Scenic Byway, include the largest remaining roadless area in southwest Montana. The eastern Pioneers rise abruptly from 6,000 to 11,000 feet. Mountain lakes and cliff-edged cirques lie hidden in the glaciated upper elevations. A massive 30-mile-long granite wall slices through the range. The craggy peaks contrast with the western Pioneers' rolling forested terrain. The wildlife alone makes this prime hiking territory. Contact the Wise River Ranger District of the Beaverhead National Forest for detailed information on hikes to the several lakes concealed in the Pioneers. The District offers a booklet describing numerous trails and including rough maps.

The Dillon Ranger District

Many trails in the Dillon Ranger District of the Beaverhead National Forest are lightly used. Consider these if you wish to really get off by yourself. The flip side: vegetation is generally sparse. The remote canyon-scored area west of I-90 and south of Hwy. 324 is split by the Big Sheep Back Country Byway, a dirt road offering access to several trails. The spacious country north of Hwy. 324 and south of Hwy. 278, encompassing the ghost town of Bannack, also includes hiking trails.

The Dillon Ranger District makes available a booklet with maps and descriptions of numerous trails traversing these areas.

The Tobacco Root Mountains

The Tobacco Root Mountains lie to the east of the Pioneers, their 10,000-foot peaks looming dizzyingly above the Gallatin and Beaverhead Valleys. Also glacially formed, these peaks harbor over 40 sparkling lakes. The range abounds with mountain goats, elk, and moose. Cutthroat and rainbow trout thrive in clear lakes and streams. This is your kind of place, if you would plant your boots where prospectors of yore once dug and departed in disappointed funks. Foothills ghost towns and other mining-era remains may tempt you to abandon more rugged hikes in favor of just poking around. If it's hiking trails you're after, the Tobacco Roots has plenty. Many are overnight or several day-hikes requiring a moderate to considerable degree of conditioning due to elevation gains in excess of 2,600 feet. The rewards: those gem-like lakes. Be aware that most trails are multiple-use, meaning that you must share with ATVs, horses, mountain bikes and motorcycles. The following two trails are open to hikers, horses and mountain bikes only.

The nine-mile **Twin Lakes Trail** #424 is rated Moderate and has an elevation gain of 1,240 feet. The trail climbs to a meadow before reentering timber and running along a steep side slope. Above a Depression era placer mining cabin, it heads through open country along a ridge top. It climbs a divide above the North Meadow Creek drainage before sidehilling down to Lower Twin Lake.

The eight-mile **Branham Lakes/Bridge Canyon Loop Trails** #15 and #610 gain 1,000 feet and are rated Moderate. Fabulous ridgetop views include distant peaks and shimmering Bell Lake. Alpine wildflowers cover the windswept ridge and songbirds abound. Mountain goats frequent the rocky peaks above the lakes.

For trailhead directions and more detailed trail information, contact the Madison and Sheridan Ranger Districts of the Beaverhead National Forest and the Jefferson Ranger District of the Deerlodge National Forest. The Madison Ranger District makes available a booklet describing trails in the Gravelly Range, the Lee Metcalf Wilderness/Madison Mountains, and the Tobacco Range.

The Anaconda-Pintler Wilderness

The headwaters of Rock Creek and branches of the Bitterroot and Big Hole Rivers rise in the mountains of this rugged 158,516-acre wilderness. Numerous feisty streams fed by the melting of perpetual above-timberline snowbanks cascade down steep canyons. No wonder mountain goats call these rocky escarpments home. Elevations range from 5,100 to 10,793 feet. Spectacular cirques, numerous lakes, U-shaped valleys and glacial moraines provide camera-ready views. Wildlife include deer, elk, moose and black bear in addition to the ubiquitous mountain goats.

Several trails access the wilderness from forest roads off US 93 on the west, MT 38 and MT 1 on the north, and MT 43 on the east and south. It's a stretch to characterize these as hiking trails. Horsepacking trails would be more to the point, this wilderness preserve being popular with local horse owners.

Hikers should be careful to avoid spooking horses. Don't make sudden noises or overtures toward horses. Step off on the lower side of the trail to allow them to pass. Bicycles and motorized vehicles are not permitted in wilderness areas.

AUTHOR TIP *If you are considering hiking here, it's imperative that you stop in at the Sula Ranger District of the Bitterroot National Forest (see Glacier Country) or the Wisdom or Wise River Ranger Districts of the Beaverhead-Deerlodge National Forest to purchase maps and discuss trail locations and conditions with the ranger on duty. Refer to Information Sources for contact information.*

Gold West Country

Hiking in the Helena National Forest

The Helena National Forest offers much diversity. The heavily forested Lincoln Ranger District lies to the north of Helena. The Missouri River/Canyon Ferry Lake/Gates of the Mountains area east of the city includes reminders of the Lewis and Clark expedition. The Elkhorn Mountains to the south, formed 75 million years ago by volcanic lava flows, remain mostly wild. As the name implies, these mountains afford refuge for a fine herd of elk.

Helena residents are to be envied for their proximity to numerous hiking trails, beginning right in town with trails up 5,460-foot-high **Mount Helena**.

Numerous trails explore the **Gates of The Mountains Wilderness**. The Helena Ranger District has compiled an information packet detailing dozens of trails ranging from the easy **Refrigerator** and **Missouri River Canyon trails** to the challenging 12-mile **Hanging Valley Trail**. **Refrigerator Canyon** is a must-see. You can reach it from the Canyon Ferry Visitor Center at the north end of the lake. Take MT 430 off I-15 to the visitor center. From there, head north to York on the Jim Town Road. Continue on to Nelson, where you'll swing a right and continue to the marked trailhead. From the visitor center, it's a 17-mile drive over unimproved roads. The trail passes through a lush forest for a quarter-mile before reaching the 10-foot-wide slit in a 200-foot-high limestone canyon enclosing a small stream. Breezes blowing over the stream and funneling through the canyon's rock walls provide the evaporative cooling that gives the canyon its name. There are many large mammals in the area, so have your camera ready.

Topographically, the **Elkhorn Mountains** resemble many other tiptilted parts of Montana. They contain seven mountain lakes and are watered by some 30 streams. **Elkhorn Peak**, a 9,381-foot volcanic mountain rising above peaceful grazing lands, keeps company with four other peaks in excess of 8,000 feet. Numerous trails and old mining roads bisect the area, looking in on mining-era reminders, crystal streams and gentle vistas. The Elkhorns include one of the country's largest winter elk ranges.

Numerous hikes are possible here. Choose the six-mile round trip hike up **Red Mountain** to put in perspective the contrast between the grandeur of Montana's wild country and its centers of civilization. From the summit, you can see the sprawling outskirts of Helena, 10 counties, nine mountain ranges, and a sprinkling of abandoned gold mines. To reach the trailhead, drive west from Helena on US 12 for nine miles to the Rimini turnoff. Hang a left and drive seven miles to Rimini ghost town, then drive south another 3.6 miles. The unsigned trail veers left after the city of Helena water ditch and cabin and just before a bend in the road.

Parts of the Helena National Forest invite a berry-picking pace. The Lincoln Ranger District makes available a print-out describing the berries and wildflowers growing in the forest, even going so far as to provide berry recipes.

MT 200 is the springboard for numerous trails accessing the **Scapegoat Wilderness** and the mountains bordering the **Blackfoot Valley** on the north. Many look in on abandoned gold diggings and such. Feeder trails access the Continental Divide Trail from Rogers, Flesher and Stemple Passes. The Lincoln Ranger District has compiled a helpful booklet describing trails with maps, as well as campgrounds. Stop in, pick one up, and discuss your hiking plans.

See *Wildlife Watching* for other Gold West Country trails.

Guided Hiking Trips

Gold West country is mostly a do-it-yourself hiking and backpacking place. Perhaps the popularity of Yellowstone and Glacier Country's mountains cause guides to focus on those. For whatever reason, they're missing an opportunity to lead treks through some of Montana's most fascinating country.

Experience Montana is owned and operated by Allen Schallenberger of Sheridan, in the heart of ghost town country. A fourth-generation Montanan, Schallenberger is a research and management biologist, licensed outfitter, former livestock rancher and range management specialist, and a longtime Montana history buff. He arranges and guides a wide variety of Montana experiences, including customized hiking trips in western Montana. 53 Elser Lane, Sheridan, MT 59749-9604; ☎ 406-842-5134.

Montana ECO Treks & Tours, aka National ECO Institute, also offers a variety of tours. These include one- and two-day watchable wildlife and photo safari nature hikes. All tours start from Helena. For information, contact S. Bud Solmonsson, PO Box 511, Helena, MT 59624; ☎ 406-442-0214.

Llama Treks

Hiking with llamas may be the best way to go. Not only are you relieved of that burdensome backpack, but you get to enjoy the company of some of the most engaging of animals. Llamas may be related to camels, but they definitely don't share camels' nasty dispositions.

Ollie Llamas guides multi-day treks in the Pioneer Mountains with Bernard, Toby, Elvis, Independence and the rest of the gang. Dick and Linda Reichle, owners of Ollie Llamas, operate as guides in the Beaverhead National Forest under licensed outfitter Tim Tollett of Frontier Anglers. PO Box 11, Dillon, MT 59725; ☎ 800-228-5263. **Montana ECO Treks & Tours** will also arrange llama treks. See address above.

Gold West Country

Caving

Lewis and Clark Caverns, 19 miles west of Three Forks on MT 2, is Gold West Country's best known cave (see *Touring*). Old timers refer to it as Morrison Cave in honor of Dan Morrison, in 1908 the first person to extensively explore it. This very accessible cave in the Jefferson River Canyon is the site of a state park (see *State Parks*) and is Montana's only fully commercial cave. If you are an experienced caver in search of a challenging exploration sans tourists, you might be tempted to bypass the caverns in favor of more stirring adventure. Don't. The tour may be guided, but the wonders of this cave cancel out that tame sheep feeling.

The cave's total length is 4,832 feet, with some 3,000 feet open to the public. It is 352 feet deep at its lowest point. Here, you'll see the best-developed cave formations in the Northwest. There are also large stalactites and stalagmites, cave popcorn and abundant flowstone. You may also see twisted helectite formations and dogtooth spar.

Developed in the Mission Canyon Formation, many passages pitch steeply downward. Lowering of the water table through downcutting by surface streams resulted in at least four levels. Water still flows into the cave and most formations continue to grow.

You can explore several other caves along the Jefferson River, albeit much smaller ones keeping lower profiles. **Oven Hole** harbors a colony of bats, while **Pigeon Cave** is home to... you guessed it.

A cave of archaeological importance is on the property of **Blacktail Ranch**, home of a horseback riding guide service north of Helena. Guided cave tours are on offer. 4440 Southfork Trail, Wolf Creek, MT 59648; ☎ 406-235-4330.

There are numerous caves in Beaverhead County, in the vicinity of **Dillon**. Many require the use of ropes. Some are on private land, so ask permission.

Southwestern Montana's complex geologic makeup results in a greater variety of caves than any other area. The region's four separate rock units are the **Cherry Creek Group** (Precambrian), the **Meagher Formation** (Cambrian), the **Jefferson Formation** (Devonian), and the **Madison Group** (Mississippian).

If you peruse the history of cave discoveries in Montana and other mountainous regions, you'll come upon instance after instance of caves discovered by happenstance as casual as a hunter's dog following a bear into a hole in a rock ledge, or a sheepherder puzzling over a disappeared ewe. Who knows? You might discover a "new" cave as you hike in these mountains.

The best place to begin searching out that great caving experience is from home, by picking up your phone and dialing ☎ 406-496-4167, the **Bureau of Mines & Geology** at Montana Tech in Butte. A credit card will get you a copy of *Caves of Montana* by Newell P. Campbell (see *Bibliography*). This excellent and exhaustive technical guide to Montana's caves may be the best $6 you ever spent.

Rock Climbing

The Humbug Spires

The monolithic granite Humbug Spires, thrusting from the surrounding Highland Mountains foothills like giant petrified trees on steroids, are both well known to climbers and easily accessed. To get there, exit I-15 at the Moose Creek interchange (Exit 99), north of Melrose. It's a four-mile hike from the Moose Creek trailhead to **The Wedge**. The Humbugs resulted from the southern rift of the Boulder Batholift, extending from Helena through Butte and Whitehall to Dillon. Crisp granite abounds in the more than 50 spires along the west to southwest flank of the range. About a fifth are in the 300- to 600-foot range. The Wedge is the largest and best known to climbers. All routes are multi-pitch.

The Continental Divide

The Continental Divide near Butte has several climbing rocks, most notably **Spire Rock** and the **Homestake Pass** climbs. Split Pinnacle, Gillette Edge, Town Pump, Hot Wings, Dragon's Back and Spire Rock offer crack and face climbing.

Helena

The Helena area also offers challenging climbing. Most popular are the granite domes and boulders on the southeast slopes of **Sheep Mountain**. The limestone cliffs of **Beaver Creek Canyon** offer multi-pitch routes.

 For detailed technical information on these climbs and others, consult *The Rock Climber's Guide to Montana*, edited by Randall Green (see *Bibliography*).

Local Climbing Equipment Shops

Montana Outdoor Sports, 708 N. Last Chance Gulch, Helena, MT 59601; ☎ 406-443-4119.

Pipestone Mountaineering, 829 S. Montana, Butte, MT 59701; ☎ 406-892-4994.

The Base Camp, 333 N. Last Chance Gulch, Helena, MT 59601; ☎ 406-443-5360.

Gold West Country

Climbing Gyms

Helena YMCA, 1200 Last Chance Gulch, Helena, MT 59601; ☎ 406-442-9622.

Pipestone Mountaineering, 829 S. Montana, Butte, MT 59701; ☎ 406-892-4994.

Guide Services

Peak Adventures, PO Box 427, Big Sky, MT 59716. No phone.

Reach Your Peak, Attn: Ron Brunckhorst, 405 S. 19th, Apt. C, Bozeman, MT 59715; ☎ 406-587-1708.

Climbing Organization

Beartooth Mountaineering and Climbing Club, 931 Ginger, Billings, MT 59105. No phone.

Rock Hounding

Rock hounding is synonomous with Gold West Country. Gold holds an allure that never tarnishes, but sapphires... ah, there's a fascination and a mystique to the glowing blue stones.

Gem Hunting at Canyon Ferry Dam/Hauser Lake

Search out gem quality stones in the Canyon Ferry Dam/Hauser Lake area east of Helena. Sapphires were first discovered here in 1865, in Missouri River terrace gravel deposits being worked for placer gold. The sapphires that turned up were dismissed as byproducts clogging the riffles. When the sapphires' value was eventually realized, the stones approached gold in importance. The introduction of synthetic corundum eliminated the need for naturally occurring abrasives, so today's commercial mining focuses on gem-quality sapphires. If you wish to dig about on the lakeshore on your own, you'll need a shovel, a pick, half-inch and eighth-inch mesh screens, a whisk broom, tweezers, and small containers for your booty.

Spokane Bar Sapphire Mine & Gold Fever Rock Shop, situated on a gravel terrace some five miles downstream from Canyon Ferry Dam on the west side of Hauser Lake, is currently the only area sapphire mine that consistently caters to rock hounders. Other mines are commercial operations. Deb and Russ Thompson charge a fee to dig and will rent equipment. Digging is reportedly in virgin ground, enhancing your chances of finding a gem quality stone or stones. If digging isn't for you, buckets of pre-screened gravel are available for purchase. "You can almost always find a gem-quality stone in a bucket – it's very rich. I've almost never seen anyone go away unhappy," says Deb. She explains that sapphires have a Coke-bottle appearance, while agates feel waxy. Garnets and bits of gold also sometimes turn up.

The gem shop is a fascinating place with stones and other curiosities on display from all over the world; even ancient mammoth teeth. From US 12/287, take Wylie Drive to York Road. Turn right and continue to Mile Marker 8. Hang a right on Hart Lane and follow signs. Open daily year-round, 9-5. Winter hours may vary. Russ and Deb Thompson, 4363 Castles Dr., Helena, MT 59602; ☎ 800-GETGEMS or 406-227-8989. gemking@crom.net. Internet www.crom.net/~gemking.

A Passion for Gems

Deb Thompson has spent her entire life literally on top of sapphire digs. Forty years ago, her mom, Ruth Castner, rowed a boat across Hauser Lake and, in true "saw and conquered"-style, bought the old gold mine and 32 acres on the spot. Now Deb and Russ's teenage children, Crystel and Cass, are growing up with gems in their blood. Cass has even demonstrated his geology knowledge in "Bill Nye the Science Guy" kids' TV programs. The Spokane Bar gem shop is a rock hounder's dream. Stones and other curiosities reflect the passion that drives this family.

Gold Panning

If you want to emulate old-time prospectors, get yourself a pan and a screen and head for just about any Gold West stream tumbling downmountain. Of course, it's not that simple, and some streams hold out better chances of your actually finding gold than others, but the fun is in the anticipation. Gold panning is a great diversion for kids. They go wild when tiny flecks of gold actually color their pans.

Much of the placer gold in streams originating in the high country got there by being washed downstream, so your chances of finding gold aren't much worse than those of prospectors of yore. You could try your luck at panning mountain streams if hiking or horsepacking in the high country. Or head for a ghost town and try panning nearby streams. Maybe **Bannack** on Grasshopper Creek, where Montana's gold rush began.

Garnet Hunting

The most exciting finds in the general vicinity of Virginia City are not gold, but garnets. Look for gem quality almandine garnets suitable for faceting along the shores of **Ruby Reservoir** above Ruby Dam, south of Alder off MT 357. You'll need screen meshes to separate the garnets from the sand. Most are small and can be identified by their deep red hue. Low water periods in early spring or late fall provide the best garnet searching. Don't even think about digging in the road cuts along the east shore of the reservoir.

Digging for Quartz Crystals

Serious diggers can find quartz crystals at **Crystal Park**, on the Pioneer Mountains Scenic Byway. These include clear, amethyst and smoky quartz crystals. Bring a shovel, a pick and assorted mesh screens. Expect to exert yourself for a couple of days if you wish to take some fine specimens home with you.

Rock shops will sometimes provide tips on where to dig. Butte and Helena boast several. Inquire at chambers of commerce.

The Mineral Museum

The Mineral Museum, on the Montana Tech campus in Butte, is a must-visit if you are at all into rock hounding. The 1,500-plus specimens on display include a 27.5-ounce gold nugget found in 1989 in the Highland Mountains south of Butte. Open daily Memorial Day-Labor Day and Mon.-Fri. the rest of the year, 9-6. ☎ 406-496-4414.

■ Adventures on Horseback

Thoughts of gold country stir up visions of riders on horseback raising dust through mountain cuts; of weary men leading wearier burros in search of an illusive bonanza. In other words, horseback adventures are as natural as gold panning in these parts.

No doubt few if any readers will trailer the family steeds out to Montana. For this reason, and because trail restrictions are subject to change from season to season, we do not provide specific horse trail information in most cases. If you do plan on bringing Old Dobbin, it's suggested that you contact the region's national forest headquarters and/or district ranger offices for current trail information. See *Information Sources* for contact numbers.

Gold West Country outfitters and guides offer horseback experiences varying from hourly trail rides to mountain pack trips to git-'em-up-dogie cattle drives. Picturesquely situated guest ranches offer days filled with riding and nights spent in comfortable, sometimes luxurious, surroundings. The choice is yours.

Outfitters & Guides

Blacktail Ranch offers hourly trail rides for ages seven and older on the 8,000-acre ranch's open hillsides and steep mountain trails. They also offer evening Steak and BBQ rides for groups of 10 or more. There's a three-day Continental Divide ride best described as a mini-wilderness trip. 4440 Southfork Trail, Wolf Creek, MT 59648; ☎ 406-235-4330.

Buffalo Jump Outfitting offers multi-day summer horse pack and fishing trips in the Gallatin and Beaverhead National Forests. PO Box 227, Cameron, MT 59720; ☎ 888-388-8840.

Centennial Outfitters has hour or day horseback rides, multi-day back country pack trips and Continental Divide horseback trips in the Centennial Mountains. Cattle drives are available on a limited basis. They also offer stream and lake fishing. Mel and Chris Montgomery, Box 92, Lima, MT 59739; ☎ 406-276-3463.

Diamond Hitch Outfitters runs two-hour rides and day trips in the Pioneer Mountains; also evening campfire cookout rides. Their multi-day horsepack trips in the Beaverhead National Forest include fishing and lots of wildlife watching. Customized trips can include Beaverhead and Big Hole River floats. 3405 Ten Mile Road, Dillon, MT 59725; ☎ 800-368-5494 or 406-683-5494.

Montana High Country Cattle Drive gives greenhorns an opportunity to participate in an authentic working cattle ranch's four-day spring cattle drive. For decades, cattle have been moved into the mountains on drives similar to this. Minimum age: 12 years. Overnight in a tent camp. Expect to spend four to six hours in the saddle each day. 669 Flynn Lane, Townsend, MT 59644; ☎ 800-345-9423. Fax 406-266-5306.

Montana High Country Tours owners Russ and Karen Kipp offer a variety of horseback experiences that include day trail rides, cattle drives in the Pioneer Mountains, and high country horse pack trips. Cattle drives involve trailing cattle between mountain meadows. 1036 E. Reeder St., Dillon, MT 59725; ☎ 406-683-4920 or 406-834-3469.

Monte's Guiding & Mountain Outfitting has one-day trail rides and customized three-day camping trips in the Big Belt and Elkhorn Mountains. 16 N. Fork Rd., Townsend, MT 59644; ☎ 406-266-3515.

Pioneer Outfitter, headquartered at Alder Creek Ranch and owned by the Page family, leads one-day and overnight pack trips in the Pioneer Mountains. Combination pack and float trips can also be arranged. 400 Alder Creek Rd., Wise River, MT 59762; ☎ 406-832-3128.

Rush's Lakeview Ranch offers three-day and seven-day pack trip vacations in the Red Rock National Wildlife Refuge and on the Continental Divide in southwestern Montana and northern Idaho. Monida Star Rt., Lima, MT 59739; ☎ 406-276-3300.

E.W. Watson & Sons has a wide variety of on-horseback, and some off-horseback, adventures. "Hands" signing on for a June or July cattle drive may choose between riding horseback or hitching a ride on a covered wagon. Multi-day pack-in high country horseback trips take guests into the Big Belt Mountains of the Helena National Forest. Also on offer are Missouri River float trips and mountain lake fly fishing trips. 152

Gold West Country

Springville Lane, Townsend, MT 59644; ☎ 800-654-2845 or 406-266-3741.

Wolfpack Outfitters offers half-day, full-day and multi-day pack trips in the Beaverhead National Forest. Jeff Wingard, Box 472, Ennic, MT 59729; ☎ 406-682-4827. Internet www.recworld.com/wolfpack.

Guest "Dude" Ranches

Guest ranches come in many guises. Some emphasize fly fishing and horseback riding, some appeal to families with children, some stress relaxation under the big Montana sky. Some offer structured activities. Others are more laid-back, allowing guests to call the shots.

AUTHOR TIP

A ranch that fits your neighbor like a well-worn saddle may rub you as raw as a horse with galls. How to find the perfect guest ranch for you and your family? Form a clear picture of what you expect from a ranch vacation. Then ask questions, questions, questions. Request photos if a ranch brochure doesn't include some. If you have young'uns, ask about kids' activities. And about the horses. Are docile kids' horses available? How much horse handling and riding instruction is given before kids and adults may hit the trail? Are helmets provided? If not, bring your own.

Refer to all six guest ranch sections of this book. Read the book through to gain insight into Montana's varied topography and geography. Having a clear vision of the area that best appeals to you will be helpful in choosing your brand of guest ranch.

C-B Ranch, in the Madison River Valley, emphasizes fly fishing and horseback riding. Weekly and daily rates include luxury log cabin lodging, all meals, riding and fly fishing Indian Creek, which runs through the ranch. Each guest has his/her personal horse. The brochure is packed with color photos that make you want to head out right now. June-September: Box 146, Cameron, MT 59720; ☎ 406-682-4608 or 682-4954. September-June: 4321 Orange Hill, Fellbrook, CA 92028; ☎ 619-723-1932.

Centennial Guest Ranch & Beardsley Outfitting & Guide Service is prettily situated at the base of the Madison Range and looks over the lovely Madison Valley. A limited number of guests is lodged in a guest house and meals in the main house are served family-style. Most of the ranch's customized activities, focussing on horseback riding and fishing, are in the Lee Metcalf Wilderness. Fly fishing the Madison is also on offer. Tim Beardsley, PO Box 360, Ennis, MT 59729; ☎ 406-682-7292.

Diamond J Ranch was established in 1920 as one of the first dude ranches in Montana. Pete and Jinny Combs purchased the ranch in 1959 and raised their children here. Placement in the Madison Mountains east of Ennis guarantees exceptionally beautiful scenery. Weekly rates include a private log cabin with fireplace, meals, horseback riding, breakfast rides and steak cookouts, square dancing, fly fishing Jack Creek, which runs alongside the ranch, and use of the tennis court. Activities are as unstructured as possible. Box 577, Ennis, MT 59729; ☎ 406-682-4867.

Horse Prairie Ranch, in Beaverhead County's historic ranch country, is both a working cattle ranch and a RanchLife Adventures, Inc. destination. Lewis and Clark descended into Horse Prairie Valley from the Continentel Divide in search of the Shoshone Indians, who would provide them with horses. It was here that Sacajawea was reunited with her brother, Cameahwait. Following the Battle of the Big Hole, Chief Joseph led his Nez Perce band through this valley. The ranch's accommodations approximate those of a luxury guest ranch. Rates for three, four or seven nights include lodging in a cabin with wood stove or fireplace, meals and on-ranch activities. A weekly schedule of activities is on offer, but flexibility is the watchword. Activites include riding, fishing, canoeing, swimming, mountain biking, line dancing and campfire sing-alongs. Off-ranch activities can be arranged. 3300 Bachelor Mountain Rd., Dillon, MT 59725; ☎ 888-RANCHLIFE or 406-681-3160. Internet www.netvoyage.com/hpr.

Rush's Lakeview Guest Ranch, surrounded by Red Rock Lakes National Wildlife Refuge in the Centennial Valley, has the usual ranch activities plus bird and wildlife watching and youth activities. Accommodations include rustic cabins. Choose from ranch packages that include Guest Ranch & Trail Rides, a Pack Trip Vacation, and a combination of the two. Keith Rush also runs an Outfitter & Guide School, a Horsemanship & Packers School, and Wildlife & Camping Skills instruction. 2905 Harrison Ave., Butte, MT 59701; winter: ☎ 406-494-2585. Summer: ☎ 406-276-3300.

White Tail Ranch, a historic spread tucked into a corner of the Blackfoot Valley at the edge of the Bob Marshall Wilderness, emphasizes fly fishing and horseback riding. Owner/operators Bill and Diana Wellman and Kurt Brekke offer guests a real Montana welcome, inviting them to feel at home in the rustic log lodge and to sit up to the table for family-style meals. Cook Judy Johnson is a sled dog musher and renowned dog artist. Per-night rates include a private log cabin (one is built right over Salmon Creek), three meals, fishing, riding to alpine lakes, hiking wilderness trails. 82 White Tail Ranch Rd., Ovando, MT 59854; ☎ 888-987-2624 or 406-793-5627. Fax 406-793-5043. Open mid-June to mid-Nov. Internet www.whitetailranch.com. E-mail whitetail@montana.com.

Gold West Country

Working Cattle/Guest Ranches

Working cattle/guest ranches differ from guest/dude ranches. These are the real item. Hosts make every effort to accommodate guests, but the emphasis must be on the daily operation of the ranch. A friendly all-in-the-family sponteneity is typical. The following ranches celebrate Montana as only working ranches can. Some offer basic downhome accommodations, others approach the ambience of dude ranches.

Bannock Pass Ranch, 30 miles southwest of Clark Canyon Reservoir, offers per-night accommodations and lots of horseback riding, hiking and fishing. Or you can help the hands for a day of branding, herding cattle or mending fences. 27200 Hwy. 324, Dillon, MT 59725; ☎ 406-681-3229. Fax 406-681-3231.

Blacktail Ranch, an 8,000-acre ranch owned and operated by Tag and Sandra Rittel, is at the base of the East Front of the Continental Divide. Tag's grandfather, Gus Rittel, homesteaded the ranch in 1886. "Modern rustic" best describes accommodation choices and they are priced on a per-day basis. Meals include ranch-grown produce, beef and chicken. Guests are invited along on the ranch's frequent cattle drives. Or ride horses, hike and explore Blacktail Cave, a cavern that includes numerous Ice Age discoveries. Native American sites can be found on the ranch and there's a ranch museum. The season runs from May 1-Dec. 1. 4440 South Fork Trail, Wolf Creek, MT 59648; ☎ 406-235-4330.

Hidden Hollow Hideaway, a 20,000-acre ranch in the Big Belt Mountains, raises cattle, sheep and horses, small grains and alfalfa. The Flynn family has lived in these mountains since the 1860s. They offer a variety of activities and tours from the ranch. Accommodations include the main ranch B&B and home-cooked meals in the historic lodge. Rose, Kelly and Jim Flynn host only a few guests each week. Box 233, Townsend, MT 59644; ☎ 406-266-3322 or 266-3580.

McCormick's Sunset Guest Ranch advertises "Bunk & Biscuit," translating as "Bed & Breakfast" and reflecting the accommodations. Guests stay in the converted bunkhouse's two family-size apartments. Breakfast-only included. Hiking, swimming and fishing the Blackfoot River and Brown's Lake, both on the ranch, are also included. Guided fishing on the Blackfoot is extra. You also pay extra for horseback riding on the ranch or on Markum and Mineral Mountains. Ranch riders must be five or older, mountain riders seven and up. Ancestors of Mike and Janice McCormick homesteaded this working cattle ranch in the 1870s. The 1,600-acre ranch borders the Blackfoot River. 50 Cutoff Rd., Helmville, MT 59843; ☎ 800-757-5574 or 406-793-5574.

Upper Canyon Outfitters, a.k.a. **Tate Ranch**, specializes in fly fishing and horseback riding. Other activites include backpacking, cross-country skiing and snowmobiling. Owners Jake and Donna McDonald are descended from Peck Tate, who homesteaded the ranch on the Ruby

River in 1910. They offer per-night pricing for log cabin or lodge accommodations with three home-cooked meals. Horseback riding and guided fly fishing cost extra. They also have an all-inclusive week of fly fishing on area streams. Box 109, Alder, MT 59710; ☎ 800-735-3973 or 406-842-5884.

ZW Ranch Vacations bills itself as a "working cattle ranch that takes in guests." And so it is, accommodating a single family in a modern two-bedroom cabin. Calvin and Lorie Zimdar's ranch is in the foothills of the Pioneer Mountains and on Grasshopper Creek, the very creek where an 1862 gold discovery led to the establishment of Bannack. Guests may choose between all-inclusive daily or weekly plans having a two-night minimum. Activities include participating in some ranch activities, riding, hiking, a picnic trail ride, fishing and swimming in a nearby hot springs pool. Family-style meals feature ranch-raised beef and pork. The guest cabin is available as a rental between November and May. 4300 Polaris Rd., Polaris, MT 59746; ☎ 406-834-3487.

■ Adventures on Wheels

OHV, 4WD & ATV Riding

Wheels are prohibited in all wilderness areas. No exceptions. Don't even think about cycling Bear Trap Canyon.

If you are a motorcyclist, make sure your bike is equipped with a spark arrestor and fire fighting equipment. Mountain country vegetation dries out quickly as summer progresses. Bring along plenty of water for both yourself and your vehicle.

AUTHOR TIP

Call ahead to the ranger district or BLM office overseeing the area in which you are thinking about riding. Some ranger districts do not permit ATVs on trails. Trail and road restrictions on other districts may vary from season to season, even week-to-week. Restrictions are usually posted on-site, but don't count on it.

The **Wise River Ranger District** of the Beaverhead National Forest is an exception to the no-ATV rule prevalent in many districts. Several trails, some affording night views of the lights of Butte, others leading to old mining areas in the Pioneer Mountains, are open to ATVs. Check with the office for an update.

Designated logging and Forest Service roads are open to licensed OHVs, ATVs and 4WD vehicles, but are subject to restrictions. While ATVs ridden on trails need not be licensed, all motorized vehicles operated on public roads must be licensed and operated only by licensed drivers.

Unlicensed ATVs and OHVs of less than 50 inches in width are permitted on so-designated trails only. ATV and OHV rules and regulations are available from Montana Fish, Wildlife and Parks (see *Information Sources*, page 66).

4WD vehicles are pretty much of a requirement on unpaved back country scenic roads. Gravel and dirt roads are subject to washing, mud and rock slides, flooding, early or late snowfalls and other hazards. Some have hairpin turns and shallow fords. All offer abundant wildlife viewing.

Mountain Biking

Bicycles are permitted on most multi-use trails. However, it's always a good idea to check in with the local BLM office or National Forest ranger district. You'll be advised of trail restrictions, offered suggestions, given an overview of mountain biking trails in the district, and given an opportunity to purchase topo maps.

Beaverhead National Forest Trails & Roads

Trails in the **Dillon Ranger District** of the Beaverhead National Forest are ideal for mountain biking. Contact the Ranger District office (see *Information Sources*) to request a booklet describing eight trails exploring old mining areas and looking in on hidden lakes.

Don't discount cycling this region's wealth of scenic byways, both paved and unpaved. Some might surprise you. Many stretches of the **Continental Divide National Scenic Trail** are open to cyclers. OHV users may also use certain stretches. Or consider cycling the **Beaverhead Loop**, a 106-mile Pioneer Mountains route traversing the Big Hole Valley, known as the "Valley of Ten thousand Haystacks." The loop bypasses snow-capped mountains and looks in on big slices of Montana history. Or cycle the scenic **Standard Creek Forest Management Road**, beginning at the West Fork of the Madison River south of Ennis off US 287. Cross the river on the Road #249 bridge.

The 54-mile **Skalkaho Pass Road** linking MT 1, below Georgetown Lakes in the Flint Creek Valley, with Grantsdale in the Bitterroot Valley is another terrific cycling route.

Helena National Forest Roads

Numerous roads in the Helena National Forest lend themselves well to cycling. Most are also open to vehicular traffic.

Alice Creek Road #293, in the Lincoln Ranger District, is a good example. The 10-mile road parallels Alice Creek (watch for beaver dams), crosses two fords, and traverses lovely mountain meadows abloom with wildflowers in June, July and August. The road begins eight miles east of Lincoln off MT 200.

You'll find the beginning of 25-mile **Beaver Creek Road #4106** two miles west of Lincoln off MT 200. The road goes to the edge of the Scapegoat Wilderness and passes through old logging areas offering huckleberry picking in late summer. Huckleberry Pass, at 5,994 feet the road's highest elevation, affords a panoramic view of Coopers Lake.

Copper Creek Road #330 begins on the north side of MT 200 near the Landers Fork Bridge. The 14.3-mile road transects the 1978 Copper burn area and parallels Copper Creek for most of its length (bring your fishing rod). There's a campground just east of Snowbank Lake. Stop in at the Lincoln Ranger District office for information on these and other area roads.

The Canyon Ferry Lake Area

The Canyon Ferry Lake area east of Helena includes two scenic roads affording great mountain biking but designed primarily for vehicular use. From the Canyon Ferry Visitor Center, drive to York. Hang a left at the York Bar (a saloon, not a sandbar) and proceed some 10 miles to Nelson. Turn left to access the **Missouri-Beaver Creek Road**, along the free-flowing section of the Missouri between Hauser Dam and the backwaters of Holter Reservoir.

A right turn at Nelson leads to the 36-mile road to **Beaver Creek-Hogback Lookout**. This road looks in on Refrigerator Canyon (see *Hiking in the Helena National Forest*) before proceeding to an open saddle dividing the Trout Creek and Beaver Creek drainages. Hang a right at the saddle and proceed another three miles to the Hogback Fire Lookout. Your reward: fabulous vistas and numerous wildlife sightings.

The Elkhorn Mountains

The Elkhorn Mountains offer ample cycling and ATV opportunities. The core of the mountain range is closed all year to motorized vehicles in order to provide seclusion and security for wildlife. But a labyrinth of tortuous old mining trails and wagon roads is open to mountain bikes and licensed OHVs.

Guided Cycling Trips

Adventure Cycling Association's seven-day "Cycle Montana VI" trip describes a loop beginning and ending in Bozeman that takes in a big chunk of Gold West Country. The trip is moderately difficult, with daily mileages ranging from 34 to 72 miles. Bikecentennial, PO Box 8308, Missoula, MT 59807; ☎ 800-755-2453 or 406-721-1776. Fax 406-721-8754. E-mail acatours@aol.com. Internet www.adv-cycling.org.

Flatline Outfitters & Guide Service's Matthew Greemore offers customized guided mountain biking trips to scenic destinations in the high country. 307 S. Main or PO Box 475, Twin Bridges, MT 59754; ☎ 800-222-5510. Fax 406-684-5638.

■ Adventures on Water

River Floating/Kayaking

The rivers running through Gold West Country inspire visions of taut fly lines shedding glistening drops of cold water. These rivers tend not to act out. Exceptions exist, notably the Madison's headlong dash through Bear Trap Canyon, but most gold country rivers are as laid back as a prospector bluffing a strike.

The Missouri River stretch that kicked up a fuss for Lewis and Clark has been tamed by Hauser, Holter and Canyon Ferry Dams.

Whitewater river runners and kayakers generally look to the rivers rushing out of **Yellowstone Park** and to Glacier Country's **Flathead River System** and **Clarks Fork**. Not that you can't hitch a ride on a wave if you have a raft or kayak handy. The **upper Madison**'s Class V-VI whitewater and the Class IV rapids through **Bear Trap Canyon** are legendary. Access points are numerous along US 287. Access Bear Trap Canyon from MT 84 east of Norris.

If you enjoy finger-dipping floats on hot summer days, you'll find peaceful waters on the **Jefferson**, **Beaverhead**, **Little Blackfoot** and smaller

Floating the Middle Fork of the Flathead River.

streams in early season high water. The **lower Boulder**, the **upper Big Hole**, the **Red Rock** and **Ruby** also offer lazy beginner and intermediate floating. Watch for fishing access signs along highways. The Missouri through Gold West Country is largely trapped by lakes. The famed Missouri Breaks are downstream, in Charlie Russell Country.

Canoeing

Tie a canoe on top of your car and you'll be ready for impromptu canoeing on Gold West Country's many accessible lakes and rivers, as well as through wildlife viewing areas (see *Wildlife Watching*).

Most rivers affording liesurely floating are good canoeing waters. Some may have diversion dams, low bridges, irrigaton pipes, fences, log jams and other obstructions that require portaging.

A chain of low profile lakes southwest of Hebgen and Quake Lakes provides a do-it-yourself canoeing adventure that includes some portaging. Straddling the divide between the Centennial and Madison Valleys, it includes **Elk, Hidden, Goose, Otter, Cliff and Wade Lakes**, all in the Ennis Ranger District of the Beaverhead National Forest. The fir-fringed lakes offer a fair amount of solitude, especially in the fall. Several Forest Service campgrounds are in the vicinity. Take the Cliff Lake Road off US 287, a couple of miles west of the Earthquake Visitor Center.

Georgetown Lakes, off MT 1 west of Anaconda, also offer canoeing, albeit with less solitude due to the lakes' runaway popularity, especially on weekends.

Spring Meadow Lake on the western edge of Helena, a day-use state park, is a good place to canoe if you don't have much time but want to dip a paddle. Motorized boats are not permitted.

Gold West Country rivers have been dammed extensively in the interests of generating electricity and trapping irrigation and drinking water. This widespread Western practice may have put a crimp in once-free rivers, but the flip side is a plethora of reservoirs, generally referred to as lakes. Some, like **Clark Canyon Reservoir** south of Dillon, are surrounded by sparsely vegetated hills. Others, like **Ennis Lake**, are set in green river valleys. The lengthy chain of lakes resulting from the damming of the Missouri, Canyon Ferry, Holter and Hauser glistens against a mountain backdrop. Canoeing the perimeters of these lakes, particularly the foot of **Canyon Ferry Lake** near Townsend, affords wonderful wildfowl watching (see *Wildlife Watching*). Campgrounds are plentiful (see *Camping*).

Canoe Rentals

Flatline Outfitters & Guide Service's Matthew Greemore has canoes for rent and will provide shuttle service. His proximity to the Beaverhead, Jefferson and Ruby Rivers makes the offer too good to pass up. 307 S. Main or PO Box 475, Twin Bridges, MT 59754; ☎ 800-222-5510. Fax 406-684-5638.

Guided Canoe/Kayak Trips

Montana River Expeditions offers guided trips on the lazy Madison River below Ennis Lake. The emphasis is on wildlife watching and the ecology. Cameras and binoculars are musts in order to capture whitetail deer browsing the river's edge, an osprey plummeting to seize a fish, or perhaps buffalo calves cavorting while moms watch indulgently. 26 Cedar Bluffs Rd., Livingston, MT 59047; ☎ 800-500-4538 or 406-222-5837. Fax 406-222-4718. Internet www.montanariver.com.

Gold West Country

Gates of the Mountains Tour Boats

The Gates of the Mountains

The Missouri ran free in 1805, when Lewis and Clark came upriver in search of a route to the Pacific. As they laboriously poled their pirogues against the current, sheer rock walls seemed to open before them like so many gates. Thus, the "Gates of the Mountains" moniker. Three dams have been constructed above and below the Gates. They generate electricity to power Helena's and Butte's mines. But the Missouri still flows, albeit wider than in the explorers' time, between the fabled cliffs.

Gates of the Mountains Tour Boats operate daily, Memorial Day weekend through September. Fares are under $10. To reach the landing, take the Gates of the Mountains exit off I-15, about 18 miles north of Helena. ☎ 406-458-5241 for tour hours.

Tour boats have been gliding through the Gates of the Mountains for over a century. From a dock at the historic Hilger Ranch, the boat begins a leisurely two-hour cruise into the canyon slicing through the Gates of the Mountains Wilderness. The scenery provides a backdrop to a narration that traces the canyon's geology and wildlife, as well as a human presence that goes back some 10,000 years.

Mountain goats and bighorn sheep pose on high escarpments. The animals were introduced in the 1950s and '70s after native Audubon sheep fell victim to over-hunting and domestic sheep diseases. Bald eagles sometimes ride the thermals. Canada geese nest in holes in the rock. Other holes access caves awaiting exploration by cavers. Osprey nest here, too.

The cliffs and canyons branching from the river contain pictographs and other evidence of Indian habitation and burial sites. Artifacts have long since been removed.

The canyon's most poignant human reminder is the Mann Gulch burn site where 13 firefighters lost their lives on August 5, 1949. The gulch looks green and innocent now, but the tragedy is imprinted on the very soil.

The boat stops at Colter Campground for a half hour. A 22-mile trail connects the campground to Refrigerator Canyon (see *Adventures on Foot*). Hikers can hop a tour boat to or from the campground. The trail follows a dry creek bed; no water on the trail in dry years. No dogs allowed on the boat, but....

It's after the boat turns back from the campground that we see the Gates of the Mountains through the eyes of Lewis and Clark. The sheer cliffs do seem to open before the boat and close on her wake.

Recreational Boating & Other Watery Fun

Canyon Ferry Lake and the Holter Lake Recreation Area are this region's premier watery fun-in-the-sun areas. Black Sandy State Park on Hauser Lake, one of Montana's most popular state parks (avoid it on summer weekends!), is a 20-minute drive from Helena.

Canyon Ferry Lake

Canyon Ferry Lake's 76 miles of shoreline undulates into quiet coves ideal for swimming and picnicking. Frequent winds attract windsurfers and sailboats. Waterskiing, tube and jet skiing are also big here. Focusing on all this fun-filled activity, you might not guess that a rich wildlife management area occupies the south end of the lake (see *Wildlife Watching*). Campgrounds, boat launch areas and marinas dot the lake's eastern shore along MT 284 north of Townsend.

Holter Lake Recreation Area

The Gates of the Mountains separates Canyon Ferry Lake from the Holter Lake Recreation Area to the north. Though smaller than Canyon Ferry, Holter Lake is no less popular. Direct access from I-15 and the Missouri River Road on the west shore contribute to this popularity. Maintained by the BLM, the recreation area includes numerous camp-

Georgetown Lake, west of Anaconda.

Gold West Country

sites and picnic areas, three designated swimming areas, boat ramps and both overnight and day use docks.

Georgetown Lakes, off MT 1 west of Anaconda, is another popular boating area.

Raft & Boat Rental

Rainbow Chasers, centrally located in East Helena, has driftboats, rafts, trailers and related equipment for rent to floaters and anglers. 3065 Moore Court, East Helena, MT 59635; ☎ 406-442-6838.

Fishing

Lake Fishing

With all the fuss over fly fishing the Blue Ribbon Madison River, you'd hardly guess that Gold West Country offers great lakes fishing with both esoteric flies and plebeian spin and bait tackle. Refer to *Fishing Mechanics* in the chapter on *How To Use This Book* (page 40) for the skinny on Montana fishing rules and regulations and where to catch which species of fish.

The **Beaverhead-Deerlodge National Forest** offers a comprehensive listing of the lakes and streams within its purview, covering such matters as access, depth, size and so forth. Available at any Beaverhead-Deerlodge ranger district office.

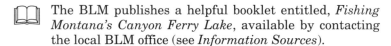 The BLM publishes a helpful booklet entitled, *Fishing Montana's Canyon Ferry Lake*, available by contacting the local BLM office (see *Information Sources*).

Most of the region's alpine lakes are aleap with hatchery-raised brook, rainbow and cutthroat trout. Many lakes in the East Pioneer, Madison and West Big Hole Mountains, are accessible only via foot or horseback.

Clark Canyon Lake, Ruby River Reservoir and **Harrison Lake** offer good fishing for browns and rainbows. **Georgetown Lake**, on MT 1 west of Anaconda, has kokanee salmon in addition to the ubiquitous brookies and rainbows. **Canyon Ferry Lake** affords shore fishing for perch, rainbow and brown trout.

Ice Fishing

Montanans are big on ice fishing. You may shiver at the very thought of cutting a hole in thick ice, dropping a line through said hole, then sitting in nose-numbing temperatures awaiting a fish's pleasure while the wind whips around your ears. But Montanans are made of stern stuff. There isn't much else to do when winter socks in, and anyway many ice fishers have heated huts.

If you're tempted to try ice fishing, **Canyon Ferry** and **Holter Lakes** are favored for trout and perch. Canyon Ferry stages an annual January Perch Festival. Contact the Townsend Chamber of Commerce (see *Information Sources*, page 255) for particulars. **Georgetown Lake** is also a popular ice fishing lake for salmon, brookies and rainbows.

Guided Ice Fishing

Tom's Fishing Guide Service, owned and operated by Tom and Chris Bugni, offers ice fishing on Clark Canyon and Canyon Ferry Lakes. Heated ice houses and hot lunches take the chill off. 3460 St. Ann's, Butte, MT 59701; ☎ 800-487-0296 or 406-723-4753.

Western Waters and Woods owner Jerry Nichols offers half- and full-day guided ice fishing on Georgetown Lake. Trips include transportation to the heated ice shelter via snowmobile. Holes are pre-drilled and poles and tackle are catch-ready. 5455 Keil Loop, Missoula, MT 59802; ☎ 800-757-1680 PIN #2060 or 406-543-3203. E-mail waters@bigsky.net. Internet www.bigsky.net/westernwaters

Fly Fishing the Rivers & Streams

The near-worshipful attitude exhibited toward the **Madison River** by fly fishers may delude you into thinking that paragon of trout streams was the one and only. But virtually every swift-flowing river and stream in Gold West Country invites fly fishing. Maybe your decision to strike out onto lesser known waters, or to join the multitudes on the Madison, depends on how serious you are about the art of fly fishing. Or how anxious you are to avoid following the crowd, both literally and figuratively. Perhaps you'd prefer to chart a middle riffle by flicking your fly over the Ruby or Big Hole.

Refer to this book's section on *Yellowstone Country Fly Fishing* for background information also relevant to Gold West Country streams. If you have the confidence and experience to head out on your own, go for it. You'll know a likely stream when you see one, and you'll have doubtless salivated over countless tomes on fly fishing streams, hatches, fly tying and other specialized information.

If you are a novice fly fisher, or if you enjoy the camaraderie and expertise of an experienced angler, you'll want to hook up with an outfitter or guide. The services listed below will get you started on your search for a guide who will best suit you. Some specialize in fly fishing, others in lure or lake fishing. Some do both. Many offer lodging or can arrange same. Many guides overlap regions, so you might also refer to this book's guide listings in *Yellowstone Country*.

Gold West Country

Gold West Country Fishing Guides & Outfitters

Diamond Hitch Outfitters offers half-day and full-day fishing floats on the Big Hole and Beaverhead Rivers. 3405 Ten Mile Rd., Dillon, MT 59725; ☎ 800-368-5494 or 406-683-5494.

Fishing Headquarters bills itself as "Beaverhead experts," but also offers guided all-day fly fishing trips on the Big Hole and Jefferson Rivers, on Clark Canyon Lake and Poindexter Slough, a spring-fed creek five minutes from Dillon. They can also arrange unguided fishing on a variety of private ponds, lakes and streams. 610 N. Montana St., Dillon, MT 59725; ☎ 800-753-6660.

Flatline Outfitters & Guide Service's Matthew Greemore offers guided wade trips on numerous rivers and spring creeks. Also, float trips on several area rivers. 307 S. Main or PO Box 475, Twin Bridges, MT 59754; ☎ 800-222-5510. Fax 406-684-5638.

Four Rivers Fishing Company is a fly shop and guide service offering full-day float trips on the Big Hole, Beaverhead, Madison and Jefferson Rivers. They also offer half- and full-day walk/wade fishing on the Ruby. 205 S. Main St., Twin Bridges, MT 59754; ☎ 800-276-8768 or 406-684-5651. Fax 406-684-5887.

Frontier Anglers is a full-service fly shop in Dillon. Owner Tim Tollett offers a wide variety of guided trips on numerous rivers and private waters that include high-mountain fishing and llama supported trips. Tackle and equipment rentals are available. Tollett can arrange accommodations at several bed & breakfasts, guest ranches and lodges. His fat catalog is to dream on. PO Box 11 (680 N. Montana St.), Dillon, MT 59725; ☎ 406-683-5276.

Gary Evans Madison River Guides' location halfway between Ennis and Yellowstone National Park affords clients instant access to the fabled Madison River fishery. On offer are half-day and full-day float or wade trips, fly fishing lessons and a fall and spring special that includes three nights lodging and two full days of guided fishing. PO Box 1456, Ennis, MT 59729; ☎ 406-682-4802.

Jack River Outfitters guides fly fishing trips on numerous waters, including the Jefferson, Madison, Yellowstone and Missouri Rivers and Harrison, Hebgen and Ennis Lakes. Use of drift boats, floats or motorboats depends on the water. Owner and guide Jim Allison specializes in fly fishing, but also uses lures. Tackle is available to rent. Box 88, Ennis, MT 59729; ☎ 406-682-4948.

John Maki Outfitters has been covering a big chunk of Western Montana since the '70s, offering fly fishing on Gold West Country's Big Hole River, Glacier Country's Blackfoot and Clarks Fork, and Charlie Russell Country's Smith and Missouri Rivers. Trips on other rivers are available. Choose between day trips and multi-day riverbank camp trips. 655 Granite, Helena, MT 59601; ☎ 406-442-6129.

Madison River Fishing Company, a full-service guide and fly shop in Ennis, conducts a fly fishing school and offers guided trips on the Big Hole, Madison and Yellowstone Rivers. They also run five-day fishing trips on the Smith River in Charlie Russell Country. PO Box 627 (109 Main St.), Ennis, MT 59729; ☎ 800-227-7127 or 406-682-4293.

Montana River Anglers' Jim Voeller fishes the Missouri and Big Hole and several Glacier Country rivers. 7742 Canyon Ferry Rd., Helena, MT 59602; ☎ 800-210-9303.

Osprey Expeditions' Gary Fritz offers float fishing on the Missouri, one of the best tailwater fisheries in the state. Box 593, Helena, MT 59624; ☎ 800-315-8502.

Paul Roos Outfitters, Inc., an Orvis-Endorsed Outfitter, fishes a dizzying number of rivers, spring creeks and small wading streams from their Helena base. Rock Creek is one of Roos's favorite Gold West Country streams. He also fishes the Blackfoot in Glacier Country and the Missouri and Smith Rivers in Charlie Russell Country. PO Box 621, Helena, MT 59624; ☎ 800-858-3497 or 406-449-2293.

Randy Brown's **Madison Fly fisher** offers walk, wade and float trips on the Madison, Big Hole and Jefferson Rivers. Randy has been fishing the Madison since 1972. He can also arrange fishing trips on the Bighorn River. A fully furnished home is available for clients to rent by the week or month. In the winters, Randy flats fishes in the Florida Keys. July-December: PO Box 444, Ennis, MT 59729; ☎ 800-417-1680 or 406-682-7481. January-June: PO Box 2624, Marathon Shores, FL 33052; 305-743-2648.

Sundown Outfitters, owned and operated by Lyle Reynolds and headquartered in Melrose, a small ranching community on the Big Hole River, offers full-day float trips on the Big Hole and Beaverhead. He also offers full-day wade trips on the Beaverhead and Spring Creek. PO Box 95, Melrose, MT 59743; ☎ 406-835-2751.

Tom's Fishing Guide Service, owned by outfitters Tom and Chris Bugni, offers guided float or wade trips on the Big Hole, Madison, Jefferson, Beaverhead and Yellowstone Rivers. They also run trips via 4WD vehicles to several mountain lakes. Trolling in a 16-foot motor boat is available on Clark Canyon Reservoir. Also on offer are wade fishing trips to mountain streams in the Big Hole Valley. 3460 St. Ann's, Butte, MT 59701; ☎ 800-487-0296 or 406-723-4753.

Troutfitters is within casting distance of the Big Hole River. Owners Frank and Edith Stanchfield specialize in float fishing the Big Hole, Jefferson, Madison, Beaverhead, Big Horn, Yellowstone and Missouri Rivers. They can custom-design trips featuring samplings of some or all

Gold West Country

of these rivers. They also offer limited accommodations. 62311 Hwy. 43, Wise River, MT 59762; ☎ 406-832-3212.

Fly Fishing Lodges/Ranches

Some fly fishing outfitters operate out of or in conjunction with lodges or ranches catering to anglers. These may be more convenient than guide services offering lodging on the side; maybe more expensive, too. Most meet every need for a complete fishing vacation.

Crane Meadow Lodge is at the edge of an 8,000-acre ranch on the Ruby River, just outside Twin Bridges where the Ruby, Big Hole and Beaverhead Rivers join to form the Jefferson. Angling adventures are offered on the Beaverhead, Big Hole, Ruby, Upper Ruby and Jefferson Rivers, and Mill and Leonard Spring Creeks and Poindexter Slough. Two- to five-day packages include lodging in private cabins, meals, guided fishing services and non-angling activites. PO Box 303, Twin Bridges, MT 59754; ☎ 406-684-5773. Fax 406-684-5772.

Madison Valley Ranch, operated under the umbrella of Eaton Outfitters, has private river access and a private stocked pond. Chris and Julie Eaton, both licensed outfitters, have a dizzying list of outdoors-related achievements under their belts. Ranch accommodations include meals and are priced by the day, with a three-day minimum stay. Guide services and fly fishing instruction are extra. Float or wade trips are offered on the Madison and several other rivers. 307 Jeffers Rd., Ennis, MT 59729; ☎ 800-755-3474.

Pioneer Outfitter's Cliff, Chuck and Carolyn Page characterize themselves as "for sure, fulltime outfitters not concerned with the fancy stuff." By-the-day clients can choose between float or wade fishing on the Big Hole and Beaverhead Rivers. Or stay in a rustic yet comfortable log cabin at the family's **Alder Creek Ranch** and enjoy three homecooked meals per day. Pricing is by the night. Guided fishing is extra. Or choose a week-long package that includes floats, guiding, meals and lodging. 400 Alder Creek Rd., Wise River, MT 59762; ☎ 406-832-3128.

The Complete Fly Fisher is just that: a luxury lodge on the Big Hole River offering discriminating anglers the ultimate fly fishing experience. Fly fishing instruction is also available. Six-night packages include private cabin lodging, gourmet meals, all transportation, fishing with one guide to every two anglers, equipment and all beverages. Custom river tours can also be arranged to the Beaverhead, Jefferson, Upper and Lower Madison, Missouri, Yellowstone or Big Horn Rivers. PO Box 127, Wide River, MT 59762; ☎ 406-832-3175.

The Old Kirby Place on the Madison is a comfortable angler's lodge that does not provide guide services. The lodge served for many years as a stagecoach stop. Travelers paid a toll to cross the bridge over the Madison River at this spot. The main lodge and bunkhouse are original hand-hewn dovetailed log structures dating to the 1880s. Guests are accommodated in these buildings and in two additional cabins. Per-day (three nights minimum) prices and seven-day packages include all meals, lodging and use of Old Kirby Place facilities. Attn: Walter Kannon, Cameron, MT 59720; ☎ 406-682-4194.

T Lazy B Ranch, owned and operated by Bob and Theo Walker, caters to a maximum of 10 fly fishers. Bob has been guiding on the Madison and other streams since 1978. Homesteaded in the late 1800s, the T Lazy B was a working sheep and cattle ranch until the 1930s when a log lodge and three log cabins were added to accomodate guests. The ranch is on Jack Creek, abounding in rainbow, brown and brook trout, and offers private fishing. Daily guided float trips are offered on the Madison. Per-day rates include lodging, meals and the use of ranch facilities. Guided float trips in McKenzie river boats cost extra. The Walkers also offer Smith River fishing expeditions. 532 Jack Creek Rd., Ennis, MT 59729; ☎ 406-682-7288.

Upper Canyon Outfitters is actually a guest ranch with per-day rates, but owners Jake and Donna McDonald are partial to fly fishing. They offer fly fishing instruction, fly fishing the Ruby River within ranch boundaries and on the ranch's private pond, and full-day guided float and walk/wade trips on the Ruby. They also offer three-day and seven-day fully guided fly fishing packages that include lodging, meals, private rod fees and all guide services. The week can be customized to suit anglers' preferences. Box 109, Alder, MT 59710; ☎ 800-735-3973 or 406-842-5884.

■ Adventures on Snow

Wintertime is snuggling-in time in Gold West Country. It's also playtime. The air has a crisp tang. Snow stacks on roofs and builds cones on fenceposts as a mantle of white shrouds the mountains and softly settles into the valleys. Cross-country skiers, snowshoers and snowmobilers awake from summer hibernation like bears in reverse. Exploring ghost towns on skis, seeing weathered buildings hoary with frost, can be a memorable adventure. Take adventure to the max by skiing, snowshoeing or snowmobiling to one of the US Forest Service's remote rental cabins or lookouts. Settle in for a few days and use it as a base for exploring the surrounding backcountry.

 Copies of the Northern Region Recreational Cabin and Lookout Directory *are available from any US Forest Service office in Montana or Idaho. Refer to* US Forest Service Cabins & Lookouts *under* Hotels, Motels & B&Bs.

Gold West Country

Gold West Country's three day-use downhill ski areas are short on pretensions, long on fun. You'll join 'boarders shredding the slopes (snowboarders are welcome at all Montana ski areas). And you'll meet Montanans having fun their way – cowboys-cum-skiers for a day. Jeans and 10-gallon hats may well outnumber Gore-Tex on these slopes.

Snowboarding

Snowboarding's acceptance as an official Olympic sport at the 1998 Winter Olympics Games at Nagano, Japan catapulted shredders onto slopes from Norway to Montana. The on-the-edge sport began riding frozen waves in the '60s, but didn't seriously catch on until the early '80s. Early 'boarders irritated skiers, who grumbled that shredders were posing a hazard and tearing up the slopes. Most resorts outlawed the reckless, baggy pants-clad daredevils. But when ski resort owners realized that 'boarders were not only here to stay, but had dollars to spend, they created playcourses just for them. Snowboarding organizations were formed along the lines of other athletic organizations, an oxymoronic move considering 'boarders' famously individualistic, anything-goes insouciance.

Practiced by the young, agile and brash (most over-30s are over shredders' hill), an insiders' lingo soon developed. *Alley oop*: any maneuver where a shredder rotates 180 or more degrees in an uphill direction. *Goofy Footed*: riding with one foot forward. *Ho ho*: two-handed handstand. *Lip trick*: a maneuver performed on or near the lip of a halfpipe wall. *Shred Betty*: a female 'boarder. *Fakie*: riding backward. *Wipeout*: you guessed it....

Named for the shape of the course, the *Halfpipe* involves defying gravity by way of acrobatic flipping, twisting and spinning within a defined area. Also called "gate-keeping," the *Giant Slalom* is similar to skiers' slalom courses.

Downhill Skiing/Snowboarding

Maverick Mountain ski area is as low-key a ski playground as you'll find anywhere. Perhaps this is due to the off-the-beaten-track location near Polaris, on the Pioneer Mountains Scenic Byway 35 miles west of Dillon. Maverick's base sits at 6,500 feet and tops out at 8,620 feet; vertical drop 2,120 feet. Chair lifts: one double, one single serving 18 runs, 20% beginner, the others evenly divided between intermediate and advanced. Average snowfall: 180 inches. Lift tickets under $25 with half price days. Open Thurs.-Sun. Elkhorn Hot Springs is nearby. Make some passes on the slopes, then cross the road for a blissful soak. ☎ 406-834-3454. Fax 406-834-3540.

Discovery Basin/Fairmont Hot Springs Resort, 23 miles west of Anaconda at Georgetown Lake, is high in the Pintlers and offers steep extreme skiing. This popular locals' ski area boasts 40 runs. Ratings are equally divided between beginner, intermediate and expert. Three double and one triple chair lift. The base elevation is 6,850 feet, the top 8,150 feet, with a vertical drop of 1,300 feet. Average snowfall: 200 inches. Instruction includes ski and snowboard beginner packages and class or private lessons. Also, a Kinderski program. Lift prices don't even begin to approach $30. Fairmont Hot Springs Motel & Resort ski packages are available. Open daily November-April, 9:30 am-4 pm.

Fairmont Hot Springs has two natural hot springs-fed Olympic-size pools and two soaking pools, plus a 350-foot year-round water slide. Add groomed and untracked cross-country ski trails and you have an all-around Montana winter vacation destination. Ski Discovery, PO Box 221, Anaconda, MT 59711; ☎ 406-563-2184. Fairmont, 1500 Fairmont Rd., Anaconda, MT 59711; ☎ 800-332-3272.

Great Divide is a smallish ski area near the sort-of-ghost-town of Marysville, 23 miles northwest of Helena. The 700-acre ski area includes a great open bowl plus trail and tree skiing. Night skiing. Caféteria and restaurant. Snowmaking equipment virtually guarantees a long season. Average snowfall: 150 inches. The base elevation is 5,900 feet, with a vertical drop of 1,330 feet from a top of 7,230. Three double lifts serve 60-plus runs. Fifty percent are rated advanced, trailed by 35% intermediate and 15% beginner. Lift rates under $25. PO Box SKI, Marysville, MT 59640; ☎ 406-449-3746. Fax 406-443-0540.

Cross-Country Skiing/Snowshoeing

Gold West Country is a wintry paradise for Nordic skiers; snowshoers, too. This type of snow country locomotion exceeds downhill skiing in popularity. Cross-country skiing and snowshoeing offer quality family time and bring nature up close and personal. A reminder: animals find it difficult to survive in winter so any exertion can make the difference between life and death. Stop or make a wide detour if you come upon a moose, deer or elk.

Snowshoes

Snowshoes, popular in the early decades of the 20th century, are enjoying a resurgence. No longer wood and rawhide relics of the kind that decorate rustic cabins, snowshoes have gone high tech. Today's shoes have lightweight metal alloy frames and synthetic decks and bindings. Snowshoes are increasingly used off-trail and in the backcountry. Some snowmobilers stow a pair on board for mushing out if their machine becomes disabled. Good idea.

Gold West Country

AUTHOR TIP

The US Forest Service has compiled a Winter Safety Guide *that should be required reading for everyone planning on venturing into the back country in winter. Copies are available for free at Northern Region National Forest headquarters and ranger district offices. Among the points covered: Identifying ski and snowmobile signs (blue diamonds mark ski trails, orange diamonds snowmobile trails). Hypothermia,what to do if you are lost or injured, avalanche danger signs, terrain and weather factors, and survival skills are emphasized.*

Avalanches

Avalanche deaths are becoming increasingly common as more people venture into the back country in winter. Montana leads the nation in avalanche deaths. The warm El Nino winter of 1997-98 resulted in a shallow, weakly bonded snowpack that triggered numerous fatal avalanches. Snowmobilers are at greatest risk of being caught in one.

The Northern Region maintains three avalanche information centers. Two cover Gold West Country. Call the center closest to your planned trip venue for the latest avalanche bulletin. Gallatin Avalanche Information Center (Gallatin National Forest): ☎ 406-587-6981. Missoula Regional Avalanche Advisory (Lolo National Forest): ☎ 800-281-1030 or 406-549-4488.

Ski Trails

Numerous groomed ski touring trails wind through the Beaverhead, Deer Lodge and Helena National Forests. Booklets listing ski trails are available at Northern Region National Forest headquarters and at ranger district offices. Dogs are usually prohibited on groomed trails, but well-controlled dogs may be permitted on ungroomed trails. The following trails don't even approach a complete listing, but will get you started.

The network of cross-country trails **off MT 1 north of Georgetown Lake** (the Phillipsburg Ranger District of the Deerlodge National Forest) affords miles of touring for all levels of expertise. The hilly terrain alternates between open meadows and trees. The ungroomed **Lodgepole Trails** vary from More Difficult to Most Difficult and are designed for one-way travel. Parking is available at the junction of MT 1 and Echo Lake Road. The intermittently groomed **Discovery Basin Trails** vary from Easiest to Most Difficult and are designed for two-way traffic. Park at Discovery Basin Ski Area, Echo Lake and Cable Mountain Campground.

For the ultimate Montana Nordic skiing adventure, check out **Mt. Haggin**. In winter, this state wildlife management area is given over to the schuss of skis on snow. Not only is the 55,000-acre area long on scenic vistas of the distant Pintler Mountains, it's strewn with relics left by prospectors and loggers of yore. Pass crumbling, snow-shrouded wood-cutter cabins on the **Little California Loop**. Parts of Allen's Flume, an 18-mile-long wooden aqueduct used to transport logs over the Continental Divide, are visible throughout the ski complex. Choose between four loop routes covering 25 km of trail. There's 10 km of skate skiing, 10 km of traditional Nordic and four km of back country skiing, plus an entire mountain basin of great Telemark snow and terrain. Check out a 15-mile forest road leading downhill from meeting Haggin to **Fairmont Hot Springs Resort**. From Anaconda, take MT 1 east for three miles to Rt. 273. Head south and look for the Mule Ranch Vista Area about 14 miles from MT 1.

The **MacDonald Pass** cross-country ski area, in the Helena National Forest 12 miles west of Helena via US 12 (a good four-lane highway), has four intermittently groomed loop trails ranging from Easiest to Most Difficult. The **Old Cabin Loop**, rated Easiest, is 2.8 miles in length. The More Difficult **Little Porcupine** and **Big Pine Loops** are, respectively, six miles and 4.6 miles in length. The 3.6-mile **Meadows Loop** is rated Most Difficult because of several steep pitches and sharp turns at the bottom of hills. Parking is off US 12.

The **Chief Joseph Pass** area, on the cusp of the Continental Divide, offers a dizzying array of groomed and ungroomed trails. The 16 groomed trails include Easiest, More Difficult and Most Difficult. These trails are fairly short, none topping three km. The eight ungroomed trails, evenly divided between More Difficult and Most Difficult, range from 1.6 km to 9.6 km. The mostly heavily forested terrain is surpassingly beautiful when winter descends. See *Glacier Country* for descriptions of **Lost Trail Pass** downhill ski area and cross-country trail complex. The Chief Joseph Pass parking area is on MT 43, 28 miles west of Wisdom. Pick up a map at the trailhead. Better yet, order one in advance from any Northern Region National Forest office.

Snowmobiling

To state that snowmobiling is big in Montana is to understate. Thinking of all that wide-open mountain terrain may make you want to jump on your sled and take off right now. But whoa! It's not that simple. This is mountain country. On one hand, mountain snowmobiling is interesting, adventurous sledding. On the other hand, it poses dangers seldom faced in prairie country. You must never, ever forget that this is avalanche country. See the preceding section on *Cross-Country Skiing/Snowshoeing* and relevant sections of other chapters in this book for valuable advice on avoiding and surviving avalanches. Montana's snowmobiling season runs from December to April, fluctuating somewhat due to snowfall and location. Snow conditions are generally powdery early in the season. Hardpack develops as the season progresses. Daytime temperatures hover in the 20 to 30° range, but can dip below zero. A six- to 15-foot snow base in the mountains is not unusual. Gold West Country has numerous designated snowmobiling areas, most maintained by local snowmobile clubs. The popular **Pioneer Mountains National Scenic Byway** closes to wheeled vehicles on December 1. From then until May 15, the section between Elkhorn Hot Springs and the Pettengail parking lot south of the town of Wise River resounds to the zruummm of snowmobiles. Snowmobile trail maps are available from the Dillon, Wise River and Wisdom Ranger Districts of the Beaverhead National Forest (see *Information Sources*, page 255).

The **Lincoln** area is also a fabulous snowmobile playground. The Ponderosa Snow Warriors Club maintains 250 miles of groomed trails and unlimited play areas through the surrounding Helena National Forest and maintains a clubhouse just outside town. From here, sledders can head over Huckleberry Pass and Dalton Mountain, through the Alice Creek trails and play areas. Climbing **Stonewall Mountain** is an advanced challenge. Eight major trails start right in Lincoln and snowmobiling is permitted on city streets. The Snow Warriors live it up all winter with poker runs, moonlight rides and social gatherings. Snowmobile rentals and licensed guide services are available in Lincoln. For more information, contact the Lincoln Ranger District of the Helena National Forest, the Lincoln Chamber of Commerce (see *Information Sources*, page 255), or the Ponderosa Snow Warriors (see *Snowmobile Clubs*).

Three major intermittently groomed snowmobile trail systems are within a 30-minute drive of Helena. The **Marysville** area has 45 miles of trails. Northeast of Helena, the **Minnehaha-Rimini** area has 120 miles of trails. The 45 miles of trails in the **Magpie-Sunshine** area afford great views of the Gates of the Mountains Wilderness. Contact the Helena Ranger District of the Helena National Forest to obtain a map of area snowmobile trails.

Georgetown Lakes, a popular winter sports area that includes a downhill ski resort, has several snowmobile trail systems. **Carp Ridge** ends at the Anaconda-Pintler Wilderness boundary. **Red Lion Racetrack Lake** affords ridgetop views of surrounding peaks. To obtain a snowmobile trail map, contact the Deer Lodge, Philipsburg or Jefferson Ranger District of the Deerlodge National Forest. Snowmobile rentals and service are available in Philipsburg and Anaconda.

Snowmobile trails in the **Madison Ranger District of the Beaverhead National Forest** traverse the **Alder Gulch/Virginia City/Nevada City** area. Contact the ranger district office for a map.

 Travel Montana's Winter Guide has a map showing snowmobile areas throughout the state.

Snowmobile Clubs

Guided tours of Georgetown Lakes area snowmobile trails can be arranged through the **Anaconda Snowmobile Club**, 150 Fireweed Ln., Anaconda, MT 59711; ☎ 406-563-7945.

Guided tours of Helena area snowmobile trails can be arranged through the **Helena Snowdrifters**, 1813 N. Oakes, Helena, MT 59601; ☎ 406-449-2685.

Contact the **Ponderosa Snow Warriors**, Box 955, Lincoln, MT 59639; ☎ 406-362-4078 or 362-4335 for the skinny on Lincoln snowmobile fun.

Guided tours of Pioneer Mountains snowmobile trails may be arranged through the **Wise River Jackpine Savages**. Box 65, Wise River, MT 59762; 406-832-3258.

Snowmobile Tours, Rentals, Lodgings & Other Services

Granite Sportland has some rental snowmobiles for riding on Georgetown Lakes trails. 728 W. Broadway, Phillipsburg, MT 59858; ☎ 406-859-3753.

Montana High Country Tours offers snowmobile packages that include lodging, meals, snowmobile and clothing rentals, guide services and airport shuttles. The lodge is in the upper Grasshopper Valley, between the east and west Pioneer Mountains. 1036 E. Reeder St., Dillon, MT 59725; ☎ 406-683-4920 or 406-834-3469. E-mail montana@mhct.com. Internet www.mhct.com.

Rush's Lakeview Guest Ranch, in the Centennial Valley, offers multi-day lodging packages that include snowmobiling and cross-country skiing over groomed trails. 2905 Harrison Ave., Butte, MT 59701. Winter: ☎ 406-494-2585. Summer: ☎ 406-276-3300.

Summit Seekers Rentals, Inc. offers snowmobile and clothing rentals in the Lincoln area. They also service snowmobiles. PO Box 487, Lincoln, MT 59639; ☎ 888-SNO-4FUN or 406-362-4078. Fax 406-362-4621.

Dog Sled Tours

Snow country looks different from a dog sled. Here's where you can hitch a ride.

Montana Mush-Sled Dog Kennels offers hour-long treks into the Scapegoat Wilderness. PO Box 217, Lincoln, MT 59639; ☎ 406-362-4004.

Pintler Sled Adventures runs hour-long to day-long dog sled trips in the Pintlers. Also moonlight rides. If you like, Bob and Nancy Davis will teach you to mush. 9010 Hwy. 1 West, Anaconda, MT 59711; ☎ 406-563-2675.

Gold West Country

Spirit of the North Dog Sled Adventures' huskies mush in the Beaverhead National Forest. PO Box 145, Cameron, MT 59720; ☎ 406-682-7994 or 406-995-3424.

Man & Dogs

Folks around Lincoln and Ovando take dog sledding seriously. Lt. Col. Terry Adkins, a retired Air Force veterinarian, raises and trains Alaskan Huskies, a hardy breed bred for running. Terry is an Alaska Iditarod veteran, having served as veterinarian in the initial running of the Iditarod, mushed in 21 Iditarods and "placed in quite a few of them". He and his dogs race in numerous races, including the Race to the Sky through Gold West Country. His dogs are his life, kind treatment his philosophy. On a training run on which I hitched a ride, he stopped when a rope got between a dog's legs, again when a harness snap came undone. Terry speaks softly as he directs his 12-dog team to gee, haw or go straight. Man and dogs, hardy as all get out, embody the best of Montana.

■ Wildlife Watching

 If you are a wildlife watcher, you'll have it your way in Gold West Country. Not only will you see Montana's native wildlife almost wherever your steps take you, but the region abounds with wildlife management areas. This, in addition to the sprawling Red Rock Lakes National Wildlife Refuge and the Rocky Mountain Front Eagle Migration Area. Have your camera and/or binoculars ready wherever you go.

Red Rock Lakes National Wildlife Refuge

Dramatic peaks in excess of 9,000 feet descending to expansive wetlands make the 13,000-acre Red Rock Lakes National Wildlife Refuge one of the most beautiful refuges you're ever likely to see. Upwards of 300 trumpeter swans, brought back from near extinction, form the largest breeding population in the lower 48 states. See them from the Upper Lake Campground and the Lower Lake turnout. Over 50,000 ducks and geese throng the refuge during fall migration. Songbirds, butterflies and moose make striking companions at Upper Lake, while sandhill cranes favor the areas west of Red Rock Lake. Numerous raptors also populate the area. If you enjoy canoeing, this refuge in the shadow of the Centennial Mountains is your kind of place. Hiking and bicycling, too. Take the Monida exit off I-15 (#0) and travel east for 28 miles on a gravel road to the refuge entrance. From West Yellowstone, follow US 20 to MT 87. Head north on MT 87 for five miles. Turn west on Red Rock Pass Road and drive about 20 miles. ☎ 406-276-3536.

The Rocky Mountain Front Eagle Migration Area

The Rocky Mountain Front Eagle Migration Area's viewing site and interpretive exhibit is on MT 200, 27 miles east of Lincoln and some nine miles past Roger's Pass. Binocular signs mark the site. This is part of a major spring migration route, primarily for golden eagles, though some bald eagles may be seen. Strong March westerly winds over the foothills boost the eagles high into the blue sky. The most eagles observed in North America in one day have been seen here. The best time to view this splendid migration is in March, but it continues through May. Also look for red-tailed hawks and northern goshawks. The land adjacent to the viewing site is private property. ☎ 406-362-4265.

Canyon Ferry Lake

The fall bald eagle migration can be viewed at the Riverside Campground on the east side of Canyon Ferry Lake, downstream from the dam. An interpretive display is available at the Canyon Ferry Visitor Center from mid-October through the first week in December. Over 1,000 bald eagles migrate through the Canyon Ferry/Hauser Lake area throughout the fall and winter. From the Riverside viewing area, it's not unusual to see 30 to 40 eagles at a single swoop. The raptors interrupt their southward flight from Canada to feed on Kokanee salmon spawning in Canyon Ferry Lake. ☎ 406-475-3319 weekdays, 8-4, for current viewing information.

Canyon Ferry Wildlife Management Area

The Canyon Ferry Wildlife Management Area is an expansive wetland and river bottom where the Missouri River enters the lake. Numerous migrating waterfowl and nesting birds favor the area. The delta also provides habitat for beavers, river otters and moose. The WMA begins one mile north of Townsend and continues for two miles along the east side of US 287. It's bisected by several gravel roads. The area is open to fall hunting. Pick up a map at Montana Fish, Wildlife & Parks or the US Forest Service office in Townsend. ☎ 406-475-3310.

Beartooth Wildlife Management Area

The 31,798 acre Beartooth Wildlife Management Area, on the east shore of Holter Lake, is a good place to see elk and bighorn sheep. The best way to spot them is by hiking up one of the creek bottoms and following a ridgeline down. Birders favor **Cottonwood Creek**. An informational sign just past the WMA boundary, on the Holter Lake Access Road, identifies a **prairie dog town**. This area is open to fall hunting, after which it is closed to public use through May 14. Exit I-15 at Wolf Creek (Exit 226). Head north on the Missouri River Road, watch for the Holter Lake Access Road and follow it about six miles to the WMA. ☎ 406-454-3441.

Gold West Country

Mt. Haggin Wildlife Management Area.

Mount Haggin Wildlife Management Area

The 54,137-acre Mount Haggin Wildlife Management Area is not only stunningly scenic, but it's a prime place to see nesting sandhill cranes, moose and elk. It also has good birding. Put on your hiking boots or hop onto your mountain bike to do justice to this area of forested mountains and rolling hills decorated with aspen and leafy willow bottoms. The lack of established trails offers scope for wandering and enjoying. Look for **Mule Ranch Vista** on RT 274, about 14 miles south of MT 1 (junction is three miles east of Anaconda). Watch for informational signs. ☎ 406-994-4042.

Clark Canyon Reservoir

A cattail marsh in Montana? Yes, indeed. The **Cattail Marsh Nature Trail** at the north end of Clark Canyon Reservoir is another of those serendipitous surprises that keep popping up in Montana. The barrier-free trail follows an old paved road below the dam. The marsh is habitat for numerous waterfowl, blackbirds, American coots, rails and common snipe. A spring on the west side of the trail affords glimpses of trout. By way of contrast, cliff swallows have made mud nests on the rocky cliffs above the marsh. You may also see yellow-bellied marmots on the rocks, basking in the sun. Exit I-15 at Clark Canyon (Exit 44). Follow Rt 324 over the dam and swing a right at the fishing access sign. ☎ 406-683-6472.

Bannack Ghost Town

Bannack Ghost Town (see *State Parks*) is bird watchers' heaven. A dizzying variety of birds can be spotted flitting through the old town and glimpsed through the foliage along Grasshopper Creek. You are invited to check out a bird book and binoculars at the Visitor Center. ☎ 406-834-3413.

■ State Parks

Gold West Country state parks include ghost towns, Lewis and Clark Expedition reminders and recreational areas for boaters and swimmers. Most are day-use areas; four offer camping.

It may stretch credulity that the **Anaconda Smelter Stack** is an official state park. There's no access to one of the world's tallest standing brick structures because it's a Superfund Cleanup Site. View Anaconda's 585-foot-tall stack from afar while imagining the pollution that once belched therefrom. Anaconda is on MT 1. ☎ 406-542-5500.

Bannack Ghost Town State Park celebrates Montana's prospecting history. Structures dating to territorial times drowse in the sun. Interpretive displays offer insight into Bannack's gold rush era. Primitive creek-side camp and tent sites make it a great destination, especially if you have young tagalongs. Drive five miles south of Dillon on I-15. Exit at #59, drive 21 miles west on RT 278 and four miles on a country road. Watch for signs. ☎ 406-834-3413.

Beaverhead Rock State Park, a day-use area, commemorates Sacajawea's recognition of the beaver-shaped rock as the beginning of her native territory. The park is 14 miles south of Twin Bridges on MT 41. ☎ 406-834-3413.

Spring Meadow Lake State Park is a 30-acre spring-fed swimming and scuba diving hole on the western edge of Helena. The day-use park is also used by anglers. A nature trail circles the lake. Non-motorized boats only. Take MT 12 west, then go north on Joslyn to Country Club. ☎ 406-449-8864.

Hauser Lake State Park (Black Sandy) is a popular weekend boating, fishing and water skiing take-off point offering primitive RV and tent camping. Drive seven miles north of Helena on I-15, four miles east on RT 453, then three miles north on a county road. Watch for signs. ☎ 406-449-8864.

Lewis and Clark Caverns State Park has unstructured RV and tent camping and rental cabins on a pleasant meadow below the caverns (see *Adventures on Foot/Caving*). The nearby mountains have numerous hiking trails. Montana's first and best known state park may be crowded in peak periods. ☎ 406-287-3541 for suggested visitation and tour times. Nineteen miles west of Three Forks on MT 2.

Elkhorn State Park includes the ghostly remains of a silver mining boom town. The day-use park has two original buildings. Exit I-15 at the

Gold West Country

Boulder exit (#164), drive south seven miles on MT 69, then 11 miles north on a county road. ☎ 406-449-8864.

Clark's Lookout State Park is a day-use area at the Beaverhead River outcrop that provided the Lewis and Clark expedition with a view of the route ahead. Exit I-15 in Dillon and pick up MT 41. Drive .5 miles east, then .5 miles on a county road. ☎ 406-834-3413.

Lost Creek State Park celebrates Lost Creek Falls, a splendid cascade plunging over a 50-foot drop. Spot mountain goats, bighorn sheep and other wildlife on the cliffs above the creek. Camping. Drive 1.5 miles east of Anaconda on MT 1, two miles north on RT 273, then six miles west. ☎ 406-542-5500.

Parker Homestead State Park is a day-use area surrounding a sod-roofed log cabin representative of homes built by pioneer homesteaders. Drive eight miles west of Three Forks on MT 2. ☎ 406-994-4042.

The **State Capitol Grounds** is a state park comprising 50 landscaped acres abloom with flowers. In Helena, at the junction of 6th and Montana Ave. ☎ 406-449-8864.

Granite Ghost Town State Park, a day-use area, is difficult to reach except in a 4WD vehicle. The ruins of a miner's hall and the superinten-dent's house are worth seeing. Lots of mining history here, five miles from Phillipsburg. Go south on Sansome Road, then east on the rough dirt road opposite Center Street. Inquire locally about road conditions. ☎ 406-542-5500.

■ Special Interest Adventures

There are times when you may feel that an expert can pro-vide more insight into Montana's wildlife, culture or history than can be gleaned from a do-it-yourself tour. One of the following specialized tours may be just what you're looking for.

Experience Montana offers customized educational tours that include history, wildlife viewing, Montana stories, photography, hiking, wild-flowers and any other Montana-related topics that may spark your curi-osity. Fourth-generation Montanan Allen Schallenberger calls on his experience as a history buff, a research biologist and former livestock rancher and range management specialist to provide insight lacking on many tours. Ride in a van or a boat with bucket seats. 53 Elser Lane, Sheridan, MT 59749-9604; ☎ 406-842-5134.

Montana ECO Treks & Tours, LLC, a.k.a. **The National ECO Insti-tute**, offers a dizzying range of trips having an ecological slant. Included are American Indian educational tours, llama treks, dinosaur dig/pale-ontology trips, photo safaris, wildland area tours, geology/mining tours, bird watching/counts, sapphire digging, history tours, archaeology trips, old mines and ghost towns. The Institute offers one to two-day treks and three-week wilderness adventures. Attn: S. Bud Solomonsson, PO Box 511, Helena, MT 59624; 800-285-8480 or 406-442-0214.

Montana ECO Treks & Tours, LLC also runs the Montana Land & River Guide School. It is certified by the National Wilderness Education Association and endorsed by the International Wilderness Leadership Foundation. The school offers three guide programs: Whitewater Rafting, Mountaineering, and Fishing. Attn: S. Bud Solomonsson, PO Box 511, Helena, MT 59624; ☎ 800-285-8480 or 406-442-0214.

North American Retreats, directed by Melane Lohmann, offers guided wilderness spiritual and educational retreats in Canada and the Continental US. Offerings vary from year to year, but generally include weekend ecological retreats at their Blackfoot River Valley ranch headquarters. They also organize Wilderwomen! Retreats for women of all ages. Horse packing on the Continental Divide is a retreat staple. PO Box 102, Ovando, MT 59854; ☎ 406-793-5824.

■ Kid Stuff

KID-FRIENDLY Show me a kid exploring a ghost town, a kid on a waterslide, or a kid panning for gold, and I'll show you a happy kid. That also goes for a kid on a horse or a kid holding a fishing rod. The folks in **Ennis** know that. That's why the Ennis Lion's Club maintains and stocks the **Community Park's kids-only pond**. Trout range up to a whopping five pounds. Kids 12 and under are invited to dip a line in their very own fishin' hole. See *Festivals & Special Events* for the lowdown on the kids' fishing derby in June.

The **Lincoln Ranger District** and Trout Unlimited sponsor an early June **fishing day** for kids six to 10 years of age in recognition of National Fishing Week. Lunch and prizes provided. Sign up by June 1. Call the ranger district (☎ 406-362-4265) if coming from out of town.

Bannack Ghost Town State Park is a great place for kids to explore, and a great place to acquaint them with a gold pan. Or pan for gold anywhere along **Grasshopper Creek**, and a myriad other creeks. Older kids will enjoy digging for sapphires and gold at **Spokane Bar** (see *Rock Hounding*). If they really dig minerals, take them to the **Mineral Museum** on the Montana Tech campus in Butte.

Kids and water go together, as you'll find if your young'uns ride the corkscrew water slide at **Fairmont Hot Springs** (see *Touring*).

Touring **Lewis & Clark Caverns** is high adventure for kids six and over who are able to handle an uphill trek of a mile or so, but not advisable for younger children; certainly not for toddlers. Youngsters who tend to freak out in enclosed places shouldn't attempt the tour.

Gold West Country

Kids and the **Grant-Kohrs Ranch National Historic Site** (see *Touring*) are perfect match-ups. Interpretive activities throughout the summer teach old-time skills. Kids can watch a blacksmith fashion horse shoes and iron tools, ride on a wagon drawn by a pair of draft horses, listen to a cowboy storyteller, pet horses and explore this hold-over from the days when cattle roamed Montana's unfenced rangelands. Hitching a ride on a horse-drawn trolley from the Prison Complex to the ranch is fun too.

Much of Gold West Country's grown-up stuff is kid stuff as well. Look for information on river floating, horseback riding and more under specific headings.

Festivals & Special Events

 Gold West Country folks take their fun seriously, and like nothing better than welcoming visitors to their do'ins. The following festivals reflect the gold country ethos: rodeos, heritage celebrations, river frolics, snowmobile events, pow-wows and ethnic foods. The dates given for the annual events listed below are approximate and subject to change. Call ahead for current dates and times.

Most festivals and such are one-day or weekend events, but a few are ongoing. Special events have a way of popping up at short notice. Contact the chamber of commerce in the area you expect to visit to learn of any newcomers to the events calendar.

Ongoing Events

Deer Lodge's Prison Players entertain from June through August. ☎ 406-846-3111.

Virginia City's H.S. Gilbert Brewery presents cabaret-style theatre with an old west flavor from May through September. ☎ 800-648-7588 for days and times.

Virginia City Players present family entertainment in the Opera House. Dial ☎ 800-648-7588 for show days, times and reservations.

January

Micro Brew Review and Cool Dog Ball, held in Helena in late January, is the kickoff for the February Race to the Sky sled dog races. Taste upwards of three dozen beers produced in Montana and the Northwest; great food, too. Jim McHugh, 736 N. Ewing, Helena, MT 59601; ☎ 406-442-3263.

Cabin Fever Days break out in Lincoln in late January with snowmobile obstacle and SnoCross races, snow volleyball, ice skating and more.

Lincoln Valley Chamber of Commerce, ☎ 406-362-4078. Fax 406-362-4621.

Winternational Sports Festival, held in the Butte area from late January into March, features 19 events that include indoor tennis, downhill skiing, speed skating and more. Butte Chamber of Commerce, ☎ 800-735-6814 or 406-723-3177. Fax 406-723-1215.

February

Moonlight Snowmobile Poker Run occurs in Lincoln at the full moon. Fun, food and door prizes. ☎ 406-362-4335 or 362-4078.

Race to the Sky Sled Dog Race, held in mid-February, includes a 300 miler and a 500 miler over the Helena-Lincoln-Seeley Lake-Missoula route. Boosters claim it's Montana's premier winter sporting event. PO Box 30-MUSH, Helena, MT 59601; ☎ 406-442-4008.

March

Equine Expo is Helena's annual horse fair featuring a stallion show and Parade of Breeds, plus booths offering a variety of horse items, Western arts and crafts, equine-related demonstrations, and food. Held in mid-March. Andrea Moody, 4925 Echo Dr., Helena, MT 59601; ☎ 406-444-6912. Fax 406-444-6973.

Snowmobile Poker Run, held in Lincoln in mid-March, is similar to February's moonlight run. ☎ 406-362-4335. Fax 406-362-4621.

St. Patrick's Day Events whoop it up in Butte, Montana's ethnic melting pot. Parade, Irish concerts, Blarney Stone Run, Friendly Sons of St. Patrick's Banquet Shillelagh Shindig. Bagpipe music all over town. Connie Kenney, 2950 Harrison Ave., Butte, MT 59701; ☎ 406-723-3177.

April

The Kite Festival & Spring Fling Runs take place in Helena in late April. The annual festival features kite flying, wagon rides, music, concessions, kite making booths. 1K Fun Run and Toddler Trot and 5K Run. Child Care Partnerships, PO Box 536, Helena, MT 59624; ☎ 406-443-4608. Fax 406-443-6186.

Annual Helena Railroad Fair occurs in late April. Billed as the largest railroad hobby event in the Northern Rockies. PO Box 4914, Helena, MT 59604; ☎ 406-442-6118.

May

Family Fun Days happen in Butte in early May. Carnival. Fundraiser for Butte Celebrations. Mollie Kirk, 1110 Caledonia, Butte, MT 59701; ☎ 406-782-1859 or 782-0742. Fax 406-782-2207.

Cinco de Mayo Festival celebrates Butte's Hispanic culture. Parade, entertainment, food. Victor Rodrigues, ☎ 406-782-6565.

Meadowlark Art Review is held in Helena in early to mid-May. Statewide show for Montana artists. Art Center, PO Box 305, Helena, MT 59624; ☎ 406-442-3342.

Gold West Country

Montana State Square and Round Dance Festival do-si-dos in Helena in late May. Lynn Conn, 2125 Villard Ave., Helena, MT 59601; ☎ 406-443-3499.

June

Governor's Cup Race, held in Helena in early June, is Montana's premier road running event and is geared toward serious runners and families out for fun. Ghost town marathon and marathon relay, 20K, 10K and 5K races. Also, music, dancing, art and food. Outdoor crafts show at the finish line. Susan Frazee, Blue Cross Blue Shield, PO Box 451, Helena, MT 59624; ☎ 406-447-3414. Fax 406-442-6946.

Powell County Ambulance Prison Break Run, held in Deer Lodge in early June, features 3K, 5K, 8K and 10K runs. W.D. Jones, PO Box 28, Deer Lodge, MT 59722; ☎ 406-846-3677.

Gold Rush Fever Day, a celebration of Virginia City's golden past, occurs in mid-June. Virginia City Chamber of Commerce, PO Box 218, Virginia City, MT 59755; ☎ 406-843-5555.

Powell County Territorial Days, in Deer Lodge in Mid-June, includes a classic car show and parade, street sales, games, food stands, pork barbeque, dance and concert. Harry Helton, 1171 Main St., Deer Lodge, MT 59722; ☎ 406-846-2094.

Pioneer Days and Kids Fishing Derby whoops it up in Ennis in mid-June. Locals don pioneer clothing. Photographs and displays celebrating pioneer families, old-timers spinning yarns, exhibits of pioneer life. Old-time children's games. Kids fishing derby awards prizes for the largest, smallest and ugliest fish. Free barbeque picnic. Ennis Chamber of Commerce, PO Box 291, Ennis, MT 59729; ☎ 406-682-4388.

Antique Show & Sale occurs in Virginia City in late June. Virginia City Chamber of Commerce, PO Box 218, Virginia City, MT 59755; ☎ 406-843-5555.

Montana Traditional Dixieland Jazz Festival rocks Helena in late June. Five nights and four days of 1920s, '40s and '50s-style jazz plus Las Vegas-style dinner shows. Dancing, arts & crafts booths, gospel services, jazz masses, food fair and a Big Band dance finale. Don West, PO Box 856, Helena, MT 59624; ☎ 800-851-9980 or 406-449-7969.

Buffalo Runners Shoot enlivens Virginia City with an Old West rifle competition in late June. Virginia City Chamber of Commerce, PO Box 218, Virginia City, MT 59755; ☎ 406-843-5555.

Annual Prison Breakout Bluegrass Festival is a late-June Deer Lodge event. Bluegrass bands, beer, food stands, craft booths, sidewalk sales. John Sanderson, 705 Washington Ave., Deer Lodge, MT 59722; ☎ 406-846-1697.

July

Freedom Festival kicks off the Fourth in Butte. Rampant patriotism and speechifying by veterans groups, lots of music, military displays. The Mississippi may be far to the east, but there's also a Huck Finn/Pollyanna Day concert, fireworks, parade, street dance, family ice cream social. Millie Kirk, 1110 Caledonia, Butte, MT 59701; ☎ 406-782-1859 or 782-0742. Fax 406-782-2207.

4th of July Rodeo and Parade is celebrated in Ennis. Rodeo events include women and kids breakaway, top six saddle bronc rideoff. Mary Oliver, PO Box ☎ 307-, Ennis, MT 59729; ☎ 406-682-4215. Fax 406-682-7417.

County Fireworks and Picnic celebrates 4th of July in Townsend with a potluck picnic and fireworks. Kathy McNulty, 223 Broadway, Townsend, MT 59644; ☎ 406-266-3325.

Butte Vigilante Rodeo celebrates the 4th. Professional riders compete in bronc riding, bull riding, bareback riding, barrel racing, calf roping and more. Lots of clowns. Lloyd Stringer, 1839 Longfellow, Butte, MT 59701; ☎ 406-494-4867.

Lincoln Rodeo and Parade kicks in the 4th with traditional Old West frolicking. Lincoln Rodeo Club, PO Box 871, Lincoln, MT 59639; ☎ 406-362-4231.

Western Heritage Days, held in mid-July on the Grant-Kohrs Ranch National Historic Site at Deer Lodge, celebrates the storied West of cowboys and cattlemen. Branding, chuckwagon cookery, blacksmithing, traditional cowboy music and poetry. Speakers and cultural demonstrators interpret the open-range cattle era at this historic working ranch. Chief Ranger, Grant-Kohrs Ranch NHS, PO Box 790, Deer Lodge, MT 59722; ☎ 406-846-2070. Fax 846-3962.

Butte Mineral and Gem Show in mid-July. Rock hounds come to the source to buy, sell and trade minerals, sapphires, gems and fossils. Demonstrations. Pete Knudsen, MT Tech West Park, Butte, MT 59701; ☎ 406-496-4395.

Square Dance and Victorian Craft Festival is a mid-July Virginia City wing-ding. Virginia City Chamber of Commerce, PO Box 218, Virginia City, MT 59755; ☎ 406-843-5555.

Townsend Quilt/Gun Show is held in late July. Quilts sewn by a local quilt group are displayed in conjunction with a gun show and arts and crafts. Kathy McNulty, 223 Broadway, Townsend, MT 59644; ☎ 406-266-3325.

Bannack Days celebrates Montana's gold rush history in late July with stage coach rides, gun fights, old time dancing, pioneer craft demonstrations and music. Dept. of Fish, Wildlife and Parks, 4200 Bannack Rd., Dillon, MT 59725; ☎ 406-834-3413.

Twin Bridges Floating Flotillas and Fish Fantasies celebrates summer in late July with fun on the Beaverhead river. Fun run, horseshoe pitching, canoe and wader races, fly casting, kids' booths, arts and crafts, barbeque dinner, river parade. Lois Smith, PO Box 426, Twin Bridges, MT 59754; ☎ 406-684-5400.

Last Chance Stampede & Fair is held in Helena in late July. Typical Western rodeo and fair with parades, carnival, professional cowboys, kids' livestock competition, live entertainment. Lewis & Clark Fairgrounds, Helena, MT 59601; ☎ 406-442-1098.

Gold West Country

Festival of Times: Victorian Weekend is a late-July Virginia City event featuring Victorian era oratory, afternoon teas and a grand ball. Virginia City Chamber of Commerce, PO Box 218, Virginia City, MT 59755; ☎ 406-843-5555.

August

Butte Silverbow County Fair, held in early to mid-August, is an old-time fair featuring 4-H animals, crafts, food booths, bull-o-rama. County Extension, 155 W. Granite, Butte, MT 59701; ☎ 406-723-8262.

Smelterman's Heritage Day is celebrated in Anaconda in early August. Historic Anaconda bar and home tours, heritage parade, ethnic food festival. Anaconda Chamber of Commerce, 306 E. Park St., Anaconda, MT 59711; ☎ 406-563-2400.

Annual Virginia City Art Festival in early August features western and wildlife art show and sale. Also a quick draw contest and auction. Virginia City Chamber of Commerce, PO Box 218, Virginia City, MT 59755; ☎ 406-843-5555.

Annual Commemoration of the Battle of the Big Hole occurs at Big Hole National Battlefield/Nez Perce National Historical Park in early August. Ceremonies, demonstrations, traditonal Nez Perce music and costumed interpretors help visitors to understand and remember the battle/massacre. Jon G. James, Superintendent, PO Box 237, Wisdom, MT 59761; ☎ 406-689-3255.

Kaleidoscope Summer Festival in Helena in mid-August features an eclectic mix of ballet, fine arts, live theater, Taste of the Capitol City/Bite of Helena, street dance, basketball tournaments, art & craft fair, music festival, 5K fun run. Greg Zeller, PO Box 1183, Helena, MT 59601; ☎ 406-442-0400. Fax 406-442-0491.

Madison County Fair at Twin Bridges in mid-August. Everything you'd expect a country fair to be: NRA rodeo, parade, petting zoo, canoe races, exhibits, duck races, talent shows, horseshoe contest, beer garden, horse show, concerts, team-roping, barbeques, carnival. Gail Banks, Drawer W, Twin Bridges, MT 59754; ☎ 406-684-5824 or 684-5631.

Tri-County Fair, in Deer Lodge in mid-August, bills itself as "an old-fashioned county fair with an up-to-date twist." Demolition derby, barbeque. Mary Tamcke, PO Box 149, Deer Lodge, MT 59722; ☎ 406-846-3680.

Montana Pioneer and Classic Auto Club Fall Tour, in Helena in mid-August, features gas-light parade, car tour and judging. Del Barnekoff, 5480 N. Montana, Helena, MT 59601; ☎ 406-458-9111.

Virginia City Heritage Day in mid-August features a parade and historic games. Virginia City Chamber of Commerce, PO Box 218, Virginia City, MT 59755; ☎ 406-843-5555.

Jefferson County Fair and Rodeo, held in Boulder in late August, is an old-fashioned county fair with all the trimmings. Terry Minow, PO Box 565, Boulder, MT 59632; ☎ 406-225-4397 or 406-933-8482.

Montana Big Sky Powwow, held in Helena, extends over three days in late August. Hundreds of Native American dancers and drummers from throughout the western states and Canada. Native crafts. Bernie Wallace, PO Box 6043, Helena, MT 59604; ☎ 406-443-5350.

Annual Madison River Run kicks off from Ennis in late August. 5K and 10K races. Susan Mercer, ☎ 406-682-5279.

September

Beaverhead County Fair and Jaycee Rodeo whoops it up in Dillon over the Labor Day weekend. Beaverhead County Chamber of Commerce, 15 S. Montana, Dillon, MT 59725; ☎ 406-683-5511.

Ennis Chamber Cowboy Poetry Gathering, held in mid-September, features music and folklore. Paula Eftee, PO Box 291, Ennis, MT 59729; ☎ 406-682-5488.

North American Indian Alliance Powwow is held in Butte in late September. This colorful contest powwow features the cream of Native American dancers. Vendors offer traditional jewelry, beadwork and other items. Debra Quellette, 100 E. Galena, Butte, MT 59701; ☎ 406-723-0461.

Annual Frontier Montana Days kicks off in Deer Lodge in mid-September. Foot stompin' parade, chili, draft horse pulls and more. Andrew Towe, 1106 Main St., Deer Lodge, MT 59722; ☎ 406-846-3111.

October

Butte Heritage Days celebrates the copper town's unique cultural, ethnic and labor history in early October. Arts and crafts, farmers market, live entertainment, lots of ethnic food. Mollie Kirk, 1110 Caledonia, Butte, MT 59701; ☎ 406-782-1859 or 782-0742. Fax 406-782-2207.

Snowmobile Swap Meet occurs in Lincoln in early October. Good chance to get in on some sled deals. April Woodhouse, PO Box 487, Lincoln, MT 59639; ☎ 406-362-4078. Fax 406-362-4621.

Oktober Fest/Bull Fest is an only-in-Montana event held in Helena in mid-October. Three days of professional bull riding, music, dance, ethnic foods, beer. Gilly Gilbreath, 920 E. Lyndale, Helena, MT 59601; ☎ 406-442-6449.

PRCA Rodeo-Corral West/Wrangler Rodeo is a professional rodeo held in Butte in mid-October. Ike Sankey, 90 Sun Set Rim, Cody, WY 82414; ☎ 307-527-6365.

Hunters Feed and Wild Game Cook-Off is in late October. Ennis merchants prepare wild game dishes for the public. Live music and raffles. Marc Glines, PO Box 291, Ennis, MT 59729; ☎ 406-682-4357.

Autumn Art & Craft Show is an annual late October Helena event featuring over 90 juried artists and crafters from Montana and the Northwest. Janet Koenig, PO Box 5414, Helena, MT 59604; ☎ 406-449-4790.

November

Downtown Helena Fall Art Walk in late November celebrates art with gallery viewing, horse-drawn carriage rides. Downtown BID Office, 225 Cruse Ave., Helena, MT 59601; ☎ 406-447-1535. Fax 406-447-1533.

Anaconda's Christmas Stroll, held in late November, begins with a tree lighting ceremony and includes a Santa-led parade with candy and hot chocolate for the kids. Barb Killow, 822 E. Park St., Anaconda, MT 59711; ☎ 406-563-2400.

Helena's Holiday Craft Fair winds up November with holiday shopping for one-of-a-kind gifts. The Art Center, PO Box 304, Helena, MT 59624; ☎ 406-443-2242.

December

Butte's Christmas Stroll in early December features a children's flashlight parade with tree lighting, horse-drawn carriage rides, petting zoo, street vendors, indoor arts and crafts show and more. Gerry Durkin, 201 W. Granite St., Butte, MT 59701; ☎ 406-723-5042.

Powell County Christmas Stroll & Festival occurs in Deer Lodge in early December. Gayle Lambert, 200 Main St., Deer Lodge, MT 59722; ☎ 406-846-2425.

Lincoln's Pancake Breakfast kicks off the snowmobile season in early December with sourdough pancakes and all the trimmings. Visit with the locals around a wood stove at the Snow Warriers clubhouse and get a fix on the Lincoln area's many trails. Charlotte Hagen, Lincoln, MT 59639; ☎ 406-362-4335.

Three Forks Christmas Stroll, held in mid-December, features Santa, horse-drawn carriage rides, crafts and other fun holiday activities. Jim Jewett, PO Box 587, Three Forks, MT 59752; ☎ 406-285-3414.

Ennis North Pole Stroll also occurs in mid-December and features lots of holiday fun. Teri Moe, PO Box 291, Ennis, MT 59729; ☎ 406-682-4388.

Lewis and Clark Caverns Holiday Candlelight Tours are conducted over December weekends, weather permitting. Reservations are required. Lee Flath, Park Manager, Dept. of Fish, Wildlife and Parks, PO Box 949, Three Forks, MT 59752; ☎ 406-287-3541.

Torchlight Parade & Fireworks Display is a New Years Eve tradition at Great Divide Ski Area. All skiers are invited to participate in the down-mountain parade, or you can watch from the restaurant or deck. Great Divide, PO Box SKI, Marysville, MT 59640; ☎ 406-449-3746. Fax 406-443-0540.

Where to Stay & Eat

■ Hotels, Motels & B&Bs

Organizing Gold West Country's lodgings into neat categories is like corralling a flock of sheep. Just when you think you have all the critters neatly compartmentalized, one breaks away and blends into another flock. So it is that this region's lodgings defy categorizing into resorts, bed & breakfast inns, lodges and so forth. Some B&Bs offer riding or other activities. Some lodges almost sneak into the guest ranch corral. Resorts range from woodsy lakeside cabins to posh. Some celebrate Montana's numerous hot springs. Rates can be equally capricious, so check prices and ask what's included before you reserve that cabin or room.

Most of the following lodgings are listed under town headings, often the nearest towns. Basic motels are not listed unless a town or area lacks alternatives.

Lodging Prices
$. . . . . .dirt cheap
$$ . . . . moderate
$$$ . . . . .pricey, but oh well
$$$$. . . . . .hang onto your checkbook

Anaconda

Fairmont Hot Springs Resort is a sizeable affair (135 rooms) built around one of Montana's most celebrated hot springs and includes four hot springs pools (two Olympic-plus size), a 350-foot waterslide, 18-hole golf course, wildlife enclosure, horseback riding, mountain biking, restaurant, and other amenities typically associated with hot springs resorts. An RV park is adjacent to the resort. $$$$. 1500 Fairmont Rd., Anaconda, MT 59711; ☎ 800-332-3272 or 406-797-3241. Fax 797-3337.

Georgetown Lake Lodge is a small (10 rooms) lodge with prices to match. $$. Denton's Point Rd., Anaconda, MT 59711; ☎ 406-563-7020.

Seven Gables Resort, at Georgetown Lake, also has 10 guest rooms. $$. MT 1, Georgetown Lake, Anaconda, MT 59711; ☎ 406-563-5052.

Boulder

Boulder Hot Springs Bed & Breakfast offers guests seven restored B&B rooms in the 100-year-old hotel (see *Touring*). Unrestored hotel rooms may be available at weekly rates. Sunday buffets. Indoor hot springs soaking pools, outdoor swimming pool. Open year-round. Children welcome, pets not welcome. $$$. PO Box 930, Boulder, MT 59632; ☎ 406-225-4339. Fax 406-225-4345.

Butte

Butte has most of the chain hostelries one might expect of a sizeable city. These include two **Best Westerns** (☎ 800-543-5814, ☎ 800-332-8600), a **Comfort Inn** (☎ 800-442-4667), a **Days Inn** (☎ 800-325-2525), and a **Holiday Inn** (☎ 406-494-6999).

Three B&Bs offer a taste of this historic copper mining community:

Copper King Mansion has four guest rooms in a splendid 1884 mansion listed on the National Historic Register. Shared baths, full breakfast. $$. 219 W. Granite, Butte, MT 59701; ☎ 406-782-7580.

Scott Bed & Breakfast has seven beautifully decorated view rooms with private baths and full breakfasts. $$$. 15 W. Copper, Butte, MT 59701; ☎ 800-844-2952 or 406-723-7030.

Victoria Joy's Bed & Breakfast, in the historic uptown area, has eight guest rooms, three with private baths. Full breakfasts. $$. 627 N. Main, Butte, MT 59701; ☎ 800-484-2258 code 3996 or 406-723-6161.

Cameron

Two of these resorts are on lakes in the Hidden Lakes chain of the Beaverhead National Forest; one overlooks the Madison River.

Cliff Lake Resort offers a four-bedroom log house, a three-bedroom house and dirt cheap rustic one- and two-bedroom cabins without running water, but with refrigerators and antique wood stoves. Common bath house. Rent a 14-foot johnboat for use on Cliff Lake. Guided horseback tours. Hiking trails include part of the Continental Divide Trail. Restaurant. $$. PO Box 267, Cameron, MT. 59720; ☎ 406-682-4982.

Madison River Cabins enjoy a secnic situation above the Madison River. The 11 shiny-new log cabins include studios and one- and two-bedroom accommodations. All have kitchenettes. There is also an RV park. A good place to stay if you wish to fish or float the Madison. $$$. 1403 Hwy. 287 N., Cameron, MT 59720; ☎ 406-682-4890.

Wade Lake Resort has five housekeeping cabins. Boats, canoes and float tubes available to rent. Fishing, hiking, cross-country skiing. $$. PO Box 107, Cameron, MT 59720; ☎ 406-682-7560.

Centennial Valley

Elk Lake Resort is salubriously situated in the Centennial Valley at the edge of the Red Rock Lakes National Wildlife Refuge. This property, now on Beaverhead National forest land, was homesteaded in 1876. The lodge and eight cabins were built in the 1940s, and had several owners before the Schofield brothers and their families purchased it. Access is by dirt road; by snowmobile in winter. Rental cabins include continental breakfasts. Lunch and dinner available. RV and tent camping is also available. Activities include fishing, boating, horseback riding, snowmobiling, wildlife refuge visits. $$$. PO Box 1662, West Yellowstone, MT 59758; ☎ 406-276-3282.

Deer Lodge

Aside from a B&B, Deer Lodge has a paucity of interesting lodgings. If you find yourself here at sleepytime and don't have a B&B reservation, you must settle for a motel.

Coleman-Fee Mansion Bed & Breakfast has five guest rooms in a handsome c.1891 Queen Anne mansion on the National Register of Historic Places. Complimentary evening social in the parlor. Full breakfasts. $$$. 500 Missouri Ave., Deer Lodge, MT 59722; ☎ 888-846-2922 or 406-846-2922.

Deer Lodge Super 8 has 54 rooms. $$. 1150 N. Main St., Deer Lodge, MT 59722; ☎ 800-800-8000 or 406-846-2370.

Scharf Motor Inn has 44 rooms and a restaurant. $$. 819 Main St., Deer Lodge, MT 59722; ☎ 800-341-8000 or 406-846-2810.

Dell

You'll know you're in cowboy country for sure if you bed down at **The Red Rock Inn**, run as a B&B. Seven guest rooms and a restaurant occupy an old hotel. $$. Box 240023, Dell, MT 59724; ☎ 406-276-3501.

Dillon

Dillon's distance from 'most anywhere, plus its proximity to I-15, make it a popular overnight spot. I can't number the times I've been thankful to bed down in Dillon when traveling this north-south corridor. The ubiquitous Best Western is augmented by guest houses on a ranch and two pleasant B&Bs.

Best Western Paradise Inn of Dillon may be wishfully named, but it does offer 65 rooms and a restaurant. $$. 650 N. Montana St., Dillon, MT 59725; ☎ 406-683-4214.

Beaverhead Rock Ranch Guest Houses, on the Beaverhead River, offers guests a choice between housekeeping in the original c.1917 farm house and in a log cabin awash with character. $$$. Gary and Sonja Williams, 4325 Old Stage Rd., Dillon, MT 59725; ☎ 800-338-0061 or 406-683-2126.

The Centennial Inn, occupying a fancied-up historic Queen Anne-style Victorian home, has four guest rooms with shared baths, full breakfasts. Dinners served nightly at this popular local gathering place except Sunday, when there's a buffet. $$$. 122 S. Washington, Dillon, MT 59725; ☎ 800-483-4454 or 406-683-4454.

Rivers Edge Lodge is 10 miles south of Dillon on the Upper Beaverhead River. Three guest rooms, one with private bath, full breakfasts. Dinners and sack lunches available. A cabin is also available. $$$$. Rod and Vicki Dickens will bed and board your horse, too. 765 Hanneberry Rd., Dillon, MT 59725; ☎ 406-683-2649. Fax 406-683-4467.

Ennis

Ennis has a predictable clutch of small motels, one with a restaurant, and three B&Bs.

Riverside Motel & Outfitters has a dozen cabins surrounding a landscaped green. $. 346 Main St. (Box 688), Ennis, MT 59729; ☎ 800-535-4139 or 406-682-4240.

Sportsman's Lodge has 29 rooms, restaurant and pool. $$. 310 US 287 N. (Box 305), Ennis, MT 59729; ☎ 406-682-4242. Fax 406-682-7565.

9T9 Ranch, a B&B, has three guest rooms, one with private bath, full breakfast, licensed guide service. $$$. 99 Gravelly Range Rd., Ennis, MT 59729; ☎ 406-682-7659. Fax 406-682-4106.

Rachie's Crow Nest has three guest rooms with shared baths, full breakfasts, swimming pool, hot tub. $$$. 100 US 287, Ennis, MT 59729; ☎ 406-682-7371.

Riverview B&B, on the Madison River, has two river view guest rooms with private baths, continental breakfast. $$$$. 321 Riverview (Box 969), Ennis, MT 59729; ☎ 406-682-4145. Fax 406-682-7402.

Grant

Horse Prairie Hilton Bed & Breakfast is about all that puts Grant on the map. The B&B with the tongue-in-cheek name is a convenient pad if you wish to hike in Big Sheep country, fish Clark Canyon Reservoir or visit Bannack Ghost Town. Monte and Charlotte Elliott's historic hotel has a variety of accommodations, including a cabin and apartments. Staying here will transport you back to the 1890s when tired travelers alighted from stage coaches. $$$. 11800 Hwy. 324, Dillon, MT 59725; ☎ 406-681-3144.

Helena

Helena has the wide choice of accommodations expected of a capitol city. Chain hostelries include a **Best Western** (☎ 800-422-1002), a **Days Inn** (☎ 800-325-2525), a **Comfort Inn** (☎ 800-221-2222), a **Holiday Inn** (☎ 800-HOLIDAY), and a **Super 8** (☎ 800-☎ 800-8000).

Five bed & breakfast inns offer heaps of Montana hospitality.

Appleton Inn, occupying a Victorian home on the National Register of Historic Places, is within walking distance to Spring Meadow Lake. Five guest rooms, all with private baths, full breakfast. $$$. 1999 Euclid Ave., Helena, MT 59601; ☎ 800-956-1999 or 406-449-7492. Fax 406-449-1261.

The Barrister Bed & Breakfast's 1874 charm is reflective of Helena's historic upscale neighborhood. Five guest rooms with private baths, complimentary evening social, full breakfasts. $$$. 416 N. Ewing, Helena, MT 59601; ☎ 800-823-1148 or 406-443-7330. Fax 406-442-7964.

Birdseye Bed & Breakfast is 10 miles from Helena on a fiber farm where llamas, cashmere and angora goats graze. Three guest rooms, two with private baths. Country breakfasts feature farm-fresh eggs. Panoramic mountain views. $$$. 6890 Raven Rd., Helena, MT 59601; ☎ 406-449-4380.

St. James Bed & Breakfast features an art gallery, a sauna, and an in-house salon offering facials and massages. Two guest rooms with private baths, full breakfast. $$$$. 114 N. Hoback, Helena, MT 59601; ☎ 406-449-2623.

The Sanders, a top-rated B&B, has seven guest rooms with private baths. $$$$. 328 N. Ewing, Helena, MT 59601; ☎ 406-442-3309. Fax 406-443-2361.

Jackson

Jackson Hot Springs Lodge's log bar and dance hall is one of those places where you wish the walls could talk. It's Western all the way, including a forest of antlers decorating the walls. Twelve of the cabins have fireplaces. Also apartments, rustic hunters' cabins and RV spaces. Natural hot springs mineral pool, restaurant. $$$. Open year-round. Cross-country skiing and snowmobiling on separate trails. On MT 278, west of Dillon. Open year-round. PO Box 808, Jackson, MT 59736; ☎ 406-834-3151.

Lincoln

Lincoln much prefers to be known as a Montana snowmobile mecca, rather than as the Unabomber's hideaway. It's not known for an oversupply of high-toned accommodations. I've listed them all, as this book goes to press, for the convenience of snowmobilers who simply want a place to lay their heads.

Blackfoot River Inn (at the 7UP Ranch) has 16 rooms and a restaurant. $$. Box 295, Lincoln, MT 59639; ☎ 800-362-4787 or 406-362-4255.

Blue Sky Motel has nine rooms. $. 328 Main St., Lincoln, MT 59639; ☎ 800-293-4251 or 406-362-4450. Fax 406-362-4354.

Leepers Motel has 15 rooms. $$. MT 200 & First Ave. (Box 611), Lincoln, MT 59639; ☎ 406-362-4433. Fax 406-362-4261.

Lincoln Lodge has 22 rooms. $. Box 757, Lincoln, MT 59639; ☎ 406-362-4396. Fax 406-362-4378.

Lumberjack Inn Bed & Breakfast is on a 390-acre wildlife refuge. Three guest rooms, one with private bath, full breakfast. Lincoln's best bet. $$$$. Box 880, Lincoln, MT 59639; ☎ 406-362-4815 or 362-4001. Fax 406-362-4827.

Sportsman Motel & RV Park has nine rooms. $. MT 200, Lincoln, MT 59639; ☎ 406-362-4481.

Three Bears Motel has 15 rooms. $. MT 200 (Box 1191), Lincoln, MT 59639; ☎ 406-362-4355. Fax 406-362-3049.

McAllister (Ennis Lake)

Lake Shore Lodge is an old-fashioned Western-style family fishing and swimming resort. Eight housekeeping cabins, full hookup RV sites and tent sites border Ennis Lake. Guided fishing available. Boats for rent. $$. Box 160, McAllister, MT 59740; ☎ 406-682-4424.

Montana City

Elkhorn Mountain Inn, in a mining-town-cum-bedroom community in the Elkhorn Mountains foothills, has 22 guest rooms, no restaurant. $$. 1 Jackson Creek Rd., Montana City, MT 59634; ☎ 406-442-6625 (collect). Fax 406-449-8797.

Nevada City/Virginia City

Just one mile separates this brace of ghost towns from Montana's fabled gold rush days. An eclectic mix of accommodations is available. Most reflect Montana's rough-and-tumble glory days.

Fairweather Inn is a rambling Victorian affair reflective of the Virginia City of rough-shod prospectors and scruffy politicians. The old hotel has 32 reasonably priced rooms, some with private baths. $$. 315 W. Wallace (Box 338), Virginia City, MT 59755; ☎ 800-648-7588 or 406-843-5377.

Just An Experience has three B&B rooms with full breakfast in a c.1864 house, comfortable log cabin rentals, day-long outdoor adventure tours. John and Carma Sinerius also offer gourmet lunches and dinners. $$$. PO Box 98, Virginia City, MT 59755; ☎ 406-843-5402.

Nevada City Hotel & Cabins will transport you back to Nevada City's heyday. The two-story log stage stop hotel is fitted out with period antiques and hand-woven rugs. The 31 rooms include 1860-style Victorian suites, hotel rooms with private baths and cozy restored miners' cabins. $$. Box 338, Nevada City, MT 59755; ☎ 800-648-7588 or 406-843-5377.

Stonehouse Inn, in the heart of Virginia City, has five B&B rooms reflecting the Victorian era. Shared baths. Full breakfast. $$. 306 E. Idaho (Box 202), Virginia City, MT 59755; ☎ 406-843-5504.

Virginia City Country Inn also has five B&B guest rooms with shared baths and full breakfast. C.1879 Victorian home harking back to Virginia City's boom days is furnished with antiques. $$. 115 E. Idaho, Virginia City, MT 59755; ☎ 888-843-5515 or 406-843-5515.

Philipsburg

Two hostelries enhance a visit to this Main Street America town.

Main Street, Philipsburg.

Blue Heron Bed & Breakfast has five guest rooms, one with private bath, full breakfast. $$$. Box 821, Philipsburg, MT 59858; ☎ 406-859-3856.

The Inn at Philipsburg has 12 guest rooms. $. 915 W. Broadway (Box 392), Philipsburg, MT 59858; ☎ 406-859-3959.

Polaris

Elkhorn Hot Springs Resort is a rustic resort with natural mineral pools for soaking, horseback riding, guided pack trips, a sauna, great hiking, snowmobiling, fishing, covered wagon and sleigh rides. Choose between the lodge or a rustic cabin. RV and tent camping available. The restaurant boasts made-from-scratch cooking. Good choice for snowmobilers, or folks wishing to explore Bannack Ghost Town. $$. Box 460514, Polaris, MT 59746; ☎ 800-722-8978 or 406-834-3434.

The Grasshopper Inn has 10 rooms, two apartments, hot tubs and a cozy restaurant with a central fireplace. Open year-round. $$. Dennis and Amy Marshall, Box 460511, Polaris, MT 59746; ☎ 406-834-3456.

Pony

The Lodge at Potosi Hot Springs is a far yippee-ki-yi from most people's idea of a Montana resort. This one, scenically situated at the foot of the Tobacco Root Mountains in the Beaverhead National Forest, is posh indeed. Accommodations include four tastefully appointed log cabins with rock fireplaces. Spring-fed hot pools feed a swimming pool and indoor soaking tub. Activities include fly fishing, horseback riding, cross-country skiing. Gourmet dining. Choose American or European plan. Three-night minimum or additional charge. $$$$. PO Box 688, Pony, MT 59747; ☎ 800-770-0088 or 406-685-3594.

Sheridan

Country Roads, Inc. has ranch home and cabin rentals. $$$ & $$$$. Box 710, Sheridan, MT 59749; ☎ 406-842-7101. Fax 406-842-7104.

Mill Creek Inn is a small (five bedroom) inn with a restaurant. $$. 102 Mill St. (Box 155), Sherican, MT 59749; ☎ 406-842-5442.

Tobacco Root Land Livestock Company rents five camping cabins. $$. Box 497, Sheridan, MT 59749; ☎ 406-842-5566.

Townsend

Three bed & breakfasts and an old-fashioned resort are in and near this pleasant town at the foot of Canyon Ferry Lake.

The Bedford Inn has two guest rooms, one with private bath. $$. 7408 US 287 (Box 772), Townsend, MT 59644; ☎ 406-266-3629.

Grassy Mountain Resort, bordering the Helena National forest west of Townsend in the Big Belt Mountains, offers a galaxy of year-round activities that include horseback riding. Choose between 12 log cabin rooms or comforatble two-bedroom log cabins. Per-night pricing with semi-

Gold West Country

American Plan meal prices. $$$. 2346 Hwy. 12 East (PO Box 489), Townsend, MT 59644; ☎ 800-226-6288 or 406-547-5263.

Lambs Rest Guest House is an entire two-bedroom, two-bath house on a working sheep and cattle ranch. Full breakfasts qualify it as a B&B. $$$. 16 Carson Lane, Townsend, MT 59644; ☎ 888-526-2778 or 406-266-3862.

Litening Lane Bed & Breakfast offers cabins, full breakfast, hot tub, fishing, horse adventures. $$. 290 Litening Barn Rd., Townsend, MT 59644; ☎ 800-654-2845 or 406-266-3741.

Twin Bridges

This town of some 400 souls is surprisingly short on lodgings, considering the proximity of three prime fishing rivers. Main Street boasts two motels. Neither has a restaurant. Both have low rates.

King's Motel has 12 rooms. $. 307 S. Main (Box 475), Twin Bridges, MT 59754; ☎ 800-222-5510 or 406-684-5639.

Stardust Country Inn & RV Park is more RV park than inn. Six guest rooms. $. 409 N. Main, Twin Bridges, MT 59754; ☎ 406-684-5638. Fax 406-684-5649.

Whitehall

This town on the Jefferson River east of Butte has a B&B and a sizeable motel.

Iron Wheel Ranch, on Little Pipestone Creek, has five guest rooms, one with a kitchenette. Full breakfast. Kennels available. Owner John Cargill is a licensed outfitter. $$$. 40 Cedar Hills Rd., Whitehall, MT 59759; ☎ 406-494-2960.

Super 8 Motel has 33 rooms. $$. 515 N. Whitehall St. (Box 1003), Whitehall, MT 59759; ☎ 800-800-8000 or 406-287-5588.

Wisdom

Wisdom, happily situated on the Big Hole River and a short drive from Big Hole National Battlefield/Nez Perce National Historical Park, is short on accommodations, but they won't drain your bank account.

Nez Perce Motel on MT 43 has nine guest rooms. $. Box 123, Wisdom, MT 59761; ☎ 406-689-3254.

Sandman Motel has nine rooms and a restaurant. $. ☎ 406-689-3218.

Wolf Creek

It's surprising, considering this charming one-street town's proximity to the Holter Lake Recreation Area, that so few lodgings are available.

Holter Lake Lodge has 12 guest rooms and a restaurant. $$. Beartooth Road (Box 7), Wolf Creek, MT 59648; ☎ 406-235-4331.

The Bungalow Bed & Breakfast is situated in a historic log lodge. There are four guest rooms, one with private bath; full breakfast. $$$$. 2020 US 287 (Box 168), Wolf Creek, MT 59648; ☎ 406-235-4376.

▪ US Forest Service Cabins

Several cabins, once used as guard stations or line cabins, are available to rent in the Beaverhead-Deerlodge and Helena National Forests. Fabulous scenery, numerous wildlife sightings and blessed seclusion thrown in for free.

Before roads were blazed through national forests, rangers' access was limited to horseback and pack animals. Cabins afforded them shelter and bases of operations as they went about the work of maintaining national forests. Passable roads and 4WD vehicles made the cabins obsolete. Some were lost to the ravages of fire and time, but an uncharacteristic burst of bureaucratic creativity resulted in the remaining cabins being made available for rent. So, for a nominal sum, usually about $20 per night, you can make like a pioneer. Some cabins are on the edges of wilderness areas. Many are isolated and reached only by horseback, shank's mare, skis or snowmobile. Others can be accessed with a 4WD vehicle.

Most have wood heating stoves and basic furniture that includes a bed or beds (bring your sleeping bags), table and chairs. The plumbing is outside and safe drinking water is seldom available. A few cabins have propane stoves and cooking utensils. Some have horse corrals. Ask what's included when making reservations.

 The US Forest Service, Northern Region, has compiled a *Recreational Cabin and Lookout Directory*, available at Forest Service and ranger district offices. Obtain a copy, look through it, make your choice and reserve it.

Recreational cabin permits are issued on a first-come, first-served basis. You can obtain a permit in person, or by contacting the Dillon, Wise River, Wisdom, Madison, Deer Lodge, Philipsburg or Jefferson Ranger District of the Beaverhead-Deerlodge National Forest or the Helena, Lincoln or Townsend Ranger District of the Helena National Forest. The maximum stay is usually 14 days, but may be less for some cabins.

▪ Camping

 Gold West Country has dozens of US Forest Service, BLM and Montana Fish, Wildlife and Parks campgrounds on rivers, lakes and forests. The more popular an area with recreationists, the more campgrounds are available.

Gold West Country

Many campgrounds are on gravel roads where conditions for RVs and trailers can be iffy, especially in wet weather.

Most public campgrounds are primitive, with pit toilets. High profile campgrounds are more apt to have showers. Some can accommodate trailers or RVs of up to 20-odd feet. Most have a 14-day stay limit. Some are no-fee campgounds, the kind of bargain that's all too scarce in these days of hiked-up public access fees. Fees are apt to be under $10. All are first-come, first-served.

Most accept dogs, but they must be leashed. I've found that one of the greatest hang-ups when traveling with my mutt, Licorice, is locating places for him to run. It takes some ingenuity, but we can often find an open field where we can play ball, or a stream or river where he can slosh and swim. It helps to travel in the shoulder seasons when fewer people are in campgrounds.

State Parks campgrounds are good bets, especially if you enjoy the interpretive programs offered by many (see *State Parks*).

Some private campgrounds are operated in conjunction with hot springs and other resorts (see *Hotels, Motels & B&Bs*). Others take advantage of river or lake locations.

Like many RVers, I like to alternate several nights of dry camping at Forest Service, BLM or state park campgrounds with overnighting at a full-hookup private campground. That gives me an opportunity to shower, do laundry and dump my holding tank.

Public Campgrounds

The BLM maintains eight year-round fee campgrounds on **Canyon Ferry Lake**. The US Bureau of Reclamation maintains nine year-round no-fee campgrounds on **Clark Canyon Reservoir**. Watch for signs.

Hauser Lake/Black Sandy Beach is a year-round lakeside campground with 30 camp sites maintained by MFWP. The BLM maintains a very popular 50-site year-round fee campground on **Holter Lake**. Come early.

There are several small public fee campgrounds in the vicinity of Bannack and the Pioneer Mountains Scenic Byway. **Bannack State Park Campground** is on Grasshopper Creek, near the Bannack Ghost Town. **Grasshopper, Fourth of July, Lodgepole, Willow, Little Joe** and **Boulder Campgrounds** are on the Pioneer Mountains Scenic Byway.

The BLM maintains a pleasant fee campground on the **Madison River** 26 miles south of **Ennis**.

The US Forest Service maintains several campgrounds in the vicinity of Georgetown Lakes. The no-fee **Flint Creek Campground**, at the bottom of the big MT 1 hill south of Philipsburg, is secluded and very pleasant. Flooding can be a problem at this below-the-dam campground.

Inquire at the Philipsburg Ranger Station regarding other **Deerlodge National Forest campgrounds**.

The BLM maintains a year-round no-fee campground at **Humbug Spires**.

The Lincoln Ranger District of the Helena National Forest has two seasonal fee campgrounds from which to enjoy area hiking trails. **Aspen Grove Campground**, off MT 200, six miles east of Lincoln, is pleasantly situated on the Blackfoot River and has spacious private camp sites. The small (seven-site) **Copper Creek Campground** is eight miles north of Lincoln. Turn off MT 200 on Copper Creek Road #330.

Inquire about undeveloped campsites at the Lincoln District Ranger's Office.

The US Forest Service and the BLM maintain numerous other campgrounds. Check with the BLM office in Butte or the local ranger district office for current information.

Private Campgrounds

Private campgrounds can be iffy; pricey, too. Some are of the trailer trash genre. Few enjoy the scenery and near-seclusion of public campgrounds. For some reason, kids love KOAs. Maybe it's the swimming pool and game room.

KOAs

Alder/Virginia City KOA is nine miles west of the twin ghost towns on MT 287. Open Jan. 15-Dec. 15. ☎ 800-KOA-1898 or 406-842-5677.

Butte KOA, conveniently situated next to the visitor center at 1601 Kaw Ave. (watch for signs) has undergone a facelift since I stayed there a few years ago and is quite nice. Open April 15-Oct. 31. ☎ 800-KOA-8089 or 406-782-8080.

Deer Lodge KOA occupies a strip of shaded grassy land beside the Clarks Fork River. Open May 1-Oct. 15. ☎ 800-KOA-1629 or 406-846-3300.

Dillon KOA, at 735 W. Park St. (watch for signs) has kamping kabins and fishing. Open April 1-Oct. 31. ☎ 800-KOA-2751 or 406-683-2749.

Anaconda

Anaconda Sportsman Park isn't in Anaconda but 25 miles away on MT 43. For a $5 per night donation you get to park your rig beside the deep-running Big Hole River. No reservations; just pull in. Definitely one of Montana's best kept, and best, camping secrets. Open May 17-Sept. 30.

Cameron

Madison River Cabins & RV Park (see *Hotels, Motels & B&Bs*).

Clinton

Ekstrom Stage Station is a resortish kind of place with horses, fishing, a pool, tepees and a restaurant. Open May 1-Sept. 30. I-90 Exit 126 then 15 miles south on Rock Creek Road. ☎ 406-825-3183.

Dillon

Southside RV Park has open campsites on a grassy acreage bisected by a swift-running irrigation ditch. Probably not safe for small children, but it's my choice when overnighting in Dillon. Open Mar. 1-Nov. 1. Exit I-15 at #62 and turn right on Poindexter. Watch for signs. ☎ 406-683-2244.

Beaverhead Marina & RV Park is a thought if you wish to be on Clark Canyon Reservoir but don't want to dry camp. 1225 Hwy. 324. ☎ 406-683-5556.

Helena

Canyon Ferry RV Park is an alternative to a public campground if you want full hookups, showers and a laundromat, but it's back from the lake. 7950 Canyon Ferry Road, Helena. MT 59601. ☎ 406-475-3811.

Lincoln Road RV Park is well run, but open sites offer little privacy. Convenient to the city and probably Helena's best bet. Open all year. Take I-15 Exit 200. ☎ 800-797-3725.

Jackson

Jackson Hot Springs Lodge (see *Hotels, Motels & B&Bs*).

McAllister

Lakeshore Lodge (see *Hotels, Motels & B&Bs*).

Townsend

Goose Bay Marina, on Hwy. 284 on the east shore of Canyon Ferry Lake, has an RV park. Open April 1-Nov. 1. ☎ 406-266-3645.

■ Where to Eat

Most Gold West Country eateries take seriously their task of turning out such Western staples as flapjacks, barbeque, steaks and home fries. A few have defected to gourmet cuisine. For the most part, "vegetarian" is a cuss word, not a dietary preference. Ethnic foods are big in melting pot mining communities such as Butte. Helena takes pride in being the flip side of Butte, both culturally and gastronomically.

If a town has no eatery that transcends ordinary, it won't get a mention here. Paraphrasing earlier chapters of this book, 'most every town has a café or a steak house and 'most every visitor can find it. Restaurants touting "family-style" and "like Mom used to make" tend toward bland and turn me off. In Gold West Country, "cowboy-style" and "authentic Western" can also be turnoffs, but not always. "Home cooking" usually delivers as expected – or hoped.

The following recommendations are admittedly subjective. Food preferences are always subjective. You may not agree with me, but here goes....

Alder

Alder Steakhouse and Bar claims to be on the "rong side of the tracks," to serve "staale beer and cheep whiskey" and have lousy service. But the popular hangout serves sizzling good steaks. Dinner daily in summer and until after the fall hunting season. Reservations suggested. ☎ 406-842-5159.

Boulder

Boulder Hot Springs Bed & Breakfast puts on thumping good summer Sunday buffets. Vegetarian entrées and special kids' meals available. In the historic hotel off MT 69. ☎ 406-225-4339.

Butte

Butte's gastronomic scene isn't what it was before the old ethnic neighborhoods gave way to the Berkeley Pit, but it still upholds a certain reputation, with pork chop sandwiches and pasties straight from the days when the hand-held meat pies went down into the mines.

John's Pork Chop Sandwich is a Butte original. Restaurants at 8 W. Mercury and 2400 Harrison Ave. serve lunch and dinner daily in addition to those famous (in Montana) pork chop sandwiches. ☎ 406-782-0812 and 782-1783.

Metals Banque Restaurant, at Park and Main, specializes in Mexican dishes with upscale flair. Lunch and dinner. ☎ 406-723-6160.

Nancy's Pasty Shop, at 2810 Pine, isn't much to look at, but the pasties are big, juicy and delicious. Don't visit Butte without munching down on one. Take-out. ☎ 406-782-7410.

The Acoma, at 60 East Broadway, is housed in an old bank whose basement boasts a capped mine tunnel. Dine in a former bank vault. Upscale cuisine; lunch and dinner. ☎ 406-782-7001.

The Uptown Café at 47 E. Broadway may have a plebeian name, but a boast of "civilized dining in the wild, wild West" earned it acclaim from *Bon Appétit* and *Gourmet* magazines. ☎ 406-723-4735.

Deer Lodge

You might expect, considering Deer Lodge's museums and such, that the town would have something other than the usual ho-hum cafés and tourist restaurants. But it doesn't, at least that I could discover.

Gold West Country

Dell

Tiny Dell, on the other hand, has two notable eateries. How can a one-horse town in the middle of nowhere support two? This is Dillon's version of a suburb, that's why.

The Red Rock Inn is known for its prime rib and fresh bread. Dinner only. ☎ 406-276-3501.

Yesterday's Café, housed in an old schoolhouse, serves up old fashioned family-style food all day, every day. ☎ 406-276-3308.

Dillon

Dillon runs heavily to chain and motel eateries, reflecting its way-stop status. But alternatives do exist.

Blacktail Station, at 26 S. Montana, is chock-a-block with mining memorabilia. No surprise that the specialties are steaks. Open daily, 11-11. ☎ 406-683-6611.

The Centennial Inn, at 122 S. Washington, serves super dinners nightly except Sunday. Daily lunch buffets and special Sunday buffets. This is THE gathering place for Dillon society. The Victorian ambience attracts locals like bees to a honeypot. ☎ 406-683-4454.

Great Harvest Micro Bakery at 23 S. Idaho. If you've never sunk a tooth into a thick slab of Great Harvest bread slathered with butter, you haven't lived. Complimentary hot-from-the-oven slices. Dillon is the headquarters of the popular Western franchised bakery chain. Usually open Mon.-Fri. I was disappointed to find it closed on a Monday in May. ☎ 406-683-5254.

Ennis

Ennis's split personality as cowboy town and fly fishing mecca is apparent in its restaurant offerings.

A big sign on Main Street announces that the **Ennis Café** serves up buffalo burgers and homemade pies. Open daily. ☎ 406-682-4442.

Bandito's Restaurant, also on Main, proudly serves homemade Mexican cuisine for lunch and dinner. Deck dining in season. ☎ 406-682-7460.

Grizzly Bar & Grill has an open pit Aspen grill. Lunch and dinner daily and nightly specials. ☎ 406-682-7103.

Grant

Centennial Livestock Recreation Cross Ranch Cookhouse, 12 miles south of Bannack State Park, recreates the ambience of an old-time cookhouse where guests and hired hands chow down together. Homemade pies and breads. Reasonably priced breakfast, lunches and dinners. 24-hour advance reservations required. ☎ 406-681-3133.

Helena

Helena's restaurant offerings are as eclectic as you might expect.

Charlie's Bagels, at 1302 Prospect Ave., specializes in gourmet bagels and coffees and fulfills every expectation of yummy made-on-the-spot bagels. Take-out, drive-through. Open daily. ☎ 406-443-5063.

The Hollow, at 26 Last Chance Gulch, is a laid-back breakfast and lunch spot offering yummy sandwiches and coffees. Open Mon.-Sat. ☎ 406-443-2288.

On Broadway, at 106 Broadway, is as upscale as Helena gets. Great pasta dishes. Dinner only, Mon.-Sat. Reservations suggested. ☎ 406-443-1929.

The River Grille, at 1225 Custer, serves up the ubiquitous steaks and prime rib, plus innovative daily specials, in elegant surroundings. Reservations suggested. Open Tues.-Sat. 11:30-10 and Sunday 4-9.

The Staggering Ox, offering Montana Muckamuck, i.e. food, at 400 Euclid, could be noted solely for the odd name, but is lauded by Helena folks for a zany creation trademarked as the Clubfoot Sandwich. Open daily. ☎ 406-443-1729.

The Stonehouse, in Reeder's Alley, offers gourmet dining in a romantic 1890s atmosphere. Locals voted it tops in a Best of Helena survey. Dining daily. ☎ 406-449-2552.

The Windbag Saloon, at 19 Last Chance Gulch, is a sort of upscale place popular with locals. Open daily. ☎ 406-443-9669.

Marysville

Marysville House, a genuine throwback to the town's red-hot mining heyday, is a popular skiers' and hikers' watering hole and dining spot. Eclectic menu. Maybe open daily. No phone.

Nevada City/Virginia City

The Star Bakery & Restaurant's pâtés, terrines and smoked salmon omelettes would shock those old prospectors right down to their boots. The elegant bistro is usually open for lunch and dinner in tourist season. No phone.

Philipsburg

Philipsburg's gastronomic scene is saved by Stephanie Burd's **Rendezvous Coffeehouse & Gallery**, at 204 E. Broadway. Open daily for breakfast, lunch and dinner, this excellent eatery features Southwestern dining, tasty veggie wraps and scrumptious pastries. Local art on display. ☎ 406-859-3529.

Gold West Country

Glacier Country

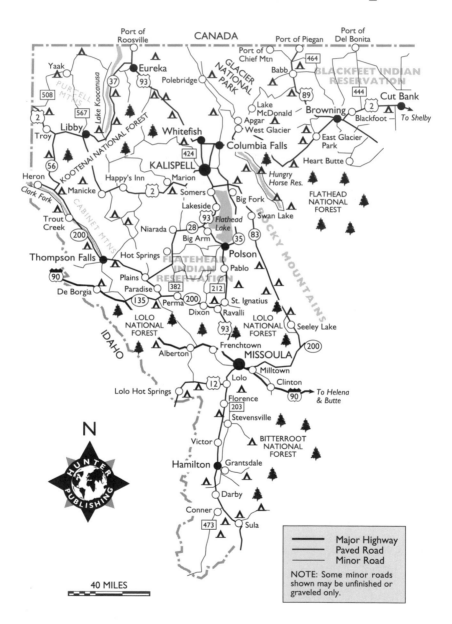

Glacier Country

Introduction

The name given the mountain landscape of western Montana celebrates the glaciers that once overlayed it. When the ice sheets retreated, roughly 20,000 years ago, they left U-shaped valleys shouldered by peaks of surpassing magnificence. Glacial remnants still hang on some north-facing slopes. Shivery mini-lakes nestle in mountain cirques. Larger lakes lie deep in glacier-ground valleys. To state that Glacier Country is an adventurer's dreamland is to belabor the obvious.

This place of soaring beauty also offers adventures of the mind and speaks to the soul. The saga of its Indian tribes, of trappers, traders and explorers, is relived through numerous museums and historic sites.

Glacier Country exerts a magnetic pull, whether seen from your car or experienced via trails winding into the high country.

Glacier National Park, tucked between the Blackfeet Indian Reservation and the Whitefish Mountain Range, is sister to Canada's **Waterton Lakes National Park**. The **Going to the Sun Road** slices through the Park's 1,600 square miles of wild beauty. The parks share some 20 miles of common border.

Two Indian Reservations occupy large tracts of Glacier Country. Their cultural contributions add to Glacier Country's fascination. The 1.2-million-acre **Flathead Reservation**, home to nearly 4,000 members of the Confederated Salish and Kootenai tribes, includes the southern half of **Flathead Lake**. The **Cabinet Mountains** overlook the reservation on the west. The **Mission Mountains** stand sentinel on the east. 52,000 acres of reservation lands have been set aside as wildlife refuges and parks. These include Ninepipe and Pablo Wildlife Refuges and the National Bison Range.

The **Blackfeet Reservation**, comprising 1.5 million acres of **Rocky Mountain Front** foothills and adjoining prairie lands, is home to some 7,300 members of the Blackfeet tribe. The reservaton is bordered on the west by Glacier Park, on the north by Canada, and on the south by the **Great Bear Wilderness**.

The **Kootenai, Flathead, Lolo** and **Bitterroot National Forests** sprawl across Glacier Country. The Kootenai and Flathead National Forests celebrate the Indian tribes that have long called the area home. The Lolo National Forest is named for an early transporation route to the buffalo hunting grounds east of the Rocky Mountain Front. The Bitterroot National Forest and the river of that name honor the Montana state flower. The roots of these showy pink and white flowers were once such an important part of Native Peoples' diets that solemn ceremonies surrounded the digging of the first roots of spring.

The Bitterroot Legend

The beautiful bitterroot flower gave birth to a beautiful legend. The name "bitterroot" was coined by Lewis and Clark, who found the root to be bitter in the extreme. Flathead legend says that the flower was created when the rising sun found an old woman weeping by a river, bemoaning the fate of her starving people. The sun sent a guardian bird to comfort her. "Your tears will cause a new plant to rise," it told her. "The flower will have the white color of your hair and the rose of my wing feathers. You will find the root bitter with your sorrow, but it will nourish you."

The First Roots Ceremony was traditionally held in early May. An elderly woman who had never tasted misfortune dug some roots and brought them to the chief who announced the arrival of root digging time. After he prayed for their safety, the women set out for the gathering site. The old woman planted her digging stick at the base of a carefully chosen plant. The women uprooted it, prompting a communal feast. It was only then that families could dig roots for their own use.

The roots were dug before the flowers appeared, when the bark layer would most easily slip off to reveal the white inner portion. Bitterroots were boiled fresh, but were more often spread on hides to dry, then cached in parfleche bags on tree platforms.

Five wilderness areas preserve Glacier Country's pristine ecology: The **Bob Marshall** and adjoining **Great Bear Wilderness**, the **Cabinet Mountains, Mission Mountains** and **Rattlesnake Wilderness ar-**

eas. Together with Glacier National Park, the areas offer virtually endless backpacking, horsepacking, primitive camping, fishing and mountain climbing opportunities.

Missoula, with just over 45,000 residents, is the region's largest city. Home to the **University of Montana** and boasting an eclectic mix of bookstores, eateries and shops, Missoula basks in a reputation as conservative Montana's most far-out city.

Kalispell ranks second, with 13,200 residents. Set in the northern end of the Flathead Valley, Kalispell is seeing an influx of wanna-be Westerners. The very people who upset the balance of nature by building where wild animals used to roam now cry foul when mountain lions stray onto their ranchettes and deer nibble their gardens. In Glacier Country, you'll find as much or as little adventure as you're up for – heart-catching vistas, grizzly bear and mountain goat sightings, churning whitewater, festival fun, colorful pow-wows... all amid scenery that will fill your reveries for years to come.

■ History

The upthrust region of Western Montana known as "Glacier Country" has never been a soft place to live.

The **Piegans**, a tribe of the Blackfeet Nation that came down from Saskatchewan, probably in the early 18th century, knew that. But they survived, even thrived.

By the late 1700s, these expert horsemen had earned a reputation as a fierce people, raiding other tribes and refusing contact with Europeans. The **Shoshone** to the south were among their enemies. Aware of the Blackfeet's fierce reputation, Lewis and Clark trod warily as they entered Piegan territory. Because their guide Sacajawea was Shoshone, they anticipated, and received, a friendly reception from her people.

By 1832, when the American Fur Company opened Fort Piegan on the Missouri River near the mouth of the Marias, the **Blackfeet** had discovered the advantages of trade goods and affected a measure of friendliness.

In the space of a few decades the tribe fell victim to smallpox, starvation and the US Army. By the end of the 19th century, the decimation of the all-sustaining buffalo had reduced the once-proud tribe to begging from their enemies. Indian agents tried and failed to make farmers of these hunter-gatherers.

Today, the Blackfeet economy is on the upswing due to improved agriculture, forest resources, tourism and cautious exploitation of the oil and gas reserves underlying parts of the reservation. However, many people remain poor and out of work. The Reservation is experiencing a resurgence of Blackfeet cultural identity. Pioneering immersion schools, in which students speak only the Blackfeet language, are meeting with heartening success.

The **Flathead** and **Pend d'Oreille**, whose descendants live on the Flathead Reservation, are thought to have begun migrating up the Columbia River system into western Montana some 5,000 years ago. The **Kootenai** may have lived in the northern valleys much longer. The three Salish-speaking peoples are linguistically related to Columbia plateau tribes.

DID YOU KNOW?

Christianity came to the Flathead and Pend d'Oreille in the 1840s when the peripatetic Fr. Pierre Jean DeSmet established St. Mary's Mission in the Bitterroot Valley.

In 1855, Isaac Stevens, superintendent of Indian Affairs in Washington Territory, proposed that the tribes move north to join the Kootenai on a reservation in the Flathead, Jocko and Mission Valleys so that the Bitterroot Valley's prime lands could be opened to white settlers. The Hellgate Treaty was signed by the Pend d'Oreille and Kootenai. Chief Victor of the Flatheads and his son Charlo refused to budge. In 1891, the Flatheads moved north on a forced march. White settlers also came to the Flathead Reservation. The 1908 Allotment Act gave each tribal member 240 acres of reservation land. A later law permitted members to sell their allotments. Many did. In 1910, Congress opened a million acres of reservation lands to homesteading. Filing was suspended in 1919, but it was too late to reverse the effects. Intermarriage, begun in fur trading days, had diluted tribal bloodlines.

The Flathead Reservation has a wealth of natural resources: forests, fertile agricultural lands, water resources. These, plus progressive tourism, contribute to a modest prosperity.

By the mid-19th century, over-trapping of beaver had put the quietus on the Mountain Man era. Settlers began trickling into Glacier Country's valleys. Today, these valleys are laced with cattle ranches and fields of small grains. Cherry orchards decorate the slopes above Flathead Lake. For decades, forestry sustained many families. Tourism and recreationism is slowly supplanting forestry.

Congress established **Glacier National Park** in 1910. The park's remoteness kept it off the mainstream tourism map until improved roads followed the Great Northern Railway, opening it to all.

■ Geography

Glacier Country is defined by mountains, rivers, valleys and lakes. In turn, these ice-age leftovers define the region's flora and fauna. This is the land of the giant grizzly, of the stealthy mountain lion, the bighorn sheep, the gray wolf, of elk, deer and moose. It's a land of abundant berries, tall conifers and showy wildflowers.

Flathead, Seeley, Koocanusa and a galaxy of smaller **lakes** shimmer invitingly under azure skies. Whitefish, yellow perch and trout swim in their clear waters. Wetlands afford habitat for waterfowl and moose.

Glacier National Park typifies all that is wild, rugged and beautiful. The Park boasts the sharpest peaks, the splashiest waterfalls, the biggest glaciers, the prettiest wildflower meadows, the clearest lakes, the most rugged backcountry, the wildest animals. The Blackfeet viewed the Park's uptilted land with awe, making forays into its fastnesses only to hunt and dig roots. We also view it with awe.

The Valleys

Three major north-to-south valleys lie in the shadows of mountain ranges whose names inspire a lust for adventure.

- The **Flathead Valley** is protected on the east by the Swan Mountains. The Cabinet Mountains stand sentinel on the west. The snowcapped peaks of Glacier Park rise to the north. The Mission Mountains seem to rise straight up from the Mission Valley floor. The Cabinets and Bitterroots define the western horizon. Flathead Lake shines like a jewel.

- Missoula heads the **Bitterroot Valley**, framed by the Bitterrroot and Sapphire mountain ranges.

- To the northeast, the Swan and Clearwater rivers bisect the 80-mile-long **Seeley-Swan Valley**. The Bob Marshall Wilderness butts up against these valleys on the east and the Mission Range protects them on the west.

The River System

Sky-piercing mountains give birth to rivers rushing down-mountain to the Columbia Basin. All of Glacier Country except slices of Glacier National Park and the Bob Marshall Wilderness, and the entire Blackfeet Reservation, lie west of the Continental Divide. The **Blackfoot**, dubbed by the Nez Perce the "River of the Road to Buffalo," feeds into the Clark Fork of the **Columbia** east of Missoula. The river that once floated Nez Perce hunters to the plains to hunt buffalo now floats recreationists and anglers.

The **Bitterroot River**, rising in the mountains of Idaho, meanders through the valley of that name to merge with the Clark Fork at Missoula. The forks of the **Flathead River**, rising in the Great Bear Wilderness and skirting Glacier National Park before heading into Canada, form the nation's longest (219 miles) Wild & Scenic River system. Numerous other rivers and streams rollick downmountain, cascading over rocks and singing through valleys. Several species of trout hide in rock-lined pools and spawn under downed tree trunks.

■ Flora & Fauna

Meadows and valleys caught among mountains soaring to 9,000 feet or more catch heavy snows and summer rains accompanying thunderstorms reverberating from mountain to mountain. This moisture permits the Bitterroot Range, defining the Montana-Idaho border, to support heavy stands of **ponderosa pine** (Montana's official tree), **lodgepole pine**, **Western red cedar** and **quaking aspen**.

Berries, the most familiar being **huckleberries** and **chokecherries**, thrive on slopes and in river valleys. Indians dried the berries to make pemmican, a sustaining cake laced with bear grease.

White settlers valued the berries for jellies and syrups. Chokecherry products are popular in Charlie Russell Country. Glacier Country's wild huckleberry jams, pies and other goodies are runaway best sellers. Somewhere on the books must be a law making it illegal to leave Montana without a jar of huckleberry jam on board.

AUTHOR TIP *Berry picking is popular with both hikers and grizzly bears. Leave Old Bruin to it, should you meet in a berry patch. Grizzlies are to be tangled with (see* Co-Adventuring With Grizzles, *page 16).*

■ Climate

Glacier Country is a meteorologist's nightmare. Winds and snows sweeping over the Rockies and down from Canada are fairly predictable over a wide area, but getting a fix on the weather in a given place on a given day can send a weatherman over the edge.

The scattershot effect of winter blizzards, summer storms and autumn frosts is difficult to second guess. Every valley, every mountain slope, every peak and canyon, has a its own weather pattern. The Kootenai area in extreme northwest Montana illustrates this, enjoying a weather pattern aping that of the Pacific Northwest. Average temperatures hover around 45°. But Arctic air masses can plunge winter temperatures to -30° and dump heavy snows in the mountains. Generally moderate summer temperatures are sometimes skewed by 90° days.

You can expect warm, sun-splashed mid-summer days in Glacier Country valleys, while thunderstorms growl through mountain passes, unleashing lashing rain and quicksilver lightning.

South-facing slopes are warmer than north-facing slopes that can retain vestiges of last winter's snows. Icy mountain streams chill the air around them. Meadows, bathed in sunlight, nurse tender grasses and delicate wildflowers.

Here, winter is truly the flip side of summer. Heavy snows settle in, insulating the ground, enabling bears and rodents to sleep snug in their dens. Winds howling over the Rockies plunge the wind-chill factor into the sub-basement. Days are short and often shrouded in fog. Then comes a rosy dawn when snow-clad peaks don splashes of gilt. The sun climbing the sky sets the snow alight with tiny crystals. Nights seem interminable. You'd think Glacier Country folks would hole up in winter, hibernating bear-like around wood burning stoves. But no: they're out skiing, snow-mobiling, ice fishing.

What to Wear

No matter what time of year you head for Glacier Country, pack warm clothing, along with swimsuits, shorts and T-shirts. Think layers even in summer; strip off or add clothing according to need. Bring a parka or insulated jacket, even in July. You may not need longjohns in summer unless you plan on hiking into the backcountry, but leaving them at home in winter is pure foolhardiness.

Don't neglect your feet, especially if you plan on strenuous hiking. Wear two pairs of wool socks under stout hiking boots. Bring extras. Melting snow oozing over trails may be hard to avoid. Warm gloves are a boon any time. If camping out, you might wish to tuck a blanket into your sleeping bag.

If you sign on for a ranch stay, river trip, fishing or horsepack trip, ask the outfitter's advice on clothing. Then follow it. He knows and respects back country weather.

Getting Around

■ Highways & Byways

Five kinds of roads criss-cross Glacier Country: Interstate 90, paved US and state highways, good gravel roads, so-so gravel roads, and logging and forest service roads mostly suitable for 4WD vehicles. Mountain country means more of the latter. Most main arteries thread the valleys.

Most Interstates are ho-hum, but the scenery along **I-90** through Glacier Country is flat-out fabulous. Entering

Montana from Idaho at Lookout Pass, I-90 follows the route of the historic Mullan Road. It glides along the St. Regis River before joining up with the Clark Fork and continuing through the heart of the Bitterroot Range. I-90 skirts Missoula, entering Gold West Country just past the Bearmouth Valley town of Clinton.

US 89 is the historic link between Glacier and Yellowstone Parks. It crosses into Glacier Country from Canada at the Port of Roosevelt and traverses the Blackfeet Reservation before entering Charlie Russell and Yellowstone Countries.

US 93 is Glacier Country's main north-south artery. Beginning at the Port of Roosville, it follows the Tobacco River for a ways before passing through the Flathead National Forest en route to Kalispell and Flathead Lake. Following the lake's western shoreline, it passes through the Flathead Indian Reservation before joining I-90 for an eight-mile scoot to Missoula. From Missoula, US 93 threads the length of the Bitterroot Valley, entering Idaho at Lost Trail Pass. **US 12** intersects with US 93 12 miles south of Missoula, shooting off into Idaho at Lolo Pass on the Lewis and Clark Trail.

MT 200 stretches the full width of Montana. It begins at the Idaho-Montana line and follows the Clark Fork River through the Bitterroots and the Flathead Indian Reservation to Missoula before checking into Charlie Russell Country.

MT 83 intersects with MT 200 33 miles east of Missoula. It follows the Swan River through the narrow Seeley-Swan Valley, ending just north of Bigfork. **MT 35** heads south from Bigfork along the east shore of Flathead Lake. **Route 206** links Bigfork with Whitefish/Columbia Falls.

US 2, the Hi-Line, traverses the northern edge of the state. It enters Glacier Country at Montana's lowest point, 1,820 feet. From here, it follows the Kootenai River, between the Purcell and Cabinet Mountains, to Libby. The highway continues on to Kalispell and Whitefish/Columbia Falls before skirting the southern boundary of Glacier National Park and crossing the Blackfeet Indian Reservation. **MT 37** leaves US 93 a mile north of Eureka and traces the length of Lake Koocanusa to Libby. The long narrow lake reaching into Canada was created by damming the Kootenai River.

MT 28 crosses the Flathead Reservation, linking MT 200 and Flathead Lake.

Routes 508 and **567** wind through the Purcell Mountains in the extreme northwest corner of the state, linking Libby with remote Yaak and numerous Kootenai National Forest campgrounds and trailheads. These routes lead to scenic detours and are punctuated with historic sites, museums, wildlife refuges and only-in-Montana small towns.

■ Road Watch

Glacier Country is a popular summer destination. Try to visit in the shoulder seasons when school is in session. Even then, you may encounter traffic gluts in Glacier National Park and the Flathead Lake area. Especially RV traffic. The popularity and ever-expanding size of RVs, and a growing number of active retirees, seem to coalesce on Montana's scenic highways.

AUTHOR TIP

Remember: you are all on vacation. Relax and be courteous. So what if you get there an hour late? It's preferable to not getting there at all.

Among the most frustrating aspects of popular vacation spots is overcrowded view areas. Taking an alternate route over Forest Service roads might ease your frustration. You won't see the same distant view or waterfall. You will see a different, maybe better, view and possibly a bigger waterfall.

Glacier Country road crews make heroic efforts to maintain roads and highways in all kinds of weather. You can expect valley highways to be fairly clear in all but the worst winter weather. Mountain roads can be another matter. Some close in winter. If in doubt, check with the Montana Highway Patrol or the Montana Road Condition Report. See *In formation Sources.*

AUTHOR TIP

Carrying adequate survival gear is a must all year out here where towns are few and far between. Mountains can shut out cell phone transmission. Carry an inflated spare tire and a jack, jumper cables, water for both yourself and your radiator, duct tape, flares, matches, blankets or sleeping bag, and food to last a couple of days. For tips on winter survival gear, see Clothing & Gear *under* Travel Strategies & Helpful Facts, *page 57.*

 The Montana Department of Transportation has available a *Take-Along Winter Survival Handbook.* Request a copy by dialing ☎ 406-444-6911.

Don't even think about driving anything other than a 4WD vehicle if you plan on exploring logging and/or Forest Service roads. Sudden rainstorms can turn a dry dirt roadway into a gooey, slippery morass. Switchback curves can be daunting for passenger cars, let alone RVs. Some paved and many gravel roads have a way of petering out into dirt tracks. Should the going look dicey, turn around and retrace your tracks.

Watch the shoulders of gravel and dirt roads, especially in steep terrain. Melting snows and heavy rains may trigger mudslides that undermine roads and/or break chunks off the downhill sides. Heed all signs. They're meant to warn you of hazards, not to decorate the roads.

Check current road conditions with the applicable national forest ranger district office before venturing onto remote forest service or logging roads. Obtaining a Forest Service travel map of a given area can mean the difference between a pleasant adventure and a disastrous experience. Check the weather report, too.

Information Sources

Getting There

Amtrak's Chicago to Portland/Seattle Empire Builder calls at Cut Bank, Browning, East Glacier, Essex (Isaac Walton Inn), West Glacier, Whitefish and Libby. Contact your travel agent for reservations or ☎ 800-USA-RAIL.

Kalispell/Whitefish is served by **Delta Airlines** (☎ 800-221-1212), **Horizon Airline** (☎ 800-547-9308), **Northwest Airlines** (☎ 800-225-2525) and **Sky West** (☎ 800-453-9417).

Missoula is served by **Delta Airlines** (☎ 800-221-1212), **Horizon Airline** (☎ 800-547-9308) and **Northwest Airlines** (☎ 800-225-2525).

Greyhound Bus Line: ☎ 800-231-2222.

Car Rentals

Columbia Falls

Payless Car Rental: ☎ 406-755-4022.

Cut Bank

Bell Motor Company: ☎ 406-873-5515.
Northern Ford: ☎ 406-873-5541.

East Glacier

Avis Rent-A-Car: ☎ 406-226-4433.
Rent A Wreck: ☎ 406-226-9293.

Hamilton

Mildenberger Motors: ☎ 800-788-2886 or 406-363-4100.
Rent A Wreck: ☎ 800-932-2642 or 406-363-1430.

Kalispell

Avis Rent-A-Car: ☎ 800-331-1212 or 406-257-2727.
Budget Rent-A-Car of Kalispell: ☎ 800-248-7604 or 406-755-7368.
Dollar Rent-A-Car: ☎ 800-457-5335 or 406-892-0009.
Enterprise Rent-A-Car: ☎ 406-755-4848.
KAC Rentals & Leasing: ☎ 406-755-7504.
National Car Rental: ☎ 406-442-8620.
Practical Rent-A-Car: ☎ 800-722-6747 or 406-755-3700.
Rent A Wreck: ☎ 800-795-3496 or 406-755-4555.
Sears Car & Truck Rental: ☎ 406-755-7507.
U-Save Auto Rental: ☎ 800-262-1958 or 406-257-1900.

Libby

Libby Auto Sales & Rental: ☎ 406-293-7717.

Missoula

Avis Rent-A-Car: ☎ 800-331-1212 or 406-252-8007.
Bitterroot Motors: ☎ 406-251-2525.
Budget Rent-A-Car of Missoula: ☎ 800-257-0700 or 406-453-7001.
Enterprise Rent-A-Car: ☎ 800-RENTACAR or 406-721-1888.
Grizzly Auto Center: ☎ 800-823-7283 or 406-721-5000.
Hertz Rent-A-Car: ☎ 800-654-3131 or 406-549-9511.
National Car Rental: ☎ 406-543-3131.
Rent A Wreck: ☎ 800-552-1138 or 406-721-3838.
Sunshine Motors: ☎ 800-735-8842 or 406-728-2626.
Thrifty Car Rental: ☎ 406-549-2257.

West Glacier

Hertz Rent-A-Car: ☎ 406-888-5427.

Whitefish

Hertz Rent-A-Car: ☎ 406-863-1210.
Rocky Mountain Transportation: ☎ 406-863-1200.

Tourism Offices

Travel Montana, Department of Commerce, PO Box 200533, Helena, MT 59620-0533; ☎ 800-847-4868 outside Montana, ☎ 406-444-2654 in Montana. Internet http://travel.mt.gov/.

Glacier Country, PO Box 1035, Big Fork, MT 59911-1035; ☎ 406-837-6211 or 800-338-5072; http://visit.com/glacier.

Chambers of Commerce

Bigfork Area, PO Box 237, Bigfork, MT 59911; ☎ 406-837-5888.

Blackfeet Country, PO Box D, Browning, MT 59417; ☎ 406-338-7406.

Columbia Falls Area, Box 312, Columbia Falls, MT 59912; ☎ 406-892-2072.

Cut Bank Area, PO Box 1243, Cut Bank, MT 59247; ☎ 406-873-4041.

East Glacier, PO Box 260, East Glacier, MT 59434; ☎ 406-226-4403.

Glacier/Waterton Visitors Association, Box 96, West Glacier, MT 59936; ☎ 406-387-4053. Fax 406-387-4982.

Bitterroot Valley & Information Center, 105 E. Main St., Hamilton, MT 59840; ☎ 406-363-2400, or 300B Main St., Stevensville, MT 59870.

Sanders County Tourist Association, PO Box 340, Hot Springs, MT 59845; ☎ 406-741-5643.

Flathead Convention & Visitor Association, 15 Depot Park, Kalispell, MT 59901; ☎ 800-543-3105 or 406-756-9091.

Lakeside-Somers, PO Box 177, Lakeside, MT 59922; ☎ 406-844-3715.

Libby Area, Box 704 (905 W. 9th), Libby, MT 59923; ☎ 406-293-4167.

Kalispell, 15 Depot Park, Kalispell, MT 59901; ☎ 406-758-2800.

Missoula Convention & Visitors Bureau, Box 7577H (825 E. Front St.), Missoula, MT 59802; ☎ 800-526-3465 or 406-543-6623.

Plains/Paradise, PO Box 714, Plains, MT 59859; ☎ 406-826-3662.

Polson Area, PO Box 667, Polson, MT 59860; ☎ 406-883-5969.

Ronan, PO Box 254, Ronan, MT 59864; ☎ 406-676-8300.

St. Regis Visitor Information Center, Box 220 (Exit 33 on I-90), St. Regis, MT 59866; ☎ 406-649-2290.

Seeley Lake, PO Box 516, Seeley Lake, MT 59868; ☎ 406-677-2880.

Superior Area, Box 383, Superior, MT 59872; ☎ 406-822-4891.

Thompson Falls, Box 493, Thompson Falls, MT 59873; ☎ 406-827-4930.

Tobacco Valley Board of Commerce, PO Box 186, Eureka, MT 59917; ☎ 406-296-2487.

Indian Reservations

Blackfeet Nation, PO Box 850, Browning, MT 59417; ☎ 406-338-7276.

Confederated Salish & Kootenai Tribes, PO Box 278, Pablo, MT 59855; ☎ 406-675-2700.

Outdoors Associations

Adventure Cycling Association, Box 8308, Missoula, MT 59807; Box 8308, Missoula, MT 59807; ☎ 406-721-1776. Fax 406-721-8754.

Fishing Outfitters Association of Montana (FOAM), Box 67, Gallatin Gateway, MT 59730; ☎ 406-763-5436.

Montana Outfitters & Guides Association, Box 1248, Helena, MT 59624; ☎ 406-449-3578.

Montana Snowmobile Association, PO Box 3202, Great Falls, MT 59403; ☎ 406-443-7350.

Montana Wilderness Association, Box 365, Helena, MT 59624; ☎ 406-443-7350.

Government Agencies

Montana Department of Fish, Wildlife & Parks, 1420 E. Sixth Ave., Helena, MT 59620; ☎ 406-444-2535. Fax 406-444-4952. TDD ☎ 406-444-1200.

Bureau of Land Management, Garnet Resource Area, 3255 Fort Missoula Rd., Missoula, MT 59801; ☎ 406-329-3914.

USDA Forest Service, Northern Region, PO Box 7669, Missoula, MT 59807; ☎ 406-329-3511.

Superintendent Glacier National Park, West Glacier, MT 59936; ☎ 406-888-7800. Internet www.nps.gov/glac/index.htm.

Bitterroot National Forest Supervisor's Office, 1801 N. 1st Street, Hamilton, MT 59840; ☎ 406-363-3131.

Bitterroot National Forest, Darby Ranger District, PO Box 388, Darby, MT 59829; ☎ 406-821-3913.

Bitterroot National Forest, Stevensville Ranger District, 88 Main St., Stevensville, MT 59870; ☎ 406-777-5461.

Bitterroot National Forest, Sula Ranger District, 7338 Hwy. 93 South, Sula, MT 59871; ☎ 406-821-3201.

Bitterroot National Forest, West Fork Ranger District, 6735 West Fork Rd., Darby, MT 59829; ☎ 406-821-3269.

Flathead National Forest Supervisor's Office, 1935 3rd Ave. E., Kalispell, MT 59901; ☎ 406-755-5401.

Flathead National Forest, Glacier View Ranger District, PO Box 340, Hungry Horse, MT 59919; ☎ 406-387-5243.

Flathead National Forest, Spotted Bear Ranger District, PO Box 310, Hungry Horse, MT 59919; ☎ 406-758-5376 (summer), ☎ 406-387-5843 (winter).

Flathead National Forest, Swan Lake Ranger District, PO Box 370, Bigfork, MT 59911; ☎ 406-837-5081.

Flathead National Forest, Tally Lake Ranger District, 1335 Hwy. 93 West, Whitefish, MT 59937; ☎ 406-862-2508.

Kootenai National Forest Supervisor's Office, 506 US Hwy. 2 West, Libby, MT 59923; ☎ 406-293-6211.

Kootenai National Forest, Cabinet Ranger District, 2693 Hwy. 200, Trout Creek, MT 59874; ☎ 406-827-3533.

Kootenai National Forest, Fisher River Ranger District and Canoe Gulch Ranger Station, 12557 Hwy. 37, Libby, MT 59923; ☎ 406-293-7773.

Kootenai National Forest, Fortine Ranger District and Murphy Lake Ranger Station, PO Box 116, Fortine, MT 59918; ☎ 406-882-4451.

Kootenai National Forest, Rexford Ranger District and Eureka Ranger Station, 1299 Hwy. 93 North, Eureka, MT 59917; ☎ 406-296-2536.

Kootenai National Forest, Three Rivers Ranger District and Troy Ranger Station, 1437 N. Hwy. 2, Troy, MT 59935; ☎ 406-295-4693.

Lewis & Clark National Forest Supervisor's Office, 1101 15th St. North (PO Box 869), Great Falls, MT 59403; ☎ 406-791-7700.

Lewis & Clark National Forest, Rocky Mountain Ranger District, 1102 Main Ave. (Box 340), Choteau, MT 59422; ☎ 406-466-5341.

Lolo National Forest Supervisor's Office, Building 24, Fort Missoula, Missoula, MT 59804; ☎ 406-329-3750.

Lolo National Forest, Missoula Ranger District, Building 24-A, Fort Missoula, Missoula, MT 59804; ☎ 406-329-3750.

Lolo National Forest, Ninemile Ranger District, Ninemile Rd., Box 366, Huson, MT 59846; ☎ 406-626-5201.

Lolo National Forest, Plains/Thompson Falls Ranger District, 408 Clayton, Plains, MT 59859; ☎ 406-826-3821 (Plains RD), ☎ 406-827-3589 (Thompson Falls RD).

Lolo National Forest, Seeley Lake Ranger District, HC 31, Box 3200 (18 Mile Marker, Hwy. 83 N.), Seeley Lake, MT 59868; ☎ 406-677-2233.

Lolo National Forest, Superior Ranger District, 209 W. Riverside, Superior, MT 59872; ☎ 406-822-4233.

Touring

■ The Bitterroot Valley

 The Bitterroot Valley extends southward from I-90 like a thumb. US 93 runs the length of it, entering from Idaho over Lost Trail Pass. You can enter Glacier Country here from the Big Hole Valley.

I've traveled the Bitterroot Valley countless times en route between central Idaho and the Idaho Panhandle. Each time, the contrast between the rural paradise it once was and today's development becomes more apparent. The river slices the valley like a knife in a ripe melon. It remains idyllic despite dewatering for irrigation.

The first 30 miles of US 93 remain a delight. They cross the Continental Divide and thread thick forests punctuated by the occasional roadside cabin complex or campground. **Lost Trail Ski Area** and **Lost Trail Hot Springs** are enhanced by a deep woods ambience. I like to visualize Lewis and Clark re-entering Montana from Idaho over Lost Trail Pass in September 1805, worrying about finding the correct trail over the mountains. They followed the route US 93 now takes to present-day Sula, then a Flathead village whose residents told them about the Lolo Trail. The party traversed the valley by floating down the **Bitterroot River**.

Conner

Four miles south of Conner, watch for the **Medicine Tree**, a historic Native American spiritual site. Gifts of tobacco are left here even today.

At Conner, Rt. 473 swings off US 93 bound for the placid **Painted Rocks Reservoir**, the state park by that name, and numerous hiking trails. The **Alta Ranger Station** is nearby. This, the country's first ranger station, dates from 1899. Alta was a gold mining tent city then.

Darby

Darby is the last and largest (population 770) forested settlement before the highway dips into the valley proper. Clothed in a piney deep-woods aura, Darby recalls a time when forestry was king and folks who came to recreate were doughty indeed.

The **Original Darby Ranger Station**, dating from the 1930s, is on the National Register of Historic Places and displays Forest Service memorabilia. Open daily, 8-6, May 8-hunting season. ☎ 406-821-3913. **Darby's Pioneer Museum**, housed in a century-old log cabin, traces the history of the area through artifacts and photographs. Open the first weekend in June-Labor Day, Tues.-Sat., 1-4 pm.

A few miles north of Darby, a gravel road heads off to **Lake Como**, a popular picnicking, camping, fishing and ice skating lake. The Skalkaho Highway travels over-mountain from the Flint Creek Valley, entering US 93 at **Grantsdale**, a side-car to heavily commercialized Hamilton.

Hamilton

The popularity of Hamilton and environs marks the Bitterroot Valley as the fastest growing area in Montana. Rampant "progress" is apparent everywhere as ranchettes fan out across the valley. From Hamilton north to Lolo, US 93 is lined with log home yards where houses in all stages of completion resemble giant Lincoln Logs. Chain saw carving shops displaying artfully posed wooden bears invite stopping.

The **Ravalli County Museum**, in Hamilton at 212 Bedford Street, charts the county seat's progress over the past 150 years or so. Open June-Oct., 10-4; Oct.-May, 1-4. Closed Tues. and Wed. ☎ 406-363-3338.

The Daly Mansion

What would Marcus Daly, the copper king who platted Hamilton, think of his lumber town now?

In the late 1880s, Daly built a summer home and thoroughbred race horse ranch overlooking the Bitterroot River. He died 12 years later. In 1910 his widow transformed the home into an extravagant colonnaded mansion. The house fell into decay after her death in 1941. It was aired out and opened to the public in 1987, but time had taken a toll.

Touring the Daly Mansion is like tip-toeing through the home of a family sunk into genteel poverty. You can appreciate the grand life that the house once knew, but you can't help but notice missing furniture, propped-up porches and patched ceilings.

The mansion is owned by the State of Montana and managed by the Daly Mansion Preservation Trust. Find it at 251 Eastside Hwy. (Hwy. 269). Open daily, April 15-Oct. 15, 11-4. Off-season tours available by appointment. ☎ 406-363-6004.

Continue north from the Daly Mansion on bucolic Hwy. 269, by-passing the US 93 sprawl. En route to Stevensville, this route passes through the pleasant agricultural town of **Corvallis**.

Victor

Halfway, take Hwy. 370 the short distance to Victor, home of Chief Victor and his people. Touring the **Victor Heritage Museum**, at Blake and Main Streets, offers a fix on the history of the Flathead Tribe and the events leading up to their forced march to the Flathead Reservation. Open Memorial Day, 1-4, then from Chief Victor Days the last weekend in June-Labor Day, 1-4. ☎ 406-642-3871.

Stevensville

Stevensville, founded in 1841, is Montana's oldest town and proud of it. White town, that is. The Salish (Flathead) Indians had for generations pitched tipi villages on the banks of the Bitterroot River. Jesuits led by Fr. Pierre Jean DeSmet arrived here in September, 1841. They constructed a log church and house and named the settlement St. Mary's. The fathers talked farming and religion to the Indians, built a grist mill and a larger church. By the end of the decade, the Jesuits lacked funds, were faced with apostasy among the converts, and suffered harassment by Blackfeet Indians. The mission closed in 1850.

Enter a trader named John Owen. He bought the mission property and renamed it **Fort Owen**. As agent to the Flathead Nation, Owen and his Shoshone wife, Nancy, maintained a fort home bustling with life. Nancy's death in 1868 precipitated Owen's inebriated slide into dementia. In 1874, Gov. John Potts had him removed from the territory.

The mission was reestablished in 1866 by Fr. Anthony Ravalli, a man of immense artistic talent who had already built and embellished Idaho's Cataldo Mission. **St. Mary's Mission** stands today as an important facet of Montana history. The chapel and Fr. Ravalli's humble home have been restored to their 1880 appearance. His handiwork is apparent in a chapel statue and the home's furnishings. The home includes Montana's first drive-in, the window where Ravalli dispensed medicines to the people. The mission is at the west end of Fourth Street in Stevensville. Open daily, April-Oct., 10:15-4:15. Modest fee. ☎ 406-777-5734.

Fort Owen eventually fell into ruin. The acre of land enclosing the fort was acquired by Montana Fish, Wildlife and Parks in 1937. Today, three original adobe and log structures remain. The locations of other structures are marked by interpretive signs. A descriptive brochure is available at the site. You can wander about at will, envisioning life in the fort.

The fort, a day-use state park, is near the river, a half-mile off US 93 and a half-mile from Stevensville. River access and picnic areas are nearby. Turn in at the Fort Owen Angus Ranch sign. The fort is adjacent to the privately owned ranch buildings. Open year-round in daylight hours.

Stevensville Historical Museum, at 517 Main, displays artifacts pertaining to the early history of the town and the Bitterroot Valley. Open Memorial Day-Labor Day, Thurs.-Sat., 11-4 and Sunday 1-4. Also open by appointment. ☎ 406-777-2269.

The **Lee Metcalf National Wildlife Refuge** encompasses 2,700 acres along the banks of the Bitterroot River on Wildfowl Lane on the north edge of Stevensville. See *Wildlife Watching*.

Today, Stevensville is a quiet town of some 1,500 souls. The era that saw both mission and fort rise and fall is amply showcased.

Hwy. 203 continues north from Stevensville to Florence, a one-time boom town long since settled into somnolence.

■ The Lolo Trail

Swing onto US 12 nine miles north of Florence. The highway parallels the Lolo Trail, trod for centuries by Indian tribes and immortalized by the 1877 flight of Chief Joseph's band and by the 1805-06 Lewis and Clark expedition.

Lolo

The **Fort Fizzle Historical Site**, five miles west of the town of Lolo, is the site of a non-battle between the Nez Perce and soldiers from Fort Missoula. Watch for signs.

Lolo town is the site of **Travelers Rest**, at the mouth of Lolo Creek. Lewis and Clark camped here en route both to and from the Pacific. After threading through a clutch of service businesses, the road climbs through thick forest. Lolo Creek chuckles down-mountain just out of sight. Watch for signs describing Lewis and Clark sites. See *Adventures on Foot* for Lolo Trail hiking trails.

The expedition passed **Lolo Hot Springs** on Sept. 13, 1805 and returned to enjoy hot baths on June 29, 1806. Indians soaked here long before that. People have been soaking here ever since. A popular resort grew up around the springs but currently shows signs of decline.

Lewis and Clark camped at **Packer Meadows** near **Lolo Pass**. A visitor information center housed in the old Mud Creek Ranger Station crowns this pass on the Montana-Idaho state line. Lewis and Clark bicentennial traffic has prompted plans for a new visitor center that may or may not be in place by the time you read this book. Displays highlight the history of the Lolo Trail. A small shop stocks books related to the area.

At this writing, the visitor center is open daily, Memorial Day weekend-Labor Day, 9-4 and Dec. 1-Mar. 31, 9-4. Operating hours may vary due to snowfall and budgets.

Missoula & Environs

Missoula has earned a reputation as Montana's most liberal-leaning city. The original name, Missoula Mills, hints at the humble beginnings of the city built where the Bitterroot and Clark Fork Rivers meet. Today the valley is packed solid with big city sprawl. For all of that, Missoula is an outdoor-oriented city whose residents take full advantage of nearby mountains and rivers. The 11,000 University of Montana students come largely for that reason. Unlike other Montana cities and towns, Missoula seems not to encourage visitors. Parking is scarce downtown and at riverside parks, especially for RVs and other large vehicles.

Getting around in Missoula is no easy trick. A city map is a must. The city's parameters are defined by mountains crowding close on the northeast and southwest and by I-90 skirting it on the north. The Clark Fork River takes a more or less diagonal course through the city, throwing into disarray any streets having grid pretensions. US 93 and 12 combine as they enter Missoula from the south. US 93 becomes Reserve Street, straight-arrowing it past Fort Missoula to I-90. US 12 slants off, skirting the University of Montana campus and crossing the Clark Fork River into a downtown squeezed between river and Interstate.

A millstone from Missoula Mills is displayed along the **Riverfront Trail**. This trail, following the south side of the Clark Fork River from the University to **McCormick Park**, has interpretive signs offering a fix on Missoula's history. Parks line the trail and foot and vehicle bridges cross to downtown. **Caras Park**, on the north side of the river, boasts the impressive **Missoula Carousel**. The congested downtown district, showing fewer signs of neglect than do many city centers, has numerous hole-in-the-wall coffee shops.

The **Art Museum of Missoula**, at 335 N. Pattee Street, celebrates contemporary art with changing exhibitions. Modest admission fee; Tuesdays free. Open Wed.-Sat., noon-6, Tues. noon-8. ☎ 406-728-0447. Most of Missoula's other attractions reflect the city's outdoor orientation.

The Rocky Mountain Elk Foundation's **Wildlife Visitor Center**, at 2291 W. Broadway, includes an elk diorama, educational displays, an art gallery featuring elk (no surprise) and a gift shop. Open daily during business hours. ☎ 800-CALL ELK, ext. 545.

Missoula is the area smokejumper headquarters. Visit the **Smokejumper and Aerial Fire Depot Visitor Center** on Airport Blvd. A video on wildland fires shows how fire fighters respond to an emergency. A replica of the Deer Lodge National Forest's Black Pine Fire Lookout is complete with locating instruments, forest diorama, and furnishings. Tours of the facility include the manufacturing building where smokejumpers pack their parachutes and make other equipment. Free admission. Open daily May 30-Aug. 1, 10-5 and noon-5 Sundays. ☎ 406-329-4900.

Fort Missoula was established in 1877 in response to requests from nervous townspeople and settlers. Their fears seemed to be realized when rumors circulated of the advance of the non-treaty Nez Perce band led by Chiefs Joseph and Looking Glass. But nothing came of it. The band continued south to the Big Hole Valley and townspeople relaxed. The Fort remained a part of Missoula life until 1947. Today, Military Row-style structures house county and federal offices. Included are the BLM's Garnet District Office, the Forest Service's Northern Region offices, the Lolo National Forest Supervisor's office and the Missoula Ranger District of the Lolo National Forest.

The **Historical Museum** of Fort Missoula is well worth a visit. Exhibits trace the Fort's checkered history. You could browse for hours and not see it all. Outdoor exhibits include an eclectic mix of historic structures moved to the museum. Interpretive signs. Summer hours: Memorial Day-Labor Day, Mon.-Sat., 10-5 and Sunday noon-5. Winter hours: Labor Day-Memorial Day, Tues.-Sun., noon-5. Modest admission. The research library is open weekdays, 8:30-5. ☎ 406-728-3476.

Fort Missoula

Fort Missoula has served many purposes. Among the most unusual was as a detention center for Italian merchant seamen, World's Fair employees and a luxury liner crew caught in the US by World War II.

For sheer quirkiness, consider the exploits of the 25th Infantry Bicycle Corps, based at the fort. Comprised of black soldiers and white officers, the Corps was organized to test the military potential of bicycles. Seems someone in Washington had a notion that bicycles might replace horses. In battle? What a thought. The 25th arrived at Fort Missoula in May, 1897. Off they went, wheeling it on errands down the Bitterroot Valley, up the Mission Valley and into Yellowstone National Park. This, before the days of feather-light frames and skinny tires. The forays must have been successful. The Corps undertook a 1,900-mile cycle trip to St. Louis. That jaunt seems not to have been successful. The cyclists returned to Fort Missoula by train. The conclusion: bicycles would never replace horses.

▪ Ghost Towns & Swans

Garnet Ghost Town

I-90 follows the Clark Fork River east from Missoula through the scenic Bearmouth Valley. Garnet Ghost Town lies secreted in the Garnet Range north of here. This not-to-be-missed mining relic can be reached via the Garnet Back Country Byway, a gnarly ribbon of dirt accessed from I-90's Bearmouth Exit on the south and MT 200 on the north.

If you choose the I-90 option, take Hwy. 10 to Bear Gulch Road. Watch for a BLM sign. Forget about driving this in an RV.

Or approach Garnet from MT 200, en route to the Seeley/Swan Valley. Pick up MT 200 at I-90's Milltown Exit. Look for the Garnet Range Road between mile markers 22 and 23, west of the Lubrecht Experimental Forest entrance. Watch for the Garnet access road sign. The Byway is closed to cars in winter, open to snowmobiles and cross-country skiers (see *Snowmobiling*).

Garnet was one of Montana's last gold camps. Prospectors jump-started it in the 1890s to work the Garnet Range's gold and silver deposits. The mountain-girt town alternately hustled and fizzled, finally folding in the 1930s.

Vying with Bannack as Montana's most intact ghost town, Garnet is maintained in a state of arrested decay by the Bureau of Land Management and the Garnet Preservation Association. A visitor center offers a fix on Garnet's colorful past. You can roam at will through once-fancy hotels and family homes. Garnet had more families than most mining camps. Frank Davey's Store and the man who owned it spanned Garnet's lifetime. The surrounding hills are carpeted with wildflowers in summer, thickly forested year-round.

You can wander about the town anytime (respect private property). The visitor center is open daily in summer, 10-6, and Sat. and Sun., 10-5 in winter.

The Seeley/Swan Valley

Fifteen miles past the Byway, MT 83 heads into the Seeley/Swan Valley. A Clearwater River river access park is just past the junction. The Clearwater-Blackfoot confluence is south of the junction.

The Seeley/Swan Valley, snuggled between the Mission and Bob Marshall Wildernesses, is 90 miles of dense conifer forests threaded by the Clearwater and Swan Rivers and peppered with lakes. No agricultural valley, this, but a late-settled slice of northwoods splendor. The forested foothills sloping to the valley floor hide hiking and pack trails and a smattering of resorts and lodges (see *Adventures on Foot* and *Hotels, Motels & B&Bs*). Summer cabins are wedged amongst the trees. The twin valleys support such quiet persuits as hiking, fishing and wildlife watching. In winter, the growl of snowmobiles shatters the stillness. Driving through these valleys is pure pleasure. Essential services are available in **Seeley Lake** and **Condon**.

First off, you come upon **Salmon Lake**, a wow! of a jewel encased in deep green larches, pines and firs. A lakeside state park can provide a base from which to enjoy the valley.

A state park on **Placid Lake** has interpretive panels describing early logging practices. A road encircles **Seeley Lake**, the largest and most populated of the chain of lakes fed by the Clearwater River. **Lakes Inez** and **Alva** hug the highway. North of here, the road rises and falls almost imperceptibly into the Swan Valley. The trees thin out as the highway follows the Swan River, flowing into highway-hugging Swan Lake. En route, pause at "**The Barn**," a gambrel-roofed barn housing a visitor center and museum opened in summer, 1999. Collapsed under the heavy snows of the winter of 1996-97, the historic Double Arrow Barn is a miracle of creative restoration. Contact the Seeley Lake Area Chamber of Commerce for current hours (see *Information Sources*, page 356).

As the valley ends, you have a choice between continuing north to Kalispell or cutting across to Bigfork on Flathead Lake via Rt. 209. It's a comedown, no matter which you choose.

The Flathead Valley: Montana's Playground

The Flathead Valley comprises the northern half of Flathead Lake, Kalispell, the overtly touristy towns of Bigfork and Whitefish, Columbia Falls and the western gateway to Glacier National Park. The southern half of the lake is on the Flathead Indian Reservation and is addressed under that heading.

At first gander the Flathead Valley may be somewhat of a turnoff, but behind the spendy façade is a trove of hiking trails, water fun, wildlife watching, skiing, horseback, backpacking and in-air adventures.

Bigfork, where the Swan River meets Flathead Lake, is a charming resort town given to art galleries, shops, and an amazing complement of top-drawer restaurants (see *Where to Eat*).

From Bigfork, MT 35 heads south along the east side of **Flathead Lake**, passing sweet cherry orchards and a lineup of summer and year-round homes. This profusion is largely responsible for an algae bloom caused by phosphorus and nitrogen pollution. Ironic, considering that homeowners came to the largest natural freshwater lake west of the Mississippi seeking pure water and air and a superior quality of life. The glittering glacial basin surrounded by sky-scraping mountains looks pristine, but arresting pollution is a serious concern. Limiting the number of marinas is one approach.

MT 82 heads west from Bigfork, bypassing the head of the lake to **Somers**. This busy lakeside town has boat rentals and one of the lake's two marinas. The other is at **Polson**, at the foot of the lake. Somers gives no hint of a time when it was a logging and railway company town and a bustling steamboat terminal. An excursion boat plies the lake from here.

US 93 heads down the lake's west shore. **Lakeside**'s clutch of bar, grill and casino enterprises seems antithetical to the condo and summer home developments arranged along the shoreline.

From the head of Flathead Lake, two routes extend north to Whitefish, Columbia Falls and Glacier National Park. **Hwy. 206** is the pleasantest of the two, leaving Bigfork to pass through semi-bucolic country. **US 93** straightlines from Somers to Kalispell.

Kalispell

Kalispell, a logging and milling town given to tourism, still carps about the Great Northern Railroad's perfidity in relocating the main line to Whitefish back in 1904. The city supports a glut of service enterprises lining the main routes. Get off these arteries and you'll find two Main Street blocks of interesting shops and restaurants. The venerable residential neighborhood east of downtown includes some fine examples of turn-of-the-century architecture.

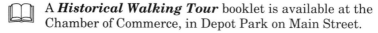 A *Historical Walking Tour* booklet is available at the Chamber of Commerce, in Depot Park on Main Street.

Kalispell's showpiece is the **Conrad Mansion**, overlooking Woodland Park at the eastern edge of the old neighborhood. Charles and Alicia Conrad were in the vanguard of a stream of outlanders coming into the Flathead Valley seeking a superior quality of life. (They're still coming; the Kalispell Chamber discourages move-ins unless they already have jobs here.) In 1895, Conrad used some of a fortune derived from commerce on the Missouri River to build the graceful Norman-style mansion.

Historic Conrad Mansion, Kalispell.

It remained in the family until 1975 when a Conrad daughter gave it to the City of Kalispell.

Touring the mansion sheds light on how the wealthy lived at the turn of the century. A bevy of servants was necessary to the smooth running of the sumptuously appointed home.

The Conrad Mansion is open daily, May 15-Oct. 15. Hours: May 14-June 14 and Sept. 16-Oct. 15, 10-5:30; June 15-Sept. 15, 9-8. Six blocks off Main Street on 4th St. East. Gift shop features Victorian reproductions and handmade items. ☎ 406-755-2166.

KID-FRIENDLY **Woodland Park**, a verdant mosquito bog-cum-parkland across from the Conrad Mansion, reflects the house's heyday with island-dotted lagoons, rustic gazebos, a swimming pool, an aviary and formal gardens. A pleasant place to picnic after touring the mansion. Heading north from Kalispell, you can take US 93 to Whitefish, or heavily traveled US 2 to Columbia Falls en route to Glacier National Park. If you wish to check out Whitefish before visiting Glacier, you can cross to Columbia Falls later via MT 40.

Whitefish

Whitefish enjoys a salubrious situation on the south shore of Whitefish Lake, snuggled picturesquely under the Whitefish Mountain Range.

This picturesque resort town is a far yodel from 100 years ago, when it went by the name of Stumptown because wagons had to avoid stumps on the harvested forest floor.

The former fur trading center boomed when the Great Northern Railroad located a division point here in 1904. The town turned trendy after 1947, when **Big Mountain Ski and Summer Resort** took up residence on a nearby mountain. Today, it's busy with shops and restaurants lining streets that could use some snow and ice clearing in winter.

Whitefish's c.1927 chalet-style **Burlington Northern Depot** (Amtrak trains stop here) houses the **Stumptown Historical Society Museum**, showcasing the town's history from Stumptown days. Free admission. Open Mon.-Sat., 11-3. ☎ 406-862-0067.

The lake shore and nearby mountainsides are a-bristle with trophy homes, quaint B&Bs and luxury lodges; all ancillary to the resort on Big Mountain.

The Whitefish area offers no end of adventure opportunities; a happy situation capped by the multiplicity of summer and winter things to do under Big Mountain Resort's capacious umbrella. See this book's activity sections for information on specific adventures.

KID-FRIENDLY From a touring standpoint, the resort's major draw has to be the **Glacier Chaser gondola**. After driving the steep winding (but paved) road to the resort and admiring Whitefish Lake views on the way up, you might think you've reached the summit. You haven't. The gondola does that, swinging up and up on a 13-minute ride to heights affording a panoramic view of the Flathead Valley. On a clear day you can see the peaks of Glacier National Park. Or ride the chairlift. Summit House has a restaurant. A USFS Environmental Education Center is open in July and August. Gondola tickets under $10. ☎ 406-862-2900 for current hours.

If you haven't caught the Glacier National Park hype yet, it'll reach out and grab you en route to Columbia Falls and beyond. Columbia Falls serves a gateway to Glacier Park.

From here to West Glacier, the grizzly-hype escalates. You may be tempted to scoot on through to the Park. Don't. Call a halt at tiny Hungry Horse. Watch for the Hungry Horse Dam sign just past the ranger station. **Hungry Horse Reservoir** interrupts the flow of the South Fork of the Flathead River, fingering deep into the Flathead Range and affording access to the Great Bear Wilderness (see *Adventures on Foot*). A paved road leads to the dam and travels about a third of the way down the lake. A gravel road continues on, circling the lake's 34-mile shoreline and giving access to numerous hiking trails and campgrounds.

Hungry Horse Dam, completed in 1953, is an arch-gravity type structure with a crest 2,115 feet in length and an elevation of 3,565 feet above sea level. Small by mega-dam standards, the Hungry Horse is nevertheless worth a gander. Looking over the top to the river roiling far below is thrilling. A visitor center offers dam tours. ☎ 406-387-5241.

■ Glacier National Park

Glacier National Park presents many faces. Sure, it's on-the-edge adventure. But the magnificent Crown of the Continent also appeals to those who prefer milder adventures. Quantifying shades of adventure, qualifying the satisfaction derived therefrom, is nigh unto impossible and probably brash in the extreme.

> *As this book goes to press, a seven-day Park permit costs $10 per vehicle; $5 for pedestrians, bicyclists and motorcyclists. An annual Park pass costs $20. US citizens may purchase a Golden Eagle Passport, a 12-month pass good at any US national park. US citizens or residents age 62 or over may purchase a Golden Age Passport for a one-time fee of $10. The Golden Access Passport is available free to US citizens with lifetime disabilities. Passholders get in free.*

Refer to the *Adventures* section for information on Glacier National Park activities. From a touring standpoint, Glacier is showy white beargrass flower clusters against deep green conifers, and waterfalls threading down granite escarpments. It's a mountain goat peering from a rocky foothold. It's rustic hotels sprawling beside glacial lakes and red Jammers (Glacier's fleet of bright red 1936-39 motor coaches) scuttling along Going-to-the-Sun-Road. It's glacier-clad peaks against the sky. It is a brace of grizzly cubs following a sow across a meadow and a bald eagle wing-spreading over a river, carrying prayers to the Creator of this indescribable place.

The Going-to-the-Sun Road is a highlight of touring Glacier National Park. You can drive it yourself if your chariot is under 20 feet long. Trailers are flat-out forbidden. From the west side, you can drive your RV as far as the Trail of the Cedars but must turn around there. From the east side, turn around at Sun Point.

I've driven the Road in a van, toured it in a Jammer, and with Sun Tours, owned by Blackfeet tribal member Ed DesRosier and employing Blackfeet guides.

View from the Going-to-the-Sun Road (west side).

AUTHOR TIP *Round-tripping the Road in your vehicle allows you to take as long as you wish to explore along the way, possibly hiking a trail or two. The disadvantages: missing the tour guides' informative narrations and having to keep your eyes on the road instead of the fabulous vistas.*

If you opt out of a guided tour, you can get a fix on what you are looking at by following the map included in the handout you received when you entered the Park. Interpretive signs are placed at some turnouts.

Jammers

Touring the Road in an open Jammer is fun and informative, but the summer employees' narrations often lack depth. Before the Jammers were refitted with new engines they could be identified by the grinding of gears as they rounded the road's sharp curves; hence the "Jammer" sobriquet.

Jammers depart at 10 am from Lake MacDonald Lodge. Reservations advised. The cost for the six-hour tour is under $40. Other Jammer tours can be arranged. They will also meet Amtrak's Empire Builder. May-Oct.: ☎ 406-226-9311. Nov.-May: 602-207-6000.

Sun Tours

Sun Tours guides offer a more personalized experience than do the Jammers. Native guides describe points of interest along the Road, offering insight from the Blackfeet perspective. A disadvantage: the bus has big windows but is enclosed, curtailing some views. The round-trip tours depart from East Glacier and St. Mary.

My guide was Raymond Croff, a teacher in Reservation schools. Ray talked about Heavy Runner, an esteemed Blackfeet warrior, and the mountain that bears his name. He made reference to Sacajawea, for whom Bird Woman Falls is said to be named. He referred to the power that Glacier has held for the Blackfeet over the centuries, and to the ways in which tribal members use the Park today. He also talked about employment on the Reservation and the opportunities opened up by the tribe's share of Glacier Park tourism.

Sun Tours' day-long tours cost under $50. Tours run June 15-Sept. 30. Reservations advised. ☎ 800-786-9220 or 406-226-9220.

Glacier's Landmark Hotels

Touring Glacier Park wouldn't be complete without visiting its three landmark hotels.

Lake McDonald Lodge was built in 1895 as a hunting lodge and still sports animal trophies on the lobby's walls. Log appointments project a rustic ambience enhanced by views of forest-girt Lake McDonald.

Glacier Park Lodge at Saint Mary, referred to by the Blackfeet as "Big Tree Lodge" for the lobby's gigantic Douglas fir pillars, reflects the grand scale of hotels built in the pre-World War I era.

Many Glacier Hotel, a chalet-style masterpiece, enjoys sumptuous views of Swiftcurrent Lake and the peaks chopping the sky beyond. A caretaker's main job in winter is to chase mountain goats off the roof of the four-story structure so they don't damage the skylights. Snowdrifts can reach 50 feet in height.

You'll find the senior bus tour contingent sitting by McDonald Lodge's big rock fireplace, or rocking on the capacious porch. Young hikers carrying bear-bell-festooned staffs group around the Many Glaciers Lodge's central fireplace. Guests at Glacier Park Lodge seem to be either coming or going.

Outside the hotels, at trailheads and points of interest, rangers and summer naturalists sporting official-looking wide-brimmed hats stand ready to answer questions and lead hikes. These men and women are often founts of Glacier knowledge. If they don't know the answer to your question, they'll look it up. That readiness to inform visitors on the myriad aspects of the Park can make the difference between admiring a wildly beautiful landscape and acquiring the depth of knowledge that leads to real appreciation. "Nature With a Naturalist" campfire programs, talks, strolls and hikes cover topics as diverse as orchids and cougars, Native American medicinal herbs and Glacier geology.

Some Glacier Facts & Non-Facts

- Bears don't eat beargrass, called Bear's Nipple by Blackfeet Indians, but sheep and goats do. Bears eat cow parsnips.
- Showy white beargrass flower stalks bloom every five to six years and are Glacier's "signature flowers."
- Waters from the Triple Divide, seen across Saint Mary Lake from Going-to-the-Sun Road, is the only place on the Continent from which waters flow into Hudson Bay, the Columbia River system, and the Missouri River.
- The mountain backdropping Wild Goose Island has been dubbed Paramount Pictures Mountain because... yes, it's the model for the famous logo.
- Though the Park has some 50 glaciers, the Blackfeet refer to the park area as "Peaks and Valleys."
- Jackson, the only glacier visible from a road, is a remnant of Blackfoot Glacier, which filled much of the Saint Mary Valley over 3,500 years ago.

The Going-to-the-Sun Road

The Going-to-the-Sun Road, winding for 52 miles over 6,646-foot Logan Pass, was blasted from rock between 1916 and 1932 at a cost of three million dollars. It's still regarded as a major engineering feat. Maintaining the road in some of the Continent's harshest winter conditions is a major feat. Snow may close it down at any time, but it's generally open June

On the Going-to-the-Sun Road (east side).

through September. Crowds can spoil the experience. The best times to go are in the shoulder seasons before and after summer school breaks.

The Road slices through the Park between Apgar on the west and the St. Mary entrance. From the west, it traverses the length of Lake McDonald, pausing at Trail of the Cedars, zig-zagging and loop-the-looping up and up to Logan Pass, then descending to St. Mary Lake. The vistas of mountains and waterfalls are indescribable. You can't get enough of looking and looking. The handicap-accessible Trail of the Cedars winds through an old-growth cedar forest carpeted with ferns and spiced with plashing streams; a gentle contrast to the Park's muscular peaks.

The **Logan Pass** parking lot and visitor center are crammed full in high summer, but worth a stop. Mountain goats, curious about camera-toting tourists, often hang out here. The visitor center has ecological displays and books. A trail leads to the top of the pass. Roadside turnouts offer opportunities to take in the scenery at leisure. Looking for grizzlies is popular, especially on meadows. Hastily pulled-over cars and clusters of gesturing people are sure signs that someone has spotted a grizzy or other animal.

AUTHOR TIP

Now that your anticipation has been whetted, be advised that weather and heavy use has taken a toll. The road is in need of serious rehabilitation. As this book goes to press, it appears that the road may be closed for extensive repairs in 2000 or 2001. Contact the Park for accurate dates: **Superintendent Glacier National Park**, *West Glacier, MT 59936;* ☎ *406-888-7800. Internet www.nps.gov/ glac/index.htm.*

Unlike Yellowstone National Park, Glacier has few in-park paved roads. The **Camas Creek Road** extends from Apgar Village to the Huckleberry Mountain Nature Trail. From there, a gravel road continues on to Polebridge and Bowman and Kintia Lakes' campgrounds and trailheads. On the east side, paved roads access the Two Medicine and Many Glacier areas. US 2 connects the west and east entrances to the Park, dipping around its south end.

Glacier National Park and Canada's Waterton Lakes National Park overlap the international border, forming the Waterton/Glacier International Peace Park. Access to Waterton Lakes is via the Chief Mountain International Highway (MT 17) branching off US 89 north of Babb.

Heading East on the Going-to-the-Sun-Road

If your vehicle is of a size to travel the Going-to-the-Sun Road (i.e., under 20 ft.), you may be tempted to drive it to reach the Park's east side. Round tripping the Road offers different perspectives going and coming. Skirt the Park later via US 2 to reach the other side.

From West Glacier, US 2 and the railroad tracks travel high above the west bank of the Middle Fork of the Flathead River. Shed-like structures covering the tracks at intervals are designed to shrug off massive snows. The **Great Bear Wilderness** wraps the highway on the west and south. The Park boundary nudges it on the east and north. After about 20 miles, watch for the **Isaac Walton Inn** sign at the non-town of Essex. The historic inn, on the National List of Historic Places, is a must if you are a rail fan fascinated by the history of the Great Northern Railway's Empire Builder. The main line passes a few yards from the inn, allowing Amtrak passengers to alight from today's Empire Builder at the historic Essex Station (see *Hotels, Motels & B&Bs* and *Where to Eat*).

Keeping the Trains Running

At first glance, the multi-tracked train yard beside the Isaac Walton Inn seems a little much. The tracks and the inn have been intertwined since 1939, when the Great Northern Railroad constructed a hotel to house railroad crews. Why were so many rooms needed out here in the sticks? And why the multiplicity of tracks? Answer: to keep trains running over Marias Pass, on the Continental Divide. Locomotives couldn't pull trains over the steep grade on the west side of the pass. A train yard was laid out to accommodate idling helper engines waiting to assist heavy eastbound freight trains over the pass. The hotel housed engine crews and work gangs who cleared snow from the tracks.

Helper engines still idle outside the chalet-style inn, ready to assist some 26 freight trains and two passenger trains rumbling through every day. But today's hostelry reflects a more leisured clientele. Umbrella tables and a riot of flowers grace the lawn beside the tracks. Inside, firelight from the lobby's rock fireplace reflects on polished pine walls. Photographs recall the glory days of railroading. Railfans can't get enough of gawking at these and a fine collection of railroad memorabilia. Even the gift shop gets into the act, offering reproductions of the "Glory of the West" china used in Empire Builder dining cars between 1940 and 1957.

Across the tracks, peeking from the trees, four restored cabooses sporting primary colors are fitted out with luxuries that 1930s brakemen could hardly imagine.

Watch for the **Walton Goat Lick Overlook** a few miles past Essex. Mountain goats are attracted to the exposed rocks along Sheep Creek by salts and minerals coming to the surface in wet seeps. The best time to see them is in late June and July when the shift to green vegetation causes them to crave minerals. One June day, I counted 10 goats lounging about on a cliff, but as many as 73 have been spotted here at a time.

Next stop is a large parking area at the summit of **Marias Pass**, known to the Blackfeet as "Backbone Pass." The headwaters of the Marias River trickle down the east side of the pass. At 5,216 feet, it's Montana's lowest Continental Divide crossing. The Blackfeet guarded the pass to prevent other tribes from using it to reach the buffalo hunting grounds to the east. The Great Northern Railroad completed tracks (now owned by the Burlington Northern Railway) over the pass in 1891. Until US 2 was built, cars were loaded onto railroad flatcars to be transported from one side to he other.

The pass attracts memorials. There's a statue of John F. Stevens, the man who engineered the tracks over the pass for the Great Northern.

Slippery Bill

A 60-foot obelisk honors Pres. Theodore Roosevelt. William H. (Slippery Bill) Morrison can be thanked for this. Slippery Bill, a trapper, prospector and frontier philosopher who would expound his favorite theories to all who would listen, died in 1932 at age 84. Before he died, the old man donated his "squatters rights" 160 acres for a memorial to his hero, Teddy Roosevelt. There's also a memorial to Slippery Bill.

From a geological perspective, the east side of Glacier Park may be more interesting than the heavily forested west side. The Rockies' bare bones are more visible here, more immediate east of the Continental Divide. At Marias Pass, the forests fall behind and grassy slopes open ahead. On the east side of the Park, foothills serve as a prelude to a marching band of dizzying peaks and hanging valleys. Lakes score this land, thrusting watery fingers into mountain fastnesses. Creeks racket down draws. Glaciers lie in mountain cirques, receding as the Earth warms.

Three paved roads enter the Park on the east side. A fourth, Chief Mountain International Highway (MT 17), clips Glacier's northeast corner before entering Canada's Waterton Lakes National Park. The Blackfeet Indian Reservation merges so seamlessly with Glacier that one may wonder why the Park boundary wasn't set farther west; say, where the mountains begin. Many service businesses outside the park are run by Blackfeet. Tribal members harbor proprietory feelings toward these foothills and the lakes scoring them. The Blackfeet presence, reflected in many place names, is palpable here.

The Blackfeet's presence isn't all that's palpable. Grizzly bears favor this foothills country. Numerous bear encounters have occurred in recent years, some with tragic results. Be careful on trails.

The southernmost road into the Park, six miles north of the cluster of services known as East Glacier, leads past **Lower Two Medicine Lake** to **Two Medicine Lake**. **Running Eagle Falls** is a lovely place of plashing water just off the road. Numerous hiking trails branch from the road (see *Adventures on Foot*). A snack bar, interpretive center and campground overlook the lake and 9,513-foot **Rising Wolf Mountain**.

Switchbacking MT 49 leads from Two Medicine Junction to US 89 at Kiowa and thence to the St. Mary Entrance to the Park. Fine, if you aren't pulling a trailer or driving an RV over 20 feet in length. RVers must make a 31-mile detour by way of Browning and Kiowa. The town of St. Mary, the Park Entrance, Saint Mary Visitor Center, Glacier Park Lodge and Park-edge shops and services are in close proximity to one another. The place can be congested, especially in summer. **Saint Mary** is the eastern terminus of Going-to-the-Sun Road. The Saint Mary Visitor Center is well worth a visit. Interpretive displays and videos are augmented by occasional dancing and drumming by members of the Blackfeet Tribe. Refer to the weekly *Naturalist Activities Guide* for current times.

After negotiating the Saint Mary congestion, a visit to a nearby **c. 1913 ranger cabin**, fitted out as a children's interpretive center, will restore your perspective. It's fun to poke about the cabin and grounds, imagining how rangers lived in the years before Park tourism heated up.

Lower Two Medicine Lake.

It's a lovely drive beside Saint Mary Lake to the Sun Point Nature Trail, but RVs must turn around here since the Going-to-the-Sun Road begins to get rough.

From Saint Mary, it's a nine-mile drive via US 89 alongside Lower Saint Mary Lake to the Reservation town of **Babb**. Here, you can pick up the road running along Swiftcurrent Creek to the **Many Glacier Entrance**. Many Glacier Hotel enjoys a spectacular setting. Lake and mountains spread before it in a visual feast. Across the lake, trails lead to famed **Grinnell Glacier** and the **Garden Wall**, a rock "wall" smack against the Continental Divide. See

Lodge Pole Gallery & Tipi Village,
Blackfeet Indian Reservation, Browning.

Adventures on Foot and *Adventures on Water* for trail and boat tour information.

■ Blackfeet Indian Reservation

The 1,525,712-acre Blackfeet Reservation is a splendid land of rolling hills and wildflower-strewn grasslands cut by creeks and rivers. Mountains tumble the Reservation's northwest corner. Glacier-created lakes reflect a sapphire sky. Wooded copses lie in the lee of hills, affording shelter for deer and elk. Sleek horses, descendants of the Spanish mustangs that carried Blackfeet warriors across the plains in past centuries, run free with the wind.

The Blackfeet Indian Nation is the largest tribe in Montana, having over 14,300 members. About half live on the Reservation. Non-Indians own some 40% of Reservation lands. The remaining property has either been allotted to tribal members or are owned by the tribe. The Reservation is crossed by US 2 and 89. A network of secondary roads, many paved, fans out from these highways. Driving aimlessly around the Reservation, exploring back roads, can be a stirring experience. The sheer beauty of the land overwhelms. Small communities like Heart Butte (watch for tepees) project a strong sense of the Blackfeet way of life.

 Blackfeet are a charming, gracious people, friendly toward visitors who respect their way of life and refrain from trespassing on private property.

Cut Bank

Cut Bank, just east of the Reservation on US 2, has basic services. The Toole County seat owes its name to a deep gorge, carved by Cut Bank Creek, clinging to the west and south edges of town. The **Glacier County Historical Museum**, next to the Sports Complex off US 2, displays artifacts reflecting area history. Open year-round, Tues.-Sat., 1-5. Weekends by appointment. ☎ 406-873-4904 or 873-4519.

Browning

Browning, at the junction of US 2 and 89, is the Reservation's principal town and the center of Reservation life. Tribal offices, Blackfeet Community College, Browning High School and Moccasin Flat School provide jobs and purpose.

The Moccasin Flat School

Browning's innovative Moccasin Flat School was founded by Blackfeet educators Darrell Kipp and Dorothy Still Smoking for the purpose of reviving the Blackfeet language among the People. Native American languages were stifled (at least 150 have been totally lost) by the US government's push to eradicate Indian culture. In the late 19th and early 20th centuries, children forced into boarding schools were punished for speaking their native tongues. The Blackfeet language, spoken by only a few elders, hovered on the edge of extinction when Kipp and Still Smoking conceived of an immersion school.

With Edward Little Plume, a rancher fluent in the language, Kipp and Still Smoking founded the Piegan Institute, a private, non-profit organization dedicated to teaching, preserving and promoting the Blackfeet language. That was in the 1980s. A decade later, after much study and focused work, the Moccasin Flat School opened. Children attending the school from age three soon learn to speak Blackfeet. They, in turn, teach their parents. In time, the language will be revived as a vibrant foundation for cultural revival. The Moccasin Flat School serves as a model for other tribes.

The **Museum of the Plains Indian**, at the western edge of Browning on US 89, showcases the artistic skills of Northern Plains tribes. The permanent exhibition gallery reflects the artistic richness and diversity created by a people who embellished articles of everyday use with intricate quillwork and beading. Historic exhibitions include the traditional clothing of men, women and children, displayed on life-size figures. Other displays are devoted to the social and ceremonial aspects of Blackfeet and other tribal cultures. Changing exhibitions include contemporary Native American arts and crafts. See *Winds of Change*, a five-screen multimedia presentation about the evolution of Indian cultures on the Great Plains narrated by Vincent Price and produced by the Museum of Montana State University. Demonstrations of Native American arts and crafts techniques are presented periodically. Special tours and gallery discussions are scheduled by appointment. The museum shop, operated by the Northern Plains Indian Crafts Association, offers authentic items unavailable in commercial shops. Open daily, June-Sept, 9-5; Oct.-May, Mon.-Fri., 10-4:30. Free admission. ☎ 406-338-2230.

The very noticeable sign atop **Bob Scriver's Museum of Montana Wildlife and Hall of Bronze** could be a turnoff. Don't let it be. The structure to the east of the Museum of the Plains Indian houses an amazing collection of fine bronze sculptures and taxidermy, the work of a remarkable artist. You'll see rooms full of sculptures celebrating the animals and people, both Indian and non-Indian, who figured in the Montana of myth and reality. There are warriors on horseback, mounted cowboys roping steers, historic figures, children and dogs, bears and cougars. Allow plenty of time to take it all in. Hours vary, but the museum is generally open daily in summer, 8-5. Best to call ahead. ☎ 406-338-5425.

Bob Scriver

Bob Scriver is self-effacing, as befits a man of artistic genius. His heroic larger than lifesize bronzes grace such places as the Lewis and Clark National Historic Trail Interpretive Center, Fort Benton's historic riverfront, the Charles Russell Museum and other Montana landmarks.

I found him in his studio, a no-nonsense place where he and his seven Blackfeet assistants create realistic works of art from clay through the bronze-firing process. Though a *National Geographic* consultant on the Blackfeet Indians, a winner of numerous artistic awards, and acknowledged as Montana's foremost sculptor of the 20th century, Scriver is little known outside Montana. He likes it that way. He once took a fling at exhibiting at a New York gallery, but disliked the pressures. "I prefer the work I love to going the marketing route."

Scriver was born in Browning in 1914, the son of a trader to the Blackfeet. He has lived on the Reservation all his life. He began sculpting late, at age 42, after a career in music. Like Charlie Russell's, Bob Scriver's art reflects the world of Montana's cowboys and Indians. Unlike Russell, whose Indian subject matter reflected the mores of his time, Scriver draws on a lifetime of association with and appreciation of the Blackfeet and their traditional way of life. "The Blackfeet people are sensitive and have much artistic talent."

■ A Circle Tour:
Tobacco Valley to Kalispell

In refreshing contrast to Glacier Park, Whitefish, Flathead Lake and the Bitterroot Valley, the northwest corner of Montana remains remote and relatively unvisited. There's a flip side: a narrower choice of accommodations and services. But the pristine beauty of the conifer-clad **Kootenai National Forest** and its coursing rivers more than cancels that out.

Coming from Glacier Park, you can pick up **US 93** at Whitefish for the jaunt to the Tobacco Valley, an intriguing place with a history and lifestyle all its own. US 93 zips through the **Stillwater State Forest** before weaving around pretty **Dickey** and **Murphy Lakes**, two of the numerous glacial remnants studding the valley and the surrounding Salish and Whitefish Mountains.

Dickey Lake has two US Forest Service campgrounds (see *Camping*, page 403). Watch for the Murphy Lake Ranger Station. Pick up hiking and sightseeing information at this attractively sited station. Hang a left a bit farther on, at the community of **Fortine**, and head for **Ant Flat Natural Resource Education Center/Historic Site**. That's a big mouthful for a historic ranger station inadvertantly built on ant condos. The old buildings now serve the Education Center, but you can wander about and walk the one-mile nature trail.

The Tobacco Valley, so-named for the tobacco-like plants once grown here by Kootenai Indians, widens out at Fortine and extends north to the Port of Roosville and west to Lake Koocanusa. This valley of rolling "drumlins" (drumlins are long, narrow hills made up of glacial drift) and verdant fields refers to itself as "Montana's banana belt" because of a modified Pacific Maritime climate.

Eureka

Eureka is the center of valley life. As you enter town, look for the **Tobacco Valley Historical Village** on your left. The cluster of structures moved here from throughout the valley reflect the self-sufficient lifestyle of the Scandinavian farmers and loggers who settled this isolated place in the late 19th century. Explore the hand-hewn log schoolhouse, the fire lookout tower, the general store and railroad depot. Local ladies still quilt in the Social Hall; quilts are on sale in the museum. The Village opens on Memorial Day, but you can wander about anytime. Living history events are held in summer. Call the Tobacco Valley Board of Commerce at ☎ 406-296-2487 for current hours and events information.

Pick up a *Tobacco Plains Heritage Tour* brochure and map at the Murphy Lake Ranger Station or the Historical Village. The tour meanders through the valley, looking in on landmarks of historical interest. Eureka seems to be in transition from a lumber town to a vaguely artsy, New Age place. People coming here for whatever reason just kinda stay, many opening businesses with such disparate names as Old World Bakery and Neon Cowgirl.

Lake Koocanusa

A mile or so north of Eureka, MT 37 swings west to Lake Koocanusa.

DID YOU KNOW? *No, it's not an Indian name. The long, narrow lake overlapping the international border, formed by damming the Kootenai River, derives its name thusly: "Koo" for the river, "can" for Canada and "usa" for the USA. Koocanusa: simple.*

Drive down either side of the lake to **Libby Dam**, a distance of some 43 miles. **MT 37** on the east side, a National Forest Scenic Byway, is the smoothest and most scenic. Since development is not permitted on the lake, thick conifer forests march unbroken to the water line. Watch for rock climbers scaling **Stone Hill**, above the Byway (see *Rock Climbing*). Watch for bighorn sheep, too.

A bridge crosses the lake eight miles south of the US 93 junction. This is decision time. You can continue south on MT 37 to Libby Dam and thence to Libby. Or cross the bridge and head south to the dam on the paved but more challenging **Forest Road #228** (closed in winter). Your chances of seeing a variety of large and small animals are better on this road.

Another alternative: cross the bridge and take **Forest Road #92**, 50 miles of paved, sharply switchbacking road traversing the Purcell Mountains to Yaak, the Kootenai word for "arrow."

AUTHOR TIP *A side trip: visit an **Amish village** by turning off FS Road #92 onto the FDR Road. There should be a sign. The Plain People make log furniture and quilts to sell at a village shop and at the annual June auction, which draws buyers from all over the Pacific Northwest. They also serve Friday night dinners to the public.*

Yaak

By taking the high road, you'll cruise into Yaak some two hours on; if you don't succumb to temptation and explore on foot. Numerous logging roads sporting "Closed" chains branch from the main road. You can walk up these roads, if you like. Remember: this is prime grizzly country. Watch for log trucks. Road not maintained in winter. You'll know you're nearing Yaak when you come to the weathered log community church. There's a one-room log schoolhouse a bit farther on. Houses? Well, they tend to be hidden in the trees or beside the Yaak River. Then "downtown

Yaak" comes into view. The Dir-T-Shame Saloon and the Yaak River Tavern & Mercantile stare each other down across the road. That's all, folks. That's Yaak.

Yaak's 150 or so souls live smack in the middle of what many consider to be the wildest area left in the Lower 48. The lush forests rising from the Yaak River and its tributaries are habitat for grizzlies, wolves, lynx, wolverines, even rare black mountain lions.

From Yaak, **Forest Road #68** follows the South fork of the Yaak River through the Purcells to Libby. It's a scenic drive, but I prefer to head west on Hwy. 508 because of fabulous **Yaak Falls**. Here, a few miles past Yaak, the Yaak River takes a spectacular rushing, foaming plunge down precipitous rocks. It then roars down a chute, racketing along to meet the Kootenai near the US 2 junction. The wide road above the river has frequent view point turnouts.

Ross Creek Cedar Grove

Northwest of the junction, US 2 and the Kootenai River enter Idaho at Montana's lowest point: 1,820 feet. Heading southeast, US 2 looks in on the small town of **Troy**. Three miles farther on, MT 56 swings south on a must-do detour past fish-rich Bull Lake to the Ross Creek Cedar Grove Scenic Area. Across the highway, a trail leads into the **Cabinet Mountains Wilderness**.

Bull lake is popular in summer, but unless you trailer a boat you're out of luck. Like many less frequently visited areas in Montana, tourist traffic isn't sufficient to support boat rentals. Campers can bed down at the **Forest Service's Bad Medicine Campground** at the foot of the lake.

Four miles of steep, twisting road leads from the campground to Ross Creek Cedar Grove. The old growth grove of Western red cedars, towering 175 feet from the forest floor, will remind you of what the entire area looked like before the logging era. A .9-mile nature trail winds alongside cold, clear Ross Creek and among ferns and wildflowers reflective of the Pacific Northwest. There are interpretive signs and it's handicap accessible.

MT 56 continues south to meet up with MT 200. Touring picks up this route in the Clarks Fork and the St. Regis section.

Kootenai Falls

Kootenai Falls is the next must-stop. Spectacular doesn't even begin to describe the wide tumbling falls interrupting the otherwise peaceful course of the Kootenai River. US 2 hugs the river all the way from the Idaho line to Libby. You can't see the falls from the highway. Watch for a sign at a turnout.

The falls thunder in a deep canyon below a woodsy park. A trail winding through the park to the canyon edge offers great views of the falls. Follow the trail down the canyon to a swinging bridge suspended above the cataract. Cross the bridge to a spacious rock ledge at river's edge.

DID YOU KNOW? *If you saw Meryl Streep outwitting the bad guys in* The River Wild, *you saw Kootenai Falls. Much of the movie was filmed on the Flathead River, but the Gauntlet scenes were shot at Kootenai Falls. Don't try it; the falls are not runnable. To film the impossible whitewater run, stunt actors were harnessed to helicopters hovering overhead so they could be snatched up should the raft capsize. Streep's scenes were shot elsewhere and spliced in. The filming caused quite a stir in nearby Libby.*

Libby

Libby owes it existence to logging. One of Montana's largest sawmills helps keep the town afloat. Libby's showpiece: the **Heritage Museum**, a spectacular 12-sided log structure 130-feet in diameter. Just touring this amazing example of lumbermens' skill is worth a visit. The museum's series of imaginatively curated galleries celebrating the area's colorful parade of Indians, trappers, miners, lumbermen, and the women who tamed the wilderness (and the lumbermen), rises to the occasion. A miner's cabin and an old forestry cookhouse grace the grounds. 1367 US 2 South. Open Mon.-Sat., 10-5; Sundays 1-5. ☎ 406-293-7521.

Libby Dam, 13 miles east of Libby via MT 37, is worth a visit. The 370-foot-high, 3,055-foot-long straight-axis, concrete gravity dam was begun in 1966 and completed in 1972. Built for flood control and to generate electricity, the dam holds back 90-mile-long **Lake Koocanusa**. A visitor center overlooks of the dam and offers explanatory material. Touring the powerhouse, seeing the five mammoth turbines up close, is a powerful experience. Tours are available for free. ☎ 406-293-5577 for current hours.

Kalispell

From Libby, US 2 rides through pretty valleys and over mountain meadows to Kalispell, a distance of 89 miles. A good road invites you to relax and enjoy the scenery. About halfway, east of the non-town of Happy's Inn, the highway passes the **Thompson Lakes** chain, **MacGregor Lake** and other remnants of the Ice Age cupped in the shelter of mountains on the Flathead and Lolo National Forests.

■ Circling the Flathead Indian Reservation

Flathead Lake's gaggle of summer homes and tourist services belie the fact that over half the lake is on the Flathead Indian Reservation. It's only south of the lake that you get a sense of being on a reservation.

This anomaly can be traced to 1910, when a million acres of Reservation land was opened to homesteaders. Filing for Reservation lands was suspended in 1919, too late to reverse a trend that allowed non-Indians to develop choice lakefront and agricultural properties. Today, only about half the Reservation's land is owned by members of the Confederated Salish-Kootenai Tribes. Some 21,259 people live within the Reservation boundaries, but only about 5,100 are Indian. Many are only a quarter- to half-Indian.

The McDonald Influence

McDonald is a prominent Flathead Reservation name. It was come by honestly, as opposed to the practice of Indians assuming anglicized names having little meaning to the bearer.

Angus McDonald, a Hudson's Bay Company employee, was born in the Scottish Highlands. In the 1840s, he helped set up a fur trading post on land that would become the Flathead Reservation. He married Catherine, whose mother came from a family of Nez Perce chiefs and whose father was part Mohawk. The couple had 12 children, many of whom married into the Salish-Kootenai tribes. Sons Joseph and Duncan were themselves fathers of numerous children. Joseph's son, Charlie, was a link between those early years and today. A founding member of the Tribal Council of the Confederated Salish and Kootenai Tribes, he died in 1995 at the age of 97.

The family remained on the Reservation, many living near Post Creek, the location of Angus's early trading post. Part of another McDonald post still stands as Montana's oldest building. There are few Reservation towns that don't figure in McDonald family history. Numerous family members, including Salish-Kootenai College President Joe McDonald, are prominent in tribal affairs. The Flathead Reservation may be the only reservation where traditional male pow-wow dancers sport tartan cloth as part of their regalia.

If you wish to learn more about this felicitous bonding of Scottish and Native American families, obtain a copy of *Scottish Highlanders, Indian Peoples* by James Hunter. See *Bibliography*.

Driving US 93 south from Lakeside, you see a seemingly endless creep of lakeside cottages and condos that continues onto the Reservation from Rollins. Summertime sprawl aside, the lake offers a procession of knock-your-socks-off vistas of blue water and green islands backed by the majestic Mission Mountains. The lake's vivid blue water is derived from suspended particles of granite.

At Dayton, a sign points to **Lake Mary Ronan** and the state park by that name. Flathead Agent Peter Ronan was highly respected by both Indians and non-Indians, an anomaly in those days of uncaring government agents. His wife loved and trusted the Flatheads and was much loved in return.

At Elmo, MT 28 swings wide to circle the west side of the Reservation, ultimately joining up with MT 200. It's a lonely drive over rolling terrain dotted with cattle and horses. This is also hot springs country. Just before you come to the twin towns of Camas/Hot Springs, you'll see the fancy **Wild Horse Hot Springs** sign. The venerable spa, developed around a thermal well sunk in 1913, has private plunges, but little else.

Head for funky **Camas/Hot Springs** to experience déja-vu straight out of the 1930s. This down-at-heels place stuck on the edge of nowhere is a part Indian, part non-Indian town reflecting the days when Eastern Montana wheat farmers would seed their fields and head for Hot Springs to soak the winter away. Now, it seems that the old place is looking up.

 KID-FRIENDLY **Symes Hot Springs** is an unlikely catalyst. The mission-style structure dates from the 1920s when this type of architecture was the in thing. The place was on the skids when Leslie and Dan Smith bought it, following the death of the original owner. The Smiths fixed it up, even installed an outdoor swimming pool. Now it's a family place with New Age overtones. You can soak in hot mineral water in an antique footed tub, get a facial or herbal body wrap, rent a bike, eat a meal, hike a trail, rent a tipi. It's a refreshing trip back to a less touristy, more ingenuous Montana.

Three miles south of Camas/Hot Springs, MT 28 angles southwest and Rt. 382 heads straight south, picking up MT 200 at **Perma**. Like most remote Reservation towns, Perma is unremarkable. At Dixon, swing north on Rt. 354. This mostly paved, part gravel road leads to the **National Bison Range** at Moise and continues on to the Pablo **National Wildlife Refuge** (see *Wildlife Watching*).

The road pulls up at **Polson**, a bustling summer resort town commanding the foot of Flathead Lake. Polson could be the clone of any lakeside resort town that jogs your memory. There are lakefront and riverfront parks, souvenir shops, hostelries, marinas, a cruise boat to Wildhorse Island, traffic lights and museums. Some businesses are operated by tribal members. MT 35 and US 93 converge here, adding to the summertime traffic crunch.

The **Polson-Flathead Historical Museum**, at 708 Main Street, show-cases area history with an authentic stagecoach, saddles and other arti-facts reflecting the Reservation's unique blend of Indian and non-Indian development. You can even gawk at Calamity Jane's last saddle. Open Memorial Day-Labor Day, Mon.-Sat., 9-6. ☎ 406-883-3049. **Miracle of America Museum**, just south of town on US 93, is a hodge podge of Americana owned by Gil and Joanne Mangels. Visualize a big, stuffed at-tic combined with the mother of all garage sales and you've got it. If you're interested in some particular facet of America's past, it's bound to be here. Modest admittance fee. ☎ 406-883-6804 for current hours.

US 93 slices through the heart of the Flathead Reservation. This is sur-passingly beautiful country; lush meadows and grasslands lying in the shadow of the Mission Mountains. The snowcapped mountain range shelters the **Mission Wilderness**. A tribal permit is required to visit the Wilderness (see *Information Sources*, page 356).

The modest Reservation towns of Pablo, Ronan, St. Ignatius, Ravalli and Arlee, strung along US 93, mix it up with souvenir shops selling Indian crafts and other items representing all shades of authenticity. You'll find some fine items made by Native artisans at the gift shop in **The Peoples' Center at Pablo**. Don't go just to shop. Designed to promote, preserve and enhance Salish-Kootenai culture, the Peoples' Center is a museum, cultural and educational center in a single attractive package. The ex-hibit gallery features audio-enhanced displays relating the saga of the Salish and Kootenai people from early times to the present. Take your time; it's a moving experience. **Native Ed-Ventures tours** originate from here. See page 456.

Six miles south of Ronan, on the east side of the road from Ninepipe Na-tional Wildlife Refuge, is a handsome log structure housing **Ninepipes Museum of Early Montana**. Opened in 1998, the museum houses a su-perb collection of artifacts and photographs relating to the Flathead Val-ley's Indian and homesteading heritage. While the artifacts, the Indian beadwork and a lifesize diorama depicting an Indian camp scene are noteworthy, the **Hall of Photographs** is a stunner. The subjects of many of these photos bear names that are familiar on the Reservation to-day. Modest admission fee. Open daily in summer, 8 am-7 pm, in winter Tues.-Sun., 11-5. 40962 US 93, Charlo, MT 59824; ☎ 406-644-3435. Fax 406-644-2928.

DON'T MISS Churches and missions may not be on your must-see list, but don't slight **St. Ignatius Mission** at the town of that name. The mission was established in 1854. The imposing church, built in 1891, seems little different from other Catholic churches. Fifty-eight striking murals painted by Br. Joseph Carignano make it a must-see.

Original log mission structures arranged in the shadow of the church offer a clearer picture of the mission's early times. A cabin operates as a museum run by volunteers who enjoy filling folks in on the history of the mission and the southern half of the Reservation. Open daily, 8-9 in summer, 9-5 in winter.

US 93 and MT 200 merge at the bottom of a steep hill at **Ravalli**. US 93 crosses the **Jocko River**, namesake of the reservation in Peter and Mary Ronan's time, before sliding through **Arlee**, site of the annual 4th of July Flathead Celebration and Pow-Wow.

■ Clark Fork & the St. Regis

MT 200 and I-90 take parallel northwesterly courses from, repectively, Ravalli and Missoula. Mt 200 rides through the Jocko and Clark Fork River Valleys. I-90 humps it through the heart of the Bitterroot Range, curving above canyons cut by the Clark Fork and St. Regis Rivers.

This is a fabulous country of gleaming rivers, towering ponderosa and lodgepole pines, formidable rock cliffs and brave wildflowers. Beauty and history tramp hand in hand here, back to Indian occupancy before David Thompson's time, to pioneering forest rangers, to loggers and the raging wildfires of 1910.

David Thompson, Explorer

A big chunk of Northwest Montana, arguably the state's wildest and most achingly beautiful, was blazed by legendary explorer and trader David Thompson on the heels of the Lewis and Clark expedition. Acknowledged as the best geographer of his day, Thompson was employed by the North West Company to survey the area with an eye to staking out British ownership. In 1809 he established a trading post, which he called Saleesh House, near the site of the present-day town of Thompson Falls. He traveled west to map the Columbia River system, east to map the site of present-day Missoula, and north to map the Flathead Lake area, returning to Canada on the eve of the War of 1812. Thompson's name remains as revered in these parts as Lewis's and Clark's are in Missouri River country.

From Ravalli, MT 200 traverses the **Jocko River Valley** for 31 miles across the southern end of the Flathead Reservation until the Jocko empties into the Clark Fork River. From here **MT 135**, richly deserving its National Forest Scenic Byway status, meanders along the Clark Fork to I-90 and the confluence with the St. Regis River.

The Byway's 21-mile length is much too brief. It's easy to become so lost in the beauty of it that the time slips away. Consider driving it in both directions to take in differing perspectives.

The roadbed clings to the side of the canyon, following the river's contours. Steep talus slopes plunge to the railroad tracks across the river. Pull-offs permit gawking and photographing. A few small oases occupy side canyons. One of these, **Quinn's Hot Springs**, a popular spa since 1899, has RV hookups and a pool. If lucky, you may spot rafters floating through the canyon. An access site and the **Cascade Trail** trailhead are a few miles past the turnoff from MT 200.

West of the turnoff, MT 200 glides through the Clark Fork Valley, a lush and productive bucolica sporting nurseries and greenhouses. The town called **Paradise** is surely that. A sign invites you to "enjoy a cheeseburger in Paradise." Corny, but nice. Railroad tracks, ubiquitous presences in many Montana valleys, run through Paradise and next-door **Plains** where a grain elevator attests to the fertile river bottom soil.

A "watch for mountain sheep next 10 miles" sign brings you up short a few miles farther on. No surprise, considering the steep Cabinet Mountains hugging the highway. A sheep-viewing turnoff has interpretive signs describing the native sheep and their habit of frequenting this area between November and April.

Thompson Falls is a beguiling town, not as much for its charm as for a small town honesty. The three-block main drag between the tracks and the river offers good RV parking, the inevitable saloons, and a couple of interesting shops; but tourist hype is refreshingly absent. Not that visitors are lacking. **Thompson Falls State Park** is a mile north of town. Thompson Falls Dam widens the Clark Fork to a series of long, narrow lakes stretching to the Idaho border; attractive to boaters and anglers. A footbridge from Maiden Lane accesses the dam and the picturesque falls (limited parking: walk from a parking spot "downtown").

The county seat is proud of its history. It shows at the **Old Jail Museum** on South Madison Street. The foursquare Sanders County Jail structure houses a collection of David Thompson artifacts, Prohibition-era stills and jail memorabilia. The stout second-story cells are still in place; one was designated for women and children. The sheriff and his family lived on the first floor. As recently as the 1950s, this was considered the finest jail in the state; a measure of Montana's nearness to frontier mores. The museum is open daily, Mother's Day-Labor Day, noon-4. ☎ 406-827-3496.

The remaining 50-mile drive on Mt 200 to deep **Cabinet Gorge** and the Idaho line is a pleasant meander in sight of long narrow lakes lying between the Thompson Falls and Cabinet Gorge Dams. MT 200 follows first the south side of the lakes, then the north. A gravel road worth exploring parallels the opposing shores. Siftings of wildflowers cover meadows and roadsides beneath the eternal presence of the Cabinet Mountains.

A few independent souls live in small lake-front towns arranged along the roads. **Noxon** seems typical. It has the essentials: a fishing/hunting outfitter, a pawn shop, a tavern, a school, a mercantile, a hardware store, two cafés, a basic motel, a few rustic dwellings and a one-lane duck-your-head bridge to the main highway. Who would guess that the white supremacist Militia of Montana is based here?

Paved **FS Road #7** leads from Thompson Falls to 4,860-foot **Thompson Pass** on the Idaho line. Since forever, a dirt track has been the only link to the old mining town of **Murray**, just down-mountain from the Pass in Idaho. The track has recently been improved, providing a convenient link from Thompson Falls to I-90 by way of Wallace, Idaho. The route makes sense if you wish to enjoy some mountain scenery while checking out old mining digs. Numerous trails accessed from it include the **Stateline National Recreation Trail** (see *Adventures on Foot*). **I-90** from the Montana-Idaho line to Missoula is a far holler from the common conception of an Interstate. The smooth four-lane seems at odds with the backcountry aspect of the forested scenery and deep-woods settlements.

The Mullan Road was blazed through here in the late 1860s; no wonder the going was so rough that the Road was never quite completed. A paved 22-mile stretch named Camels Hump Road (**FS Road #10**) for the pack camels once used experimentally on the Mullan Road, follows the original Mullan Road from St. Regis to I-90 Exit 22.

Each of the very small towns along I-90, De Borgia, St. Regis, Superior, Alberton, Huson, owes its livelihood to logging, the railroad, the US Forest Service and tourism. The latter two, though low-key, offer today's best job prospects. St. Regis and Superior have gas and other services.

Residents of **St. Regis**, at the western end of the St. Regis-Paradise Scenic Byway (MT 135), have a deep sense of place and history. A statue of John Mullan, builder of the road bearing his name, occupies a place of honor in (what else?) Mullan Square. **Kielty Hill**, above the town center, belies its once-raucous collection of beer halls, bawdy houses, rooming houses and cabins.

Superior is the jumping-off place for the paved **North Fork Adventure Road** (FS Road #250) leading into Idaho from Hoodoo Pass. It's also known as the Trout Creek Road. Take I-90 Exit 47 to MT 287, and thence to FS Road #250. Beautiful as the I-90 corridor may be, getting off into the "bush" stokes the sense of adventure. The **Stateline Trail** can be accessed from this road. Check with the Superior Ranger Station for other area adventure drives, many requiring a 4WD vehicle.

Leave I-90 at **Huson** for a look into the early years of the 20th century when the Forest Service was young and rangers relied on horses and pack animals to penetrate the new national forests' deep wilderness.

The historic **Nine Mile Remount Station** has been preserved as an outpost of those times. It remains a remount facility with some 30 pack mules and horses quartered here, plus 225 over-wintered mules from other ranger districts. Education is the Station's primary thrust. The

Nine Mile Wild Lands Training Center operates traveling clinics relevant to minimal impact camping in bear country. Region Pack Train Director Bob Hoverson offers Mule packing classes in late May and early June. Classes in historic building preservation (including log cabins) are also offered. ☎ 406-626-5427 or 626-5201 for information.

The spit-and-polish Station includes a visitor center, horse barns and ranger housing set in the folded meadows of the Ninemile Divide. The visitor center offers insight into the history of the Station. Open daily, Memorial Day-Labor Day, 9-5.

You can wander about the Station, reading interpretive signs and getting a feel for what a ranger's life must have been like back then. Up-trail from the Station, you'll find the grove-like **Grand Menard Picnic Area** and a pleasant interpretive trail.

Montana's splendid northwest country pulls into focus a quote from Chief Joseph of the Nez Perce: "The Earth was created with the assistance of the Sun, so it should be left as it was." Outdoorsman Bob Marshall, for whom the Bob Marshall Wilderness was named, said in more contemporary terms, "This is the last stand for that glorious adventure into the physically unknown that was commonplace in the lives of our ancestors.... It is vast panoramas, full of height and depth and glowing color, on a scale so overwhelming as to wipe out the ordinary meaning of dimension."

Adventures

■ Adventures on Foot

Hiking opportunities abound in Glacier Country. There's a trail for everyone who's curious about this spacious and often wild chunk of Montana and enjoys putting one foot in front of the other. These include interpretive trails, nature trails, hikes of but a few hours duration, and backpacking trails demanding a high level of conditioning.

Most trails on national forest lands do not require permits. Check with the local ranger station if your plans include backpacking in a wilderness area. Glacier National Park requires backpackers to obtain a back country permit. Hiking on the Blackfeet and Flathead Indian Reservations, including the Mission Wilderness, is by permit only. This chapter's section on *Hiking* covers interpretive trails and day-hikes. The section on *Backpacking* covers trails requiring two or more days.

Even if you have a hike of only a few hours in mind, be sure to refer to *Backpacking* as well. Short segments of longer trails often lend themselves to day-hikes. These can usually be accessed from a trailhead or via a connecting trail. This advice also holds true in reverse: backpackers may wish to use linked trails mentioned under *Hiking*.

Hiking

Missoula Area

Most Montana cities have access to a hiking trail or two, but Missoula boasts the most. A situation near the confluence of two rivers might give most cities boasting room, but that's just a beginning for Missoula. The city is situated at the southern edge of the Rattlesnake National Recreation Area and Wilderness, and next door to the Blue Mountain Recreation Area.

Mount Sentinel, Missoula's pet mountain, crowds the city. The **"M" Trail**, gaining 620 feet via 11 switchbacks, begins right in town. The **Hellgate Canyon Trail** climbs the less precipitous north side of Mt. Sentinel and continues on to access the **Pattee Canyon Recreation Area** southeast of the city.

This is horse country, so many trails within hollering distance of Missoula are multiple-use trails permitting horses. Many permit bicycles. ATVs are permitted on some.

> *Missoula Trails*, a booklet produced by the Missoula Trails Project in cooperation with state and national agencies, describes over 100 miles of trail within a few miles of Missoula. It's available through the Missoula Ranger District of the Lolo National Forest, from Travel Montana, or from the Missoula Convention & Visitors Bureau.

The 61,000-acre **Rattlesnake National Recreation Area and Wilderness** has 33,000 acres of designated wilderness. The South Zone's 28,000 acres have been designated a National Recreation Area. The main entrance is accessed from Missoula via Van Buren Street, which becomes Rattlesnake Drive. The South Zone is for day-use only. Camping is permitted in the Wilderness Area North Zone, making it good for backpacking. Horses are permitted on these trails. Bicycles are permitted on South Zone trails (no bicycles on the Woods Gulch/Sheep Mountain Trail). Horses have the right of way. Should you not want to hob-nob with horses, you might give the **Rattlesnake Valley** a try. This green corridor following Rattlesnake Creek, and traversing natural riparian habitats, includes paved paths for both hikers and bicyclists and unpaved paths for hikers only. Greenbelt paths also follow Missoula's Clark Fork Riverfront. The 2.5-mile **Kim Williams Nature Trail** takes advantage of an abandoned railroad bed on the south side of the Clark Fork River. It connects with the Hellgate Canyon Trail to Mt. Sentinel.

The **Pattee Canyon Recreation Area**, accessed via the Pattee Canyon Road, includes a network of one mile- to 3.4-mile combined foot, bicycle and horse trails.

The **Blue Mountain Recreation Area**, a former US Army Military Reservation, comprises 5,500 acres of valley bottom and mountain top. Reach it by making a right turn off US 93 onto Blue Mountain Road (County Road #30). The area includes the eight-mile **Blue Mountain National Recreation Trail**, a .4-mile nature trail, and the 1.4- and 1.8-mile **Maclay Flat Trails** paralleling the Bitterroot River.

The Lolo National Forest

The Lolo National Forest, comprising big chunks of Montana and Idaho and overlaying the Bitterroot Range, includes some of Montana's densest forests, highest mountain pitches and most inspring scenery. This country conceals numerous old mining camps and dry digs. Logging has long been a money maker here. Rivers and streams scoring the valleys and mountainsides make soft music blending with bird song and the faint rustle of forest creatures.

The **Lolo Trail**, winding through eastern Idaho and entering Montana some 33 miles west of Missoula at Lolo Pass, is part of a network of ancient Indian trails. Much of the original Lolo Trail has been obliterated by road building, logging and other exigencies of progress. But portions of this trail, once trod by moccasined feet, survive to be trod by hikers. From US 93, turn onto US 12 at Lolo and drive 18.5 miles to the Howard Creek Road. From here, you can trace the Trail via a steep, rocky 0.4 mile loop.

You can access a longer section of the Trail via the Lee Creek Road off US 12, 26.5 miles west of Lolo. **Wagon Mountain Trail** #300 begins at the Lee Creek Campground and continues for five miles to Lolo Pass. The terrain may have remained pretty much as Lewis and Clark found it when they passed this way in September, 1805, and again in the summer of 1806, but not so the vegetation. The dense stands of youngish trees you see today have replaced the scattered stands of mature trees that Lewis and Clark saw. Those trees have fallen victim to successive forest fires, the most destructive having occurred in 1910.

The 2.5-mile **Lee Creek Interpretive Trail** also begins at the Lee Creek Campground. The nature trail features interpretive stations explaining the life cycle of the forest and defining the differences between old, young and logged forests.

The **Reservation Divide** area, accessed via Forest Road #456 and Ninemile Road, above and beyond the Ninemile Ranger Station, includes several day-hike trails leading to the much longer **Reservation Divide Trail**. The Divide area consists of 16,000 acres of prime high elevation back country along the divide between the Flathead Indian Reservation and the Lolo National Rorest. Contact the Ninemile Ranger Station for a map and detailed directions.

Watch for a sign to the 1.4-mile (round trip) **Cascade Falls Nature Trail** on MT 135, a few miles west of Paradise. The pleasant walk up one of the canyon's oasis-like side canyons leads to a cooling waterfall. Contact the Plains Ranger Station for an interpretive brochure.

The route of the Hiawatha Railroad shot southwest from Taft, entering Idaho via the St. Paul Pass Tunnel. The track bed has been cleared and opened as the **Route of the Hiawatha Rail-Trail**. As of this writing, the Idaho side has been completed and the completion of the Montana side awaits tunnel work. ☎ 208-245-4517 or 744-1392 for information on the current status of the Montana link. The Superior Ranger District office will also have current Rail-Trail information.

The Superior Ranger District maintains numerous trails in the mountainous country surrounding the l-90 corridor between the Ninemile/ Reservation Divide area and the Idaho line. Terrain is varied, ranging from river bottoms to a subalpine environment. Valley bottoms, dense forests, meadows and barren ridges mix with streams, rivers and lakes. Most of these trails lend themselves best to two- to three-day backpacking trips, but many are suitable for day-hikes. The Superior Ranger District office makes available a descriptive listing of these trails. Included are two day-hike trails in the Ward-Eagle Lake Area of the South St. Regis Area: the 3.2-mile **Ward Creek Trail** and the three-mile **Hazel-Hub Lakes Trail**. Short portions of these primitive back country routes may be obscured by vegetation. Topographic maps are advised.

The easily negotiated 4.1-mile **Crystal Lake Trail** west of De Borgia looks in on an abandoned mining camp and links up with the Stateline Trail. The 2.8-mile **St. Regis Lakes Trail**, mostly over a primitive road, also visits an abandoned mine.

The South Superior Area also includes several day-hike trails. The 1.2-mile **Cliff Lake Trail** offers quick access to one of several alpine cirques on the Superior Ranger District. The short (0.8-mile) **Lower Oregon Lakes Trail** packs a steep workout as it climbs through a narrow gorge to the twin Oregon Lakes. A cold-water swim is a just reward for the climb.

Kootenai National Forest

The ranger districts on the Kootenai National Forest maintain numerous day-hike trails with low to moderate elevation gains and offering some truly wonderful scenery. Many trails offer sightings of deer, elk and black bear; grizzlies, too. You may spot moose in the marshy areas of subalpine lakes.

You'll find a very special nature trail at **Ross Creek Cedar Grove**, south of Bull Lake in the Troy Ranger District of the Kootenai National Forest. Access MT 56 from either US 2 or MT 200. Watch for signs identifying the road to the Grove. Deep in the Cabinet Mountains, in the extreme western portion of the state, the Grove celebrates the magnificent Western red cedars growing along Ross Creek. Many of these trees are as much as 175 feet tall and measure upwards of eight feet in diameter. A 0.9 mile nature trail describes a winding loop through this old growth forest.

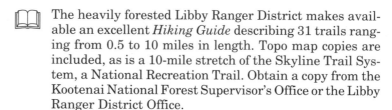 The heavily forested Libby Ranger District makes available an excellent *Hiking Guide* describing 31 trails ranging from 0.5 to 10 miles in length. Topo map copies are included, as is a 10-mile stretch of the Skyline Trail System, a National Recreation Trail. Obtain a copy from the Kootenai National Forest Supervisor's Office or the Libby Ranger District Office.

Other National Recreation Trails on the Kootenai National Forest include the 22-mile **Trout Creek Loop Trail** and the 19-mile **Boulder-Vinal Trail**. The five-mile **Pulpit Mountain Trail** north of Troy is more to the liking of day-hikers (all Three Rivers/Troy Ranger District). The **Little North Fork Trail**, leading to a plashing waterfall near Koocanusa Lake (Rexford Ranger District), is so short it hardly merits the trail designation. But it's very pretty.

The **Yaak River area**, tucked into the Purcell Mountains of extreme northwest Montana, is a place of deep glaciated valleys surrounded by rounded mountain "islands." This is logging country. It's also grizzly country. Always be alert to the possibility of encountering a grizzly, even on short hikes up forest roads (see *Co-Adventuring With Grizzlies* under *Montana Fauna*, page 16).

The **Northwest Peaks Scenic Area** can be reached via Forest Roads off US 2 and MT 508. Tucked into a corner bordered by Canada and Idaho, the area encompasses deep valleys broken by the sky-brushing peaks of the Selkirk Range. Northwest Peak and Davis Mountain, both in excess of 7,000 feet, command a wildly beautiful area of alpine forests and lakes. Unpredictable weather at high elevations puts it out of bounds for all but the hardiest trekkers. Mid-summer is about right. Only a few miles of trail penetrate this area.

The two-mile-plus **Northwest Peak Trail** gains 1,615 feet as it climbs up the 7,705-foot peak. Extend the hike by exploring alpine lakes mothered by the peak. An unmanned fire lookout tower tops this peak. To access the trailhead, take Pete Creek Road (#338) off MT 508, two miles west of Yaak. Drive 13 miles north, turn west onto the West Fork Road, go two miles, then turn right onto the Winkum Creek Road. Proceed for seven miles to the trailhead on the south side of the road at the edge of a clearcut. Contact the Three Rivers Ranger District for current conditions.

The **Rexford Ranger District** also has available a descriptive trail guide with topo map copies defining individual trails. Eleven trails ranging from 0.5 to eight miles offer plenty of day-hike choices. The District encompasses the splendid country surrounding Koocanusa Lake. The **Fortine Ranger District** encompasses the popular **Ten Lakes Scenic Area** and the **Tobacco Valley**. This ranger district also makes available a descriptive listing of hiking trails with maps. The Ten Lakes Scenic Area enjoys a runaway popularity, largely due to an easy access gravel and dirt road from US 93, but also due to its wild beauty. This was one of the original areas designated for special wilderness evaluation under the Montana Wilderness Study Act. Rangers with whom I spoke feared for the area's pristine viability. Though it's most suitable for backpacking, several short trails can be accessed from Grave Creek Road.

If a nature ramble better fits your mood, set out on the **Ant Flat Nature Trail** near the village of Fortine. Yes, you'll see ant hills. You'll also learn about area history and trees.

The Flathead National Forest

The 2.3 million-acre Flathead National Forest covers some very popular territory. This includes the **Tally Lake/Glacier View Ranger District** near Whitefish, the **Jewel Basin Hiking Area** in the Swan Mountain Range, the **Hungry Horse Reservoir area** and the **Bob Marshall** and **Spotted Bear Wildernesses**.

 The Flathead National Forest Supervisor's office makes available a helpful booklet describing the numerous trails on the forest. Included are day-hikes and backpacking adventures on trails maintained by the Swan Lake, Spotted Bear, Glacier View, Tally Lake and Hungry Horse Ranger Districts. Obtain a copy from the Flathead National Forest Supervisor's Office or from any Flathead Ranger District office. The Swan Lake Ranger District has compiled a Trails Inventory that includes descriptions and topo map copies ranging from short Jewel Basin trails to the 53-mile Alpine Trail.

The Jewel Basin has become so well-traveled that rangers wince when questioned about it. That doesn't mean you should avoid these 15,349 acres of high mountains, alpine lakes, mountain streams and meadows. It does mean you should observe responsible back country behavior when hiking here. The Basin is at the north end of the Swan Mountain Range, 17 miles east of Kalispell and 14 miles south of Hungry Horse. You can access the area from the west via the Seeley/Swan Highway (MT 83) or from the east by way of the Hungry Horse Dam. Contact the Swan Ranger District for detailed hiking information and to purchase a topographical map of the area.

If you're on for a strenuous, non-technical Class I (cross-country hiking, hands not needed) mountain climb, consider **Great Northern Mountain** east of Hungry Horse Reservoir (take the East Side Road). The eight-mile round trip hike offers a good day's workout. Approach this climb in mid-summer's maximum daylight. The reward: fabulous views of Glacier National Park peaks, the rugged Middle Fork (of the Flathead) Divide, and Hungry Horse Reservoir far below. Mountain goats, black bears and elk frequent this area. Contact the Hungry Horse Ranger station for information on current conditions.

Three nature trails are at the other end of the hiking spectrum. **Bigfork's Wild Mile Trail** parallels the Swan River for two miles before it empties into Flathead Lake. The river below the trail kicks up a fuss here (see *Kayaking* in *Adventures on Water*), so there's plenty to watch. Access is a mile above the dam at the Swan Bridge off Hwy. 209, or in Bigfork near the power plant.

The 2.1-mile **Sprunger-Whitney Nature Trail** in the Swan Valley covers terrain used for thousands of years by the Pend d'Oreille and Salish peoples to fish, hunt and gather berries. Entire families would move camp to the valley for an extended period of time. Their ancestors still come to gather huckleberries and to hunt. Take MT 83 south from Swan Lake. Turn right at the Point Pleasant Campground, a half-mile south of mile marker 64. Follow signs to the Trail. Pick up a brochure describing plants on the trail on-site or at the Swan Lake Ranger station.

The 5.6-mile **Danny On Memorial Trail** is dedicated to a Forest Service silviculturist whose impact on the Tally Lake and Whitefish area yet lingers. The trail begins at the 7,000-foot summit of Big Mountain at the ski resort of that name (you can take the gondola or chairlift to the summit). Hike all or part of the trail. Brochures are available at the Tally Lake Ranger station or Big Mountain Ski and Summer Resort.

Hiking in Glacier National Park

One of the best things about visiting Glacier National Park is availing yourself of the numerous trails leading from gorgeous vistas to more gorgeous vistas; along lakeshores, to Grinnel Glacier and to plunging waterfalls. While many trails into the wild heart of the park require several days to cover, others fill just a few hours or a day. You can hike on your own, or choose from numerous naturalist-led hikes, walks and strolls. Permits are not required for day-hikes, but are necessary for overnight hikes. Hiking alone is discouraged because of grizzly bear activity in the Park.

Your first stop should be at a Glacier Park visitor center to get a fix on the numerous hiking trails in this mountain-girt chunk of parkland. Helpful rangers will point you in the direction you want to go; even in directions you never dreamed of going.

AUTHOR TIP *The day-hike trails you choose largely depend on the length of time you intend to spend in the Park. Some misguided folks set aside only a couple of days to visit Glacier. Better plan on at least a week; longer if possible. There's more to see and do than you can possibly imagine and much of depends on your two boot-clad feet.*

The **Firebrand Pass** (9.6 round trip miles), **Piegan Pass** (12.8 miles to Many Glacier Hotel), **Highline Trail** (15.2 miles from Logan Pass to Swiftcurrent Motel), and **Garden Wall** (11.6 miles from the Logan Pass Visitor Center to The Loop on the Going-to-the-Sun Road) are great day-hikes if you are in peak condition.

Numerous shorter hikes offer a chance to do two, even three, separate hikes in a single day. Some samples:

The **Avalanche Lake Trail**, above **Trail of the Cedars** off Going to the Sun Road, offers a leg-stretch while driving the scenic road. The 6.1-mile trail begins with one of the boardwalks dear to the heart of national parks developers. This peters out after a short distance, as do most of the peo-

Lake McDonald, Glacier National Park.

ple. The trail traverses the North American Continent's farthest inland rain forest before coming in sight of the rounded red rock walls of **Avalanche Gorge**. More forest shade preceeds the thrill of discovering **Avalanche Lake**, a sheet of sheer beauty framed by glaciers leaking waterfalls.

Taking a boat to a trailhead is a fun way to go. The **Grinnell Glacier hike**, accessed via tour boats up the lengths of two lakes from Many Glacier Hotel, is a favorite, which is good because grizzlies are active in this area and there's safety in numbers. The **Two Medicine hike** involves taking a tour boat up Two Medicine Lake to the trailhead. A low-key trail winding along the north shore of **Lake McDonald** offers an opportunity to unwind and enjoy frequent lake views.

Backpacking

Glacier Country's tumbled mountains offer backpacking adventures fit to work out the bod and capture the imagination. Fully experiencing the unpeopled wild calls for overnighting it with a sleeping bag.

The sense of aloneness out here in the wilderness puts your workaday life into sharp perspective. The clear air is the present reality. Hurry-up city life evaporates into unreality. The music of a freshet dancing over polished stones so far surpasses more mundane music that you yearn to capture it on tape. But it belongs to the wild.

Awakening to see a doe gazing at you with liquid eyes while her fawn capers trustingly nearby captures the essence of this wild place as surely as do wildflowers carousing across a meadow. Winds sigh through fir trees, mocking the groans of a distant, over-stressed world. You tread a trail into deeper wilderness. At trail's end, you return to real life refreshed, sustained until next time.

Backpacking in mountain country isn't just a long walk in the outdoors. It's a walk on the wild side. You must observe special concerns for your safety, for the quality of your trip, and for the protection of the environment. Safely co-existing with grizzly bears, mountain lions and other wild creatures must also be taken into consideration.

CAUTION

Refer to Special Concerns under Adventures on Foot in the Yellowstone Country chapter (page 166) for advice that applies to backpacking in all of Montana's back country and wilderness areas. Some ranger districts and wilderness areas impose additional rules and restrictions. Check with the ranger district maintaining the area you wish to explore for current conditions and restrictions. A topographical map of your target area is a must. Refer to the sections on grizzlies and mountain lions (page 15-19) for life-saving information.

The Continental Divide Trail

The Continental Divide National Scenic Trail, fully described in the *Gold West Country* chapter (page 279), follows the Divide through a challenging portion of Glacier Country. Beginning at the Canadian border, the Trail follows a route near the Divide through Glacier National Park and part of the Blackfeet Indian Reservation to 5,280-foot Marias Pass. The Trail then threads the continent's rocky spine through the Great Bear, Bob Marshall and Scapegoat Wilderness Areas, skirting the storied Chinese Wall.

The Stateline Trail

The Stateline Trail, designated a National Recreation Trail in 1981, threads the Bitterroot Divide through mountainous country splashed with lakes and high meadows. This is not a trail for the unadventurous, or for hikers lacking orienteering skills. Some stretches, looking into Montana on the east and Idaho on the west, are clearly marked. Others are faint at best. The Trail gives equal exposure to both states. Portions lend themselves well to day-hikes and one- to two-day backpacking trips. Backpacking the Trail in its entirety requires a commitment of a week to 10 days or longer. Contact the Lolo and Bitterroot National Forests' Supervisors Offices for detailed information on the Trail's Glacier Country sections, and to learn how to access sections of it from wherever you happen to be.

The Reservation Divide

The Reservation Divide, in the Ninemile Ranger District of the Lolo National Forest, consists of 16,000 acres of back country between Ninemile Creek and the Flathead Indian Reservation. Two trail systems traversing the Divide can be reached from the Ninemile Ranger Station off I-90 (Exit 82).

The **Squaw Peak Trail** wraps up an extravaganza of vistas. The 7,994-foot peak affords a 390° panorama that includes the Cabinet Range, Flathead Lake, the National Bison Range and the distant Mission Mountains. On a really clear day you can see the peaks of Glacier National Park. McCormick, Josephine and Three Lakes Peaks also afford great views. These trails involve considerable elevation gains, most in excess of 1,800 feet. Contact the Ninemile Ranger Station for directions, current conditions and maps.

The Kootenai National Forest

The wildly beautiful Kootenai National Forest includes the 94,360-acre **Cabinet Mountains Wilderness**, the 15,700-acre **Ten Lakes Scenic Area** and the 19,100-acre **Northwest Peaks Scenic Area**. The Cabinet Mountains Wilderness has over 20 trails offering access to dozens of vest-pocket lakes and alpine meadows. Plant life is numerous and varied according to elevation and terrain. Best to hike here between late June and early September in order to avoid sudden snowstorms. Contact the Trout Creek Ranger Station for detailed trail information.

The Ten Lakes Scenic Area, just south of the Canadian border and east of the Tobacco Valley, was one of the original areas designated for special wilderness evaluation under the Montana Wilderness Study Act. The "Ten Lakes" appellation doesn't begin to describe this area of numerous glacier-sculpted lakes dominated by the high ridge of the Whitefish Mountains. Wildflowers bloom and huckleberries ripen amongst several varieties of spruce, fir and pines. This is one of the few areas supporting the rare alpine larch. The confusion of trails criss-crossing the area, many to **Little** and **Big Therriault Lakes**, can be combined. There are campgrounds at the above-mentioned lakes. Contact the Fortine Ranger District for specific trail information.

Bob Marshall, Great Bear & Scapegoat – Montana's Ultimate Wilderness Areas

The adjoining Bob Marshall, Great Bear and Scapegoat Wilderness Areas offer the ultimate in back country expeditions. These combined wildernesses comprise an astonishing 1,535,063 acres of wild beauty butting up to Glacier National Park on the north and dipping into the Helena National Forest on the south. On the west, the tumbled mountains of the Great Bear and the "Bob" merge with the Swan Mountain Range. The Rocky Mountain Front, distinguished by the 22-mile-long, 1,000-foot-high Chinese Wall, comprises the eastern edge of the Wilderness Areas and marks the beginning of broken prairie stretching to the North Dakota Badlands.

These areas afford unlimited opportunities to view wildlife in its natural habitat – elk, wolverine, moose, cougars, grizzly and black bears, mountain goats and sheep, plus bevies of birds. There should be a law mandating cameras in backpacks and gear bags.

These primitive areas are off-limits to anything with wheels, but open to travel by horseback, backpacking and horse packing. Permits are not required for travel within wilderness boundaries. Camping is limited to a maximum of 14 days in one campsite. When the maximum is reached, campers must move at least five miles to another campsite. Pets are permitted, but must be restrained as a courtesy to others, for your pet's safety, and to minimize stress on wildlife. It's a given that "no trace" camping is required.

 This is prime grizzly bear country. Take care! See pages 15-17 for precautions.

The **Great Bear Wilderness** contains alpine basins and broad U-shaped valleys. Elevations range from 4,000 feet along the Middle fork of the Flathead River to 8,705 feet atop Great Northern Mountain. Most valleys are heavily forested. High ridges and peaks poke above timberline. The weather can be charitably described as unpredictable. Sudden rain and snowstorms are possible throughout much of the year. Trails access this wilderness from Hungry Horse Reservoir, Spotted Bear River, Two Medicine River and from trailheads off US 2 between Glacier National Park and the Great Bear.

Much of the interior is without trails and can be hazardous, meaning that unless you are an experienced orienteer you had best hire a licensed outfitter/guide. Don't even think of backpacking in the Great Bear without first checking in with the Hungry Horse Ranger District of the Flathead National forest for current trail conditions and restrictions and a topo map.

The **Bob Marshall Wilderness** is the largest of the three with 1,009,356 acres, the most awe-inspiring and the most visited. Montanans regard it as their last best place, affectionately referring to it as "The Bob." Sandwiched between the Great Bear and the Scapegoat, The Bob straddles the Continental Divide and includes the headwaters of the Flathead River to the west and the Sun River to the east. Elevations range from 4,000 feet to over 9,000 on the Divide. Numerous peaks brush the sky at 8,000 feet or better. The Bob's most famous geologic feature is the huge escarpment known as the Chinese Wall, for its resemblance to China's manmade wall. This wilderness is a serendipitous extravaganza of precipitous ridgetops, gently sloping alpine meadows, forested river bottoms, mountain lakes and meandering streams and rivers. All of this adds up to difficult terrain traversed by over a dozen trails. Unless you are an experienced backpacker and orienteer, you might wish to use the services of a licensed guide.

Numerous access routes extend from forest roads off US 2 on the north, US 89 and 287 on the east, and MT 200 and 83 on the south and west. Contact the Hungry Horse Ranger District of the Flathead National Forest, the Seeley Lake Ranger District of the Lolo National forest, and/or the Rocky Mountain Ranger District of the Lewis & Clark National Forest for specific access information. You'll need to check in with one of the above for answers to the numerous questions you might, or should, have before venturing into this wilderness area, for current trail conditions and restrictions, and to purchase topo maps.

The **Scapegoat Wilderness**, the smallest of the three, straddles the Continental Divide to the south of The Bob. It's also the loftiest of the three, lying between 5,000 feet at the Blackfoot River and 9,400 feet on Red Mountain. Scapegoat Mountain's massive limestone cliffs are an extension of the Chinese Wall. The topography mirrors the other wilderness areas, with rugged ridgetops, alpine meadows, forested slopes, 14 lakes and 89 miles of streams. Many miles of trails wind through the Scapegoat, affording a prime backpacking adventure. These trails can be accessed via trails originating from forest roads on the Wilderness perimeter. Contact the Seeley Lake Ranger district of the Lolo National Forest, the Hungry Horse Ranger station of the Flathead National Forest, the Lincoln Ranger station of the Helena National Forest, or the Rocky Mountain Ranger District of the Lewis & Clark National Forest in Choteau for specific access points, current trail conditions and restrictions, and to purchase topo maps.

Jewel Basin

The Jewel Basin Hiking Area on the Flathead National Forest affords attractive hiking and backpacking, though use may be heavy along the lakes closest to the road access. This 15,349-acre area at the north end of the Swan Mountain Range is a designated back country use area. Wheeled vehicles and equine/llama stock are prohibited. The mountainous area includes 27 alpine lakes, picture-perfect streams, and drifts of wildflowers decorating meadows nestled under rocky peaks. Thirty-five miles of trails connect most of the lakes. Access on the west is via an unimproved road off MT 83. Not recommended for trailers, RVs or other low-clearance vehicles. Check with the Swan Lake Ranger District of the Lolo National Forest for particulars. Access from the east is from Hungry Horse Dam. Several roads lead from the dam to trailheads off Forest Service Road #895. Check with the Hungry Horse Ranger Station of the Flathead National forest for the current open road status. Rangers will also apprise you of current trail conditions and/or restrictions.

Glacier National Park

You'll need a permit to backpack in Glacier National Park and will have to confirm that a camping site or Glacier Chalet space is available at your destination. A $4 per night back country permit fee was instituted in 1998 ($50 a season). There's also a $20 advance reservation processing fee. But Glacier Park's beauty and outstanding hiking opportunities are so overwhelming that you'll take these regulations in stride.

 AUTHOR TIP *It's essential that you obtain a copy of Glacier National Park's* Back Country Guide, *preferably before leaving home. Read it through to familiarize yourself with the permit application process, the necessary equipment and other vital considerations. See* Information Sources.

Upon your arrival, huddle with a ranger at either the **Apgar Wilderness Information Center** or the **St. Mary Visitor Center.** He or she will help to map out your trip. At the same time you can obtain a permit and topographical maps and learn of current trail conditions, restrictions and grizzly sightings. You can reserve a camp site or chalet space in advance (after April 15) by mail.

The following trails are but a beginning. Inquire about customizing your trip over several trails. See *Guided Hiking Trips* for information on guided backpacking trips in the Park.

- ■ The 15.2-mile **Highline Trail** has a difficulty rating of 4 on a scale of 5. This high alpine walk along the Continental Divide on the west side of the Garden Wall looks in on the Granite Park Chalet and offers great views of Heaven's Peak and the Livingstone Range as well as waterfalls and alpine lakes. Beginning at the Logan Pass Visitor Center, the trail ultimately traverses Swiftcurrent Pass, ending at the Swiftcurrent Motel. This trail is largely in the Many Glacier area, noted for a high number of grizzly bears. Make noise and don't hike alone or after dark.

- ■ The 14.4-mile **Triple Divide Pass Trail** is rated 3 on a scale of 5 and covers a part of the Park that's well off the beaten path. Here's your chance to stand on the pass where water divides into three major watersheds: the Gulf of Mexico, the Pacific Ocean and Hudson's Bay. The trail starts at the Cut Bank Creek Campground on the east side of the Park. Several trails branching from the main trail present extended hike possibilities. Climbing Triple Divide Peak affords experienced hikers an added adventure.

- ■ The 18.8-mile **Dawson-Pitamakan loop** in the Two Medicine Area is rated 4 on a scale of 5. The highlight: a traverse around 9,513-foot **Rising Wolf Mountain**. This hike affords splendid views of the Park's interior.

- ■ The easy **Red Eagle Trail**, originating at St. Mary Ranger Station, takes you over 15 miles of an old buffalo hunters' route behind the St. Mary Mountains. This trail connects with higher routes, offering a fine multi-day backpacking adventure.

Guided Hiking Trips

The following guides/outfitters offer hiking and/or backpacking trips in Glacier Country.

Backcountry, Ltd. leads six-day inn-to-inn hikes beginning in Whitefish and traversing Glacier National Park. The last night is at Waterton Lakes National Park's Prince of Wales Hotel before hiking to one of Waterton's famous lakes. Intermediate to advanced hikers. PO Box 4029, Bozeman, MT 59772; ☎ 800-575-1540 or 406-586-3556. Fax

406-586-4288. E-mail vacation@bckcntry.com. Internet www.backcountrytours.com.

Glacier Wilderness Guides is authorized by the National Park Service to conduct ecologically sensitive backpacking trips in Glacier National Park. Trips accommodate all ability levels and range from three days to a week. Customized trips and inn and hut hikes are available. Ask about combination hiking/rafting trips. Box 535, West Glacier, MT 59936; ☎ 800-521-RAFT or 406-387-5555. Fax 406-387-5656. E-mail glguides@ cyberport.net. Internet glacierguides.com.

Off the Beaten Path offers deluxe multi-day hiking adventures featuring a naturalist-led trip through Glacier and Waterton Lakes National Parks. Wider-ranging trips wrap up Glacier, Banff, Lake Louise, Jasper and the Icefields Parkway; or Glacier, Flathead Lake, Yellowstone, Jackson and the Grand Tetons. 27 E. Main St., Bozeman, MT 59715; ☎ 800-445-2995 or 406-586-1311. Fax 406-587-4147.

Silver Box Outfitters owner Leonard Howells, a licensed outfitter, leads backpacking trips into roadless areas of the Cabinet Mountains. He also offers guided day-hikes. 500 E. Fisher Rd., Libby, MT 59923; ☎ 406-293-9497.

Wilderness River Outfitters has combination eight-day backpacking/ rafting and hiking with horse support/rafting trips in the South Fork of the Flathead River area of the Bob Marshall Wilderness Area. PO Box 72, Lemhi, ID 83465; ☎ 800-252-6581. E-mail wro@wildernessriver.com. Internet www.wildernessriver.com.

Hiking near Swiftcurrent Lake in Glacier National Park.

The Montana Wilderness Association schedules guided wilderness walks/hikes in Glacier Country. Contact them for a current schedule. PO Box 635, Helena, MT 59624; ☎ 406-443-7350.

Wild Rockies Tours runs three-day and four-day backpacking/mountaineering trips in the Selway-Bitterroot Wilderness and the Cherry Peak Roadless Area. Unscheduled backpacking trips are also on offer. PO Box 8184, Missoula, MT 59807; ☎ 406-728-0566.

Llama Treks

So you enjoy hiking, but aren't thrilled about shouldering a backpack. Or perhaps the weight of a backpack might aggravate a back or other problem. Or you are an animal lover who craves a hiking companion you can cozy up to.

For all of the above, and a number of other very good reasons, you might want to consider hiking with a llama. These docile, woolly, intelligent, long-necked camel relatives make perfect hiking companions. Used for 5,000 years in the Andes Mountains, llamas are sure-footed and ecologically responsible. Like deer, they browse on whatever happens to be growing nearby. Unlike sharp deer hooves, padded llama feet have little or no impact on fragile terrain. Llamas lack camels' nasty dispositions. Rather than spit or bite as camels are wont to do, your pack llama will likely mooch cuddles and ear rubs.

These gentle animals will carry your gear, and they are easy to lead. My daughter Amy will attest to that. While llama-trekking as a nine-year-old, she soon had "her" llama following sans lead rope. The owners of the llama trekking companies listed below claim that hiking with llamas is the very best way to experience Glacier Country's splendid backcountry.

Ecollama, a Missoula-based llama trekking company owned and operated by David and Amy Rubin Harmon, offers a variety of multi-day llama treks in the Bob Marshall Wilderness and along the Stateline Trail. They also offer customized treks, day treks, fishing treks, women-only treks, and a kids' wilderness journey for ages 9-13 (see *Kid Stuff,* page 457). Hikes cover five to seven miles per day at elevations of 4,000 to 8,000 feet. David's background in natural history, animal ecology and environmental studies permits him to offer guests an ecologically sensitive perspective. Amy manages the llama breeding business and practices law. PO Box 8342, Missoula, MT 59807; ☎ 406-542-1625.

Great Northern Llama Company, situated in the Flathead Valley, is a llama breeding and trekking company owned and operated by Steve and Sue Rolfing. Their multi-day llama treks along the Swan Divide of the Flathead National Forest offer the best of the backcountry: hiking through wildflower-strewn meadows, panoramic views, fishing and swimming in alpine lakes, slding down a snowfield in August. 600 Blackmer Lane, Columbia Falls, MT 59912; ☎ 406-755-9044. Fax 406-755-4652.

Teton Canyon Llama Livery offers day and overnight hikes with llamas. Paul Wick, 961 Teton Canyon Rd., Choteau, MT 59422; ☎ 406-466-5709.

Caving

Most Glacier Country caves are on Flathead National Forest lands and deep within the Bob Marshall, Great Bear and Scapegoat Wilderness Areas. Many are near the tops of high peaks. Most require ropes and/or other special equipment to explore because of steep vertical entrances and the presence of water. Most are unexplored, unsurveyed or unexplorable.

Among the most intriguing are the **Yaak Creek Caves**, on Yakinikak Creek (some maps show this creek as Tuchuck Creek) some 60 miles north of Columbia Falls. Contact the Flathead National Forest Supervisor's Office to obtain an area map. Three of the four caves lie virtually atop one another and contain underground streams. If you are fascinated with ice caves, you might want to explore the **Little Bitterroot Canyon Ice Cave**, 26 miles west of Kalispell on the Hubbart Reservoir Road. Lying in a small gully, the cave has two vertical entrances that connect about 50 feet down. At this level, the floors and walls are coated with ice and feature ice stalactites and crystals.

 If you are a serious caver, you will find plenty of scope for your obsession in Glacier Country. A specialized guidebook is a must. *Caves of Montana*, by Newell P. Campbell, describes every known cave in Montana and includes diagrams and map references. See *Bibliography*.

Rock Climbing

The following information is designed to point you toward Glacier Country's rock climbing areas, not to provide technical input. Rock climbing requires expert instruction, rigorous conditioning and specialized knowledge.

 The Rock Climber's Guide to Montana, edited by Randall Green (see *Biblography*), provides in-depth information.

The **Lolo Pass area**, in the Bitterroot Mountains off US 12, about 40 miles west of Missoula, has numerous coarse-textured granitic rock domes ranging from 40 to 300 feet in height. These climbs are popular, though 62 routes provide some spread. Most are on private land, meaning that locked gates, road closures and other restrictions must be respected. Depending on snowfall and temperatures, the climbing season generally runs from late March to November. The proximity to Lolo Hot Springs makes them especially attractive. Domes having established routes include The Heap (8), Bonsai Rock (6), Elk Rock (18), Tor Rock (12), That Rock and Random Events Wall (4), and Crystal Theatre, a.k.a Babcock Spires (14).

Kootenai Canyon is a popular climbing area, even though most of the established routes are on private land. According to *The Rock Climber's Guide to Montana*, the landowner generously allows access and has expressed support of the local climbing community. For this reason, it is suggested that you check with one of the climbing equipment shops listed at the end of this section for information on the routes' current status. Access to Kootenai Canyon is via the North Kootenai Road off US 93, just north of Stevensville.

Hamilton, some 40 miles south of Stevensville, is the gateway to **Mill Creek** and **Blodgett Creek Canyons**. Both offer numerous routes, many on south-facing walls.

Stone Hill, overlooking the east shore of Lake Koocanusa, is a well-known sport and practice climbing area with routes for climbers of all levels of expertise. The area is readily accessible from MT 37.

Glacier National Park's numerous peaks and spires might seem like a rock climber's paradise. Not so. Mountain/rock climbing and off-trail scrambling are discouraged because Glacier Park rock is of sedimentary origin, mostly metamorphorsed mudstone and limestone. Often loose and unstable, it is generally unsuitable for rock climbing.

Local Climbing Equipment Shops

Canyon Critters, 235 W. Main, Missoula, MT 59801; ☎ 406-728-9157.
Pipestone Mountaineering, 101 S. Higgins, Missoula, MT 59801; ☎ 406-721-1670.
Rocky Mountain Outfitter, 135 Main, Kalispell, MT 59901; ☎ 406-752-2446.
The Trailhead, 110 East Pine, Missoula, MT 59802; ☎ 406-543-6966.

Climbing Gyms

Hold-On, 235 W. Main, Missoula, MT 59801; ☎ 406-728-9157.
University of Montana, Outdoor Recreation Dept., Fieldstone Annex, S. 6th, Missoula, MT 59801; ☎ 406-243-5172.

Rock Hounding

Gold West Country lays claim to Montana's most productive gold and silver mines, but Glacier Country is no slouch. It stands to reason that the creek beds and gulches of Western Montana would also conceal all that glitters. So they have, and still do. The catch is that most claims are privately owned, making access at the pleasure of the landowners. Others are deep in national forests and difficult to find, or iffy if you do find them.

 If you're serious about rockhounding, it's recommended that you obtain a copy of *Rockhounding Montana* by Robert Feldman (see *Bibliography*). This excellent resource includes geological and map information and locations where specific rocks and minerals might be found.

Sometimes it may seem that all roads lead to the **Lolo Pass area**, so much does this area have to offer adventurers with different interests. It should, then, come as no surprise that the area conceals quartz crystals ranging in color from clear to dark smoky. Extensive logging has uncovered outcrops of Idaho Batholith. Crystals may be found in cavities in rocks and sometimes even loose in the soil. Quartz crystals are being mined commercially in the area, so be sure to honor No Tresspassing signs. The collecting area is reached via the Granite Creek Road, off US 12 about 1.5 miles south of Lolo Hot Springs.

Some $100,000 in copper, silver, lead and gold has been mined in the **Clinton Mining District**, some two miles northeast of Clinton. No bonanza, as such matters go, but enough to turn up recently mined dumps yielding chalcopyrite, tetrahedrite, galena, pyrite, bornite, barite, siderite, hematite, calcite and quartz. The catch: many of the mines are on private land; some are on BLM lands. The area is reached by a mountain road leading north from Clinton. Refer to BLM Public Lands in Montana map: 21 Granite or US Geological Survey Clinton and Mineral Ride Quadrangles.

The **Libby Creek Gold Panning Area** has been set aside specifically for recreational gold panning. Take the Bear Creek Road off US 2 about seven miles south of Libby. Drive another 18 miles to the Area on a paved and gravelled road. Pick up a brochure describing the Libby Creek area at the Libby Ranger station on MT 37. The Howard Lake Campground is a mile from the panning area. The historic mining area includes several old cabins. A considerable amount of gold remains in gravel piles created by early mining operations.

Visitors to **Garnet Ghost Town** can hunt for sapphires in the vicinity, at **Gem Mountain Sapphire Mine** on the West Fork of Rock Creek.

■ Adventures on Horseback

Horse packing into the wilderness is a rock-solid Montana tradition; an inalienable right forged by a vanquished way of life. Time was when Indians packed over the Nez Perce Trail to hunt buffalo. Mountain Men packed through streambeds and river valleys to trap beaver. Prospectors packed through the mountains in search of pay dirt. Ranchers and homesteaders alike packed into the back country to hunt winter meat supplies.

With all this tradition, it's as natural as a bear grows hair that Montanans should regard their back country and wilderness areas as personal last best places. To most, the only way to experience it is on horseback while trailing a string of pack horses or mules. It follows that a pack trip is among the most authentic of Montana adventures, ranking right up there with cowboys and cattle drives; maybe ahead of them.

Laying no bets on the likelihood of readers trailering Old Dobbin to a Montana trailhead, this book skips do-it-yourself horse packing in favor of insight into guided trips available to both greenhorns and experienced riders. On the off-chance that you do want to go horsepacking with the family steeds, it's recommended that you contact the supervisor's office of the national forest in which you plan to travel, or Glacier National Park if you want to ride there. They all have reams of very specific information, including rules and regulations on back country horsepacking.

Trekkers might refute riders' opinion that the only way to fully see and appreciate Glacier Country's glorious wilderness areas, and the animals who live there, is from a horse's back. But it's true that the views and your sense of space are greatly enhanced when elevated to horseback height. And you'll cover more ground; penetrate more deeply into mountain fastnesses and perhaps catch sight of more wildlife.

The outfitters and guides below will take you there – some in-style, some not. Prices range from $100 per day to more than double that. Most outfitters are native Montanans with years of experience in guiding folks to their favorite places. Most also guide hunting trips in season. It follows that some place more emphasis on lucrative hunting safaris. Ask about priorities. Also refer to *Guest Ranches*; some offer pack trips in addition to or instead of ranch activities.

All spin yarns around a campfire while sparks fly up to touch the stars. Some Montana is bound to rub off on you, perhaps change your perspective on life. Pretty profound, but the wilderness does that to folks.

Choosing a Horse Outfitter

■ When choosing a wilderness outfitter, you should delve deeper than going for the outfit whose brochure has the prettiest horse pictures. Much deeper. Ask questions. Consider what you want your back country experience to be, what you want it to do for you.

■ If you have young tagalongs, inquire into the outfitter's track record with kids. Does he offer special **kid-friendly** activities? Will other kids be on the trip? What's the minimum age? How about gentle kids' horses?

■ If you ride seldom or not at all, you'll need time to accustom your **muscles** to the saddle. Riding involves muscles you never knew you had. An hour or two is plenty for starters. Ask how long the first day's ride will be. It might be a good idea, if possible, to arrive a couple of days before the trip and sign on for trail rides at a riding stable. Will there be time during the first day's ride to dismount, walk around and stretch your legs?

■ Must you be an **experienced** rider, or is it okay to be as green as a willow shoot in May? Will you receive some riding instruction prior to hitting the trail? Does someone in the party have CPR and First Aide training? What's the scenario in the event of an accident or **medical emergency**?

■ Assess your **timidity** quotient. Wilderness rides can be over steep terrain. No matter how trail-wise your horse is, and these horses are chosen for sure-footedness, there will be times when you are very much aware that one misplaced hoof could send you both head over rump into the gorge below. I've had that feeling many a time, and it's scary, even though statistics indicate that such accidents are rare. There are other choices if you think these momentary scares would cancel out the positive aspects of a back country pack trip. Ask about the route; the elevation gain. If it seems dicey, you might opt for a less strenuous trip. Glacier Country has areas with more gradual terrain that may be more to your liking.

■ **Camping** arrangements are important. Some outfitters maintain base camps that may include walled tents with cots, even shower and cook tents. Others go the tent pitching and sleeping bag route. Some guides utilize a base camp, riding to a different locale each day. Others ride progressively, setting up a different camp each afternoon. Decide which option most appeals to you.

■ **Meals** are important. Fresh air breeds big appetites. You can expect solid Western fare such as steaks, fresh-caught trout, perhaps Dutch oven-baked cobblers. Fruits and vegetables are seldom slighted. Ask about the food. Most outfitters will oblige your special dietary concerns or restrictions.

■ You will have many more questions. Think them out, discuss them, and don't be afraid to ask no matter how trivial a question or concern may seem. Remember: they've heard everything.

Pack Trip Outfitters

KID-FRIENDLY **A Lazy H Outfitters** is a family outfit run by Allen and Sandy Haas and their grown children, Joe, Pete and Ann. Allen has 20 years of outfitting behind him. The Haas family offers seven- to 10-day trips in the Bob Marshall Wilderness, using mules to pack gear. Trips are scheduled from June through September. Parts of most days are spent on the move to new campsites, but some layover days are included to allow for hiking, fishing and relaxing. Tents with foam pads, portable toilet facilities and sun showers are provided. Camps are set up beside streams or alpine lakes. You need not be an experienced rider. Children as young as six may sign on. A naturalist guide is on hand. One of the highlights of each trip is riding to the Chinese Wall (it really does look like its namesake). Another is angling for trout on tributaries of the Sun and Flathead Rivers. PO Box 729, Choteau, MT 59422; ☎ 406-466-5564.

American Wilderness Experience (dba AWE!) is a Boulder, Colorado-based resource that arranges a wide variety of trips in numerous locales down to the last detail. They offer several June-August wilderness pack trips led by hand-picked guides. The advantage of arranging a trip through AWE! is being able to discuss individual trips with an objective resource. I have found AWE!'s David Wiggins to be extremely helpful on a number of occasions. 2820-A Wilderness Place, Boulder, CO 80301; ☎ 800-444-0099 or 303-444-2622, fax 303-444-3999.

Bear Creek Guest Ranch offers pack trips in the Bob Marshall Wilderness. See *Guest Ranches*.

Bill Mitchell has been leading customized pack trips in the Bitterroot Mountains for 25 years. Trips are generally of four to six days duration. Bill and his wife Karen maintain base camps at their ranch near Hamilton and over the Bitterroots in Idaho. Pack trippers sleep under the stars or in a tent. Children welcome. 364 McCarthy Loop, Hamilton, MT 59840-9146; ☎ 406-363-4129.

Bitterroot Outfitters' Tom Henderson offers multi-day pack trips in the Selway-Bitterroot Wilderness. Trout fishing is a big part of these trips. Children under 16 are half-price when accompanied by an adult. 1842 Hwy. 93 South, Hamilton, MT 59840; ☎ 406-363-0403.

Bob Marshall Wilderness Ranch owners and operators Virgil and Barbara Burns have been in the outfitting business for over 20 years. They offer five- to 10-day Bob Marshall Wilderness mule pack trips, using either established or moveable camps. Possibly a tad more deluxe and pricier than some. Many trips emphasize trout fishing. The 10-day Chinese Wall trip offers an opportunity to ride to the top of the wall. Business office: St. Ignatius, MT 59865; ☎ 406-745-4466.

Great Divide Guiding & Outfitters' host Richard Jackson has worked as a professional outfitter since 1980 and guides all trips. His son, Cody, is a wrangler for the outfit. Five-day June through September pack trips meander through a scenic corner of the Lewis & Clark National forest tucked between Glacier National Park, the Blackfeet Indian Reservation and the Great Bear and Bob Marshall Wilderness Areas. Activities include a cattle drive plus fishing, hiking and other fun stuff. Tent camps are set up in storied places, including the banks of the Two Medicine River, featured in Ivan Doig's *Dancing at the Rascal Fair*. PO Box 315, East Glacier, MT 59434; ☎ 800-421-9687 or 406-226-4487.

JM Bar Outfitters' Jeff and Maria Freeman's principal business is, like many outfitters, hunting in season. Outfitters since 1975, they offer reasonably priced summer pack trips in the Long John Mountains with opportunities for fishing, photography and just getting away. Comfortable back country camps. 23945 Bonita Rd., Clinton, MT 59825; ☎ 406-825-3230.

Lion Creek Outfitters' Cecil and Isabel Noble have been guiding rugged, ecologically sensitive outdoor adventures for over 20 years. They offer multi-day trips into Lion Creek Country between the Swan and Mission Mountain Ranges, on the western boundary of the Bob Marshall Wilderness. They also offer half-day guided rides. 610 Patrick Creek Rd., Kalispell, MT 59901; ☎ 406-755-3723. E-mail horses@ montanaadventures. Internet www.montanaadventures.com.

L Diamond E Ranch Outfitters, owned by Dan and Retta Ekstrom, offers multi-day sapphire mining pack trips to their streamside high mountain meadow claim. Dan says that guests have yet to leave empty handed. The many-colored gems can be up to two to four carats in size. The claim's established camp assures guests of comfortable tent camping on foam mattresses. An extended trip includes a ride to the Ekstroms' Stony Lake Camp. They also offer guided trail rides ranging from an hour to all day – a good idea if you want to break your rump in easy before tackling the 11-mile ride to Sapphire Camp. PO Box 855, Clinton, MT 59825; ☎ 406-825-6295.

Montana Safaris, owned and operated by Rocky and Lorell Heckman, specializes in customized multi-day summer horse and mule pack trips in the Bob Marshall Wilderness. Fishing is an important part of these trips. Access is from the east side of the Bob. PO Box 1004, Choteau, MT 59422; ☎ 406-466-2004. Internet www.montanasafaris.simplenet.com.

Rich Ranch is the umbrella moniker for Jack and Belinda Rich's Double Arrow Outfitters and Pinto Horse Guest Ranch. They take a maximum of 10 guests at a time into the Bob Marshall Wilderness on multi-day pack trips. The numerous trips offered between late June and mid-September emphasize fishing, photography or just riding. Sleep in tipi-style tents with floors. They also offer half-day and all-day trail rides. PO Box 495, Seeley Lake, MT 59868; ☎ 406-677-2317.

Rugg's Outfitting is the granddaddy of Montana outfitters, the family having been outfitting since 1947. This full-service outfitting business, now run by third generation Ruggs, offers a wide range of pack trips, customized or not. The family's Dry Creek Ranch and their guest lodge on Fish Creek afford ready proximity to Bitterroot Mountains trails on the Lolo National Forest. They also offer day rides and whitewater and fly fishing floats. 50 Dry Creek Rd., Superior, MT 59872; ☎ 406-822-4240. Mobile: ☎ 406-728-5203 unit 1137. E-mail spr4240@Montana.com.

Silver Bow Outfitters, owned and operated by Leonard Howells, offers customized multi-day pack trips in the Cabinet Mountains on the Kootenai National Forest between Kalispell and Libby. Choose between a comfortably furnished established camp complete with shower and cooking/dining tent, or impromptu back country camps. 500 E. Fisher Rd., Libby, MT 59923; ☎ 406-293-9497.

White Tail Ranch Outfitters, Inc. offers a variety of multi-day pack trips in the Bob Marshall Wilderness Complex. Owner/operators Jack and Karen Hooker have guided in the area since 1955. They bill their trips as "educational," offering insight into horsemanship, wilderness survival skills and Montana lore. Also on offer is a women-only trip. 520 Cooper Lake Rd., Ovando, MT 59854; ☎ 800-WTR-5666 or 406-793-5666.

Wilderness Connection, Inc., based in Gardiner and owned by Gary and Sam Duffy, offers five- to 10-day pack trips in the Bob Marshall Wilderness. Rides tend to be lengthy and quite rigorous. They also offer seven-day horse and raft fly fishing trips in the Bob. Customized trips are also on offer. 21 Shooting Star Trail, Gardiner, MT 59030; ☎ 800-285-5482 or 406-848-7287.

Day Trail Rides

Visiting Montana without mounting a horse is like ordering a Western breakfast without eggs and hash browns. If you don't have time to devote to a pack trip, a trail ride is the next best choice. In Glacier Country, riding stables are thick as flies on a swishtail horse. Ergo: you can sign on for a trail ride almost at the drop of a 10-gallon hat. But it's good form to call at least a day ahead to reserve your steed. The following stables are for starters.

Big Mountain Ski & Summer Resort's Horsepower Adventures offers guided half-day trail rides. PO Box 1400, Whitefish, MT 59937; ☎ 406-862-1949. Fax 406-862-2955.

Big Sky Rides cooperates with Kalispell's Parks & Recreation Department to offer trail rides along pretty Ashley Creek. They also do hayrides, cookouts and dinner rides. 750 Foy's Lake Rd., Kalispell; ☎ 406-755-RIDE.

Elkhorn Guest Ranch, four miles up-creek at the Rock Creek Exit off I-90, 30 miles east of Missoula, offers trail rides wrangled by Jeff Freeman. Choose from one-hour, two-hour, half-day or full-day rides, or an evening steak ride to a back country camp. Ride along Rock Creek where wildlife sightings are common. Jeff also offers overnight pack trips. Address: Clinton, MT 59825; ☎ 406-825-4004 or 825-3230.

Gaynor's Riverbend Ranch, at 1992 KM Ranch Road, Whitefish, offers guided and unguided trail rides. ☎ 406-862-3802.

Glacier Outback Rides, at Loon's Echo Resort, offers one-hour to full-day rides and dinner and sunset rides by reservation. 1 Fish Lake Road, Stryker; ☎ 800-956-6632.

High Country Trails offers one-hour to all day guided trail rides in the high country near Kalispell. Also on offer are breakfast and supper rides, riding lessons, wagon train rides, cattle drives and overnight camping trips. 2800 Foy's Lake Rd., Kalispell, MT 59901; ☎ 406-755-1283 or 755-4711.

L Diamond Ranch Outfitters: see *Pack Trip Outfitters.*

Lion Creek Outfitters: see *Pack Trip Outfitters.*

Lonesome Dove Ranch near Whitefish offers one-hour to half-day guided trail rides through wooded foothills; riding lessons, too. ☎ 800-949-4169 or 406-862-0899.

Montana Ranch Adventures is off Hwy. 464, on the northwest shore of Duck Lake, on the Blackfeet Indian Reservation near Babb. Owners Don, Pat and Brent Compton claim that "real cowboys don't ride single file" in describing their half-day and full-day rides between the Rockies and the plains. The Comptons also offer one-day steak fry and entertainment rides and two-day steak rides that include sleeping in a tipi. RR HC 72 Noffsinger Rd., Browning, MT 59417; ☎ 406-338-3333.

Mule Shoe Outfitters, owned by Paul and Ginny DeToni and authorized by the National Park Service, offers one-hour to all-day trail rides to scenic areas of Glacier National Park from June 1-Sept. 15. Rides originate from corrals at Apgar (☎ 406-888-5010), Lake McDonald (☎ 406-

Horseback riding near Glacier National Park.

888-5121) and Many Glacier (☎ 406-732-4203). Summer: PO Box 322, West Glacier, MT 59936; Winter: PO Box 174, Kila, MT 59920.

Rawhide Trail Rides offers rides through country near Glacier National Park. 1200 US 2 E.; ☎ 800-388-5727 or 406-387-5999.

Rich Ranch: see *Pack Trip Outfitters*.

Ruggs Outfitting: see *Pack Trip Outfitters*.

St. Regis Riding Stables off MT 135 in St. Regis (take Exit 33 off I-90) offers one-hour, half-day and full-day trail rides on the Lolo National Forest. ☎ 406-649-2110 or 822-3384.

Wagon Tracks, near Trego, offers half-day or full-day guided trail rides and dinner rides. 933 Edna Creek, Trego (seven miles off US 93); ☎ 406-882-4933.

W/J Ranch has half-hour, one-hour and two-hour horseback rides. Stagecoach rides and ranch-style barbeques are also possible. 36085 Washo Rd., Potomac, MT 59823; ☎ 406-244-5523.

Working Cattle/Guest Ranches

Glacier Country is longer on dude ranches than on working cattle/guest ranches – to be expected, considering the mountainous topography and the region's runaway attraction for tourists. But if you are drawn to this fabulous area, and wish to experience a working cattle ranch, you can have it both ways.

Hargrave Cattle & Guest Ranch has graced the Thompson River Valley since the turn-of-the-century homesteading era. Leo and Ellen Hargrave assumed ownership of the 87,000-acre ranch when the property's original homesteader retired. The Charolais ranch includes log buildings crafted by the homesteader's own hands. The Hargraves keep the guest list to 15, assuring all guests personal attention. Children are welcome, but must be over seven to go on trail rides. A children's program is available in July and August for kids through age 12. In May, the Hargraves host a women's week and a singles' week. Activities at the year-round ranch vary according to season. Guests may join spring cattle drives to green pastures or help with summer herd management. There's lots of riding, fishing and other activities. Accommodations include three Western theme cabins, rooms in the Headquarters building and a new four-bedroom executive log home. By-the-week rates are all-inclusive except for pack trips and other outfitted excursions. Winter cabin rental and a B&B plan are also available. 300 Thompson River Rd., Marion, MT 59925; ☎ 800-933-0696 or 406-858-2284.

Hayes Ranch has been on the Montana map since 1888, when the Hayes family's great-grandparents came over from Britain to raise draft horses here. Today's crops are Angus-Hereford cattle, horses, hay, grain, and guests wishing a taste of Montana ranch life. The 3,300-acre ranch is situated along the Blackfoot River. Guests are put up in private apartments in the ranch house. Horses are put up in cozy box stalls with paddock access. Guests may help with cattle tending chores when not river rafting, fishing and horseback riding. Per-day rates are all-inclusive except for guided trail rides and raft trips. Discounts are available for stays longer than three days, and for non-riding guests who wish to spend a couple of days relaxing at the ranch. Star Route Box 208, Bonner, MT 59823; ☎ 406-244-5573 or 224-5224. E-mail ptm5224@montana.com. Internet www.montana.com/hayes/ranching.htm.

Pepperbox Ranch, situated in the Bitterroot Mountains, raises a small herd of Texas Longhorn cattle. Guests can ride the range helping to check on the cattle, or participate in a range of activities that includes horseback riding, mountain biking and games. Sleep in log cabins, each having a fireplace or wood-burning stove. Open year round; sleigh rides in winter. 9959 West fork Rd., Darby, MT 59829; ☎ 406-349-2920.

Guest Ranches

The old fashioned dude ranch concept fits Glacier Country as snugly as a lariat around a dogie's neck. Early in the 20th century, the glories of Glacier National Park began attracting tourists. Northern Pacific passenger trains came on line, linking Chicago with points west. Trains stopped in a hiss of steam at East Glacier and Columbia Falls, disgorging wanna-be cowboys eager to sample life in the Wild West. Without the discomforts, of course.

Today's dude ranches still honor that wanna-be yen. Things have changed over the years. Most early ranches were long on mountain country atmosphere and short on amenities, by today's standards. The current crop achieves a workable combination of yuppie amenities, back country atmosphere and horses, horses, horses. The challenge is enough to put any host in a lather.

Get a fix on just what you want in a guest ranch. Do you visualize sleeping in a log cabin and pretending you're roughing it like those early homesteaders did? Or would you rather sleep in a pretentiously "Western" log lodge? Or would something in-between suit you? Are you wild about horseback riding? Do you want to spend every available minute in the saddle, riding into the sunset through scenery you could only imagine back home? Do the rich aromas of horse sweat, leather and manure and the squeaky creak of the saddle satisfy some atavistic longing within you? If so, you need to make sure riding is the main focus of a ranch's activities.

Maybe riding isn't for you. Perhaps you'd rather wander about, soaking in the beauty of the surroundings; maybe fish, swim, take pictures, relax. If so, you must keep that preference in mind when choosing a vacation ranch.

AUTHOR TIP *Many ranches are flexible, combining riding with other activities. Others emphasize riding to the near-exclusion of other activities. The key is to ask questions. Ask, too, how structured activities will be. If you envision a laid-back week, you'll be an unhappy camper if you are handed an hour-by-hour schedule.*

Most ranches are on the American Plan, charging by-the-week or by-the-day rates that include meals, horseback riding and other activities, with specific exceptions. A few include meals, but not activities, in their rates. The line between guest ranches and lodgings can be as thin as a winter-starved wolf. Just because "guest ranch" appears on a business's brochure doesn't mean it is one. I've tried to sort them out. Genuine guest ranches are listed below. Others are listed under *Hotels, Motels & B&Bs* or *Resorts*. Be sure to inquire, if in doubt; you don't need those kinds of surprises.

Each ranch reflects the personality and philosophy of the hosts. All have two things in common: knock-your-socks-off scenery and a string of horses managed by a wrangler who may or may not be the owner or a member of his or her family.

The following guest ranches are as authentic as a Montana sunrise and as individualistic as a Montana cowboy.

Averill's Flathead Lake Lodge & Dude Ranch offers the best of two vacation worlds: dude ranching and water-oriented activities. The ranch's 2,000 acres of rolling, forested terrain hug a bay on the east shore of Flathead Lake. The Averill family has owned and operated the ranch since 1945. The "help" consists mostly of college students – a tradition as old as dude ranches. Accommodations include rooms in log lodges oozing country atmosphere, and rustic family-size log cabins. The setting is pure north country. Fir forests fringe lawns sweeping to the lake. The log structures look as if they grew there. The Sunday-to-Sunday rates may seem a tad pricey at first glance, but the full seven-day stay includes meals, lodging, horseback riding and other traditional ranch activities, plus all sorts of on-water activities – more fun than any one person could possibly cram into a single week. Box 248, Bigfork, MT 59911; ☎ 406-837-4391. Fax 406-837-6977.

Bear Creek Guest Ranch owners Bill and Lora Beck insist that theirs is not a dude ranch in the current sense of the word, and want no part of that lifestyle. Bear Creek is a down-to-earth guest ranch that trades fancy digs for neat, clean and comfortable. The ranch is on the site of a wide-open c.1890 railroad town where anything went, and usually did. Bear Creek is tucked between Glacier Park and the Bob Marshall-Great Bear Wilderness. This intensely horse-oriented ranch has been welcoming wanna-be cowboys since 1933. Accommodations include rooms in the main lodge and picturesque log cabins. Monday-Saturday rates are all-inclusive. The Becks also offer multi-day scheduled and custom Bob Marshall Wilderness pack trips. They will also arrange for May cattle drives on working ranches, dependent on how many people are interested. PO Box 151, East Glacier, MT 59434 (April 1-Sept. 30). PO Box 386, Cut Bank, MT 59427. (Oct. 1-Mar. 31); ☎ 800-445-7379.

Bull Lake Guest Ranch, hosted by Alex and Eileen Thompson, is in the gorgeous Bull River Valley of northwestern Montana. The Thompsons have run this downhome-style ranch since 1980. Horseback riding is the main attraction, but Blue Ribbon trout fishing, mountain biking, swimming, canoeing, wildlife watching and more are available at this unstructured ranch. In winter there's cross-country skiing, ice fishing and snow shoeing. There are several lodgings packages to choose from. Self-contained RV parking is also available. 15303 Bull Lake Rd., Troy, MT 59935; ☎ 800-995-4228 or 406-295-4228.

Diamond R Guest Ranch enjoys a splendid situation on the Flathead National Forest, 70 crow miles south of Glacier National Park. Meals are served in a lodge overlooking the Spotted Bear River. Accommodations include c.1926 cabins, cabins of more recent vintage, and a bunkhouse accommodating 12 (bring your sleeping bags). Per-day cabin and bunkhouse rates include meals. Trail ride and float/fishing trip prices are à la carte. Or choose an overnight combo horseback and float trip, or a three- to seven-day Summer Adventure Trip that includes trail rides, fishing, float/fish and a photography or sightseeing trip by van to Glacier National Park or another destination. PO Box 1419, Kalispell, MT 59903-1419; ☎ 800-597-9465 or 406-756-1573 (9-5).

Klick's K Bar L Ranch is on the edge of the Bob Marshall Wilderness, at the confluence of the North and South Forks of the Sun River. Access is by jetboat up Gibson Lake or by saddle horse and pack mule over a mountain trail. The log buildings owe their comfortable rusticity in part to tasteful Western decor, in part to the absence of conventional electricity. Lighting is by hydroelectric power, heat from wood stoves, transportation via horses and mules. The phone is battery operated. Shades of old Montana! Daily trail rides, fishing, swimming and other fun. Family-style meals taste better for having been cooked on a wood stove. One of Montana's most venerable ranches, the K Bar L has been putting guests up in log cabins since 1927. All-inclusive rates. PO Box 287, Augusta, MT 59410; ☎ 406-562-3589 (winter and spring), ☎ 406-562-3551 (summer and fall).

RJR Ranch, owned and hosted by Dick and Gail Reilly, is in the Tobacco Valley area. Open year-round, ranch packages include a wide range of activities, even tennis and cross-country skiing. Horses are an important part of ranch life. Wranglers introduce horses and guests with lessons on horsemanship and by matching saddles and horses to each rider. The ranch's nine luxurious log structures were built in the 1980s by a wealthy oil family. The Reillys offer activities that keep parents and children together, but special kids' activities can be arranged. PO Box 117, Eureka, MT 59917; ☎ 406-889-3395. Fax 406-889-3829.

Rich Ranch, hosted by Jack and Belinda Rich, combines RR Pinto Horse Guest Ranch and Double Arrow Outfitters. The former offers traditional dude ranch activities. The latter offers custom and scheduled multi-day summer pack trips in the Bob Marshall Wilderness. The Rich family's Montana roots go back five generations. The ranch is open year-round for riding in summer, cross-country skiing and snowmobiling in winter. Accommodations include lodge rooms and cozy cabins. Two per-day rate schedules are offered. Both include room, meals and the use of ranch amenities. *The Cowboy* is for horseback riders. *The Westerner* is a non-horse package. *The Winter Fun Package* includes meals, lodging, a horse-drawn sleigh ride and access to miles of trails. Snowmobiles can be rented in Seeley Lake. PO Box 495, Seeley Lake, MT 59868; ☎ 406-677-2317.

Rising Wolf Ranch, an unstructured retreat on the South Fork of the Two Medicine River, offers traditional guest ranch activities. Accommodations include tent houses, cabins and bedrooms in the rustic lodge. Pack trips can be arranged. PO Box 66, East Glacier, MT 59934; ☎ 406-226-4478.

Triple J Wilderness Ranch, owned by the Barker, is on the Rocky Mountain Front near the east side of the Bob Marshall Wilderness. Ranch vacation packages include horseback riding, hiking, simple mountain climbing, fly fishing, volleyball, evening firesides and more. Guests sleep in cozy cabins and eat family-style in the log main lodge. A kiddie wrangler is on hand to supervise kids' rides and other fun. Multi-day pack trips in the Bob Marshall Wilderness. PO Box 310, Augusta, MT 59410; ☎ 406-562-3653. Fax 406-562-3836.

■ Adventures on Wheels

ATVs & High Clearance 4WD Vehicles

 The explosion of OHVs and ATVs has taken Montana's national forest supervisors by surprise. ATVs are permitted on some trails, but most rangers with whom I spoke expressed doubts about their viability for three reasons: The extreme mountainous terrain is not suitable for ATVs. They tear up fragile trails. They disturb wildlife.

As this book goes to press, travel management plans for five Montana national forests are being redone. Conservationists want the US Forest Service to drastically limit trail access by off-road vehicles. ATV users are crying foul. It's a good bet that when the dust settles more trails will be closed to off-road vehicles. If you wish to take your ATV or other off-road vehicle on Glacier Country trails, you should first contact the Forest Service Ranger district maintaining the area where you want to ride. A ranger will tell you which, if any, trails are open to your type of vehicle.

Among areas that are open are the **Blacktail Wild Bill Off Road Vehicle National Recreation Trails** west of US 93 on the Flathead National Forest. Trails traverse the slopes of Eagle Mountain, offering views of the Flathead Valley, Flathead Lake and Lake Mary Ronan. Contact the Flathead National Forest Supervisor's Office or Montana Fish, Wildlife and Parks for a descriptive brochure.

If ATVing is an important part of your vacation, consider riding on Forest Service and/or logging roads. The drawback: These roads are considered public highways, so you must have a valid driver's license and your ATV must be licensed in Montana or in the state in which you live.

AUTHOR TIP *Glacier Country is pack horse- and backpacker-friendly and has more acres of designated wilderness than any other region in Montana. Designated wilderness areas are off-limits to all wheeled vehicles, motorized or not.*

The region's non-wilderness national forest lands include many miles of logging and Forest Service roads that are iffy for passenger vehicles but passable by high clearance 4WD vehicles. "Passable" is the key word. Four-wheeling is frowned upon for numerous reasons, among them rider safety and damage to roadbeds often weakened by heavy snows and melting ice. Riding a 4WD vehicle or ATV on low-maintenance gravel or dirt roads can enhance your enjoyment of this big beautiful chunk of landscape. But save your cowboying for horseback riding.

Most roads leading to trailheads and campgrounds are passable by most vehicles, but many roads extending deeper into the back country are not. You may want to use these roads to reach a specific trailhead, wildlife area or campground, or simply to enjoy the scenery. Montana traffic laws apply to national forest roads unless otherwise specified. Avoid driving on unpaved roads when they are wet or muddy. Observe all signs. Some roads are closed to vehicular traffic, other than snowmobiles, in winter.

AUTHOR TIP *Your first stop should be the ranger district office maintaining the area of interest to you. Ask about points of interest, road conditions and current restrictions. Forest Service Travel Maps are available for free at some ranger stations. Or you can purchase a topographical map for a nominal charge.*

It's not unusual to drive for miles in the back country without seeing another vehicle, let alone another human being. For that reason, you should stow emergency rations, extra water, basic camping supplies, warm clothing and blankets and/or sleeping bags, spare tire or tires, and an emergency repair kit. Traction devices are also a good idea.

Guided ATV Rides

Bitterroot Adventures offers guided ATV tours in the Bitterroot Mountains. 566 Queens Way, Hamilton, MT 59840; ☎ 406-961-3392.

Adventure Motorsports runs guided ATV tours in the Flathead Valley area and rents new Polaris ATVs. 1805 9th St. West, Columbia Falls, MT 59912; ☎ 406-892-2752. www.adventuremotorsports.com.

Cycling & Mountain Biking

Glacier Country byways and highways are wide open to bicyclists. Riding valley roads is usually a piece of cake, but only experienced high altitude cyclists should consider mountain routes.

Glacier Country figures prominently in the **National Bicycle Route Network** mapped out by the Adventure Cycling Association, based in Missoula. The route enters Montana from Washington State and loops through Glacier National Park before heading over the plains. The Great Parks Route, linking Glacier, Waterton Lakes and other Canadian parks with Yellowstone and Teton, traverses Glacier Country. Pedaling a part or all of this amazing route is the ultimate cycling adventure. Waterproof maps detailing the routes can be ordered from **Adventure Cycling Association**, PO Box 8308, Missoula, MT 59807; ☎ 800-721-8719 or 406-721-1776. Fax 406-721-8754. E-mail acatours@aol.com. Internet www.adv-cycling.org.

The Association has also mapped the **Great Divide Bike Trail**, a route paralleling the Continental Divide from Montana to Mexico. The 2,500-mile trail is the world's longest mountain bike route. Like the Continental Divide National Scenic Trail, the Great Divide Bike Trail traverses an assortment of existing dirt roads and single-track trails running along or near the Divide.

Adventure Cycling sponsors and/or leads multi-day cycling trips in Glacier Country. Call for current information.

Town-to-town rides are a great way to acquaint yourself with Montana at ground level. Pick any two or more small towns, estimate the distance between them, and take off. An especially easy and enjoyable ride takes you through the history-rich **Flathead Valley** on US 93. The distance between **Arlee and Polson**, at the foot of Flathead Lake, is 41 miles.

The **Bitterroot Valley** is great for cycling. Get off US 93 onto less traveled roads. The **Eastside Road** across the Bitterroot River from the highway offers an enjoyable ride through rolling farmland. The

Skalkaho Road linking Hamilton with MT 1 in the **Flint Creek Valley** affords an extreme aerobic challenge.

MT 83 threading the **Seeley/Swan Valley** could have been designed with cyclists in mind. You could spend a week cycling here, exploring side roads looping around lakes.

Glacier Park's **Going-to-the-Sun Road** is popular with cylists, but poses a serious aerobic challenge. Other Glacier Park routes are less strenuous.

Bicycling accidents are often caused by discourteous drivers. But an only-in-Montana traffic hazard unseated a man cycling the Going-to-the-Sun road one clear autumn day. Joel Rosenberg collided with a bear (make unknown). He was hauled off to the hospital with a broken collarbone. The bear departed in haste.

Hwy. 508 between the US 2 junction and Yaak Falls is one of the most enjoyable biking routes you'll find anywhere. The road paralleling the Yaak River is wide enough for safety. The scenery is world class.

Many of the trails in recreation areas near Missoula (see *Adventures on Foot*) have been designated for non-exclusive bicycle use.

The **Kreis Pond Mountain Bike Trails** are 23 miles west of Missoula via I-90. Take Exit 82 and follow signs to the Ninemile Ranger Station. Stop here for maps and trail information. The multi-use trails cover 35 miles and include a range of difficulty ratings.

Cautions

Many multi-use trails on national forest lands permit mountain bikes. Multi-use means you will encounter hikers and possibly horses. Announce your approach with a bell or greeting and pass slowly. Move off the trail to make way for less mobile trail users. Ride in control at all times. Travel at a safe speed, taking into consideration the terrain and your ability. Use caution on blind corners and unfamiliar trails, especially when visibility is limited. Avoid harsh skids and any action that might destroy trail surfaces. Much of Glacier Country is also grizzly bear country. By observing basic precautions, you and Bruin should keep a safe distance from one another. Most grizzly encounters result from a bear being startled by the sudden appearance of a human. Refer to *Co-Adventuring With Grizzles* (page 16) for basic behavior in bear country. An added caveat for bikers: make noises on a regular basis by attaching noise makers to your bike. Talking or singing is a good idea, too. Calling, "hey bear!" as you ride along may seem silly, but your life could depend on it.

Mountain Bike Trails

Several ranger districts maintain trails that are especially friendly to mountain bikes. The **Tally Lake Ranger District** in the Whitefish Lake area is outstanding in this regard. Four dollars gets you a detailed mountain bike trail map of the area. Included are trails rated from Easiest to Expert. The proximity to Big Mountain Ski & Summer Resort makes this area of lakes and meadows quite popular. The **Rexford Ranger District** maintains several mountain biking trails, ranging from Easy to Strenuous, in the vicinity of Eureka and Lake Koocanusa.

Several trails in the popular **Jewel Lake Hiking Area**, north of the Seeley/Swan Valley, are also open to mountain bikes.

Other ranger districts also maintain trails where mountain biking is permitted. Check with the ranger district in the area of interest to you for current trail information. Local cycle shops are also good sources of trail information.

As you drive through Glacier Country, you'll see the occasional dirt road sporting a chain with a "Closed" sign on it. These roads are closed to vehicles for wildlife protection, because of poor road surfaces or for other reasons, but are open to hikers and mountain bikers.

Mountain biking is big at **Big Mountain Ski & Summer Resort**. The entire mountain is laced with single and double track trails. The nine-mile **Big Mountain Bear Grinder Race Loop** has 1,500 feet of climbing per lap. The **Huckleberry Downhill Race Course** descends eight miles from the Big Mountain summit to the village.

Bicycle Shops/Rentals

Rental reservations are recommended at all bike outlets.

Flathead Valley:

Big Mountain, ☎ 406-862-1995.
BikeRite, 2181 US 2 East, Kalispell; ☎ 406-756-0053.
Bikology Cycling Fitness, 155 N. Main, Kalispell; ☎ 406-755-6748.
Glacier Cyclery, 336 E. 2nd St., Whitefish; ☎ 406-862-6446.
Wheaton's, 214 First Eve. W., Kalispell; ☎ 406-257-5808.

Missoula:

Bicycle Hangar, 1801 Brooks; ☎ 406-728-9537.
Open Road, 517 S. Orange; ☎ 406-549-2453.
New Era Bicycle, 741 S. Higgins; ☎ 406-728-2080.

Hamilton:

Bitterroot Bicycle Works, 162 S. 2nd St.; ☎ 406-363-0665.
Valley Bike & Ski, 219 S. 1st St.; ☎ 406-363-4428.

Guided Mountain Biking Trips

Adventure Cycling offers several cycling adventures each summer. The 75-day, 2,468-mile *Great Divide Expedition* averages 40 miles per day. This is an Advanced difficulty trip and self-contained mountain bike experience is required. The trip starts in Whitefish and ends at Antelope Wells, New Mexico. Also on offer are *East Coast to West Coast Trans-America* and *Northern Tier* expeditions. Contact them for information on other trips. PO Box 8308, Missoula, MT 59807; ☎ 800-721-8719 or 406-721-1776. Fax 406-721-8754. E-mail acatours@aol.com. Internet www.adv-cycling.org.

Backroads, a bicycle touring company headquartered at Berkeley, California, offers several multi-day Glacier and Waterton Lakes National Parks trips designed for all ability levels. They include both lodge or inn and camping tours. 801 Cedar St., Berkeley, CA 94710-1800; ☎ 800-462-2848 or 510-527-1555. Fax 510-527-1444. E-mail goactive@backroads.com. Internet www.backroads.com.

Backcountry, Ltd. offers five-day combination biking, hiking, rafting and horseback riding inn trips in Glacier National Park. Biking averages 15-35 miles per day over mostly level to rolling terrain. Shuttles available. PO Box 4029, Bozeman, MT 59772; ☎ 800-575-1540 or 406-586-3556. Fax ☎ 406-586-4288. E-mail vacation@bckcntry.com. Internet www.backcountrytours.com.

Big Fork Outdoor Expeditions' Larry Shanks was a state game warden for 20 years and has been an outfitter since 1990. He offers mountain biking, nature hikes, photographic trips and non-technical peak climbs. PO Box 213, Big Fork, MT 59911; ☎ 406-837-2031.

Grizzly Country Tours' Ken Justus offers custom bicycle tours on the backroads and trails of the West Kootenai region and the Purcell Range. He also leads hiking and snowshoe trips. 5611 W. Kootenai Rd., Rexford, MT 59930; ☎ 406-889-5240.

■ Adventures on Water

Rafting, Kayaking, Floating

 Glacier Country offers rafters and kayakers some gnarly whitewater runs, but an equal number of riparian stretches are best suited to family floating. The high profile lower Middle Fork of the Flathead and Clark Fork through **Alberton Gorge** leave veteran rafters wondering what all the fuss was about while neophytes whoop and holler with glee (the ructious Upper Middle Fork is another matter). Rapids and water levels are dependent on snow melt and other factors, so a river that's feisty in spring may be ho-hum later on.

The scenery along these rivers is unparalleled. Wildlife is often abundant. Waterfowl are more than abundant. Even sections of river following highways are generally well below and out of sight of whizzing cars and trucks, permitting a sense of remoteness from civilization.

Commercial rafting companies offer floats on the upper and lower Middle, North and South Forks of the Flathead, on the Clark Fork through Alberton Gorge, the main Flathead south of Flathead Lake, the Blackfoot, and the peaceful Bitterroot. Some floats appeal to the adventurous; others to families. Gnarly rivers like the Yaak and Kootenai are strictly do-it-yourself.

The **Yaak River** starts out ho-hum, but gains quite an attitude before meeting the Kootenai near the junction of US 2 and Hwy. 508. The river is canoeable above the 17-mile Road Bridge. Below the bridge you can expect Class III rapids to the Falls. Below the falls, nine miles of serious whitewater includes two Class IV-V drops. This last stretch is for highly skilled kayakers or rafters only! Don't do this one alone. Informal access along Forest Service Road #92. Access points at the Yaak Bridge and several marked points on Hwy. 508.

The **Kootenai River** flows through Koocanusa Reservoir to Libby Dam. It's floatable from the dam to the Idaho border but releases from the dam cause fluctuating flows. The stretch from the dam to Libby can be floated (beginner to intermediate skill levels) in moderate-size craft. Only skilled kayakers or rafters need apply between Libby and the gorge below Kootenai Falls. **China Rapids**, named for the break-up of a Chinese mining party's gold-loaded raft (the gold has never been found), can be dangerous due to heavy dam discharges. (☎ 406-293-3421 for recorded dam release information.) **Kootenai Falls** (see *Touring*, page 382) thunder below these rapids. Below here is a sheer-walled mile-long gorge with Class III and IV stairstep rapids. Once into the gorge, you're committed. From here, it's placid floating to the Idaho line. Access points are below the dam, at the Libby Bridge, the Troy Bridge and at the mouth of the Yaak.

The **Middle Fork of the Flathead** rampages through the Bob Marshall Wilderness before settling down to run obligingly below US 2, between Glacier National Park and the Great Bear Wilderness. Like the rest of the Flathead system, this river enjoys a Wild & Scenic River designation. The "Bob" section must be accessed via horseback or airplane to the Schaeffer Meadow Ranger Station and Airstrip. This is Montana's biggest whitewater run, having 27 miles of almost continuous whitewater. Only highly skilled rafters need apply. **Moccasin Creek** to the West Glacier Bridge is the stretch most commonly run by commercial rafting companies. It's a piece of cake for experienced kayakers or rafters. Access points are numerous along US 2.

The **North Fork of the Flathead** runs along the west boundary of Glacier National Park. Except for a few Class II and III rapids, this river is swift and floatable except in spring when snow runoff speeds things up. **Fool Hen Rapids**, at Miles 8 and 7.2, offer the biggest challenge. Intermediate skills are called for on most of this river. Access points are at the Canadian border, the Glacier Park bridge at Polebridge, and at several points below Camas Bridge.

The **South Fork of the Flathead** is largely inaccessible except by horse or foot. Forty miles of the river's 100 miles are in the Bob Marshall Wilderness. The lower part of this stretch has several Class II to IV rapids, followed by the legendary Meadow Creek Gorge. Unless you have the skill and experience to deal with on-the-edge drops and chutes you'd best portage. There are 20 miles of easy floating between the Wilderness boundary and where the river enters Hungry Horse Reservoir. Three miles of whitewater churns the river below the dam. Several access points below the Wilderness boundary can be reached from the reservoir's West Side Road.

The **main Flathead River** begins with the joining of the Middle and North Forks north of Columbia Falls and extends through Kalispell to be swallowed by **Flathead Lake** at Bigfork. These 55 miles or so offer pleasant floating. Six miles south of Polson, the rejuvenated river is interrupted by the Kerr Dam. The river gets serious below the dam with seven miles of Class III to IV rapids. Only experienced kayakers and rafters should consider shooting these rapids. After these tantrums, the river flows quietly through the Pablo National Wildlife Refuge and the National Bison Range. Access points are at MT 40 near Columbia Falls, at Kalispell and at Sportsman Bridge near Bigfork; also at Polson, Kerr Dam and Dixon.

The **Clark Fork** is one lengthy river, extending for 333 miles from Warm Springs, near Anaconda, to the Idaho line above Cabinet Gorge Dam. Three diversion dams within the first 100 miles and major dams at Thompson Falls and Noxon require portages. Except for 20 miles of Class III to IV whitewater in Cyr Canyon and Alberton Gorge, and a couple of Class III rapids at Miles 102 and 80, the Clark Fork is ideal for canoeing and family floating. Intermediate to experienced kayakers can play happily in the **Cyr Canyon-Alberton Gorge** stretch. There are numerous marked access points along I-90 between Deer Lodge and Missoula, and from Frenchtown to St. Regis. At St. Regis, the river veers sharply east, flowing alongside MT 135 to Paradise and affording access at three points. From here to the Idaho border, the river follows MT 200. Access points are frequent and well marked.

The **Blackfoot River** rises at Rogers Pass in Gold West Country and enters Glacier Country west of Ovando. The 25-mile stretch from Clearwater Junction to Sheep Flats provides kayakers a playground full of drops and rapids. Intermediate to experienced rafters can have a ball, too. Frequent access points line Ninemile Prairie Road, looping north of MT 200. Take-out is at Bonner Dam at the confluence of the Clark Fork River.

The **Bitterroot River** flows quietly through the Bitterroot Valley, paralleling US 93 for most of its 80-mile length to meet the Clark Fork at Missoula. Lewis and Clark called it "this handsome stream." And so it is, allowing for a pleasant float through the bucolic landscape. Access points are numerous from US 93.

The **St. Regis**, a short but feisty river, rises near Lookout Pass and parallels I-90, entering the Clark Fork at the town of St. Regis. In high water, experienced kayakers and rafters can get quite a joyride on this rocky river's Class II and III rapids. To catch the best waves, put in at the rest area four miles west of Saltese. Whitewater rafts and kayaks are sometimes available for rent at sporting goods stores and marinas.

The **Swan River** is generally considered a lazy floating or canoeing river, but the **Wild Mile**, the stretch between a dam and the river's entrance into Flathead Lake spits out Class IV and even V rapids. This is kayakers' heaven, so much so that kayakers come from afar to Bigfork to participate in May's Wild Mile races and attendant fun. Put-in is on MT 209 below the dam.

Canoe & Kayak Rental

Pipestone Mountaineering rents kayaks and canoes in addition to rock climbing equipment, tents, backpacks and other outdoor items. 101 S. Higgins, Missoula, MT 59801; ☎ 406-721-1670.

Commercial River Rafting Companies

Decide whether you want a whitewater experience or a quieter float before plunking your money down. Many of the following rafting companies offer both whitewater trips and scenic floats. The latter may be more to the liking of young children and first-time floaters. Ask for trip descriptions before committing. Also refer to *Fishing* Guides, some of whom offer scenic float trips.

Flathead Raft Company offers twice-daily half-day whitewater/scenic trips on the Lower Flathead River below Kerr Dam. Trips originate at Polson. They also offer twice-monthly June-August afternoon barbeque dinner trips. PO Box 1596, Polson, MT 59860; ☎ 800-654-4359 or 406-883-5838. Fax 406-745-4862. E-mail frc@bigsky.net.

Glacier Raft Company has half-day and full-day floats on the Middle Fork of the Flathead. They also lead multi-day scenic/whitewater/fishing trips on the Middle and North Forks of the Flathead, multi-day *Great Bear Wilderness Whitewater* trips on the Upper Middle Fork, and one-day and multi-day *Ride and Raft* trips in the Great Bear Wilderness.

Daring Duckies (inflatable kayaks) are available as an alternative to riding on a raft. They also have rental rafts for self-guided river trips. Also available are half-day and full-day fly fishing trips, multi-day custom fishing trips and a five-day fly fishing school. PO Box 218D, West Glacier, MT 59936; ☎ 800-235-6781 or 406-888-5454. Fax 406-888-5541. E-mail grc@digisys.net. Internet www.montanamall.come/glacier.

Glacier Wilderness Guides/Montana Raft Company runs half-day and full-day floats on the Middle Fork, plus *Dinner on the River* trips and *Overnight River Adventures* on the North or Middle Fork of the Flathead. This company, designated by the National Park Service as the exclusive backpacking guide service in Glacier National Park, offers one-day to eight-day combination *Hike & Raft Adventures* in the Park. One-day and four-day *Ride & Raft* trips are also available. Box 535, West Glacier, MT 59936; ☎ 800-521-RAFT or 406-387-5555. Fax 406-387-5656. E-mail glguides@cyberport.net. Internet www.travelfile.com/get?glguides.

Great Northern Whitewater runs half-day, full-day and BBQ dinner trips on the Middle Fork of the Flathead. They also offer multi-day Middle Fork trips, plus guided and self-guided canoe trips on quiet stretches of the Middle Fork. Their half-day *Whitewater Funyak* trips are designed for adventurous adults with previous river experience. Half-day and full-day *Raft & Ride* trips are also offered. Guided half-day and full-day fly fishing trips are available. Also, an all day fishing school and custom fishing trips. PO Box 278, West Glacier, MT 59936; ☎ 800-735-7897 or 406-387-5340. E-mail whiteh20@netrix.net. Internet www.gnwhitewater.com.

Lewis & Clark Trail Adventures leads full-day, overnight and dinner trips on the Clark Fork through Alberton Gorge and day floats on the Blackfoot River. Box 9051, Missoula, MT 59807; ☎ 800-366-6246 or 406-728-7609. Internet www.montana.com/lcta.

Montana River Guides offers half-day and full-day trips on the Blackfoot River and through Alberton Gorge, twilight floats on the Clark Fork and Bitterroot Rivers, plus *Scenic Sunrise* floats on the Bitterroot. They also do custom trips. 210 Red Fox Rd., Lolo, MT 59847; ☎ 800-381-RAFT or 406-273-4718. E-mail rivers@montana.com. Internet www.montana.com/rivers.

Pangaea Expeditions offers half-day, full-day and overnight trips on the Clark Fork through Alberton Gorge and on the Blackfoot River. They also have sunset wine & cheese and brunch floats on the Clark Fork through Hellgate Canyon into Missoula. They do customized trips for parties of six or more, and women-only trips. PO Box 5753, Missoula, MT 59806; ☎ 406-721-7719. E-mail pangaeaexp@aol.com.

R.O.W. Inc. offers one-day trips through Alberton Gorge on the Clark Fork. Trips begin at St. Regis. Daring Duckie inflatable kayaks are an option. PO Box 579, Coeur d'Alene, ID 83816-0579; ☎ 800-451-6034 or 208-

765-0841. E-mail rowinc@aol.com. Internet www.rowinc.com. or www.gorp.com/row.htm.

10,000 Waves-Raft & Kayak Adventures offers sit-on-top kayak trips on the Blackfoot River and through Alberton Gorge or Hellgate Canyon into downtown Missoula. They also have half-day and full-day rafting trips through Alberton Gorge and on the Blackfoot River. Combination trips include touring Garnet Ghost Town with Blackfoot River kayak and rafting trips. Owner-operator Deb Moravec also leads customized trips which include women-only, elders-only, bird watching and other special interests. Deb also operates a kayak school. PO Box 7924, Missoula, MT 59807; ☎ 800-537-8315 or 406-549-6670.

Wilderness River Outfitters' trips are for the truly adventurous. The five-day Middle Fork of the Flathead trip includes the gnarly upper section in the Bob Marshall Wilderness. Two eight-day South Fork of the Flathead trips in the "Bob" include a backpacking/river combo and a hike with horse support/river combo. PO Box 72, Lemhi, ID 83465; ☎ 800-252-6581. E-mail wro@wildernessriver.com. Internet www.wildernessriver.com

Wild River Adventures has half-day and full-day oar raft trips and dinner trips on the Middle Fork of the Flathead. Folks desiring full participation can choose a half-day whitewater trip in inflatable kayaks or 12-foot paddle rafts. They also offer half-day scenic floats on a quiet stretch of the Middle Fork. Also available are multi-day rafting trips on the Middle or North Fork, *Saddle & Paddle* combinations and four-day *Horseback & Raft Adventures* in the Flathead National Forest and on the Middle Fork of the Flathead. Guided fly fishing trips are also offered. PO Box 272B, West Glacier, MT 59936; ☎ 800-700-7056 or 406-387-9453. Fax 406-387-9454. E-mail wildriver@riverwild.com. Internet www.riverwild.com.

Canoeing

Canoers can get lost in Glacier Country's wilderness backpacking and whitewater rafting hype. Too bad. Numerous streams, rivers, lakes and wildlife refuges offer memorable canoeing.

Canoeing whitewater is not a swift idea, but every Glacier Country river has a few quiet stretches ideal for exploring by canoe. The **Bitterrroot and Clark Fork** below Thompson Falls come to mind. Some river stretches are recommended for experienced canoers, so check with the local ranger district office before putting in.

Lake shorelines afford great canoeing, especially smaller lakes such as **Dickey** and **Murphy** in the Tobacco Valley, and the **Thompson Lakes chain**.

Some canoe rentals are available (see above, page 427), but traveling with your canoe atop your car will give you more options. The following suggestions will get you started. Refer also to *Wildlife Viewing*, page 451 – wildlife refuges often lend themselves to canoeing.

Marshy, slow-moving streams can offer pleasant canoeing with world class wildfowl watching. Such a one is **Ashley Creek**, at the south end of Smith Lake. Watch for the Kila Turnoff west of Kalispell on US 2. Put in at the county bridge, two miles from the turnoff. Much of the wetland bordering the creek is a wildfowl production area managed by the US Fish and Wildlife Service. The lands bordering the creek are closed in spring and summer, but the creek remains open.

The **Bull River**, flowing east of Bull Lake and not related to it, empties into the Clark Fork above Cabinet Gorge and Dam. It may look marshy and uninteresting from MT 56, but it's actually quite deep and is popular with local canoers. Put in at one of two MT 56 bridges. Be warned that the last three miles can have Class III rapids in high water. The river's slow middle portion offers lazy canoeing suitable for beginners.

The **Clearwater Canoe Trail**, in the Seeley/Swan Valley, is 3.5 miles of canoeing heaven. The slow-moving Clearwater River is wildlife heaven, too. No telling what you'll see: beaver dams for sure, musical loons, comical moose, curious white-tailed deer. The marked access road is about a mile north of the Seeley Lake Ranger Station, off MT 83. The take-out is at the head of Seeley Lake. A 1.5-mile trail links the take-out with the Seeley Lake Ranger Station.

Guided Canoe Trips

Guided canoe trips are scarce, no doubt due to the popularity of Glacier Country's more macho adventures.

Wild Rockies Tours partners Dan Ward, Matt Thoms and Gail Gutsche are canoeing specialists. They offer multi-day canoe trips on the Lower Clark Fork and Blackfoot Rivers. While descending these glorious rivers, Matt shares his considerable knowledge of Montana's ecosystems and often controversial environmental concerns. Dan teaches trippers a variety of primitive skills, such as fire making with native materials. PO Box 8184, Missoula, MT 59807; ☎ 406-728-0566. E-mail gutsche@ wildrockies.org.

Sea Kayaking

Sea kayaking in land-locked Montana? You bet! Flathead Lake and Lake Koocanusa are big enough to be considered inland seas; so it's not as far-fetched as it sounds. Sea kayaking is easier to get the hang of than river kayaking and no Eskimo roll skills are needed. One- and two-person sea kayaks are larger and more stable than river kayaks and have foot-operated steering, permitting you to concentrate on the scenery. Previous experience not required.

Glacier Sea Kayaking! offers tours of Flathead and Koocanusa Lakes' interesting shorelines that include overnight lake expeditions, *Full Moon Adventures, Summer Solstice Selebrations, Bed & Breakfast Tours* and custom trips. Owner and operator Bobbie Gilmore also offers educational excursions arranged through Flathead Valley Community College. The three-day Women's Sea Kayaking Retreat is popular. 390 Tally Lake Rd., Whitefish, MT 59937; ☎ 406-862-9010.

Lake Boating

Anything you can do on a lake, you can do on Flathead Lake; to a somewhat lesser degree on other Glacier Country lakes. Boat motors are limited to 10 hp or less on many small lakes and on some Glacier National Park lakes. Personal watercraft may or may not be permitted. Check with the local ranger district office or a marina to be sure you're in accordance with the law.

> Everything you ever wanted or needed to know about boating in Montana is included in the Montana Department of Fish, Wildlife & Parks' *Safe Boating Manual*. Request a copy from FWP before your trip, or pick up a copy at any FWP office or marina.

Water skiing is permitted between sunrise and sunset on Glacier Park's **Lake McDonald** and **St. Mary Lake**. So much for the Park's pristine reputation. **Lake Koocanusa**'s strict boating rules help keep it delightfully clean. Water skiing and personal watercraft are big on **Flathead** and **Whitefish Lakes**. The operation of personal watercraft is coming under fire nationwide, so check before you slip your toy into the water.

Several islands seem to float on Flathead Lake. The largest and best known is **Wildhorse Island**, 2,163 acres of wild mountain beauty. The entire island is a primitive day-use state park accessible only by boat. Wild horses, Rocky Mountain bighorn sheep, bald eagles and song birds are only a few of the wildlife species living here. Hiking trails lace the island. There are limited docking facilities on the west side of the island.

Flathead Lake's winds are just right for **sailing**. If you enjoy skimming along sans noise, this lake's for you.

Numerous marinas and watercraft rentals operate on and near Glacier Country's larger lakes. It makes sense, even if you trailer your own craft, to call ahead or stop in to check current boating rules and regulations on a particular body of water. Refer also to *Hotels, Motels & B&Bs* and *Campgrounds* for rental information.

Flathead Lake Marinas & Rentals

Ace Power Sports offers free delivery of personal watercraft, ski boats, fishing boats and luxury boats to all area lakes. ☎ 406-257-4400.

Flathead Boat Rentals, at Somers and Polson, rents personal watercraft, ski boats, jet boats, fishing boats, canoes, paddle boats and kayaks. Somers: ☎ 406-857-3334. Polson: ☎ 800-358-8046 or 406-883-3900.

Marina Cay Resort at Bigfork rents paddle boats, aluminum fishing boats, pontoon and ski boats, Waverunners, pleasure boats, canoes and rafts, knee boards and water skis. ☎ 406-837-5861.

Power Play Water Sports, on the west shore at Lakeside, rents Sea-Doos, wetsuits, tubes and inflatables, ski boats, and fishing boats. ☎ 406-844-2400 or 406-752-4909.

Quiet World, at Dayton on the lake's west shore, rents sailboats having overnight accommodations. Sailing lessons available. ☎ 406-849-5423.

Wild Wave Watercraft Rentals, at the Lakeside Bay Marina on the west shore of Flathead Lake, rents personal watercraft. ☎ 406-257-2627.

Whitefish Lake Marinas & Rentals

Adventure Motor Sports, at 1805 9th St. West in Columbia Falls, has personal watercraft and trailers, water skies, wetsuits, life jackets, knee boards and tubes for rent. ☎ 406-892-2752.

Big Mountain Adventures rents ski boats with skis, pontoons and personal watercraft. ☎ 406-862-9191.

Rising Sun Outdoor Adventures in Columbia Heights rents whitewater rafts, paddle rafts, canoes, kayaks and sailboats. Shuttle service available. ☎ 406-862-5934 or 892-2602.

Whitefish City Beach has paddleboats, rafts, innertubes and kayaks for rent. ☎ 406-863-2470.

Whitefish Lake Lodge Marina rents ski boats, personal watercraft, canoes, paddleboats, knee boards, water skis, tubes and fishing boats. ☎ 406-862-9283.

Lake Koocanusa Marinas & Rentals

Lake Koocanusa retains its pristine ecology by permitting only two marinas, one in Canada and one in the US, and restricting water craft. No vacation homes clutter the shore of this pine-girt lake.

Dream Marine, Inc. rents canoes, personal watercraft and fishing boats. 1001 N. Hwy. 37, Libby, MT 59923; ☎ 406-293-8142. Fax 406-293-6800.

Koocanusa Resort, just north of Libby Dam, is a catch-all marina and resort with boats for rent. 23911 Scenic Highway 37, Libby, MT 59923; ☎ 406-293-7474.

Seeley & Swan Lakes Marina & Rentals

Arburtec Rentals rents several sizes of outboard boats, canoes and paddleboats on Seeley Lake. Rainbow Drive, Bigfork, MT 59911; ☎ 800-525-3344 or 406-837-4608. Fax 406-837-2468.

Glacier National Park Marinas & Rentals

Glacier Park Boat Co. has outlets at Apgar, Lake McDonald Lodge, Two Medicine Lake and Swiftcurrent Lake. Motorboats, rowboats, kayaks and canoes are available to rent. ☎ 406-257-2426.

Tour Boats

Tour boats offer enjoyable and informative cruises on Flathead and Whitefish Lakes and on Glacier National Park lakes.

Classic Cruisin' Charters schedules daily Flathead Lake cruises from Marina Cay Resort at Bigfork aboard the *M/V Seafarer*, a 56-foot 1926 wooden motor yacht. Private charters available. Summer: ☎ 406-837-2544. Winter: ☎ 406-676-8593. Fax 406-676-8524. E-mail tlc@ronan.net.

The Far West, a 64-foot two-level vessel, cruises the northern end of Flathead Lake from Somers. Daily half-hour cruises. Ask about sunset cruises. Charters available. ☎ 406-857-3202.

Flathead Tours, Inc. offers several cruises on the southern half of Flathead Lake from KwaTaqNuk Resort in Polson. Included are three-hour narrated cruises around Wild Horse Island, bay cruises and twilight cruises. KwaTaqNuk Princess, 303 US Hwy. 93 E., Polson, MT 59860; ☎ 406-883-2448.

Pointer Scenic Cruises has small inboard/outboard boat custom charter cruises of Flathead Lake that include a hiking cruise to Wildhorse Island. Custom charters include anywhere you want to go, including a lift to a dinner venue. East Shore Rt., Bigfork, MT 59911; ☎ 406-837-5617.

Questa Yacht Charters and Chandlers offers daily cruises aboard two vintage Class Q sailing ships, the 1928 *NorEaster* and the 1929 *Questa*. Charter cruises are also available. Cruises depart from the Flathead Lake Lodge, a mile south of Bigfork. PO Box 248, Bigfork, MT 59911; ☎ 406-837-5569. Fax 406-837-6977.

Whitecap Sailing, Inc. has charters, leases, rentals and lessons aboard 25-foot sailboats on Flathead Lake; Memorial Day-Sept. Box 528, Lakeside, MT 59922; ☎ 406-844-3021 summers, ☎ 406-844-3977 winters.

Whitefish Lake Lodge Marina schedules 90-minute twilight cruises of Whitefish Lake, beginning May 15. ☎ 406-862-9283.

Glacier Park Boat Co. offers cruises of Lake McDonald, Many Glacier, St. Mary Lake and Two Medicine. Most cruises feature Park naturalists explaining the lakes' ecology and wildlife. Refer to your Park information packet for scheduling information. PO Box 5262, Kalispell, MT 59903; ☎ 406-257-2426. Fax 406-756-1437.

Diving

Certified divers wishing to dive Flathead or other Glacier Country lakes are invited to contact Steve and Renee Golleher at **Bighorn Divers** north of Kalispell. They rent diving equipment and conduct evening Flathead Lake dives and weekend dive trips to other lakes. 2490 US 93 N., Kalispell; ☎ 406-752-4970.

Fishing

Get a firm fix on Montana fishing rules and regulations if you want to fish Glacier Country's rivers, streams or lakes. You'll need other sets of rules for fishing in Glacier National Park and on the Flathead or Blackfeet Indian Reservation. A non-member fishing permit and a tribal recreation and conservation tag are required for recreating on the reservations.

Knowing the rules is imperative if you plan on acting as your own guide; less so if you'll be hiring a guide/outfitter licensed by the Montana Board of Outfitters. The guide will look out for catch limits and other such matters and help you obtain a fishing license. Montana Fish, Wildlife & Parks makes available a fishing regulations booklet covering the entire state, a Montana Fishing Access Sites brochure, and a helpful stream-by-stream Fishing Guide offering a fix on which species of fish swims where. See *Information Sources*, page 357. A copy of Flathead Indian Reservation recreation regulations is available by contacting the office of the Confederated Salish and Kootenai Tribes at Pablo. Inquire also about tribal members who work as guides. See *Information Sources*.

A copy of *Non-Member Sportsman Regulations* is available by contacting the Blackfeet Fish and Wildlife Department (PO Box 850, Browning, MT 59417; ☎ 406-338-7207). Some tribal members act as fishing guides. The BFWP will provide that information.

AUTHOR TIP *A Montana fishing license is not necessary in Glacier National Park, but anglers must obtain Park fishing permits. Copies of fishing regulations are available on request. These are subject to change from year to year.*

Your next decision is whether you want to flick a fly over a river or stream, or if you prefer to cast a lure into a lake.

A River Runs Through It hype has splashed the **Blackfoot River** into the mainstream of famous fly fishing rivers, but it's not the only river with great trout fishing. The **Flathead River System** hosts spawning runs of westslope cutthroat and the endangered bull trout – native species held in near-reverance by Montana anglers. Mountain whitefish are also numerous in these rivers. The **Kootenai River**'s wild rainbow trout fishery is world class. Rainbow and brown trout swim in the **Bitterroot** and **Clark Fork Rivers**. The Clark Fork and the Flathead System are also notable largemouth bass and northern pike fisheries. Almost every sizeable river and stream in the region harbors cold water mountain whitefish. Exceptions are the Tobacco River and the South Fork of the Two Medicine River.

Lake fishing is a stand-out, too. **Flathead Lake** yields trophy lake trout, lake whitefish and yellow perch. Predictably, **Whitefish Lake** harbors lake whitefish; also golden and lake trout. **Lake Mary Ronan** has Kokanee salmon, cutthroat and rainbow trout, largemouth bass and yellow perch. **Lake Koocanusa** is a renowned Kokanee salmon, mountain whitefish and cutthroat trout fishery. And so it goes, with most other Glacier Country lakes following suit. Some high mountain lakes are limited to non-native rainbow trout and a few are fishing duds. Upward of 50 lakes in Glacier National Park offer good fishing for ling, northern pike, grayling, rainbow, mackinaw and the ubiquitous brookies. "The bigger the lake, the bigger the fish," seems to be the rule. Mackinaw in the 30-pound range hang out in **Lakes McDonald** and **St. Mary**. Forget stream fishing. Some are fishless and some are closed to fishing to protect bull trout and native cutthroat. Bears like to fish, too. Observe bear-awareness fishing practices and keep an eye open lest you and Old Bruin opt for the same fishery. Refer to *Co-Adventuring With Grizzlies* (page 16).

Fishing Outfitters & Guides

Glacier Country fishing outfitters and guides are as numerous as bears around a honey tree. Guides must operate under the auspices of an outfitter licensed by the Montana Board of Outfitters. Fly fishing's popularity has escalated sharply in recent years, leading to a moratorium on new licensees except when slots open due to attrition. This has spawned a school of rogue guides who flout a law that mandates licensing for any guide baiting a hook or shooting a gun. The best way to guard against inadvertently signing up with a rogue guide is to request a copy of the current licensed outfitters list from the Montana Board of Outfitters. See *Information Sources*, page 66. Some licensed outfitters operate independently with the help of hired guides. A few operate under a fly shop's umbrella. Some offer lake charters. Yet others operate out of or in conjunction with a fishing resort or lodge. The following categories attempt to sort these out, but expect some overlap. Refer also to *Commercial River Rafting Companies*. Some offer fishing floats in addition to scenic and whitewater trips. The following outfitters are among the best.

Independent Fishing Outfitters/Guides

Big Fork Outdoor Expeditions' Larry Shanks was a state game warden for 20 years and has been an outfitter since 1990. He offers fly fishing instruction and fly fishing river trips and mountain lake float tubing. He also has mountain biking, nature hikes, photographic trips and non-technical peak climbs. PO Box 213, Big Fork, MT 59911; ☎ 406-837-2031.

Bill Abbot's Trout Fishing Only offers fly fishing experiences on the Bitterroot and other southern Montana rivers. He also runs six-day guided float/walk/wade trips on the Bitterroot, Beaverhead and Big Hole Rivers. PO Box 1332, Hamilton, MT 59840; ☎ 800-363-2408 or 406-363-2408.

Bitterroot Anglers' Andy Carlson has fly fishing schools and float and wade trips on the Bitterroot West Fork, Clark Fork, Blackfoot and other Montana rivers. He also leads overnight camping trips. Box 433 (300 College St.), Stevensville, MT 59870; ☎ 406-777-2341.

Bitterroot Outfitters' Tom Henderson offers guided float trips on the Bitterroot River and pack trips in the Selway-Bitterroot Wilderness that emphasize fishing mountain lakes and streams. 1842 Hwy. 93 So., Hamilton, MT 59840; ☎ 406-363-0403.

Crain Guide & Outfitting Service's Dick Crain leads a variety of customized one-day and multi-day fishing trips on the Clark Fork, Thompson and Flathead Rivers. PO Box 1221, Plains, MT 59859; ☎ 406-826-5566.

Diamond N Outfitters' Brian Nelson offers guided day floats and multi-day river camping/fly fishing floats on the Clark Fork, Bitterroot, Blackfoot and other Montana rivers. PO Box 1982, Missoula, MT 59806; ☎ 800-308-FISH. Fax 406-543-3887. E-mail diamondn@montana.com. Internet www.montana.com/dno/dno.htm.

Flat Iron Outfitting's Jerry Shively is primarily a hunting guide, but he also offers high mountain lake fishing in the Cabinet Mountains. 3 Golf Course Rd., Thompson Falls, MT 59873; ☎ 406-827-3666.

Fly fishing Adventures' Richard Thomas offers half-day and full-day float fishing on the Bitterroot River. 702 N. 1st St., Hamilton, MT 59840; ☎ 888-363-6158 or 406-363-6158. E-mail fishaus@montana.com. Internet www.montana.com/fishaus.

John Maki Outfitters runs multi-day fly fishing camp trips on the Blackfoot, Clark Fork and other Montana rivers. They also offer lodge accommodations on the Blackfoot. 655 Granite, Helena, MT 59601; ☎ 406-442-6129.

John Perry's West Slope Outfitters leads one-day walk-in and float fly fishing trips on the Clark Fork, Bitterroot, Blackfoot and other Montana rivers. They also have three-day Clark Fork and Bitterroot trips. PO Box 20080, Missoula, MT 59801; ☎ 800-580-9703 or 406-258-2997. E-mail sherlock@bigsky.net

K & N Outfitting's Wade Nixon mostly offers hunting trips, but he does have per-day fishing trips as well. PO Box 418, Libby, MT 59923; ☎ 406-293-9488.

Kootenai River Outfitters, Inc.'s Gary McCabe gives fly fishing instruction and runs half-day and full-day McKenzie River drift boat fly fishing and/or spin fishing trips on the Kootenai and Yaak Rivers. He also leads sightseeing/photography float trips. PO Box 1115, Troy, MT 59935; ☎ 800-537-8288 or 406-295-4615.

Lineham Outfitting Co./Kootenai River Guide Service's Tim Lineham runs an Orvis Endorsed guide service employing experienced guides. He offers float and wade trips on the Kootenai and Yaak Rivers and float tubing on low elevation and alpine lakes in Western Montana. He also gives personalized instruction. 472 Upper Ford Rd., Troy, MT 59935; ☎ 406-295-4872.

Montana Adventures in Angling's Jim McFadyean, a member of the Blackfeet Tribe, guides primarily on the Blackfeet Indian Reservation and on Custer Country's Big Horn River. Most of his guides are Blackfeet or Crow Indians. McFadyean also arranges guided lake and stream fishing trips in the Bob Marshall Wilderness and Glacier National Park. 1845 Bannack Dr., Billings, MT 59105; ☎ 406-248-2995.

Montana Experience Outfitters' Carl Mann offers float fishing on the Clark Fork, butterroot and Blackfoot Rivers. Choose between fly fishing or light spin casting. He also runs family charter boat fishing trips on Flathead Lake. 15440 Thayer Rd., Lolo, MT 59847; ☎ 800-435-4651 or 406-273-6966 or 837-5632 (lake).

Montana Fly Fishing Company's Kirk Johnston, a native Montanan and quarter-century fly fishing guide, offers drift, walk-wade and float-tube fishing on the Blackfoot, Clark Fork, Bitterroot and other Montana rivers. He also fishes small streams and lakes. 1204 Powell St., Missoula, MT 59802; ☎ 406-549-4822. Fax 406-549-2220. E-mail fishingMT@ aol.com.

Montana River Anglers' Jim Voeller runs half-day and full-day drift boat and wade trips on the Flathead River System. He also does fishing trips on other Montana rivers. 7742 Canyon Ferry Rd., Helena, MT 59602; ☎ 800-210-9303.

Outlaw River Runners' Steve Armstrong leads fly and spin fishing trips on the Swan River. 814 Cascade Ave., Bigfork, MT 59911; ☎ 406-837-3529 or 837-4337.

Paul Roos Outfitters: see *Fishing Lodges/Ranches*, page 439.

Rainbow Guide Service's Joseph Biner offers half-day, full-day and multi-day raft float fishing trips on the Bitterroot, Clark Fork, Blackfoot and other Montana rivers. They also run scenic float trips. 5424 West Fork Rd., Darby, MT 59829; ☎ 406-821-4643. To leave a message, dial 821-3541.

The Northern Rockies Outfitter's Richard Birdsell welcomes anglers of all abilities on his fly and spin fishing trips on the Flathead River. 2775 Dillon Rd., Whitefish, MT 59937; ☎ 406-758-6649.

Treasure State Outfitting's Mike Canavan and guides offer fly fishing opportunities on the Kootenai and Yaak Rivers. He also does cast and troll fishing on Lake Koocanusa. 259 Shalom Dr., Libby, MT 59923; ☎ 406-293-8666. Fax 406-293-9518.

Western Rivers' Fred Tedesco has combination float/camping trips on the lower Clark Fork, Blackfoot and Bitterroot Rivers. He also fishes and offers package tours on other Montana rivers. PO Box 772, East Helena, MT 59635; ☎ 406-227-5153.

Western Timberline Outfitters' Jammin and Dawn Krebs have customized half-day, full-day and three-day wade and drift boat fishing on the Clark Fork. They also run high mountain pack-in fishing trips and scenic float trips on the Clark Fork. PO Box 839, Plains, MT 59859; ☎ 406-826-3874.

Western Waters & Woods' Jerry Nichols does daily and extended fishing trips on the Clark Fork River and other Montana rivers. He also has a charter boat on Noxon Rapids Reservoir and on other lakes. 5455 Keil Loop, Missoula, MT 59802; ☎ 800-757-1680 Pin# 2060 or 406-543-3203. E-mail waters@bigsky.net. Internet www.bigsky.net/westernwaters.

Fly Shops

Fly shops can supply you with flies, rods and a wide range of accessories plus guided fishing trips. It's a good idea to stop in at a local shop, even if you intend to fish on your own. You can glean valuable insight into local fisheries, plus scuttlebutt on hatches and other matters. The following shops are owned and operated by licensed outfitters.

Fishaus Tackle, serving the Bitterroot Valley, has been in the same Hamilton location for 20 years. Owners Bill and Lucy Bean offer anglers of all ability levels guided half-day and full-day floats on the Bitterroot, Clark Fork, Rock Creek and Blackfoot. 702 N. First St., Hamilton, MT 59840; ☎ 406-363-6158.

Lakestream Fly Fishing Shop works with Big Mountain Ski and Summer Resort, conducting summer flycasting classes. They also offer individual and group casting sessions on a city park pond just outside the shop. Guided float tubing, river floating and wading trips are available on area rivers and streams. 15 Central Ave., Whitefish, MT 59937; ☎ 406-862-1298. Fax 406-862-6521. Internet www.lakestream.com.

The Grizzly Hackle's owner Jim Toth employs a staff of experienced guides to lead fly fishing trips on the Clark Fork, Blackfoot and other Missoula area rivers, lakes and spring creeks. The shop in downtown Missoula stocks name brand apparel and gear. Toth offers accommodations at his house on Butler Creek, a short drive from Missoula. Packages available. 215 W. Front St., Missoula, MT 59802; ☎ 800-279-8996 or 406-721-8996.

Fishing Charters

Landing Flathead Lake's trophy-size mackinaw (lake trout) requires heavy tackle and a boat larger than a rental put-put. Several charter services combine guides and charter boats for a memorable fishing experience.

A-Able Fishing, owned by "Shorty" George and Jeannie Goggins, offers covered and heated charter boats out of Marina Cay near Bigfork for year-round fishing on Flathead Lake. They also operate on other lakes, as well as Flathead Rivers. 63 Twin Acres Dr., Kalispell, MT 59901; ☎ 800-231-5214 or 406-257-5214. Fax 406-752-2166.

Babcock Creek Outfitters owner LeRoy Brooks runs half-day and full-day charter boat fishing trips on Flathead Lake. Boats and tackle are hefty enough to land 35 lb. lake trout. Brooks also offers drop floats in the Bob Marshall Wilderness. 280 Twin Lakes Rd., Whitefish, MT 59937; ☎ 406-862-7813.

Bagley Guide Service's Dusty Bagley guarantees a catch on his year-round half-day or full-day Flathead Lake charters. 171 Terrace Hill, Bigfork, MT 59911; ☎ 406-837-3618 or 250-3161.

Glacier Fishing Charters owner Jim Landwehr has three boats available for half-day and full-day fishing charters on Flathead Lake. Large parties accommodated. 375 Jensen Rd., Columbia Falls, MT 59912; ☎ 800-735-9244 or 406-892-2377.

Fishing Lodges/Ranches

Staying at a lodge or ranch dedicated to housing anglers offers total immersion in the sport you love best. The following are stand-outs.

Bar-One Ranch, a 30-minute drive from Missoula, gives accommodations in a splendiferous log lodge or a private cottage. Customized fly fishing itineraries on the Clark Fork, Blackfoot, Bitterroot, Rock Creek and other waters are arranged with licensed guides for a first class experience. Non-fishing activities are also available. The ranch is represented by Frontiers International, 305 Logan Rd., Wexford, PA 15090-0959; ☎ 800-245-1950 or 412-935-1577. Fax 412-935-5388. E-mail info@frontierstrvl.com.

Spotted Bear Ranch is an Orvis Endorsed lodge perched above the South Fork of the Flathead River, 60 miles from the nearest highway and near the boundary of the Bob Marshall Wilderness. Log cabins are rustic on the outside, modern on the inside even to showers and flush toilets – no small deal in the wilderness. Horseback riding is available, but fishing is the ranch's focus. Kirk and Cathy Gentry offer several multi-day packages that include packing and fishing in the "Bob" and a ranch experience with fishing the South Fork. 2863 Foothill Rd., Kalispell, MT 59901; ☎ 406-755-7337.

Paul Roos Outfitters, a long-time Montana outfitter and guide service, welcomes anglers to North Fork Crossing, a unique lodge on the North Fork of the Blackfoot River. A spacious lodge for meeting and dining is augmented by heated luxury wall tents complete with wood floors, screened windows and doors, oversized cots, electricity and decks. A shower/bathhouse is nearby. They also offer fishing on other area rivers. PO Box 621, Helena, MT 59624; ☎ 800-858-3497 or 406-442-5489. Fax 406-449-2293.

Wilderness Lodge & Guest Ranch, in the Bitterroot Mountains near Cabinet Gorge and Dam, is a no-nonsense anglers' and hunters' retreat. Licensed outfitter Tom O'Brien leads multi-day fishing trips to high mountain lakes or has ranch-based fishing on area streams and creeks. O'Brien also runs an outfitters & guides school. 620 Elk Creek Rd., Heron, MT 59844; ☎ 406-847-2277 or 847-2398.

Ice Fishing

Most Glacier Country lakes freeze over enough to allow fishing through the ice. Lakes on the Blackfeet Reservation provide especially good ice fishing. An ice hut and other special equipment shut out the casual visitor who wants to try his or her hand. If you really want to ice fish you can contact one of the fishing or back country outfitters listed above to see if someone will take you out. Or contact the Blackfeet Fish and Wildlife Department to inquire about a guide.

■ Adventures on Snow

You can either stay indoors by the fire and look at the snow through a window, or get out in it. The latter is the choice of most Montanans; who wants to sit indoors for half the year?

If the thought of visiting Montana in winter gives you the shivers, skip this section. If it makes you want to snap on your skis or rev up your snowmobile, read on.

Snow adventures come in three main guises: downhill skiing, cross-country skiing/snowshoeing and snowmobiling. Dogsledders are out there too, nipping at skiers' heels. Glacier Country has the best of each.

Downhill Skiing & Snowboarding

If you associate downhill skiing with full-service resorts you'll not be disappointed. Ditto, if you prefer low-key ski venues. All Montana ski resorts permit snowboarding.

Big Mountain

Big Mountain is big business – full-service destination skiing with all the frills and winter fun you'd expect of a high profile ski resort. Average snowfall: 300+ inches. The base elevation is 4,700 feet, top 7,000 feet, adding up to a vertical drop of 2,300 feet. The 64 runs are rated 25% beginner, 55% intermediate and 20% advanced. The longest run is 2.5 miles. Unlimited tree skiing. Per-day lift tickets around $40 (children under $30, six and under free) make Big Mountain Montana's priciest ski venue after Big Sky. A gondola lifts skiers to Big Mountain. Lifts include three quads, four triple chairs, one double chair and two surface lifts. Telemark and mono-skiers are welcome in addition to snowboarders. Guided snowcat skiing. Ten km of groomed cross-country trails. Instruction includes skill-builder, snowboard, telemark and cross country, plus a Women's Week snowboard camp. Kids' day care and ski school. Ask about ski/lodging packages. A Snow Bus shuttle schedules regular runs between Whitefish and Big Mountain. PO Box 1400, Whitefish, MT 59937; ☎ 800-858-3913 or 406-862-1900. Fax 406-862-2955. Internet www.bigmtn.com/resort.

Blacktail Ski Area

Blacktail Ski Area, above Lakeside on the Flathead National Forest, opened for the 1998-99 ski season in response to a perceived need for a new family ski area in the Flathead Valley. It projects a low key, laid-back ambience reflective of rural Montana. Families may find it a comfortable alternative to the much larger Big Mountain Aki Resort. The handsome lodge at the upper terminal has a lounge, two restaurants, daycare, ski rental and ski school. Average snowfall: 250 inches. Under $25 per-day lift tickets (students and juniors $15, age seven and under free); short or no lines. Family passes. Base elevation: 5,236 ft., top 6,676 ft. with a vertical drop of 1,440 feet. The longest of the 24 groomed runs is 6,229 feet. Ratings include 15% beginner, 70% intermediate, 15% expert runs. Two double lifts, one triple lift and a beginner's platter. The season runs from mid-November to approximately April 1. Open Wed.-Sun. and holidays, 9:30-4:30. Ask about ski-lodging packages offering lodgings at **Cavanaughs at Kalispell Center** or **Cavanaughs Outlaw Hotel**. PO Box 1090, Lakeside, MT 59922; ☎ 406-844-0999. Fax 406-257-8543. E-mail skiing@blacktailmountain.com. Internet www.blacktailmountain.com.

Lost Trail Powder Mountain

Lost Trail Powder Mountain, off US 93 on the Continental Divide, is an informal place where the dress code is jeans and a parka. Average snowfall: 300+ inches. Under $20 full-day lift tickets (kids half price, five and under free) and short or no lines. Family discounts. Base elevation is 6,600 feet, top 7,800, with a vertical drop of 1,200 feet. The 18 runs are rated 20% beginner, 60% intermediate and 20% advanced. Two double lifts and two surface chairs. Ski school. The season is December-April (great spring skiing). Open Thurs.-Sun. and holidays, 9:30-4. **Camp Creek Inn** at Sula offers *Ski & Stay* packages. A mogul freestyle competition is held in February. PO Box 311, Conner, MT 59827; ☎ 406-821-3211 or 821-3508. Fax 406-821-350. Internet www.bitterroot.net/lostrail/lostrail.html.

Marshall Mountain

Marshall Mountain is a day-use ski area near Missoula with bargain per-day lift tickets at under $20. Average snowfall: 150 inches. Base elevation is 3,900 feet, top 5,400 with a vertical drop of 1,500 feet. The 22 runs are rated 15% beginner, 65% intermediate and 20% advanced. 5250 Marshall Canyon Rd., Missoula, MT 59802; ☎ 406-258-6000.

Montana Snowbowl

Montana Snowbowl, 12 miles northwest of Missoula on the Lolo National Forest, has 700 acres of "extreme" skiing, 30+ trails and groomed runs, open powder bowls and tree skiing. Average snowfall: 300 inches. The vertical drop: 2,600 feet from a top of 7,600 feet to a 5,000-foot base. Runs are rated 20% beginner, 40% intermediate, 40% advanced. Per-day lift tickets under $30 (kids half-price, five and under free). Two high-capacity double chairs and two surface lifts. Beginner's, downhill, snowboard and Pee-Wee instruction. Season: late November-early April, Wed.-Mon. On-mountain hotel/hostel lodging at Gelandsprung Lodge. PO Box 8226, Missoula, MT 59807; ☎ 800-728-2695 or 406-549-9777.

Turner Mountain

Turner Mountain is a day-use ski area in the Purcell Mountains 22 miles north of Libby, half-way to Yaak on Rt. 567. Bargain basement per-day lift ticket prices at well under $20 (kids under $15, six and under free). Average snowfall: 200 inches. The base is at 3,842 feet, top 5,942 with a vertical drop of 2,110 feet. The 26 runs are rated 5% beginner, 20% intermediate and a whopping 75% advanced. One T-bar lift. If you like a serious challenge, this mountain is for you. ☎ 406-293-4317.

Cross-Country Skiing/Snowshoeing

Glacier Country's national forests and Glacier National Park offer some of the state's finest cross-country skiing. It doesn't come without hazards, namely avalanche and hypothermia. Refer to pages 46 and 200 for valuable information on clothing, emergency supplies and avalanche awareness. The Northern Region National Forests makes available a *Winter Safety Guide*. See *Information Sources*, page 357.

AUTHOR TIP *The Northwest Montana Avalanche Warning System assesses avalanche conditions. Forecasts are updated weekly each Friday morning during avalanche season. Forecasts are broadcast by local radio stations. The call-in numbers are ☎ 406-257-8402 or 800-526-5329. The National Avalanche Center's Internet address is http://csac.org/Bulletins/ or http://avalanche.org/.*

Glacier National Park Nordic Skiing

If you think of Glacier National Park as a fair weather destination, you'll be pleased to learn that the Upper Lake McDonald, Polebridge, Apgar-West Glacier, Marias Pass, St. Mary and Two Medicine Valley areas offer some wonderful cross-country skiing trails. Most trails are not marked. Stop at a ranger station or the Apgar Visitor Center to learn of current conditions and to obtain a topo map – a necessity unless the trail is on an unmaintained road. Skiers and snowshoers are asked to register at the trailhead registration boxes. The Park has available a Cross-Country Skiing brochure that includes descriptions of the aforementioned trails.

Glacier Park Ski Tours offers guided day-long or extended snowshoe or ski tours in Glacier National Park. 728 Kalispell Ave., Whitefish, MT 59937; ☎ 800-646-6043, ext. 3724 or 406-862-2790.

National Forest Nordic Skiing

The four national forests sprawled across Glacier Country offer some of the West's finest ski touring trails. Some are intermittedly groomed, most not. Trail ratings include Easiest, More Difficult, and Most Difficult. Mountain Touring trails are challenging and best left to highly skilled skiers. Dogs are prohibited on groomed trails. The Forest Service, Northern Region, makes available a brochure describing trails on the Bitterroot, Lolo, Flathead and Kootenai National Forests. Some ranger districts have put together detailed descriptions, including maps, of ski trails in their districts. You can request copies, or pick one up at a ranger station when in the area.

Lolo National Forest Ski Trails

If you are in Missoula and desire a day of close-in skiing, check out the **Pattee Canyon Ski Trails** maintained by the Missoula Ranger District. The trailhead (four miles up Pattee Canyon Drive from the corner of Higgins and Southwest Higgins) accesses two trail systems. A map is available. Included are 1.6 km Easiest, 4 km More Difficult, 5.4 km Most Difficult trails. Intermittent grooming.

The **Holloman/Plant Creek Loop** 13 miles southeast of Missoula has 12.9 km of ungroomed More Difficult trail. Contact the Missoula Ranger District of the Lolo National Forest.

Lolo Pass ski trails are popular with Missoulians and visitors alike. US 12 is well maintained, offering easy access. Trails are on both the Idaho and Montana sides of the Pass. An Idaho Park `N' sticker is required to park at Lolo Pass; obtain one at the pass visitor center. On the Montana side, choose between the ungroomed **Lee Creek** and Wagon Mountain Trails. Lee Creek Trail offers 10.6 km of More Difficult terrain between Lolo Pass and Lee Creek. **Wagon Mountain Trail**, 11.4 km of Most Difficult trail, is a Mountain Touring route having intermittent steep sections. Climbing skins are recommended. **Lookout Pass Recreation Area**, in the Superior Ranger District and also on the Montana-Idaho state line, is accessed via I-90. Park at Lookout Pass Ski Area. Ski trails include 3.6 km Easiest, 3.5 km More Difficult and 4.5 km Most Difficult. No grooming. Portions of some trails are shared with snowmobiles. Maps are available at the trailhead and at the Superior Ranger District office.

The **Seeley Lake** area, on the Seeley Lake Ranger District, offers beautiful Nordic skiing. A trail complex from a trailhead on the Cottonwood Lakes Road, one mile north of Seeley Lake via US 83, includes a network of trails through mixed terrain. Included are three km Easiest, 12 km More Difficult and three km Most Difficult intermittently groomed trails. Maps are available at the trailhead and at the district office.

Bitterroot National Forest Ski Trails

Lost Trail and **Chief Joseph Pass trails**, accessed via US 93, offer numerous options on both the Montana and Idaho sides of the Continental Divide. A brochure with maps is available from the Sula Ranger District office. There are 27.9 km of ungroomed Mountain Touring trails in the **Saddle Mountain area of Lost Trail Pass**, and a whole bunch of intermittently groomed trails for all skill levels, none exceeding 2.6 km, in the Chief Joseph Pass Area. The **North Big Hole** area has 51.2 km of serious ungroomed Mountain Touring trails. Contact the Bitterroot Cross-Country Ski Club for more area ski trail information. PO Box 431, Corvallis, MT 59828.

Kootenai National Forest Ski Trails

The **Libby Ranger District** has numerous ski trails for all abilities in the **Purcell and Cabinet Mountains**. The **Timberline Campground**, nine miles north of town, is a wonderful family area with 2.5 km of intermittently groomed Easiest and .8 km More Difficult ski trails, a sledding and ski play hill, fire ring and firewood.

Bear Creek, seven miles south of town, has 2.3 km Easiest, 1.8 km More Difficult and 1.4 km Most Difficult trails. Contact the ranger district office for detailed information on these and other area ski trails.

The **Murphy Lake Ranger Station** also maintains numerous ski trails. Most popular are the **Grave Creek Road trails** 16 miles southeast of Eureka off US 93. Maintained by the Ten Lakes Snowmobile Club, the complex has 35 km Easiest and 10 km More Difficult trails. The **Therriault area**, having 16 km of intermittedly groomed More Difficult and two km Most Difficult trails, is accessed from a trailhead at the junction of FS Roads 756 and 7077. Contact the ranger station for detailed information on these and other area ski trails.

Flathead National Forest Ski Trails

Skiing the **Essex Trail Complex** from the famed Isaac Walton Inn (see *Hotels, Motels & B&Bs*) can be very enjoyable, especially if you combine it with a stay at the inn, or at least a warming bowl of soup. Park at the inn. There's a $5 per-person trail fee. The trails are maintained and groomed by the inn. The seven trails include 16.3 km Easiest, 12.5 km More Difficult and two km Most Difficult.

Glacier Wilderness Ranch, 20 miles east of Hungry Horse on US 2, has 20.2 km of intermittently groomed trails over old Hwy. 2. They range from Easiest to Most Difficult.

Round Meadows, 15 miles northwest of Whitefish on the Star Meadows Road (Tally Lake Ranger District), has 5.9 km intermittedly groomed Easiest and 1.5 km Most Difficult trails.

Blacktail Mountain X-Country Ski Trails, on Blacktail Road eight miles west of Lakeside above the west shore of Flathead Lake, has 10 km Easiest and 29.5 km More Difficult intermittently groomed trails. For grooming information, call Flathead County Parks at ☎ 406-758-5800. A map is available from the District Ranger office in Bigfork (☎ 406-862-2508).

Big Mountain Ski & Summer Resort has 10 km of groomed cross-country ski trails.

Cross-country skiing or snowshoeing to **Garnet Ghost Town** over a groomed road offers a memorable experience. See *Snowmobiling*.

Snowmobiling

If you enjoy sledding, Glacier Country is your kind of place. Gravel and dirt Forest Service and logging roads become winter snowmobile routes. Sure, there's a faction in favor of cutting the noisy machines way back in Montana's national forests, but it seems unlikely that such a popular form of recreation will suffer serious setbacks. Be aware that snowmobiles, like wheeled vehicles, are off-limits in designated Wilderness Areas.

Observing safety rules, wearing proper snowmobile garb, avoiding avalanche danger areas and being prepared for emergencies are hallmarks of safe and enjoyable sledding. See avalanche warning information on pages 46 and 200 for advice regarding these and other vital concerns.

The US Forest Service, Northern Region, makes available descriptive brochures listing marked snowmobile trails on the Lolo, Flathead, Kootenai and Bitterroot National Forests. Copies are available at ranger district offices or by contacting the Northern Region Supervisor. Contact Travel Montana to request a copy of *Montana Snowmobiling Guide* describing trail systems throughout the state. See *Information Sources*, page 64.

DON'T MISS So many hundreds of square miles of prime snowmobiling terrain are out there that you may wonder where to begin. A suggestion: start with a visit to **Garnet Ghost Town** (see page 454) over the **Garnet National Winter Recreation Trail System**. The road linking Garnet with MT 200, and the upper portion of Bear Gulch Road from I-90, are groomed but not plowed in winter. Snowmobilers, cross-country skiers and snowshoers, rejoice! Garnet Ghost Town, tucked away in the Garnet Range, is well worth a visit anytime. In deep winter, when snow piles up around the old cabins and kisses the eaves, you can get a real feel for what it must have been like to live there year-round. Miners of yore seem to speak in the silence and the night sky is a'glitter with stars. Staying in one of the old cabins, made cozy by wood stoves, is a memorable experience (see *Hotels, Motels & B&Bs*). A few Garnet trails are for skiers only; be sure to observe signs. The Garnet System has 110 miles of groomed and ungroomed trails offering a variety of riding conditions. Some climb to 7,000 feet and offer splendid views. Contact the Garnet Resource Area, Bureau of Land Management, 3255 Fort Missoula Rd., Missoula, MT 59801 (☎ 406-329-3914) to obtain a Garnet area map and brochure, and to be apprised of snow conditions.

The **Seeley Lake** area has over 250 miles of groomed trails forking in all directions from the town of Seeley Lake and the Clearwater Valley floor. A trail connects with the Missoula Trail System to the southwest and another connects with the Lincoln Trail System to the southeast. Seeley Lake itself is unsafe for snowmobiling. Maps and brochures are available from the Seeley Lake Ranger District, the Seeley-Condon Chamber of Commerce, the Drift Riders Snowmobile Club (PO Box 174, Seeley Lake, MT 59868), and area businesses. Contact one of the above for information on special winter events.

Missoula sits in the middle of three major snowmobile systems offering over 75 miles of groomed trails: the **Lolo Pass Sports Area**, the **Miller Creek** area and **Blue Mountain**. Contact the Missoula Ranger District of the Lolo National Forest or the Missoula Snow Goers (Rt. 2, Mallard Estates No. 20, Missoula, MT 59801) for trail maps and other information.

The **Superior Ranger District of the Lolo National Forest** maintains over 150 miles of snowmobile trails in the rugged Bitterroot Mountains. Trails for all skill levels range from groomed family trails to difficult signed-only trails. Obtain a detailed brochure and map from the district office.

The scenic **Skalkaho Pass** area, in the Sapphire Mountains, offers virtually unlimited play for all skill levels. The trailhead is 15 miles east of Hamilton. You can also reach the pass from MT 1 below Georgetown Lakes. For further information, contact the Darby Ranger District of the Bitterroot National Forest.

The **Kootenai National Forest** has over 350 miles of groomed snowmobile trails. Many more miles of ungroomed terrain make this a sledder's dream. Tiny **Yaak** (see *Touring*) sits smack dab in the middle of some of the best snow you'll ever rev a sled over. Another big trail system surrounds **Turner Mountain Ski Area**, between Yaak and Libby in the Purcell Mountains. Yet more terrain awaits in the **Cabinet Mountains** and the **Ten Lakes Area** southeast of Eureka. Obtain a map from the Kootenai National Forest Supervisor, Montana Department of Fish, Wildlife & Parks or the Libby, Tobacco Valley or Troy Chambers of Commerce (see *Information Sources*, pages 357, 66, 356 respectively).

*You may also wish to contact the **Lincoln County Sno-Kats** (PO Box 1180, Libby, MT 59923; ☎ 406-293-8644 or 295-5858) or the **Ten Lakes Snowmobile Club** (PO Box 131, Fortine, MT 59919; ☎ 406-882-4474). Special rides and events are held throughout the season.*

The **Stillwater State Forest** offers little recreation in summer, but comes into its own in winter. The popular snowmobiling area includes an extensive system of groomed trails winding through the Forest and the Whitefish Divide area north of Big Mountain Ski Resort. A smaller trail system, ungroomed or intermittently groomed, covers rugged terrain between Hungry Horse and the Great Bear Wilderness. Yet another is east of Polson and Flathead Lake. A map/brochure can be obtained by contacting the Flathead National Forest Supervisor's office, the Hungry Horse/Glacier View Ranger District or the Tally Lake Ranger District.

*Area snowmobile clubs include **Flathead Snowmobile Association** (PO Box 5041, Kalispell, MT 59903; ☎ 406-752-0827), **South Fork Snowmobile Assoc.** (PO Box 190250, Hungry Horse, MT 59919; ☎ 406-387-5514) and the **Mission Mountain Snowmobile Club** (2375 Mud Lake Trail, Polson, MT 59860).*

Glacier Country

The **Skyland-Two Medicine Trail System**, south of Marias Pass on US 2, includes 34.3 miles of easily accessed groomed trails and 27.3 miles of ungroomed trails east of the Great Bear Wilderness on the Flathead and Lewis & Clark National Forests. Trailheads are at the Summit of Marias Pass and at the Skyland Parking Area west of the Pass. Contact the Hungry Horse Ranger Station to obtain a map/brochure.

Snowmobile Tours, Rentals, Lodgings & Other Services

See *Hotels, Motels & B&Bs* for other lodgings offering convenience for snowmobilers.

Adventure Motorsports offers snowmobile and accessory rentals seven days a week. 1805 Hwy. 2 West, Columbia Falls, MT 59912; ☎ 406-892-2752. www.adventuremotorsports.com.

Bitterroot Adventures has guided snowmobile rides and rentals in the Bitterroot Valley. 566 Queens Way, Hamilton, MT 59840; ☎ 406-961-3392.

Canyon Creek Cat House, at the Canyon Creek Trailhead on the North Fork Road up from Columbia Falls, rents Arctic Cats, clothing and other necessities for a memorable ride. PO Box 381, West Glacier, MT 59936; ☎ 800-933-5133 or 406-888-5109.

Columbia Saw & Skidoo leads guided snowmobile tours on the Flathead Trail System, rentals and park & ride service. 30 9th St. East, Columbia Falls, MT 59912; ☎ 800-221-5098.

Double Arrow Resort offers snowmobiling from your cabin or room. Snowmobile rentals available. Dog sled and horse-drawn sleigh rides are also available. PO Box 747, Seeley Lake, MT 59868; ☎ 800-468-0777 or 406-677-2777. Fax 406-677-2922.

McAfée Lodge offers guided snowmobile tours, rentals and park & ride service in the Libby Trail System. Rt. 1, Yaak River Rd., Troy, MT 59935; ☎ 406-295-4880.

Middlefork Outdoor Recreation runs guided snowmobile tours on the Flathead Trail System, rentals and park & ride service. PO Box 395, Martin City, MT 59926; ☎ 406-387-5556.

Seeley Lake Fun Center rents Arctic Cats. PO Box 1200/Hwy. 83 N., Seeley Lake, MT 59868; ☎ 406-677-CATS. Fax 406-677-3692.

Sno-Slip Rentals offers guided snowmobile tours on Marias Pass trails, and rentals. 12 Luedtke Rd., Cut Bank, MT 59427; ☎ 406-873-4780.

Summit Station, on the Marias Pass Trail System, has guided tours, rentals and park & ride service. Box 167, East Glacier, MT 59434; ☎ 406-226-4428.

Tamaracks Resort, in the Lolo National Forest at the north end of Seeley Lake, has snowmobile rentals and packages. PO Box 929, Seeley Lake, MT 59868; ☎ 406-677-2433.

Unlimited Fun runs guided snowmobile tours on the Flathead Trail System, and rentals. 1805 Hwy. 2 West, Columbia Falls, MT 59912; ☎ 406-892-7676.

Dogsledding

Sledding at the speed of dog is one of the pleasantest ways to enjoy snowtime. The speed is slow enough to enable you to really see the land and the creatures of winter. The gentle shhhh shhh of sled runners over snow and the barking of dogs reflect the aura of winter. If you are a dog lover like me (four Humane Society "finds" at last count), you'll get into interacting with these enthusiastic canines. The following dog sledders offer rides.

Dog Sled Adventures' lead dog Phazer and team of husky, wolf, greyhound and shepherd mixes mush a 12-mile loop through the Stillwater State Forest. Reservations required. Box 34, Olney, MT 59927; ☎ 406-881-BARK.

Snowcrest Dog Sled Adventures' Alaskan huskies will take you on day-long and overnight trips. PO Box 935, Seeley Lake, MT 59868; ☎ 800-677-3004 or 406-677-3025.

Ice Skating

Whitefish Ice Rink, operated by the Whitefish Parks & Recreation Dept., offers public skating seven days a week. Also, skating lessons. For current rink times, ☎ 406-863-2470 or 863-2477.

Blade Running

It's a toss-up whether to list this far-out on-the-edge new sport under *Adventures on Snow* or *In the Air*. It's not for everyone. Only expert skiers with at least 5,000 parachute jumps under their belts need apply. As a spectator sport, it's a wow a minute. What these guys do is jump out of a helicopter wearing skis and activating a parachute-like canopy. Once on the ground, they thread a slalom course, soaring back into the air and down again, skiing downslope to a finish line. In a Glacier Country sanscopter version, blade runners soar from the top of Big Mountain Ski Resort's Inspiration ski run, run the slalom and soar into the air again before skiing downslope. Watching these guys soar overhead with colorful canopies eating the air is thrill city.

You can trek to **Big Mountain** in early April to watch a annual blade running competition, or contact technical director B.J. Worth at ☎ 406-862-5484 (fax 406-862-9020) to find out how you can qualify to become a blade runner.

■ Adventures in the Air

Flightseeing

Flightseeing permits wide-angle views of Glacier Country's fabulous scenery. Plane and chopper flights are popular over Glacier National Park. Flights are generally under $100 per hour for fixed-wing craft, over $100 for helicopters. The following firms offer scenic flights. Some also offer charter flights.

Glacier Heli-Tours leads scenic helicopter tours and half-hour and one-hour narrated flights over Glacier National Park in four-seat and six-seat Bell helicopters; also, custom sightseeing flights and drop-offs outside the Park and in wilderness areas. PO Box 528 (11950 Hwy. 2 East), West Glacier, MT 59936; 800-879-9310 or 406-387-4141.

Hamilton Aviation has scenic flights of the Bitterroot Valley. They also have rental planes. C8 Hamilton Airport Road, Hamilton, MT 59840; ☎ 406-363-3833.

Holman Aviation, based at Glacier National Park International Airport, offers scenic overflights of Glacier Park and the Bob Marshall Wilderness in Cessna 172s and twin-engine 340s. ☎ 406-755-5362.

Homestead Helicopters, Inc., based at Missoula International Airport, offers scenic tours and charter services. ☎ 406-544-0402.

Kruger Helicop-Tours offers half-hour and one-hour flights over the Park in four-passenger choppers. Box 235, Lakeside, MT 59922; ☎ 406-387-4565 or 857-3893.

Minuteman Aviation, Inc., based at Missoula International Airport, offers Lear Jet charter service anywhere in the Lower 48, Alaska and Canada. They also offer scenic helicopter tours. ☎ 800-926-7481 or 406-728-9363.

Red Eagle Aviation, operating out of Kalispell City Airport, offers 70-minute flights over Glacier National Park. Rentals available. ☎ 406-755-2376.

Western Montana Aviation offers scenic flights of the Bitterroot Valley. they also have rental planes. 3925 Flying Lane, Stevensville, MT 59870; ☎ 406-777-2410.

Hot-Air Balloon Rides

Take a spacious valley surrounded by high mountains, combine it with the right humidity and wind currents, add a popular tourist area, and you'll find hot-air balloons. Three hot-air balloonists take passengers on rides over the Flathead Valley. Advance reservations are advised, but spur-of-the-moment requests may be honored. Most flights end with traditional champagne or cider toasts.

Air Big Sky Balloon Adventures' pilot Darren Kling of Whitefish has two balloons ready to lift you off into the wide blue. ☎ 406-862-3432.

Fantasy Flights offers daily one-hour flights in early morning and before sunset. 107 W. Bluegrass Dr., Kalispell; ☎ 406-755-4172.

Let's Go Ballooning! owner John Warren brings his colorful craft to whatever launch site customers request. Flights last about an hour. ☎ 406-387-4646.

Gliding

Gliding isn't for everyone, but if you are so inclined you can test your mettle with one of two Kalispell soaring clubs.

Glacier Eagle Soaring Club uses a Blanik L-13 with a 54-foot wing-span. The club operates out of the Kalispell Airport and offers demonstration rides. ☎ 406-881-2440.

Flight Training, also operating out of the Kalispell Airport, schedules flights until the end of October. Weekends are favored. ☎ 406-755-8095.

■ Wildlife Watching

Designated wildlife watching sites and refuges may seem redundant when wildlife turn up virtually everywhere in Glacier Country. Refuges exist primarily for wildlife protection, secondarily for wildlife watching.

Viewing wildlife is much like taking a peek at people through the windows of their homes. The wildlife you watch are doing their thing and could care less about you unless you disturb them, and that's a no-no. Serendipitous encounters are wonderfully rewarding.

AUTHOR TIP *The safest way to view wildlife is through binoculars or spotting scopes. If the animal stops feeding or resting, you've come too close. Ditto, if it moves either toward or away from you, if it makes unusual sounds, if it paws the ground or swings its head, if its neck hair or feathers stand up, or if it appears uneasy or stressed in any way.*

Glacier Country has four national wildlife preserves and a national fish hatchery.

The National Bison Range

The National Bison Range, on the Flathead Indian Reservation near Moise, was established in 1908 to preserve remnants of the buffalo that once roamed the prairies of the West in seas of black. The Range's 18,500 acres of steep grassy hills and coniferous forests support some 300-500 buffalo. You also may see elk, pronghorn antelope, white-tailed and mule deer, mountain goats and more than 200 species of birds. You can drive a half-hour loop, but you'll see more on the 19-mile loop. No off-road hiking except on designated trails. You may see newborn calves in mid-April through May, bugling elk in September and bighorn sheep in summer. The visitor center has wildlife exhibits. Open daily in summer, 8-8; weekdays only in winter, 8-4:30. Per-vehicle entrance fee. ☎ 406-644-2211.

Ninepipe National Wildlife Refuge

Ninepipe National Wildlife Refuge, FWP & Tribal Wildlife Management Areas is a wetland complex containing over 800 glacial potholes and a 1,770-acre reservoir. Birds love it! A viewing area is off US 93 on the east side of the reservoir. An access road and barrier-free paved trail offer waterfowl and shorebird viewing. To see nesting great blue herons and cormorants, follow SR 212 to a dirt road on the west side of the reservoir. Turn west off US 93 a mile north of SR 212 to get a good look at curious glacial pothole ponds and the myriad wildfowl inhabiting them. Raptor viewing is good in winter. Be aware that the area is open to fall hunting. ☎ 406-644-2211.

Swan River National Wildlife Refuge

Swan River National Wildlife Refuge's swampland and coniferous forest seem as undisturbed as it was centuries ago. Elk, moose, deer, grizzly and black bears browse the forest while 171 bird species, including bald eagles and great blue herons, inhabit both forest and wetlands. A Swan River canoe trip (see *Canoeing*) is the best way to see wildfowl. The refuge is closed March 1-July 1 but canoeing is permitted. Watch for the Swan River National Wildlife Refuge sign on MT 83, at the southern end of Swan Lake. Access is via Bog Road. Expect it to impassable in spring. You can hoof it year-round. ☎ 406-755-7870.

Lee Metcalf National Wildlife Refuge

Lee Metcalf National Wildlife Refuge, in the Bitterroot Valley, is 2,800 acres of wetlands, river bottom woodlands and open fields hospitable to migratory wildfowl, owls, muskrats, otters, beavers, white-tailed deer, coyotes and a chorus of songbirds. Foot trails from a day-use area on Wildfowl Lane meander through pine and cottonwood stands to the Bitterroot River. At Stevensville, turn east onto MT 203 (Eastside Highway) to Wildfowl Lane. ☎ 406-777-5552.

While in the vicinity, stop in at the Stevensville Ranger Station for interpretive trail guides to the nearby **Willoughby Environmental Education Area** and **Charles Water Nature Trail**. ☎ 406-777-5461. **Creston National Fish Hatchery** raises rainbow, cutthroat and bull trout and kokanee salmon. Raceways adjacent to the building allow for fish viewing. Spawning occurs inside. Displays explain how fish eggs are fertilized and how they develop and hatch. Kokanee salmon spawning is between early November and the end of January. Not surprisingly, fish-eating birds such as osprey, great blue herons and belted kingfishers are seen in the vicinity. Canada geese broods frequent the picnic area in summer. The hatchery is off MT 35, just east of Creston. Open daily, 7:30-4. ☎ 406-755-7870.

Wild Horse Island State Park (see *Boat Tours*) is a big, fabulous wildlife viewing site boasting some 100 bighorn sheep, a few wild horses, coyotes, nesting bald eagles, osprey, waterfowl, songbirds and solitude. Rent a boat at Big Arm and beach it on the island, but be careful not to intrude on private property. Hike the numerous wildlife trails circling the island and climbing into the hills. ☎ 406-752-5501.

Kookoosint Sheep Viewing Area is a meadow adjacent to MT 200, eight miles east of Thompson Falls. Watch for interpretive signs along the highway. Herds of as many as 100 bighorn sheep are often seen here between Oct. 15 and May 1. Peak viewing is during the breeding season, Nov. 15-Dec. 31. Sheep may also be seen in an area about seven miles on either side of the area. ☎ 406-826-3821.

Vinal Creek, near Yaak on the Kootenai National Forest, is in a moist, coastal climate zone that supports old-growth forests. A stand of Western larch boasts trees four feet in diameter. Red cedars at the creek crossing measure over 25 feet around, providing habitat for pileated woodpeckers, barred owls, goshawks and warblers.

Summer on Seeley Lake.

The marked trail is off FS 746 paralleling the upper Yaak River. ☎ 406-293-6211.

Seeley Lake supports a large colony of nesting common loons. If you've never heard loon calls, you have a treat in store. The calls resounding over the lake are the quintessential sounds of the north country. Penetrating the clear air, hanging hauntingly, each call has a distinctive meaning. Signed loon viewing stations on MT 83 are at the north end of Salmon Lake, at the Seeley Lake Ranger Station, and at the northern end of Lake Alva. Another viewing area is at a campground where the Clearwater River leaves Seeley Lake. Obtain a *Loons of Seeley Lake* brochure at the Ranger Station. ☎ 406-677-2233.

Murphy Lake, 14 miles south of Eureka on US 93, is also a nesting area for common loons. Pick up a brochure at the trailhead and hike a mile to an observation platform from which you may see loons, horned grebes, bald eagles, osprey, and waterfowl. The area is heavily forested with adjacent marshland where moose are sometimes spotted. Take FS 7008 off US 93. ☎ 406-882-4451.

Kootenai River below Libby Dam (see *Touring*) is a prime bald eagle and osprey nesting area and migration viewing site. The birds are especially numerous in the fall when the raptors gather below the dam to catch spawning kokanee salmon. Eagle migration begins in October, peaks in mid-November and tapers off in late December. Large waterfowl overflights pass through in March. ☎ 406-293-5577.

Kelly Island proves that, in Montana, you needn't go far afield to view wildfowl. This popular wildfowl habitat is reached from Missoula by taking Mullan Road (about four miles west of Reserve Street) to the Kelly Island Fishing Access Site. Backwater sloughs provide resting spots for large concentrations of wildfowl. Great blue herons and Canada geese nest here, as well as red-tailed hawks, American kestrels and great horned owls. You can boat or wade to the island, but don't attempt to wade in periods of high water. ☎ 406-542-5500.

Skalkaho Wildlife Preserve is in the Skalkaho Basin, reached from US 93 via MT 38 and FS Road 1352 from the top of Skalkaho Pass. The Preserve turns up moose, elk, mule deer, badgers, coyotes, black bears and bevvies of birds. Mountain goats frequent a ridge around the basin. Look for a wildlife interpretive sign and orientation maps as you turn off MT 38. Numerous hiking trails offer good wildlife spotting. ☎ 406-363-7161.

Garnet Ghost Town (see *Touring* and *Snowmobiling*) isn't a designated wildlife viewing area, but you're bound to spot some of the small mammals that have burrowed their way into the lore of the West. Stomping noises inside abandoned buildings may indicate a nest of packrats. Pine squirrels skitter through conifers and northern pocket gophers and Columbian ground squirrels scurry about on the ground; chipmunks, too. In winter, you may see snowshoe hares. Did you know that porcupines climb trees? Yellow bellied marmots like to den in hillside rocks.

■ State Parks

Most Glacier Country state parks offer opportunities to enjoy the region's runaway beauty. Many are beside lakes or rivers and have boat ramps and swimming areas. These parks emphasize recreation rather than human or natural history, strong features of parks in other travel regions. **Flathead Lake's six state parks** are the showpieces of the parks system. Five have campgrounds and boating facilities. **Wild Horse Island** (see *Boat Tours* and *Wildlife Watching*) is the exception. See *Camping* for information on full-service state parks.

AUTHOR TIP

Purchase a parks pass if you plan on using the parks system often, perhaps swimming or boating at lakeside parks or visiting day-use parks. Non-residents can purchase permits at any FWP office or park visitor center for, at this writing, an annual fee of $25. Montana residents pay $20. Day-use fees for vehicles not displaying a sticker are about $3.

Day-use state parks appealing to recreationists include **Frenchtown Pond** (see *Kid Stuff*) and **Lone Pine**. The latter is a 200-acre park overlooking Flathead Lake and the Big Mountain Ski Area. On tap are a visitor center with interpretive displays, a picnic area, an archery range and hiking trails. Lone Pine State Park is four miles south of Kalispell on Foy Road, then one mile east on Lone Pine Road. ☎ 406-755-2706.

Day-use state parks celebrating places or events with historical significance include **Fort Owen** (see *Touring*) and **Council Grove**. The latter is on the site of the 1855 Hellgate Treaty signing that established the Flathead Reservation. Interpretive signs. On Mullan Road, 10 miles west of Missoula. ☎ 406-542-5500.

■ Special Interest Adventures

Most adventure trip guides are eager to share their knowledge of Glacier Country's ecology, wildlife, history and culture. But perhaps you want a deeper understanding. The following farms, organizations, excursions and outfitters will help.

Montana Rockies Rail Tours

Montana Rockies Rail Tours offers the ultimate special interest experience: a seven-day, six-night rail tour beginning and ending at Spokane that describes a circle route whose highlights include Glacier National Park, the Plains Indian Museum in Browning, the Lewis and Clark Interpretive Center in Great Falls, a Gates of the Mountains cruise and a wealth of other museum visits and cultural experiences. The tour features two full days aboard the Montana Daylight train and overnights at Glacier Park Lodge and other fine hostelries. Contact your travel agent or write: Montana Rockies Rail Tours, Inc., 1055 Baldy Park Ave., Sandpoint, ID 83864. ☎ 208-265-8618 or 800-519-RAIL.

Native American Experiences

Blackfeet Historic Site Tours and Tipi Village, offered by Curly Bear Wagner, cultural officer for the Blackfeet Nation, and traditionalist Blackfeet artist Darrell Norman, provides an in-depth look at Blackfeet life ways and traditions. Guests stay in a tipi circle encampment on Norman's ranch near Browning. Meals, including fry bread and other traditional foods, are served family-style at a nearby ranch home housing artisans' workshops.

"We give people a very clear understanding of who the Blackfeet people are and what we are doing as a modern people, not just as antiques of the past," says Norman in explaining the program. Several choices are available. The Cultural Camp Package includes two nights in the tipi village, a full-day tour of Blackfeet historic sites and a full-day workshop on beading, leather work and other traditional arts and crafts. Special activities packages include a full-day arts & crafts workshop, telling campfire stories by Blackfeet elders, and a mini-pow-wow. Blackfeet Tours & Encampment, Box 271, Babb, MT 59401; ☎ 800-215-2395.

Native Ed-Ventures offers a variety of culturally appropriate tours and experiences on the Flathead Reservation. Customized itineraries include a homestay with a Native family, full-day *Walk Through Time* tours and half-day *History, Heritage and Culture* tours led by tribal guides. Tours visit important sites on the Reservation and offer insight into the history, culture and lifeways of the Salish, Kootenai and Pend d'Orielle people. Highlights are **The People's Center** (see *Touring*) and the **National Bison Range** (see *Wildlife Watching*).

If you want to attend one of the Flathead Reservation's two July pow-wows but feel timid or out of place, Native Ed-Ventures will arrange a personal guide to clue you in on pow-wow etiquette, the meanings of the various dances, and other aspects of a pow-wow. Traditional encampments beside Flathead Lake, complete with stories, drumming and dancing, are also available. Native Ed-Ventures will also arrange for guided fishing trips or other outdoor activities on the Reservation. Box 278, Pablo, MT 59855; ☎ 800-883-5344 or 406-883-5344. Fax 406-675-0260.

Farm Tours

Echo Lake Llama Farms' Reece family welcome visitors to Pet, brush or walk a llama on their small farm on Echo Lake. ☎ 406-837-5869 for directions and to arrange a visit.

Royal Tine Elk Farm owner Justin Haveman offers tours of his 600-acre elk farm near Woods Bay. Admission. ☎ 406-837-3557 for directions and to arrange a tour.

Historical & Naturalist Tours

Garnet Historical Tours & W/J Ranch serves up tours of Garnet Ghost Town with their horseback, surrey, hay wagon and stagecoach rides. The ghost town (see *Touring*) is a fascinating place made doubly interesting by a guided tour. 36085 Washo Rd., Potomac, MT 59823; ☎ 406-244-5523.

Glacier Institute is a private, non-profit outdoor education organization designed to promote understanding of the cultural and natural resources of the Crown of the Continent/Glacier National Park Ecosystem. Over 100 youth and adult courses are offered annually. Seminars take a closer look at the Park's many features than Park naturalists are able to provide. Programs are designed to satisfy your curiosity about the Park's wildlife, geology, flora, birds – even the stars in the sky over the Park. Seminars lasting from a single day to several days begin in March and extend into September. Catalogs are available. Instructors are specialists in their respective fields. Enrolled students can stay dirt cheap at Glacier Park Field Camp, a rustic facility just inside the west entrance to the Park. PO Box 7457, Kalispell, MT 59904; ☎ 406-755-1211.

WW Outfitters runs special wildlife and photography tours of the Bitterroot Valley via 4X4 vehicles. 1313B Old Darby Rd., Darby, MT 59829; ☎ 406-821-3648.

■ Kid Stuff

KID-FRIENDLY Kids have it good in Glacier Country. 'Most anything grownups can do, kids can do too. Parents know what their offspring like to do and will find it under *Horseback Riding, Guest Ranches, River Floating* and other adventure headings. Some adventures may be too extreme for your tagalongs; ask just how extreme when researching a trip or stay. Some guides and ranches set minimum age limits. Know your young'uns and what they're up for.

Water and kids go together like peanut butter and jelly. River floats are obvious child-pleasers, but sometimes a simple fun time splashing and swimming is in order. Most towns have a municipal pool. **Kalispell's Bruckhauser Pool** in Woodland Park (see *Touring*) is a stand-out. The **Columbia Falls pool** is in Pinewood Park, just off US 2. **City Beach in Whitefish** is apt to be crowded, less so the **park below Polson's Flathead River Bridge**. We took our crew there one afternoon and had a high old time swimming, splashing and picnicking. Waterslides are always fun. **Big Sky Waterslides**, just east of Columbia Falls on US 2, has four twister slides, two 200-foot kiddie slides, an inner tube River Ride slide, water balloon games, a picnic area and more. ☎ 406-892-2139.

If you are in the **Missoula** vicinity and yearn for a splashing good time, hie to **Frenchtown Pond State Park** off I-90 West. No dogs allowed, but otherwise this sizeable pond is reminiscent of an old-time swimming hole. ☎ 406-542-5500.

Every lakeside state park has a swimming area shallow enough for young children. See *State Parks*.

Kids can be educated the fun way by visiting the **Rocky Mountain Elk Visitor Center** in Missoula, the **People's Center** at Pablo, and any number of other museums (see *Touring*).

The hands-on **Big Mountain Environmental Education Center** at Summit House, staffed by naturalists from the Tally Lake Ranger District, is a fascinating way for kids to learn about local animals. Special programs may be offered in summer.

In 1998, **Glacier National Park** turned a c. 1913 ranger cabin at St. Mary into a hands-on just-for-kids educational center. Special programs were on offer. Hopefully, the center caught on and is still operating. Glacier Park has several on-going programs tailored for youngsters. The **Junior Ranger program** for ages six-12 is a tried-and-true winner. Inquire at Apgar or St. Mary Visitor Centers about Junior Ranger and other kid-related programs.

If you've reached the point where your tagalongs need a silly break, check out the **KIDZ Fun Center** at Northgate Plaza off North Reserve Street, south of I-90, in Missoula. ☎ 406-549-7720.

Kids-only camps or trips are sometimes appealing to both kids and parents.

Ecollama Wilderness Llama Trips offers June and July three-day Children's Wilderness Journeys for boys and girls aged 9-13. PO Box 8342, Missoula, MT 59807; ☎ 406-542-1625.

Glacier Institute's week-long youth programs include *Young Naturalist* for ages 9-11, *Wild Glacier Adventures* wherein young teens learn back country skills, *Ecology Afield* for older teens and young teen girls' *Naturalist Adventures*. Numerous day programs are also available. See *Special Interest Adventures* above for more information. PO Box 7457, Kalispell, MT 59904; ☎ 406-755-1211. **Rich's Double Arrow Outfitters** offers week-long *Youth Horsemanship Camps*, for ages 9-18, in June, July and August. Basic Western horsemanship and outdoor ethics are taught. Jack and Belinda Rich, PO Box 495, Seeley Lake, MT 59868; ☎ 406-677-2317.

Festivals & Special Events

 Glacier Country comes alive with musical, theatrical and just plain fun events. Annual events are listed below. Contact the planners for exact dates. Ongoing events and theatre companies are listed at the end of this section. Contact the chamber of commerce in the area you plan on visiting for information on other festivities, many of them spur-of-the-moment. Contact Big Mountain Ski & Summer Resort's Recreation and Events Department for ski race and workshop dates (☎ 800 858-3913 or 406-862-1900).

On-Going Events

Bigfork Summer Playhouse: Memorial Day and Labor Day bracket performances presented by this accomplished theatre company. Most seasons include five plays/Broadway musicals. The venue: a 430-seat theatre on Electric Avenue. Box 456, Bigfork, MT 59911; ☎ 406-837-4886.

Depot Park in Kalispell is the scene of Wednesday lunchtime music between noon and 1 pm in the months of June, July and August.

The **Flathead Music Festival** sprawls over three summer weeks in venues that include Whitefish, Kalispell and Bigfork. Musical styles run a gamut from jazz to classical to old-time fiddlin'. ☎ 406-257-0787 to request a current schedule.

The **Fort Missoula Amphitheatre** is the place for an assortment of July and August events that include Charlie Russell's *Montana!*, an extravagant production highlighting the state in the artist's lifetime. ☎ 800-655-3871 to request a current schedule of events.

Out to Lunch is a weekly Wednesday performing arts festival featuring musicians, choirs, dancers, theatre plus food vendors. Missoula Downtown Assoc., 101 East Main, Missoula, MT 59802; ☎ 406-543-4238.

Riverbend Concert Series present concerts in the park every Sunday. Elna Darrow, PO Box 400, Bigfork, MT 59911; ☎ 406-837-4848.

Shakespeare in the Parks performs statewide. SUB Room 354, Montana State University, Bozeman, MT 59717; ☎ 406-994-3901.

Whitefish Theatre Company has been presenting popular plays for over 20 years. Productions span the calendar year. PO Box 1463, Whitefish, MT 59937; ☎ 406-862-5371.

January

Winter Microbrew Festival, featuring seasonal beers and great food, is held at Big Mountain in late January. ☎ 406-862-2905. Fax 406-862-2955.

Western Montana Wine Festival is held in Missoula in late January. Nate Kohler, 100 Madison, Missoula, MT 59802; ☎ 406-728-3100.

AUTHOR TIP *Seeley Lake Winterfest, a week-long late-January hoop-de-do, kicks off with a Christmas tree bonfire and includes motorcycle ice drags, sled dog races and rides, a softball tournament snow country-style, fireworks, Driftriders snowmobile poker run, horse drawn sleigh rides, snow sculpture competition, a sanctioned Rocky Mountain Snowcross Race, a Nordic ski race. Seeley Lake Area Chamber of Commerce, ☎ 406-677-2880.*

February

Whitefish Winter Carnival, held in early February, is a three-day celebration of winter that includes parades, dinners, sidewalk sales and other fun activities. Kris Fuehrer, PO Box 1120, Whitefish, MT 59937; ☎ 406-862-2597 or 862-3501. Fax 406-862-9494.

Snowboard Jam, at Montana Snowbowl in early February, features two days of on-the-edge snowboard events that include Giant Slalom, Slope-Style Jam and Monster Air contest. Cash purse and prizes. PO Box 8226, Missoula, MT 59807; ☎ 406-549-9777.

Race To The Sky Sled Dog Race in mid-February emulates Alaska's Iditarod and is Montana's premier winter sporting event. The 300-mile and 500-mile races criss-cross the Continental Divide at elevations up to 7,000 feet as they traverse the Helena-Lincoln-Seeley Lake-Missoula distance. Pam Otto, PO Box 30-MUSH, Helena, MT 59601; ☎ 406-442-4008.

Snowbowl Cup Gelande Championship, held at Montana Snowbowl in late February, is a major alpine ski jumping event. PO Box 8226, Missoula, MT 59807; ☎ 406-549-9777.

March

Northern Division Freestyle Championship, held at Montana Snowbowl in early March, is a USSA-sanctioned event drawing skiers to compete at moguls, freestyle and jumping. PO Box 8226, Missoula, MT 59807; ☎ 406-549-9777.

Annual Marshall Mountain Snowmobile Hillclimb Championship, held at Missoula in early March, is just what it sounds like. Bruch Doering, 5250 Marshall Canyon Rd., Missoula, MT 59802; ☎ 406-258-6000. Fax 406-259-2900.

Grape Expectations Wine & Food Festival at Big Mountain in early March benefits the American Cancer Society. Wine tasting and gourmet foods. ☎ 406-862-2900. Fax 406-862-2955.

Big Mountain Doug Betters Winter Classic in mid-March benefits children in need of medical care. The fun weekend features NFL players, actors and rodeo cowboys. Lots of activities and a country western dinner. ☎ 406-862-2900. Fax 406-862-2955.

Irish Fair and Music Festival celebrates St. Patrick's Day in Libby with a parade, Irish music and step dancers, Irish foods, Friday and Saturday night concerts featuring Irish performers and dancers. David. F. Latham, PO Box 946, Libby, MT 59923; ☎ 406-293-8202.

Spring Art & Craft Show kicks off Kalispell's arts & crafts season in mid-March. Janet Randall, PO Box 1684, Kalispell, MT 59903; ☎ 406-881-4288.

Snowbowl Hexathlon, held at Montana Snowbowl in mid-March, is a family event open to all ages and abilities. Appropriately modified events include downhill, ski jumping, slalom, giant slalom, bobsled and target shooting. PO Box 8226, Missoula, MT 59807; ☎ 406-549-9777.

Waitress Cup, held at Big Mountain in mid-March, is a zany ski race and skit put on by local waiters and waitresses. ☎ 406-862-2900. Fax 406-862-2955.

Annual Snow Rodeo and Spring Ski Race, held at the Izaac Walton Inn in late March, features hilarious family-oriented snow rodeo events. PO Box 653, Essex, MT 59916; ☎ 406-888-5700. Fax 406-888-5200.

April

Run For The Trees, an early April event in Missoula, celebrates Arbor Month with a 5K fun race and 5K walk for all ages. Kids games, door prizes and more. Missoula Parks & Recreation, 100 Hickory St., Missoula, MT 59801; ☎ 406-721-7275. Fax 406-523-2765.

Annual Furniture Race, at Big Mountain in mid-April, features competitors attaching skis or sleds to pieces of furniture and racing down a snow slope. Helmets required! ☎ 406-862-2911. Fax 406-862-2955.

International Wildlife Film Festival, held in Missoula in mid-April, is a juried film competition featuring wildlife films. Also workshops and panels on wildlife filmmaking. Amy Sperry, 802 East Front, Missoula, MT 59802; ☎ 406-728-9380. Fax 406-728-2881.

Annual Story Telling Conference, at Cut Bank in mid-April, features Blackfeet stories, chalk talking, ghost stories, folk music, cowboy poetry, top story tellers. Jewel Wolk, 326 5th Ave. S.E., Cut Bank, MT 59427; ☎ 406-873-2039. Fax 406-873-3341.

Bitterroot Horse Expo & Carnival is held in Hamilton in late April. Gary Wiley, ☎ 406-363-3411.

Annual Spring Cowboy Poker Ride, also in Hamilton in late April. Thadd Turner, PO Box 381, Hamiltin, MT 59840; ☎ 406-363-3059.

A Taste of Bigfork, a late April event, features a stroll through the resort town sampling restaurant offerings and dropping in on galleries and specialty shops. Laura Barrett, 408 Bridge St., Bigfork, MT 59911; ☎ 406-837-5507 or 837-5825.

May

Cherry Blossom Festival kicks off Bigfork's summer season in early May with a farmer's market, homes tour, arts & crafts and cherry desserts. Bigfork Chamber of Commerce, Bigfork, MT 59911; ☎ 406-837-5888.

AUTHOR TIP *Buffalo Feast & Pow-Wow, at St. Ignatius on the Flathead Indian Reservation, is a three-day mid-May pow-wow featuring war dances and stick games. Free feasting on a pit-roasted buffalo. Doug Allard, PO Box 460, St. Ignatius, MT 59865; ☎ 745-2951. Fax 406-745-2961.*

Kite Festival! Missoula Parks & Recreation throws a mid-May family party at Frenchtown. Bring your kites. Prizes and fun for all. ☎ 406-721-7275. Fax 406-523-2765.

Mullan Day is a mid-May St. Regis event featuring insight into the Mullan Road between Walla Walla, Washington and Fort Benton, Montana. Cathryn Strombo, 140 Mullan Rd. W., Superior, MT 59872; ☎ 406-822-4626.

Annual Whitewater Festival is a mid-May Bigfork event featuring down river and slalom kayak racing, wild mile triathlon and more. Garden Bar & Grill, 451 Electric Ave., Bigfork, MT 59911; ☎ 406-837-9914.

Stumptown Days, held in Whitefish in mid-May, celebrates the town's original name with sidewalk sales, chicken barbeque, live music and more. Whitefish Chamber of Commerce, 500 Depot St., Suite #303, Whitefish, MT 59937; ☎ 406-862-3501. Fax 406-862-9494.

NCHA Cutting Horse Show is held at Hamilton in late May. Sherry Lee, Hamilton, MT 59840; ☎ 406-363-5246.

AUTHOR TIP *Loon & Fish Festival is a late May event at Seeley Lake. Loon viewing with biologists on area lakes, early morning bird walks, educational loon and fish programs by Watchable Wildlife and US Forest Service, art show, kids' games, crafts, wildlife film festival. Dorothy Boulton, HC 31 Box 2995, Seeley Lake, MT 59868; ☎ 406-677-3276.*

St. Regis Flea Market, billed as Montana's largest flea market, is held at St. Regis Community Park over Memorial Day weekend. St. Regis Community Club, PO Box 278, St. Regis, MT 59866; ☎ 406-649-2342 or 649-2727. Fax 406-649-2300.

Garden City Microbrew Fest is an annual late May event in Missoula. Kevin Head, 158 Ryman, Missoula, MT 59807; ☎ 406-721-6061.

June

Whitefish Summer Games, in early June, is a mini-Olympics featuring a variety of sporting events. Visiting participants welcome. Whitefish Chamber of Commerce, PO Box 1120, Whitefish, MT 59937; ☎ 406-862-3501.

Annual Collector Doll Show & Competition is held at the Marcus Daly Mansion in early June. Doug Johnson, PO Box 223, Hamilton, MT 59840; ☎ 406-363-6004.

Wildhorse Plains Days is a three-day early June rodeo event. Mike Hashisaki, 141 River Rd., Box 9, Plains, MT 59859; ☎ 406-826-3202. Fax 406-826-3674.

Stevensville Western Days features arts, crafts, dining and dancing in mid-June. Bitterroot Chamber, 105 E. Main St., Stevensville, MT 59870; ☎ 406-363-2402.

Big Sky Fiber/Arts Festival is an unusual event held in Hamilton in early June. Sheep and angora goat exhibits, llama pack demo, working dogs, fashion show, skein contest, demos of spinning, weaving and other fiber arts. D. Hachenberger, 419 Dutch Hill Rd., Hamilton, MT 59840; ☎ 406-961-3058.

Montana Senior Games, for adults 50 and older, are held in Missoula in mid-June. Missoula Parks & Recreation, 100 Hickory St., Missoula, MT 59801; ☎ 406-721-7275. Fax 406-523-2765.

Lake to Lake Canoe Race starts on the Whitefish River and finishes in Kalispell. Whitefish Chamber of Commerce, PO Box 1120, Whitefish, MT 59937; ☎ 406-862-3501.

Annual Bitterroot Day celebrates Montana's state flower in late June with related presentations, bitterroot tastings and potted plants. Helen Ann Bibler, 205 Bedford, Hamilton, MT 59840; ☎ 406-363-3338.

Darby Fun Day is a Darby event held in late June. Debra Ragello, ☎ 406-821-4770.

July

The Annual Arlee Celebration has been going non-stop for over 100 years. This big three-day 4th of July competition pow-wow features a military veterans' parade of honor, traditional drumming, singing, dancing and games, rodeo, softball tournament, arts, crafts and food vendors. Well over 600 dancers, including the author of this book, danced in the 100th Anniversary pow-wow's Grand Entry. Les Bigcrane, PO Box 579, Pablo, MT 59855; ☎ 406-675-2700. Fax 406-675-2806.

4th of July Celebration – Seeley Lake-Style includes a parade, games for all, dog show, bed races, pig roast and fireworks. Seeley Lake Chamber of Commerce, PO Box 516-Seeley Lake, MT 59868; ☎ 406-677-2880.

Celebrate the 4th – An Art Affair is the theme of this Plains celebration. Arts & crafts sales and demonstrations, live music, team roping, rodeo, bull riding. Mike Hashisaki, 141 River Rd., Box 9, Plains, MT 59859; ☎ 406-826-3202. Fax 406-826-3674.

Free Pig Roast & Craft Show is an annual Essex 4th of July event. Stanton Creek Lodge, HC 36 Box 1C, Essex, MT 59916; ☎ 406-888-5040.

St. Regis July 4th Festivities include logging contests and games reflecting this small mountain town's culture. Paula Mintz, ☎ 406-649-2463.

Whitefish Annual Arts Festival is an early July event featuring children's activity booths, entertainment and art. Cross Currents School, 820 Ashar Ave., Whitefish, MT 59937; ☎ 406-862-5875.

Libby Logger Days, held in mid-July, celebrates logging traditions with contests, food booths, kids' events, logging demonstrations and more. Libby Chamber of Commerce, PO Box 704, Libby, MT 59923; ☎ 406-293-4167. Fax 406-293-3222.

North American Indian Days is looking at its 50th year. The three-day mid-July Browning celebration features a pow-wow, traditional dancing and drumming, crowning of Miss Blackfeet, parade, fun run and more. Blackfeet Tribe, PO Box 850, Browning, MT 59417; ☎ 406-338-7179. Fax 406-338-7501.

Chief Victor Days, a mid-July Victor event, features activities, fun, food and entertainment, all in the name of Chief Victor. Sheila Veerkamp, ☎ 406-363-1250.

Senior Pro Rodeo, held in Hamilton in mid-July, is a nationally sanctioned event drawing contestants from 12 states and Canada. Western and wildlife fine art show, cowboy poetry and music, local crafts, draft horse contests, quick draw auction, back country horsemanship clinic, raffles, kids' carnival. Steve Benedict, PO Box 668, Hamilton, MT 59840; ☎ 406-363-3010.

Summer Artists and Craftsmen of the Flathead Summer Show is a mid-July Kalispell event. Janet Randall, PO Box 1684, Kalispell, MT 59903; ☎ 406-881-4288.

Senior Pro Rodeo/Junior Rodeo is held at Cut Bank in mid-July. Cut Bank Area Chamber of Commerce, PO Box 1243, Cut Bank, MT 59427; ☎ 406-873-4041.

Taste of Missoula is in mid-July. Local restaurants feature food specialties from traditional to exotic. Music, clowns and more. YWCA, 1130 W. Broadway, Missoula, MT 59802; ☎ 406-543-6691. Fax 406-543-6777.

Bitterroot Valley Bluegrass Festival is a mid-July Hamilton event. This nationally recognized family festival features workshops on banjo, mandolin, fiddle and guitar. Parking lot picking. Bands, arts, crafts. Mark Dickerson, PO Box 1371, Hamilton, MT 59840; ☎ 406-363-2575 or 363-5450. Fax 406-363-2796.

Western Montana Arabian Horse Show is held in Hamilton in late July. G. Wiley, 100 Old Corvallis Rd., Hamilton, MT 59840; ☎ 406-363-3411.

Herron Park Horse Trials is a late July Kalispell event featuring dressage, cross-country and stadium jumping. Susan Smyth, PO Box 428, Whitefish, MT 59937; ☎ 406-862-6890. Fax 406-862-1318.

Lakeside Community Fair is a late July fun event. Kids' parade, arts & crafts, barbeque, silent auction, attic treasures, talent contest, duck races, farmers' market, live music. Jane Bennett, ☎ 406-844-2133.

Railroad Days in Alberton in late July features a parade, craft fair and celebration of Alberton's railroad past. Sandy Pocci, 103 River Rd., Alberton, MT 59820; ☎ 406-722-3316.

Darby Strawberry Festival, held in late July, is an old fashioned ice cream social with music by local musicians. Annual fundraiser for the Darby Fire Department. Janet Brock, Darby, ☎ 406-821-3480.

Standing Arrow Pow-Wow, at Elmo on the Flathead Indian Reservation, is a traditional pow-wow held in late July. Doug Juneau, PO Box 93, Elmo, MT 59915; ☎ 406-675-0160.

Summerfest/Squawfish Days is a two-day late July event in Thompson Falls. River races, games, crafts, melodrama, fun run and more. ☎ 406-827-4930.

Montana State Fiddlers Contest is a two-day late July event held in Polson. Watch and listen to kids and old-timers fiddling; street dance. Fred Buckley, 319 Old divide Rd., Roundup, MT 59072; ☎ 406-323-1198.

Arts In The Park is a two-day late July Kalispell juried art and crafts show with live music, food. Hockaday Art Center, 2nd Ave. East & 3rd St., Kalispell, MT 59901; ☎ 406-755-5268.

Bitterroot Valley Good Nations Pow-Wow, an annual late July event held in Hamilton, features all the color and excitement inherent in Native American pow-wows. T. Ghosthawk, PO Box 1421, Hamilton, MT 59840; ☎ 406-961-4705 or 642-3769.

Country Music Campout is on the shores of Bull Lake in late July. Similar campout in mid-August. B.J. Davis, 14799 Bull Lake Rd., Troy, MT 59935; ☎ 406-295-4358.

Lewis & Clark Days, at Cut Bank in late July, features a parade, free barbeque, Lewis & Clark costume contest, farmer's market, quilt show, kids' games, crafter's fair, lawnmower races and more. Cut Bank Area Chamber of Commerce, PO Box 1243, Cut Bank, MT 59427; ☎ 406-873-4041.

Art In The Park, sponsored by the Bitterroot Arts Guild, occurs in Hamilton in late July. Carolyn Kissil, PO Box 582, Victor, MT 59875; ☎ 406-642-3600.

Skydive Lost Prairie Annual Jump Meet, from late July through early August, is the largest gathering of skydivers in the northwestern US. It draws jumpers from around the world. Instruction. Fred Sand, 3175 Lower Lost Praire Rd., Marion, MT 59925; ☎ 406-858-2493.

Garnet Appreciation Days is a late July event. Homemade pie auction, raffles, children's games, door prizes, concessions. BLM, 3255 Fort Missoula Rd., Missoula, MT 59801; ☎ 406-329-3914. Fax 406-549-1562.

August

Creamery Picnic, an old fashioned Stevensville event held in early August, features a parade, crafts, firemen's competitions, homemade ice cream, street dance. R. Stout, ☎ 406-777-2685.

Polson's Annual Outdoor Arts Festival is a well-established early August event drawing over 100 artisans and crafts people. Sandpiper Gallery, 2 First Ave. East, Polson, MT 59860; ☎ 406-883-5956.

Bigfork's Annual Festival of the Arts, also held in early August, has been going since 1979. Upwards of 100 booths on the shore of Flathead Lake. Bigfork Retail Merchants Assoc., PO Box 1892, Bigfork, MT 59911, ☎ 406-881-4636.

Western Montana Fair & Rodeo, held in Missoula in early August, is a typical farm and ranch country fair with horse racing, 4-H exhibits, free stage acts, antique engine displays, country western concert, rodeo and more. Sam Yewusiak, 1101 S. Ave. W, Missoula, MT 59801; ☎ 406-721-3247. Fax 406-728-7479.

Flathead Rendezvous, held in Kalispell in mid-August, is a juried arts and crafts show benefiting Big Brothers and Big Sisters of the Flathead. Mary Lou Sennett, PO Box 1053, Lewistown, MT 59457; ☎ 406-538-2212.

Huckleberry Days is an early August Whitefish event celebrating local wild huckleberries with a pie-eating contest, huckleberry cook-off, arts & crafts and more. Whitefish Chamber of Commerce, PO Box 1120, Whitefish, MT 59937; ☎ 406-862-3501. Fax 406-862-9494.

Huckleberry Festival, at Swan Lake in early August, also celebrates Montana's favorite berry. Food booths, arts & crafts carry the huckleberry theme. Swan Lake Chamber of Commerce, PO Box 5199, Swan Lake, MT 59911; ☎ 406-886-2345.

Northwest Montana Fair is held at Kalispell in mid-August. PRCA rodeo, horse racing, 4-H exhibits and more. Flathead Country Fairgrounds, 265 N. Meridan Rd., Kalispell, MT 59901; ☎ 406-758-5810. Fax 406-756-8936.

Annual Bigfork Charity Antiques Show and Sale in mid-August includes nationally known antiques dealers displaying 18th and 19th century country and period antiques. Appraisal Service. Patricia Lamb, PO Box 486, Bigfork, MT 59911; ☎ 406-982-3570.

Hot August Nights in Libby in late August features a classic car show, rod runs, dance, food and vendor booths. Libby Chamber of Commerce, PO Box 704, Libby, MT 59923; ☎ 406-293-4167. Fax 293-3222.

Big Mountain Microbrew Festival is held in late August. Beers, finger food, dancing. Matt Mosteller, PO Box 1400, Whitefish, MT 59937; ☎ 406-862-2905. Fax 862-2955.

Ravalli County Fair, at Hamilton in late August, is an old-fashioned Montana fair. G. Wiley, 100 Old Corvallis Rd., Hamilton, MT 59840; ☎ 406-363-3411.

Sanders County Fair & Rodeo is another typical country fair, this at Plains in late August. Mike Hashisaki, 141 River Rd., Box 9, Plains, MT 59859; ☎ 406-826-3202. Fax 406-826-3674.

Annual Show and Shine Car Show in late August features a poker run, barbeque and dance. Stanton Creek Lodge, HC 36 Box 1C, Essex, MT 59916; ☎ 406-888-5040.

September

Wild West Days is celebrated in Bigfork over the Labor Day weekend with Native American dancers, carriage rides, gunfighters in the street, line dancing, Western art. Linda J. Anderson, PO Box 663, Bigfork, MT 59911; ☎ 406-837-5861. Fax 406-837-1118.

Taste of Whitefish takes off in early September with cuisine from area restaurants, Montana-made products. Whitefish Chamber of Commerce, PO Box 1120, Whitefish, MT 59937; ☎ 406-862-3501. Fax 406-862-9494.

Libby Nordic Fest in mid-September celebrates the Scandinavian heritage of many area residents with an International Fjord horse show, Scandinavian foods, country entertainers, homes tour and more. Libby Chamber of Commerce, PO Box 704, Libby, MT 59923; ☎ 406-293-4167. Fax 293-3222.

Flathead International Balloon Festival, held in the Kalispell area in mid-September, features mass balloon inflations, skydivers, evening balloon glow-off, barbeque, music. Flathead Convention & Visitor Assoc., 15 Depot Park, Kalispell, MT 59901; ☎ 800-543-3105 or 406-756-9091. Fax 406-257-2500.

AUTHOR TIP *Testicle Festival (yes, you read that right), held in late September at the Rock Creek Lodge at I-90 Exit 126 near Clinton, is a Rocky Mountain oyster feed with cowboy beans on the side. Upwards of 10 tons of this gourmet delight are served each year. Have a ball! Rod Lincoln, PO Box 825, Clinton, MT 59825; ☎ 406-825-4868. Fax 825-4062.*

Annual MacIntosh Apple Day, a late September Hamilton event, is billed as the biggest bake sale under the Big Sky. Apple butter bubbling over an open fire, cider pressing, apple baked goods, arts & crafts. Helen Ann Bibler, 205 Bedford, Hamilton, MT 59840; ☎ 406-363-3338.

October

Glacier Jazz Stampede is an early October Kalispell event featuring jazz bands PLAYING jazz, big band, swing and modern music. Karla West, PO Box 9524, Kalispell, MT 59904; ☎ 406-862-3814.

Alta/Mont Railfan Weekend is an annual mid-October event at the Izaac Walton Inn at Essex. Stories and local railway history, train excursions on the Burlington Northern/Great Northern line to sites of interest for railroad fans. Karen Kibbee, PO Box 653, Essex, MT 59916; ☎ 406-888-5700. Fax 406-888-5200.

Fiesta Days, in Whitefish in mid-October, is a chili cook-off on Central Avenue. Whitefish Chamber of Commerce, PO Box 1120, Whitefish, MT 59937; ☎ 406-862-3501. Fax 406-862-9494.

Tamarack Time is a mid-October Bigfork harvest festival featuring harvest foods, entertainment, art show and sale. Elna Darrow, PO Box 400, Bigfork, MT 59911; ☎ 406-837-4848.

Christmas at the Mansion, held in late October, pushes the holiday season at Kalispell's favorite mansion. The Conrad mansion is festooned with Victorian Christmas decorations including a two-story decorated tree. Music, food, arts and crafts. Lynn Redfield, PO Box 1041, Kalispell, MT 59903; ☎ 406-755-2166.

Glacier Golden Autumn Arts & Crafts Show is a late October event at the Izaac Walton Inn featuring local artists and craftsmen. Frank Krshka or Lynda Wielleux, PO Box 653, Essex, MT 59916; ☎ 406-888-5700. Fax 406-888-5200.

November

Annual Holiday Art & Craft Show, an early November Kalispell event, features over 50 juried artists and craftsmen from the Northwest. Janet Koenig, PO Box 5414, Helena, MT 59604; ☎ 406-449-4790.

Annual Holiday Marketplace is a late November event in Missoula. Convention & Visitor Association, 825 E. Front St., Missoula, MT 59807; ☎ 406-721-FAIR.

Bigfork Elves Decorate for Christmas, held in late November, involves elves dispersed throughout the village, decorating for Christmas. Sleigh rides. Bigfork Chamber of Commerce, PO Box 237, Bigfork, MT 59911; ☎ 406-837-5888.

Christmas City of the North Parade in late November brings Santa to town. Kalispell Chamber of Commerce, 15 Depot Park, Kalispell, MT 59901; ☎ 406-758-2800. Fax 406-758-2805.

Renaissance Fair, a late November Missoula event, features over 65 top artists from five states. Convention & Visitor Assoc., 825 E. Front St., Missoula, MT 59807; ☎ 406-538-2212.

Artists & Craftsmen Christmas Show is a late November event. Janet Randall, PO Box 1684, Kalispell, MT 59903; ☎ 406-881-4288.

December

Christmas Comes to Life & Festival of Trees is an early December event in Libby wherein business windows sport live Christmas scenes; carolers, horse-drawn wagons, roasted chestnuts and hot apple cider on street corners. Libby Chamber of Commerce, 905 W. 9th, Libby, MT 59923; ☎ 406-293-4167. Fax 406-293-3222.

Stevensville Christmas Gift Fair is an early December event. Bitterroot Valley Chamber of Commerce, 105 E. Main St., Hamilton, MT 59840; ☎ 406-363-2400.

Catch the Magic in early December with a champagne reception, music, arts & crafts boutique, walk-through tours of Daly mansion. Doug Johnson, PO Box 223, Hamilton, MT 59840; ☎ 406-363-4218.

Holiday Stroll takes place in Missoula in early December with food vendors, entertainers, special downtown events. Missoula Downtown Assoc., 101 E. Main, Missoula, MT 59802; ☎ 406-543-4238.

Annual Magical Holiday Stroll, Artwalk & Tree Lighting Ceremony is an early December Bigfork event. Bigfork Chamber of Commerce, PO Box 237, Bigfork, MT 59911; ☎ 406-837-5888.

Kick-Out-The-Kinks Ski Race, at the Isaac Walton Inn in early December, benefits the Middlefork Quick Response Unit. Cross-country ski race and Huckleberry Hustle progressive lunch-on-skis. Isaac Walton Inn, Essex, MT 59916; ☎ 406-888-5700. Fax 406-888-5200.

Whitefish Christmas Stroll in mid-December includes Santa's arrival, carolers, chestnuts roasting, hot cider, horse-drawn wagon rides, street vendors. Whitefish Downtown Merchants Assoc., 141 Central Ave., Whitefish, MT 59937; ☎ 406-862-3516. Fax 406-862-9494.

Race By The Lake, a mid-December event in the Swan Valley, is an 80-mile mid-distance staged race; ski joring, mushers. Werner Probst, PO Box 922, Seeley Lake, MT 59868; ☎ 406-677-3434.

Christmas Eve Torchlight Parade with Santa is an annual Big Mountain event featuring Santa's arrival. Big Mountain Ski Resort, PO Box 1400, Whitefish, MT 59937; ☎ 406-862-2900. Fax 406-862-2955.

Root Beer Classic, in late December, is a 60-mile, mid-distance staged sled dog team race in Polebridge at the western boundary of Glacier National Park. Jack & Laurie Beckstrom, 4108 Hwy. 93 N., Kalispell, MT 59901; ☎ 406-752-2929. Fax 406-752-2989.

First Night Missoula is an annual community New Year's Eve celebration of the arts. Performing, visual and literary artists showcase their talents in over 100 events. Alcohol and drug free. Jennifer Gibson, PO Box 8183, Missoula, MT 59807; ☎ 406-549-4755.

New Year's Eve Torchlight Parade down Big Mountain ends with fireworks. Big Mountain Ski Resort, PO Box 1400, Whitefish, MT 59937; ☎ 406-862-2900. Fax 406-862-2955.

Where to Stay & Eat

Glacier Country has the most eclectic assortment of lodgings and eateries of any Montana travel region. Prices are mostly reasonable even in the upscale Whitefish-Bigfork area, though there are exceptions. Throughout Glacier Country, numerous B&Bs, resorts, lodges and eateries offer memorable lodging and dining experiences, prices you can live with, and genuinely friendly hosts. This section attempts to sort the gold from the dross.

Lodging Prices	
$	dirt cheap
$$	moderate
$$$	pricey, but oh well
$$$$	hang onto your checkbook

■ Hotels, Motels & B&Bs

The lodgings embrace everything from hostels to luxury lodges. Hicktown motels are not included here unless they are a town's only choice. Guest ranches are listed under that heading (see *Adventures on Horseback*) unless run as a lodge.

Alberton

Hole In The Wall Lodge is a smallish affair with 11 guest rooms and a restaurant. $$$. Box 326, Alberton, MT 59820; ☎ 800-669-2421 or 406-523-6145. Fax 406-722-3152.

Montana Hotel is a restored c. 1909 hostelry run as a B&B. 10 guest rooms, full breakfast. $$. 702 Railroad Ave. (Box 423), Alberton, MT 59820; ☎ 800-564-4129 or 406-722-4990.

Big Arm

Big Arm Resort & Marina, on the west shore of Flathead Lake, offers lakeside housekeeping units, RV spaces and typical marina-oriented activities. $$. Box 99, Big Arm, MT 59910; ☎ 406-849-5622.

Bigfork

Bigfork is awash in B&Bs, some high-toned, some not; also luxury lodges and such.

B&Bs

Burggraf's Countrylane B&B, in a charming log home on Swan Lake, has five guest rooms with private baths, full breakfast, canoeing and paddleboating; picnic baskets available. $$$. Rainbow Dr., Bigfork, MT 59911; ☎ 800-525-3344 or 406-837-4608.

Cherry Way Inn Family B&B, overlooking Flathead Lake, has four guest rooms with private baths and serves full breakfast. $$. 26400 East Shore Rt., Bigfork, MT 59911; ☎ 800-837-6803 or 406-837-6803.

Coyote Roadhouse Inn offers two suites with private baths, one suite with shared bath, cabins with private river frontage; full breakfast. Nightly Roadhouse Restaurant gourmet dinners prepared by owner/chef Gary Hastings are by reservation only and cost extra. $$$. 602 Three Eagle Lane (Box 1166), Bigfork, MT 59911; ☎ 406-837-4250. Fax 406-837-0048.

Deck House has a private suite on Flathead Lake and continental breakfast. $$. 298 Pierce Lane (Box 865), Bigfork, MT 59911; ☎ 406-837-6174.

Jubilee Orchards Lake Resort B&B, on Flathead Lake, has three guest rooms with kitchens and private baths, man-size continental breakfast. There are 220 feet of private beach, cherry orchards for snacking, extensive library. $$$. 836 Sylvan Dr., Bigfork, MT 59911; ☎ 406-837-4256.

O'Duachain Country Inn is a luxury log home with five guest rooms, private baths, full breakfast include delicious baked treats. The atmosphere is pleasantly homey and the hosts warm and welcoming. $$$. 675 Ferndale Dr., Bigfork, MT 59911; ☎ 800-837-7460 or 406-837-6851. Fax 406-837-4390.

Schwartz's B&B has two guest rooms with shared bath, full breakfast, private lake, canoeing, swimming. $. 890 McCaffery Rd., Bigfork, MT 59911; ☎ 406-837-5463.

Other Lodgings

Bayside Resort offers a rustic four-bedroom home and six one-bedroom log cabins with kitchens and showers on Bigfoot Bay. One of Bigfork's original accommodations. $$$. Del Ivey, 155 Bay Dr. #14, Bigfork, MT 59911; ☎ 406-837-4551.

Bayview Resort & Marina has kitchenette accommodations, marina, boat rentals, in-lake swimming area. $$$. 543 Yenne Point Rd., Bigfork, MT 59911; ☎ 800-775-3536 or 406-837-4843.

Holiday Resort, an intimate hostelry on Flathead Lake, has eight guest rooms and a restaurant. $$$. 17001 E. Shore Rt., Bigfork, MT 59911; ☎ 800-421-9141 or 406-982-3710.

Marina Cay Resort is a biggie situated where the Swan River enters Flathead Lake. 120 guest rooms, restaurants, pool, numerous other amenities. $$$. 180 Vista Lane (Box 663), Bigfork, MT 59911; ☎ 800-433-6516 or 406-837-5861. Fax 406-837-1118.

Swan River Inn defies classification. Three sumptuously appointed suites opening onto the Swan River reflect distinct themes: Western Montana at its most imaginative, elegant Victorian complete with antiques, and romantic art deco. Breakfast is not included in the rate, but the upstairs Swan River Café is open for wakeups. $$$. 360 Grand Ave., Bigfork, MT 59911; ☎ 406-837-2220. Fax 406-837-4618.

 The Last Best Place offers a unique overnight experience in an authentic Plains tipi on a meadow seven miles from Bigfork. $. ☎ 406-837-1443.

Browning

Browning, at the junction of US 89 and 2, has more choices than most Indian reservations. Best bets:

Lodge Pole Gallery & Tipi Village. See Special Interest & Cultural Activities.

Old Nine Mile Inn, a B&B between East Glacier and St. Marys, has three guest rooms with private baths, full breakfast. $$$. Box 1763, Browning, MT 59417; ☎ 800-775-1355 or 406-338-7911. Fax 406-338-3672.

War Bonnet Lodge offers convenient on-Reservation lodging with 40 rooms and a restaurant. $$. Jct. US 2 & 89, Browning, MT 59417; ☎ 406-338-7610. Fax 406-338-2142.

Charlo

Ninepipes Lodge has 25 comfortable guest rooms, but that's just for starters. On the lodge property is the **Ninepipes Museum of Early Montana**, an outstanding collection of historical artifacts pertaining to the Flathead Valley's Indian and European-American traditions. A restaurant and trading post round out the lodge. Easy access to numerous wildlife watching sites (see *Wildlife Watching*). $$. 41000 Hwy. 93, Charlo, MT 59824; ☎ 406-644-2588. Fax 406-644-2928.

Clinton

The following are in the lovely Bearmouth Valley.

Ekstrom Stage Station on Rock Creek is a century-old stagecoach stop. Restaurant, rock shop, playground, RV hookups. $$. 81 Rock Creek Rd., Clinton, MT 59825; ☎ 406-825-3183.

Elkhorn Guest Ranch offers trail rides, has a restaurant, heated pool, convenience store, one mile private Rock Creek fishing access. $$$. 408 Rock Creek Rd., Clinton, MT 59825; ☎ 406-825-3220. Fax 406-825-3224.

Rock Creek Lodge, visible from I-90, is the home of the Testicle Festival. Okay rooms, free RV park for patrons, Wild West museum, fishing. Hokey, but fun. $$. Box 835, Clinton, MT 59825; ☎ 406-825-4868.

Columbia Falls

Columbia Falls' proximity to Glacier National Park has prompted a rash of B&Bs and other assorted lodgings.

B&Bs

Bad Rock Country B&B, on 30 scenic acres, has seven luxury guest rooms with private baths, full breakfast, spa. $$$$. 480 Bad Rock Dr., Columbia Falls, MT 59912; ☎ 800-422-3666 or 406-892-2829. Fax 406-892-2930.

Mountain Timbers Lodge, a mile outside Glacier National Park, has seven guest rooms, four with private baths, full breakfast. $$$. 5385 Rabe Rd., Columbia Falls, MT 59912; ☎ 800-841-3835 or 406-387-5830. Fax 406-387-5835.

Park View Inn Bed & Breakfast, done in the Victorian-style, has seven accommodations that include log cabins and a honeymoon cottage with Jacuzzi. Full breakfast. $$$. 904 4th Ave. West (Box 567), Columbia Falls, MT 59912; ☎ 406-892-7275.

Plum Creek House has five guest rooms with private baths, full breakfast, swimming pool, riverside Jacuzzi. $$$$. 985 Vans Ave., Columbia Falls, MT 59912; ☎ 800-682-1429 or 406-892-1816. Fax 406-892-1876.

Other Lodgings

Columbia Mountain Cabins consists of five log cabins with kitchenettes in a secluded woodsy setting. Separate bathhouse. Playgound, archery range. Three-night minimum. $$. Sissy Girtman, 890 Jensen Rd., Columbia Falls, MT 59912; ☎ 406-892-3005. Fax 406-892-4280.

Meadow Lake Resort has 24 guest rooms, restaurant, pool, hot tub. $$$. 100 St. Andrews Dr., Columbia Falls, MT 59912; ☎ 800-321-4653 or 406-892-7601. Fax 406-892-0330.

Ol' River Bridge Inn has 31 guest rooms, restaurant and pool. $$. 7358 US 2 East, Columbia Falls, MT 59912; ☎ 406-892-2181.

Condon

Swan River Valley Lodge offers riverfront log cabins with kitchens on 15 acres of timber and meadowlands. Open year-round. $$$. 1171 Jette Rd., Condon, MT 59826; ☎ 406-754-2780.

33-Bar Ranch Bed & Breakfast is on a historic ranch between the Mission and Bob Marshall Wilderness Areas. Two guest rooms with private baths, continental breakfast. $$$. Hultman Rd. (Box 1068), Condon, MT 59826; ☎ 406-754-2820.

Coram

A Wild Rose B&B has four luxury guest rooms done up in Victorian style, three with private baths, whirlpool suite, full breakfast, spa, massage. $$$$. 10280 US 2 East (Box 130396), Coram, MT 59913; ☎ 406-387-4900.

Heartwood. Fully equipped vacation cabins and a studio apartment nestled among tall trees on a 200-acres of meadows and woodlands, seven miles from Glacier Park's West Entrance. $$$. Joe or Linda Rogers, Box 130187, Coram, MT 59913; ☎ 406-387-4151.

Corvallis

Daybreak Bed & Breakfast, in a historic log home, has four guest rooms, three with private baths, full breakfast. $$$. 616 Willowcreek Rd., Corvallis, MT 59828; ☎ 406-961-4530.

Cut Bank

Northern Motor Inn may be your best bet in a town having several motels but few real choices. 61 guest rooms and a pool. $$. 609 W. Main St., Cut Bank, MT 59427; ☎ 406-873-5662.

Glacier Motor Inn is another possibility. 53 guest rooms and a restaurant. $. 15 1st Ave. SW, Cut Bank, MT 59427; ☎ 406-873-5555.

Darby

Here in the Bitterroots, lodgings tend to be as rustic as the wooded terrain and night unto as numerous as the trees.

Alta Meadow Ranch, a historic ranch splendidly situated in the Bitterroot Mountains, offers three fully equipped family-size log homes, visiting horse facilities, RV hookups. Gourmet meals, horseback rides and other activities by arrangement. $$$. 9975 West Fork Rd., Darby, MT 59829; ☎ 800-808-2466 or 406-349-2464. Fax 406-349-2018.

Nez Perce Ranch has three two-bedroom streamside log cabins; maid service. $$$. 7206 Nez Perce Rd., Darby, MT 59829; ☎ 406-349-2100.

Painted Rocks Lodge has rustic log homes on the Bitterroot River. Can accomodate large groups. $$$. 791 West Fork Rd. (Box 791), Darby, MT 59829; ☎ 406-349-2146.

Rye Creek Lodge offers fully equipped modern two-bedroom log cabins with rock fireplaces in a secluded setting. $$$$. 458 Rye Creek Rd. (Box 877), Darby, MT 59829; ☎ 888-821-3366 or 406-821-3366.

Triple Creek Ranch, more an exclusive resort than a ranch, is open year-round for seasonal activities. The variety of luxury cabins and suites are available by the day. Rates include all meals, drinks, on-ranch trail rides, winter activities, gourmet picnics, fly-casting lessons, tennis and more. $$$$. 5551 West Fork Stage Rt., Darby, MT 59829; ☎ 406-821-4600. Fax 406-821-4666.

Wilderness Motel, RV and Tent Park. Bunkhouse has 12 assorted accommodations. An economical and convenient choice; $. 308 S. Main St. (Box 431), Darby, MT 59829; ☎ 800-820-2554 or 406-821-3405.

DeBorgia

Hotel Albert, a renovated 1911 railroad hotel, is a B&B oozing Old Montana ambience. Shared baths, full breakfast. $. #2 Yellowstone Trail (PO Box 300186), DeBorgia, MT 59830; ☎ 406-678-4303.

East Glacier

B&B

Bison Creek Ranch has six guest rooms, each with private bath. Continental breakfast; dinners on request. $. 20722 US 2 W. (Box 144), East Glacier, MT 59434; ☎ 406-226-4482.

Hostels

Backpacker's Inn has dorm-style accommodations. Bring your sleeping bag. Under $10. 29 Dawson Ave., East Glacier, MT 59434; ☎ 406-226-9392.

Brownies Grocery and AYH Hostel is in a 1920s-era log building; grocery, bakery & deli on main floor, hostel & kitchen upstairs. $. Off US 2 on MT 49. Box 229, East Glacier, MT 59434; ☎ 406-226-4426.

Essex

Essex is known for the Isaac Walton Inn, but other area choices are available.

Isaak Walton Inn is a historic railway crew hotel (see *Touring*) restored to reflect a rustic alpine ambience. Over 30 guest rooms reflecting a railroading theme, plus four antique cabooses gussied up to a fare-thee-well. The Dining Car Restaurant has old railroad photos on the walls, delectables on your plate. Great cross-country skiing and snowshoeing from the door or via Glacier Park ski packages. Amtrak's Empire Builder stops at the door. $$$$. Box 653, Essex, MT 59916; ☎ 406-888-5700. Fax 406-888-5200.

Paola Creek Bed & Breakfast has four guest rooms with private baths, serves full breakfast; sack lunches and dinners on request. $$$$. HC 36, Box 4C, Essex, MT 59916; ☎ 406-888-5061. Fax 406-888-5063.

Stanton Creek Lodge offers four cabins; bathhouse, community fire pit, café. $. US 2 E. Milepost 170 (HC 36, Box 1C), Essex, MT 59916; ☎ 406-888-5040.

Eureka

Eureka is gaining popularity. Make reservations.

Huckleberry Hannah's Montana Bed & Breakfast, on 50 prime view lakeside acres, has five guest rooms with private baths and serves full breakfast. $$$. 3100 Sophie Lake Rd., Eureka, MT 59917; ☎ 888-889-3381 or 406-889-3381.

Ksanka Motor Inn has 30 guest rooms and a restaurant. Junction US 93 and MT 37. $$. Box 959, Eureka, MT 59917; ☎ 406-296-3127. Fax 406-296-3337.

Willow Fire Lodge offers country hospitality in a five-bedroom lodge with shared baths. Meals optional. $$. 1866 West Rd., Eureka, MT 59917; ☎ 406-889-3344.

Fortine

Laughing Water Ranch has family accommodations and activities. $$$. 20 Deep Creek Rd. (Box 157A), Fortine, MT 59918; ☎ 800-847-5095 or 406-882-4680.

Florence

Green Thumb Bed & Breakfast offers a two-bedroom apartment near the Bitterroot River; full breakfast. $$$. 5311 Leaning Tree, Florence, MT 59833; ☎ 406-273-6522.

Greenough

Loran's Clearwater Inn has four guest rooms and a restaurant. Convenient to fishing and river put-in, Garnet Ghost Town and the Seeley Valley. $. Junction MT 200 & 83. Box 20, Greenough, MT 59836; ☎ 406-244-9535.

Glacier National Park

Glacier National Park lodgings include high-profile historic hotels, but the several motor inns are less expensive and very nice, albeit with less atmosphere.

Apgar Village Lodge has 50 rustic rooms, many with views of Lake McDonald, plus the Cedar Tree Deli. $$$. Box 398, West Glacier, MT 59936; ☎ 406-888-5484.

Glacier Park Lodge is a grand full-service hotel with 161 guest rooms, restaurants, pool, golf course. $$$$. Box 147, East Glacier, MT 59434; ☎ 602-207-6000.

Lake McDonald Lodge, a wonderful old hotel in the best rustic turn-of-the-century tradition, has 100 guest rooms and cabins, restaurants. $$$$. Box 147, East Glacier, MT 59434; ☎ 602-207-6000.

Many Glacier Hotel, a fine example of north country chalet architecture in a splendid lakeside setting, has 208 guest rooms, a restaurant and easy access to some of Glacier Park's most popular hiking trails. $$$$. Box 147, East Glacier, MT 59434; ☎ 602-207-6000.

Rising Sun Motor Inn, on the Park's east side, has 72 motel-style rooms and a restaurant. $$$. Box 147, East Glacier, MT 59434; ☎ 602-207-6000.

Swift Current Motor Inn, in the Many Glacier Valley, has 88 motel-style rooms and a restaurant. $$$. Box 147, East Glacier, MT 59434; ☎ 602-207-6000.

Village Inn is a more intimate lodging (36 rooms) at the Park's West Entrance. West Glacier, MT 59936; ☎ 602-207-6000.

Hamilton

Hamilton's trendiness tends toward numerous B&Bs, some posh indeed.

B&Bs

The Bavarian Farmhouse Inn B&B, a remodeled 1890 farmhouse, has five guest rooms with private baths, full breakfast. $$. 163 Bowman Rd., Hamilton, MT 59840; ☎ 406-363-4063.

Deer Crossing Bed & Breakfast also has five guest rooms with private baths. Hearty ranch breakfast. $$$. 396 Hayes Creek Rd., Hamilton, MT 59840; ☎ 800-763-2232 or 406-363-2232.

Heavenly View Hideaway Bed & Breakfast, in a luxurious log home, has three guest rooms, one with private bath, full breakfast, hot tub, king-size beds. $$$. Box 313, Hamilton, MT 59840; ☎ 406-961-5220.

Ranch Bed & Breakfast has two guest rooms, one with private bath, full breakfast. $$. 1615 US 93 S., Hamilton, MT 59840; ☎ 406-363-4739.

Trout Springs Bed & Breakfast has four guest rooms with private baths, pretty gardens. Full breakfast include fresh-caught trout from inn's private ponds. You can even catch your own breakfast trout! $$$. 721 Desta St., Hamilton, MT 58840; 888-67TROUT or 406-375-0911. Fax 406-375-0988.

Other Lodgings

Hamilton has three sizeable chain motels: **Best Western** (☎ 800-HAMILTON), **Comfort Inn** (☎ 800-442-4667), **Super 8** (☎ 406-363-2940).

Lost Horse Creek Lodge has both rustic cabins and hotel-style suites. Log cabin eatery, trail rides. $$. 1000 Lost Horse Rd. (Box 381), Hamilton, MT 59840; ☎ 406-363-1460. Fax 406-363-3059.

Starfire Farm Lodge offers three luxury condos with fireplaces in a wooded setting; private decks, stocked trout pond, picnic area. $$$$. 401 Fleet St., Hamilton, MT 59840; ☎ 800-757-2041 ext. 5720 or 406-363-6240.

Haugan

Silver $ Inn, off I-90 near the Idaho line, has 40 guest rooms and a restaurant. $$. Box W, Haughan, MT 59842; ☎ 800-531-1968 or 406-678-4242.

Heron

Wilderness Lodge offers secluded weekly accommodations near the Clark Fork River in motel units and cabins with wood stoves. Guided pack trips, fishing, cross-country skiing. $$. 620 Elk Creek Rd., Heron, MT 59844; ☎ 406-847-2277.

Hot Springs

Symes Hotel & Mineral Baths (see *Touring*) is a funky family-run art deco/New Age kind of place in a constant upgrade mode. Outdoor mineral pool, 26 guest rooms, private spa facilities, café. $. 109 Wall St. (Box 632), Hot Springs, MT 59845; ☎ 406-741-2361.

Hungry Horse

Glacier Bed & Breakfast is a log home on US 2 East; five guest rooms, four with private baths. Full breakfast. $$. Box 1900-10, Hungry Horse, MT 59919; ☎ 406-387-4153.

Historic Tamarack Lodge & Hotel includes a c. 1907 log lodge, eight-unit motel and cabin with kitchen. $$. 9549 US 2 East (Box 190236), Hungry Horse, MT 59919; ☎ 406-387-4420. Fax 406-387-4450.

Huson

The Schoolhouse and The Teacherage B&B. Four guest rooms with shared baths in an old teacherage have feather beds and down comforters; full breakfasts in old schoolhouse. Near Nine Mile Ranger Station (see *Touring*) $$. 9 Mile, Huson, MT 59846; ☎ 406-626-5879.

Kalispell

Kalispell also spawns numerous B&Bs ranging from expensive to very pricey. Other choices are equally unaffordable.

B&Bs

Blaine Creek Bed & Breakfast has three guest rooms, one with private bath, full breakfast, sauna, hot tub. $$$. 727 VanSant Rd., Kalispell, MT 59901; ☎ 800-752-2519 or 406-752-2519.

Bonnie's Bed & Breakfast has three guest rooms, one with private bath, full breakfast. $$$. 265 Lake Blaine Rd., Kalispell, MT 59901; ☎ 800-755-3778 or 406-755-3776. Fax 406-752-5544.

Creston Country Inn B&B is a classic farmhouse; four guest rooms with private baths, full breakfast. $$$. 70 Creston Rd., Kalispell, MT 59901; ☎ 800-257-7517 or 406-755-7517.

Logan House Bed & Breakfast, a turn-of-the-century mansion near Woodland Park in Kalispell's carriage district, has four guest rooms with private baths, full breakfast. $$$$. 528 Woodland Ave., Kalispell, MT 59901; ☎ 800-615-5588 or 406-755-5588. Fax 406-755-5589.

River Rock Bed & Breakfast, in a sunny luxury home, has three guest rooms with private baths, full breakfast. $$$$. 179 Schrade Rd., Kalispell, MT 59901; ☎ 800-477-0699 or 406-756-6901.

Stillwater Inn's four guest rooms, two with private baths, reflect a turn-of-the-century ambience; full breakfast. $$$. 206 4th Ave. E, Kalispell, MT 59901; ☎ 800-398-7024 or 406-755-7080. Fax 406-756-0020.

Switzer House Inn, a 1910 Queen Anne Revival home, has four guest rooms with shared baths, full gourmet breakfast. $$$. 205 5th Ave. E, Kalispell, MT 59901; ☎ 800-257-5837 or 406-257-5837.

Other Lodgings

Kalispell has seven sizeable chain motels: **Best Western** (☎ 800-237-7445), **Days Inn** (☎ 800-329-7466), **Four Seasons** (☎ 800-545-6399), **Super 8** (☎ 800-800-8000), **Motel 6** (☎ 800-440-6000), **Ramada** (☎ 406-857-2200), **Red Lion** (☎ 800-547-8010).

Cavanaugh's at Kalispell Center is a 132-room, full-service luxury hostelry. $$$$. 20 N. Main, Kalispell, MT 59901; ☎ 800-843-4667 or 406-752-6660. Fax 406-752-6628.

Kalispell Grand Hotel has 40 guest rooms and a restaurant in a historic building. $$$. 100 Main St. (Box986), Kalispell, MT 59901; ☎ 800-858-7422 or 406-755-8100. Fax 406-752-8012.

The Outlaw, a Cavanaugh's hotel, is a luxury full-service hotel with 220 deluxe rooms and suites, two indoor swimming pools, sauna, full-service restaurant, fitness center, tennis, racquetball courts. 1701 Hwy. 93 S., Kalispell, MT 59901; ☎ 800-325-4000 or 406-755-6100. Fax 406-756-8994. www.cavanaughs.com.

Lakeside

Angel Point Guest Suites reflects traditional lakeside resort ambience; it has luxury suites with kitchens and balconies, beach toys, fishing platforms, beach pavilion, boat rentals and more. $$$$. 829 Angel Point Rd. (Box 768), Lakeside, MT 59922; ☎ 800-214-2204 or 406-844-2204.

Bayshore Resort Motel on Flathead Lake has 14 units. $$. 616 Lakeside Blvd. (Box 375), Lakeside, MT 59922; ☎ 800-844-3132 or 406-844-3131.

Edgewater Motel & RV Park is a tad more upscale with 20 units. $$$. 7145 US 93 S (Box 312), Lakeside, MT 59922; ☎ 800-424-3798 or 406-844-3644. Fax 406-844-3840.

Shoreline Inn is a B&B with a dock on Flathead Lake, three guest rooms with private baths, continental breakfast. $$$. 696 Lakeside Blvd. (Box 568), Lakeside, MT 59922; ☎ 800-645-0255 or 406-844-3222.

Libby

Libby has a raft of so-so motels that include a **Super 8** with pool (☎ 800-800-8000). Other lodgings include a B&B and a motor inn with a pool for the tagalongs.

Koocanusa Resort is low key, but the location on Lake Koocanusa makes up for any perceived lack of comforts. $$. 23911 MT 37, Libby, MT 59923; ☎ 406-293-7548.

The Kootenai Country Inn, a five-bedroom (three private baths) guest house on a 40-acre ranch, serves full breakfast. $$$. 264 Mack Rd., Libby, MT 59923; ☎ 406-293-7878. Fax 406-293-5918.

Venture Motor Inn has 72 guest rooms, a restaurant and pool. $$. 443 US 2 W, Libby, MT 59923; ☎ 800-221-0166 or 406-293-7711.

Lolo

Days Inn of Lolo offers an alternative to downtown Missoula. 40 guest rooms but no restaurant. $$$. 11225 US 93S., Lolo, MT 59847; ☎ 800-325-2525 or 800-329-7466. Fax 406-273-0712.

Holt Ranch B&B, a B&B in a turn-of-the-century home on a working cattle ranch, has three guest rooms, one with private bath, full breakfast. $$$. Box 869, Lolo, MT 59847; ☎ 406-273-0268.

Lolo Hot Springs Resort has fallen on hard times, but may be an option if you wish to soak in the hot springs, climb the nearby rocks, tramp the Lewis & Clark Trail, snowmobile, or be near Lolo Pass. Restaurant. $$$. ☎ 800-273-2290 or 406-273-2290. Fax ☎ 406-273-3677.

Marion

Hilltop Hitchin' Post has seven guest rooms and a restaurant. $$. 8225 US 2 W., Marion, MT 59925; ☎ 406-854-2442.

Martin City

Abbott Valley Homestead offers five fully furnished guest houses sleeping two to eight near Glacier Park's West Entrance. Three-night minimum. $$$. Edna Foley, 837 Spotted Bear Rd., Martin City, MT 59926; ☎ 406-387-5330. Fax 406-387-5457.

The Little Matterhorn Cabins are old-fashioned one and two-bedroom cabins. $$. 167 Martin Lane (Box 260124), Martin City, MT 59926; ☎ 406-387-5072.

Missoula

Missoula has some pricey B&Bs, a hostel reflecting the city's counter-culture image, and the usual complement of chain hostelries.

B&Bs

Foxglove Cottage Bed & Breakfast has two guest rooms with shared bath, continental breakfast, in a century-old house with gardens and a swimming pool. $$$. 2331 Gilbert Ave., Missoula, MT 59801; ☎ 406-543-2927.

Goldsmith's Inn, on the Clark Fork River near downtown, has seven guest rooms with private baths and serves full breakfast. $$$$. 809 E. Front St., Missoula, MT 59801; ☎ 406-721-6732.

Gracenote Garden has two guest rooms with private baths, continental breakfast, bookish comfort. $$$$. 1558 S. 6th St. W., Missoula, MT 59801; ☎ 406-543-3480. Fax 406-549-3630.

The Greenough Bed & Breakfast has three guest rooms with full baths and serves full breakfast. $$$$. 631 Stephens St., Missoula, MT 59801; ☎ 800-718-3626 or 406-728-3626.

Hostel

Birchwood Hostel has 22 beds in four bunk rooms and one private room. Kitchen, dining room/lounge, inside bicycle storage, laundromat. Bring your sleeping bags; rentals available. Convenient to downtown, riverfront and U of M. Under $10 & $. 600 S. Orange, Missoula, MT 59801; ☎ 406-728-9799.

Other Lodgings

Some of Missoula's chain hostelries are on the Clark Fork River; some on or near Reserve Street on the west side of town. Chains include a downtown **Best Western** (☎ 800-528-1234), a **Best Western** at I-90 and Reserve Street (☎ 888-543-0700), a **Comfort Inn** (☎ 406-542-0888), a **Days Inn** (☎ 800-DAYSINN), a **Hampton Inn** (☎ 800-HAMPTON), a riverside **Holiday Inn** (☎ 406-549-7600), a parkside **Holiday Inn** (☎ 800-399-0408), two **Red Lion Inns** (☎ 800-547-8010), a **Rodeway Inn** (☎ 800-247-2616), two **Super 8**s (☎ 800-800-8000) and a **Travelodge** (☎ 800-578-7878).

Noxon

Bighorn Lodge is a B&B having four guest rooms with private baths, full breakfast. Fishing, canoeing, trail rides. $$$$. #2 Bighorn Lane, Noxon, MT 59853; ☎ 406-847-5597. Fax 406-847-5502.

High Country Connection is a mountain country log B&B with two guest rooms with private baths; full breakfast. Activities include llama hikes, trail rides, canoeing, fishing the Clark Fork River. 345 Pilgrim Creek Rd. (Box 1608), Noxon, MT 59853; ☎ 888-643-1565 or 406-847-2279.

Paradise

Quinn's Hot Springs on MT 135, overlooking the Clark Fork River (see *Touring*), is a Montana tradition. 16 cabins and trailer units, RV sites, store, bar & supper club, outdoor pool and hot tub, private Jacuzzis. Open year-round. $. Box 219, Paradise, MT 59856; ☎ 406-826-3150 or 826-3157.

Polebridge

North Fork Hostel & Square Peg Ranch, just outside Glacier Park's western boundary, is a rustic old lodge accommodating 15 people. No electricity, but hot showers are available. Kitchen facilities; bring food, towels, flashlights, sleeping bags. Also, log homes and small cabins for rent. $. 80 Beaver Dr. (Box 1), Polebridge, MT 59928; ☎ 800-775-2938 or 406-888-5241.

Polebridge Mercantile & Cabins has rustic cabins available year-round. $. Box 280042, Polebridge, MT 59928; ☎ 406-888-5105.

Polson

B&Bs and a full-service resort dominate Polson's choices.

B&Bs

Hammond's Bed & Breakfast, a summer cabin on Flathead Lake, has two guest rooms with shared bath, full breakfast. $$$. 10141 East Shore, Polson, MT 59860; ☎ 406-887-2766.

Hawthorne House is off the lake, has five guest rooms with shared baths, full breakfast. $$. 304 3rd Ave. E, Polson, MT 59860; ☎ 800-290-1345 or 406-888-2723.

Hidden Pines has a hot tub, nearby boat docking, four guest rooms, two with private baths. $$. 792 Lost Quartz Rd., Polson, MT 59860; ☎ 800-505-5612 or 406-849-5612.

Ruth Bed & Breakfast has two guest rooms with shared bath, full breakfast. $. 802 7th Ave. W, Polson, MT 59860; ☎ 406-883-2460.

Swan Hill Bed & Breakfast, in a woodsy view setting, has four guest rooms with private baths; full breakfast. $$$$. 460 Kings Point Rd., Polson, MT 59860; ☎ 800-537-9489 or 406-883-5292.

Other Lodgings

Best Western KwaTaqNuk Resort, a development of the Confederated Slaish and Kootenai Tribes, commands a gorgeous lakeside location. This very nice full-service resort has 112 guest rooms, most with lake views, restaurant, pool, access to lake cruises (see *Adventures on Water*). $$$$. 303 US 93 E, Polson, MT 59860; ☎ 800-882-6363 or 406-883-3636. Fax 406-883-5392.

Port Polson Inn, on Flathead Lake, has 44 guest rooms, some with kitchens; no restaurant or pool. $$$. US 93 (Box 1411), Polson, MT 59860; ☎ 800-654-0682 or 406-883-5385. Fax 406-883-3998.

Schiefelbein Haus has 11 guest rooms and a restaurant. $$. 6395 East shore Rt., Polson, MT 59860; ☎ 406-887-2431.

Mission Mountain Resort offers cabins plus rooms in the main lodge, traveling horse facilities. $$. 257 Fulkerson Lane (Box 456), Polson, MT 59860; ☎ 406-883-1883.

Proctor

Camp Tuffit has cabins on Lake Mary Ronan; fishing, boat rentals, nightly campfire. $$. Box 196, Lake Mary Ronan, Proctor, MT 59929; ☎ 406-849-5220.

Lake Mary Ronan Resort has 12 cabins, RV spaces, restaurant, marina. Small grocery sells homemade baked goods. $$. Star Route, Proctor, MT 59929; ☎ 406-849-5454.

Ronan

The Timbers Bed & Breakfast, on 21 acres of timbered Reservation land, has two guest rooms, one with private bath, full breakfast. $$$. 1184 Timberline Road, Ronan, MT 59864; ☎ 800-775-4373 or 406-676-4373.

St. Ignatius

B&Bs

Mandorla Ranch Retreat B&B, a spacious designer log home, has four guest rooms/deluxe suites with private baths, full breakfast. $$$$. 6873 Allard Rd., St. Ignatius, MT 59865; ☎ 406-745-4500. Fax 406-676-8524.

Mission Falls Ranch Vacations offers B&B or B&B + Supper options on a working cattle ranch in the shadow of the Mission Mountains.

Choose between a comfortable bedroom with bath or a tipi with kitchen. $$. 15338 Hillside Rd., St. Ignatius, MT 59865; ☎ 406-745-3375.

Stoneheart Inn takes its name from a legend that says finding a heart-shaped stone brings great fortune. You may not find one, but you will find a choice of four theme guest rooms with private baths. Gourmet breakfast, feather beds, bedside refreshments, pleasant common room with fireplace. Sack lunches available. $$. 26 N. Main (PO Box 236), St. Ignatius, MT59865; ☎ 888-291-4960, Pin #7038 or 406-745-4999.

Hostel

Biking Bunks Hostel-St. Ignatius Camping has tent camping and sleeps 16 dormitory-style. Indoor bicycle storage, laundromat. $. Junction US 93 & Airport Rd. (Box 91), St. Ignatius, MT 59865; ☎ 406-745-3959.

St. Mary

St. Mary Lodge & Resort, near the east entrance to Glacier Park and Going to the Sun Road, has 76 guest rooms and a restaurant. $$$. St. Mary, MT 59417; ☎ 406-732-4431 (summer), ☎ 406-726-6279 (winter).

Seeley Lake

Seeley Lake's popularity is reflected in a wide choice of B&Bs, resorts and other fun country lodgings.

B&Bs

The Emily A. Bed & Breakfast has a cabin and a family suite in a log lodge on the Clearwater River. Full breakfast. $$$$. MT 83, Milepost 20 (Box 350), Seeley Lake, MT 59868; ☎ 800-977-4639 or 406-677-FISH.

Kozy Kountry Bed & Breakfast has five guest rooms, one with private bath; full breakfast. $$$$. Box 1160, Seeley Lake, MT 59868; 406-677-3436. Fax 406-677-3355.

Other Lodgings

Double Arrow Resort is situated on 200 acres surrounded by the Flathead National Forest. Traditional old-fashioned resort has an indoor pool, fine dining, tennis courts, horseback rides, wagon & sleigh rides, cross-country skiing, snowmobiling and more. $$. Box 747, Seeley Lake, MT 59868; ☎ 800-468-0777 or 406-677-2777. Fax 406-677-2922.

Elkhorn Motel & Café has 27 guest rooms. $$$. MT 83 at Milepost 16 (Box 565), Seeley Lake, MT 59868; ☎ 800-867-5678 or 406-677-2278. Fax 406-273-2640.

The Lodges at Seeley Lake, centered around a historic lodge, has cabins with kitchens among old-growth larches and a sandy beach on Seeley Lake. Open year-round. $$$$. Box 568, Boy Scout Rd., Seeley Lake, MT 59868; ☎ 800-900-9016 or 406-677-2376.

Tamaracks Resort, on the north end of Seeley Lake, is one of those old-time family resorts that are far too scarce in this glitzy age. The 13 woodsy lakefront housekeeping cabins, some historic, sleep from one to 10. Also a large log recreation building, camping/RV sites. Boat, canoe, hydro-bike, cross-country ski, skate and snowmobile rentals. Swim from the beach. $$-$$$. Box 812, Seeley Lake, MT 59868; ☎ 800-447-7216 or 406-677-2433.

The Center at Seeley Lake is hardly a drop-by lodging, but the big log conference center owned by the University of Montana hosts family re-unions and other gatherings in complete luxury. Situated on an island in Salmon Lake, the 8,000 sq. ft. log "cabin" was built as a private home. In summer guests are ferried to the island by boat. In winter, an ATV ferries guests across the ice on a sled. Flexible lodging and meal packages. $$$$. HC 31, Box 800 South Seeley Lake, MT 59868; ☎ 406-243-5556 or 406-677-3620. Fax 406-677-3846. E-mail ifisher@selway.umt.edu Internet www.salmonlakecenter.org.

Wapiti Resort, a mile north of Seeley Lake, features a reproduction Old West town. Modern and rustic cabins with kitchens, motel rooms, RV and tent sites. Restaurant, boat dock and rentals. $$$. MT 83 Milepost 16 (Box 565), Seeley Lake, MT 59868; ☎ 800-867-5678 or 406-677-2775. Fax 406-273-2640.

Somers

Osprey Inn B&B has a dock on Flathead Lake, two guest rooms with private baths, a two-room suite with private bath, and a log cabin for two with separate private bath; full breakfast. $$$$. 5557 US 93 S., Somers, MT 59932; ☎ 800-258-2042 or 406-857-2042. Fax ☎ 406-857-2019.

Outlook Inn Bed & Breakfast, steps from Flathead Lake and enjoying a superb view, has four themed guest rooms with private baths and decks. Families welcome. Full breakfast. $$. PO Box 177, Somers, MT 59932; ☎ 888-857-VIEW or 406-857-2060. E-mail outlook@digisys.net. Internet www.webby.com/montana/outlook

Stevensville

Stevensville is following Hamilton's lead with a rash of B&Bs. **Big Creek Pines Bed & Breakfast** advertises "casual elegance" and "candlelit gourmet breakfast." Also afternoon tea trays. Four guest rooms with private baths. $$$. 2986 US 93, Stevensville, MT 59870; ☎ 888-300-6475 or 406-642-6475.

The Country Cabooose boasts a guest room with bath in a genuine 1923 caboose; refurbished, of course. Full breakfast. $$. 852 Willoughby Lane, Stevensville, MT 59870; ☎ 406-777-3145.

Haus Rustika Bed & Breakfast has four bedrooms with shared baths, full country breakfast, other meals by prior arrangement, kitchenette/ sitting room, loads of charm. $$. 396 Dry Gulch, Stevensville, MT 59870; ☎ 406-777-2291.

Schoolhouse B&B has a guest room with bath in a restored 1918 schoolhouse. Full breakfast. $$$. 2853 Eastside Hwy., Stevensville, MT 59870; ☎ 406-777-3904.

Glacier Country

Stryker

Loon's Echo Resort & Fish Farm on 40-acre Fish Lake in the Stillwater State Forest offers fully equipped vacation houses and cabins. Lodge dining room overlooks private 14-acre trout pond. Indoor pool. Open year-round. $$$$. 1 Fish Lake Rd. (Box 98), Stryker, MT 59933; ☎ 800-956-6632 or 406-882-4791. Fax 406-882-4676.

Sula

Sula's way-back-in-the-woods ambience is reflected in its lodgings. **Broad Axe Lodge** is on the Bitterroot River and is surrounded by the Bitterroot National Forest. Cabins have queen beds, full baths, kitchens. Restaurant. Open year-round. A designated Montana Wildlife Viewing area. $$. 1237 East Fork Rd., Sula, MT 59871; ☎ 406-821-3878.

Camp Creek Inn B&B has two housekeeping cabins and three guest rooms, two with private baths, country breakfast. Horse boarding for overnight guests, horseback riding, cross-country skiing. $$. 7674 US 93 S., Sula, MT 59871; ☎ 800-351-3508 or 406-821-3508.

Lost Trail Hot Springs Resort has 23 guest rooms, family restaurant, natural hot mineral pool, sauna, hot tub; a cross-country ski mecca. $$. 8321 US 93 S., Sula, MT 59871; ☎ 800-825-3574 or 406-821-3574. Fax 406-821-4012.

Superior

Sheep Mountain Lodge reflects the classic rusticity for which Montana resorts are known. Scenically situated on the Clark Fork River, the lodge offers numerous activities, including fishing and games. Private river access. Guided fishing trips available. By-the-day rates include lodging and three meals. $$. 29 Sverdsten Lane (PO Box 787), Superior, MT 59872; ☎ 800-668-8366 or 406-822-3382.

Swan Valley

Holland Lake Lodge offers both lodge rooms and cabins, restaurant, sauna, canoeing, fishing, cross-country skiing, snowmobiling, pack trips, horseback riding. $$$. 1947 Holland Lake Rd., Swan Valley, MT 59826; ☎ 800-648-8859 or 406-754-2282. Fax 406-754-2208.

Thompson Falls

Prospect Creek Bed & Breakfast's log lodge is on Flatiron Ridge; it has 10 guest rooms with private baths, full sourdough pancake breakfast. $$. 26 Crown Terrace, Thompson Falls, MT 59873; ☎ 406-827-9888.

The Riverfront offers one- and 2-bedroom vacation homes on the Clark Fork River and five log-style cabins with kitchens, screened porches, river access; fire pit, horseshoes, nature trail. $$$ & $$. 4907 MT 200 (Box 22), Thompson Falls, MT 59873; ☎ 406-827-3460.

Trego

Tucker's Inn Resort and Conference Center has a honeymoon Jacuzzi suite in the lodge, four tastefully appointed cabins, a family-style restaurant and access to year-round fun. This is a property that straddles the line between lodge and guest ranch. All-inclusive summer packages include horseback riding. Winter snowmobile or ski packages are available. Adventure trips are also possible. $$$. PO Box 220, Trego, MT 59934; ☎ 800-500-3541 or 406-882-4200.

Trout Creek

Blue Spruce Lodge is a gorgeous log complex on 200 acres overlooking Noxon Reservoir. Home cooked family-style meals included in price, or choose breakfast-only rate. Truly delightful getaway. $$. 451 Marten Creek Rd., Trout Creek, MT 59874; ☎ 406-827-4762.

Lakeside Motel has eight guest rooms and a hot tub. $$. 2957 MT 200 (Box 1489), Trout Creek, MT 59874; ☎ 406-827-4458.

Troy

Kootenai River Vacation Homes offers a furnished A-frame home and two log homes on the river; spa and indoor pool. $$. 1815 River Rd., Troy, MT 59935; ☎ 800-558-VIEW or 406-295-4630.

Victor

Bear Creek Lodge is on 72 acres at the mouth of Bear Creek Canyon. Log lodge has understated elegance, gourmet cuisine, eight guest rooms with private entrances. $$$$. 1184 Bear Creek Trail, Victor, MT 59875; ☎ 800-270-5550 or 406-642-3750. Fax 406-642-6847.

Duck Creek Bed & Breakfast is a two-bedroom cottage featuring a fridge stocked with breakfast goodies. $$$$. Box 818, Victor, MT 59875; ☎ 406-642-☎ 307-3.

Time After Time B&B, in a wooded setting with a pond, has three guest rooms, two with private baths, full breakfast. $$$. 197 Pistol Lane, Victor, MT 59875; ☎ 406-642-3258.

West Glacier

There are so many lodging choices in and around West Glacier that you'd expect a glut of available rooms. There isn't. Make reservations, especially in high summer.

B&Bs

Glacier-West Chalet has five guest rooms with shared baths, full breakfast. $$$. 125 Edgar Lane (Box 43), West Glacier, MT 59936; ☎ 406-888-5507.

Mountain Timbers Lodge, situated on 220 acres near Glacier Park, has seven guest rooms with shared baths, full breakfast, Jacuzzi. $$$. Box 94, West Glacier, MT 59936; ☎ 800-841-3835 or 406-387-5830. Fax 406-387-5835.

Silverwolf Chalets. Fully equipped designer chalets for two in a forested setting; log interiors, fireplaces, decks, barbeques, maid service, muffin & juice breakfast delivered each morning. $$$$. Box 115, West Glacier, MT 59936; ☎ 406-387-4448.

Other Lodgings

Belton Chalet & Lodge, the first Great Northern Railway chalet, has been restored to its original Mission-style ambience. First opened in 1910, the year that Glacier was designated as a national park, the lodge is pleasantly situated on a hillside across from the historic train depot and West Glacier village. Belton Chalet's 25-room lodge and two cabins are ready for guests while an expansion effort continues. Open year-round, there's ample opportunity for cross-country skiing from the door and in Glacier Park. The Belton Taproom offers rib-sticking soups and luscious treats. Nostalgia trippers will be impressed by this landmark inn. $$. 12575 Hwy. 2 East, West Glacier, MT 59936; ☎ 406-888-5000. Fax 406-888-5005. E-mail belton@digisys.net.

Glacier Highland Motel has 33 guest rooms and a restaurant. On US 2 East. Box 397, West Glacier, MT 59936; ☎ 800-766-0811 or 406-888-5427. Fax 406-888-5764.

Glacier Raft Company has five log cabins sleeping two to six in a wooded setting a half-mile from Glacier Park's West Entrance. $$$. #6 Going to the Sun Road (Box 218), West Glacier, MT 59936; ☎ 800-332-9995 or 406-888-5454.

Glacier Wilderness Resort offers luxury log homes with Jacuzzis on decks, fireplaces, washer/dryers. Five-night minimum. $$$. Box 295, West Glacier, MT 59936; ☎ 406-888-5664.

Great Northern Chalets has 12 chalet-style units, restaurant, pool. $$$. Box 278, West Glacier, MT 59936; ☎ 800-735-7897 or 406-387-5340. Fax 406-387-9007.

Great Northern Whitewater offers five log chalets a mile from Glacier Park; fireplaces, upper and lower decks, barbeques, hot tub/swim spa on site. $$$. Box 278, West Glacier, MT 59936; ☎ 800-735-7897 (outside MT), 800-535-0303 (in MT) or 406-387-5340.

Lake Five Resort has lakeside cabins, RV and tent sites, swimming, boating, sandy beach. Nice family place. $$. 540 Belton Stage Rd. (Box 338), West Glacier, MT 59936; ☎ 406-387-5601.

River Bend Motel has 33 guest rooms and a restaurant; close to the Park. 200 Going to the Sun Road (Box 398), West Glacier, MT 59936; ☎ 406-888-5662.

Vista Motel has 26 guest rooms and a pool. On US 2. Box 98, West Glacier, MT 59936; ☎ 800-831-7101 or 406-888-5311.

Whitefish

The Whitefish area is as high-toned as Glacier Country gets, but the people are invariably friendly and downhome.

B&Bs

The Crenshaw House is a ranch house situated on a pretty meadow. Three guest rooms with private baths, full breakfast. $$$. 5465 US 93 S., Whitefish, MT 59937; ☎ 800-453-2863 or 406-862-3496. Fax 406-862-7640.

Duck Inn has 10 guest rooms with private baths, continental breakfast; Amtrak meet/depart service. $$$. 1305 Columbia Ave., Whitefish, MT 59937; ☎ 800-344-2377 or 406-862-3825.

Eagle's Roost Inn Bed & Breakfast has three guest rooms with in-room Jacuzzis, one with private bath, full gourmet breakfast. $$$. 400 Wisconsin Ave. (Box 518), Whitefish, MT 59937; ☎ 406-862-5198.

Edgewood Bed & Breakfast, a historic home decorated with antiques, has three guest rooms with shared baths. Full breakfast often include sourdough waffles made from a Yukon starter. $$$. 12 Dakota Ave., Whitefish, MT 59937; ☎ 406-862-9663.

The Garden Wall Inn, in a charming historic house in town, has five guest rooms with private baths; full breakfast. $$$$. 504 Spokane Ave., Whitefish, MT 59937; ☎ 406-862-3440.

Gasthaus Wendlingen has three guest rooms with private baths. Full breakfast includes German specialties. $$$$. 700 Monegan Rd., Whitefish, MT 59937; ☎ 800-811-8002 or 406-862-4886.

Good Medicine Lodge, an environmentally sensitive pro-earth inn whose decor projects a Native American ambience, has nine tastefully appointed guest rooms with private baths, balconies, hearty European breakfast. Kids 10 and under stay free in parents' room. $$$. 537 Wisconsin Ave. (Box 562), Whitefish, MT 59937; ☎ 800-860-5488 or 406-862-5488.

Hidden Moose Lodge, a gorgeous log-faced chalet at the base of Big Mountain, offers rooms with private entrances, private balconies, Montana-size breakfast, free use of mountain bikes in summer. The decor is quintessential mountain country Montana. Owners/Innkeepers Kent and Kim Taylor built and decorated the inn themselves and have a keen eye for the whimsical. $$$. 1735 E. Lakeshore Dr. (Box 344), Whitefish, MT 59937; ☎ 800-862-6516. Fax 406-862-6514.

La Villa Montana, a spacious new chalet, has four guest rooms with private baths, full breakfast. $$$$. Box 4390, Whitefish, MT 59937; ☎ 800-652-8455 or 406-892-0689. Fax 406-892-0690.

Big Mountain Ski & Summer Resort Lodgings

Alpinglow Inn at the Big Mountain has 54 guest rooms and a restaurant. $$$. 3900 Big Mountain Rd. (Box 1770), Whitefish, MT 59937; ☎ 800-754-6760 or 406-862-6966. Fax 406-862-0076.

Hibernation House is an economical choice with 42 rooms, no restaurant. $$. 3812 Big Mountain Rd. (Box 1400), Whitefish, MT 59937; ☎ 800-858-5439 or 406-862-1982. Fax 406-862-1956.

Kandahar Lodge, with 50 guest rooms and a restaurant, is Big Mountain's priciest. $$$$. Big Mountain Rd. (Box 1659), Whitefish, MT 59937; ☎ 800-862-6094 or 406-862-6098. Fax 406-862-6095.

The Big Mountain Alpine Homes has 40 condos and alpine homes for rent. Box 1400, Whitefish, MT 59937; ☎ 800-858-5439 or 406-862-1982. Fax 406-862-2955.

Condo Rentals

Anapurna Properties, 3840 Big Mountain Rd. (Box 55), Whitefish, MT 59937; ☎ 800-243-7547 or 406-862-3687. Fax 406-862-0586.

Bay Point Estates, 300 Bay Point Dr. (Box 35), Whitefish, MT 59937; ☎ 800-327-2108 or 406-862-2331.

Edelweiss Condominiums, 3898 Big Mountain Rd. (Box 846), Whitefish, MT 59937; ☎ 800-228-8260 or 406-862-5252. Fax 406-862-3009.

Ptarmigan Village, 3000 Big Mountain Rd. (Box 458), Whitefish, MT 59937; ☎ 800-552-3952 or 406-862-3594. Fax 406-862-6664.

Whitefish Lake Lodge Resort Condominiums, 1399 Wisconsin Ave. (Box 2040), Whitefish, MT 59937; ☎ 800-735-8869 or 406-862-2929. Fax 862-3550.

Other Lodgings

Best Western Rocky Mountain Lodge is upscale with 79 guest rooms, swimming pool. $$$$. 6510 US 93 S., Whitefish, MT 59937; ☎ 800-862-2569 or 406-862-2569. Fax 406-862-1154.

Comfort Inn also has a pool, 65 guest rooms. $$$. 6390 US 93 S., Whitefish, MT 59937; ☎ 800-888-4479 or 406-862-4020. Fax 406-862-4115.

Gaynor's RiverBend Ranch has a four-room suite in a ranch setting, horseback riding, riding lessons, horse boarding. $$. 1992 KM Ranch Rd., Whitefish, MT 59937; ☎ 406-862-3802. Fax 406-862-4158.

Crestwood Resort, in a wooded setting across from Whitefish Lake, has one and two-bedroom condos with fireplaces; swimming pool. $$$. 1301 Wisconsin Ave. (Box 1000), Whitefish, MT 59937; ☎ 800-862-7574 or 406-862-7574. Fax 406-862-0491.

Grouse Mountain Lodge has it all: 144 guest rooms, lobby with stone fireplace and Montana-style decor, restaurant, swimming pool. $$$. 1205 US 93 W., Whitefish, MT 59937; ☎ 800-321-8822 or 406-862-3000. Fax 406-862-0326.

Kristiana offer ski-in, ski-out lodging on Big Mountain. two- ,three- , and four-bedroom units, private decks, dry sauna/hot tub, wood stoves or gas fireplaces, kitchenettes. $$$. 3842 Winter Lane, Whitefish, MT 59937; ☎ 800-754-0040 or 406-862-2860. Fax 406-862-0782.

Mountain Harbor offers two- to four-bedroom rental properties on Whitefish Lake. Tennis court, pool, Jacuzzi, marina. $$$$. 1750 E. Lakeshore Dr. (Box 4389), Whitefish, MT 59937; ☎ 800-883-2506 or 406-862-5511. Fax 406-862-5574.

North Forty Resort has 22 fully equipped, log-furnished cabins convenient to both Whitefish and Columbia Falls; kitchens, fireplaces, barbeques, covered porches, down comforters, hot tub, campfire, vollwyball. $$. Box 4250, Whitefish, MT 59937; ☎ 800-775-1740 or 406-862-7740. Fax 406-862-7741.

Quality Inn - Pine Lodge offers more luxury than one might expect; 76 guest rooms, pool. $$$$. 920 Spokane Ave. (Box 2069), Whitefish, MT 59937; ☎ 800-305-7463 or 406-862-7600. Fax 406-862-7616.

The Non-Hostile Hostel, at 300 E. Second St., has large, clean dorm-style rooms with rows of bunk beds and mattresses. Laundry facilities, café (see *Where to Eat*). Bring your bedroll. $. ☎ 406-862-7383.

Woods Bay

This non-town on the east side of Flathead Lake a few miles south of Bigfork boasts a family-style resort.

Woods Bay Resort has motel units and comfortable cabins with kitchens, barbeques with picnic tables, nice pebble beach. $$. Also RV hookups (see *Camping*). 26481 E. Lakeshore Rt., Woods Bay, MT 59911; ☎ 406-837-3333.

Yaak

Overdale Lodge is on a c.1918 homestead; many original buildings and barns remain standing. The five-bedroom lakeside lodge was built in the 1920s. Two new log cabins accommodate up to four persons. Minimum stay two days. Open year-round. Great wildlife watching. $$. 1076 Overdale Lodge Rd., Yaak-Troy, MT 59935; ☎ 406-295-4057.

Yaak River Lodge has pleasant guest rooms with private baths, dorm accommodating up to nine with own bath. Dining room, hot tub, sauna. Open year-round. $. 2774 Yaak River Rd., Troy, MT 59935; ☎ 800-676-5670 or 406-295-5463.

■ US Forest Service Cabins

When being pampered won't do; when you want to get away from civilization, yet want a roof over your head, consider renting an old line cabin, fire lookout or historic miners' cabin. The Forest Service or the Garnet Preservation Association may have just the thing, guaranteed to spirit you back to when life in Montana was, well... more elemental.

Time was when the back country had numerous fire lookout towers manned by lonely smoke spotters. Scores of cabins were used by rangers while maintaining their districts. Enter fire spotting planes and 4WD vehicles; exit the useful lives of most lookout towers and cabins. Many deteriorated beyond redemption or were purposely destroyed before preservationists and Forest Service honchos came up with the brilliant concept of renting them to recreationists. Meanwhile the BLM, together with the Garnet Preservation Association, had undertaken to preserve the Garnet Ghost Town (see *Touring*). While most structures not privately owned were better looked at than slept in, a couple of old miners' cabins had lodgings appeal.

Fire lookouts, perched on top of peaks, offer wide-angle views that bring back country grandeur up close and personal. Cabins are the flip side, nestled as they are in trees, by streams or in the lee of hills.

Generally, these digs define basic. Some are accessible by car or 4WD vehicle, but most require walking, riding, snowmobiling or skiing in. Some are available year-round, some not. Most have wood stoves and basic furnishings; virtually none have electricity. Some lack potable water. "Bathrooms" are out back. Some have horse corrals. What these digs lack in conveniences, they make up for in delicious solitude. When reserving your cabin or lookout, ask what's supplied and what you'll need to bring.

 A booklet is available listing and briefly describing rental lookouts and cabins in Northern Region National Forests. Request a copy by contacting any ranger district.

The **Bitterroot National Forest** has a lookout tower, a guard station and four line cabins.

The **Flathead National Forest** rents two lookouts and six cabins. The **Kootenai National Forest** maintains five former fire lookouts. The **Lolo National Forest** has four lookouts, a homestead cabin, a guard station, a cookhouse/bunkhouse and a line cabin.

Rental fees are usually in the $25-$30 range and stays are limited to 14 days. Obtain a permit and reserve your get-away by contacting the ranger district having responsibility for the lookout or cabin of your choice.

The **Garnet Preservation Association** has two former miners' cabins. The **Dahl Cabin** is great for groups, having three full-size beds and two hide-a-beds. It rents for $40 the first night and $35 for subsequent nights. The **Wills Cabin** is a single room with two double beds renting for $30 the first night and $25 for each night thereafter. Access is by ski or snowmobile in winter.

Reservations are determined by a drawing. Applications are accepted between November 1 and 14. Obtain a permit and application form by contacting Garnet Preservation Association Cabin Rental Program, Box 20029, Missoula, MT 59801; ☎ 406-329-1031 prior to November 1.

■ Camping

 Campgrounds and places to park your RV for the night are thick as scales on a fish in Glacier Country. They sort out into state parks, US Forest Service campgrounds, commercial RV and camping parks, RV spaces next to hot springs, motels and other combinations thereof (see *Hotels, Motels &*

B&Bs). It's nigh unto impossible not to find a campsite here. Riding on the premise that any traveler can locate an unremarkable overnight pad, the campgrounds listed below fall into four categories: State Parks, Forest Service campgrounds, Glacier National Park campgrounds, and commercial RV and camping parks – all having something special to recommend them. That lets out parks where RVs are lined up side-by-side in the broiling hot sun.

State Parks

Fees vary, but Montana State Parks campsites are generally in the $10-$15 per-night range, less if you display an annual pass ($25 for non-residents). Campsites are generally available on a first-come, first-served basis. Those accepting reservations are noted below. With the exception of the West Shore Unit, state parks on Flathead Lake are among Montana's best. There are five, conveniently spaced around the lake. Wildhorse Island makes six, but it's a day-use park only accessible by boat. Finley Point has RV hookups; others offer dry camping.

Wayfarer's Unit, a half-mile south of Bigfork on MT 35, has easily accessible well-shaded RV and tent sites above the lake, hiking trails, picnic spots, a boat ramp and a large sunny meadow that's ideal for ball games. Summer: ☎ 406-837-4196. Winter: ☎ 406-752-5501. **Yellow Bay Unit** is farther south on MT 35; 15 miles north of Polson. Prettily situated in sweet cherry country, the park has a walk-in tent area and a wide gravelly beach. ☎ 406-752-5501.

Finley Point Unit, 11 miles north of Polson on MT 35 and four miles west on a county road, is the aristocrat of Montana's state parks. Surrounded by a mature conifer forest, it boasts full hookup RV sites with a 40-foot capacity, slips for boats up to 25 feet long, a boat pump-out station and overnight boat slips with utilities. The good news: RV sites right on the lake. The bad news: sites are close together with no private green space. Summer: ☎ 406-887-2715. Winter: ☎ 406-752-5501.

Big Arm Unit, 12 miles north of Polson on US 93, is a jump-off point for boating to Wildhorse Island. Lakeside campsites extend for quite some distance along the shore and are staggered along two hillside roadways to allow a maximum number of campers to enjoy close-up lake views. Sites closest to the lake have lake access virtually at their doors. Lots of Canada geese and other wildfowl. Reservations: ☎ 406-755-2706.

West Shore Unit, hidey-holed in a mature forest above the rocky lakeshore, is woodsy-pretty but has little or no room for RVs over 20 feet. Summer: ☎ 406-844-3901. Winter: ☎ 406-752-5501.

Lake Mary Ronan State Park, seven miles northwest of Dayton, offers a charming alternative to the big lake. The 76-acre park has pleasant campsites sheltered by Douglas fir and western larch. Swimming, fishing, boating, bird watching. ☎ 406-752-5501.

Whitefish Lake State Park's pleasant situation on a popular lake is marred by the close proximity of a heavily traveled railway line. All night, I just knew the next train was going to fall and squish me – RV, dog and all. The 10-acre park is one mile west of Whitefish off US 93. Summer: ☎ 406-862-3991. Winter: ☎ 406-752-5501.

Beavertail Hill State Park enjoys a half-mile of frontage on the Clark Fork River with campsites in the shade of cottonwoods. 26 miles east of Missoula; take the Beavertail Hill exit off I-90. ☎ 406-542-5500.

Salmon Lake and **Placid Lake State Parks** are prettily situated on the Clearwater River chain of lakes at the south end of the Seeley Valley. Both have tent and RV sites and are good wildlife watching and fishing venues. Salmon Lake Park is on MT 83. Placid Lake Park is on a county road three miles west of MT 83. ☎ 406-542-5500.

Logan State Park is a pleasant way-stop on US 2, 45 miles west of Kalispell and some 60 miles east of Libby. Situated in a western larch and ponderosa pine forest, the park is on the north shore of Middle Thompson Lake. Swimming, boating, waterskiing, fishing. Dump station available. Reservations: ☎ 406-755-2706.

Thompson Falls State Park, a mile northwest of Thompson Falls on MT 2, offers tent and RV camping on the shores of Noxon Reservoir. Bird watching and nature walks augment fishing for bass, trout and ling. ☎ 406-752-5501.

Painted Rocks State Park, on Rt. 473 some 40 miles southwest of Hamilton, is tucked away in the scenic Painted Rocks area of the Bitterroot Mountains. Tent and RV camping on a reservoir whose clear water reflects colorful rocks reminiscent of the Southwest. ☎ 406-542-5500.

US Forest Service Campgrounds

The US Forest Service seems to make an extra effort in Glacier Country, maintaining several exceptional campgrounds convenient to major routes and places of interest. These are established campgrounds, not to be confused with back country camping areas accessible by foot or horse. For information on these, contact the ranger district maintaining the trail system or designated wilderness area through which you plan to hike or horse pack.

Developed Forest Service campground fees are about $8 per night, with a 14-day limit. Golden Age card holders pay half-price. Many campgrounds have RV dumps and flush toilets. All have drinking water. Many have paved interior roads and campsite pads. Unless otherwise noted, these are fairweather campgrounds open between mid-May and Sept. 30.

First-come, first-served is the rule. Exceptions are Quartz Flat on the Lolo National Forest, McGillivray and Rexford Bench on Lake Koocanusa on the Kootenai National Forest, Tally Lake and Big Creek on the Flathead National Forest, and Warm Springs and Spring Gulch/ Spring Gulch Bicycle Group Site on the Bitterroot National Forest. Sites in campgrounds other than Tally Lake can be reserved by calling ☎ 800-280-2267 (TTY 1-800-879-4496). Fax 301-722-9802. ☎ 800-416-6992 to reserve a Tally Lake campsite.

The following campgrounds are stand-outs I've enjoyed at one time or another. For information on others, contact the Lolo, Kootenai, Flathead and Bitterroot National Forests Supervisors Offices. The Lolo National Forest maintains several campgrounds convenient to, or on, the I-90 corridor between Missoula and the Idaho line, in the Lolo Pass area, and in the Seeley-Swan Valley. The Forest has available a booklet describing these and other campgrounds.

Quartz Flat, at the rest areas on both sides of I-90 11 miles east of Superior, is within walking distance of the Clark Fork River. Level campsites long enough for all RVs are shaded by large conifers. Kids enjoy collecting pine cones here. A road tunnel connects the two sides. **Slowey**, on I-90 midway between Superior and St. Regis, has fairly secluded campsites and horse camp facilities. Volleyball net, horseshoe pits, sandbox.

Two campgrounds on US 12 east of Lolo Pass, **Lewis & Clark** and **Lee Creek**, offer pleasant, convenient camping. Creekside and hillside sites under mature trees are close to the Lewis & Clark Trail.

Four developed campgrounds in the vicinity of MT 83, in the Seeley-Swan Valley, offer access to fishing, boating, hiking, wildlife watching and other fun activities. **River Point, Seeley Lake** and **Lake Alva** are open between Memorial Day and Labor Day. **Big Larch** is open year-round.

The **Kootenai National Forest** maintains two campgrounds on Lake Koocanusa. The **Rexford Bench Complex**, west of Eureka, offers several camping options. It's larger than it seems because of winding interior roads. Several short hiking trails lead to lake view areas. **McGillivray Campground** is a large affair on the west shore of the lake north of Libby Dam. **North Dickey Lake Campground** sites are tucked under sheltering trees, among thick clumps of descendants of the wild Wood Roses admired by Lewis and Clark. Nice swimming area. **Bad Medicine Campground** is convenient to both Bull Lake and Ross Cedar Grove.

The **Flathead National Forest** maintains numerous campgrounds, most having just a few sites, in the **Tally Lake Ranger District** north of Whitefish, in the **Swan Lake Ranger District**, the **Glacier View Ranger District** east of Glacier Park, and the **Hungry Horse Ranger District** along Hungry Horse Reservoir and the South Fork of the Flathead River. **Tally Lake Campground**, on Montana's deepest natural lake, is very popular, but worthwhile because of the great natural beauty and proximity to hiking trails. This mostly rugged country is accessible by 4WD vehicle, horseback or shank's mare. A booklet obtainable from these ranger districts describes these and other campgrounds. The **Bitterroot National Forest** maintains fewer campgrounds. Contact the Supervisors Office for a list.

Campgrounds in Glacier National Park

Glacier Park campgrounds fall into three categories: developed campgrounds accessible via paved roads, less structured campgrounds on gravel roads and back country camping. Refer to *Adventures on Foot* for information on the latter.

With the exception of St. Mary and Fish Creek Campgrounds, sites in developed campgrounds are available on a first-come, first-served basis. Sites in the aforementioned campgrounds may be reserved through the National Park Reservation Service by dialing ☎ 800-365-2267 well in advance of your visit. A limited number of tent sites can be reserved by pedestrians, bicyclists and motorcyclists by dialing ☎ 406-888-7800. Camp site registrations are on a day at a time basis. These campgrounds offer dry camping, meaning no electric and water hookups. Fresh water is available and larger campgrounds provide washrooms and dump stations. Trailer spaces are available at all but Sprague Creek. Campground fees are in the $10-$12 range. Campers without cars pay $5. Golden Age card holders pay half-price.

Campgrounds Reached by Paved Roads

Apgar, near Apgar Village at the West Entrance, is a sizeable campground shaded by tall trees.

Avalanche Creek, off the Going-to-the-Sun Road near Trail of the Cedars.

Fish Creek is in a heavily wooded area on the northwest shore of Lake McDonald.

Sprague Creek, a mile south of Lake McDonald Lodge, is favored by tent campers.

On Glacier's East Side

St. Mary's (owned by the Blackfeet Nation) has campsites on an open meadow.

Many Glacier offers access to numerous hiking trails.

Rising Sun is adjacent to St. Mary Lake.

Two Medicine is attractively situated near the lake by that name in the southeast corner of the Park.

Campgrounds Reached by Gravel Roads

Campgrounds reached by gravel roads provide fireplaces, tables and pit toilets; no running water. These are found at **Cut Bank** (not to be confused with the town of that name), **Kintla** and **Bowman Lakes** in the Polebridge area, **Quartz Creek** and **Logging Creek**. Roads to these tend to be rough and narrow. Inquire at a ranger station before attempting to reach these campgrounds if you are driving an RV or towing a trailer.

Campgrounds Adjacent to Glacier Park

Campgrounds close to the Park offer alternatives to the Park's first-come, first-served, one-day-at-a-time rule. These are more expensive, but they offer full hookups; and you can reserve a space.

Campgrounds East of the Park

Chewing Blackbones Campground & RV Park, scenically situated on St. Mary's Lake six miles north of the St. Mary Entrance, is Indian-owned. Attractive 120-site park has lakefront tent sites, children's playground, marina, coffee shop, laundromat. Open May 15-Sept. 15. John and Mona Horn, St. Mary, MT 59417; ☎ 888-360-0547 or 406-360-4547 year-round.

Other Blackfeet-owned campgrounds on the east side of the Park: **Duck Lake Campground** has great trout fishing, campsites on the lake shore, tribal boat dock. ☎ 406-338-5042. **Red Eagle Campground**, on Two Medicine Lake has good fishing in summer, ice fishing in winter. Open year-round. ☎ 406-226-5512.

Campgrounds West of the Park

Glacier Campground, a mile from the Park entrance on US 2, has sites on 40 timbered acres; also rustic cabins. General store, playground, dump station, laundromat, nightly barbeques. PO Box 447, West Glacier, MT 59936; ☎ 406-387-5689.

San-Suz-Ed RV & Tenters Park, 2.4 miles west of West Glacier on US 2, has pull-through spaces, TV, laundry, breakfast. Box 387, West Glacier, MT 59936; ☎ 406-387-5280.

Other Commercial Campgrounds

Arlee

Jocko Hollow Campground is one of those serendipitous finds one comes across all too seldom. Unstructured grassy spaces with electric and water hookups on gurgling Jocko River; trout ponds, kids' playground. The hollow, sheltered by huge cottonwoods, is a safe place in a storm. We found that out when a terrific wind storm blew in. Dump station. Open May-Oct. On US 93, a mile north of Arlee. ☎ 406-726-3336.

Big Arm

Big Arm Resort & Marina (see *Hotels, Motels & B&Bs*).

Bigfork

Outback Montana, south of town on Flathead Lake, has 40 full hookup pull-through RV sites, tent sites with water and power, in a shady setting under tall trees. 27202 E. Lakeshore, Bigfork, MT 59911; ☎ 888-900-6973 or 406-837-6973. E-mail outback@cyberport.net.

Clinton

Elkhorn RV Ranch has 120 wooded RV and tent sites on Rock Creek, pool, general store, restaurant. Open May-Sept. Four miles south of I-90 Exit 126 on Rock Creek Rd. Clinton, MT 59825; ☎ 406-825-3220.

Essex

Stanton Creek Lodge (see *Hotels, Motels & B&Bs*).

Hamilton

Lick Creek Campground has 20 tent and 34 RV spaces, fishing pond, full hookups, store; adjacent to Lick Creek and the Bitterroot River. 2251 US 93 S., Hamilton, MT 59840; ☎ 406-821-3840.

Libby

Koocanusa Resort (see *Adventures on Water* and *Hotels, Motels & B&Bs*) has RV hookups and dry camp sites on the shore of Koocanusa Lake. Restaurant, general store, fishing licenses, horsehoes, etc. 23911 Scenic Hwy. 37, Libby, MT 59923; ☎ 406-293-7474.

Woodland RV Park is prettily situated in a wooded area off the main drag. Convenient to town and local attractions. 185 Woodland Rd. (PO Box 1152), Libby, MT 59923; ☎ 406-293-8395.

Missoula

Missoula KOA is very large, clean and well run, but spaces are much too close together. Kamping Kabins. Okay if you must overnight in Missoula. Open year-round. 3450 Tina Ave., Missoula, MT 59802; ☎ 800-KOA-5366 or 406-549-0881.

Paradise

Quinn's Hot Springs (see *Touring* and *Hotels, Motels & B&Bs*) has 30 tent spaces and 38 RV sites overlooking the Clark Fork River. Open year-round. Box 219, Paradise, MT 59856; ☎ 406-826-3150 or 826-3157.

Ronan

Diamond `S' RV Park is on a working ranch (tours offered). It has 22 full hookup pull-through spaces and 15 tent sites. Hot showers, laundry, tipi rental. Open April-Nov. Box 792, Ronan, MT 59864; 676-3641.

Sula

Lost Trail Hot Springs Resort (see *Hotels, Motels & B&Bs*) has a few tent spaces and RV hookups; also mineral hot springs pool. 8321 US 93 S, Sula, MT 59871; ☎ 406-821-3574.

Woods Bay

Woods Bay Resort, on Flathead Lake's east shore, a few miles south of Bigfork, has full RV hookups, pebble beach. 26481 E. Lakeshore Rt., Woods Bay, MT 59911; ☎ 406-837-3333.

■ Where to Eat

Recommending restaurants is subjective. I might come away from an eatery raving about the delicious viands. You might dine there tomorrow and wonder what all the fuss was about. So I offer the following listings with a degree of trepidation.

As stated in previous chapters of this book, any traveler can find a café or a ho-hum family restaurant. Only places offering something special are listed here. If a town doesn't appear here it's because I found no eatery with that special zing. Some of the most memorable munching can be found at dine-in hostelries such as guest ranches, lodges and B&Bs. Some serve drop-ins by reservation.

Glacier Country, perhaps more than other Montana regions, offers an eclectic array of cuisines ranging from typical Western beef and beans to high-toned culinary creations. Some towns are in transition from small town basic to New Age trendy. Eureka is a good example. Heavily visited areas, notably the larger Glacier Park area, including Bigfork and Whitefish, take trendy to Elysian heights. If you travel by RV, you may be on the lookout for quality baked goods. These "finds" are also noted. Not listed are bars and casinos; call this a personal quirk, but you can find these on your own if you are so inclined.

AUTHOR TIP *Missoula and the Flathead Valley are noted for trendy brewpubs whose beers and ales have way-out labels such as Scud Runner Dark and Flathead Lake Monster Ale. The Great Northern Brewing Company in Whitefish turns out brews with such monikers as Wild Huckleberry (reportedly good with chocolate), Big Fog and Wheatfish.*

Bigfork

Bigfork, not known for modesty, claims to have the mostest of the bestest restaurants in Montana. See what you think.

Bigfork Inn resembles one of those kitchy Swiss clocks that produces yodeling figurines when the hour strikes. The menu tends to basic Montana fare, but includes several upscale selections. Patio dining. The venerable Company Brass Dance Band plays on weekends. Open nightly, 5-10, for dinner. 604 Electric Ave.; ☎ 406-837-6680.

Brookies Cookies is THE place to indulge in toothsome cookies and breakfast cinnamon rolls. You can't get within a mile of this charming cookie shack without your nose leading you on. They also do a mail order business and will deliver anywhere in the Flathead Valley. Open Mon.-Sat., 6:30 am-5 pm, Sun. 7:30-2. 191 Mill St., Bigfork, MT 59911; ☎ 800-697-6487. Toll-free fax 800-700-8017. E-mail brookies@ptonet.net.

Bridge Street Galley serves up art with your dinner. Open Tues.-Sat., 5:30-9. Sunday brunch, 10:30 am-2. Reservations suggested. ☎ 406-837-5826.

Coyote Roadhouse Inn (see *Hotels, Motels & B&Bs*) serves up nightly dinners by reservation only. Eclectic cuisine spans national borders and includes Southwestern, Mayan and Tuscan dishes. A Gourmet Diners Society "restaurant of distinction." 602 Three Eagle Lane. ☎ 406-837-4250 or 837-1233.

Del Norte, at 355 Grand Ave., claims to serve the best Mexican food in the valley. They are also known for two favorite Montana treats: buffalo burgers and huckleberry ice cream. Open Mon.-Thurs. 11:30-11, Fri. & Sat. 11:30-2 am, Sun. 11:30-8. ☎ 406-837-0076.

Quincy's at Marina Cay (see *Hotels, Motels & B&Bs*) serves dinner from 5:30 Wed.-Sun. and features live music on weekend nights and during the day at the Tiki Bar, Bigfoot's only bar on the lake. ☎ 406-837-5861.

Tuscany's Ristorante serves up delicious Northern Italian cuisine in a warm Old Country atmosphere. Meals prepared to order. Outdoor dining and live music in summer. Open daily for lunch and dinner. Reservations suggested. 331 Bridge St.; ☎ 406-837-6065.

ShowThyme's digs are in an old bank building next to Bigfork's popular playhouse. The fare defines innovative and upscale. Open for lunch Tues.-Fri., 11:30-2:30; dinner Tues.-Sat. from 5 pm. Deck seating. ☎ 406-837-0707.

Swan River Café's name might offer the impression of just another café, but no such thing. The food can hold its own against any California upscale restaurant. Succulent seafood is a specialty. Breakfast and lunch are served in the café-style lunchroom, dinner in the cozy Grotto. Open daily, 8-3:30; dinner 5-10. Dinner reservations suggested. 360 Grand Ave.; ☎ 406-837-2220.

Browning

Red Crow Kitchen is the place to go for slurpy-sloppy-delicious Indian tacos and other dishes. Open daily for breakfast and lunch. In Teepee Village Shopping Center; ☎ 406-338-7626.

Charlo

Ninepipes Lodge is more than a pleasant restaurant overlooking a pond teeming with waterfowl and a wildlife meadow (see *Hotels, Motels & B&Bs*). Lunch and dinner offerings include sourdough rolls and huckleberry crisp. Open daily for breakfast, lunch and dinner. 41000 US 93; ☎ 406-644-2928.

Darby

Montana Café is what's needed in every small town. Buffalo burgers remind you that this is the woolly West. Also, homemade soups and pastries. Open for breakfast, lunch and dinner Mon.-Sat. 614 N. Main; ☎ 406-821-1931.

East Glacier

Serrano's serves up great Mexican food and imported beers at reasonable prices. Open daily for dinner. Across from the depot on US 2 East; ☎ 406-226-9392. Also in Whitefish at 10 Central Ave.

Essex

The Dining Car isn't on-track, but it's close. Trains rumble just outside the windows. The walls are lined with old Empire Builder menus and the placemats depict historic trains. The china is the "Glory of the West" mountain goat pattern used in the original Great Northern dining cars. Situated in the Isaak Walton Inn, the former railway crew dining room serves up viands the likes of which those gandy dancers never imagined. Upscale dishes incorporate local trout, lamb, beef and huckleberries in imaginative ways. A tad pricey, perhaps, but not when you consider the whole dining experience. Open year-round for breakfast, lunch and dinner. ☎ 406-888-5700.

Eureka

Bullwinkle's is one of those holes in the wall that surprise you. Offerings include lunch and dinner pastas, pizzas, scampi, steaks, sandwiches. Sunday brunch. No alcohol, but diners who want wine are urged to order their meals from the bar next door! Open daily from 11 am. On the main drag. ☎ 406-296-3932.

The Antler Inn Restaurant, in a cozy log home surrounded by daisy-strewn meadows, is owned and operated by Susan Ennenbach and Ken Renaud. The Home Comfort wood-burning kitchen range that greets you just inside the door hints of the antiques decorating this restaurant "find." Reasonably priced entrées include favorites prepared with imaginative style; even liver! Also pastas and yummy desserts. Open nightly for dinner. Reservations suggested. One half-mile off US 93 south of town; watch for sign. ☎ 406-882-4408.

Sunflower Bakery is a homestyle bakery the likes of which are found all too seldom. Breads include healthy seven-grain loaves. Goodies vary from day to day, but you're sure to like them. Open whenever. On the main drag. ☎ 406-296-2896.

Glacier National Park

Apgar Village, Lake McDonald Lodge and other Glacier Park gathering areas have eateries serving light meals. All the high profile hotels and lodges (see *Hotels, Motels & B&Bs*) have quality full-service restaurants.

Hamilton

The Grubstake Restaurant is one of those hokey "wild West" places that may turn you off at first, but will end up hooking you. After negotiating the twisty five-mile dirt and gravel road up Downing Mountain, you'll be ready to settle in by the center fireplace and order up some steak, barbeque and buttermilk pie. Prices aren't bad, considering that supplies and victuals must be brought up-mountain by pack train (that's a joke). Open daily for dinner, year-round (4WD vehicle required to get there in winter). 1017 Grubstake Road; ☎ 888-363-GRUB or 406-850-3068.

La Tratorria Italian Restaurant serves up Northern Italian specialties in a turn-of-the-century Victorian home. Dine outdoors, or in one of several rooms graced by fireplaces and bay windows. The sizeable menu offers a good variety of dishes at surprisingly reasonable prices, considering the trendiness of the area. Reservations advised. Open for dinner Tues.-Sun. 315 S. Third St.; ☎ 406-363-5030.

Morning Glory Coffee House bills itself as "a relaxing European-style coffee house in an elegant Victorian home." And so it is, serving toothsome breakfasts and lunches, plus tasty baked goods and gourmet coffees and teas. Open daily. 111 Fourth St.; ☎ 406-363-7500.

Stone Point Bakery & Café is easy to overlook if you're not watching for it. Gourmet bakery goods and coffees. Open for breakfast and lunch, Tues.-Sun. 310 S. First; ☎ 406-375-0381.

The Sundance specializes in Mexican food and homemade desserts. Open for lunch and dinner, Mon.-Sat. Reservations. 900 S. First St. at Hamilton Stage Stop; ☎ 406-363-2810.

Hot Springs

Corn Fish Café is tucked away in Symes Hotel & Mineral Baths (see *Hotels, Motels & B&Bs*). Vegetarian and New Age type dishes prepared by a former Moosewood chef are on offer. Call for current meal availability and times. 109 Wall St.; ☎ 406-741-2361.

Hungry Horse

Huckleberry Patch has anything and everything that can be made from Montana's favorite berry; even huckleberry hotcakes and waffles with guess what flavor syrup. Also, huckleberry pies, cheesecakes, yogurt, ice cream. Also, Made in Montana gifts. Open daily, all day. 8868 US 2 East; ☎ 406-387-4444.

Kalispell

Big League Bagels & Deli boasts 17 kinds of bagels and 15 homemade cream cheeses. Deli fare of sandwiches, soups, salads and homemade breads come in a close second to the bagels. 1645 US 93 S. (a mile north of the US 2 and MT 5 intersection); ☎ 406-752-4700.

Café Max, at 121 Main St., is Kalispell's soup kitchen, and I don't mean charity. The hearty homemade soups and yummy focaccia are real tummy warmers. Lunch is served Mon.-Sat. and dinner by reservation. ☎ 406-755-SOUP.

Fenders is into cars, old-timers that is, with antique car booths. Weekday offerings are average Montana fare, but Sundays they put on the cackle with reasonably priced all-you-can-eat pan fried chicken dinners and all the trimmings. Open daily for lunch and dinner. On US 93 between Kalispell and Whitefish; ☎ 406-752-3000.

Lakeside

Rosario's is known for Italian food, steaks and seafood. Located on the lake, the restaurant has a dock for diners arriving via boat. Deck seating. US 93 S.; ☎ 406-844-2888.

Libby

Hidden Chapel Restaurant, in a former chapel, is a pleasant surprise in this lumber town. A wide range of dishes reflects the chef's flair. The

Beef Bourgignon is especially tasty. Great prime rib Saturday and Sunday. Sunday champagne brunch. Specialties include Swedish knot bread with huckleberry butter. Victorian carriage rides available from your lodging to the restaurant. Open daily for lunch and dinner. Reservations recommended. 1207 Utah Ave.; ☎ 406-293-2928.

The Libby Café feeds lumberjack appetites on traditional Montana café fare while tickling your funny bone with the menu's tongue-in-cheek logger country sayings. Burgers, flapjacks, chicken-fried steak and other loggers' favorites plus pies, pies, pies. Open for breakfast and lunch. 411 Mineral Ave. ☎ 406-293-3523.

Lolo

Guy's Lolo Creek Steakhouse serves Western-style steaks cooked over an open-pit wood barbeque. Open for dinner Tues.-Sun. 6600 US 12W; ☎ 406-273-2622.

Missoula

Missoula is Montana's counter-culture city. As such, it boasts an eclectic range of eateries. The following suggestions are but samplings.

El Cazador, at 101 S. Higgins, serves up lunches and dinners featuring authentic Mexican fare. Open daily for lunch and dinner. ☎ 406-728-3657.

Goldsmith's Riverfront Café & Bakery has a patio right on the river, an ideal spot to enjoy healthy homemade dishes and local microbrews. Open daily for breakfast, lunch and dinner. 809 E. Front St.; ☎ 406-721-6732.

Great Harvest Bread Co., at 1407 S. Higgins, convenient to downtown and the U. of M., has all the wonderful breads, buns and other delights that have made this bakery chain one of the West's best bakery bets. ☎ 406-728-4549.

Hong Kong Chef owner Shawn Lee and his wife Lili, natives of China, offer authentic cuisine such as you would find if you were to visit Hong Kong. Made to order dishes arrive at tableside in splendid presentations. Emperor Delight in a Dragon Boat arrives in an 18-inch-long wooden boat and includes an assortment of toothsome delights. No MSG. Take-out and delivery service. Open daily for lunch and dinner. 2009 Brooks St. (in the Fairway Shopping Center); ☎ 406-549-6688.

McKay's on the River serves a well-prepared range of Montana staples in a splendid near-downtown riverfront setting. No pretense at gourmet trendy, just darned good food. Open daily for lunch and dinner. Sunday brunch. 1111 E. Broadway; ☎ 406-728-0098.

Perugia, at 1106 W. Broadway, offers authentic Mediterranean cuisine; Italian, Greek, Spanish and Middle Eastern. Open for dinner Tues.-Sat. from 5 pm. ☎ 406-543-3757.

Thai Spicy Restaurant, at 206 W. Main, is generally acknowledged as Missoula's best Thai eatery. Take-out available. Open Mon.-Thurs 11-9, Fri. & Sat. 11-10. ☎ 406-543-0260.

The New Black Dog Café, at 138 W. Broadway, specializes in organic vegetarian dishes, but does serve organic meats and chicken. Open Mon.-Sat. for lunch, 11-3 and Tues.-Sat. for dinner from 5 pm. ☎ 406-542-1138.

Tipu's Tiger, in the university area's "hip strip," serves East Indian cuisine. Take-out. Open for lunch and dinner. 531 S. Higgins; ☎ 406-542-0622.

Polebridge

Northern Lights Café, next door to the Polebridge Mercantile, is closed Mondays, but serves dinner all other evenings between June 15 and Sept. 15 (approximately). No phone.

Polson

Richwine's Burgerville isn't much to look at, but they serve the best hamburgers this side of hog heaven. In fact, their praises have been sung by restaurant reviewers from San Diego to Denver. Also burritos, foot-long hot dogs, seafood and more. Take-out. Open daily, all day from 9 am. US 93 East.; ☎ 406-883-2620.

Ronan

Cappucino Cowboy has homemade ice creams, breads and pastries, specialty coffees and teas and juices as well as Western clothing and a gallery of local artists' works. Sidewalk café. Main St. & 4th; ☎ 406-676-8593.

St. Mary

Snowgoose Grill is well known for Montana specialties such as range-fed buffalo, St. Mary Lake whitefish and huckleberry goodies. Open daily for breakfast, lunch and dinner. In St. Mary Lodge & Resort; ☎ 406-732-4431.

Seeley Lake

Lindey's Prime Steak House, on MT 83, offers lakeside dining with sunsets thrown in. Arrive by car, boat or seaplane. Open daily from 5 pm in summer; Thurs.-Mon. in winter. ☎ 406-677-9229.

Somers

Montana Grill has fabulous lake views, eclectic menu offerings and ribs to die for. The downstairs Grill is famous for grilled pizza made with micro-brew beer. Open daily for lunch and dinner. Dinner reservations suggested. On US 93 S.; ☎ 406-857-3889.

Tiebuckers Pub and Eatery is a popular dinner house offering Saturday night entertainment – so popular that a traffic light in the parking lot signifies how long you must wait to be seated. Northern Italian fare rubs ribs with meats prepared on a wood-fired grill. Prime rib Fri. & Sat. Open for dinner Tues.-Sun., 5-9. 75 Somers Rd.; ☎ 406-857-3335.

Stryker

Loon's Nest Restaurant at Loon's Echo Resort, in the Stillwater State Forest, is open for dinner year-round. Cuisine is best described as middle-of-the-trail gourmet. Always a vegetarian entrée. Reservations requested. 1 Fish Lake Road; ☎ 800-956-6632 or 406-882-7676.

Victor

Victor Steak House serves up no-nonsense Western open pit charbroiled steaks. Open for dinner Mon.-Sat., from noon Sundays. 2426 Meridian Rd.; ☎ 406-642-3300.

West Glacier

Heaven's Peak Kaffee Haus is more than a place to get a cup of java. Nicely situated in (what else?) a log house, this eatery specializes in fresh pastas, charbroiled steaks and nifty desserts. Great Glacier Park views; outdoor dining in summer. Open daily for lunch and dinner. 12130 US 2 East; ☎ 406-387-4754.

Whitefish

Whitefish's dining out offerings reflect the ambience of a casual rail-to-ski town with upscale tastes and downhome friendliness. It's virtually impossible to get a bad meal here. The following restaurants represent a sampling of the numerous offerings in this destination resort town.

Big Mountain Ski & Summer Resort's three eateries, **Moguls, Stube & Chuckwagon Grill** and **Summit House**, offer a wide range of hearty viands and light snacks appreciated by skiers and hikers. Also on Big Mountain are **Hellroaring Saloon**, serving nifty tummy-warming après-ski viands and **Café Kandahar**, offering an upscale menu at reasonable prices (☎ 406-862-6247).

Buffalo Café, at 514 Third St., proves the adage that breakfast is an event in Whitefish. The huevos have been the foundation of many a skiers' day. Ditto, the breakfast pies. Noontime brings out soup 'n salads and great Mexican fare. Open Mon.-Fri, 6:30-2, Sat. 7-2, Sun. 9-2. ☎ 406-862-BUFF.

Café Al Dente, at 6479 US 93 S., is, as the name implies, a dedicated Italian restaurant. Traditional menu items represent a range of Italian fare from Tuscany to Sicily. Open daily for lunch from 11 and for dinner from 5. ☎ 406-862-3131.

Dire Wolf Pub offers hand-tossed pizza and calzone, and a wide selection of Northwest microbrews. Open daily for lunch and dinner. 845 Wisconsin Ave.; ☎ 406-862-4500.

Hot Chili Mama's Cocina & Gift Shop, in the Alpine Village Center, is a Southwestern restaurant whose decor reflects the cuisine. The story behind the warm ambience and tasty food is that of owner Kimmy Romero Davis. Kimmy's odyssey traces a path from a New Mexico ranch where her grandmothers taught her to prepare the traditional foods of her Hispanic-Indian heritage, to Whitefish, where a divorce left her to support three children. She went on welfare, but not for long. Bartering salsa made from a grandmother's recipe led to a sales boom. That led to an award from the State of Montana for the year's best off-welfare achievement, an appearance on the Rosie O'Donnell Show, and the January, 1999 opening of a restaurant whose motto is "made to be shared." Hot Chili Mama's is open daily except Monday, 6:30 am-9:30 pm winters, 7-9:30 summers. ☎ 406-862-8776.

Swift Creek Café, at ☎ 307- E. 2nd St., was named for an old Big Mountain ski run. breakfast are big in Whitefish, and this eatery's cinnamon rolls are bigger yet. The cozy café has an innovative breakfast and lunch menu. Open for breakfast and lunch. ☎ 406-862-9136.

The Wrap & Roll Café, in the Non Hostile Hostel (see *Hotels, Motels & B&Bs*) at 300 E. 2nd St., is your basic skiers' and hikers' eatery serving up tasty wraps, burritos and such with reasonable price tags. Open Mon.-Sat., 11-9. ☎ 406-862-7383.

Tupelo Grille, at 17 Central Avenue, offers casual dining in an unpretentious yet upscale ambience. While Cajun fare is a specialty, other offerings are straightforward tasty. The pastas are great. Open for dinner Tues.-Sun. from 5:30. ☎ 406-862-6136.

The Whitefish Times Coffee House, in a cozy vintage home, offers homemade pastries and desserts, plus quiches in addition to the usual light coffee house fare. A relaxing place to munch and read. Open Mon.-Sat., 7-10, Sunday 10-5. 334 Central Ave.; ☎ 406-862-2444.

Charlie Russell Country

Introduction

Charlie Russell Country is a big chunk of broken prairie land interspersed with mountain "islands" – truly Montana's heartland. The touristy allure of Glacier, Yellowstone and Gold West Countries are far away. Here, hard working folk live close to the land, not far removed from a many-faceted heritage that defines the West. The people include descendants of homesteaders, members of several Indian tribes, Hutterites, stockmen for whom "Old West" is a present reality – all threads in the colorful tapestry of the Plains.

The Hutterites

A "Fresh Vegetables" sign pointing down a gravel road may lead to one of Russell Country's several Hutterite colonies. You'll be greeted hospitably, perhaps shown around if someone can take the time.

I was invited to tour a colony set in a sea of ripening grain. Everything, the well-weeded gardens and hog pens, the plain church and simple homes, gleamed with care. My guide exhibited modest pride as he showed off a new computerized feed mixing mill. A gaggle of curious barefoot children tagged along.

These plain-living people adhere to religous tenets set forth by Leonhard Hutter, a super-orthodox 17th-century Lutheran theologian. The German-speaking Hutterites (most also know English) live in agricultural colonies based on worship, communal ownership and hard work. Men are bearded and both men and boys wear suspended trousers and caps or straw hats. Women and girls are quaintly modest in ankle-length aproned dresses and head kerchiefs.

Hutterites are superb farmers who embrace modern farming technologies. Most colonies raise food for themselves, plus a large surplus to sell. They are a self-suffcent people, making furniture, clothing, soap, butter and other necessities.

They adhere to old customs, women eating on one side of the dining hall, men on the other, children after the adults. The sexes are segregated in schoolhouse and church as well. Work is assigned on a rotating basis. Necessities are apportioned as needed and money goes into a common pot.

Big families are encouraged. When a colony's population grows too large for the land to support, it splits and a new colony is formed, perhaps as far away as the Dakotas or Saskatchewan. I spoke with a mother of 13 who told me that some of her older ones had recently left to form a new colony in Canada.

This land's beauty lies in rolling fields of grain ripening under a sky big as infinity and in mountains rising like exclamation points above the prairie. The Big Belts and Little Belts, the Big Snowies and Little Snowies, the Judith, Castle and Bears Paw Mountains, are pikers by a Rocky Mountain rulestick. The Little Belts, the last "real" mountains on the cusp of the prairie, are the most extensive of these mini-ranges, and the highest. **Big Baldy Peak** tops out at 9,191 feet.

Mega-Monsters

Agriculture is Montana's premier industry. The 3,400 really big farms in the Golden Triangle, an area loosely bounded by Browning, Havre and Cut Bank, represent Montana's breadbasket. Some 200 mega-monster tractors crawl across Golden Triangle fields. Just how monstrous is monstrous? Take the Big Bud 747, the largest farm tractor ever built. From the front, it looks like a road rig on steroids. Eight fat black tires, each eight feet tall, support a 14-foot-high cab. Boasting a 900-horsepower, 16-cylinder Detroit Diesel engine, the tractor weighs in at 100,000 pounds. It can cover an acre a minute pulling a wide-angle cultivator. That's farming!

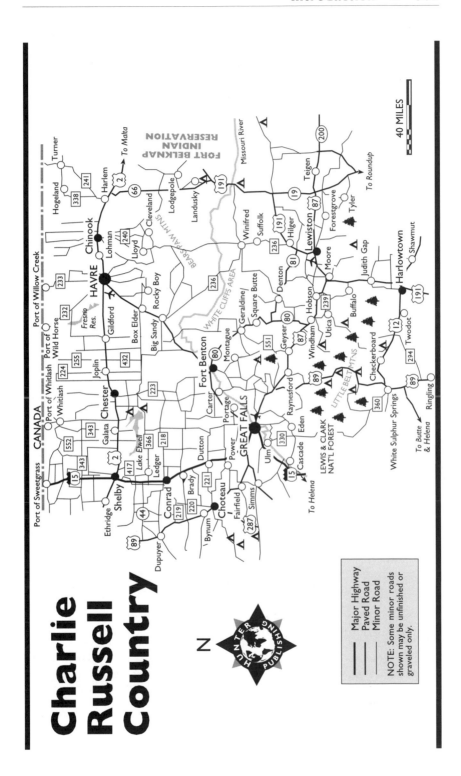

Charlie Russell Country

The **Rocky Mountain Front** brushes the sky on the region's western edge, both weather-maker and historic barrier. This region of brawn and plenty butts up against the golden prairies of Alberta and Saskatchewan on the north and merges seamlessly with Missouri River Country on the east and Yellowstone Country on the south.

The **Missouri River**, carving a deep, inscrutable channel between dramatic "breaks," carries the waters of many rivers and the sagas of many peoples clear across the center of the region. Other rivers, the Sun, the Marias, the Milk, the Judith, the Smith, feed the historic waterway. The river that beckoned Lewis and Clark into the unknown vies with Great Falls and Fort Benton as the region's biggest tourist draw. The ol' Missouri hasn't seen such traffic since steamboats brought prospectors and flim-flam artists up-river to Fort Benton. Russell Country's three major cities, **Great Falls**, **Havre** and **Lewistown**, form points of a triangle. Great Falls is the largest with some 58,200 residents. Here, artist Charles Russell (Montanans refer to him affectionately as "Charlie") and explorers Lewis and Clark face off. Numerous points of interest celebrate the lives and exploits of these larger-than-life figures.

The region includes two Indian reservations, **Fort Belknap** and **Rocky Boy's**, each differing markedly from the other. The reservations are interesting to visit, though tourism is less developed than on the larger and higher profile Blackfeet and Flathead Reservations. However, Fort Belknap's Tribal Council is moving in that direction with exciting results.

The **Lewis and Clark National Forest** maintains the "rough" land in and around the Little Belt, Highwood, Big Snowy and Castle Mountains. Plenty of adventure awaits in Russell Country. Adventures of the mind explore a past that steered the West's destiny. More strenuous adventures include cattle drives, horseback riding, hiking, river floating, cross-country skiing and snowmobiling.

 It is fitting that this chunk of Montana be named after Charlie Russell, the famed Western artist who lived and worked in Great Falls and whose youth was spent "cowboying" in the Judith Basin.

■ Russell Country's Epochal Past

A procession of larger-then-life peoples has for centuries trod the riparian corridors and prairie pathways of the travel region known as Russell Country.

Buffalo once roamed these plains, attracting hunters from Indian tribes living both east and west of the Continental Divide. Prior to obtaining horses, probably in the 1700s, hunters harried bison over high and steep ulms, or jumps. Ulm Pishkun, southwest of Great Falls, celebrates that era. So important were the buffalo to the plains peoples' survival and culture that a worshipful mystique surrounded, and still surrounds, these animals.

Traders, offering Indians beads, iron pots, blankets and "firewater" in exchange for pelts, began trickling down from Canada at about the time that Lewis's and Clark's Voyage of Discovery toiled up the Missouri. Trappers followed traders, fanning out along rivers and creeks to feed Europe's beaver hat craze.

Lewis & Clark - 100 Years Later

Not everyone is cheering the bicentennial of Lewis and Clark's Voyage of Discovery. Native Americans don't regard the anniversary of the exploration that opened the West to white settlement as cause for celebration. Observance, yes. Celebration, no.

Indian peoples were decimated, their land stolen and their culture nearly destroyed. The Nez Perce, having rendered assistance that furthered the company's progress over the Rocky Mountains, may well feel a sense of betrayal. The Blackfeet, having exhibited hostility toward the company, may well feel vindicated.

It can be argued that, had Lewis and Clark not shown the way, British interests soon would have. Perhaps England would have claimed the northern Rocky Mountains and the Pacific Northwest, both outside Louisiana Purchase boundaries. Indians might even have had a fairer shake, but that's doubtful. Conjecture aside, the Lewis and Clark bicentennial "celebration" is best approached with sensitivity toward the people who in large part made it possible, and in the end suffered because of it.

The beaver supply had no sooner been over-exploited than rich gold diggings began to attract prospectors. As the Civil War ended, the trickle became a flood as disaffected Southerners, gold-hungry Northerners and mining camp hangers-on headed for the digs. Many traveled on steamboats up the Missouri to Fort Benton, from whence they made their way over the recently completed Mullan Road to Alder Gulch, Last Chance Gulch and numerous digs in-between. The steamboat era lasted until the 1880s, when railroads proved faster and more convenient. Fort Benton remains a fascinating microcosm of Montana's no-holds-barred past.

Chief Joseph's 1877 surrender in the Bears Paw Mountains, followed by the last of the Indian wars, opened the plains to stockmen. The slaughter of the buffalo, the banishing of Indians to reservations, the laying of railroad tracks across the prairie, furthered cattlemen's and sheepmen's interests. Cattle barons such as Charles M. Bair enjoyed a heyday.

Charlie Russell Country

Enter the cowboy. Rugged, hard working, hard drinking, profane, seemingly indestructible, the Western cowboy swaggered into history through the aegis of countless dime Westerns. More than most who peopled Montana's colorful procession, cowboys shaped the public's conception of the Old West. That this conception was largely erroneous didn't factor in. Cowboys actually led hard, dangerous lives relieved only by an occasional chance to hit town and blow their meager earnings on drink and floozies. Charlie Russell bought the legend, as evidenced by his large body of work romanticizing cowboy life.

Homesteaders, eyes alight with hope, came at the turn of the 20th century. They prospered, then failed. Their descendants who stuck it out, aided by modern irrigation and farming technology, justified their hopes by proving that Montana's high plains could produce unprecedented yields of wheat and other grains.

Read the Montana sagas authored by native Montana novelists A. B. Guthrie Jr. and Ivan Doig. These writers, expressing viewpoints formed by their personal Montana perspectives, illuminate this past and its people in ways that bring the present into focus.

■ Geography & Fauna

Mountainous "islands" dominate the southern portion of Russell Country. Lapping these "islands" are fertile, glacially formed basins and valleys. To the north, the high plains undulate under the legendary big sky.

The Missouri, known locally as the "Big Muddy," runs deep and slow through Russell Country. The sandstone and shale Missouri River Breaks, especially in the Wild and Scenic corridor between Fort Benton and Fort Peck Reservoir, present tumbled masses of stone and surrealistic pinnacles. These are remnants of layered sediments and shorelines of the inland sea that once covered most of the Great Plains. The layers have been folded, faulted and uplifted by volcanic eruptions and sculpted by glaciers. Erosion smoothed these layers, forming the Missouri River Breaks. Nineteenth-century German artist Karl Bodmer's obsession with these Breaks produced eerily accurate portraits of the Breaks as they look today.

The Eye of the Needle

In the summmer of 1997, vandals knocked off the top of the 10-foot Eye of the Needle, a Missouri River Breaks landmark shaped like an inverted V. The act brought outrage statewide. What to do? Could it be repaired? Should it be repaired? The Bureau of Land Management hemmed and hawed before deciding to leave the shorn-off rock pillars as they stand. A replica is to be built on the Fort Benton levee at a cost of some $44,000.

With the partial exception of the Smith, the rivers flowing into the Missouri tend to be slow and sluggish, weaving lazily through grasslands and clumps of cottonwoods.

Some rivers have been dammed to provide irrigation water and sport reservoirs. Some wetlands include prairie potholes, remnants of the prehistoric inland sea. Natural lakes are few.

Russell Country's mountains are habitat for deer, elk, mountain lions, black bears and numerous small mammals and birds. Grizzlies sometimes wander down from the Front Range. Pronghorns, blending as one, flow with liquid swiftness over the grasslands. Moose favor the woods and wetlands. Coyotes play no favorites.

Wild animals and civilization sometimes clash. Moose have been known to wander onto Great Falls' Northwest Bypass, with fender-thumping results. The Great Falls Airport erected eight miles of eight-foot-high chain link fence to keep high-jumping antelope and meandering moose off the runways.

■ Climate

Dramatic weather frequently swoops down on the Northwest Chinook Zone characterizing Russell Country's western counties. Intense cold spells are often broken by Chinook winds sweeping over the Front Range, raising temperatures by as much as 50° in as many minutes. The reverse effects of Arctic fronts can be equally dramatic.

Russell Country's eastern portion represents a climactic transition from the milder Chinook Zone to the typically colder winter weather of the Great Plains. Snowfall is less heavy than west of the Continental Divide, but can be considerable.

Spring, summer and fall weather can be dramatic too, especially as warm and cold fronts collide. Mid-summer heat lightning plays sky tag – preludes to the main act. Watching an approaching priairie boomer is to be swept up in one of Nature's most spell-binding sound and light shows. Incandescent slivers split the sky. Growls rumble across the plains, deepening as the lightning arcs brighter, closer. Your skin prickles as light and sound merge, reaching a clashing crescendo of white light and earth-shaking booms. Wind whips the storm, sheets the rain.

Wind is a present reality in every season. It sweeps across the land, sustaining a steady velocity. Other times, it plays capriciously, whooshing clumps of sagebrush high in the air, slamming debris into fences, causing birds to fly backwards.

Charlie Russell Country

One June day, heading north out of Great Falls on I-15, a tangle of sagebrush flew skyward some 200 feet in front of me like a plane taking off. I slowed, gripped the steering wheel and braced for the inevitable. Sure enough, it hit me broadside. The RV remained upright and the micro-burst departed without incident, but it was scary. Moral: driving a high profile vehicle on the high plains can be hazardous to your health. Be vigilant.

You can generally expect winter temperatures to be well below freezing, springs to come in bashfully, summers to be hot and dry, autumn days to be pleasantly warm with crisp nights. Nature's colors are intense. Deep golden wheat and bright yellow canola meet the horizon under a sky so intensely blue and cloudless that it hurts your eyes. Snow cover reflects the sun so intensely that the glare assumes a golden hue. Turning leaves cast a red and gold spell over the land.

Preparing for weather extremes in Russell Country should emulate common sense preparedness elsewhere in Montana. Visualize the unexpected when packing. May and early June might be balmy where you live, but don't expect them to be so here. By July, the weather heats up and dries out. Hot weather clothing is a must. Bring out the layers for winter visits. If your plans include a Missouri River float, a ranch visit or a pack trip, ask your outfitter for guidelines on appropriate clothing. Then follow them.

Getting Around

■ Highways & Byways

Several US and Montana highways form a network linking Russell Country towns.

I-15 enters the region north of Helena at Craig, follows the Missouri River to Great Falls, then angles north to Alberta. It'll get you where you're going pronto, but the scenery gives out at Great Falls. **US 89**, entering the region south of Ringling (north of Livingston), crosses the Little Belt Mountains via the Kings Hill National Forest Scenic Byway before pulling up at Great Falls. This highway connects the I-90 Corridor with Glacier National Park. A short section of **US**

287 enters Russell Country at Augusta and meets US 89 at Choteau for the last lap before entering the Blackfeet Indian Reservation. **US 2** enters the region between Cut Bank and Shelby and bee-lines east across the high prairie, following the Milk River between Havre and the Fort Belknap Indian Reservation and on to Missouri River Country. This highway is referred to as the **Hi-line** because it parallels the Great Northern Railroad's "high line" across the plains.

US 87 heads due north from Billings and hangs a left before scooting through Lewistown. The highway crosses the storied Judith Basin, then takes a sharp northerly turn at Great Falls before heading for Havre. **US 191** heads north from Big Timber, looks in on Lewistown, then skirts the Judith Mountains before swinging north into Missouri River Country.

Unlike most highways in mountainous areas, Russell Country highways tend not to follow rivers. An exception is **US 12**. This route follows the Musselshell River west from Deadman's Basin Reservoir to Checkerboard. The highway looks in on Harlowton and White Sulphur Springs before angling southwest, crossing the Big Belt Mountains, and leaving Russell Country east of Townsend.

Russell Country's state highways compare to wealthier and more heavily populated states' secondary roads. They mostly link towns whose heydays got up and went. An exception is **MT 66**, slicing through the Fort Belknap Indian Reservation from south to north. Paved roads linking yet smaller towns are indicated on the *Official Montana Highway Map* as solid black lines. The map's broken grey lines indicate gravel or dirt roads that may not be maintained in winter. These lead to really tiny towns and private ranches. Two such roads provide the only vehicle access to the National Wild and Scenic stretch of the Missouri River between Fort Benton and the US 191 bridge. Roads indicated by parallel faint grey lines are dirt tracks.

▪ Road Watch

The most frequent view through your windshield in Russell Country may well be the outline of a 10-gallon Stetson worn by the driver of the pickup in front of you. The sight may prompt some ruminating: Every male plains dweller comes equipped with such a hat. They needn't be cowboys to wear one. They seem never to remove these hats, even indoors. How do they keep them on in high winds? Are their heads conical? Some mysteries are never meant to be solved.

If your idea of US highways includes wide roadways with ample shoulders, forget it. While this region's US highways are in generally good repair and are maintained in winter, they receive no special consideration just because of their exalted status. Though exceptions exist near cities and larger towns, roadways tend to be no wider than Montana's state highways and shoulders are often non-existent. This situation could soon change. In 1998, Montana was awarded a large block of money for highway improvements.

Some US Forest Service roads in the Little Belts, Big Snowies and Highwoods may require 4WD vehicles. All other roads are suitable for passenger vehicles and some RVs. When in doubt and before venturing onto them in winter, call the State Highway Patrol Road Report (see *Information Sources*).

The three greatest hazards to watch out for are black ice, animals in the road and high wind gusts. All are discussed in preceding chapters of this book.

Blizzards are very real hazards in winter. Carrying adequate survival gear can let you live to tell about the adventure of being trapped in a snow storm. See *Survival Gear* under *Travel Strategies & Helpful Facts* (page 55) in the opening chapters of this book.

Information Sources

Getting There

Amtrak's Chicago to Portland/Seattle Empire Builder calls at Havre and Shelby. Amtrak buses run between Shelby and Great Falls. (☎ 800-USA-RAIL).

Havre and Lewistown are served by **Big Sky Airline** from Billings (☎ 800-237-7788).

Great Falls is served by **Delta Airlines** (☎ 800-221-1212), **Horizon Airline** (☎ 800-547-9308), **Northwest Airlines** (☎ 800-225-2525) and **Sky West** (☎ 800-453-9417).

Greyhound buses link the region's cities and towns (☎ 800-231-2222).

Car Rentals

Great Falls

Allstar/Practical: ☎ 800-722-6704 or 406-727-1711.

Avis Rent-A-Car: ☎ 406-761-7610.

Budget Rent-A-Car of Great Falls: ☎ 800-527-0700 or 406-454-1001.

DBW Auto-Limo: ☎ 406-727-5440.

Enterprise-Great Falls: ☎ 800-RENTACAR or 406-761-1600.

Haggerty Motors: ☎ 800-523-7779 or 406-761-1260.

Hertz Rent-A-Car: ☎ 800-654-3131.

National Rent-A-Car: ☎ 406-453-4386.

Rent A Wreck: ☎ 800-962-5344 or 406-761-0722.

U-Save Auto Rental: ☎ 800-622-5291 or 406-771-1111.

Havre

Budget Rent-A-Car of Havre: ☎ 406-265-1156.
Enterprise Rent-A-Car: ☎ 800-RENTACAR or 406-265-1177.
Rent A Wreck: ☎ 406-265-1481.

Lewistown

Budget Rent-A-Car of Lewistown: ☎ 800-823-3326 or 406-538-7701.

Shelby

Ford-Mercury: ☎ 800-823-3767 or 406-434-5593.

Tourism Offices

Travel Montana, Department of Commerce, PO Box 200533, Helena, MT 59620-0533; ☎ 800-847-4868 outside Montana, ☎ 406-444-2654 in Montana. Internet http://travel.mt.gov/.
Russell Country, Box 3166, Great Falls, MT 59403; ☎ 800-527-5348 or 406-761-5036.

Chambers of Commerce

Most towns post signs indicating the location of Visitor Centers beside highways entering town. Chamber mailing addresses are listed below.

Chester, Box 632, Chester, MT 59522; ☎ 406-759-5215. Fax 406-759-5392.
Chinook, Box 744, Chinook, MT 59523; ☎ 406-357-2100.
Choteau, Rt. 2, Box 897, Choteau, MT 59422; ☎ 406-466-5316. Fax 406-466-5317.
Conrad, Box 1480 (406 1/2 S. Main), Conrad, MT 59425; ☎ 406-278-7791.
Fairfield, Drawer 9, Fairfield, MT 59436; ☎ 406-467-2531. Fax 406-467-2505.
Fort Benton Community Improvement Assoc., Box 879, Fort Benton, MT 59442; ☎ 406-622-3864. Fax 406-622-3425.
Great Falls, Box 2127 (710 1st Ave. N.), Great Falls, MT 59403; ☎ 406-761-4434. Fax 406-454-2995.
Harlowton, Box 694, Harlowton, MT 59036; ☎ 406-632-4694. Fax 406-632-5633.
Havre, Box 308, Havre, MT 59501; ☎ 406-265-4383. Fax 406-265-7451.
Lewistown, Box 818, Lewistown, MT 59457; ☎ 800-216-5436 or 406-538-5436. Fax 406-538-5437.
Shelby, Box 865, Shelby, MT 59474; ☎ 406-434-7184.
Stanford, Box 102, Stanford, MT 59479; ☎ 406-735-6949.
White Sulphur Springs, White Sulphur Springs, MT 59645; ☎ 406-547-3928.

Indian Reservations

Fort Belknap Tourism Office and Information Center, RR 1, Box 66, Harlem, MT 59526; ☎ 406-353-2205.

Fort Belknap Agency, Harlem, MT 59526; ☎ 406-353-2205.

Rocky Boy's Reservation: The Chippewa-Cree Business Committee, Box 544, Rocky Boy Route, Box Elder, MT 59521; ☎ 406-395-4282.

Outdoors Associations

Fishing Outfitters Association of Montana (FOAM), Box 67. Gallatin Gateway, MT 59730; ☎ 406-763-5436.

Montana Outfitters & Guides Association, Box 1248, Helena, MT 59624; ☎ 406-449-3578.

Montana Snowmobile Association, PO Box 3202, Great Falls, MT 59403; ☎ 406-443-7350.

Government Agencies

Montana Department of Fish, Wildlife & Parks, Region 4, PO Box 6610 (4600 Giant Springs Rd.), Great Falls, MT 59406; ☎ 406-454-5840.

Bureau of Land Management Offices

Great Falls Resource Area, 1101 15th St. N., Great Falls, MT 59401; ☎ 406-791-7700.

Havre Resource Area, PO Box 911, Havre, MT 59501; ☎ 406-265-5891.

Lewistown District Office, PO Box 1160 (Airport Rd.), Lewistown, MT 59457; ☎ 406-538-7461.

Lewis & Clark National Forest Supervisor's Office, PO Box 869 (1101 15th St. N.), Great Falls, MT 59403; ☎ 406-791-7700.

Lewis & Clark National Forest, Augusta Information Station, PO Box 365 (405 Manix St.), Augusta, MT 59410; ☎ 406-562-3247.

Lewis & Clark National Forest, Belt Creek Information Station, Hwy. 89 (5 miles north of Neihart), Neihart, MT 59465; ☎ 406-236-5511.

Lewis & Clark National Forest, Judith Ranger District, PO Box 484, Stanford, MT 59479; ☎ 406-566-2292.

Lewis & Clark National Forest, Kings Hill Ranger District, Box A (204 West Folsom), White Sulphur Springs, MT 59645; ☎ 406-547-3361.

Lewis & Clark National Forest, Musselshell Ranger Station, 809 2 NW, Box 1906, Harlowton, MT 59036; ☎ 406-632-4391.

Lewis & Clark National Forest, Rocky Mountain Ranger District, PO Box 340 (1102 Main Ave. NW), Choteau, MT 59422; ☎ 406-466-5341.

Touring

Russell Country isn't just fields of waving wheat and cowboys wrangling horses. Epochal events occurred here – events that shaped the nation. Touring Russell Country, planting your feet on the sites where it all happened, is to come face to face with the real West.

■ Ulm Pishkun

Following signs along a series of gravel roads and up a steep incline gets you to Ulm Pishkun, one of the world's largest and best documented buffalo jumps. Archeological studies indicate that native people drove millions of buffalo over these cliffs between 500 AD and the 1700s, when the acquisition of horses changed harvesting methods. Standing at Ulm Pishkun's edge, with the Missouri River Valley spread out before you, is a humbling experience.

The Buffalo Hunt

It's no stretch to "see" a buffalo hunt as enacted thousands of times in the past. Men disguised as buffalo harry the animals toward the cliffs. Other men, stationed at the sides of the drive, head them over the rocky cliffs to their deaths. Women and children wait below to dress out the carcasses, saving every scrap for use as food, robes and bone tools. They cut the meat into strips and dry it for future use. Feasting and celebrating continues into the night, for once again Brother Buffalo had assured his people of a winter of plenty.

Long a stepchild of the Montana State Parks system, the Ulm Pishkun site is being developed to include an educational center, interpretive trails, story and pow-wow circles, and visitor facilities. The opening is projected for summer, 1999. The State of Montana, archaeologists and local Indian tribes are working together to showcase this important pishkun while preserving artifacts as yet uncovered.

■ The Great Falls of the Missouri

Ten miles and two centuries separate Ulm Pishkun and the Great Falls of the Missouri, as experienced by Meriwether Lewis, William Clark, Sacajawea and the soldiers of the Voyage of Discovery. Hydroelectric dams have tamed the series of five falls – falls so formidable that the expedition was forced to portage around them. They felled a cottonwood tree to fashion wheels for the canoes. On June 22, they dragged the

Ulm Pishkun State Park, near Great Falls.

heavily loaded canoes up Portage Creek and over the river's steep breaks to commence the 17-mile portage.

That scene, reproduced in lifesize, gut-straining reality at the **Lewis and Clark National Historic Trail Interpretive Center**, might serve as a symbol for the city that came to be named Great Falls. Those 17 days in June of 1805 could have spelled the end of Lewis and Clark's ambitions, but they didn't. A mere 52 years later, railroad tracks followed where they toiled.

Great Falls

Great Falls' original townsite rose where the Missouri and Sun River (aka Medicine River) meet. Today's city sits above the Missouri and straggles onto the prairie. It's a handsome city of riverside parks, world class museums and well preserved historic structures and homes.

The **Great Falls Visitor and Information Center** affords a fine view of the city from the Broadwater Overlook above 10th Ave., east of the I-15 Interchange. A heroic Bob Scriver bronze depicting the famous explorers stands on the grounds. Stop here to pick up brochures and get a fix on the city and its points of interest. The **Great Falls Historic Trolley** leaves from here in summer for two-hour narrated tours of the city. Pick-ups at many motels can be arranged. ☎ 406-771-1100 for times.

This city, lapped by the prairie clear to its fast food and housing development shoals, is easy to get around in. I generally take a dim view of cities, but quite enjoy Great Falls. The proximity of the Missouri and the **River's Edge Trail** and adjacent points of historical interest may account for that. River Drive, the Trail and a series of parks wrap the city on the west and north. Huge General Mills and Pasta Montana grain elevators set off views of the river and the altered Falls. The former serve as reminders that Great Falls is surrounded by some of the world's most productive wheat farms. The Montana Refining Company's "farm" north of the 10th Street Bridge is a reminder of the state's oil and natural gas fields.

Lewis & Clark

Industry is a fact of 21st century life, but here it's overshadowed by reminders of the epic journey that put the Great Falls on the map. **West Bank Park** features a commemorative sign describing Meriwether Lewis's close call with a grizzly. The **Sulphur Spring**, from which Lewis ordered water drawn for the relief of Sacajawea, who had fallen alarmingly ill, is a lesser known landmark.

The falls described by Lewis as "a sublimely grand specticle" are now the site of **Ryan Dam**, which raises the water level to form a 152-foot cascade. The continuous five-mile rapid of Lewis's time is no more. **Black Eagle** and **Rainbow Falls** still present a pleasing appearance, but purists mourn changes wrought by the dams.

On the south bank of the river, about halfway between these falls, is the **Giant Springs Heritage State Park and Fish Hatchery**. These springs, putting out 7.9 million gallons of water per hour, are among the world's largest. The 201-foot **Roe River**, the shortest river in the US, carries the Springs' output into the Missouri. The day-use park offers pleasant picnicking. Walks wind among trout pools fed by the springs. Wild geese and fluffy goslings are everywhere, a pleasure or a nuisance depending on your point of view. The fish hatchery is open during business hours. ☎ 406-454-3441 or 538-5588. The **Region 4 Montana Fish, Wildlife and Parks Headquarters**, nearby at 4600 Giant Springs Road, has a splendid taxidermy display of area wildlife. Open during business hours.

The **Lewis and Clark National Historic Trail Interpretive Center**, opened in July, 1998, is the focal point of the riverside drive and trail. The 25,000-square-foot museum structure hugs a cliff above the river, a symbolic tribute to the historic portage. Enormous windows afford sweeping views of the river. A 25-minute film by Ken Burns and Dayton Duncan highlighting the Lewis and Clark journey begins your self-guided tour.

The portage tableau is the focal point for interpretive displays retracing the Journey and honoring the Native peoples who helped Lewis and Clark on their way west. Included are examples of the flora and fauna encountered by Lewis and Clark, and actual and replicated maps, charts and artifacts used by them. Many exhibits are interactive, such as the rope you are invited to pull to see how far you could budge a canoe upstream.

Fees and seasonal hours of operation have yet to jell as this book goes to print, but the museum is open year-round. Inquire at the Great Falls Visitor Center or call the museum at ☎ 406-727-8733 for current hours.

Charlie Russell

Lewis and Clark may be the focus of attention during these bicentennial years, but Charlie Russell endures as the city's favorite son. The **C.M. Russell Museum Complex**, at 400 13th Street North, showcases the world's most complete collection of the artist's original art and personal objects. Gallery after gallery shows off oils, sculptures and drawings expressing Russell's infatuation with the West of his youth. His human side is apparent in illustrated cards and letters sent to friends and family. The Browning Firearms Collection is also on permanent display.

Russell's c. 1903 log cabin studio stands beside the museum, unchanged since he last stepped out the door. Here, where the cowboy artist created most of his work, you can see his brushes and palette, his signature "half breed" sash, plus the frontier-style artifacts with which he loved to surround himself.

The Russell home, designed by Nancy Cooper Russell and built in 1900, is revealing of the driven woman who promoted Russell to fame. The modest two-story clapboard house reflects the couple's lives and tastes in numerous small ways. They lived here until Russell's death in 1926, after which Nancy moved to California.

Whether or not you're a Charlie Russell fan, a visit to the museum complex honoring the man and his work gives insight into the artist who kept the hell-for-leather Old West of buffalo hunts, Indian wars and range-riding cowboys alive in the public imagination well past its heyday.

Modest entry fee. Summer hours: Mon.-Sat. 9-6, Sun. 1-5. Winter hours: Tues.-Sat. 10-5, Sun. 1-5. ☎ 406-727-8787.

The Cowboy Artist

The "cowboy artist" wasn't born or bred to the West he came to love and celebrate in his work. He was born in St. Louis in 1864. At age 16, Charlie left home for Montana and the seductions of life on the range. He found work as a cowboy, lived among the Blackfeet Indians for several months, all the while honing his considerable artistic talents. His fellow cowboys were amused by Charlie's habit of drawing scenes of what they considered the everyday grind, and that he considered to be high drama.

Charlie was 31, a seasoned cowboy and full time artist when he met 17-year-old Nancy Cooper, a hired girl at the home of friends. She and the artist were married on September 9, 1896.

Nancy had been orphaned and abandoned. The experience must have toughened her, for she set about making a success of her footloose husband. Art historians generally agree that, without Nancy, fondly nicknamed Mamie, Charlie would doubtless not have created the large body of artwork that he did. And it's a cinch that the work he did create would never have received recognition.

Charlie acknowledged Nancy's contribution by stating, "The lady I trotted in double harness with was the best booster an' pardner a man ever had.... If it hadn't been for Mamie I wouldn't have a roof over my head."

Nancy not only reigned in Charlie's carousing, she set out to promote his work with a zeal that would have done a 21st-century public relations firm proud. Charlie continued to slip out to The Mint, his favorite watering hole, but Nancy's vigilance kept the visits brief. Should a crony drop in to invite Charlie downtown for a tipple when he was working on a painting, Nancy refused to let him out. She was not admired by Great Falls saloon-hoppers.

Nancy's determination landed Charlie exhibits at the country's, then Europe's, most prestigous galleries. The good life was theirs. They built a lodge on Lake McDonald, in Glacier National Park, calling it Bull's Head Lodge for the signature symbol on Charlie's work. The couple had no children and the lack rode heavily on Charlie. In 1916, they adopted a baby named Jack. Nancy was a casual mother, to put it kindly; Charlie was a doting father.

Nancy's fondness for material things kept Charlie in working harness even after he began feeling poorly. He was diagnosed with goiter, but refused surgery until it was too late. On October 24, 1926, Charlie died of a heart attack while checking on his sleeping son. Nancy continued to promote Charlie's work, moving to Pasadena, California and refusing two marriage proposals so she could remain Mrs. Charles M. Russell. As for her son Jack, Nancy gave him every advantage but a mother's love. She died in 1940 and was interred beside Charlie in Great Falls.

Great Falls isn't all Lewis and Clark, the Missouri River and Charlie Russell. **Paris Gibson Square Museum of Art**, named for Paris Gibson, the official founder of Great Falls, is housed in a historic landmark building at 1400 First Avenue North. The museum, part of a regional culture center, displays contemporary Northwestern art. The building also houses the **Cascade County Historical Museum**, a museum store and café. Open year-round, Tues.-Fri. 10-5, Sat. & Sun. 12-5, Tues. evenings 7-9. Free admission. ☎ 406-727-8255.

■ On the Whoop-Up Trail

US 87 crosses the Missouri and hurries northeast from Great Falls, riding across 42 miles of high prairie farmland before a sign directing drivers to Fort Benton heaves into view.

Fort Benton

Fort Benton, population 1,650, has stood at the crossroads of Montana progress almost since Lewis and Clark passed that way in 1805. Today, Fort Benton slumbers quietly on a ledge of land between the Missouri and steep gear-grinding breaks. Tree-lined streets set off modest homes of a certain age. Two or three blocks of storefronts face the long park-like levee, seemingly little changed since the end of the rip-roaring steamboat era. But Fort Benton has seen layers of change, apparent along the levee and in the town's several excellent museums.

The History of Fort Benton

The shelf of riverfront land that became Fort Benton was originally Blackfeet country. In 1830, the Blackfeet signed a treaty permitting trading posts on their lands. In 1846, the American Fur Company built Fort Benton. The c. 1850 blockhouse stands as Montana's oldest structure. In 1855, the US government established the first Blackfeet Agency here. It was moved to Old Agency when reservation boundaries were changed.

A town began to straggle up outside the fort. In 1864, the American Fur Company was dissolved. In 1866, with the Civil War over and the Indian Wars heating up, Army troops arrived at Fort Benton. By then, the fort was so dilapidated that the garrison was quartered in the town. Nevertheless, it remained a military post until 1881, at the close of the Indian Wars.

Meanwhile, in 1860, steamboats began venturing as far as the end of Missouri River navigation at Fort Benton. Tiny Fort Benton became Montana's most important city, a center of transportation until railroads pushed through in 1883. Travelers headed for the Northwestern US debarked at Fort Benton and continued their journey via the Mullen Road. Western Canada-bound passengers struck out on the Whoop-Up Trail, prosaically known as the Old Forts Trail. The procession passing through Fort Benton colored those two decades with as diverse a bunch of characters as imagination can conjure up. Prospectors came, bound for the goldfields via the Mullan Road. Whiskey and gun runners came, bound for profits at the end of the Whoop-Up Trail linking Fort Benton with Canada's Fort Walsh. Mule skinners offloaded heavy mining machinery onto wagons for the last lap to Last Chance Gulch. Gamblers, flim flam artists and ladies of the night crowded into town. Settlers came, seeking they knew not what.

Saloons and brothels set up shop in the blocks facing the levee. Wild goings-on peppered with gunfire earned one block the sobriquet, "bloodiest block in the West." The Grand Union Hotel, a fine brick structure that still stands, provided sumptuous accommodations. Fort Benton was as wide open as any frontier town from the Arizona Strip to Dodge City.

The Great Northern and other railroads put the quietus on Fort Benton's heyday. Travelers could now circumvent a lengthy steamboat trip and grueling traverses over bad-awful rutted roads. Now they could ride the entire way in comfortable coaches, even in winter. The floozies and gamblers left for richer pickin's. But vestiges of the old ways lingered. A new version of the Whoop-Up Trail surfaced in the Prohibition era. Fort Benton went to sleep, until struck by the realization that it slept on a tourism gold mine.

Fort Benton Today

Strolling the Fort Benton levee is one of Montana's most enjoyable and rewarding time line adventures. Stop at the Visitor Center to pick up a walking tour brochure of the Historic Landmark town. The tourism season kicks off on Mother's Day with a community breakfast at the Oddfellows Hall and the official opening of the vest pocket visitor center.

The contrast between the town's lush lilacs and the river rolling beneath the levee is telling. Just as Fort Benton once signalled the limit of steamboat navigation, so it marks the beginning of the Wild and Scenic stretch of the Missouri River. The corridor extends through the White Rocks and Badlands Areas to the Charles M. Russell National Wildlife Refuge, a distance of some 147 river miles. No Carl Bodmer painting and no photograph can do justice to the **Upper Missouri River Wild & Scenic Corridor**. It projects a wild, sweeping beauty blending sky and river in a symphony of clouds and coursing water, the melody playing counterpoint to the rhythm of the Breaks' ever changing light.

 A fine new MT 80 bridge spans the river at Fort Benton. The old bridge was left in place so that visitors can walk out onto it to view the Missouri in mid-stream.

Lewis and Clark saw this river corridor much as we see it today. The levee holds numerous reminders of their epic journey. Foremost is the State of Montana's **Lewis and Clark Memorial Statue**, "The Explorers at the Marias," by Bob Scriver. Sacajawea rests as the explorers take a sighting of the river. Nearby is a replica of the keelboat *Mandan* that brought the Corps upriver. The replica was featured in a movie based on A.B. Guthrie Jr.'s novel, *Big Sky*.

Information on the Missouri's Wild and Scenic portion, and how it figured in the Lewis and Clark journey, is available at the BLM office across Front Street from the levee.

The levee is a natural place for memorials. There's one commemorating the Whoop-Up Trail, an obelisk honoring John Mullan of Mullan Road fame, a World War I Doughboy statue. Perhaps the most poignant is a statue, also by Bob Scriver, of a dog named Shep. Some people come to Fort Benton just to see it.

The Story of Shep

Shep was helper and companion to a sheepherder who died in a Fort Benton hospital in 1936. The dog watched as his friend's body was loaded onto a train for shipment back East. For over five years, Shep kept vigil, meeting every train in the hope that his master would return. Fed and cared for by railroad personnel, the dog became a Fort Benton fixture. On a winter day in 1942, Shep slipped on the rails and fell beneath an oncoming train. His death generated an outpouring of sympathy the world over. In the midst of a world war, a dog's loyalty touched people's hearts.

The handsome three-story **Grand Union Hotel** remains the most prominent of the structures harking back to Fort Benton's heyday. Seemingly in a constant state of restoration, the hotel gazes over the river with empty eyes. Fort Benton folks aren't holding their breath waiting for a grand opening.

Many of the Front Street stores facing the levee once housed the most flagrant of the saloons and brothels of Fort Benton's wild salad days. But today it may be a stretch to connect, say, the L&R Sandwich and Bakery, with goings-on that would chill your blood.

Fort Benton's Museums

The sagas reflected in Fort Benton's brace of museums are as telling as the transformation of bawdy house to sandwich shop.

The Museum of the Upper Missouri, flanked by the historic **Blockhouse** in Old Fort Park, encapsulates the frontier experience with dioramas depicting major events and picture walls of Fort Benton life in former times. Artifacts include such diverse items as the rifle surrendered by Chief Joseph of the Nez Perce, china from the Grand Union Hotel, Shep's collar and dish, Blackfeet artifacts, a genuine fur trade cabin, a saloon back bar and a fine collection of saddles. These displays, presented in chronological order, relate the saga of the Upper Missouri in a manner that appeals to folks of all ages and interests. Nominal admission fee. Open mid-May-mid-October. Call the Fort Benton Chamber of Commerce (see *Information Sources*) for current hours.

The State of Montana's **Museum of the Great Plains**, at 20th and Washington Streets, brings to life the history of Plains agriculture with one of the most exhaustive collections of farming machinery extant. To walk through this museum is to follow the Homestead years right up to the present. Cropping methods and seed development augment tractors. The human side of agriculture is represented by displays showcasing the progression of three generations of hypothetical families on the land. Outside, a Homestead Village offers additional insight into agrarian life in a bygone time. A grouping of six bison, collected in 1886 by conservationist William T. Hornaday for the National Museum in Washington, D.C., came from the last of the great herds that once roamed the Plains. The impressive grouping represents bison ranging from an adult bull and cow down to a four-month-old calf.

Modest entry fee includes both museums. Open daily, Memorial Day-Labor Day 10-5; mid-May and late September, 11:30-4:30. ☎ 406-622-5316.

The **Benton Belle trolley** stops at major points of interest and both museums. The two-hour trolley ride costs about $5. Summers only. ☎ 406-622-BOAT for reservations.

AUTHOR TIP *Take a summertime cruise on the **Benton Belle**, a scaled-down replica of a river boat by that name that once plied the Upper Missouri. Today's Belle, a 55-foot confection sporting an upper deck for spotting riverside wildlife, departs from the levee daily except Wednesdays at 10 am and 2 and 6 pm. Cruises last one hour. Fare: under $15. Reservations suggested. ☎ 406-622-BOAT.*

■ A Tame Look At The Wild & Scenic Missouri

By far the best way to experience the Upper Missouri River Wild & Scenic Corridor is by canoe (see *Adventures on Water*). No road follows this stretch of river. To see snatches of it by car you must travel the few gravelled and unsurfaced roads leading to ferry crossings and put-ins. Most involve long prairie miles.

The **Missouri Breaks National Back Country Byway**, originating north of Lewistown at **Winifred**, makes a passing acquaintance with the Missouri, but mostly traverses the prairie via gravelled and dirt roads that are impassable when wet and require a 4WD vehicle even in dry weather. A booklet with background on the Byway is available from the

BLM's Lewistown District Office (see *Information Sources,* page 516). The **Marias River** enters the Missouri at **Loma,** a couple of miles up US 87 from Fort Benton. Lewis and Clark camped here, naming the smaller river for Lewis's cousin, Maria Wood.

Two landings can be reached via roads heading riverward from US 87, northeast of Loma. Two roads a few miles apart join at **Virgelle,** site of an old mercantile, currently a B&B and canoe rental outfit. The more easterly road looks in on **Coal Banks Landing Recreation Area,** a popular put-in point for canoers. A ferry links Virgelle with an unsurfaced road meandering to **Geraldine,** once a stop on the Milwaukee Railway. The free ferry runs between May and October, Mon.-Sat. 7-7 and Sundays 9-5.

Rt. 236, partly paved and partly gravelled, extends for 44 miles from Big Sandy to the Judith Landing Recreation Area, halfway between the White Rocks and Badlands Areas. A bridge crosses the river here and Rt. 236 continues on to Winifred and the beginning of the Missouri Breaks National Back Country Byway. You can also access the river and the Byway via Rt. 240 from Chinook, crossing the river for free on the McClelland Ferry between May and October. This lengthy, mostly gravelled route, running partially through the Bears Paw Mountains, is lightly traveled. From Winifred, Rt. 236 continues on to US 87 at Lewistown. Lest you feel confused, a glance at a map will reveal that US 87 describes a rough triangle with Great Falls at the apex.

■ Bull Hook Siding, now Havre

US 87 enters **Rocky Boy's Indian Reservation** at tiny Box Elder. The 121,000-acre reservation, Montana's smallest, is home to bands of the Chippewa and Cree tribes. The reserve's name is a corruption of Stone Child, the Chippewa leader for whom it was named.

There's a ski area (see *Adventures on Snow,* page 558), but no tourism on this reservation, a beautiful and remote place of cropland interspersed with rolling Bears Paw Mountain foothills. The principle town, **Rocky Boy's Agency,** is at the center of the reservation. The winter sports area at the reserve's southern edge attracts Havre skiers and snowboarders.

DID YOU KNOW?

*Havre, 12 miles northeast of the reservation, once wore the unappetizing name of Bull Hook Siding. Jim Hill sought a more dignified name as his Great Northern Railway pushed through the townsite. He found it in the French birthplace of one of the original homesteaders. So it was that a town bearing a Frenchified name came to be established on a wild and lonesome Montana prairie. The fast-growing town soon learned to kick up its heels, Wild West-style. The **Havre Beneath the Streets** tour testifies to that.*

Fires were major hazards in the frontier era, often racing through entire blocks. When fire decimated a Havre block at the turn of the century, businesses simply moved underground. Many continued to do business in these basement warrens even after a new block of buildings rose overhead. Reminders of this "underground mall" remained even after the saloon and butcher shop, the Chinese laundry and bordello, the blacksmith and barber shops ceased to operate. Enter an enterprising group of Havre folks. Following a lengthy spate of researching, cleaning and artifacts collecting, Havre Beneath the Streets opened for business. The hour-long underground tour offers a fascinating look at Havre in its salad days, and by extension at other Montana frontier towns. Tours cost around $5, less for children. ☎ 406-265-8888 for reservations and a current tour schedule.

With over 10,000 residents, Havre is the largest city on the Hi-Line (US 2), and the trading center for a wide-flung agricultural area where wheat is king. Prior to assuming the name Bull Hook Siding, the townsite was a way station on the Old Forts Trail, also known as the **Whoop-Up Trail**, between Fort Benton and Canada. Watch for signs depicting a covered wagon sprouting US and Canadian flags along US 87 and Rt. 233 leading to the Port of Willow Creek.

The Trail looked in on **Fort Assinniboine**, situated just south of the junction of US 87 and 2. Established in 1879 to monitor the "Indian situation" and to put a stop to bootlegging and gunrunning, the fort was, for a time, the largest military post in Montana. Over 500 soldiers bunked here, including units of the famed African-American Buffalo Soldiers and 1st Lt. John J. Pershing, later of World War I fame. The surviving 16 of the original 104 structures are on the National Register of Historic Places. The site currently houses the Northern Agricultural Research Center, operated by Montana State University. The Fort Assinniboine Association conducts guided tours during the summer months. Contact the Havre Chamber of Commerce for tour schedules (see *Information Sources*).

The **H. Earl Clack Museum**, at the Hill County Fairgrounds (on US 2 just after the US 87 junction), has displays highlighting the history and development of the Havre area. Included is a diorama depicting the strong Indian influence on the area. Open May 15-Sept. 15. Free admission. Call the Havre Chamber of Commerce for current hours.

Wahkpa Chu'gn, a 2,000-year-old archaeological site, is in an unlikely location behind the Holiday Village Mall, across US 2 from the Fairgrounds. Used as a bison kill site and campground from approximately 2,000 to 600 years ago, the site has yielded up numerous projectile points and other artifacts. Many are on display at five interpretive locations throughout the site. Nominal admission fee. Open for tours mid-May-Labor Day, Tues.-Sat. 10-5, plus one 7 pm tour. Also open Sunday, 10-5. ☎ 406-265-6417 or 265-7550.

Charlie Russell Country

■ Surrender in the Bears Paws

US 2 follows the Milk River east from Havre to Fort Belknap Indian Reservation and Missouri River Country, first looking in on **Chinook**. This pleasant prairie town serves as the gateway to the Bear's Paw Battleground, site of the sad surrender of Chief Joseph and his Nez Perce band. The town takes note of its proximity to the Battleground with the dignified restraint mandated by such a tragic chapter in history.

Stop at the **Blaine County Museum** before continuing on to the Battleground. No collection of pioneer attic gleanings this, but a small, tastefully curated museum giving pride of place to Native American artifacts and culture, including an early photographic record of Nez Perce life. A deeply moving video explaining the 1877 Nez Perce flight and surrender serves as an introduction to a Battleground visit. Free admission. Guided tours available. Gift shop stocks relevant books. Battleground information available. Open daily, Memorial Day-Labor Day and weekdays in the off-season. The museum is off US 2, on the route to the Battleground. Watch for signs. ☎ 406-357-2590 for current hours.

The **Bear's Paw Battleground** is 16 miles south of Chinook on Rt. 240. The paved route leaves the Milk River Valley and climbs through hilly grasslands to the lower slopes of the Bears Paw Mountains. Standing on a hill, the battleground's folded hills are spread before you. The eternal wind hints at the late September and early October cold endured by the survivors of the trek from Oregon's Wallowa Country. No visitor center, no foot-worn trails disecting the Battleground; only a monument to a people's courage, plus a self-guided interpretive trail with nine unobtrusive exhibits describing the battle and seige.

Driving away toward Chinook, I spotted three pronghorns gliding across the prairie from the surrender site, their feet seeming not to touch the ground. Like swift spirits, they appeared to take flight.

Chief Joseph & the Nez Perce

Five bands of Nez Perce, some 800 men, women and children, had spent the summer traveling eastward from their Wallowa Country homelands. The trek was interrupted by battles at White Bird in Idaho and Big Hole south of Missoula. Referred to as Non-treaty Nez Perce, these followers of chiefs Joseph, Looking Glass and White Bird agreed with their chiefs' refusal to sign a treaty surrendering their sacred ancestral lands. Pushed toward a deadline, they chose flight over capitulation. Their numbers decimated by US military attacks, Chief Looking Glass killed, hopes of finding acceptance among the Crow Indians dashed, they now hastened to join Chief Sitting Bull in Canada.

Fleeing the Big Hole in disarray, they had left behind tipis, blankets and food. By the time they crossed the Bears Paws, summer's warmth was gone and the people were cold and hungry. Children and old people were suffering greatly. On September 29, they camped just 30 miles, a two-day trek, from sanctuary in Canada.

Early on the frigid morning of September 30, the 7th Cavalry under Col. Nelson A. Miles attacked the camp, separating the warriors from their horses after a spate of hand-to-hand combat. Despite heavy losses, the Nez Perce held their position. A siege ensued. Gen. Oliver O. Howard, having been in pursuit all summer, arrived with reinforcements on October 4. The Nez Perce fought fiercely despite numerous losses. During the night, Chief White Bird and some 150 followers escaped camp and fled to Canada. The seige continued, but Chief Joseph's heart was touched by the suffering of his people. On the afternoon of October 5, he surrendered his rifle to Col. Miles. The words of this great man ring as poignantly today as they did from that windswept hill in 1877: "Hear me, my chiefs, I am tired; my heart is sick and sad. From where the sun now stands, I will fight no more forever."

The trek of Chief Joseph and the 430 persons who survived was not over. During the surrender negotiations, Col. Miles agreed to their return to the Nez Perce Reservation in Idaho. Miles meant well, but was overruled by his superiors. The Nez Perce began a circuitous route to Indian Territory in Oklahoma that took them first to the Tongue River Indian Cantonment, then to Fort Abraham Lincoln in North Dakota and to Fort Leavenworth, Kansas. By 1885, the band numbered only 268. That year Col. Miles, an honorable man whose tongue was not forked like others', was able to oversee the return of 118 Nez Perce to Idaho. Chief Joseph and the remaining 149 were sent to the Colville Reservation in Washington State.

Chief Joseph died there in 1904. Never again did he lay eyes on his sacred homeland.

■ Fort Belknap Indian Reservation

Harlem

Harlem, Fort Belknap Indian Reservation's principal town, is 25 miles east of Chinook. US 2 traverses the northern edge of the 650,000-acre reservation, a panorama of plains and grasslands taking in a rough rectangle stretching south to the Little Rocky Mountains.

Some 4,000 members of the Assinniboine and Gros Ventre (pronounced "gro-von" with a soft n) tribes reside here. Their historical backgrounds differ, but they've lived together since before the 1888 establishment of the Fort Belknap Reservation.

The Assinniboine & Gros Ventre Tribes

The Assinniboine split from the Yanktonai Sioux in the early 1600s and allied with the Cree in Lake of the Woods country. The tribe divided at least twice as they moved westward to the Plains. Decimated by smallpox epidemics, the once sizeable tribe numbered only about 400 lodges (families) by the mid-19th century. These excellent buffalo hunters and horsemen prospered, until the end of the buffalo era forced them to accept government protection. The Gros Ventre are descended from the Algonkian speaking Arapaho, splitting off in the late 1600s. By the late 1800s, they had migrated to Montana's northern plains and allied with the Blackfeet. Smallpox and alcohol hit both tribes hard and they became enemies. In 1867, the Gros Ventre lost a final battle to the Blackfeet. Retreating to the Milk River country, they allied with the Assinniboine to occupy the Fort Belknap Reservation.

French speakers will recognize that "Gros Ventre" means "big belly." The Blackfeet called the Gros Ventre by a similar name, but the reason remains elusive.

Both the Assinniboine and Gros Ventre tribes regard the buffalo as central to their cultural identity. Over 10,000 acres support the reservation's herd of 300 bison. Tribal fish and game director Mike Fox estimates that herd numbers will eventually exceed 1,000 animals on 30,000 acres. The tribes released black footed ferrets onto the range in a further effort to bring back the buffalo culture. Buffalo, prairie dogs and ferrets complete an ecological circle. Ferrets keep prairie dog numbers down, ensuring a diversity of healthy plants to sustain the bison.

AUTHOR TIP

The buffalo reserve is open to guided tours departing daily from the Fort Belknap Tourism Office and Information Center. Tours of ancient tipi rings and other Reservation landmarks are also available. ☎ *406-353-2205 for current information.*

George Shields, the reservation's developer of tourism, states that the tribes are making a serious effort to help non-Indians understand the culture. Pow-wows and ceremonies are open to the public. This hospitable attitude extends to the attractive information center complex on US 2, in Harlem. Every effort is made to welcome visitors who may not be familiar with Native American culture. A small museum features some fine taxidermy specimens. A gift shop sells handcrafted Native American arts and crafts. The adjacent **Buffalo Robe Campground** has RV hookups and showers.

A nearby shopping center includes a tribal-run grocery and **Cowboys & Indians**, a custom leather and jewelry shop featuring the work of George Chub Snell, an Assinniboine whose ancestors include Pennsylvania Dutch.

MT 66 bisects the reservation, linking US 2 with US 191 and leading to **Old Mission Church** at Hays, and the scenic **Mission Canyon/Natural Bridge** recreational area in the Little Rocky Mountains. This small mountain range was part of the reservation in its entirety until prospectors discovered gold here. In 1896, the tribes were persuaded to sell a seven-by-four-mile parcel of land to the US government. Industrial gold mining in the vicinity of nearby Zortman continues to spark periodic protests.

■ Riding The Hi-Line

Riding the Hi-Line (US 2) between Chinook and Shelby is a time warp experience. Great Northern trains rumbled across the Hi-Line at the turn of the 20th century, bringing hopeful homesteaders to towns they named Kremlin, Gildford, Hingham, Rudyard, Inverness, and Joplin. Russian, British, Scottish, the names reflect the origins of families who battled the elements and grasshoppers where Blackfeet and Gros Ventre Indians once battled the whites and each other.

The towns sprang suddenly to life, hovered on a precipice of prosperity, then slid downhill when the wind went out of the homestead era's overinflated hopes. A few survive as agricultural centers. Chester is atypical, having begun as an 1880s rest stop for ranchers driving their cattle to the railhead at Minot, North Dakota. Vast wheatfields billow across a landscape that failed to support small diversified farms better suited to the Midwest and East.

Shelby

Shelby has hung on where others couldn't. Born as a station on the Great Northern Railway, Shelby soon became the distribution center for a trade area extending over 50 miles in every direction. The raw town opened its saloon doors to both cowboys and sheepherders. The country around Shelby was one of the last prairie grasslands to be settled by homesteaders.

By 1921, most of the homesteaders, done in by drought, had packed up and left. Instead of dying as so many towns did, Shelby plunged into boom times. Danged if the town wasn't sitting smack dab on an oilfield stretching clear to the Canadian border. Shelby rode so high that it hosted the 1923 fight in which Jack Dempsey successfully defended his World Heavyweight Boxing Champion title. The oil boom went bust, slowing

Shelby's high ridin' ways. Oil explorations are again being proposed in the Sweetgrass Hills north of town, but conservationists and the Blackfeet Nation oppose any new drilling. Where's that leave Shelby? The rough-edged town of some 2,800 residents takes it as it comes.

■ Facing Up To The Rocky Mountain Front

The towns, ranches and Hutterite colonies lying west of I-15 and south of the Hi-Line cozy up to the Rocky Mountains' Front Range. This country will feel familiar to readers of Ivan Doig's *Dancing at the Rascal Fair* and his other Montana novels. Numerous back roads invite leisurely drives through a more hospitable landscape than the windswept prairie of the Hi-Line. This country butting up to the Rockies is rich in wildlife; always has been. Today it's grizzlies and mountain goats; many yesterdays ago it was dinosaurs. Several roads straight-arrow to trailheads accessing the Front Range. Small towns reflect pride of place and their ranching origins.

Developers on the Way?

Developers are seeking to capitalize on the area's proximity to Great Falls. Big city rat race escapees have pretty near saturated the Bitterroot and Flathead Valleys. Conservationists fear that the lands lapping the Front Range could be next.

As aging ranchers contemplate selling out, the possibility of developers carving historic spreads up into ranchettes is real. It's happened elsewhere; conservationists don't want it to happen here. Developers are being cut off at the pass by Conservation Easements. Backed up with federally allocated dollars, these agreements between sellers and buyers assure that the property will never be developed. Some lands are being put in trust for wildlife conservation. This rolling landscape fronting the Rocky Mountains stands a good chance of remaining unspoiled and unchopped for future generations to enjoy.

To get here from Shelby, you must first endure 15 miles of I-15. Cross the fledgling Marias River, take Exit 348, and head west on MT 44 to US 89. Hang a left here.

Choteau

The 43-mile stretch to Choteau runs through Dupuyer, an old ranching town that's slipped a bit, but holds its own. **Dupuyer** is typical of the galaxy of towns outflung from Choteau; drowsing, but beginning to awaken to tourist possibilities.

Choteau, the Front country's principal town and the Teton County seat, lives up to most folks' image of Western small town America. Even its history fits. From trading post to agricultural trading center, the town named for American Fur Company president Pierre Chouteau (they dropped the first u from his name for convenience!) has continued to thrive.

 DID YOU KNOW? *A.B. Guthrie, Jr., the author who coined Montana's "Big Sky" sobriquet with his novel by that name, was a lifelong Choteau resident. His best selling books celebrated Montana and the West as no others had. From the vantage point of his Front Range home, he glorified a Montana that was 90% grit, toil and heartache. The Pulitzer Prize-winning author died in 1991.*

Choteau showcases the town's and the Front Range's wide-ranging history at the **Old Trail Museum Complex**, on US 89 at the north edge of town. Choteau's **Information Station** is adjacent to the museum. Museum displays are arranged in a series of Old West-style structures and include a log cabin grizzly bear exhibit, a Metis cabin, the A.B. Guthrie exhibit, dinosaur exhibits, a pioneering guest ranch exhibit. An ice cream parlor and antique shop round out the complex. Open daily, May 15-Sept. 15, 9-6; winter hours are Tues.-Fri., 10-3. Nominal admission fee. ☎ 406-466-5332.

Refer to *Special Interest Adventures* (page 564) for information on the Museum's summer Paleontology Field School.

If you wish to see how a cattle ranch operates, **Teton County Cattle Women** will arrange a ranch tour for you. ☎ 800-823-3866 or 406-466-5316.

US 89 and 287 meet at Choteau, US 89 swinging southeast to Great Falls by way of the **Freezeout Lake Wildlife Management Area** (see *Wildlife Watching*, page 562). The route passes through **Fairfield**, the self-proclaimed malting barley capital of the world. The distinction may mean little to casual visitors, but it's cause for celebration among barley growers and the businesses that support them. US 287 beelines south to I-15 and Helena, entering Gold West Country near Augusta.

Choteau and **Augusta** are jumping-off points to the Bob Marshall Wilderness. The Lewis and Clark National Forest's Rocky Mountain Ranger District is headquartered in Choteau, the Augusta Information Station in Augusta. Choteau's access follows the Teton River, rising out of Pine Butte Swamp Wildlife Viewing Area, and culminates at the Rocky Mountain Hi Ski Area. Augusta being closer to the Front, the access is shorter and leads to numerous Forest Service campgrounds. A part-gravel, part-

Charlie Russell Country

At the Augusta American Legion Rodeo.

unsurfaced road meanders between US 287 and the Front Range, linking access roads between the two towns.

Augusta's 500 residents celebrate the cowboy era; but not to the exclusion of catering to Wilderness-bound backpackers. The town has thrown a major rodeo for nigh unto 65 years.

▪ Riding High in the Little Belts

Most Russell Country highways radiate from **Great Falls**. In racking up 10,000 miles on this book's final research stint, I returned again and again to Great Falls. I came to welcome the sight of this city rising straight up from the prairie.

MT 21 straight-arrows between Augusta and Great Falls, joining MT 200, then I-15 for the last 24 miles. After exiting I-15, take the 10th Avenue Bypass to US 87/89. Some 23 miles down the highway and over the prairie, US 87 forks off and zips through the Judith Basin to Lewistown. More about that later.

US 89 heads straight for a riseable clump of mountains wearing a "hat" of dark green jackpines. These are the Little Belts, Montana's last sizeable mountains before the plains grip the land in earnest. Watch for a sign to **Sluice Boxes State Park** at the base of a long steep incline. Hang a right and drive a short distance to a most unparklike park. Visiting this park, the northern eight miles of Belt Creek Canyon along an abandoned railway, takes a fair amount of walking and stream fording. Licorice and I had a ball exploring this once busy route to a gaggle of old mining towns. You will find brochures stashed at the parking area.

At the incline, US 89 becomes the 71-mile-long **Kings Hill Scenic Byway**. Slicing through the Little Belts' midsection, the route follows energetic Belt Creek to the summit at King's Hill Pass. Several Forest Service campgrounds line the Byway, a boon if you're tempted to linger and maybe hike a bit.

To state that these mountains are very beautiful is to understate. A few aggressively new log homes contrast with the old mining towns of Monarch and Neihart. **Neihart** is a pleasing jumble of weathered log cabins, fallen-down shacks, summer cabins, and homes bearing sad signs of past pretensions. **Showdown Ski Area** tops the summit. Numerous logging roads lace the Little Belts; tempting trails to old mining sites and other traces of man's presence here. Some of these roads may be okay for passenger cars in dry summer weather, but a 4WD vehicle is the better choice. Obtain back country travel maps from the **Lewis and Clark National Forest's Belt Creek Information Station**, five miles north of Neihart on US 89, or from the **King's Hill Ranger District office** in White Sulphur Springs.

White Sulphur Springs

White Sulphur Springs anchors the southern end of the Byway. The town is a staging area for Smith River Canyon floats. It isn't much to look at today, but the quiet main drag harbors reminders of its rip-roaring heyday.

DID YOU KNOW? *The **Stockmen Bar** in White Sulphur Springs was a favorite hangout of cowboys, sheepherders and prospectors working nearby lead and silver mines who shouldered into town of a Saturday night. What stories its log rafters could tell! Its dank recesses will be recognized by readers of Ivan Doig's* This House of Sky.

The namesake medicinal springs once attracted Indians and whites alike, but never achieved the popularity of other Montana hot springs. The **Spa Hot Springs Motel** straddles one spring. The other is covered over by a baseball diamond. So much for convivial soaking. A stern stone edifice referred to as **The Castle** crowns a hill overlooking the business section. Stockman and mine owner B.R. Sherman built the structure in 1892, positioning it to overlook his extensive holdings. The Meagher County Historical Association has made a valiant stab at restoring and refurbishing the mansion. It's worth a visit if only for the magnificent cherry wood stairway and the views from the third story windows. The carriage displays old buggies and such. Modest admission fee. Open daily, May 15-Sept. 15, 10-6, and other times by appointment. ☎ 406-547-3666.

■ Discovering The Judith Basin

The Judith Basin, a spacious expanse of prime grassland, occupies an area roughly bounded by the Missouri Breaks on the north, the Little Belt and Highwood Mountains to the south and west, and the Judith Mountains on the east. Wolf Creek and the Judith River run through the Basin, merging before emptying into the Missouri River. **Lewistown**, a historic city with an over-active public relations approach, is the Basin's self-proclaimed hub. **Stanford**, plunk in the center of the Basin, meets the needs of local farmes and ranchers.

DID YOU KNOW? *The Judith Basin was named by Meriwether Lewis for his cousin, Judith Hancock. She would doubtless be amazed, could she realize the scope of these fabled grasslands.*

To reach the Basin, head east on US 12, shooting off US 89 three miles north of White Sulphur Springs. The route traverses a valley between the Little Belt and Castle Mountains, then follows the Musselshell River eastward from Bair Reservoir.

Charles M. Bair Family Museum

A visit to the Charles M. Bair Family Museum near **Martinsdale** offers insight into the life of the railway conductor who came to own one of the world's largest sheep herds. As Bair accrued land, sheep and wealth in the final decades of the 19th century and the early decades of the 20th, he became friends with such diverse shapers of Montana's future and the mythical West as Charlie Russell and Chief Plenty Coups. In 1913, Bair purchased a Musselshell Valley spread. He enlarged the ranch house many times over, making it into a suitable home for a family of means.

From the outside, the white clapboard house appears fairly modest, despite its size. Inside, it's a showcase for eclectic acquisitions ranging from museum-quality Indian beadwork to furniture, silver and objets d'art purchased by Mrs. Bair and the girls on trips to Europe. The house remains a fascinating portrait of a privileged family's life on the Montana frontier.

Modest admission fee. Open May 1-Sept. 30, Wed.-Sun. 10-5. Special hours by appointment. ☎ 406-727-8787.

Harlowton, 23 miles downriver from Martinsdale, is notable for two things: entire blocks of locally quarried sandstone structures, and its role as the once busy terminal for an electrified section of the Milwaukee Railroad. The county seat projects a prosperous appearance. Enormous General Mills silos further that image.

The **Upper Musselshell Museum**, displaying items of historical interest from the Upper Musselshell river country, occupies a landmark sandstone structure. A replica of an Avaceratops skeleton found near Shawmut, plus numerous dinosaur bones and gizzard stones, prove how far back area history extends. Free admission. Open May 1-Oct. 31, Tues.-Sat. 10-5, Sunday 1-5. ☎ 406-632-5519.

From Harlowton, US 191 heads north to Judith Gap and the Judith Basin. This 39-mile stretch through some of Montana's finest grasslands links up with US 87.

Blackfeet buffalo hunters, trappers, Chief Joseph and his fleeing Nez Perce band, cattle drovers, wolfers, cattlemen and sheepmen – the Judith Basin has seen them all. Had it not been for the vivid paintings of a cowboy artist named Charlie Russell, the Basin might not have become synonymous with Wild West history, heroics and antics. Russell's paintings recorded the Old West's poignant side, too. "White Man's Buffalo," depicting a trio of mounted Indians sadly contemplating a longhorn steer, contrasts with "In Without Knocking" depicting a bunch of liquored-up cowboys spurring their horses through a saloon door.

The *C.M. Russell Auto Tour*, a souvenir-quality descriptive booklet illustrated with several Charlie Russell paintings, is available free of charge at the C.M. Russell Museum in Great Falls, the Judith Ranger District office in Stanford, and through area chambers of commerce. Through representative Russell oils, the booklet identifies points of interest to both Russell buffs and history buffs. It covers the Charles M. Russell Trail along US 87, and the Memorial Way through Utica and the South Fork of the Judith River.

The small towns up the line between the US 87 junction and the US 89 junction near Belt drowse among memories of the Basin's heyday. **The Belt Museum**, at 37 Castner Street, offers a look at local mining history through displays housed in a c.1895 jail. Open Sat., Sun. and holidays, 12-4. ☎ 406-227-3616 or 227-3366.

Stanford

Stanford predates and has outlasted them all. On the main freight line between Judith Gap and Fort Benton, the town was Antelope Butte Springs until 1880. That's when Calvin and Edward Bowers trailed in 1,000 head of sheep, acquired 100,000 acres of land, and named the town for their New York State hometown. Stanford's watering holes soon attracted cowboys and sheepherders. When it became the Judith Basin County Seat, it's future was assured. The town boasts only 524 residents, but has two museums.

Judith Basin Museum, next to the Court House, is a repository of a telling collection of homestead-era artifacts. Open June 1-Aug. 31, 9-12 and 1-5. Other hours by appointment. ☎ 406-566-2281.

Prairie Past Museum, at the county fairgrounds on US 87, offers a look at the Basin's past through an array of historic agricultural equipment displayed in an outdoor setting. Open year-round in daylight hours. ☎ 406-566-2428.

Charlie Russell Country

The White Wolf

Time was when wolves roamed the Judith Basin, preying on cattle and sheep after the buffalo, their principal dinner entrée, had been killed off. Stockmen hunted these wolves to extinction, often hiring "wolfers" to kill the predators by whatever means necessary. One wolf remained – a big old white wolf whose elusive ways earned him a grudging respect. The wolf did in over a thousand dollars worth of young stock in a time when a calf wasn't worth a whole lot. A bounty was placed on his head, attracting hunters from all over. Poison bait traps were set. For 15 years, the canny wolf eluded all efforts to bring him down. Then he made a mistake. He could have bolted when a pair of dogs and two men surrounded him, but instead stood his ground and snarled. A rifle shot ended the life of one of the West's most prolific killers. Yup, the White Wolf was big: 83 pounds and measuring six feet from nose to tip of tail. He can be seen, mounted up real pretty and snarling, at the Basin Trading Post in Stanford, Mon.-Sat. from 8-5.

Utica

The Memorial Way featured in the *C.M. Russell Auto Tour* booklet describes a loop south of US 87 via County Routes 541 and 239 to the Judith River town of Utica.

The annual roadside hay bale contest engenders big excitement along the loop. In early September, ranchers and farmers compete over who can best turn bales of hay into fanciful creations. Entries get downright zany; punny, too. Take BumbleBale, a giant bee with flapping hay wings. Or Moby Dick and the Great White Bale. Life was a tad wilder in days gone by. Perhaps more than any other Montana town, Utica embodies the rip-roaring Old West. Charlie Russell painted the area's hell-for-leather doings, not needing to put on any dog. The goings-on were wilder than any of the yarns the artist was known to spin. His oil, "Quiet Day in Utica," depicting mounted cowboys funning it up on the town's dusty street while a tin-canned dog hock-hobbles a bucking horse and chickens scatter, tells it like it was.

How Utica Got its Name

The story goes that Utica was named for a city in New York State by four prospectors-cum-settlers who, holed up in a blizzard fit to freeze the tail off a rattlesnake, decided they had been crazy to come here. So they named the place Utica for their hometown, that being the site of the New York Insane Asylum.

The **Utica Museum** is a repository of artifacts relating the story of the town's exciting past. Open weekends, Memorial Day-Labor Day, 8-5. Other hours by appointment. ☎ 406-423-5208.

Lewistown

Lewistown makes hay out of being at the geographic center of Montana. The wildness that beset the town in the late 19th century has long since been toned down. Today, it's a peaceful county seat town in the lee of the Judith Mountains. Four vest-pocket districts are listed on the National Register of Historic Places: the Silk Stocking and Judith Residential Districts and the Downtown and Courthouse Square Districts. The Lewistown Area Chamber of Commerce makes available a brochure describing them.

The **Central Montana Historical Association Museum**, at 408 NE Main in Symmes Park, presents a pageant of the artifacts, antiques and guns that served to mold the town and the area. Free admission. Open year-round, Mon.-Fri., 8-noon & 1-5. Also open Sat. & Sun. between Memorial Day and Labor Day, 10-4. ☎ 406-538-5436.

The **Lewistown Art Center**, at 801 West Broadway, has changing exhibits and a shop featuring original Montana arts and crafts. Free admission. Open Tues.-Sat., 11:30-5:30. ☎ 406-538-8278.

AUTHOR TIP *If you're here the first Saturday after Labor Day you can take in the annual* **Chokecherry Festival***. The sour chokecherry is the area's counterpart to the ubiquitous wild huckleberry of Western Montana.*

The town's biggest attraction is the **Charlie Russell Chew Choo**, a two-car lunch or dinner tour train that round-trips between Spring Creek Junction, just outside Lewistown, and the small agricultural community of Denton. The four-hour run includes a heap of Western high-jinks, even a train robbery. Summer weekends; call for reservations and current schedule. ☎ 406-538-5436.

Driving the Lewistown area's back roads offers insight into the area's diverse geology and visits numerous old mining sites. Brochures describing four off-the-beaten-track auto tours are available from the Lewistown Area Chamber of Commerce. Some tours are over fair weather roads. Translation: a 4WD vehicle isn't a bad idea. Closest in is the **Spring Creek Tour**, taking in some local landmarks and the Montana State Fish Hatchery. The hatchery is open in business hours for self-guided tours. Numerous springs rise in Lewistown area hills. Spring Creek flows through town from Big Spring, the world's third largest fresh water spring. It's also on the tour.

The **North and South Moccasin Mountains Tour** looks in on the Kendall Mining District, in the mountains north of Lewistown. The once bustling turn-of-the-century mining town is a ghostly place today, drowsing among its ruins.

The **Judith Mountains Tour** also looks in on mining camp sites. Few reminders remain, most buildings having been moved off by local ranchers when the mining boom went bust. **Judith Peak**, once the site of an Air Force radar facility, is the highest point at 5,808 feet. The BLM maintains a recreation site here. The drive is worthwhile for the views alone. On a clear day, you can see the Snowy Mountains, 30 miles to the south, the Little Belts, 70 miles to the southwest, the Moccasins, 20 miles to the west, the Highwoods, 70 miles to the west, the Bears Paws and Little Rockies, 70 miles to the northwest, and the Missouri River Breaks, 50 miles straight north.

The **Crystal Lake/Big Snowy Mountains Tour** accesses several hiking trails (see *Adventures on Foot*) in the Snowies, plus 6,000-foot-high Crystal Lake.

West of Lewistown, US 87 snakes across the prairie to Missouri River Country as the last of the mountains fall behind in the rear view mirror.

Adventures

■ Adventures on Foot

Hiking & Backpacking

Russell Country's prairie-isolated mountain ranges offer some wonderful hiking and backpacking. Special concerns and conservation practices applicable to hiking in other regions also apply here.

The **Rocky Mountain Front, the Little Belts, Big Snowies** and **Highwood Mountains** are in the Lewis and Clark National Forest and include numerous hiking and multi-use trails. The **Bear Paws** consist largely of privately owned ranchlands used by hunters.

Wildlife

Grizzly bears are a concern along the Rocky Mountain Front, less so or not at all in the Little Belts, Big Snowies, Highwoods and Bear Paws. Mountain lions can be a very real concern.

Reclusiveness is in the big cats' nature. Nevertheless, they seem to be losing their fear of humans and are spotted increasingly. Two factors contribute to these sightings: a decrease in the deer population and human population creep. When a wild animal, especially a hungry wild animal, loses its fear of humans it becomes dangerous. Stories of close encounters of the cat kind are becoming more common. Typical is that of a father out hunting with his nine-year-old son. Dad's sixth sense kicked in. He turned to see a mountain lion headed straight for the boy. Dad shot. The lion dropped just 30 feet from the kid.

The moral of the story: be careful. Refer to *Mountain Lions* on page 19.

Beaver Creek Park

Beaver Creek Park, 12 miles south of Havre via County Route 234 (take 5th Ave. south from Main Street) affords pleasant day hiking. The 10,000-acre park extends south along Beaver Creek and is sandwiched between the Rocky Boy's Reservation and the western slopes of the Bears Paws. It includes two lakes and several developed campsites.

Rocky Mountain Ranger District

The Rocky Mountain Ranger District is the eastern gateway to the **Bob Marshall Wilderness Area** (the "Bob"). As such, the district has more trails than you could ever hope to hike in a summer: 179, covering over 1,000 miles. Many trails tend to be heavily traveled. Three, **Wood Lake #263**, **Our Lake #194**, and **Mt. Wright #160**, are restricted to hikers only. All others are open to horses, mules, llamas and mountain bikes as well as hikers. Mountain bikes and motorized vehicles are not permitted in the Bob. The latter are also prohibited on many of the trails accessing the Wilderness. The District makes available a *Hiking and Horse Trail Guide* listing trail difficulty ratings and easily referenced restrictions.

If you wish to hike or backpack the Front, check in at either the **Rocky Mountain Ranger District office** in Choteau or the **Augusta Information Station**. Don't show up on a Saturday morning; ranger districts generally observe weekday office hours. Do check in during the week or before 4 pm on a Friday so you'll have plenty of time to go over the topo map with a knowledgeable ranger. He or she will steer you in the direction you want to go.

Little Belts Trails

The Little Belts have the largest variety of hiking/backpacking trails after the Rocky Mountain Front. The *Lewis and Clark National Forest Trail Guide* is a freebie describing trails in the Little Belt, Big Snowy and Highwood Mountains. Obtain a copy from the Judith, Kings Hill or Musselshell Ranger District offices.

Charlie Russell Country

Topo maps are recommended and can be obtained from the aforementioned ranger districts, or from Castle Mountain Sports in White Sulphur Springs (☎ 406-547-2330).

Many Little Belts trails are accessed from the Kings Highway Scenic Byway (US 89). Others are accessed from gravel roads branching off US 12. Some samples:

- The 3.3-mile **Bear Gulch Trail #310** is a little-used access trail to the Smith River, where there's a pleasant camp site. Access is two miles west of Monument Peak on Forest Road 268; 6.2 miles west on Trail #301.

- The 6.1-mile **Old Baldy Trail #301** into the Deep Creek area is one of the Little Belts' most popular trails and a good backpacking choice. Most of this trail runs along ridge tops and affords great views. The trailhead is at Daisy Spring via FS Road #268.

- The 5.2-mile **Dry Wolf Trail #401** takes off from the Dry Wolf Campground, traversing meadows and timber and climbing a slope to a ridge. The reward: a gorgeous panoramic view from the Jefferson Divide. At Stanford, take US 87 to Dry Wolf Road #251; follow it to the campground.

- The one-mile **Lost Stove Trail #346** to the upper part of Tenderfoot Creek not only has an intriguing name, it's easily accessed from US 89. Take Forest Road #3484 at the Kings Hill junction of #839 and #3484.

Crystal Lake Area

The Big Snowy Mountains' Crystal Lake Area has a trail for everyone who enjoys hoofing it. Many loop off from pretty Crystal Lake. Watch for the Crystal Lake sign on US 87, 12 miles west of Lewistown. Head south on the gravel road for 16 miles, then drive nine miles on FS Road #275. Surrounded by dense stands of conifers, the rainbow trout-stocked shallow alpine lake sparkles at an altitude of 6,000 feet.

Shoreline Loop Trail #404 is an easy loop around the lake. Signs identify points of interest regarding the lake's history and flora. The **Hidden Basin Wildflower Trail**, north of the loop trail, has signs identifying species of trees and flowers indigenous to the area. **Grandview Trail #403** climbs 3.5 miles, with a 1,000-foot elevation gain, to a lofty viewpoint overlooking the lake and the Judith Basin. You can continue another 1.5 miles on **West Peak Trail #490**, along the ridge running the length of the Snowies. Short, easy **Promontory Peak Trail #491** gains 400 feet to a view of the lake, Hidden Basin and the Snowy Crest. **Crystal**

Cascades Trail #445 follows the east fork of Rock Creek for five miles, gaining 1,000 feet in elevation. A short side trail leads to a waterfall emerging from a cave and cascading some 100 feet down stairstep ledges.

Possibly the best known of the Crystal Lake trails is the **Ice Caves**, or **Ulhorn, Trail #493**. This trail climbs five miles to permanant ice caves on the Snowy Crest and gains 2,200 feet in elevation. After a difficult first half, the trail follows the open top of the Snowy Crest along West Peak Trail #490 to the ice caves (see *Caving*, page 544). On a clear day, you can see the Absarokee Range, Grand Tetons, Little Belts and Crazies from the crest.

Several combinations of the above described hikes are possible, offering scope for several days of pleasant backpacking. These trails are open to mountain bikes and equestrian travel, as well as hikers.

The Highwood Mountains

The compact bump on the prairie east of Great Falls known as the Highwood Mountains has several trails in the vicinity of Thain Creek Campground open to mountain bikers, equestrians and hikers. To reach the campground, on the northwest edge of the Highwoods, take paved Route 331 off US 89, southeast of Great Falls. Watch for a gravel road on your right, just south of the town of Highwood. Ranging from two to 6.5 miles and gaining from 150 to 900 feet over saddles to creek drainages, these make good family hiking trails. Info and maps are available at the Judith Ranger District office in Stanford.

Guided Hiking/Backpacking Trips

Montana Wilderness Association offers a variety of *Wilderness Walks* throughout the state every summer. Contact them for a current schedule. PO Box 635, Helena, MT 59624; ☎ 406-443-7350.

High Country Adventures' Lester Lobie leads backpacking trips on Rocky Mountain Ranger District lands. 3316 Hackberry, Bismark, ND 58501-0240. Call Rick Graetz at ☎ 406-442-9277.

Caving

Russell Country offers plenty of scope for serious cavers. Numerous caves are found in the Big and Little Belt Mountains, the North and South Moccasins, the Big Snowy Mountains, the Judiths and Little Rockies. These mountains have been formed by vertical uplift. The host rock for all these caves is the **Mission Canyon Formation** of the Madison Group (Mississippian).

Many of these caves have steep drops. Do not attempt to explore any cave unless you are an experienced caver, have caving equipment and know how to use it. Never enter a cave by yourself; teamwork is the key to a safe

Charlie Russell Country

and successful caving expedition. The following cave descriptions represent a sampling of the region's more accessible caves.

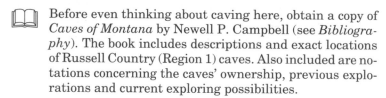 Before even thinking about caving here, obtain a copy of *Caves of Montana* by Newell P. Campbell (see *Bibliography*). The book includes descriptions and exact locations of Russell Country (Region 1) caves. Also included are notations concerning the caves' ownership, previous explorations and current exploring possibilities.

Lick Creek Cave in the Little Belts 10 miles west of Monarch on Logging Creek, has a two-by-three-foot entrance into passages leading to the Cathedral Room via a 40-foot pit. This, Montana's largest cave room, measures 405 by 465 feet. The cave's popcorn, flowstone and small stalactites have been vandalized.

Snowy Mountain Ice Cave is at the summit of the Big Snowy Mountains, about a half-mile east of West Peak. Two large south-facing entrances slope to a 100-by-75-foot room filled with ice and presenting ice stalactites and stalagmites. Rusty pieces of pipe remain from a system of pipes once used to raise water to troughs used for watering sheep. **Devil's Chute Cave** is about a half-mile east of Snowy Mountain Ice Cave. A sizeable walk-in entrance slopes steeply to a room containing a lake. A vertical entrance opens to the opposite side of the lake. **Snow Chute Cave**, at the summit of West Peak, is also in this area. The north entrance opens to the top of a 30-by-82-foot room, accessible via a steep snow and ice slope.

Dry Wolf Cave in the Judith Basin, on the north side of Dry Wolf Creek Canyon some 15 miles southwest of Stanford, is about 340 feet long in its entirety. A small crawlway at the base of a hoodoo opens to a passage about six feet high. After 100 feet, this passage, apparently part of an old stream bed, splits into smaller passages. Bat guano indicates that the cave is home to numerous bats. South Fork Cave is under a road bordering South Fork Creek, some 30 miles south of Stanford. The one-foot-square entrance is in a ditch at the side of the road and may be covered over to prevent livestock from falling in. The cave opens into a fissure that can be climbed without rope. Inside is a stream falling 100 feet to the bottom of the cave. More cave may exist beyond a small opening at the bottom.

Rock Hounding

While not as rich as Gold West Country, Russell Country nevertheless has some pockets of interest, especially in old gold and silver mining areas, where you may spot some ore. The **Zortman-Landusky area**, in the Little Rocky Mountains south of Fort Belknap Reservation, comes to mind. Unfortunately, the Landusky Mining District's old placer mines are being aggressively mined, making access to tailings and dumps doubtful at best.

Area **fossil collecting** presents a brighter picture. Search road cuts for fossiliferous rock, notably oyster *Gryphaea*, star-shaped crinoid *Pentacrinus* columnals and less common species of ammonites and brachiopods.

AUTHOR TIP

*"**Montana diamonds**" may be found above the old mining camp of **Maiden**, in the Judith Mountains. Drive 10 miles north of Lewistown on US 191. Hang a right on Maiden Road and proceed to the ghost camp. Four miles past Maiden, up a steep winding road, is an outcrop of quartz porphyry, a.k.a. Montana diamonds. Look in road cuts for doubly terminated quartz crystals. Generally, these are smoky in color and opaque, about a quarter-inch to an inch in diameter. Small light-colored terminated feldspar crystals are also found here. Pan for gold in small streams in the Maiden vicinity. There are several private claims in the area, so be careful to pan only on BLM land.*

Yogo Gulch has long been synonymous with **sapphires**. Nineteenth-century prospectors came to the Little Belt Mountains' Yogo area to pan for placer gold. But blue stones shone among the flecks of gold caught in their pans. Someone thought to ascertain if the pretty stones had any value. Darned if they didn't! When cut, the stones' deep cornflower blue rivaled highly prized Ceylon stones. Commercial sapphire mining continues.

Chances of finding rough Yogo sapphires are doubtful, since the four-mile igneous dike containing the sapphires is off-limits to collectors. However, panning area streams is permitted, as long as they're not on private land or claims. Pan local gift shops for a reliable, though expensive, source of faceted Yogo sapphires.

Mississippian Madison Limestone is often exposed in the Big Snowy Mountains south of Lewistown. Ergo: marine type fossils are not uncommon. These may consist of brachiopods, corals and crinoids. Search for fossils in road cuts and cliffs along the road to Crystal Lake (see *Hiking & Backpacking*).

Rockhounding Montana by Robert Feldman is a recommended reference for serious rockhounders (see *Bibliography*).

Charlie Russell Country

■ Adventures on Horseback

Horseback riding and horsepacking are natural reflections of the cowboy ethos for which Charlie Russell Country is famous. Rocky Mountain Front trails into the Bob Marshall Wilderness offer almost unlimited scope for Montana's favorite outdoor recreation. The Little Belts also afford great riding and horsepacking.

AUTHOR TIP

If you plan on trailering your personal steeds to Montana, there are rules and regulations that you need to be aware of. As few readers will fall into that category, and as Forest Service equestrian regulations and restrictions are subject to change, this book doesn't go into detail on the issue. Contact the Lewis and Clark National Forest Supervisors Office well in advance of your trip for permit requirements, if any, and to get a fix on laws pertaining to bringing horses into Montana. Also request equestrian regulations and lists of trails and campgrounds open to horses.

If you want to make riding the focus of your visit, you must decide between roughing it on a mountain pack trip or cattle drive and enjoying the comparative luxury of a guest ranch.

If you opt for a pack trip, be sure that the outfitter you choose is licensed, insured and bonded. As mentioned in earlier chapters of this book, rogue outfitters are a problem. Illegal outfitters violate the law. You will be in violation if you hire one.

Horsepacking Outfitters

The following outfitters offer horsepacking trips in Charlie Russell Country. Most have horses suitable for inexperienced as well as experienced riders, but discourage riders weighing over 250 pounds. Most prefer that children be at least six years old. Refer to the *Glacier Country* chapter of this book for additional outfitters offering trips into the Bob Marshall Wilderness.

A Lazy H Outfitters, owned and operated by Allen and Sally Haas and their three grown children, offers multi-day horse and mule pack trips to several very special areas of the Bob Marshall Wilderness. PO Box 729, Choteau, MT 59422; ☎ 406-466-5564.

Beaver Creek Outfitters' Clayton Barkhoff offers a choice between five-day fixed camp trips and five-day progressive pack trips in the Little Belt Mountains. Customized trips can also be arranged. Rt. 1, Box 1732, Lewistown, MT 59457; ☎ 406-538-5706.

Lass & Ron Mills Outfitters runs five-day to eight-day horse and mule pack trips in the Bob Marshall Wilderness Complex. Guides pride themselves on teaching conservation ethics on their trips. PO Box 2, Augusta, MT 59410; ☎ 406-562-3335.

Little Rockies Outfitting offers trail rides, breakfast and steak rides from Zortman. PO Box 200, Zortman, MT 59546; ☎ 406-673-3559.

Miller Outfitters' Bob Miller and P.K. and Anita Williams lead multi-day summer pack trips to a comfortable tent camp in the Little Belt Mountains. Guests ride smooth-gaited Tennessee Walkers. 663 Vaughn So. Frontage Rd., Great Falls, MT 59404; ☎ 406-738-4281.

Montana Safaris' Rocky and Lorell Heckman have numerous Rocky Mountain Front equestrian trips that include overnight and extended pack trips. They also offer riding lessons, photography safaris and day trail rides along Spring Creek. 21 Airport Rd., Choteau, MT 59422; ☎ 406-466-2004.

Seven Lazy P Guest Ranch owners and outfitters Chuck and Sharon Blixrud lead multi-day pack trips in the Bob Marshall Wilderness in addition to guest ranch stays. PO Box 178, Choteau, MT 59422; ☎ 406-466-2044.

Cattle Drives

No experience is more authentically Montana than joining a cattle drive. The following outfits will be happy to oblige. Yee-ha!

Chase Hill Outfitters' Bill and Renita Brown run six-day spring cattle drives, three-day summer range rider drives, and five-day fall ranch roundups from their ranch between the foothills of the Bears Paw Mountains and the Missouri River Breaks. These are real working ranch roundups. HC77, Box 851, Big Sandy, MT 59520; ☎ 406-386-2447. Fax 406-386-2435.

Laredo Enterprises, owned by Judy and Bob Sivertsen, takes would-be cowboys on multi-day May, June and September cattle drives on the Rumney Ranch in the foothills of the Rockies bordering Glacier National Park, and the X Hangin' H Ranch in Eastern Montana. PO Box 2226, Havre, MT 59501; ☎ 800-535-3802 or 406-357-3748.

O Circle Bar Guest Ranch offers six-night cattle drives. See *Guest Ranches.*

Guest Ranches

No two guest ranches are the same. Perhaps more than any other kind of outfit catering to outlanders, guest ranches reflect the personalities and philosophies of their owners. Some are working ranches accepting guests as a sideline. Others are out-and-out dude ranches. Most fall somewhere in-between and are owned and operated by the folks who'll meet you at the door. The one thing common to all: warm Western-style hospitality.

Abbott Guest Ranch is a historic working cattle ranch 18 miles east of Lewistown, in the foothills of the Judith Mountains. Dating back to 1880,

Charlie Russell Country

the ranch was part of the DHS Cattle Ranch owned in part by Granville Stuart, Darrell Abbott's great-grandfather. Stuart, legendary pioneer, prospector, stockman, vigilante and president of the Territorial Council, was a bigger-than-life character in a state known for that breed. The Abbotts invite guests to view a collection of artifacts pertaining to their famous ancestor. Of course, there's the guest ranch experience to enjoy as well. Lodgings are private cabins with showers, or tents with wood stoves. Two-day and three-day packages include lodging and meals. HC 85 Box 4190, Lewistown, MT 59457; ☎ 800-870-8807 or ☎ 406-538-8605.

Bonanza Creek Country's Voldseth family offers year-round comfort and seclusion with horseback riding and other typical working cattle ranch activities. As they welcome no more than 16 guests at a time, the Voldseths can give guests individual attention. Accommodations include private log cabins and a tipi. A sheepwagon is available for overnighting kids. All-inclusive four-night and seven-night packages. Lennap Route, Martinsdale, MT 59053; ☎ 800-476-6045. Fax 406-572-3366. www.avicom.net/bonanza.

Ford Creek Guest Ranch owners Liz Barker and son Travis offer a comfortable guest ranch experience featuring plenty of horseback riding, a whitewater river trip and area sightseeing tours. Accommodations include creekside cabins. The Barkers also run wilderness flyfishing and horsepacking trips. PO Box 329, Augusta, MT 59410; ☎ 888-46-359-3474 or 406-562-3672. Internet www.goflyfish.com. E-mail catchtrout@goflyfish.com.

Hill Country Expeditions' John and Lois Hill welcome a single party at a time to their 16,000-acre working family ranch near the Highwood Mountains. Vacations designed around guests' preferences include lots of horseback riding, hayrides, backpacking, hiking, photo safaris and more. Guests choose between a three-bedroom house and a one-room cabin. Children under 12 are put up for free with an accompanying adult. PO Box 108, Geyser, MT 59447; ☎ 800-531-4484 or 406-735-4484. Fax 406-735-4487.

O Circle Bar Guest Ranch, owned and operated by Sarah Hollatz, is a longtime dude outfit on the Judith River. The ranch supports a herd of registered Angus cattle. Activities include loafing by the pool, trail riding, helping with ranch chores and moving cattle. Popular horseback rides lead to an old homestead and a Blackfoot cave. Log cabins accommodate guests in comfort. All-inclusive weekly rates. The O Circle Bar has cattle drive adventures in June and October, plus a five-day September *Ride The Russell Trail* experience. HCR 81 Box 61, Utica, MT 59452; ☎ 406-423-5454. Fax 406-423-5686.

Pine Butte Guest Ranch, owned by the Nature Conservancy, combines a guest ranch experience featuring daily horseback rides with natural history tours and workshops (see *Special Interest and Cultural Activities* for details). The ranch is idylically situated on the South Fork of the Teton River, in the shadow of the Front Range. Guests are put up in rustic cabins shaded by aspens, cottonwoods and firs. All-inclusive weekly rates in summer, choice of daily or weekly rates in May and September; group rates in May, September and October. Lee Barhaugh, Manager,

Pine Butte Guest Ranch, HC58, Box 34C, Choteau, MT 59422; ☎ 406-466-2158.

Seven Lazy P Guest Ranch, owned and operated by Chuck and Sharon Blixrud, is a laid-back outfit focusing on trail riding. Cozy log cabins have porches overlooking gorgeous vistas. The main lodge's library features books about Montana. Choose between all-inclusive daily or weekly rates. PO Box 178, Choteau, MT 59422; ☎ 406-466-2044.

Wickens Salt Creek Ranch is a family operated working farm and ranch in the lee of the Judith Moutains north of Lewistown. No frills, just a good feel for what ranch life is all about. Guests are invited to lend a hand with chores, explore the surrounding country on horseback, and fish for rainbow trout in the ranch's private stocked ponds. Guests lodge in a two-bedroom house and take meals with John and Diane Wickens and their family. 1030 Salt Creek Rd., Hilger, MT 59451; ☎ 406-462-5618.

■ Adventures on Wheels

Off-Highway Vehicles

OHV riders have two options here: using Forest Service and/ or logging roads, or riding trails open to ATVs, OHVs and such. All vehicles and riders operating on roads must be street legal.

Lewis and Clark National Forest ranger districts have leaflets offering OHV tips. Montana Fish, Wildlife and Parks publish a booklet, *Off-Road! Montana*, with detailed information and regulations on OHV riding.

ATVs and their OHV relatives are kicking up more than dust in the Little Belts. Conservationists and OHV riders are facing off in a seemingly unwinnable battle. Opponents want the noisy machines banned. ATV users want greater access.

Conservationists are in a lather over what they consider to be the Forest Service's failure to properly maintain wilderness study areas, such as the Yogo Creek area, by allowing ATV access. Opines John Gatchell, conservation director of the Montana Wilderness Association, "Their (ATVs) impact is way out of proportion to their numbers... they don't belong in the backcountry." He and other critics claim that ATVs disturb wildlife, emit toxic fumes, spread noxious weeds and promote soil erosion.

Russ Ehnes, president of the Montana Trail Riders Association, concedes that "there's an element that doesn't understand they're supposed to stay on the trails." It's understood that this represents only a small percentage of ATV users. Nevertheless, the problem is real and can't help but have an impact on responsible ATV users. What the brouhaha will mean to ATV riders is unclear at this time. There's talk of widening some existing trails to accommodate OHVs' wider wheelbases. Building new trails is also an option. Your best bet is to check with the Forest Service ranger district or BLM office maintaining the area in which you wish to ride. They will advise you of trails open to ATVs, and any current restrictions.

Mountain & Road Biking

Riders of non-motorized mountain bikes get a better shake than do ATVers. Generally, trails open to hikers and equestrians are also open to bikers. Some restrictions exist, and some trail conditions are not bike-friendly. Check with the local ranger district office for an update on current trail conditions and restrictions before taking off.

I needn't tell cyclists that town-to-town rural roads make great biking trails. This is especially true of **Judith Basin roads** and roads striking out from **US 89 and 287 to the Front Range**.

Many of these roads are shoulderless wonders exacerbated by local ranchers' less than sedate driving habits. If you see a pickup wearing a dust halo approaching at a speedometer-busting speed, its no angel. Dive for the ditch.

The Judith and Kings Hill Ranger Districts of the Lewis and Clark National Forest offer a nifty brochure, complete with maps, describing 17 mountain biking trails on and off the **Little Belts' Kings Hill Scenic Byway**, in the Highwood Mountains, and in the Judith River Country.

These routes include improved gravel roads, primitive roads and single track trails. Some describe loops. **Kings Hill Byway** trails offer the most scope, including some extremely technical trails. It's possible to ride from Showdown Ski Area at the summit of the Kings Hill Byway clear east across the Little Belts to the Judith Ranger Station on the Middle Fork of the Judith River. The **Highwoods** have fewer miles of trails, but some of the terrain is challenging, with fun descents. The scenery surpasses description and the wildlife viewing is superb.

Don't discount **Great Falls** when seeking a route. The five-mile **River's Edge Trail** is well suited for family biking.

■ Adventures on Water

Floating & Canoeing Prairie Rivers

Most Russell Country rivers are floatable in canoes or rafts. The Sun River excepted, whitewater river rats had best seek excitement elsewhere. The Missouri and the Smith are the region's headliners; the Missouri for its unspoiled beauty and its association with the Lewis and Clark Expedition, the

Smith for its feeling of remoteness and not a little curiosity engendered by mandated float permits. The Teton, Judith, Musselshell and Milk Rivers run placidly through some lovely prairie country and offer pleasant family floating and/or canoeing. Canoes are good choices on these relatively slow-moving rivers. Beginner to intermediate skill levels should suffice. Shuttle services for these rivers are nigh unto nonexistent, but by asking around in nearby towns you might find someone willing to pick you up for a fee at a prearranged time and place.

Rafting the Sun

The Sun River turns prairie rivers' placid reputation upside-down. The Blackfeet Indians refer to it as the Medicine because minerals found along the upper river reportedly have healing properties. The upper Sun has two whitewater stretches. Only expert kayakers and rafters should attempt the 2.5 miles of Class V whitewater below Gibson Dam. This consists mainly of two eight-foot drops in a 15-foot-wide canyon. A mile of relatively calm water separates this section from a nine-mile stretch of nearly continuous Class III whitewater below the Sun River Dam. The former is accessed from a trailhead near Gibson Dam, the latter from an access point just below the Sun River Dam. Take Willow Creek Road west from Augusta, then bear right on Sun River Road.

As is typical of most rivers used for irrigation, a minefield of diversion dams below the Sun's whitewater sections interrupts the flow and sometimes mandates portages. Largely for this reason, it's a good idea to obtain topo and/or river maps before launching your canoe on any Russell Country river. They are available from Forest Service ranger stations and BLM district offices.

Floating the Smith

The Smith River mainstem begins near White Sulphur Springs. It wiggles northward to the Missouri for 124 miles. The 61-mile stretch between the Camp Baker put-in and the Eden Bridge take-out flows through a roadless landscape of wide vistas interrupted by canyon walls. A rich variety of wildlife abounds. Remote is the key word, though you are unlikely to be alone on this popular river. The optimum float season is June and July. April, before irrigation draw-downs, and September when draw-downs cease, are good times, too. Numerous boat camps are spaced so floaters can take the three or four days necessary to do the river justice. Canoes, rafts... anything goes. One factor that makes the Smith so great for family floats is its undemanding character. Though beginners can doubtless navigate successfully, intermediate skills are recommended because of frequent tight turns and the utter remoteness.

Charlie Russell Country

AUTHOR TIP

The 61 miles between Camp Baker and Eden Bridge delineate one of Montana's more unusual state parks. You must have a permit to float the Smith. Request an application from Montana Fish, Wildlife and Parks (see Information Sources). Applications must be in no later than February 1 of the float year. Permit drawings are held February 15. You can request preferred dates. The permit process involves a fee. Should your application be drawn, you'll be assigned campsites for four nights, maximum.

Jay and Shawn Paulsen at **Castle Mountain Sports** in White Sulphur Springs have topo and Smith River maps for sale. They also rent rafts and canoes and provide a Smith River shuttle service. ☎ 406-547-2330. Refer to page 556 for information on guided Smith River trips.

Exploring the Mighty Missouri

Permits are required between the weekend before Memorial Day and the weekend after labor Day to float the Missouri River between Fort Benton and James Kipp State Park. They can be obtained from the BLM at major launch points. Other than obtaining these free seasonal permits, you are free to float the river made famous by the Lewis and Clark Voyage of Discovery without restrictions other than common courtesy and a respect for the environment.

From the hoopla surrounding the progress of Lewis and Clark up the Missouri, you'd think they'd invented the river. The role the river has played in the migrations of native peoples for centuries preceding the famous voyage has been overlooked by many. The most recent Native migration of note was the 1877 crossing by Chief Joseph's Nez Perce band during its unsuccessful attempt to reach Canada.

Better understood is the role the river played in the movement of fur trappers and traders following Lewis' and Clark's 1805-06 travels. After these Mountain Men came steamboats carrying a colorful assortment of people and goods to the end of navigation at Fort Benton. But the Lewis and Clark voyage is the glass through which most of today's floaters prefer to see the Upper Missouri Wild & Scenic River.

 Taking along one of the several Lewis and Clark Trail guides and books flooding the market will assist you in locating the Corp's campsites and other landmarks pertaining to the famous voyage. Refer to *Bibliography* for suggestions.

The 149-mile Wild & Scenic section stretches from Fort Benton to the James Kipp Recreation Area above Fort Peck Reservoir. Running wide

The 149-mile Wild & Scenic section stretches from Fort Benton to the James Kipp Recreation Area above Fort Peck Reservoir. Running wide and deep between "breaks" caused by some 10 million years of erosion, this stretch can easily be negotiated by neophytes. Canoes are the preferred craft, though other person-propelled craft will work. Vehicle access points are at Fort Benton, Loma, Coal Banks Landing, Judith Landing and the McClelland Ferry landing. Take-out is at the James Kipp Recreaton Area boat ramp at US 191.

The Wild & Scenic Corridor is maintained by the Bureau of Land Management (BLM). Contact the Lewistown District Office (see *Information Sources*) to purchase a four-map *Upper Missouri National Wild & Scenic River Floater's Guide*. A booklet detailing common hazards that may be encountered on the river, and other free brochures pertaining to the Missouri's human and natural history, can be obtained from the Lewistown office or at the BLM Visitor Center in Fort Benton. The visitor center is open from Memorial Day to shortly after Labor Day.

The BLM has placed registration boxes at major launch sites. They request that you register so that you may be located in case of emergency. Designated campsites are identified in the *Floater's Guide*, but primitive camping is permitted anywhere on Federal land, islands excepted, on a first-come, first-served basis. Rangers are on hand at various points to provide interpretive insights or to lend a hand.

Floating the Wild & Scenic Missouri can be the trip of a lifetime. The beauty is wild, wonderful and sometimes weird. The remoteness makes you to as if you're freefalling through centuries gone by. The "real" world matters not a whit.

Little has changed since the time of Lewis, Clark and Sacajawea. The buffalo are gone. So are the grizzlies. But the rattlesnakes are still coiled to strike. The Breaks are eternal.

Shuttle Services & Canoe Rentals

Getting your car from put-in to take-out can be a major problem. Several shuttle services are available for Missouri River floaters. Many also have canoes to rent.

Adventure Bound Canoe & Shuttle Co. offers shuttle service between Fort Benton and James Kipp Recreation Area and points between. They also rent canoes. 607 E. Blvd. St., Lewistown, MT 59457; ☎ 406-538-4890.

Dale and Shirley Robertson are at your disposal to either shuttle you to and from put-in and take-out, or to store your car while you're on the river, then bring it to meet you at take-out. Box 786, Fort Benton, MT 59442; ☎ 406-622-5653 (evenings).

Missouri River Outfitters offers customized shuttle services. They also have 17-foot aluminum Michi Craft canoes for rent. Rentals include life jackets and paddles. PO Box 762, Fort Benton, MT 59442; ☎ 406-622-3295.

Virgelle Merc. & Missouri River Canoe Company provides shuttle service from Fort Benton to James Kipp Park or points in-between. They will also pick you up at the Amtrak station in Havre, or at the Great Falls International Airport. They rent 17-foot Michi Craft two-person canoes and 17-foot Mad River Royalex Revelation canoes. Rentals include life jackets and paddles. They will also provide full outfits for those who wish to canoe the river on their own, but don't care to tote camp gear from home. HC 67 Box 50, Loma, MT 59460; ☎ 406-378-3110.

Guided Missouri River Trips

The BLM issues Missouri River permits to qualified companies. These vary considerably in their approach to experiencing the Missouri's Wild & Scenic Corridor. Before signing on, think about your expectations. Choices include journeys by canoe, jetboat or riverboat. Do you want to canoe lazily downriver while spotting and photographing wildlife? Or will a quick historic overview do you? Do you prefer to focus on the Lewis and Clark voyage? Is geology your main interest? Do you envision a trip offering fun times for your kids? Call around and inquire. Be selective. Refer to *Guided Fishing Trips* for outfitters who specialize in fishing trips but welcome non-anglers.

American Wilderness Experience, Inc. (A.W.E.!) is a kind of adventure travel clearing house. Owner Dave Wiggins is careful about the trips he offers. A.W.E.'s catalog includes an eight-day Missouri River canoe trip from Coal Banks Landing to James Kipp Recreation Area. The provider: Wild Rockies Tours. A.W.E.!, 2820-A Wilderness Place, Boulder, CO 80301; ☎ 800-444-0099 or 303-444-2622. Fax 303-444-3999.

Lewis & Clark Canoe Adventures offers a choice between five-day trips on the Upper and Lower Missouri River. The Upper trip journeys between Coal Banks and Judith Landings, the Lower from Judith Landing to James Kipp Park. Some trip dates coincide with Lewis and Clark's 1805 campsite dates. 1627 W. Main, Suite 106, Bozeman, MT 59715; ☎ 888-595-9151 or 406-585-9151. Internet www.lewisandclarkguide.com.

Lewis & Clark Trail Adventures has three-day canoe trips in the White Cliffs section of the Missouri. Campsites coincide with Corps of Discovery campsites. Attn: Wayne Fairchild, Box 9051, Missoula, MT 59801; ☎ 800-366-6246 or 406-728-7609. Internet www.kire.com/l&c.html.

Missouri Breaks River Company has an option for those who prefer not to go the canoe route. Their jetboat trips offer a fast-forward look at milestones along the river's upper 50 miles between Fort Benton and the beginning of the "wild" designation. Other trips include a jetboat ride up the Marias River from Loma to the next access point; a trip upstream from Fort Benton to Belt Creek where Lewis and Clark began their portage around the Great Falls of the Missouri; upstream from Great Falls' Broadwater Bay past White Bear islands to a Lewis and Clark canoe camp; up Holter Lake through Gates of the Mountains. Attn: William Marsik, 2409 4th Ave. North, Great Falls, MT 59401; ☎ 406-453-3035.

Missouri River Canoe Company, headquartered in the old Virgelle Mercantile building, offers four- to 12-day guided Missouri River eco-tours covering geology, flora and fauna as well as history. Trips include pre- and post-trip accommodations in a restored homestead cabin or a B&B room in the mercantile. Attn: Don Sorenson or Jim Griffin, HC 67, Box 50, Loma, MT 59460; ☎ 406-378-3110.

Missouri River Outfitters provides a choice between seven-10 day outfitted canoe trips on the Missouri and Marias Rivers and one- to five-day outfitted river boat trips on the Missouri. The 32-foot boats accommodating 18 resemble scows with canopies. All trips include opportunities to hike to vantage points and historic sites. Larry and Bonnie Cook, PO Box 762, Fort Benton, MT 59442; ☎ 406-622-3295.

Montana River Expeditions styles their trips as "quiet adventures for discriminating explorers." Translated, that means they offer one- to 10-day canoe trips on the Missouri and other historic Montana rivers that weave wildlife watching and the rivers' epochal history in with responsible ecological practices. Russell Young, 26 Cedar Bluffs Rd., Livingston, MT 59047; ☎ 800-500-4538 or 406-222-5837. Fax ☎ 406-222-4718.

Montana River Guides specializes in whitewater rafting trips, but also offers four-day and seven-day Missouri River canoe trips. Michael Johnston, 210 Red Fox Rd., Lolo, MT 59847; ☎ 800-381-RAFT or 406-273-4718.

Wilderness Inquiry, Inc. is a non-profit organization providing outdoor adventures for people of all ages and abilities. They offer several eight-day canoe trips each summer between Coal Banks Landing and the James Kipp Recreation Area. One of their campsites is a Lewis and Clark campsite at the mouth of the Slaughter River. 1313 Fifth St. SE, Box 84, Minneapolis, MN 55414-1546; ☎ 800-728-0719 (Voice or TTY). Internet www.wildernessinquiry.org.

Lakes Fun

Here, most lakes are reservoirs resulting from damming rivers for irrigation. The two largest, **Elwell Lake** damming the Marias River and **Fresno Reservoir** damming the Milk River, host campgrounds and lend themselves to boating, swimming and fishing. Smaller lakes, some prairie potholes left by retreating glaciers, offer fishing and wildlife watching.

Fishing

If you have a rod and a tackle box, you're in luck. The **Smith River** fly fishery is one of the finest in the state. Other top trout streams include the tailwater stretches of the **Missouri** and **Marias Rivers**, the lower reaches of the **Sun River** and **Big Spring Creek**. Warm water gamefish abound in downstream sections of the Marias, **Milk** and **Judith Rivers**. The Wild & Scenic Missouri River is known for warm water gamefish such as walleye, northern pike and channel catfish. Several lakes, including the smaller reservoirs, offer fine fishing for both coldwater and warmwater species.

AUTHOR TIP *Request a free fishing guide with information on which fish swim in which waters along with a copy of Montana Fish, Wildlife and Parks' Montana Fishing Regulations. Both are indispensible. FWP also has a Fishing Access Sites brochure pinpointing sites in Montana sporting the distinctive sign depicting a fish taking a hook. Refer to* Information Sources *for ordering information. The brochures are also available wherever fishing licenses are sold.*

Unlike angling in some parts of the state, particularly fly fishing in Yellowstone and Gold West Travel Regions, Russell Country fishing is fairly straight forward. However, guide services are available for those who prefer to go that route. Outfitters tend to concentrate on fly fishing the Smith – quite a commitment of time, considering the lack of road access for 61 miles.

Some anglers prefer a complete experience created around a fly fishing lodge. The outfitters and lodges listed below offer a variety of choices. Some offer float trips for non-anglers. Many also guide fishing trips on rivers in other travel regions. Refer to *Fishing* in this book's other regional chapters.

Fishing Outfitters In Russell Country

Avalanche Outfitters' Doug and Zita Caltrider offer fishing trips on the Smith and Missouri Rivers and on private lakes, plus individualized family-oriented vacations. PO Box 17, White Sulphur Springs, MT 59645; ☎ 406-547-3962.

John Maki Outfitters, guiding anglers since the 1970s, leads five-day fly fishing trips on the Smith River for wild browns and rainbows. Also offering fishing trips on other rivers. 655 Granite, Helena, MT 59601; ☎ 406-442-6129.

John Perry's West Slope Outfitters leads five-day fly fishing packages through the Smith River Canyon. Trips on other rivers are available. PO Box 20080, Missoula, MT 59801; ☎ 800-580-9703 or 406-258-2997. E-mail sherlock@bigsky.net.

Madison River Fishing Company offers five-day Smith River fishing trips. The company's fly shop is in Ennis and they publish a catalog. They also have fly fishing schools. 109 Main St., Ennis, MT 59729; ☎ 800-227-7127 or 406-682-4293.

Montana River Outfitters offers five- to seven-day fly fishing trips on the Smith River that include luxury camping, if that's not an oxymoron. Three- or four-day Smith River trips are available on request. Cabins, a motel and RV hookups are adjacent to the company's Wolf Creek fly shop. Fly fishing instruction can be arranged. Half-day and full-day float fishing on Missouri River tailwaters are also offered. Mailing address: 1401 5th Ave. S., Great Falls, MT 59405; ☎ 800-800-8218 or 406-761-1677. Fax 406-452-3833. Summer phone: ☎ 800-800-4350 or 406-235-4350.

Montana Riverworks' Gary Padgham offers single- and multi-day river trips throughout Central Montana that include five-day and six-day Smith River trips. This may be the outfitter for you if someone in your family chooses not to fish. Fishing and non-fishing rates are offered; the spread is around $600 per head. Padgham also offers fly fishing instruction and half-day to multi-day fishing and non-fishing trips on other rivers. 520 N. Grand Ave., Bozeman, MT 59715; ☎ 888-744-FISH or 406-586-4826. E-mail RIVERWRX@aol.com.

Paul Roos Outfitters offers tailwater fishing on the Missouri and five-day Smith River trips accommodating both anglers and non-anglers. PO Box 621, Helena, MT 59624; ☎ 800-858-3497 or 406-442-5489.

T Lazy B Ranch owner and operator Robert Walker offers five-day fly fishing trips on the Smith River. 532 Jack Creek Rd., Ennis, MT 59729; ☎ 406-682-7288.

Western Rivers' outfitter/guide Fred Tedesco offers four- to six-day fly fishing floats on the Smith River, plus daily, overnight and base camp floats on the Missouri below Holter Dam. Tedesco claims to have over 25 years and 15,000 miles of float fishing and guiding experience on Montana rivers. PO Box 772, East Helena, MT 59635; ☎ 406-227-5153.

Western Waters & Woods owner Jerry Nichols offers charter boat fishing for northern pike, walleye and perch on Lake Elwell (also known as Tiber Reservoir). Choose between day trips or extended trips. Boats are Alumacraft and Alumaweld inboard, outboard and jet units. Everything is provided. They also offer ice fishing. 5455 Keil Loop, Missoula, MT 59802; ☎ 800-757-1680 PIN #2060 or 406-543-3203. E-mail waters@bigsky.net. Internet www.bigsky.net/westernwaters.

Fly Fishing Lodges

Fly Fishers' Inn, on the Missouri River at Hardy Creek, offers anglers' lodging packages that include gourmet breakfast and five-course dinners. Multi-day and single-day guided fishing packages with lodging and meals are also available. 2629 Old US Hwy. 91, Cascade, MT 59421; ☎ 406-468-2529.

Golden Bear Enterprises provides anglers with rustic log cabin lodging (bring your bedroll), homecooked meals and guided fly fishing on private ranches. HC 60 Box 348, Judith Gap, MT 59453; ☎ 406-473-2312.

H Lazy 6 Ranch Fly Fishing Lodge, on a 7,000-acre cattle ranch owned and operated by Hank and Laura Bouma, borders the Nature Conservancy's Pine Butte Preserve. Fish in alpine lakes for rainbows, browns and brooks. One- to six-day packages include rod fee, lodging and meals. Guides and rental equipment are available. PO Box 971, Choteau, MT 59422; ☎ 406-466-2550 (ranch), ☎ 406-466-2552 (lodge).

■ Adventures on Snow

Downhill Skiing & Snowboarding

"Trendy" doesn't describe Charlie Russell Country's three downhill ski areas. "Family-oriented" does. If it's a destination ski resort you're after, better check out Big Sky or Big Mountain. If you want good powder skiing in a relaxed down-home atmosphere, these day-use ski areas are for you. Snowboarders are welcome.

Bear Paw Ski Bowl on the Rocky Boy's Indian Reservation, 29 miles south of Havre via Rt. 234, has nine runs and a vertical drop of 900 feet from a 4,200-foot base elevation. Average snowfall: 140 inches. Ten lifts mean no lift lines. Runs are rated 25% each beginner and intermediate, 50% advanced. Lift tickets are in the $15 range and kids under eight ski free with accompanying adult. ☎ 406-265-8404.

Showdown Ski Area, in the heart of the Little Belts on King's Hill Scenic Byway (US 89), has been central Montana's winter playground for over 60 years. Here, ski togs are as likely to be farm and ranch coveralls as pricey ski bibs. Showdown has 34 runs and a vertical drop of 1,400 feet from a 6,800-foot base elevation. Average snowfall: 240 inches. Two surface lifts and one each triple and double chair lifts. Runs work out to 30% each beginner and advanced, and 40% intermediate. Lift tickets around $25; over 70 and ages six-12 discounted, under six free. Downhill and snowboard instruction. Long season: early December-early April, 9:30-4. Rental shop, base lodge, eateries, area lodgings. Inquire about special fun ski events. ☎ 800-433-0022 or 406-236-5523.

Teton Pass, in the Front Range west of Choteau, is another high spirits ski and 'boarding area. The 30 runs have a vertical drop of 1,100 feet from a 3,842-foot base elevation. Average snowfall: 300 inches. One double chair lift, one surface lift. Runs are rated 20% beginner, 50% intermediate, 30% advanced. Lift tickets under $25, less for kids; under six free. Lessons, rentals, lounge, concessions; all services in Choteau. Numerous races and special events. Open Thurs.-Sun. and holidays, 9:30-4. ☎ 406-799-6833 or 406-278-7904 or 278-7855.

Cross-Country/Nordic Skiing & Snowshoeing

Great Falls Nordic skiers and snowshoers are to be envied. The city sits mid-way between two prime cross-country ski areas on the Lewis and Clark National Forest: the Little Belts and the Rocky Mountain Front west of Choteau. Lewistown folks kick snow on trails near Crystal Lake in the Big Snowy Mountains.

Refer to previous chapters of this book for suggestions regarding survival gear, preparedness and avalanche awareness. Most of these trails traverse remote country where snow conditions can be treacherous. Being prepared to spend the night makes good sense. Never underrate the ferocity of Montana's winters.

Several ungroomed trail systems on the **Rocky Mountain Front** offer challenging cross-country skiing. Contact the Choteau Ranger District office for trail descriptions and current conditions. Snowshoeing or cross-country skiing and wildlife watching make good winter companions here (see *Wildlife Watching*).

Skiing the Little Belts

The **Little Belts** are area residents' favorite winter playgrounds. "Popular" might be a turn-off in most cases. Here, it assures skiers of help in case something goes wrong. Four trail systems branch of of US 89. These offer a dizzying range of conditions and terrain. All can be accessed from the snowmobile parking lot off US 89 near Kings Hill, north of Showdown Ski Area. All trails are either intermittently groomed or not groomed at all; unless you count the impact of frequent traffic. Most trails are well marked with blue diamond signs. Kids? Teens, yes; younger kids, no. For further information, contact the Kings Hill District Ranger office in White Sulphur Springs (☎ 406-547-3361) or the Belt Creek Information Station in Neihart (☎ 406-236-5511). In addition, **Showdown Ski Area** includes 12 miles of groomed cross-country ski trails; a boon for those who prefer groomed tracks to taking their chances with non-groomed trails. Kids can usually negotiate these trials. The **Silver Crest Trail** system's four loop trails offer 18 km of interesting skiing over a variety of terrains. This intermittently groomed trail system is ideal for accomplished skiers, with 14.5 km rated More and Most Difficult.

Mizpah Ridge Trail runs along a ridge for 5.5 km and is ungroomed. An Easiest rating accounts for just under half the distance, with the majority being More Difficult and 1.2 km Most Difficult.

The popular **O'Brien Creek Trail** goes from exhilarating heights in the vicinity of the Showdown Ski Area to a couple of miles along a creek bed and through beaver meadows, crossing back and forth on snow bridges (use caution!). Total distance: 6.7 km, 2 km rated Easiest and the balance teetering between More Difficult and Most Difficult. For a great back country ski experience, embark on a **Deadman Creek Ridge** cross-country ski trip. Intermediate-plus skill levels are advised for this 6.3-km trek. The trail begins with a steep 500-foot climb before attaining a ridge affording fabulous views in all directions. Open slopes are ideal for telemarking. The trail descends steeply to an old logging road paralleling

Charlie Russell Country

Deadman's Creek. Watch for blue diamonds at all times; they are sometimes elusive.

The Judith Ranger District of the Lewis and Clark National Forest makes available clear description sheets with maps of two cross-country ski trails in the Crystal Lake area. Contact the district office to obtain these sheets, plus detailed directions to access points.

The two-mile (four miles round trip) **Green Pole Canyon Trail**, following an open grassy creek bottom, is ideal for snowshoers, novice skiers and kids.

The three-mile **Rock Creek Trail**, rated Novice to Intermediate, follows the creek bottom and offers an opportunity to continue on to Crystal Lake where you might rent the Crystal Lake Cabin (see *Forest Service Cabins*).

Snowmobiling

Though less extensive than some Montana snowmobiling areas, the **Little Belts** offer some fine snowmobiling. The area includes a veritable maze of over 200 miles of groomed trails, many having big powder play areas.

Refer to previous chapters of this book for valuable snowmobile survival and avalanche information.

The 25-mile Judith Ranger District's **South Fork Lodge Loop Snowmobile Trail** connects with snowmobile trails originating at King's Hill Pass on US 89. The latter include three loop trails: **Divide Road, King's Hill and Big Loop**. All have powder play areas.

Little Belts trails can be accessed from the snowmobile parking lot off US 89 near Kings Hill, north of Showdown Ski Area.

For detailed trail information, contact the Judith Ranger District at Stanford and Kings Hill Ranger District in White Sulphur Springs (see *Information Sources*, page 516).

Snowmobile Rental

Montana Snowmobile Adventures has a full line of Arctic Cat rental snowmobiles and clothing available at Showdown Ski Area. PO Box 5, Neihart, MT 59465; ☎ 406-236-5358.

■ Wildlife Watching

The peak time for summer visitors isn't necessarily peak wildlife watching time. Wildfowl and raptor migrations occur in spring and fall. Winter's snows and thinner vegetation make elk, deer, mountain goats, sheep and their tracks, and a bevy of birds more visible along the Rocky Mountain Front. Pack binoculars or a spotting scope when setting out on that cross-country ski trip. The following sites offer rewarding wildlife watching year-round.

Sun River Canyon northwest of Augusta has numerous opportunities for skiers to spot animals. Several gulches branching off the main canyon provide good skiing and wildlife spotting. Watch for deer and elk as you drive past the nearby Sun River Wildlife Management Area. Take Willow Creek Road west from Augusta and hang a right on Sun River Road.

Teton Canyon west of Choteau is a good place to catch sight of moose, and bighorn sheep if deep snow has driven them down from the higher elevations. Take the Teton Canyon Road, five miles north of Choteau off US 89.

The nearby **Pine Butte Swamp Preserve**, managed by the Nature Conservancy, is a great place to view ring-necked pheasants and sharp-tailed grouse, roosting bald and golden eagles, and a variety of waterfowl. The 18,000-acre preserve's varied terrain is habitat for most of the animal species living along the Front; even grizzly bears. Over 44 species of mammals frequent the preserve. More than 150 bird species have been recorded here. ☎ 406-466-5526. Refer to *Special Interest Adventures* (page 563) for extended tour information.

Skiers and snowshoers can sometimes see big game animals along the 3.5-mile trail to **Our Lake**, on the South Fork of the Teton River. This alpine lake, one of only a few along the Rocky Mountain Front, is a sure bet for spotting mountain goats year-round. Due to the lake's popularity, the animals have adapted to people and should not be approached or fed. It's fun to watch pikas and yellow bellied marmots scampering in the rocky scree. Take the Teton Canyon Road west of US 89 for 15 miles to the Ear Mountain Ranger Station sign. Turn left on County Road 109 and drive nine miles to the end of the road. For further information, contact the Rocky Mountain Ranger District office in Choteau.

West of Bynum via the Blackleaf Road, the 19,430-acre **Blackleaf Wildlife Management Area** protects winter range for elk and deer. Off-road travel is prohibited between December 1 and May 15, but you may spot animals from the road. In summer, the WMA's marshes and ponds offer good waterfowl, shorebird and songbird viewing. The trail up **Blackleaf Canyon** is for spotting bighorn sheep and a herd of some 75 mountain goats year-round. The canyon, at the base of sheer orange, red and yellow rock walls, is alone worth a look-see. Raptors nest in depressions in the canyon walls. ☎ 406-454-3441.

West of Dupuyer, as many as 2,000 deer and elk winter on the **Theodore Roosevelt Memorial Ranch**, owned by the Boone & Crockett Club (☎ 406-472-3380). The 6,040-acre ranch includes wet meadows, cottonwood river bottoms and shortgrass prairie below limestone reefs. The varied terrain is habitat for numerous other animals and birds. A kiosk and a 0.5-mile trail overlook the ranch; closed during hunting season, mid-Oct. to Dec. 1. The ranch is otherwise closed to public access except by written permission. Foot and horseback access on the road is open year-round, but vehicle access is restricted to May 15-Oct. 15. From US 89, take the Dupuyer Creek Road west for 8.5 miles. Take the left fork and go south 0.5 mile to a T, then left some three miles to another T, then right about two miles to the top of the hill past the cattle guard.

March through May, and Sept. through Nov., are the times to see migrating snow geese and tundra swans winging it over the 11,350 acre **Freezeout Lake Wildlife Management Area** and touching down to feed. Legend has it that the lake's shivery name comes from a poker game called "Freezout" played by travelers putting up at a stagecoach station here. Bevies of birds and many small mammals can be seen year round. The series of natural and artificial lakes and marshes offer leisurely watching from a canoe or on foot. The WMA is closed during the Oct.-Dec. waterfowl hunting season to provide a waterfowl resting area. The Headquarters office, just off US 89 north of Fairfield, has maps and bird lists. ☎ 406-454-3441.

Benton Lake National Wildlife Refuge, north of Great Falls, is also a refuge for migrating snow geese and tundra swans. The 12,383-acre refuge is recognized by the Western Hemisphere Shorebird Reserve Network as a significant area for migrating and nesting shorebirds. Here, far from the mountains, you can see wildlife native to the prairie environment. These include upland sandpipers, burrowing owls, badgers and white-tailed jackrabbits. A brochure interprets the nine-mile auto route. The four-mile route is self-interpretive. The refuge is nine miles down Bootlegger Trail, off US 87 north of Great Falls. ☎ 406-727-7400.

Prairie potholes are intriguing leftovers from when a huge lake covered what is now prairie. They are sprinkled over the prairie as though a giant hand had let loose of a fistful of confetti; a few landed here, lots more there. **Lonesome Lake** is one of these. Once used heavily by Native Americans, the area around the wetland complex has one of Montana's highest concentrations of tipi rings. Treat them as though a big "Don't Disturb!" sign hangs there. The shallow lake is favored by migrating shorebirds and waterfowl. The lake may dry up in summer. Prairie wildlife are often spotted here. Turn west off US 87 onto MT 432 at Big Sandy. After four miles, turn left on a gravelled county road and continue for 5.5 miles. The lake is about a quarter-mile down an undeveloped trail. ☎ 406-265-5891.

To describe **Square Butte** as a landmark is to understate by a prairie mile. The volcanic laccolith, a bubble of molten rock that penetrated the earth's crust to form a domed tower, rises 2,400 feet above the prairie. Watch for Rocky Mountain goats taking a stroll along vertical cliffs that seem to offer no footholds whatsoever. You'll no doubt see deer and pronghorn antelope near the base of the butte. Raptors nest in declivities in the steep cliffs. You can hike from the end of the road to the top of the butte, a distance of about a mile. The butte is owned by the BLM but the access is on private property. Instructions and a check-in box are at the ranch gate. The road to the butte is closed during hunting season. Take MT 80 to the town of Square Butte. Drive west on a county road for 2.5 miles, following Square Butte Natural Area signs. ☎ 406-538-7461.

The 5,000 acre **Judith River Wildlife Management Area** must seem like heaven for upwards of 100 species of birds and for coyotes, bobcats, red foxes and other denizens of the forests fringing the plains. Hiking along the road bisecting the WMA is possible in summer and fall. Be on the alert for beavers, identified by river dams resembling untidy heaps of sticks. Be aware that the WMA is open to fall hunting, and that the land along the river is private. The WMA is closed between Dec. 1 and May 14, but viewing is possible from the road. From Utica, follow the gravel road for 12 miles to Yogo Creek Road. Drive 1.3 miles to the WMA. Owned by Montana FWP; ☎ 406-454-3441.

In these Lewis and Clark sesquicentennial years, most visitors want to see the wildlife that Lewis and Clark saw. The **Upper Missouri National Wild and Scenic River** remains rich in wildlife. Spotting descendants of the animals and birds seen and identified by Capt. Meriwether Lewis can be a heady experience. The grizzly bears and buffalo that captured the imaginations, and furnished the dinner entrées, of expedition members are gone. But over 200 species of songbirds, wild turkeys, white-tailed deer, great blue herons, raptors and prairie dogs remain as reminders of wildlife's persistence when left undisturbed. American white pelicans afloat on the river are as idyllic a sight as you'll see anywhere. You must rent a canoe and float/paddle the 149-mile stretch of river in order to see this abundance of wildlife.

 Consult river maps (see *Adventures on Water*) for areas of major wildlife concentrations. Taking along copies of Stephen E. Ambrose's *Undaunted Courage* and Carol and Hank Fischer's *Montana Wildlife Viewing Guide* will enhance your viewing experience (see *Bibliography*). The former describes many of the areas where species of wildlife were seen by members of the Voyage of Discovery.

■ Special Interest Adventures

 Charlie Russell Country's Native American plains culture, its dinosaur digs, its Lewis and Clark lore and a treasure trove of natural wonders provide the focus for several guided off-the-beaten track adventures.

Fort Belknap Reservation Buffalo Tours offer more than just watching buffalo graze. The Gros Ventre are known as "Ah-ah-ne-nin," meaning "White Clay People." The Assiniboine are known as

"Nakota," meaning "the Generous Ones." These tribes sharing the Fort Belknap Reservation once depended on buffalo for food, clothing, tipis, tools and weapons. Buffalo continue to be important to their cultural and spiritual beliefs. Virtually extinct 100 years ago, the buffalo are making a comeback. Since 1974, the Fort Belknap tribes have included a buffalo herd in their wildlife management program. Today over 300 bison graze the 10,000-acre tribal buffalo preserve. Viewing is limited to guided tours departing daily from the Visitor Center at Harlem from May 1 through September 30. Tours include insight into the sacred relationship between Native Peoples, the buffalo and the prairie that sustains them. In addition to the buffalo reserve, you will visit a prairie dog town and perhaps catch sight of a swift pronghorn. Tribal Buffalo Tours, RR1, Box 66/Fort Belknap Agency, Harlem, MT 59526; ☎ 406-353-2205.

As this book goes to press, a new venture, **Traveling Wind, Inc.**, is being developed by noted Fort Belknap artist and cultural promoter George Shields and a group of fellow tribal members. For current information, contact the address and telephone number listed above. The **Buffalo Robe Cultural Camp** promises to be a five-day immersion experience involving all but the most sacred aspects of Plains Indian culture. Guests will learn skills that once were, and in many cases still are, central to Native life. Discussions with tribal elders will enrich the program. Included will be pow-wow dancing and drumming. The **Western Theme Adventure** promises to be five days of Western adventures that will include stagecoach rides, a cattle drive, campfire yarn-spinning, country dances and a tour of the Chief Joseph Battleground.

Off The Beaten Path and Special Expeditions have joined up to offer *Following in the Trail of Lewis and Clark*, a nine-day adventure highlighting the section of the explorers' trek between Great Falls and the Lemhi Valley. Led by historian guides, the trip begins in Great Falls with a buffalo roast dinner on the banks of the Missouri and ends with a stay at Horse Prairie Ranch, near the place where Lewis was befriended by Chief Cameahwait, Sacajawea's brother. The days between are filled with visits to noteworthy Lewis and Clark sites and discussions centered on the Voyage of Discovery. ☎ 800-445-2995 for detailed trip descriptions.

Choteau's **Old Trail Museum & Paleontology Field School** offers a variety of summer paleontology programs. Popular two-day *Family Programs* are designed for families with children and include fossil preparation, badlands walks, site work and prospecting for new finds. Classes are offered June through August. Minimum age requirements are determined case by case. The week-long *Family Course Package* expands on the shorter course with hands-on field work and lectures. An *Advanced Course*, a college credit course, and Elderhostel courses are also offered. They also conduct a paleontology related kids day camp. 823 N. Main, Choteau, MT 59422; ☎ 406-466-5332.

Pine Butte Ranch, owned and operated by the Nature Conservancy, offers a variety of spring and autumn workshops reflecting the natural riches of the Rocky Mountain Front. These may include *Blackfeet Indians in Life and Legend, A Naturalist's Tour of the Rockies, Montana Grizzly Bears, Birds of the Rockies and Prairies, Mammal Tracking, Nature Photography* or a *Dinosaur Workshop.* Participants lodge at the ranch. Lee Barhaugh or Amy Stevens, HC 58 Box 34C, Choteau, MT 59422; ☎ 406-466-2158.

Springtime Ranch, a working cattle ranch bordering the Missouri River, specializes in kids' camping (see *Kid Stuff* below) but offers a three-day *Ladies Retreat, a Parent / Child Retreat* and a *Family Retreat.* All are packed with outdoor activities and include gifted speakers. 147 Springtime Rd., Ulm, MT 59485; ☎ 406-866-3222.

Timescale Adventures has one-day, two-day and 10-day hands-on dinosaur field programs emphasizing field experience and insight into area geology. Staff members include professionals in the paleontology field. Business office: PO Box 356, Choteau, MT 59422; ☎ 406-466-5410. Field station: Bynum, MT 59419; ☎ 800-238-6873. E-mail timescale@timescale.3rivers.net.

Tour de Great Falls owner and operator Carol T. Place offers a variety of tours of cultural, historical and natural attractions in the Great Falls area. Ask about customized tours. PO Box 27, Ulm, MT 59485; ☎ 406-771-1100.

■ Kid Stuff

KID-FRIENDLY Kid-friendly tours and a day camp are offered by Choteau's **Old Trail Museum & Paleontology Field School**.

Springtime Ranch Camp, on the Shortridge family's working cattle ranch near Ulm, is a summer camp for girls and boys aged seven-12. The stated purpose of the camp is to help young people develop an appreciation of nature by working with animals. Camp director Sally Shortridge offers canoeing, hiking, fishing, archery, woodworking and crafts in addition to a basic horsemanship program. One-week programs. 147 Springtime Rd., Ulm, MT 59485; ☎ 406-866-3222.

Festivals & Special Events

Rodeos, county fairs, pow-wows and hometown celebrations head Russell Country's annual events. Hard working people living on farms and in small towns energetically organize festivals reflective of the area's agricultural heritage. Aggressively touristic areas of the state may throw festivities designed to attract visitors, but for the most part Russell Country's downhome folks enjoy kicking up their heels just for the fun of it. Visitors are made to feel welcome, but getting hold of tourist dollars is secondary to hometown fun.

The festivities listed below are established annual events. Dates are approximate. Call for current dates.

If you plan on being in a given area at a certain time, contact the local chamber of commerce to inquire about additional events.

January

Montana Pro Rodeo Circuit Finals is an exciting mid-January event in Great Falls featuring 12 pro rodeo contestants testing their abilities against Montana's finest rodeo stock. Barbeque, rodeo dance, auction. Duane Walker, 111-2nd Ave. South, Great Falls, MT 59405; ☎ 406-727-8115. Fax 406-791-9655.

Magie Montana Agricultural and Industrial Expo is a mid-January Great Falls event. Exhibitors from throughout the Pacific Northwest, Montana, the Dakotas and Canada show up to present exhibits and information on every agricultural topic from vegetable gardens to large-scale wheat growing. Jim Senst, PO Box 3309, Great Falls, MT 59403; ☎ 406-761-7600. Fax 406-761-5511.

February

Regional Special Olympics at Showdown Ski Area in mid-February includes Nordic and alpine skiing races. Kate Willett-Gold, PO Box 92, Neihart, MT 59465; ☎ 406-236-5522. Fax 406-236-5523.

Great Falls Wine and Food Festival is a mid-February event featuring an evening of food, wine and beer sampling. Robert Dompier, 1700 Fox Farm Rd., Great Falls, MT 59404; ☎ 406-761-1900. Fax 406-761-0136.

Kids Carnival at Showdown Ski Area in late February includes sledsful of fun stuff: face painting, obstacle course, three-leg races, snowball toss, ski lessons, slalom race and hot dog barbeque. Kate Willett-Gold, PO Box 92, Neihart, MT 59465; ☎ 406-236-5522. Fax 406-236-5523.

March

Custom Car Show, held in Great Falls in mid-March, celebrates Montanans love of classic cars. Galin Bredesen, 530 Jay Court, Great Falls, MT 59404; ☎ 406-453-8808.

C.M. Russell Auction of Original Western Art is a late March event in Great Falls. Two major auctions, chuckwagon brunch, over 100 exhibitor rooms, seminars, artist autograph party, three receptions, two quick draws and auctions. Ad Club, 1301 12th Ave. South, Suite 202, Great Falls, MT 59404; ☎ 800-803-3351. Fax 406-453-1128.

Jay Contway and Friends Art Show, held in Great Falls in mid-March in conjunction with the C.M. Russell Auction, rates among the country's finest Native American art shows. Jay Contway, 434 McIver Rod., Great Falls, MT 59404; ☎ 406-452-7647.

Western Invitational Tournament, in Lewistown in late March, is a 12-team amateur basketball tournament featuring top-ranked college seniors from all over the US. Three days of continuous play from 9 am to midnight. Championship game Saturday night. Central Montana Jaycees, PO Box 401, Lewistown, MT 59457; ☎ 406-538-7629.

April

Mannequin Jumping in early April, part of the Great Falls Ski Club Fun Day at Showdown Ski Area, includes an obstacle course, slalom race and Mannequin Jump. Corporate Cup, a dual slalom, includes team categories for families and ski professionals. Kate Willett-Gold, PO Box 92, Neihart, MT 59465; ☎ 406-236-5522. Fax 406-236-5523.

Great Falls Homebuilders Home Show in mid-April is Montana's largest. Raffle ticket proceeds go to student scholarships. Sue Hennessy, PO Box 2724, Great Falls, MT 59403; ☎ 406-452-4663.

Lewiston Art Auction in mid-April features local and regional art displays and a juried sale. Ellen Gerharz, 801 W. Broadway, Lewistown, MT 59457; ☎ 406-538-8278.

Annual Ice Breaker Road Race, a late April Great Falls event, features runs, walk/jog and walk races for both families and experienced runners. Before-race fitness routine and a feed at the fairgrounds after the races. Awards to elite racers and winners in each age group. Park & Recreation Dept., 1700 River Drive North, Great Falls, MT 59401; ☎ 406-771-2165. Fax 406-761-4055.

May

Bull Dazzle is the fetching name for a rodeo held annually in Great Falls in mid-May. This rodeo features bull riding by talented Montana contestants. John Carroll, PO Box 7382, Great Falls, MT 59403; ☎ 406-727-1048. Fax 406-727-7200.

Great Falls Pow-Wow in late May features hundreds of Native Americans representing numerous tribes dancing in tribal regalia, drumming and singing. Vendors offer Native American items not found elsewhere. James Parker Shields, 700 10th St. South, Great Falls,. MT 59405; ☎ 406-761-3165.

Fresno Walleye Challenge, at Fresno Reservoir/Havre in late May-early June, is a North American Walleye Circuit Tournament featuring 100 of the top walleye fishing teams from throughout the Northwest. Thousands of dollars worth of prizes. Jim Rettig, PO Box 529, Big Sandy, MT 59520; ☎ 406-378-2176.

Charlie Russell Country

June

Big Sky Tour Master Mortorcycle Rally, a mid-June Lewistown event, features a parade, barbeque, fun runs. Jackalee Leap, Rt. 2, Box 2264, Lewistown, MT 59457; ☎ 406-538-8369.

Montana Junior Beef Expo, held in Lewistown in late June, includes a purebred cattle show and seminar. Marty Linhart, Rural Route, Hobson, MT 59452; ☎ 406-423-5445.

Great Falls' late June **Lewis and Clark Festival** highlights the events that occurred during the summer of 1805 when the Expedition was in the Great Falls area preparing for their portage around the Great Falls of the Missouri. Reenactors in historic garb, tours of Lewis and Clark sites, demonstrations, seminars, children's day camp, exhibits, float trips, buffalo roasts, college courses. Phil Scriver, 1104 Ave. CNW, Great Falls, MT 59404; ☎ 406-727-8314.

Fort Benton Summer Celebration in late June showcases its famous levee as it presents a weekend of hometown fun; parade, art show, fishing derby, fun run/walk, street dance, fireworks, volleyball and basketball tournaments, Cottonwood Antiques and Crafts Show. The swimming pool is open and parkside camping is available. Connie Jenkins, First National Bank, PO Box 279, Fort Benton, MT 59442-0279; ☎ 406-622-3351. Fax 622-3657.

The **Augusta American Legion Rodeo** in late June is a PRCA rodeo and one of the largest one-day rodeos in the state. Augusta has been rodeoing for upwards of 65 years! Ben Arps, PO Box 58, Augusta, MT 59410; ☎ 406-562-3477.

July

Lewistown 4th of July Celebration kicks off with a wagon train rumbling into town. Contact Collie or Dorinda Bass, 501 1st Ave. South, Lewistown, MT 59457; ☎ 406-538-8709 or 538-5915. The celebration includes a Shrine Circus and fireworks. Lewistown Area Chamber of Commerce, PO Box 818, Lewistown, MT 59457; ☎ 406-538-5436.

The **Harlowton Rodeo** is the main event at this town's 4th of July celebration. Also parades, fireworks. Susan Beley, PO Box 694, Harlowton, MT 59036; ☎ 406-632-4894. Fax 406-632-5644.

The **Four-County Marias Fair** in Shelby in mid-July features typical county fair fun, an NRA rodeo, horse racing, 4-H and open exhibits, pet and doll parade, theme parade, nightly shows, fireworks. Kari Frydunlund, Marias Fair, Hwy. 2 East, Shelby, MT 59474; ☎ 406-434-2692.

Central Montana Horseshow, Fair and Rodeo is Lewistown's big late July event. Horseshow, three rodeo sessions, carnival, 4-H and open exhibits, night shows, bump-n-run auto race. Central Montana Fair, Alan Fisk, PO Box 1098, Lewistown, MT 59457; ☎ 406-538-8841. Fax 406-538-3860.

The **Montana State Fair** in Great Falls is the late July-early August event where Montanans really kick up their heels. Pro rodeo, superstar entertainment, carnival, livestock shows, exhibits, food, free entertainment. Montana State Fair, PO Box 1888, Great Falls, MT 59404; ☎ 406-727-8900. Fax 406-452-8955.

August

Rocky Boy's Annual Pow-Wow is presented at Rocky Boy in early August. Pow-wow begins with a walk for sobriety. The competition pow-wow includes colorful dancing, drumming, cultural demonstrations, ethnic foods. Havre Area Chamber, 518 1st St., Havre, MT 59501; ☎ 406-265-4383. Fax 406-265-7451.

The **Great Northern Fair** in Havre in early August includes NRA and youth rodeos, 4-H fair, night shows, carnival, open talent stage, auction, petting zoo, great country food. Mike Spencer, Great Northern Fairgrounds, 1676 Hwy 2 West, Havre, MT 59501; ☎ 406-265-7121.

Dinosaur Days is an early August Harlowton event celebrating area dinosaur discoveries. Activities include a dinosaur bone hunt, crafts, parade, educational presentation. Susan Beley, PO Box 694, Harlowton, MT 59036; ☎ 406-632-4894. Fax 406-632-5644.

Big Sky Arts and Crafts Show is an early August Lewistown event featuring a variety of art forms, performing and culinary arts. Linda Edwards, 301 8th Ave. South, Lewistown, MT 59457; ☎ 406-538-9078.

Montana Cowboy Poetry Gathering is a mid-August Lewistown event. Cowboy poetry, Western music, juried Western art and cowboy gear show. Workshops, kids' classes, jam session. Lewistown Area Chamber of Commerce, PO Box 818, Lewistown, MT 59457; ☎ 406-538-5436.

The **Choteau County Fair** is held at Fort Benton in late August. Rodeo, dance, concert, demolition derby, livestock shows, arts & crafts, garden and wheat production entries. Gene Chapel, PO Box 549, Fort Benton, MT 59442; ☎ 406-622-3821. Fax: 406-622-3758.

Great Falls Dixieland Jazz Festival in late August features red hot mamas and upwards of 10 Dixieland bands. Jazz bands playing music of the 40s and 50s; special dinner show. Finale features big band dance and jam session. Don West, PO Box 856, Helena, MT 59624; ☎ 800-851-9980 or 406-449-7969.

Dog Obedience Trials are held in Great Falls in late August. Sara McLaughlin, PO Box 395, Vaughn, MT 59487; ☎ 406-965-3570.

Winnett Fun Day in late August offers small town fun for all ages. Sponsored by the Winnett Lions Club. Tug-o-war, dunking booth, motorcycle barrel races, messy bossy contest, hail storm hysteria, pig mud wrestling contest. Luann Knutson, PO Box 21, Winnett, MT 59087; ☎ 406-429-6361.

September

Crossroads Classic Barrel Racing Futurity, held in Shelby in early September, is for young horses aged four-seven. Helen Brown, PO Box 5, Whitlash, MT 59545; ☎ 406-432-5100.

Great Falls Cottonwood Festival, held in early September, celebrates those big trees found growing along prairie rivers. Over 50 old time activities include basket weaving, horse shoeing, toy making, gold panning, cow milking, making apple head dolls. Old time entertainment, ethnic and folk foods. Cascade County Historical Society, 1400 First Ave. North, Great Falls, MT 59401-3299; ☎ 406-452-3462.

Montana State Chokecherry Festival is Lewistown's early September blowout. Tastings of jams, jellies, wines and other chokecherry delights. Pancake breakfast, race and run/walk, farmers market, art festival, Taste of Lewistown, 100-mile bike-a-thon. Lewistown Area Chamber of Commerce, PO Box 818, Lewistown, MT 59457; ☎ 406-538-5436.

Utica Day Fair, in Hobson in early September, features numerous arts & crafts booths, raffles. Homemade pies are a fair specialty. The Fair date coincides with the area's annual hay bale decorating contest. Carol Campbell, HC 81 Box 19, Hobson, MT 59452; ☎ 406-423-5364.

Montana Trappers Assoc. State Convention comes to Lewistown in mid-September. Trappers gather to show and trade. Visitors welcome. Trappimg demonstrations, contests, rifle/pistol shoot, fur fashion show, dealer booths, raffle, auction. Fran Buell, PO Box 133, Gilford, MT 59525; ☎ 406-376-3178.

Montana Old Time Fiddlers' Show in Lewistown in mid-September features Montana's top fiddlers. Fred Buckley, 319 Old divide Rd., Roundup, MT 59072; ☎ 406-323-1198.

Big Sky Tour Master Motorcycle Poker Run for charity at Lewistown in mid-September. Jackalee Leap, Rt. 2, PO Box 2264, Lewistown, MT 59457; ☎ 406-538-8369.

Havre Festival Days in late September features such high jinks as bed races, 5K run, parade, arts & crafts show, local food booths, quilt show, Saturday night dance, Sunday in the park barbeque and pie social, kids' games, entertainment. Havre Chamber of Commerce, PO Box 308, Havre, MT 59501; ☎ 406-265-4383.

October

Pioneer Power Day Threshing Bee, an early October Lewistown event, features operating steam engines, threshing machines, antique farm machinery, crafts, flea market. Central MT Flywheelers Assoc., Brian H. Sallee, 1015 W. Washington, Lewistown, MT 59457; ☎ 406-538-5236.

St. Jude's Circle Fall Antique Show & Sale is a mid-October Great Falls event featuring dealers from throughout the Northwest. Larry J. Milot, Tracy Rt., PO Box 37, Sand Coulee, MT 59472; ☎ 406-736-5201.

Forest Grove Arts & Crafts Show is an annual mid-October event. May Charbonneau, PO Box 6, Forest Grove, MT 59411; ☎ 406-538-3510.

Winnett's Hunters Banquet is a free wild game feed; raffle, dance. Ben Busenbark, Winnett, MT 59087; ☎ 406-429-6251 evenings.

November

Choteau Winter Fair, held in early November, features crafts, bake sale, homemade pies. Sally Haas, PO Box 729, Choteau, MT 59422; ☎ 406-466-5564.

Havre Art Association Annual Show & Sale in early November features the work of local and state artists. Vicky Campbell, 1252 Washington Ave., Havre, MT 59501-4855; ☎ 406-265-8450.

Great Falls Christmas Collection gets a festive jump on the holidays in mid-November with crafts, ornaments and goodies. Kathy Schermele, 1400 1st Ave. North, Great Falls, MT 59404; ☎ 406-727-2353 or 45206024.

Great Falls Holiday Antique Show is a late November event featuring over 35 dealers from five states. Janine Chesko, 117 Central Ave., Great Falls, MT 59401; ☎ 406-727-5150. Fax 406-453-0736.

December

Harlowton's Christmas Stroll kicks off the Christmas shopping season in early December with lights decorating the town's historic electric railway engine and strung along Main Street. Parade, hayride, chili supper. Susan Beley, Harlowton Chamber, PO Box 694, Harlowton, MT 59036; ☎ 406-632-4694.

Conrad Christmas Stroll is an early December event featuring carollers, barber shop quartet, tree lighting ceremony, wagon rides, children's carnival, food vendors, Santa. Pam Marsh or Bob Beck, 410 South Main, Conrad, MT 59425; ☎ 406-278-5343.

Great Falls Christmas Stroll is also held in early December. City Center Assoc., 600 Central Plaza 336, Great Falls, MT 59401; ☎ 406-453-6151. Fax 406-761-0103.

Havre Christmas Stroll, held in early December, features a tree lighting ceremony, parade of lights, over $10,000 in gift certificates to give away, free sleigh rides, children's activities, food vendors. Havre Chamber of Commerce, PO Box 308, Havre, MT 59501; ☎ 406-265-4383.

Lewistown Christmas Stroll, also in early December, features a Christmas parade, tree decorating contest, Santa's arrival, food booths, horse and wagon sled rides, prizes, Christmas Art & Craft Show. Lewistown Area Chamber of Commerce, PO Box 818, Lewistown, MT 59457; ☎ 406-538-5436.

Stanford Christmas Stroll in early December features a crafts show and Christmas wreath fundraiser auction. Tess Brady, PO Box 315, Stanford, MT 59479; ☎ 406-566-2633.

Where to Stay & Eat

Dining and lodging in Charlie Russell Country doesn't approach the sophistication and trendy ambience of many Glacier and Yellowstone Country establishments. That's just as well; pretentiousness is foreign to most people living under the big prairie sky.

Every town has ma and pa motels seemingly cloned from some invisible parent. Most are adequate, if not exactly an adventure in lodging. Larger towns and Great Falls have sizeable chain hostelries. Bed & breakfast inns are on the increase and are generally good bets. Cabins can be okay, too – especially Forest Service cabins. Eateries are most apt to offer stick-to-your ribs fare topped off with pies, upholding the reputation of a state that sets great store by them. Pie popularity no doubt dates from the homestead era when farm wives and their daughters vied to see who could bake the most toothsome pies to take to pie socials.

Lodging Prices
$ . . . . dirt cheap
$$. . . . . moderate
$$$. . . . . .pricey, but oh well
$$$$ .hang onto your checkbook

■ Hotels, Motels & B&Bs

Except in smaller towns without alternatives, this book skips over basic motels in favor of more adventurous accommodations and some chain hostelries – the latter for the swimming pools enjoyed by families with kids, and for the predictable comforts so welcome after days of hiking or canoeing. Sometimes, given a couple of small town motel choices, this book opts for the one having an eatery.

Big Sandy

Raven Crest Bed & Breakfast, on a working grain ranch, has two guest rooms and provides full breakfast. $$$. RR1, Box 662, Big Sandy, MT 59520; ☎ 406-378-3121. Fax 406-378-2655.

Cascade

Badger Motel is the best bet because it has an eatery; five guest rooms. $$. 132 1st. Ave. N., Cascade, MT 59421; ☎ 406-468-9330.

Chester

MX Motel has 17 rooms and a restaurant. $. On US 2; ☎ 406-759-7176.

Chinook

Chinook Motor Inn has 38 rooms and a restaurant. $$. 100 Indiana Ave.; ☎ 800-642-7053 or 406-357-2248. Fax 406-357-2261.

Choteau

Choteau runs more to B&Bs than to big motels.

Best Western Stage Stop Inn has 43 rooms, a pool and hot tubs. $$$. 1005 N. Main Ave., Choteau, MT 59422; ☎ 888-466-5900 or 406-466-5900. Fax 406-466-5907.

Styren Ranch Guest House rents three bedrooms by the day or week; kitchen, laundry facilities. 961 20th Rd. NW, Choteau, MT 59422; ☎ 406-466-2008 or 466-5698.

B&Bs

Country Lane Bed & Breakfast has five guest rooms, one with private bath, full breakfast and an indoor heated pool. $$$. Rt. 2, Box 232, Choteau, MT 59422; ☎ 406-466-2816. Winter: 404 Luscombe, Los Lunas, NM 87031; 505-865-4412.

Great Bear Gallery and Bed & Breakfast offers three guest rooms with shared bath in a fine turn-of-the-century home; full breakfast. $$. #4 Second Ave. SW, Choteau, MT 59422; ☎ 406-466-5345.

Gunther Bed & Breakfast offers former studio apartments in the old Gaylord Hotel, each with private bath. Continental breakfast. $$. 415 N. Main, Choteau, MT 59422; ☎ 406-466-5370.

Conrad

Conrad Super 8/Townhouse Inn has 49 rooms and a restaurant. $$. 215 N. Main, Conrad, MT 59425; ☎ 800-442-4667 or 406-278-7676. Fax 406-278-5370.

Dupuyer

Inn Dupuyer Bed & Breakfast, a hand-hewn log structure, has five guest rooms, four with private baths; full breakfast. $$$$. 11 Jones Ave. W. Dupuyer, MT 59432; ☎ 406-472-3241.

Fort Benton

Fort Benton's lodgings have yet to catch up with the towns's tourism boom.

Pioneer Lodge has nine guest rooms and a levee-view location. $$. 1700 Front St., Fort Benton, MT 59442; ☎ 800-622-6088 or 406-622-5441.

Long's Landing Bed & Breakfast has three charming guest rooms, one with a private bath, and serves continental breakfast. $$. 17th and Washington Sts., Fort Benton, MT 59442; ☎ 406-622-3461.

Grassrange

Roy's Motel & Bar is the only show in town with nine rooms and an eatery. $. US 87, Grassrange, MT 59032; ☎ 406-428-2242.

Great Falls

Montana's second largest city has the expected complement of chain hostelries. 10th Avenue is practically lined with motels, most acceptable if predictable. Several nice B&Bs round out the offerings.

Best Western Heritage Inn has restaurant, pool, 240 rooms; the works. $$$. 1700 Fox Farm Rd., Great Falls, MT 59401; ☎ 800-548-0361 or 406-761-1900. Fax 406-761-0136.

Best Western Ponderosa Inn has 105 rooms and a restaurant. $$. 220 Central Ave., Great Falls, MT 59401; ☎ 800-528-1234 or 406-761-3410.

Budget Inn has 60 rooms and a pool. $$. #2 Treasure State Dr., Great Falls, MT 59401; ☎ 800-362-4842 or 406-453-1602.

Comfort Inn has 64 rooms and a pool. $$. 500 13th Ave. S., Great Falls, MT 59401; ☎ 800-228-5150 or 406-454-2727.

Holiday Inn Great Falls has 170 rooms, restaurant, pool, convenient location; the works. $$$. 400 10th Ave. S., Great Falls, MT 59401; ☎ 800-626-8009 or 406-727-7200.

Townhouse Inns of Great Falls has 109 rooms, restaurant, pool and more affordable rates than some having all the frills. $$. 1411 10th Ave. S., Great Falls, MT 59401; ☎ 800-442-4667 or 406-761-4600. Fax 406-761-7603.

B&Bs

Murphy's House Bed & Breakfast, the city's first B&B, has two guest rooms with shared bath and serves full breakfast. $$. 2020 5th Ave. N, Great Falls, MT 59401; ☎ 406-452-3598.

Old Oak Inn occupies a restored Victorian mansion; has six charming guest rooms, one with private bath; full breakfast. $$. 709 4th Ave. N, Great Falls, MT 59401; ☎ 406-727-5782.

Sun River Ranch Bed, Breakfast & Bale has three guest rooms, one with private bath, full breakfast, indoor swimming pool, outdoor hot tub and horse corrals for traveling steeds. $$. 18 Manchester Lane, Great Falls, MT 59401; ☎ 888-761-1940 or 406-761-1940.

Three Feathers Inn. Elegant home furnished with English antiques has a private library and lovely gardens; five guest rooms, two with private baths, full breakfast. $$$. 626 5th Ave. N, Great Falls, MT 59401; ☎ 406-453-5257.

Harlowton

Corral Motel has 18 rooms and a restaurant. $. Jct. US 12 & 191; ☎ 800-392-4723 or 406-632-4331. Fax 406-632-4748.

Havre

Havre has more choices than one might expect. Its situation on the Hi-line might account for this.

Duck Inn has 20 guest rooms and a restaurant. $$. 1300 1st St., Havre, MT 59501; ☎ 800-455-9615 or 406-265-9615. Fax 406-265-4448.

Park Hotel has 29 rooms and a restaurant in Havre's historic downtown. $$. 335 1st St., Havre, MT 59501; ☎ 406-265-7891.

Townhouse Inns of Havre. 104 rooms, pool, hot tub. $$. 629 W. 1st. St., Havre, MT 59501; ☎ 800-442-4667 or 406-265-6711. Fax ☎ 406-265-6213.

B&Bs

Our Home Bed & Breakfast has views of the Bears Paw Mountains, two guest rooms, one with private bath, full breakfast. $$$. 66 65th Ave. NW, Havre, MT 59501; ☎ 406-265-1055.

West Prairie Inn Bed & Breakfast, in a restored c. 1920 home on 29 acres, has three guest rooms, one with private bath, full breakfast, horse corral for peripatetic steeds. $$. 9855 US 2 NW, Havre, MT 59501; ☎ 800-268-3645 or 406-265-7281.

Hobson

Meadow Brook Farm Bed & Breakfast Inn, in a restored 1908 ranch house, has five guest rooms with shared baths, full breakfast. An opportunity to browse through old barns reminiscent of Montana's past. $$. Box 271, Hobson, MT 59452; ☎ 800-318-6423 or 406-423-5637.

Judith Gap

Golden Bear Enterprises rents bring-your-own-food-and-bedroll log cabins. Heated bathhouses. $. HC 60 Box 348, Judith Gap, MT 59453; ☎ 406-473-2312.

Lewistown

Trail's End Motel has 18 rooms and a pool. $. 216 NE Main, Lewistown, MT 59457; ☎ 406-538-5468.

Yogo Inn of Lewistown has 124 rooms, a restaurant and pool. $$. 211 E. Main, Lewistown, MT 59457; ☎ 800-860-9646 or 406-538-8721.

B&Bs

Downey's Bed & Breakfast, in the foothills of the Big Snowy Mountains, has two guest rooms with shared bath and serves full breakfast. $$. Rt. 1, Box 1675, Lewistown, MT 59457; ☎ 406-538-7048.

Robertson's Spring Creek Bed & Breakfast has two guest rooms with shared bath, serves full breakfast. $. HC 87, Box 5050 (Burly Beach Rd.), Lewistown, MT 59457; ☎ 406-538-9548.

Symmes-Wicks House, in Lewistown's historic Silk Stocking district, has three guest rooms with shared baths, full breakfast. Reservatons only. $$. 220 W. Boulevard, Lewistown, MT 59457; ☎ 406-585-0567. Fax 406-538-5133.

Martinsdale

Crazy Mountain Inn is the only lodging in town; has 10 guest rooms and an eatery. $. 100 Main St., Martinsdale, MT 59053; ☎ 406-572-3307.

Monarch

Cub's Den Motel/Restaurant/Bar/Grocery has all the bases covered with 14 poolside guest rooms and all of the above; continental breakfast included in rates. $$. 5012 US 89 S., Monarch, MT 59463; ☎ 406-236-5922.

Rocking 3 Cabins & Campground has creekside cabins with kitchenettes. $. Box 24, Monarch, MT 59463; ☎ 406-236-5535.

Neihart

Bob's Bar & Beds has 12 rooms (with beds) and an eatery. Vacation packages. $. US 89; ☎ 406-236-5955 or 236-5936.

Shelby

Comfort Inn has 72 rooms and a pool. $$. 50 Frontage Rd., Shelby, MT 59474; ☎ 800-442-4667 or 406-434-2212. Fax 406-434-2493.

Crossroads Inn has 52 rooms and a pool. $$. US 2 & I-15, Shelby, MT 59474; ☎ 406-434-5134. Fax 406-434-2937.

Stanford

Sundown Motel has 11 Guest rooms and an eatery. $. MT 200 W., Stanford, MT 59479; ☎ 800-346-2316 or 406-566-2316.

Valier

Atkins Inn is this town's only lodging; 12 guest rooms. $. 411 Teton, Valier, MT 59486; ☎ 800-551-8332 or 406-279-3476.

Virgelle

Virgelle Merc. & Missouri River Canoe Co. has four guest rooms with shared baths in the old mercantile building, plus cabins. Hearty continental breakfast. This is a popular pad for folks embarking on Missouri River floats. $$ & $$$. HC 69 Box 50, Loma, MT 59460; ☎ 800-426-2926 or 406-378-3110.

White Sulphur Springs

Spa Hot Springs Motel has a corner on the town's elusive hot springs, being built over the only known surviving mineral spring. The motel has two natural hot mineral pools that are drained, cleaned and refilled every night; no chemicals added. 21 geothermally heated rooms. A bargain at $. 202 W. Main St., White Sulphur Springs, MT 59645; ☎ 406-547-3366.

B&Bs

The Columns, occupying a restored Victorian home, has three guest rooms with shared baths, full breakfast. $$. 19 E. Wright St., White Sulphur Springs, MT 59645; ☎ 406-547-3666.

Foxwood Inn occupies an 1890 inn, has 14 guest rooms with shared baths. $$. 52 Miller Rd., White Sulphur Springs, MT 59645; ☎ 406-547-2224.

Montana Mountain Lodge is out in the country, has five guest rooms with private baths and serves full breakfast. $$$. 1780 US 89 N., White Sulphur Springs, MT 59645; ☎ 800-631-4713 or 406-547-3773.

Sky Lodge, east of town on US 12, has four guest rooms with private baths and serves full breakfast. $$. 4260 US 12 E, White Sulphur Springs, MT 59645; ☎ 406-547-3320.

■ Forest Service Cabins

Five former line cabins in the Lewis and Clark National Forest can be rented. These were once used by mounted forest rangers who were out on multi-day patrols. The Northern Region, US Forest Service, has available a *Recreational Cabin and Lookout Directory*. Pick up or order a copy at all Montana Forest Service offices. Cabins may be reserved on a first-come, first-served basis by contacting the Lewis and Clark National Forest Supervisors Office (see *Information Sources,* page 516). Per-day rental fees are in the $20-$40 range.

Cabins are minimally furnished with bunk beds, table, chairs and a wood stove. Firewood is usually provided. Ask about water availability when reserving your cabin. The Kings Hill and Crystal Lake Cabins have electricity, but others do not. The Dry Wolf and Hunters Spring Cabins have propane cookstoves.

Crystal Lake Cabin, in the Judith Ranger District, available from mid-October to the end of April, is popular with cross-country skiers. The road is plowed to within six miles of the cabin.

Dry Wolf Cabin, also in the Judith Ranger District, is available all year. 4WD vehicle access.

Hunters Spring Cabin, in the Musselshell Ranger District, is available from December 1 through March. The road is plowed to within seven miles of the cabin.

Calf Creek Cabin, in the Kings Hill Ranger District, is available all year and can be accessed via unplowed Forest Service Road #119. **Kings Hill Cabin** is also in the Kings Hill Ranger District and is available all year. Roughing it is easy at this cabin situated a mere 100 yards from US 89.

■ Camping

It can be tricky finding a place to park your RV or pitch your tent. Many small towns, especially those having few or no private campgounds, allow free overnight camping at parks or other designated sites. Fort Benton allows RVs to overnight near the levee. I had to wonder if Lewistown's roadside park, away from town and adjacent to the airport, was entirely safe. If in doubt, ask at the police station.

Public Campgrounds

I've found that US Forest Service campgrounds are often the best choices. The Lewis and Clark National Forest maintains several scenic campgrounds in the Little Belts, the Big Snowies and along the Rocky Mountain Front. The Forest Supervisors Office has compiled a Campground Information brochure describing these and including maps. Pick a copy up at any ranger district office. These fair weather campgrounds are closed in winter. All are primitive, with water only, but most have pads adequate for RVs up to 30 feet in length; some can accommodate larger rigs.

Ackley Lake State Park, in the Judith Basin, has 18 primitive campsites and a boat ramp for anglers and boaters. From Hobson, take Secondary Route 400 south for five miles, then drive two miles on a county road.

The BLM maintains primitive campgrounds at **Coalbanks, Judith Landing** and **James Kipp Recreation Area**. All are on the Missouri River and all are open year-round. Refer to *Adventures on Water* for information sources. The US Bureau of Reclamation maintains numerous primitive free campsites on Fresno Reservoir and Lake Elwell (Tiber Reservoir). Open all year, these are primarily for the use of anglers. Potable water is iffy; bring your own.

Private Campgrounds

Like other services, the quality of these vary by a cow-country mile. Some motels and truck stops permit overnight camping; some even have hookups. The following are the best choices.

Chester

Crazy Joe's Tiber Marina is so-so, but if fishing is your thing you'll appreciate the proximity of a full-service marina. Five RV sites. Open May 1-Sept. 30. ☎ 406-759-5200.

Choteau

Choteau KOA fills the bill if the kids are clamoring for a pool and you need to do laundry. 20 tent sites, 55 RV sites. Open May 1-Sept. 30. East of town on Rt. 221. ☎ 800-KOA-4156 or 406-466-2615.

Harlem

Fort Belknap Agency Rest Stop (see *Touring*) has a small seasonal campground with RV sites. Grocery store nearby. ☎ 406-353-2537.

Great Falls

Great Falls KOA is a stunner. In summer, there's horseback riding and water-sliding into the pool. I found the wide open spaces behind the park perfect for playing ball with my dog. Shrubbery divides the 22 tent spaces and 116 full hookup RV sites. Kamping Kabins overlook prairie farms. Lots of flowers, even a vegetable garden. Open all year. 10th Ave. S. and 51st St. ☎ 800-KOA-6584 or 406-727-3191.

Harlowton

Chief Joseph Park, at the west end of town on US 12, has unlimited tent spaces and eight RV sites. Playground, fishing pond, BBQs. Open April 1-Oct. 31. ☎ 406-632-5522.

Havre

Beaver Creek Park, 10 miles south of town (see *Adventures on Foot*), has room for 100 tents. Open year-round. ☎ 406-395-4565.

Clack Campground, at the fairgrounds on US 2 west of town, has 15 tent sites and 23 full hookup RV spaces; grass and shrubs. There's always something going on at the fairgrounds. Open May 15-Sept. 15. ☎ 406-265-4000.

Lewistown

Mountain Acres RV Park & Campground, north of town on US 191, has 50 full hookup RV spaces; no tenting. Open April 1-Nov. 30. ☎ 406-538-7591.

White Sulphur Springs

Conestoga Campground, four blocks west of US 89 on South Street, has 36 tent sites and 41 full hookup RV spaces, trout pond, hot mineral baths. Open year-round. ☎ 406-547-3890.

■ Where to Eat

You seldom need a guide to find hearty down-home food in Charlie Russell Country. As stated in previous chapters of this book, any visitor can locate a café. The trick is finding an outstanding café. The tastiest vittles and the juiciest steaks are often found in a bar. Almost every town boasts a watering hole named "Stockman" or "Mint" that's seen generations of grizzled cowboys bellying up to the bar.

The following represent acceptable, sometimes unusual or outstanding, restaurants and bakeries discovered or recommended in my travels. If no eatery is listed for a given town, it doesn't mean there's not one. It's because I haven't come across a notable one.

Charlie Russell Country

Choteau

Buckaroo Eatery & Coffee House, at 202 N. Main, mixes cow country ambience with espresso and light fare. Open daily, 7 am to 10 pm. ☎ 406-466-2667.

Choteau Trading Post, at 106 N. Main, is a one-stop ranch wear and lunch stop with some cool Montana books and collectibles added for good measure. Weekday ranch-cooked lunch specials. Open Mon.-Sat., 9-5:30. ☎ 406-466-5354.

Outpost Deli & Ice Cream Shoppe serves up homemade pies, cinnamon rolls and other sweets along with soups and sandwiches. At the north end of town across from the museum. Open daily. ☎ 406-466-5330.

Conrad

Durango Dining Room & Red Garter Casino adds an 11-4 Sunday buffet to its predictable fare of steaks, burgers, chicken, etc. Open 11-10 weekdays, 5-10 Saturdays. ☎ 406-278-5477.

Fairfield

Fairfield Bakery & Diner, at 205 1st Ave. N., is known for homemade breads, cinnamon rolls and cookies. Good food, too. Open 7-3 Mon., Wed. & Sat., 7-7 Tues., Thurs., Fri. ☎ 406-467-3443.

Pendroy

The Rose Room, one of the Rocky Mountain Front area's few fancy dining places, serves complimentary wine and fry bread and honey with every carefully prepared entrée. This is the locals' choice for special occasions. Reservations requested. Open nightly. ☎ 406-469-2205.

Fort Benton

Bob's Riverfront Restaurant is one of those surprising gems that you come upon unawares. A hangout for the local coffee crowd, the walls are lined with old Fort Benton photos. Bob bakes toothsome pies and cinnamon rolls and cooks up a variety of innovative specials. Open daily for breakfast, lunch and dinner. ☎ 406-622-3443.

Great Falls

Borrie's, at 1800 Smelter Ave. in Black Eagle, has Italian dishes, prime rib every Tuesday. Dinner served from 5 pm Mon.-Fri., from 4 Sat. and 3 Sun. ☎ 406-761-0300.

Eddie's Supper Club, at 3725 2nd Ave. N., is locally famous for fabulous steaks. Not just a supper club, Eddie's serves breakfast, lunch and dinner. Open 9:30 am-11 pm, Sun.-Thurs., til midnight Fri. & Sat. ☎ 406-453-1616.

Elmer's Pancakes & Steaks, at 1600 Fox Farm Rd., serves breakfast all day. Western-style food. ☎ 406-761-2400.

Great Harvest Bread, at 511 1st. Ave. N., is the place to stock up on healthy, hearty wholegrain breads and cookies. Open daily except Sunday. ☎ 406-452-6941.

Havre

Uncle Joe's Steak House and Restaurant, at 1400 First St., may well be the best feedbag in town. Broasted chicken a specialty; varied menu, daily specials. Restaurant open 11-11 Tues.-Sat., 5-11 Sun. Steak house open 5-11 Tues.-Sat. ☎ 406-265-5111.

Lewistown

Poor Man's Southwestern Café, at 413 W. Main, is a laid-back kind of place where it's okay to eat and read one of the café's previously owned cut-rate books. The homemade Southwestern cuisine is the real item. Lunch served daily; dinner Thurs., Fri., Sat. Call-ahead seating and orders to go. ☎ 406-538-4277.

Monarch

The Lazy Doe offers fine dining in a gold town atmosphere. Reservations suggested. Hours vary. ☎ 406-236-9949.

White Sulphur Springs

Stockman Saloon & Steakhouse, at 117 E. Main, exudes the if-only-walls-could-talk ambience expected of saloons that have seen a procession of old Montana's elbow-bending cowboys, sheepherders, wheelers and dealers. The place seems not to have changed since Ivan Doig described it in *This House of Sky*. Fare includes smoked ribs, steaks and burgers. Daily lunch specials. Open daily, 11-midnight. ☎ 406-547-9995.

Charlie Russell Country

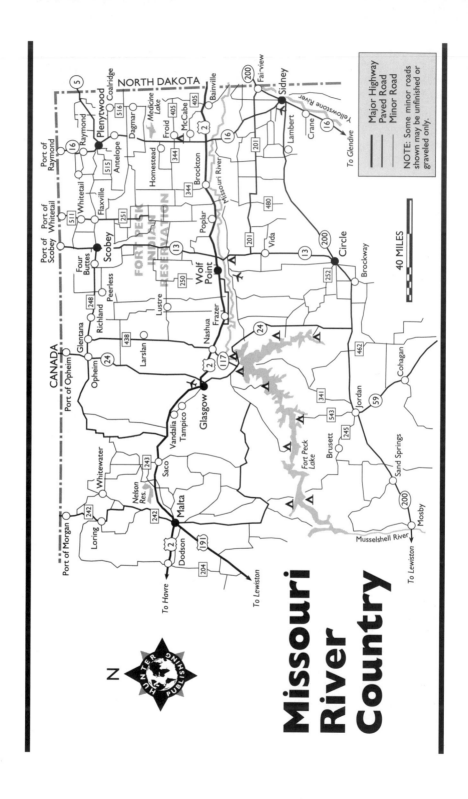

NORTH DAKOTA

CANADA

Missouri River Country

N

Major Highway
Paved Road
Minor Road

NOTE: Some minor roads shown may be unfinished or graveled only.

40 MILES

To Glendive

To Havre

To Lewiston

To Lewiston

Port of Morgan
Port of Opheim
Port of Scobey
Port of Whitetail
Port of Raymond

FORT PECK INDIAN RESERVATION

Fort Peck Lake

Missouri River

Yellowstone River

Musselshell River

Nelson Res.

Coalridge
Plentywood
Raymond
Antelope
Dagmar
Medicine Lake
McCabe
Froid
Bainville
Fairview
Sidney
Lambert
Crane
Homestead
Brockton
Poplar
Vida
Circle
Brockway
Scobey
Flaxville
Whitetail
Four Buttes
Peerless
Lustre
Nashua
Frazer
Wolf Point
Richland
Glentana
Opheim
Larslan
Glasgow
Tampico
Vandalia
Saco
Whitewater
Loring
Malta
Dodson
Brusett
Jordan
Cohagan
Sand Springs
Mosby

5
516
515
16
511
251
248
438
13
250
117
24
2
2
201
201
480
462
252
200
200
200
16
16
405
405
405
344
344
405
191
204
242
242
243
245
245
341
543
59

Missouri River Country

Introduction

 **T**his is an area where you keep expecting something to happen, but it seldom does; where you expect the next town to be a whopper, but it never is.

"Big" is the operative word in this chunk of prairie Montana. Sprawling Fort Peck Lake, created from the first dam on the Missouri River, is one of the biggest things that ever happened to the people of the region. It once spelled big jobs. Now it's big fish, big fun. Fort Peck Indian Reservation, Montana's second largest, is a big part of the region.

The dinosaurs and buffalo that once roamed across this land were big. The sweep of open prairie is big. The aspirations of the people who tried to tame the land were big. That some succeeded and more failed somehow fits the scheme of life here.

Adventure on this undulating prairie reflects life: cattle drives, rodeos, pow-wows. Wildlife watching affords a special brand of adventure. Missouri River Country has no national forests, no mountains. On Foot adventures are limited to rock hounding and wildlife watching.

Touring, taking in the windswept beauty and the life history of this place, can be an adventure, albeit a tame one. The massive dam halting the downriver rush of the Missouri is well worth a look-see. But it's small town museums, reflecting a hardy people's pride of place, that best grab the imagination.

Homestead

Many people come to northeastern Montana seeking their roots, with parents or grandparents yanked from the soil when homesteading went bust. One day, I turned off MT 16 to check out a has-been place intriguingly named Homestead, announced by a sign depicting a homesteader's shack. The town wasn't much – two grain elevators, false fronts with wind-slapped windows staring down a hollow-eyed depot, a grass-grown railway siding. A pickup drove up and slid to a stop. An elderly man, face etched by the elements, wanted to know if I was looking for anyone or anyplace in particular. "No, just moseying," said I.

"Lots of folks come by here, looking," he said, clearly disappointed. "Thought your folks might have been from around here." I wished I had been seeking out the place where my family's roots once clutched this land.

On the west, Missouri River Country seamlessly picks up where Charlie Russell Country leaves off. The region blends with Saskatchewan's wheatlands on the north and North Dakota's on the east. On the south, an arbitrary, invisible line separates Missouri River Country from Custer Country.

This region has no town even approaching city status. The largest are **Sidney** with some 5,200 residents and **Glasgow** with some 3,500. **Wolf Point**, population some 2,800, comes in third.

The **Missouri River** slices through the center of the region. About half its length is swallowed by **Fort Peck Lake**. The **Yellowstone River** slants across the region's southeast corner. It enters the Missouri just off-stage, a few yards east of the North Dakota state line. Other rivers are inconsequential, from a recreationists' standpoint. The Milk, Frenchman, Redwater and Poplar flow into the Missouri. Access and camping areas are limited or nonexistent.

■ History

Plains Indian tribes once roamed this land, hunting buffalo but never settling in any particular place. Lewis and Clark, Sacajawea and members of the Corps of Discovery slogged up the Missouri in the spring of 1805. Few physical reminders of their progress remain, but their impact is indelible. Fur traders set up business shortly thereafter, establishing riverbank forts.

The Fort Peck Agency was established in 1871, one of three overseeing reservation lands lying north of the Missouri River and extending from the eastern border of Montana Territory west to the Continental Divide.

These lands were whittled down again and again as white settlers filtered in and the Great Northern Railroad pushed through. Fort Peck Reservation's current boundaries had been defined by 1890. Residents include the Lower Band of the Assinniboines and members of the Yanktonai, Sisseton Wahpeton, Ogalala and Hunkpapa Sioux bands.

Homesteaders thirsted for land. The Great Northern's president, Jim Hill, was pleased to oblige. His PR effort made him one of the biggest flim-flam artists of all time. The Allotment Act of 1908 opened the reservation to homesteading. Today, some 56% of reservation lands are owned by non-Indians.

The reservation covers some 65 miles along the Hi-Line, so-named for the Northern Pacific route slicing across the northern plains. Homesteaders rushed to take up lands, founding Culbertson, Glasgow, Malta, Saco and a rash of other towns. Families toting livestock, plows and high hopes also fanned out into the extreme northeast corner of the state. The communities they founded embodied the virtues that defined rural America in the early decades of the 20th century. Life was hard, but it was good.

Then the rains stopped. The bottom fell out of the grain market. Small farmers couldn't make it any longer. The Great Depression hit. Things got so bad that Plentywood residents took up with the Communist Party, going so far as to publish a newspaper advocating collective farms and organizing a Young Pioneers cell. Discouraged farmers packed up and left. Many didn't go far. In 1933, President Franklin D. Roosevelt authorized the building of a dam to hold back the waters of the Missouri River. The Fort Peck Project prompted a stampede rivaling that of the homestead era. Nearby Glasgow swelled with importance. Thousands of down-and-out farmers and others found work on the project. Fort Peck town was built to house US Corps of Engineers brass and their families. Eighteen satellite shantytowns sprang up, spawning goings-on that would put a trail-weary cowpoke to shame. In 1936, at the peak of construction, 11,000 workers were employed here.

The dam was completed in the fall of 1940. The workers dispersed. Few stayed in Montana. A year later, the United States' entry into World War II solved the unemployment problem.

Wartime demands for wheat and other grains and improved dryland farming techniques transformed northeast Montana into a land overspread with large small grains farms and cattle ranches. Today, fewer people live here than 75 years ago ago. The surviving towns continue to reflect the lifestyles of the tight homesteading communities of past times.

■ Weather

This is a land of extremes – the driest droughts, the loudest thunderstorms, the heaviest hailstorms, the hottest summer days, the coldest winter winds, the most brutal blizzards.

Missouri River Country

Warm chinook winds seldom make it here. Westby has the distinction of claiming Montana's coldest winters with January temperatures averaging 5.7°. Most of the area can expect 40 to 50 summer days when the mercury rises to 90 or above.

Watching a summer thunderhead approaching over waves of wheat ripening on the plains is a sight to delight the casual visitor, and to bring a farmer to his knees. Thunderstorms pack hail. Hail shreds crops.

Spring is as unpredictable as it is 'most anywhere, so pack for anything from sunny and 65° to a sudden snowstorm. Summers are generally hot and dry, but many days are warm, golden and pleasant. Fall can stretch summer out most agreeably, but early frosts are common. Winter calls for longjohns and the whole range of chill-fighters.

Getting Around

■ Highways & Byways

Getting around here is easy, but slow. The few main highways cover a heap of distance. It's a far-flung place with far-flung towns linked by lonely stretches of road. Virtually every town can be reached via a paved highway. Gravelled and/or dirt roads access Fort Peck Lake recreation areas and ranches.

US 2, the region's main artery, makes its entrance at the eastern edge of Fort Belknap Indian Reservation and highlines it clear to North Dakota, paralleling the Missouri for over half the distance. En route, it makes the passing acquaintance of a straggle of struggling towns.

North of US 2, four highways, **RT 242, MT 24, MT 13** and **MT 16**, head for Canada. RT 242 connects Malta with the Port of Morgan. MT 24 connects Glasgow with the Port of Opheim. MT 13 junctions with US 2 just east of Wolf Point and connects with the Port of Scobey. MT 16 connects Culbertson with the Port of Raymond.

MT 5 crosses part of the region in the far north, entering from North Dakota at Westby, looking in at Plentywood, and petering out at Scobey.

To the south, **MT 200** strikes westward from Sidney, riding across a whole lot of emptiness to Mosby, where it leaves the region. Fort Peck Lake and the Fort Peck Indian Reservation take up a big swath of Missouri River Country. **MT 24** slides down the eastern arm of Fort Peck Lake and circles across the dam, but other access is via seasonally iffy roads. Fort Peck Reservation is split by **MT 13**. US 2 crosses the reservation's southern edge.

▪ Road Watch

Missouri River Country roads are generally quite good, though they tend to be narrow. Most roads are banked up from the surrounding terrain and have no shoulders. None. Period. Driving a large vehicle such as an RV can be scary, especially if the wind is blowing (it usually is). Meeting a semi rig is a real white-knuckle experience, a prime Missouri River Country adventure.

Paved roads are generally well maintained and plowed in winter. Be alert for black ice if the mercury is below freezing and there's fog, or the temperature has dropped during the night. You can't see black ice, but you sure can feel the effect when your car slides into a ditch.

4WD vehicles are required only on gravelled and dirt roads in wet weather. A light rain can turn a road into a slough.

Because of the distances involved in touring, it makes sense to carry survival equipment. This is especially true in winter. Blizzards can come up fast and bury your car in a wink. A cellular phone makes really good sense here, where no mountains interfere with reception.

Information Sources

Getting There

Amtrak's Chicago to Portland/Seattle Empire Builder stops at Wolf Point, Glasgow and Malta. ☎ 800-USA-RAIL.

Glasgow, Wolf Point and Sidney are served by **Big Sky Airline** (☎ 800-237-7788). Connecting service is available to Billings, served by **Delta** (☎ 800-221-1212), **Northwest** (☎ 800-225-2525) and **United Airlines** (☎ 800-241-6522).

Greyhound buses link the region's towns (☎ 800-231-2222).

Car Rentals

Glasgow

Budget Rent-A-Car of Glasgow: ☎ 406-228-9325.

Sidney

Avis Rent-A-Car: ☎ 800-331-1212 or 406-482-4402.
Larson Motors: ☎ 406-482-1810.

Missouri River Country

Tourism Offices

Travel Montana, Department of Commerce, PO Box 200533, Helena, MT 59620-0533; ☎ 800-847-4868 outside Montana, ☎ 406-444-2654 in Montana. Internet http://travel.mt.gov/.

Missouri River Country, Box 387, Wolf Point, MT 59201; ☎ 800-653-1319 or 406-653-1319.

Chambers of Commerce

Circle, PO Box 38, Circle, MT 59215; ☎ 406-485-2414.

Daniels County, PO Box 91, Scobey, MT 59263; ☎ 406-487-5502.

Glasgow, PO Box 832, Glasgow, MT 59230; ☎ 406-228-2222.

Jordan, PO Box 49-MR, Jordan, MT 59337; ☎ 406-557-6158.

Malta Area, Box GG/MR, Malta, MT 59538; ☎ 800-704-1776.

Plentywood, 501 1st Ave. West, Plentywood, MT 59254; ☎ 406-765-1607.

Sidney, 909 S. Central Ave., Sidney, MT 59270; ☎ 406-482-1916.

Wolf Point, PO Box 237, Wolf Point, MT 59201; ☎ 406-653-2012.

Indian Reservation

Fort Peck Assinniboine and Sioux Culture Center and Museum, Poplar, MT 59255; ☎ 406-768-5155.

Fort Peck Assinniboine and Sioux Tribes, PO Box 1027, Poplar, MT 59255; ☎ 406-768-5155.

Outdoors Associations

Montana Outfitters & Guides Association, Box 9070, Helena, MT 59620; ☎ 406-449-3578.

Government Agencies

Montana Department of Fish, Wildlife & Parks, 1420 E. 6th Ave., Helena, MT 59620; ☎ 406-444-2535. Hearing impaired #: ☎ 406-444-1200. Regional Headquarters FWP: RR 1-4210, Glasgow, MT 59230; ☎ 406-228-9347.

US Department of the Interior Bureau of Land Management (BLM): Malta Office: 501 S. 2nd St. East, Malta, MT 59538; ☎ 406-654-1240. **Glasgow Office**: Rt 1-4775, Glasgow, MT 59230; ☎ 406-228-4316. US Army Corps of Engineers, PO Box 208, Fort Peck, MT 59923; ☎ 406-526-3411.

US Department of the Interior Bureau of Reclamation, Milk River Field Office, PO Box 700, Malta, MT 59538; ☎ 406-654-1588.

Montana Board of Outfitters, Dept. of Commerce, 111 N. Jackson, Helena, MT 59620; ☎ 406-444-3738.

Montana Dept. of Transportation: Highway Information, 2701 Prospect Ave., Helena, MT 59620; ☎ 406-444-6200. Recording: ☎ 406-

444-6339. **Montana Highway Patrol**, 303 N. Roberts, Helena, MT 59620; ☎ 406-444-7000.

Touring

Punch in a country music station and put the pedal to the metal. You're cruisin' Missouri River Country, your car a craft floating on a gold and green sea reaching for a hard blue horizon. You're a fly caught in a spider's spell woven of endless miles of grain broken only by the occasional belt of trees sheltering a farmstead. Anything astir on this land looks insignificant. Behemoth tractors trail git-along harrows over chocolate springtime fields. Later, monster combines spew golden rivers of wheat into trucks drifting in tandem. How, you'd like to know, did homesteaders dependent on horses achieve a sense of proportion in all this vastness? The occasional weather-worn house, an escapee from the merciless plow, stares vacantly, offering no clue.

■ 200 Miles on the Hi-Line

US 2 leaves the Fort Belknap Indian Reservation behind as it slides into Missouri River Country. The highway follows the river Lewis and Clark named "Milk" because the water resembled tea with milk. It veers off to rendezvous with the Missouri east of Glasgow. Tiny Dodson and once-bustling Glasgow anchor a 110-mile string of homestead-era towns: Malta, Saco, Hinsdale, Vandalia, Tampico.

Malta

Malta predates the homestead era. Its name, bestowed on it by a Great Northern Railroad big-wig, seems an odd moniker for the one-time hub of a cattle empire covering a chunk of prairie stretching from Glasgow to Havre, from the Missouri Breaks to Canada. Today, its claim to fame is one of the country's last Carnegie libraries, now the **Phillips County Museum**. Indian artifacts, fossils and cattle era mementoes mix freely. Free admission. Open the week before Memorial Day to the week after Labor Day, Tues.-Sat., 10-12 and 1-5. ☎ 406-654-1037.

US 191 slants southwestward from Malta, connecting with MT 66 leading to the mining communities of Landusky and Zortman on the edge of the Fort Belknap Indian Reservation.

Look sharp some 20 miles east of Malta, at the **Cree Crossing of the Milk River**, and you'll see a herd of sleeping buffalo. Well... not real live buffalo, but glacial boulders that, from a distance, resemble the real items. Indians have long regarded this place as sacred. Even today, offerings of tobacco or sweetgrass are placed here.

Nearby **Sleeping Buffalo Resort** has hot mineral pools and a waterslide. Refer to *Kid Stuff* and *Hotels, Motels & B&Bs*. Just up the road from the resort is **Nelson Reservoir**, a pleasant place to camp, picnic, fish or just play in the water.

Glasgow

Glasgow had big city aspirations in the 1930s, when the Fort Peck Dam was a'building. The town went back to sleep after the completion of the dam and the exodus of the thousands of workers. Today's visitors come to see the largest embankment dam in the US and to fish the lake behind the dam.

The **Valley County Pioneer Museum** on US 2 is an ambitious affair with exhibits on the dinosaur remains found in the area, the Indian presence, Lewis and Clark's journey up the Missouri, old Fort Peck (it fell into the Missouri), the homestead and dam building eras. Free admission. Open Memorial Day-Labor Day, 9-9 weekdays, 1-9 Sundays. ☎ 406-228-8692.

Fort Peck

Fort Peck Lake.

From Glasgow, MT 24 heads south to skirt the blufftop town of Fort Peck, loops over the dam, and continues south to MT 200. Recreation sites on the east shore of **Fort Peck Lake** can be accessed from MT 24. This may be the most direct route to the dam from Glasgow, but I prefer MT 117 from Nashua, 12 miles east on US 2.

MT 117 travels through a slice of **Fort Peck Dam** building history. Today, the banks of the dredge cuts, now backwater "lakes," are invitingly green. Back in the '30s, raw earth piled up as dredges chewed through, gobbling up fill to pile onto the massive embankment dam. Scattered modest homes and a townlet named Parkdale are all that remain of a confusion of tossed-together shanty "towns" bearing names like New Deal, Delano Heights, Square Deal.

What appears to be an unnaturally long, high river break comes into view. This is the dam, so colossal that it's difficult to take in the enormity of it. The **Powerhouse**, no mean structure, crouches insignificantly below the dam. Statistics boggle the imagination: 250.5 feet high, 21,026 feet long, 3,500 feet wide at the base. It took 125,628,000 cubic yards of fill, 1,200,000 cubic yards of concrete and four years to build. A massive slide a year after construction was completed set the project back two years. The **Power Plant Museum** displays over 400 specimens taken from the prehistoric graveyard excavated from the Fort Peck Fossil Field. Models and exhibits also focus on the building and operation of Fort Peck Dam. Free admittance. Open daily, 9 am-8:30 pm. Powerhouse tours are conducted hourly from 9-5. ☎ 406-526-3421.

Fort Peck townsite crowns a hill overlooking the dam. The anachronistic **Fort Peck Hotel** dominates the town. Many structures remain from the 1930s, incongrous reminders of a time when the woodsy Adirondacks-style was synonymous with the boonies, whether indigenous to it or not.

The **Fort Peck Indian Reservation**'s southwestern corner abuts Nashua. US 2 streaks across the reservation to Culbertson, pulling up at Wolf Point and Poplar, following the Missouri River all the way. Not much to see here.

Wolf Point

Wolf Point got its name from several hundred frozen grey wolf carcasses stacked beside the Missouri by 19th-century wolfers. Seems they intended to skin the wolves in the spring and sell the pelts, but Indians got to them first. A wolf statue near the tracks is a pale reflection of those hell-for-leather days. The town went from fur trading post to cow town. Its present-day trading center brings it full circle.

Wolf Point's **Historical Society Museum** has artifacts dating back to early settlers and Indians. Free admittance. Open Memorial Day-Labor Day, Mon.-Fri., 10-5. ☎ 406-653-1912.

Detour to Lustre, 15 miles north of Wolf Point on Rt. 250, then west on a gravel road, to see **Taovs' Tractors**. Way out here in homestead country is an extensive collection of John Deere tractors dating from the earliest models. ☎ 406-392-5224.

Poplar

Poplar, 21 miles east of Wolf Point, is the center of Reservation life. You may or may not find the **Fort Peck Assinniboine and Sioux Culture Center and Museum** open. Best to call ahead: ☎ 406-768-5155. The **City Museum** has displays reflecting area history. Free admission. Open June 15-Sept. 15, Mon.-Fri. 11-5. ☎ 406-768-5212.

Culbertson

Culbertson really has its act together. Only some 800 people live in the cow town-cum-farming community, but there's no lack of fun goings-on. Rodeos, a pow-wow, an annual wagon train, a mid-summer river float, the Roosevelt County Fair, even a community threshing bee (see *Festivals & Special Events*) keep folks on the jump. Like every self-respecting

Missouri River Country

Missouri River Country town, Culbertson has a museum highlighting its history. Unlike others, this one is combined with a State Information Center on US 2. Free admittance and guided tours. Open daily, May-Sept., 8-5 and until 8 pm in June, July and August. ☎ 406-787-6320.

Bainville

The community of Bainville, 16 miles east of Culbertson, has also joined the museum sweepstakes. Its **Pioneer Pride Museum** features a typical pioneer era bedroom, kitchen and music room. Also on display is an old jail moved from Mondak, a "wet" town just over the line from "dry" North Dakota. Mondak died when Prohibition put a lid on its reason to exist. The museum is open Memorial Day-Labor Day, Tues.-Sun., 1:30-4:30. Free admission. ☎ 406-769-3102.

■ Where the Rivers Meet

Mondak

The Mondak townsite is near **Fort Union Trading Post**, now a national historic site. It's doubtful if, in Mondak's heyday, anyone gave a thought to the crumbling fort near the confluence of the Missouri and Yellowstone Rivers and just over the state line in North Dakota (the parking lot is in Montana). A visit is a must if you would get a fix on Montana's fur trading history. RT 327 slants southeastward from Bainville for 11 miles, pulling up at the Fort.

The walled fort rising above the Missouri dominated the fur trade on the Upper Missouri between 1828 and 1867. Built by John Jacob Astor's American Fur Company, it hosted a roster of Indian chiefs, statesmen, frontiersmen and artists come to paint the wonders of the West. Indians and trappers did a brisk business with the Fort's traders, exchanging pelts for necessities. Illegal firewater, smuggled upriver on steamboats, caused many a fracas. Dominating the fort was a large home where the Fort's bourgeois, or commandant, lived and entertained illustrious guests. Workmen and their mostly Indian wives occupied a straggle of structures inside the palisades. A trade house just inside the main gate served as a buffer between Indians and the Fort's residents. Hangers-on camped outside the walls.

Only four low ridges on a grassy bluff indicated the fort's location when the National Park Service acquired the site in 1966. After extensive excavations, the NPS reconstructed the walls, the stone bastions, the Indian trade house and the Bourgeois' House to their 1851 appearance. The latter reflects a lavish lifestyle that equaled that of 19th-century St. Louis and amazed visitors who expected much less in a wilderness outpost. The structure has a museum and a book store with a good selection of Western books.

Fort Union Trading Post National Historic Site is open daily year-round. Hours are 8-8, CDT, Memorial Day-Labor Day and 9-5:30 CST the remainder of the year. Special tours can be arranged by calling the park: ☎ 701-572-9083.

The **Fort Buford State (North Dakota) Historic Site** is two miles east of Fort Union. This fort was built with wood from Fort Union when the latter was dismantled. It was used to house Indian prisoners, among them Chief Joseph of the Nez Perce. Not much to see; only a houselike structure containing a small museum. The confluence of the Missouri and Yellowstone is a half-mile farther on. Here, separate parties led by Lewis and Clark were reunited before continuing their 1806 return trip to St. Louis.

■ Farm & Ranch Country

Sidney

MT 16 is the main north-south artery linking Sidney and northeast Montana with I-94 at Glendive. From Culbertson, MT 16 continues north past the Medicine Lake National Wildlife Refuge (see *Wildlife Watching*) to a swarm of towns dating from the homestead era. A more interesting route to Sidney is MT 58, which crosses the Missouri south of Fort Union and continues through Fairview, the sugar beet capitol of Montana and North Dakota. Fueled by oil and sugar beets, Sidney is a thriving Yellowstone River town and home of the truly remarkable **MonDak Heritage Center, Museum and Art Gallery**. The Center's ground floor is given over to galleries hosting permanent and changing exhibits, many by local artists. The Historical Reference Library attracts those who wish to study the area's fur trading history, pioneer diaries, old newspapers and such. The Center also has an art reference library.

A curving staircase leads to a "town" lifted from the homestead era. No attic collections here, but "buildings" lining "streets" and inhabited by mannequins dressed in period attire. Homes, a church, school, soda fountain, depot, leather and tack shop, dentist and sheriff offices, bank; each has been curated by persons whose hearts were engaged. Older folk will recognize many items from their childhoods.

The Center, at 120 3rd Ave. S.E., is open year-round, Tues.-Sun. from 1-5. Expanded Monday and morning openings during the summer. Modest admittance fee. ☎ 406-482-3500.

South of Sidney, MT 16 trails the Yellowstone River before slipping into Custer Country a few miles south of Savage. East of Sidney, MT 200 heads west across close to 100 miles of farm and ranch country, pulling up at crossroads named Lambert, Enid, Richey, Circle, Jordan, and Sand Springs, before sliding into Charlie Russell Country at Mosby. Each community, whose populations number in the low hundreds or less, is a microcosm of farm and ranch life. The few roads leading from the highway connect with the Charles M. Russell Wildlife Refuge, Fort Peck Lake and remote ranches.

East of Sidney

Museums at **Jordan, Circle, Richey** and **Lambert** reflect residents' pride in their ranching and homestead heritage. All offer free admittance. Jordan's **Garfield County Museum** is open daily, June 1-Labor Day from 1-5. ☎ 406-557-2517. **McCone County and Circle Museum** is open year-round, 9-5 weekdays; other times by appointment. ☎ 406-485-2414. The **Richey Museum** is open Memorial Day-Labor Day, Mon., Wed. and Fri., 2-5; other times by appointment. ☎ 406-773-5656. **Lambert's Historical Society Museum** is open May-Sept., Tues. & Thurs., 9-3. ☎ 406-774-3439.

Extreme northeast Montana, wrapped around Fort Peck Indian Reservation on the east and south and reached via highways branching north from US 2, is an enclave unto itself. A network of roads extend from MT 16, MT 5 and RT 248, most leading to sleepy homestead era towns set in rich farmland.

Open range until about 1900, the country soon became thickly settled with towns and farms. The Soo Line and the Great Northern built branch lines with sidings and depots placed at six-mile intervals. Towns serving newly arrived homesteaders rose around them. Folks lived out the rural American dream; a dream that lasted but a few decades. Wheat and cattle continue to fuel the economy. Homesteads of a few hundred acres have been swallowed by farms and ranches now measuring in the thousands of acres. Townsfolk remain friendly and close-knit.

Here, as elsewhere in Missouri River Country, people take pride in celebrating the "good old days." **Plentywood** and **Scobey**, towns that have managed to hang in there, have museums to prove it. Those that fell by the wayside after homesteading went bust are museums in themselves. Wandering the back roads, exploring dusty ghost towns, is the other side of adventure's coin.

Plentywood's **Sheridan County Museum**, at the fairgrounds, is dedicated to the preservation of Montana's pioneer heritage. That noble sentiment may have sounded a mite specious during Plentywood's flirtation with Russian Communism, but it fits today. The museum boasts the longest mural in the state and hundreds of antique threshers and tractors. Free admission. Open Memorial Day-Labor Day, Tues.-Sun., 1-5. ☎ 406-756-2219.

Scobey's **Pioneer Town Museum** is just that: a complete town lifted from the homestead era. Some 50 old buildings have been authentically fitted out. There's a general store stocked with merchandise sought by homesteaders in town to trade. An authentic, fully furnished homesteader's shack contrasts with a fine town home. Three churches and the Dirty Shame Saloon illustrate the extremes of town life. You can tour the 20-acre museum any day in summer, but it comes to life during June's Pioneer Days. Modest admittance fee. Open daily, Memorial Day-Labor Day. Call for current hours. ☎ 406-487-5965.

Adventures

■ Adventures on Foot

Rock Hounding

The **Montana moss agate** is an official state gemstone. While prime agate hunting grounds are found along the **Yellowstone River** and its tributaries in Custer Country, you may have happy hunting along the last 50 miles or so before the Yellowstone merges with the Missouri. Alluvial gravels above and adjacent to rivers and streams offer the best chance of picking up one of these prized stones. Be aware of private property and always ask permission before setting foot thereon. For more information on agates and how to identify them, refer to *Rock Hounding* in this book's Custer Country chapter. **Harmon's Agate and Silver Shop**, on MT 16 in Crane, is a good place to become informed about the various grades of agates, and to acquire an agate the easy way. Tom, Cheryl, Jim and Deanna Harmon, in business for over 25 years, graciously share their knowledge. The shop offers an extensive collection of agate jewelry carved and set in gold or silver by the Harmons, as well as moss agate cabochons, scenic slabs and rough agates sold by the pound. PO Box 94, Crane, MT 59217; ☎ 406-482-2534 or 406-798-3624. Fax 406-798-3624. Internet www.inetco.net/harmons. E-mail harmons@servco.com.

The Badlands of the Cretaceous Hell Creek Formation between Fort Peck Lake and Jordan have yielded up numerous **bones and fossils** from the dinosaur age that include a nearly complete Tyrannosaurus rex skeleton, Triceratops skulls, Hadrosaurs remains and more. If you wish to launch your own fossil hunt, be sure to get permission to dig on private lands. Public lands adjacent to **Fort Peck Lake** offer good digging, with some restrictions. It's illegal to remove dinosaur or other vertebrate fossil remains from public land. Finds should be reported to the Museum of the Rockies in Bozeman (see *Yellowstone Country Touring*) or to the BLM office listed below. Plant or shell fossils may be removed. Should you come across Indian artifacts, leave them where you found them and report your find to Doug Melton, Highline Zone Archeologist for the BLM, Bureau of Land Management, 501 S. 2nd St. E., Malta, MT 59538; ☎ 406-654-1240.

■ Adventures on Horseback

 Kids raised in northeast Montana just naturally fit rump to horse. Rodeo fun begins before kindergarten and riding herd on Dad's cattle isn't far behind. By the time a kid dons grownup spurs he's a wrangler trailing cattle like his forebears did and loving every minute of it. Well... maybe not pitching hay in the teeth of a blizzard.

Visitors can get a taste of the authentic farm and ranch life that folks hereabouts wouldn't trade for a million dollars worth of big city glitz. You can join a wagon train or cattle drive or book a stay at a working ranch. These are spread more thinly than in more heavily populated parts of Montana, but the welcome you'll receive reflects the warm downhome spirit of folks hereabouts.

Some of the ranches listed below offer multiple adventures crossing a line between cattle drives or wagon train treks that may involve sleeping under the stars, and farm/ranch stays with soft beds. They are as different as their hosts, so do some research before making a choice. Most have brochures.

Cattle Drives, Wagon Trains & Farm/Ranch Stays

Bar Y 7 Ranch in the amazing Missouri Breaks country is owned and operated by Claude and Meredith Saylor. Claude is a licensed outfitter and guide. The couple offers riding, a day-long covered wagon ride, hiking and fishing for walleye in Fort Peck Reservoir. They also run fishing-only trips in summer and ice fishing in winter. Lodgings are rustic cabins with separate shower rooms, plus one modern cabin. Meals are served family-style in the old ranch house. HC 60 Box 10, Brusett, MT 59318; ☎ 406-557-6150. Fax 406-557-6199.

Foss Cattle Drive & Wagon Train Trail Rides is operated by Marcia and Gene Foss from their ranch on the rolling prairie near Culbertson. A five-day stay includes a wide range of cowboying experiences. The cattle drive/wagon train season begins in May and runs through mid-September. HC 69, Box 97, Culbertson, MT 59218; ☎ 406-787-5559.

Hell Creek Guest Ranch is a cattle, sheep and grain operation in the Missouri River Badlands on land homesteaded in 1913 by Elmer Trumbo. Owners John and Sylvia and Mike and Maribeth Trumbo provide guests with plenty of horseback riding, plus fishing, fossil digging and ranch activities. Lodgings are rustic yet modern cabins. A bed and breakfast alternative is available. PO Box 325, Jordan, MT 59337; ☎ 406-557-2224 or 406-557-2864.

High Plains Escape is the moniker that Gary and Barbara Anderson have given their wagon train trips, combined with cattle drives or watchable wildlife treks. PO Box 1622, Malta, MT 59538; ☎ 406-654-2881.

Montana Harb Prairie Adventures & Beaver Creek Trail Rides is a mouthful describing the guest ranch side of the Bruckner family's 10,000-acre cattle and sheep ranch. The men run the ranch while Eva and the kids host a single family or group, giving them a real taste of ranch life. Eva also offers trail rides by the hour. Bunkhouse and cabin accommodations. Meals are taken with the family and the hired hands. An overnight 4x4 back country trip is an option. Rates are on a per-day basis. A B&B rate is also available. Eva Bruckner, HC 65 Box 6180, Malta, MT 59538; ☎ 406-658-2111.

Murdock Ranch hosts Bill and Jeanette Murdock offer wagon trains, trail rides and working vacations on their 20,000-acre Red Angus cattle ranch near Malta. HC 82, Box 9050, Malta, MT 59538; ☎ 406-658-2303.

Prairie Schooners High Plains Cruises' Ronnie Korman has a variety of wagon train treks, trail rides and cattle drives from his working cattle ranch near Saco. 3H Ranch, Saco, MT 59261; ☎ 406-648-5536.

Rock Creek Lodge is run by Dean and Patti Armbrister as an adjunct to their remote Limousin cattle ranch. Horseback riding is the focus of a vacation here, but area activities and wildlife watching are also offered. The new lodge has comfortable accommodations. Meals are served family-style at the ranch and lunches are packed for the trail. PO Box 152, Hinsdale, MT 59241; ☎ 406-648-5524. E-mail rock-creek-lodge1@juno.com. Internet www.finditlocal.com/rockcreek.

■ Adventures on Water

Fort Peck Lake

Fort Peck Lake (locals prefer "reservoir" to "lake") is the largest body of water in northeast Montana and the only one allowing for extensive boating, waterskiing and such. Houseboating is popular and rentals are available. The reservoir is Montana's foremost warm-water fishery. Given this frolic-on-the-lake image, it's hard to believe that the Missouri River runs underneath somewhere. The 185 miles of river between the Fort Peck Dam and the North Dakota line offer pleasant floating and canoeing. Access points are few: ramps at the dam, at Wolf Point's MT 13 bridge campground, at the Poplar Bridge and campground at Mile 77, at Brockton, and difficult access and egress at the Culbertson Bridge. If you choose to canoe or float all the way to North Dakota, you can continue on for three miles to the ramp and campground at the confluence with the Yellowstone near Fort Buford.

The US Army Corps of Engineers, the BLM and the State of Montana maintain 19 camgrounds with boat ramps and/or docks at various points around the lake. Boat rentals are available at the Fort Peck Marina just west of the dam, and at Rock Creek Marina on the east shore. A brochure with a map showing recreation sites, and including dam and reservoir information, is available from the US Army Corps of Engineers (see *Information Sources,* page 66).

Exploring the lake's many arms and coves by boat can be endlessly absorbing. Wierd, tumbled badland formations rise on every side, offering a perpsective on what Lewis and Clark saw. A houseboat is the perfect craft. You can cruise in comfort and the shallow draft permits pulling onshore when you wish to explore.

Marinas & Boat Rentals

Fort Peck Houseboat Rentals has three houseboats sleeping six or more equipped with bath, galley, BBQ grill, VHF radio, depth finder and swim platform. Weekend or weekly rentals. PO Box 1013, Glasgow, MT 59230; ☎ 406-228-8709 or 888-554-8125.

Fort Peck Marina offers fishing and houseboat rentals, plus a full range of marina services. Also, campsites with hookups. Fort Peck, MT 59223; ☎ 406-526-3442.

Rock Creek Marina offers boat rentals and marina services. Fort Peck, MT 59223; ☎ 406-485-1560.

Hell Creek Recreation Area has boat rentals, cabins and RV hookups. Sand Springs, MT 59077; ☎ 406-557-2345.

Fishing

If you are hooked on game fishing, you'll hook champs in Missouri River Country's warm water fisheries. **Fort Peck Reservoir** is nationally famous for walleye weighing two to four pounds. There's always a chance you'll hook a lunker in the 10-pound class. Several walleye tournaments are held during the summer. Contact Montana Fish, Wildlife and Parks for current dates and other info. Be sure to request or pick up a copy of *Montana Fishing Regulations*, available at FWP and at stores and marinas where fishing licenses are sold. Fishing regulations can change from year to year, so be sure to obtain a current issue.

The sprawling lake also has thriving populations of sauger, a walleye relative. Unlike walleye, the smaller sauger can be caught by bank anglers. Northern pike were first stocked here in 1951 and have adapted well. They generally ranging from four to eight pounds, but there's an outside chance you'll hook a 20-pounder. Feisty smallmouth bass are caught in rocky areas around points and islands. Lake trout, also an introduced species, are best caught in spring and fall when water temeratures are cooler.

Burbot, commonly known as ling and the only freshwater member of the cod family, are also found in Fort Peck Lake. Some people shy away from burbot because of their resemblance to eels, but they make good eating. Chinook salmon, a cold water fish unable to naturally reproduce in the lake, are stocked periodically.

Nelson Reservoir, off US 2 between Saco and Malta, is Montana's number one walleye fishery. Northern pike taken from the 4,000 acre reservoir often outsize Fort Peck northerns. The reservoir also has a good population of yellow perch, at their most catchable through the ice in February and March.

Smaller reservoirs scattered throughout the region also offer fishing for various species. Refer to *Montana Fishing Regulations* for detailed information.

The **Yellowstone and Missouri Rivers** harbor paddlefish, prehistoric fish found only here and in China's Yangtze River system. Refer to *Touring* and *Fishing* in this book's Custer Country chapter for insight into paddlefish and how to catch them. This region's Missouri River snagging spots are between the Fred Robinson Bridge on US 191 south of Malta and the head of Fort Peck Reservoir. Or try your hand at snagging one in the Yellowstone near Sidney. Refer to *Montana Fishing Regulations* for paddlefishing rules.

Walleye, sauger, catfish, northern pike and burbot are also caught in these and other regional rivers.

Ice Fishing

Ice fishing is popular on Fort Peck, Nelson and other reservoirs.

Guided & Charter Fishing

Several licensed outfitters and guides offer guided gamefishing trips on Fort Peck Lake and other reservoirs. Most also offer ice fishing excursions. It makes sense to hire a guide if you want to go where the fish are. These guys make it their business to know where the big ones are, and to be current with the FWP's limits and regulations.

Billingsley Ranch Outfitters' Jack and Andie Billingsley offer fishing trips on Fort Peck Lake. Box 768, Glasgow, MT 59230; ☎ 406-367-5577.

Kibler Outfitting and Charter Fishing, owned and operated by Myron and Mary Beth Kibler, offers Fort Peck Lake fishing excursions from Hell Creek using the latest craft, tackle and equipment. An angler's angler, Myron has been credited with catching the World All Tackle Record Saugeye, weighing in at 15.66 pounds. Myron also offers ice fishing on the west end of the lake. The Kiblers put ice fishing clients up and feed them. As this book goes to press, Mary Beth is going through the final

Missouri River Country

hoops prior to offering lake excursions for non-anglers. Box A-6, Sand Springs, MT 59077; ☎ 406-557-2503.

Marvin Loomis offers trophy Fort Peck Lake fishing under the auspices of John E. Trumbo, co-owner of Hell Creek Guest Ranch. Rather than making clients pack along a cold lunch, Connie Loomis cooks hot meals in a houseboat moored in a nearby cove. Box 312, Jordan, MT 59337; ☎ 406-557-2727 or 557-2224.

Triple Creek Outfitters and Whitcomb Lodge offer fishing for walleye and rainbow trout on a reservoir on the 25,000 deeded acres at the lodge's disposal. Licensed outfitter and guide Roy Ereaux also offers guided fishing on Fort Peck Reservoir. The log lodge, built and operated by Roy and brothers Ezzie and Carroll, offers anglers and hunters a restful retreat. Box 1173, Malta, MT 59358; ☎ 406-654-2089 or 658-2550.

■ Wildlife Watching

Missouri River Country is a treasure trove of wildlife refuges and waterfowl production areas affording viewing opportunities. Many areas incorporate the region's numerous prairie potholes, freshwater depressions and marshes left from when glaciers periodically advanced and retreated across the prairie provinces of Canada and the northern plains states. Many privately owned wetlands are managed and developed through cooperative landowner agreements to protect existing wetlands, restore drained wetlands, and protect nesting cover.

Medicine Lake National Wildlife Refuge

Medicine Lake National Wildlife Refuge is 31,000 acres of potholes and wetlands. It hosts Montana's largest nesting population of white pelicans. Over 2,000 of the graceful white birds nest here, along with over 100,000 ducks, geese and the rare piping plover. Migrating raptors, upland game birds and whitetail deer may also be seen. Medicine Lake also boasts Montana's smallest wilderness area; some 10,000 acres that include the refuge's main lake and a sandhill prairie ecosystem area. May and October are the peak wildlife watching months, though birds and wildlife can be seen throughout the year. An 18-mile auto tour is open May-September. You can hike and canoe in the wilderness areas all year. A concealed blind is available on a sharptail grouse lek throughout April for viewers who wish to watch the birds' mating dance from as close as five feet. Reservations are necessary. The Refuge is off MT 16, about 15 miles north of Culbertson. Watch for signs. ☎ 406-789-2305.

Charles M. Russell National Wildlife Refuge

The Charles M. Russell National Wildlife Refuge extends for 125 miles from the Fred Robinson Bridge on US 191 south of Malta to Fort Peck.

The best way to see wildlife is by boat. However, you can view the area and its varied terrain from gravelled roads and hike all but the elk area. The 20-mile CMR National Wildlife Refuge Tour route begins on US 191, 55 miles south of Malta (watch for signs), and ends at the Fred Robinson Bridge. This wild remnant of the Great Plains is replete with prairie wildlife including prairie dogs, deer, pronghorns, raptors. Between mid-March and mid-May, sharp-tailed grouse perform their mating dances near post #10. In September, the nation's largest prairie elk herd perform fall mating rituals along the Missouri River. It's a restricted area, but you can see and hear the animals from the road. ☎ 406-538-8706.

UL Bend National Wildlife Refuge

UL Bend National Wildlife Refuge, a prairie grasslands habitat giving way to Missouri River breaks, has one of the country's highest densities of black-tailed prairie dogs. The dog towns attract numerous predators: badgers, coyotes, burrowing owls, golden eagles, ferruginous hawks. Brandon and Mickey Buttes are good places to see bighorn sheep. Hiking is a viewing option, but watch out for prairie rattlesnakes. Roads through the refuge are impassable when wet and nearly so when dry. A 4WD vehicle is a must. From Malta, follow US 191 south for 24 miles to Dry Fork Road. Turn left and head east for 15 miles to Refuge Road #212. Continue south for 1.5 miles, then turn left onto Refuge road #201. ☎ 406-538-8706.

Bowdoin National Wildlife Refuge

Bowdoin National Wildlife Refuge, six miles east of Malta on old US 2, includes an hour-and-a-half self-guided auto tour. Pick up a tour brochure and bird identification check list at the starting point. This refuge is known for exceptional colonies of nesting ducks, geese, black-crowned night herons, white-faced ibis and American white pelicans. Over 236 different bird species have been seen here. Also, pronghorn antelope and whitetail deer. The roads are impassable when wet. ☎ 406-654-2863.

Fox Lake Wildlife Management Area

Fox Lake Wildlife Management Area is a cattail and bullrush marsh set amid rolling hills off MT 200 near Lambert. The area is used by waterfowl and shorebirds for nesting and resting during migration. Sandhill cranes migrate through here in October. Tundra swans and American white pelicans are often seen. Dikes divide the lake. Prairie mammals can be seen in the upland habitat. You can hike the dikes. The area is open to hunting in the fall. ☎ 406-228-9347.

Elk Island

Elk Island, maintained by FWP and BLM, is a Yellowstone River island near Savage. It's accessible by boat, 0.75 miles downstream from the Elk Island Fishing Access on Rt. 344 off MT 16. The island's ash and cotton-

Missouri River Country

wood trees loom above a thick underbrush supporting a high density of whitetailed deer. There are beds of freshwater mussels along the river, and painted and snapping turtles are common. Fireflies, unusual in Montana, are also seen here. Fox squirrels, racoons and beavers enjoy this verdant habitat. Exploring the island's wildlife trails is a made-for-kids adventure. ☎ 406-232-4365.

Missouri River Downstream Recreation Area

The Missouri River Downstream Recreation Area below Fort Peck Reservoir includes ponds, cottonwood bottoms and willow thickets affording habitat for waterfowl that include three species of loons, surf scoters, and snow geese. Migrating warblers may be glimpsed on the Beaver Creek Nature Trail in Kiwanis Park. See bald eagles in late fall. Bison, pronghorn, elk and deer disport at the Leo B. Coleman Wildlife Exhibit, just south of the dredge cuts. ☎ 406-526-3464.

The Pines Recreation Area

This is an area of ponderosa pines providing habitat for elk, mule deer, coyotes and red foxes. Numerous raptors and shorebirds can also be seen. Sage grouse mating rituals are often be seen at dawn from April through May. On the west shore of Fort Peck Lake via a gravelled road 26 miles off MT 24 north of Fort Peck. ☎ 406-526-3411.

Jordan to Hell Creek Drive Route

Jordan to Hell Creek Drive Route passes through sagebrush grasslands with deep draws and coulees. Watch for wild turkeys in early morning or late afternoon, also sage and sharp-tailed grouse. Look sharp to see pronghorn, mule deer and golden eagles. Songbirds abound in the ponderosa and limber pine at the end of the road adjacent to the reservoir. In the bay, you may see nesting Osprey, American white pelicans and Canada geese. ☎ 406-232-4365.

■ Special Interest Adventures

Farms and ranches are the mainstays of Missouri River Country life, the engines that run the economy. How country folks live and how they care for their animals and till the soil may be a mystery. One way to clear up that mystery is to book a stay at a working ranch or a farm or ranch B&B. Or take a farm tour. Some of these operations go beyond cattle, sheep and hogs, raising such exotics as fainting goats and ostriches. The following farms host visitors. Call ahead to make arrangements.

Bar Y Seven Ranch owner Claude Saylor offers both day tours and overnight accommodations on his cattle and small grains ranch near Fort Peck Lake. HC 60, Box 10, Brusett, MT 59318; ☎ 406-557-6150.

Billingsley Ranch Outfitters' Jack Billingsley offers day tours of his mixed cattle, sheep and alfalfa ranch. He also leads fishing trips (see *Adventures on Water*). Box 768, Glasgow, MT 59230; ☎ 406-367-5577.

Beebe & Son's Farming, owned and operated by Jim and Deb Beebe, raises hogs and small grains and will conduct day tours. Box 161, Malta, MT 59358; ☎ 406-654-1909.

Montana Ostrich Ranch's Jerry Wiedebusch offers day tours of his most atypical Montana ranch. Plentywood, MT 59254; ☎ 406-765-1897.

Rolling Hills Llamas & Exotics owners Bazil and Marlene Anderson offer day tours of their operation which includes Australian cashmere goats, yaks, llamas, Tennessee fainting goats and Vietnamese potbellied pigs. Tucked into a corner between North Dakota and Saskatchewan, this is Montana's most northeastern ranch. HCR 276, Box 51, Westby, MT 59275; ☎ 406-385-2597.

DID YOU KNOW? *Three F's Unique Breeds, owned by Dave and Sheila Friedrich, raises Tennessee fainting goats and Dexter cattle. This breed of goats has myatonia, a condition that causes them to keel over in a 10-15 second faint when startled. Dexters, a breed of small Irish cattle, mature when they reach about 40 inches at the shoulder. RR1, Box 17, Antelope, MT 59211; ☎ 406-286-5219.*

Spoklie Elk Ranch offers day tours. The Spoklie family raises some 125 elk and specializes in velvet antler harvesting and breeding stock. Box 143, Antelope, MT 59280; ☎ 406-286-5280 or 765-2065.

Dot & Lin's Exotic Animals has miniature horses and donkeys and fainting goats. Owners Dorothy Brockmier and Linda Halland offer day tours. Plentywood, MT 59254; ☎ 406-765-2914 or 895-2219.

■ Kid Stuff

KID-FRIENDLY Farm and ranch tours are great kid stuff. So are fishing, wagon rides and horseback riding. Then there's this scenario:

The kids are loaded into the car and you're driving a seemingly endless stretch of US 2. The troops are in an insurrection mode. Then "Dad, I'm bored" segues to "Hey, Mom, I see a waterslide!" It's no mirage. Plunk in the middle of the prairie between Saco and Malta is a waterslide for sure.

Sleeping Buffalo Resort (see *Touring*) has been a parents' sanity saver for years. The outdoor pool, fed by a thermal mineral well, has a nifty corkscrew water slide. Also, an indoor pool and a hot (106°!) soaking pool. Also a café, tent spaces and RV sites with hookups, lodgings, horsehoe

Missouri River Country

pits, volleyball court and more. HCR 75, Box 13, Saco, MT 59261; ☎ 406-527-3370.

Festivals & Special Events

 It's no accident that rodeos, county fairs and fishing tournaments top this region's events roster. These are the real items, put on for the home folks and not for tourists, though visitors are made to feel welcome. Dates listed below are approximate. Call for current dates. Check with chambers of commerce for additional events.

On-Going Events

Fort Peck Summer Theatre presents theatrical and musical events throughout the summer in a theatre dating from 1930s dam construction days. Glasgow Chamber of Commerce, PO Box 832, Glasgow, MT 59230; ☎ 406-228-2222. Fax 406-228-2244.

January

AG Days and Trade Show starts the year off right in Sidney in early January with ag seminars, livestock judging, petting zoo, video farm tour and a Saturday night banquet featuring a top ag speaker. Red Lovec, 123 W. Main, Sidney, MT 59270; ☎ 406-482-1206.

February

Fort Peck/Glasgow Ice Fishing Tournament is held in Marina Bay in late February. Prize money and merchandise prizes, hot beverages. Glasgow Chamber of Commerce, PO Box 832, Glasgow, MT 59230; ☎ 406-228-2222. Fax 406-228-2244.

March

Sidney Home and Garden Show gets a jump on spring in late March. Libby Berndt, 310 2nd Ave. NW, Sidney, Mt 59270; ☎ 406-482-2403.

May

Peter Paddlefish Day & Kite Festival is a mid-May Sidney event celebrating the running of the paddlefish. Paddlefish soapbox derby, casting contests for adults and kids, the Great Fish Frenzy involving chances on numbered vinyl fish dropped from a crane, kite festival, concessions. Sharon Rau, Chamber of Commerce, 909 S. Central Ave., Sidney, MT 59270; ☎ 406-482-1916.

Fresno Walleye Challenge, a North American Walleye Circuit Tournament, is held from Havre/Big Sandy (Fresno Reservoir) over Memorial Day weekend. Jim Rettig, PO Box 529, Big Sandy, MT 59520; ☎ 406-378-2176.

Heirloom Quilters Quilt Show is held in Glasgow over Memorial Day weekend. On-going demonstrations and quilters' market. Mrs. Lea Hagen, HCR-217 1063, Glasgow, MT 59230; ☎ 406-228-4051 or 228-2675.

June

Western Days & Cowboy Poetry Gathering is an early June Sidney event. Weekend of events include a pet parade, kids' events, family entertainment, evening barbeque, cowboy poetry, country music.

The Richland County Youth Rodeo goes on Sat. & Sun. Sharon Rau, Chamber of Commerce, 909 S. Central Ave., Sidney, MT 59270; ☎ 406-482-1916.

Border Sports Ranch Rodeo is held in Scobey the first Saturday in June. Area towns compete in old-time rodeo events reminiscent of early days ranch rodeos. Ed Hinton, Border Sports, Scobey, MT 59263; ☎ 406-893-4462.

Frontier Days is an early June Culbertson event featuring a parade and rodeo both days, community follies and other fun stuff. Ila May Forbregd, Culbertson Chamber of Commerce, PO Box 639, Culbertson, MT 59218; ☎ 406-787-5821. Fax 406-787-5271.

Peerless Prairie Days is a mid-June old-fashioned town festival. Games, goodies, chili contest, pig feed and dance. This event usually welcomes the Northeast Montana Wagon Train to town. Mary Machart, Peerless Community Club, PO Box 594, Peerless, MT 59253; ☎ 406-893-4445. Fax 893-4399.

Fort Union Rendezvous, a colorful event held at Fort Union in late June, is an authentic recreation of early trading and trapping days. Authentically garbed "Mountain Men" and their families camp on the site, some in tipis. Trade goods for sale. Demonstrations using tools of the era include beading, cooking, weaponry, musical instruments. Paul Hedren, Fort Union, Buford Rt., Williston, ND 58801; 701-572-9083.

Longest Dam Run, held in late June, is a run/walk across the face of Fort Peck Dam. Sanctioned 10k, 5k run and 5k or 1 mile walk. Open to Olympic and marathon runners as well as amateurs. Glasgow Chamber of Commerce, PO Box 832, Glasgow, MT 59230; ☎ 406-228-2222. Fax 406-228-2244.

Annual Carp Shoot in Nelson Reservoir tests archery skills in late June. Carp average 20 lbs. Buddy Lundstrom, PO Box 1119, Malta, MT 59538; ☎ 406-654-1041. Fax 406-654-1050.

Pioneer Days and Antique Show is held annually in Scobey the weekend before July 4th. Pioneer Town comes to life with family vaudville show featuring the Dirty Shame Belles and Dixieland Band, antique car and tractor parade, threshing, threshermen's breakfast and art show. Edgar Richardson, PO Box 133, Scobey, MT 59263; ☎ 406-487-5965 or 487-2224.

Opheim Rodeo in late June features a parade "with horses, wagons and whatever" and NRA rodeo. Ken Floyd, Opheim, MT 59250; ☎ 406-724-3295.

Missouri River Country

July

Milk River Days and Rodeo, held in Hinsdale over July 4th, is an open rodeo followed by a street dance. Games, barbeque and fireworks on the 4th. Bill Schultz, Hinsdale, MT 59241; ☎ 406-364-2310 or 364-2223. Fort Kipp Pow-Wow is held at Fort Kipp, west of Culbertson, over the July 4th weekend. Dancers in full tribal regalia, drumming, vendors selling authentic items. Culbertson Chamber of Commerce, PO Box 639, Culbertson, MT 59218; ☎ 406-787-5821.

Poplar Wild West Days, held over July 4th, includes a parade, community picnic, fireworks, craft sale, two days of rodeos, street dance. Jerry Seaman, PO Box 527, Poplar, MT 59255; ☎ 406-768-5502 or 768-3483. Fax 406-768-3422.

Sandcreek Clydesdales Annual Wagon Train is an annual early July sign-on cattle ranch ride. Bev Harbaugh, PO Box 330, Jordan, MT 59337; ☎ 406-557-2865.

Montana's Governor's Cup Walleye Tournament attracts anglers from far and wide to Fort Peck Lake in early July. $10,000 first place. Fish fry, barbeque, Guys & Gals Tournament, youth fishing tournament, entertainment. Glasgow Chamber of Commerce, PO Box 832, Glasgow, MT 59230; ☎ 406-228-2222. Fax 406-228-2244.

Wolf Point Wild Horse Stampede, held in mid-July, is a three-day PRCA-Wrangler sanctioned rodeo. This, Montana's oldest rodeo, dates from the 19th century. Also, parade, street dance carnival and world famous wild horse race. Wolf Point Chamber of Commerce, PO Box 293, Wolf Point, MT 59201; ☎ 406-653-2012.

Sunrise Festival of the Arts is a mid-July affair in Sidney. Arts and crafts booths, pottery demonstrations, food fair, kids' activities, live entertainment. Sharon Rau, Chamber of Commerce, 909 S. Central Ave., Sidney, MT 59270; ☎ 406-482-1916.

Walleye In-Fisherman Professional Walleye Trail brings professional anglers to Fort Peck Lake in mid-July. Glasgow Chamber of Commerce, PO Box 832, Glasgow, MT 59230; ☎ 406-228-2222. Fax 406-228-2244.

Richey Rodeo is a late July amateur rodeo featuring a bunch of rodeo fun. Nancy Verschoot, HCR 80 Box 5, Lambert, MT 59243; ☎ 406-774-3467.

Northeast Montana Fair is held in Glasgow in late July. Two nights of rodeo, family entertainment, demolition derby, livestock exhibits, 4-H, crafts, food booths, carnival. Jenny Reinhardt, 501 Court Square #14, Glasgow, MT 59230; ☎ 406-228-8221.

August

Richland County Fair and Rodeo is held in Sidney in early August. PRCA rodeo, power pull, livestock, 4-H and FFA exhibits, carnival, petting zoo, big name entertainment. Kris Weltikol, HCR 89, Sidney, MT 59270; ☎ 406-482-2801.

Daniels County Fair is held in Scobey in early August. NRA rodeo, concert, demolition derby, 4-H events, petting zoo, carnival, parade, kids' entertainment. Phyllis Kaul, PO Box 734, Scobey, MT 59263; ☎ 406-487-5581 or 487-2468. Fax 406-487-5541.

Roosevelt County Fair, held in Culbertson the third weekend in August, features all the fun and excitement of a typical farm country county fair. Culbertson Chamber of Commerce, PO Box 639, Culbertson, MT 59218; ☎ 406-787-5821.

Demolition Derby, Rolling Thunder Car Show, Jaycees River Run is held in Sidney in late August. The run crosses the Yellowstone River on the Lewis and Clark Bridge. Tammi Christensen, HC 89 Box 5164, Sidney, MT 59270; ☎ 406-482-4400.

September

Saco Fun Days in early September includes a fiddler contest, barbeque, street dance, craft show, parade, farmers market, kids' games, homemade pie social, demolition derby. Saco Chamber of Commerce, Betty Copple, PO Box 485, Saco, MT 59261; ☎ 406-527-3218.

Milk River Wagon Days has, for over a quarter-century, been an annual Malta Labor Day celebration highlighting the entrance of the Milk River Wagon Train to town. Fun and high jinks. A bring your own horse event. Malta Chamber of Commerce, PO Box 850, Malta, MT 59538; ☎ 406-654-1776.

Threshing Bee and Antique Show is a Culbertson event held the fourth weekend in September. Parade featuring 80+ tractors, bundle threshing by 1897 hand-feed thresher, lumber sawing, slow races, straw scramble for quarters by kids 12 and under, barbeque, fiddlers' music. Rodney Iverson, PO Box 168, Culbertson, MT 59218; ☎ 406-787-5265.

October

Northeast Montana Exposition, held in Wolf Point in mid-October, is billed as northeast Montana's biggest trade show. Livestock judging. Jerald Petersen, 200 Eureka, Wolf Point, MT 59201; ☎ 406-653-1951.

November

Wine and Food Festival is an early November event in Sidney. Food samplings from area restaurants. Live and silent art auction. July Held, PO Box 443, Sidney, MT 59270; ☎ 406-482-2120. Fax 406-482-5023.

Christmas Parade of Lights brings Santa to Sidney in late November. Night parade, carolers. Sharon Rau, Chamber of Commerce, 909 S. Central Ave., Sidney, MT 59270; ☎ 406-482-1916.

December

Malta's Christmas Stroll Parade of Lights is held in early December. Curtis Star, Malta Chamber of Commerce, PO Box 850, Malta, MT 59538; ☎ 406-654-1776.

Wolf Point's Annual Christmas Parade is held in early December. Wolf Point Chamber of Commerce, PO Box 293, Wolf Point, MT 59201; ☎ 406-653-2012.

Missouri River Country

Mon-Dak Heritage Center Ethnic Christmas Celebration is an early December Sidney event. Sue Moore, PO Box 50, Sidney, MT 59270; ☎ 406-482-3500.

Where To Stay & Eat

Missouri River Country lodgings are gradually moving to B&Bs and lodges. High profile chain hostelries have yet to find northeastern Montana worth their while, but larger towns such as Malta and Glasgow have modern motels with pools. Small motels are noted here only when a town has no alternative.

As elsewhere in Montana, you can be assured of hearty rib-sticking viands. Don't expect gourmet. Country cooking has a well-earned reputation, especially for homemade pies. Just dig in. Forget the calories and remember you're on vacation.

Lodging Prices
$ . . . . dirt cheap
$$. . . . . moderate
$$$. . . . . .pricey, but oh well
$$$$ .hang onto your checkbook

■ Where To Stay

Bainville

Montana River Ranch is a country inn on a four-generation ranch. Five ranch-style guest rooms have private sinks and shared showers. Cozy new log cabin. Full home cooked breakfast. Private dinners on request. $$. HC 58 Box 9, Bainville, MT 59212; ☎ 406-769-2127 or 769-2404. Fax 406-769-2200.

Circle

Travelers Inn, on MT 200, has 14 rooms, no restaurant. $. Box 78, Circle, MT 59215; ☎ 406-485-3323.

Culbertson

The Kings Inn Motel, at 408 E. 6th, has 20 units and advertises winter car plug-ins to keep your battery from freezing. You know you're in the polar regions when you see this claim. $. Box 665, Culbertson, MT 59218; ☎ 800-823-4407 or 406-787-6277. Fax 406-787-6177.

Dodson

Stage Road Inn is a B&B offering one guest room with private bath, Western art decor, full ranch breakfast. Also B&B lodging for your horse. $$$. Box 6, Dodson, MT 59524; ☎ 406-383-4410.

Fairview

Korner Motel, at 217 W. 9th, has four guest rooms. $. Box 13, Fairview, MT 59221; ☎ 800-6-KORNER or 406-747-5259.

Fort Peck

Missouri River Country's entry in the Historic Hotel sweepstakes reflects a unique chapter in Montana history.

Fort Peck Hotel is a rambling frame structure that seems not to have changed since the 1930s when dam construction was in full furor. The 38 guest rooms are plain but adequate. The restaurant is a cut above most. $$. Box 168, Fort Peck, MT 59223; ☎ 800-560-4931 or 406-526-3266.

Glasgow

Glasgow has numerous basic lodgings, some seemingly left over from dam building days.

Cottonwood Inn, on US 2 East, is Glasgow's largest hostelry with 92 rooms, a restaurant and pool. $$. Box 1240, Glasgow, MT 59230; ☎ 800-321-8213 or 406-228-8213. Fax 406-228-8248.

Koski's Motel, with 24 roms, accepts patrons by reservation only. $. 320 US 2 E., Glasgow, MT 59230; ☎ 800-238-8282 or 406-228-8282. Fax 406-228-2002.

Lakeridge Motel & Tackle, 17 miles east of Glasgow near Fort Peck Lake on MT 24, has 12 rooms. $$. HCR 1660, Glasgow, MT 59230; ☎ 406-526-3597.

Jordan

Fellman's Motel, on MT 200, has 16 units. $. Box 463, Jordan, MT 59337; ☎ 406-557-2209.

Garfield Hotel & Motel, at MT 200 and Main, has 13 guest rooms. $. Box 374, Jordan, MT 59337; ☎ 406-557-6215.

Malta

Edgewood Inn, at the junction of US 2 and Rt. 242, has 32 guest rooms and a pool. Restaurant across the street. $$. Box 1630, Malta, MT 59538; ☎ 800-821-7475 (MT) or 406-654-1302.

Great Northern Motel, at 2 S. 1st Ave. E., has 29 rooms and a restaurant. $$. Box 190, Malta, MT 59538; ☎ 406-654-2100. Fax 406-654-2622.

Medicine Lake

Club Bar, Hotel & Restaurant, at 202 W. Main, has seven guest rooms. $. Box 17, Medicine Lake, MT 59247; ☎ 406-789-2208.

Plentywood

Sherwood Inn, an attractive structure on West 1st Ave., has 69 guest rooms and a restaurant. $$. 515 W. 1st Ave., Plentywood, MT 59254; ☎ 406-765-2810.

Poplar

Lee Ann's Motel, on US 2, has 15 units. $. Box 205, Poplar, MT 59255; ☎ 406-768-5442.

Saco

Big Dome Hotel B&B, at 121 Taylor, occupies a restored historic hotel with period decor. The six guest rooms share baths. Full gourmet breakfast. $$. Box 382, Saco, MT 59261; ☎ 406-527-3498.

O'Brien's Motel, at 203 Taylor, has eight units. $. Box 556, Saco, MT 59261; ☎ 406-527-3373.

Sleeping Buffalo Resort (see *Touring* and *Kid Stuff*) on US 2 has 33 motel units and three large cabins, plus waterslide, hot pools, café, steakhouse. $. HC 75, Box 13, Saco, MT 59261; ☎ 406-527-3370.

Scobey

Cattle King Motor Inn, on MT 13 South, has 29 guest rooms, hot tub, continental breakfast. $$. Box 750, Scobey, MT 59263; ☎ 800-562-2775 or 406-487-5332.

Sidney

Camel Hump Bed & Breakfast has two guest rooms with shared bath, recreation room with ping pong, exercise equipment, full breakfast. $. 1313 22nd Ave. N.W., Sidney, MT 59270; ☎ 406-482-6184.

Lalonde Hotel, Restaurant & Casino is a full-service hotel with 32 guest rooms. $. 217 S. Central, Sidney, MT 59270; ☎ 406-482-1043.

Richland Motor Inn has 62 rooms with breakfast. $$. 1200 S. Central, Sidney, MT 59270; ☎ 406-482-6400.

Vandalia

Double J Bed & Breakfast near Fort Peck Lake has five guest rooms with shared baths, full breakfast, pool and hot tub. $$. Box 775, Glasgow, MT 59230; ☎ 406-367-5353.

Westby

Hilltop House B&B is situated on a hill overlooking two states and Canada. Three country decor guest rooms, one with private bath, full breakfast. $$. 301 E. 2nd St., Westby, MT 59275; ☎ 406-385-2533. Fax 406-385-2508.

Wolf Point

Forsness Farm Bed & Breakfast has two guest rooms with shared bath, serves full breakfast. $. HC 33, Box 5035, Wolf Point, MT 59201; ☎ 406-653-2492.

Grain elevator, Vendalia.

Homestead Inn has 47 guest rooms. $. 101 US 2 East, Wolf Point, MT 59201; ☎ 800-231-0986 or 406-653-1300. Fax 406-653-3685.

Sherman Motor Inn, at 200 E. Main, has 46 rooms and a restaurant. $. Box 879, Wolf Point, MT 59201; ☎ 800-952-1100 or 406-653-1100. Fax 406-653-3456.

■ Camping

Missouri River Country's public campgrounds are mostly limited to those around Fort Peck Reservoir. Managed by the US Army Corps of Engineers, most are primitive campsites with drinking water available. Most have boat launch ramps. Contact the Corps of Engineers (see *Information Sources*) to request a map with detailed camping information.

The Downstream Campground, in a grassy setting shaded by large trees, is especially attractive and has electrical hookups and showers. The Dredge Cuts Swim Beach is just across the road. West End Campground, below Fort Peck Dam via Hwy. 24, and Rock Creek Marina, on the east shore of Fort Peck Lake, also have RV hookups. ☎ 406-526-3411.

Hell Creek State Park, 25 miles north of Jordan on Fort Peck Lake, is the region's sole state park. Boat launch and rentals. ☎ 406-232-0900.

Nelson Reservoir Campground, managed by the US Bureau of Reclamation, offers grassy camp-where-you-please no-fee camping on the east shore of this popular fishery. The close proximity to swimming makes this a good place to camp if you have children or dogs. My dog Licorice had a fine time here, playing stick and swimming. Take Forest Road #4780 off US 2 for some three miles past Sleeping Buffalo Resort. No phone.

Some towns permit free camping in or around their parks. Such a one is **Malta's Trafton Park**, north of the junction of US 2 and 191. I found more free camping under big cottonwood trees beside the Yellowstone River, east of Fairview off Hwy. 200, a few miles over the line in North Dakota.

Private Campgrounds

Private campgrounds offering pleasant camping are less than plentiful here. Motels flanked by a few afterthought spaces do not come under the "pleasant" umbrella. Ranches with camping do.

Glasgow

Shady Rest RV Park is quiet and has trees, four tent sites and 45 pull-thru RV sites. Open year-round, it has full hookups, a laundry and store. US 2 and Lasar Drive; ☎ 800-422-8954 or 406-228-2769.

Trails West Campground has a swimming pool and playground, 15 tent spaces and 35 full hookup RV spaces. Open year-round. 1.5 miles west of Glasgow on US 2. ☎ 406-228-2778.

Jordan

Kamp Katie has 10 tent sites and 10 RV sites with electrical hookups. On MT 200 at west end of bridge. Open June 15-Sept. 1. ☎ 406-557-2851.

Malta

Edgewater Campground has 19 full hookup RV spaces and an indoor pool (extra $), hot tub, laundry. Open May-Sept. Junction US 2 and Rt. 242; ☎ 800-821-7475 or 406-654-1302.

Plentywood

Bolster Dam Campgrounds, at the north edge of town, has informal camp sites, boat launch, fishing. No fee. Open year-round. ☎ 406-765-1700. Fax 406-765-2738.

Saco

Sleeping Buffalo Resort. Refer to *Touring*, *Kid Stuff*, *Hotels*, *Motels & B&Bs*. Open year-round.

Scobey

Lion's Campground, a mile west of town near the golf course, has nearby swimming, unstructured spaces, water, electricity. Open May-Sept.

Sidney

Sandcliff Ranch, Inc., 10 miles from Sidney on a foothills creek, offers quiet, private tent camping. Cook on a campfire near the creek. Guided trail rides available. 621 4th St. NE, Sidney, MT 59270; ☎ 406-482-6239.

Wolf Point

Rancho Motel & Campground, two miles west of town on US 2, is a pleasant exception to motels with spaces tacked on as an afterthought. The 20 tent sites and 29 full hookup RV spaces are arranged in a shady park-like area. Open April-September. ☎ 406-653-1940.

■ Where to Eat

As I've stated before, any traveler can find a café in Montana. Same thing goes for steaks and pies. Bars sometimes serve the best food. This book skips over the mundane, mentioning a café or small town eatery only when something special is on offer.

Fort Peck

Fort Peck Hotel dining room combines interesting historic surroundings with reasonably priced breakfasts, lunches and dinners. Hearty ranchhand breakfasts, a varied sandwich menu and Montana-raised steaks and walleye straight from the lake raise this restaurant above the mundane. Porch dining in summer. The dining room is open daily except Mon. and Tues. from Oct. 15-June 15. ☎ 800-560-4931 or 406-526-3266.

Four Buttes

Whiskey Buttes, on US 2 west of Scobey, claims it's "not far from anywhere," a far-fetched statement in these open spaces. Typical Montana ranch country ambience with lunch and dinner on the side. ☎ 406-783-5318.

Reserve

Reserve Bar specializes in broasted chicken, has 11:30-1:30 lunch specials and Wednesday dinner specials. Menu changes weekly. ☎ 406-286-5416.

Sidney

Sadie's, in the Sidney Livestock Center, serves hearty breakfast and has dinner specials (dinner's at noon, for you greenhorns' information). Stockmen don't load up their trailers without first tucking into a slab of Sadie's homemade pie. Mon.-Fri., 5:30 am-4 pm. ☎ 406-482-9949.

South 40 Restaurant, at 207 2nd Ave. NW, a Montana Beef Backer Award winner, serves burgers and steaks to match. Also, Mexican fare, soup & salad bar and a kids' menu. Lunch and dinner. Open daily, 10-10. ☎ 406-482-4999.

Triangle Nite Club, in southeast Sidney, is also a Beef Backer Award winner. Montana Cowbells, the cattlemen's wives association, awards the honor to restaurants that come up with unique beef dishes. Restaurant open Sun.-Thurs., 5-10, Fri. and Sat. til 11. ☎ 406-482-4709.

Westby

Rainbow Shack II specializes in homestyle lunches and dinners and has a Sunday smorgasbord from 11-1:30. ☎ 406-385-7404.

Wolf Point

Old Town Grill, at 400 US 2 East, spices up its chicken and steak menu with Mexican dishes and stir-fries. Open daily for breakfast, lunch and dinner. ☎ 406-653-1031.

Bibliography

Bad Land: An American Romance by Jonathan Raban, Pantheon Books.

Caves of Montana by Newell P. Campbell, Montana Bureau of Mines and Geology, Room 206, Main Hall, Montana College of Mineral Science and Technology, Butte, MT 59701.

Floating and Recreation on Montana's Rivers by Curt Thompson, published by Curt Thompson, Box 392, Lakeside, MT 59922.

Montana: A History of Two Centuries by Michael P. Malone, Richard B. Roeder and William L. Lang, University of Washington Press.

Montana's Indians Yesterday and Today by William L. Bryan, Jr., American and World Geographic Publishing, PO Box 5630, Helena, MT 59604.

Montana-Yellowstone Earthquake: The Night the Mountain Fell by Edmund Christopherson, Yellowstone Publications, Box 411, West Yellowstone, MT 59758.

Names on the Face of Montana by Roberta Carkeek Cheney, Mountain Press Publishing Company, PO Box 2399, Missoula, MT 59806.

Undaunted Courage by Stephen E. Ambrose, Touchstone, Simon & Schuster.

Very Close to Trouble: The Johnny Grant Memoir edited by Lyndel Meikle, Washington State University Press, PO Box 645910, Pullman, WA 99164-5910.

The following books are published by Falcon Press, PO Box 1718, Helena, MT 59624, ☎ 800-582-2665:

Hiking Montana by Bill Schneider.

Montana Campfire Tales by Dave Walter.

Montana Wildlife Viewing Guide by Carol and Hank Fischer.

More Than Petticoats: Remarkable Montana Women by Jayle C. Shirley.

Rockhounding Montana by Robert Feldman.

The Rockhounder's Guide to Montana, edited by Randall Green.

Under the Chinook Arch by R. W. "Rib" Gustafson, D.V.M.; published by R. W. Gustafson and distributed by Falcon Press.

The following books are published by Montana Historical Society Press, PO Box 201201, Helena, MT 59620-1201:

Montana Native Plants and Early Peoples by Jeff Hart.

Montana's Historical Highway Markers, compiled by Glenda Clay Bradshaw.

Perilous Passage: A Narrative of the Montana Gold Rush, 1862-1863 by Edwin Ruthven Purple, edited by Kenneth N. Owens.

Scottish Highlanders, Indian Peoples: Thirty Generations of a Montana Family by James Hunter.

The Montana novels and remembrances of Ivan Doig:
English Creek, Penguin Books.
Heart Earth, Penguin Books.
Ride with Me, Mariah Montana, Penguin Books.
Bucking the Sun, Scribner Paperback Fiction, Simon and Schuster.
This House of Sky: Landscapes of a Western Mind, Harcourt Brace & Company.

The Montana novels of A. B. Guthrie, Jr.:
The Big Sky, Houghton Mifflin.
Fair Land, Fair Land, Houghton Mifflin.
Arfive, Houghton Mifflin.
The Last Valley, Houghton Mifflin.

Index